The Games That Weren't

Words and concept Frank Gasking
Foreword David Crane
Design Sam Dyer & Frank Gasking
Artist's impressions & pixel work Trevor Storey
Hardware blueprints Adam Rufino
Publisher Bitmap Books

This book is dedicated to:

My wife, Natasha, and daughter, Jessica – for all their support and love throughout writing the book and being the best thing to have happened in my life. My parents, Christine and Charlie, who always encouraged me, teaching me valuable life lessons and providing some of the best childhood memories – the best parents I could ever wish for. My sister, Anne, who first introduced me to the Commodore 64, igniting my career path in life. My other siblings, John, Bev, Ellis and Colin, for putting up with me over the years. My best friends, Vinny Mainolfi, Michael Errington and Brian O'Neill, who, for years, have always given constant encouragement for everything I've done and whose friendship I value very much.

Finally, to all those involved in the process of digital preservation, in particular, with unreleased prototypes and games. An often undervalued and unrecognised process which has made it possible for others to continue enjoying classic games on new and old platforms, as well as helping to preserve the history of the games industry for future generations.

**Ran out of tim
changed mind
bankruptcy, to
quality issues,
on, legal wran
delays, develo
failed location
bombed, infigh
leaving, comp.**

, publisher
licensing,
o ambitious,
market moved
lings, time
ment issues,
test, console
ting, staff
ny buyout...

Contents

Foreword by David Crane

Video games are entertainment, so it may be somewhat pretentious of me to use the term 'tragic' when describing any aspect of the video game business. That said, in my opinion, the greatest tragedy in video games is the institutional lack of preservation in the industry.

Film vaults contain films going back over 100 years, and electronically recorded music has been preserved for nearly that long. Video games are every bit as influential to our culture, but, due to the obsolescence of electronic systems, it is very difficult for current generations to enjoy playing games from past eras.

Thankfully, as of this writing, greater effort is being made to preserve video games – primarily by recreating and emulating game console systems. Emulate one game console, and you are well on your way to reviving thousands of games that were originally available for that console.

Unlike console video games, arcade games are often built around custom circuitry specific to a single game. So while it can be difficult to play classic console games, it can be doubly challenging to enjoy arcade games of the past. In many cases, arcade cabinet games have to be preserved in ones and twos or be lost forever.

And what of games that reached completion but were never actually published? As a pioneer in the video game business, I can tell you that this happened more times than you might imagine. While the reasons that a game wasn't published can vary, many of those games deserved attention then and deserve preservation now.

The Games That Weren't is a valuable collection of games that never quite reached the game-playing public. Many such games are included, with stories relating to their conceptualisation, design, and implementation from the games' creators themselves. And while we regret that some of these gems were never made available, at least the creativity behind each game's design has been preserved in this volume.

Enjoy this glimpse of some of the games that might have been.

David Crane
Games industry veteran

Welcome by Frank Gasking

Over the years, I've often been asked why I have such a fascination with unreleased games. It is indeed a strange infatuation to have, especially when there are so many wonderful 'released' games out there to enjoy instead. So I'll attempt to explain why...

My own fascination began at the age of 11, reading an issue of *Commodore Force* magazine (once known as *Zzap!64*), where writer Ian Osborne had created an article looking at unreleased Commodore 64 games (only briefly released in the case of *The Great Giana Sisters*). The accompanying screenshots teased me, and the frustration of being denied access to these games made the desire to want to play them stronger.

After some digging around, I was surprised when I was able to obtain many of the games that Ian had written about. I also discovered that he'd only really scratched the surface and that many more lost titles were out there waiting to be found. From that point on, I began researching and collating, initially resulting in a regular article for a fanzine called *Commodore Zone* in 1998.

The Internet boom during the mid-to-late 1990s gave an opportunity to expand and create an online presence to share all the information and games I was finding. The Games That Weren't archive was born in 1999, going strong ever since with the help of Andrew Fisher, David Simmons, Alex Ross, Peter Weighill and Adrian Simpson, as well as our visitors.

When our 20th anniversary neared, I wanted to try and mark it in a special way. So I had the crazy idea of writing a book, covering unreleased games across different platforms and multiple decades. Not realising the effort required, it has been a journey lasting five years, where I have talked to many people and have aimed to solve some mysteries along the way. It's impossible to cover everything, but I've aimed to give a good flavour, covering a mixture of known titles as well as some never heard of or never investigated in detail until now.

I'll conclude by saying that, although generally rewarding, the games industry can be quite tough and ruthless too. So many person-hours are lost on games never seen by the public, for various reasons that you will discover shortly. Although some unreleased games are not particularly great, there are many which clearly could have been very special. We hope that you enjoy this book and our showcase of some of the games that weren't.

Frank Gasking
Games That Weren't

Nineteen Seventy Five — Nineteen Seventy Nine

Trying to cover unreleased games during the 1970s is no easy feat, with only a handful of home computers available at the time and the games industry very much in its embryonic stages. Arcades were the main place to play new and fresh microprocessor-based games, where Atari was the big arcade player, along with companies such as Dave Nutting Associates, Cinematronics, Taito and Bally, to name but a few.

Monochrome display was as good as you were going to get for some titles, though this changed rapidly over time, especially with the introduction of home consoles, such as the Atari VCS (later 2600) and Mattel Intellivision, providing a much-needed colour explosion. It was an exciting era, one which would change the lives of many people over the years that would follow.

Blackjack
Too many hurdles

Year: 1975
Developer: Dave Nutting Associates
Platform: Arcade

Available to play
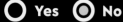 Yes No

Starting our journey through the early era of unreleased video games, you may wonder why the first title covered is a gambling machine and not some *Pong* or *Space Invaders* clone. Before shouting for a refund, *Blackjack* was on the cusp of being one of the first gambling machines to include a microprocessor and graphical display. Where cheap microprocessors kick-started the video games industry, they also served to rejuvenate pre-existing concepts, including gambling machines, sharing almost identical technology to early arcade games being produced at the time.

Gambling machines during this era were nothing new, with some of the first developed as early as the 1800s. However, before the days of microprocessors and graphical displays, they were all pretty much electromechanical-based from the 1960s onwards. With a complex nature to them and intricate components, there was more that could go wrong.

During the early 1970s, Dale Electronics released a video poker machine using standard integrated circuits when microprocessors were not yet a viable option but gave a glimpse of what was on the horizon for future gambling machines. When the cheap microprocessors arrived, Dave Nutting Associates felt there were benefits to be had – not just for saving money, but with more sophisticated implementations of products that could separate them from the competition at the time.

It all began with the introduction of Jamie Fenton (born Jay Fenton) at Dave Nutting Associates in 1974. Jamie was working as a research assistant within the AI lab at the University of Wisconsin, Milwaukee, when a former student came to the lab looking for developers. Jamie and her colleagues were sent over as contractors and became the first employees at Dave Nutting Associates. "It was fun, despite my friends thinking I joined the Mafia. Bally had a reputation, then undeserved, that they were trying to live down, which came from making slot machines," explained Jamie.

Jamie was primarily employed to develop microprocessor-based pinball machines, of which Dave Nutting Associates was one of the first to develop (via Jeff Frederiksen, converting Bally's *Flicker* in 1975 to use an Intel 4004 microprocessor). However, with all the excitement coming from video games, Jamie desired to be more involved in that area. She pursued her interest by looking to develop their second arcade video game, following on from the recently released *Gun Fight*.

Not quite getting a new video game to work on, Jamie was still given an opportunity to produce something with both a microprocessor and visual display. "I got Jamie Fenton working on a video slot machine to show Bally management the video technology available for its mechanical slot machines," Dave Nutting recalled. "Jamie on her own would develop *Video Blackjack*, with video animation of dealing the cards. We were going to really impress Bally management with the future of video gambling devices."

Other companies were likely already experimenting with video game technology, but, at the time, there was nothing else like it on the market. Dave sensed a major opportunity for his company to lead the way forwards, which would mean making sacrifices to ensure that they were not pipped to the post. "Over a Christmas holiday, David and I built *Blackjack* in a cocktail table format," Jamie recalled. "It just used a single deck of cards and classic Blackjack rules overall. David drew all of the card images; Jeff Frederiksen did all of the hardware."

"It was fun, despite my friends thinking I joined the Mafia."

The prototype was similar-looking physically to the Blackjack games that you see all over Las Vegas today. The game pitted one player against a computerised dealer, and things were kept deliberately simple whilst Jamie got to grips with the new hardware, hence just a single deck of cards being developed to start with. It was just enough to demonstrate the concept.

Development was swift, taking less than a month in total, according to Jamie. The game would utilise the very same hardware that was used for *Gun Fight*, with an Intel 8008 processor and a 512×384 screen capable of displaying 1-bit black-and-white pixels. The game also came with simple mono sound – just as *Gun Fight* did.

The cabinet was tidied up and prepared for field testing, with a makeshift payout chute and a 'cash out' button added. It's important to note that the inclusion of both could have qualified the game as the very first computer-controlled card game gambling device. "The godmother of all Video Poker and Blackjack games in Las Vegas and Atlantic City!" Jamie declared proudly. Unfortunately, it would be an accolade that it would, in the end, never officially get to receive.

Field testing consisted of guests at a party house in Milwaukee, where Jamie lived at the time. The feedback was extremely promising. "Everyone played it and loved it," Jamie recalled. "We turned the payout chute off to avoid breaking the gambling laws in Wisconsin."

Only having a single deck of cards meant that more work was required to turn it into a commercially viable product. "This would have been a fatal mistake if it went into production as it was, as card-counters would have been able to milk it dry by merely counting the face cards," explained Jamie. "I knew this then but was told to stick with a single deck for now. That made sense for a demo, where making the player feel like a winner was part of the pitch."

Part of the plan would be to later increase the number of card decks from one to six, and reshuffling long before you ran out of cards. "This would have made card-counting harder to do," Jamie added. "However, it still would have required the game to be installed in a casino with security staff as, even today, casinos have problems with card-counters with six decks. Most casino card games tweak the rules so as to generate a higher 'house percentage'. We would have needed to do that too, in order to match the earnings of slot machines."

As the prototype had proved popular and tested well, the team had been confident that Bally would take the game on. What they didn't anticipate was that Bally was already looking into a similar route. "Bally management had moved forwards on their own course," Dave explained. "We never had the opportunity to present our future video gambling devices."

"There was never any serious plan to release the game as a result," added Jamie. "Producing an electronic game then, as now, involved getting approval from the Nevada State Gaming Commission, among many other hurdles. You needed to earn the confidence of game operators too." Those extra hurdles would put off the team from trying to pursue the development any further. *Blackjack* was assigned to the development scrapheap as quickly as it had been developed.

However, the experience led to Jamie working on famous arcade titles, such as *GORF* and *The Adventures of Robby Roto*, making her well-known in the games industry today. No doubt though, *Blackjack* was a missed opportunity and could have gone down in history as being the first of its kind, but it wasn't to be. Around a year later, United Games released its *Video Card World* cabinet, containing various card games, including its own *Video Blackjack*.

"We were going to really impress Bally management with the future of video gambling devices."

For something that could have been the first of its kind, there is a curiosity as to what happened to the field test prototype developed. Could it someday become a museum piece of interest? Unfortunately, Jamie and Dave never kept anything of the development, even photos or documentation in relation to it due to the short period of time spent on the game.

"Eventually, the prototype wound up in a Midway storage area, like the lost Ark of the Covenant from *Indiana Jones*. Will it ever be found? Will it still boot up?" wrote Jamie on her website. We may never know the answer, with the likelihood of the game turning up becoming lower as the years pass by. Strange things can happen; so we can, at least, dream that something will someday surface to experience or see of what could have been the first of its kind.

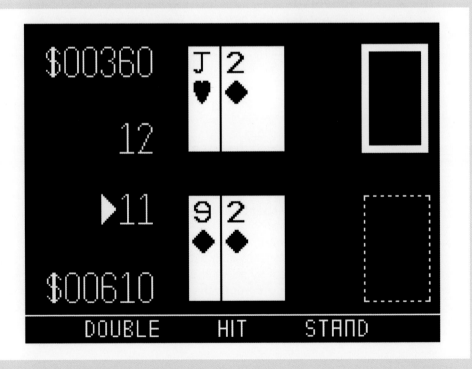

Above: Two artist's impressions of how *Blackjack* (arcade) may have looked – based on Jamie's recollections – showing a single deck and monochrome display.

AVAILABLE FOR SHIPMENT JAN. 1, 1977
ORDER NOW!
VIDEO CARD WORLD

FEATURES:
- *Color or Black & White Monitor*
- *1-2-3-4 Player*
- *25¢ Per Player*
- *Illuminated Coin Entry*
- *Warranty on Monitor & Logic Board*
- *Accepts Both American & Canadian Coins*
- *19" Table Model*

DIMENSIONS & WEIGHT
35" x 35" x28¼"
Net Weight Approx. 145 lbs.
Shipping Weight Approx. 170 lbs.

UNIT CONTAINS
VIDEO BLACKJACK PLUS OTHER CARD GAMES

DISTRIBUTED BY:

UNITED GAMES, INC.
7831 S.E. Stark
Portland, Oregon 97215
(503) 255-8042

Above: This flyer shows a microprocessor arcade implementation of *Blackjack* that was released not long after the cancellation of Jamie's project. One of the first of its kind.

Cannonball
Too violent?

Year: 1976
Developer: Atari
Platform: Arcade

The first game from Owen Rubin (of *Major Havoc* fame), where you fire a human cannonball through a hole in a wall at different heights. Featuring background music (the first game to do so), it annoyed arcade owners in tests. Annoyances plus concerns over its 'splat' sounds would condemn it. It was later reworked for the Atari 2600 as *Human Cannonball* in 1978, simplifying and replacing the wall with a water bucket.

"I was hired in 1976, right out of college, put into a small lab and told to make a game. On paper, I designed the idea of a man shot from a cannon, aiming for a hole in a wall. When he misses, he splats and slides down, before limping away (no people death in Atari games back then). For sounds, I wanted a splat sound, so I went into the work showers and recorded tossing wet paper towels onto the floor – resulting in a bone-crunching splat. I loved it, but management said no way.

Graphics were designed on graph paper and the program assembled by hand, entered via teletype and saved onto tapes. During review, I was asked to show my 'listings'. Listings? What listings? Turns out, there were two computer operators and a system for assembling my code, supplying printouts and paper tapes, but I never knew."

Owen Rubin, developer

Available to play

 Yes No

Time Bomb

Failed testing

Year: 1977
Developer: Atari
Platform: Arcade

Available to play

 Yes ⊙ No

Avoiding exploding bombs in games is something we're all very familiar with, thanks to titles such as *Bomberman* and even *Super Mario Kart*. You could well have been avoiding them way back in 1977, had things gone to plan with a new game concept concocted within the doors of Atari.

Steve Calfee, one of the team leaders at Atari, needed a new development from his coin-op group to keep things moving on the arcade 'conveyor belt'. Lyle Rains (head of development for all the teams) came up with a unique idea which showed some promise. "The concept was for a tension-packed battle as bombs ticked down, with opposing bulldozers trying to outwit each other to move or block bombs," said Chris Downend, describing Lyle's concept.

Fresh from receiving a degree in electrical engineering at the University of California, Berkeley, Chris got his first employment gig at Atari. After first working on a title called *Snakey*, Chris was then assigned as the developer for Lyle's new game, working under his guidance. "Lyle coached me on the implementation and the gameplay mechanics," explained Chris, working closely together on what was to become known as *Time Bomb*.

Whilst acting as the main designer for the game, Lyle would also be involved on all of the pixel work. Although much of Lyle's memory of *Time Bomb* has since faded, he was keen to describe the process back then for developments such as this. "We always wanted a basic prototype with minimal tuning, just to see if it was fun," he said. "If it was 'fun' or 'sorta fun', we would work on it a bit more, putting additional design resources into it and eventually testing it in an arcade. If not, we moved on to another idea."

As with most titles at this time, *Time Bomb* was monochrome-based, with players represented in white and black respectively, and with the field of play split into two halves to represent each player's area. The game was similar in many ways to *Combat* on the Atari 2600, with the aim to score as high as possible within a set time limit. Bombs would frequently appear on the map, and you would have to move them into your opponent's area as quickly as possible to score points once they had exploded. The player with the most points at the end would be declared the winner.

Unfortunately, *Combat* had been a two-player-only game but, if you were a bit of a 'billy no mates' like the author as a child, then *Time Bomb* was ideal. "It was one- or two-player, with the robot AI doing duty in the one-player mode," Chris explained – making the game appealing for those with a lack of friends.

Aiding rapid production, the game made use of pre-existing *Sprint 4* hardware (released the same year), powered by a MOS 6502 CPU and discrete circuitry for sound handling. "These were still the early days of microprocessor-based game hardware," Lyle explained. "Our 8-bit microprocessors were running at clock speeds near 1MHz rather than several GHz. The processor and memory (RAM and ROM) were the most expensive components on the boards, and we tried hard to minimise memory usage. So, even though the games were 'programmable', the available processing and storage resources were limited."

"Game graphics were designed on graph paper and transferred one bit at a time to a ROM emulator."

The system was part of a Motion Object Count family (motion object = sprite), utilising a MOC 4 system. "MOC 4 had four motion objects that could be positioned at precise X-Y coordinates on the screen, with a whopping 256×256 coordinate space, give or take a few lines – my recollection is fuzzy," Chris explained. "The hardware also supported an independently generated playfield that allowed the programmer to place 8×8 pixel tiles on the 32×32 grid (8×32=256). The tiles were loaded from a separate graphics memory, where the wall piece segments and numerics for scores and time clock digits were also stored."

"Game graphics were designed on graph paper and transferred one bit at a time to a ROM emulator," Lyle added. "There were no artistic development applications or tools. Powerful paint and 3D programs, music synths and programmable audio chips did not exist." Graphically, the game was functional, with some well-drawn bulldozer and bomb sprites.

The game was played across a single static map, compared with *Sprint 4* (which had several tracks available to play on), with just a few plain wall segments in both areas. Sound was impressive due to its discrete circuitry, allowing for robust engine and explosion noises. *Sprint 4*'s pre-existing sound system was simply adjusted via noise generator parameters to produce new effects.

Towards the end of development in summer 1977, Atari added John Ray to its team of arcade engineers and developers, so he was a latecomer to the *Time Bomb* project. "I was hired to work on hardware for the team. *Time Bomb* was a project I was hired into, and it was wrapping up when I joined Atari," John recalled. "I helped out with the field test duties – accompanying marketing to observe players – and I offered gameplay suggestions, but I did not do any programming or other engineering on it. I was just excited to be a part of Atari and learn everything as quickly as I could."

In the end, development was swift as a result of the pre-prepared hardware. Although the exact time period couldn't be recalled, maximum development time was usually six months, and Chris suggested it was probably less than this.

Complete and playable, it was time for the game to be put into field testing. Full cabinet art was produced with a vibrant orange and black colour scheme and cartoon-based bezel artwork emblazoned across the sides. The controls consisted of two four-way joysticks and a button for each to grab bombs when contact was made. It looked great overall, but now its fate was out of Atari's hands and in the hands of the gaming public.

It is almost an anticlimax, as *Time Bomb* wouldn't have otherwise featured in this book if the game had been successful. Unfortunately, the game didn't perform well. "Well, it is easy to quip that it 'bombed'!" Chris jumped in quickly, clearly anticipating our probable and predictable wordsmanship. "The problem was that it was too simple, and there were no strategies or tactics to learn and master that would give it depth and replayability. We wanted to keep it as a head-to-head battle, but it was not fun enough to want to play again and again." Apart from seeing bombs appear and pushing those bombs into the opposition's play area, Chris was right – there wasn't much to do.

The map was also sparse with a lack of obstacles, and the computerised player was pretty ropey, often getting stuck in places during play. Really, it needed an injection of something more, such as varied maps, different obstacle types and other elements to challenge and get players thinking more about how to outwit their opponent. In its current state, players would play for a single game, and that was the whole game experienced within a few short minutes. Before there was time to reflect on the poor field test, the developers were straight onto a new project to find that next magical hit.

"These were still the early days of microprocessor-based game hardware."

So would the developers have done things differently in hindsight? "Maybe evolve it into *Time Bomb* meets *Canyon Bomber*!" Chris joked. "Seriously, in 1977, game design was a bit like building a sandcastle: there was as much enjoyment in the creating as in the playing. If something failed: no harm, no foul. No big investment to worry about. We moved on to creating and dreaming up the next bigger and better sandcastle. We were inventing a whole new form of game (video games in general) with remarkable freedom to create and try just about anything with a whole new medium."

"There wasn't a lot of cost in the prototype, and no huge stigma attached to the failure of any single project," added Lyle. "We were using light resources to prototype a lot of ideas and had great fun. A failed field test, therefore, implies that *Time Bomb* was a 'sorta fun' project that did not resonate with players when tested. As the hardware advanced and the artistic and strategic content of games increased, this style of rapid prototyping faded, and a different (resource-heavy) model of game development eventually replaced it." If anything, *Time Bomb* was part of the learning process for everyone involved – it taught lessons which would be used when developing future titles.

With the cancellation of *Time Bomb*, there was now a prototype with no purpose. Luckily, one of the team saw value in keeping it for posterity. "Chris did not have room at home, so I ended up with it," John informed us. "That eventually went to Scott Evans (who runs the Atari Games Museum) along with all my other proto games when I moved away from the SF Bay Area. I believe I had the one and only cabinet prototype, which was the game on field test. There were probably other PCBs that somebody might have ended up with."

"Chris did not have room at home, so I ended up with it."

Scott Evans posted a video of the game in 2014. It is hoped that, someday, the game will be preserved for others to play. We conclude with some final words from Chris about what was an exciting time for all back then. "Applaud us for giving every idea a shot. It was an amazing time, full of creativity and excitement. We were all fresh out of college, inventing the foundation of what was to grow to a multi-billion-dollar industry. Wow!"

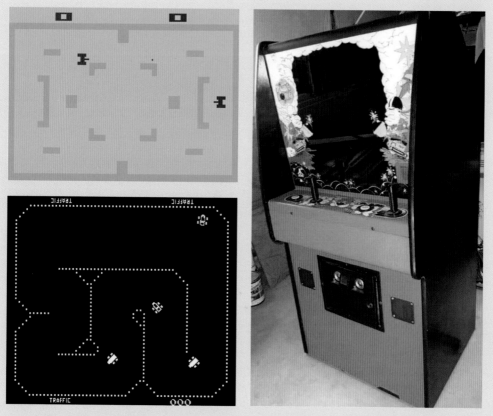

Top: Similar to but not directly inspired by *Combat* (Atari 2600). Bottom: *Sprint 4* (arcade), the starting point for *Time Bomb*. Right: The wonderfully vibrant and orange cabinet from John Ray.

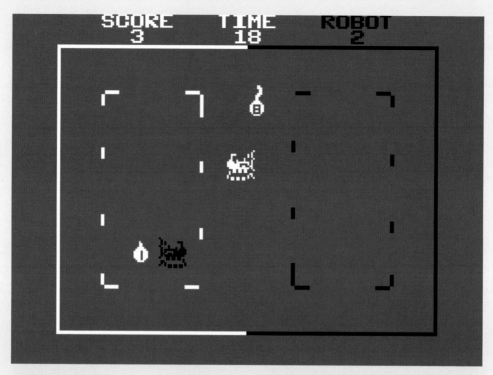

Above: An artist's pixel recreation of *Time Bomb* (arcade) from video footage Scott Evans posted of the game to YouTube in 2014, showing the game in action.

The Atari Game Brain
Outdated hardware

Year: 1978
Developer: Atari

The Atari Game Brain was initiated whilst the Atari 2600 (then VCS) was well underway, with all the circuitry to run each game found within the cartridges themselves. Controls consisted simply of two paddles and directional buttons built into the machine rather than being separate. The intentionally limited shelf life meant that only a handful of games were intended for release, most being replacements for stand-alone systems released earlier by Atari, including titles such as *Stunt Cycle* and *Super Pong*.

Only a few working prototypes were ever created (one recently displayed at the National Videogame Museum). Its conception just didn't make sense at a time when programmable ROM cartridges were the future; the system was cancelled as a result. Atari would put all of its focus into its recently released 2600 console, which contributed to moulding the games industry into what we know today.

PLAYER 1 PADDLE

LEFT FIRE BUTTON

LEFT DIRECTIONAL CONTROLS

GAME CARTRIDGE

POW

RE

DISCONNECT

CONNECT

V

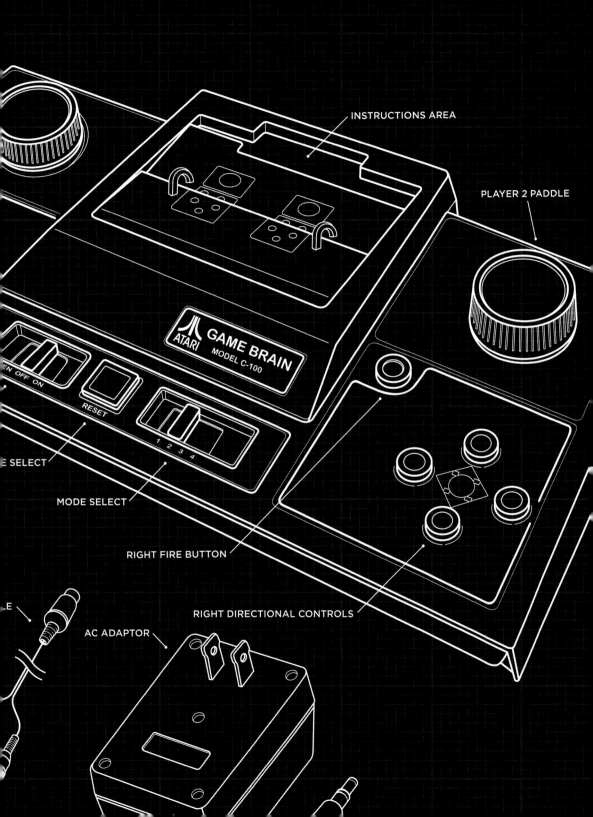

INSTRUCTIONS AREA

PLAYER 2 PADDLE

ATARI GAME BRAIN
MODEL C-100

EN OFF ON

RESET

1 2 3 4

E SELECT

MODE SELECT

RIGHT FIRE BUTTON

RIGHT DIRECTIONAL CONTROLS

E

AC ADAPTOR

Boggle Licensing issues

Year: 1978
Developer: Atari
Platform: Atari 2600

Available to play
 Yes No

The Atari Video Computer System (VCS, later renamed the 2600) is where it all began for many home video gamers, with its interchangeable cartridge system allowing gamers to purchase new games instead of a whole new system to play something different each time. The console had an impressive shelf life, released in 1977 and discontinued in 1992.

The architecture of the machine was primarily modelled so that it could produce decent home representations of *Pong* and *Tank*. The hardware included two 'player' sprites, two 'missile' sprites and one 'ball' to help make the task of replicating those games more straightforward. Initially, this seemed to limit what was possible with the console, but, as developers got to grips with the hardware and the Atari's TIA chip (the graphics and audio chip), various tricks were discovered which could expand the types of games possible.

"Every technique developed for the 2600 at Atari (and then Activision) expanded the base technology available to the game designers," explained David Crane. "The original *Video Chess* Venetian Blind technique was added to and expanded upon a dozen times, creating new categories of games we could make. When one of us came up with a new idea, it only took seconds for another to think, 'that's a cool technique – I can use the same technique in a different way and make something new'."

David was one of the original Atari 2600 developers, creating well-known early titles, such as *Outlaw* and *Canyon Bomber*. After not being properly recognised for their work, David, Larry Kaplan, Alan Miller and Bob Whitehead left Atari to set up Activision in 1979 – becoming the first independent developer for game consoles. However, whilst at Atari, one of David's first-ever 2600 developments was aiming to push yet more boundaries with a popular word game being the focus.

"One common method I used in making games for the 2600 was to experiment with new ways to manipulate the system hardware – always trying to expand the breadth of games we could make," David told us. "I took the Venetian Blind concept (pioneered by Activision co-founder Bob Whitehead for *Video Chess*) and made it work for eight alphanumeric characters in a line, or more by adding flicker. Staring at a character grid made me consider a word game like *Boggle*, which I had played around the kitchen table with my family."

Boggle was another example of a project born from a developer and not assigned by a manager. "There wasn't a lot of 'assigning' of game projects at Atari. Each project was so complicated that management realised they had to leave a lot of decisions up to the technical people who knew what the Atari 2600 could do. With that new display technique, I proposed testing out making a game like *Boggle*, and I was approved to spend a few weeks on the concept."

If you're not familiar with the game *Boggle*, here is a brief lesson: you first start with a 4×4 grid of letters, randomly allocated by shaking a plastic container of letter cubes. From the assignment of letters, you must form as many words as possible in various directions before the timer runs out. You can only use each letter once, and the more letters a word uses, the more points you receive. The winner is the player with the highest tally of points at the end.

"Once the display was worked out, the game was trivial."

With an obvious lack of keyboard to enter words, *Boggle* wasn't necessarily the first title you would envisage working on the Atari 2600. But David was sure that it could work and began a journey of squeezing the complex word game into just a 2K ROM cartridge (which was the standard at the time – not expanded to 4K until a year later). However, David made little work of the development.

"Once the display was worked out, the game was trivial. With a little work on a good random number generator and a shuffle routine, the game was virtually complete," he explained. "In the game of *Boggle*, the player does most of the work. All that was required on the game was creating the board, navigating the grid with a cursor, score, timer and rule-checking the player's clicks. My best guess would be that I spent no more than three weeks developing the game to that point." So David had a complete and functioning game of *Boggle*, something never previously thought possible on the hardware.

Boggle would certainly win no awards for its graphic display, but then the focus was just on getting the text display working. With an understanding of the limitations, it could be overlooked very quickly and admired for what was present. Starting a game required you to flick the reset switch several times for all of the letters to appear – a quirky and effective way of replicating the 'shuffle' of the original plastic shaker.

The game's interface built by David was simple and ingenious. You moved a cursor over the letters, pressing 'fire' to select a letter to add on to your word. Once finished, you would press 'fire' on the letter you last chose (where a dot displays to indicate that you are ready to finish) and press again. Both players would not play simultaneously against a timer like with the original game, but each player had 99 seconds to construct as many words as possible, taking turns to construct individual words. For each player's turn, the timer would start counting down for as long as they would take, and the time remaining would resume once it was their turn again.

As you would expect, there were cutbacks imposed due to the hardware constraints. Firstly, you could only get a maximum of eight words each per player, and you could only play with two players. "I don't think I ever considered making it a one-player game at any stage," David mused. "Besides the difficulties of a computer algorithm and a dictionary, the 2600 was primarily a two-player console in that era. Most families had the machine in their living rooms attached to their only television, and the games were played by fathers and sons or two siblings. The era of kids sequestered in their bedrooms with their game machines 24 hours a day (playing one-player games) came later."

When you consider that the original game had to be played with a minimum of two players, then this wouldn't have been seen as an issue at the time at all. As David alludes, you had to do some of the work yourself to make each game valid and crucially legitimate. With the enforced 2K ROM limit, there was no chance of the game ever being able to check if words were actually valid or spelt correctly. Even with double the ROM, it would have been hard.

Therefore, it was possible to just assign any old random letters, so each player would have to validate words manually, like with the real game. To prevent your opposition from just copying your words, they would have to be made to look away whilst it was your turn, or you just poked them in the eyes or something to get a similar effect. This was not damaging to the video game as these issues were also prevalent with the original game. If anything, it was just the eight-word limit that was a bit unfortunate overall. "It was never really a game, just a fully functional demo," David reflected. "I would have dressed the display up with other graphic elements, maybe added text messages, etc. So I would never call *Boggle* a 'complete' game."

"I don't think I ever considered making it a one-player game at any stage."

Although fully playable, there were still a few bugs to iron out, but it wasn't too far away at all from being in a release candidate state. Minor flaws aside, it was a bizarre decision when Atari decided not to pursue development of the game, especially one which was technically very impressive. Perhaps it was due to the two-player-only limitation, but then other games suffered the same issue at the time. It was actually a completely different reason, and one which could have been trivial had the game been developed just a few years later.

"In 1978, the idea of licensing a property from outside the games industry was unheard of. Atari had never licensed a property to that point, and it would be years before they did so," explained David. "When my boss took the idea of a *Boggle* game up the chain for approval, the almost immediate answer was '*Boggle* is a Parker Brothers product. We can't put out a game based on someone else's product!?!' I pointed out that, yeah, you'd have to license the property. The thought of paying someone for the rights to make a game was foreign to them, and, besides, *Boggle* wasn't a really well-recognised product, so licensing it probably didn't make a lot of sense anyway."

With no route to negotiation over licensing costs, the proverbial 'brick wall' was hit and the game was swiftly laid to rest. David was quickly moved on to new projects and, just a year later, faced new adventures with Activision, going on to create brilliant and innovative titles, such as *Pitfall!* and *Ghostbusters*. In the decades that followed, David would go on to create almost 100 games across virtually every genre on computers, consoles, mobiles and online.

Many developers will tell you that any development experience is never wasted, and, whilst at Activision, David actually had another attempt at a word game, inspired by his earlier efforts with *Boggle* at Atari. "I developed a *Cryptograms* game a few years later at Activision. For that game, I made what I called the 'Filled Venetian Blind' technique," he explained. "The basic Venetian Blind technique displayed the odd lines of objects 1, 3, 5, etc., shifted the sprite objects and then the even lines of objects 2, 4, 6, etc. Filled Venetian Blind then filled in the gaps. On alternate frames, it displayed the even lines of objects 1, 3, 5, and the odd lines of objects 2, 4, 6, outputting graphics where there would otherwise have been background showing through. This had a strange effect. If you looked directly at it, the text appeared solid but translucent. When you moved your eyes, you would catch a glimpse of the dashed Venetian Blind letters."

With *Cryptograms*, there was a little more intelligence compared with *Boggle*, due to a 4K ROM now being available. Development was swift and relatively painless for David, and it wasn't long until there was something tangible for publication. "*Cryptograms* was complete. I entered the text for 2K bytes of famous quotes, like an Indy 500 winner saying 'All I had to do was keep turning left'. A scrambled version appeared on the screen. The player could experiment with letter substitution guesses, and every place a letter appeared in the quote, the guess was shown above it. Since there were a limited number of canned quotes, I added the ability to enter your own. You could enter a quote and shuffle it for a friend, or you could enter a cryptogram and use the 2600 to help solve it."

However, as with *Boggle*, *Cryptograms* also never made it out of the door. "Ultimately, our CEO, Jim Levy, decided the game didn't have the mass appeal to ship," David recalled. "It was cool for wordies but not for the mass game market. Activision could only support the marketing of so many releases at once, and he would rather not put out a title than put it out without marketing support."

Unfortunately, *Cryptograms* has since been lost to time and is yet to be digitally preserved at the time of writing. David confirmed that he no longer had anything of either *Cryptograms* or *Boggle*. "Sadly, for video game archivists, when a games professional leaves a company, they are not allowed to take any materials with them. When you couple that with an institutional disregard for obsolete games, the company doesn't save that stuff either. I left Atari in 1979, and Activision eight years later with nothing but the skill of my art," he confirmed.

Miraculously, *Boggle* has surfaced by other means, via a series of disks recovered from the Atari vaults. The disks contained the complete source code for *Boggle* and were found by Curt Vendel from the Atari Museum (www.atarimuseum.com) around 2005 whilst archiving a bunch of recovered Atari materials. The dates on the files indicate that development was from around August 1978.

"It was cool for wordies, but not for the mass game market."

No actual physical cartridge prototype was ever found of the game though, and David wasn't 100% certain if it ever got burned onto one. "I may have put it on an EPROM cart to play at home or take on a visit to my family during a holiday trip. However, most of the discussions centring on the game were done on a development system in the lab," he recalled.

It is thanks to the sterling efforts of Atari historians, Curt Vendel and Matt Reichert (www.atariprotos.com) that *Boggle* is available for people to experience and have the chance to view some of David's earliest magic on the Atari 2600. It is hopeful that perhaps, someday, *Cryptograms* will meet a similar fate, and fans of the iconic console will be able to enjoy it as intended.

Above: A typical original *Boggle* set that the Atari 2600 game was based upon.

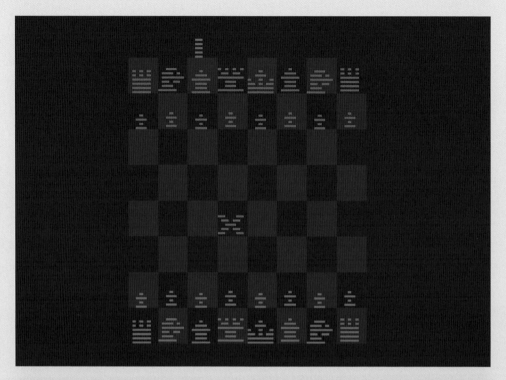

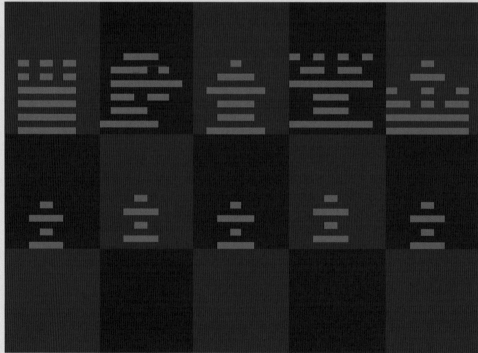

Top: *Video Chess* (Atari 2600) paved the way for games like *Boggle*, thanks to its Venetian Blind technique. Bottom: A 'zoomed-in' view to show the Venetian Blind technique more clearly.

```
05    KVTᶜ     00
21    ITLN     86
GO    DGOE
      LAOE
1. LAG
2. LAD
3. LOG
4. LENT
5. LOO.
```

```
00    AELG     00
93    OGOR     99
GO    LYWT
      ARLA
1.
```

Above: *Boggle* (Atari 2600) in action, utilising the Venetian Blind technique with an interlace effect so the words appear full. Screenshots have been tidied up slightly so you can see the final result properly.

Boxer
Poor testing

Year: 1978
Developer: Atari
Platform: Arcade

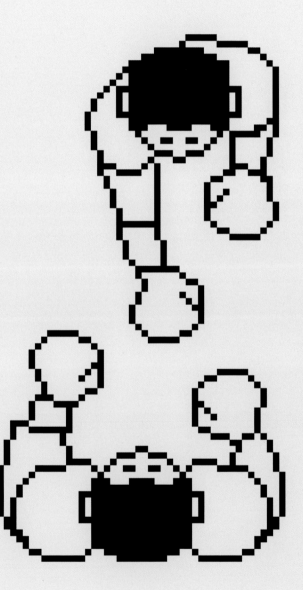

Available to play
◉ Yes ◯ No

Many enjoyed Activision's *Boxing* released in 1980 on the Atari 2600, not knowing its inspired, unreleased arcade origins. Created by Mike Albaugh, controls went through changes to keep the game physical and fun but also more durable. Poor testing performance saw it dropped. Activision's effort simplified and rotated everything by 90 degrees, giving players something close to the original game.

"*Boxer* (also known as *Boxing*) was the third game I worked on at Atari. There were two different revs on the hardware. We were looking for a sports simulation game with high physical involvement for the player and a pop/camp presentation influenced by the 1966 Batman TV series (with Adam West). Alas, the 'physical involvement' part was too successful, and players tended to thrash the controls to destruction fairly quickly.

Originally, the controls were sort of an analogue joystick with a rotating top, so three axes (X, Y, Rotate), but, by Rev 14 or so, they did not move in Y (towards/away from the screen). This was still prone to failures, and the compromise left the machine less engaging. It was never produced. Later, I got closer to my goal with *Atari Football*."

Mike Albaugh, developer

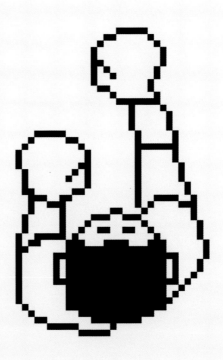

Captain Seahawk
Failed field test

Year: 1978
Developer: Atari
Platform: Arcade

Available to play
 Yes No

With the Atari Video Computer System (VCS) picking up a head of steam towards the end of the 1970s, it was not uncommon for Atari to pick from its very own arcade back catalogue for inspiration on what to release next. This meant that many of us had the ability to play conversions of classic arcade titles within our own homes, though with obvious compromises due to the vast differences in technology.

Taking a VCS title and creating an arcade conversion, on the other hand, was unheard of at the time but was exactly what Dave Stubben asked his team to do with *Captain Seahawk*. "At the time, I was the leader of a team that included some of the best developers – Mike Albaugh, Ed Logg and Dennis Koble," reflected Dave. "I think *Captain Seahawk* was my game idea, but I can't recall much from so long ago – now over 40 years."

You may not recognise the title in the VCS library, and this is because the game was based on a game called *Air-Sea Battle*, itself inspired by Atari's *Destroyer* and *Anti-Aircraft* arcades. *Air-Sea Battle* was one of the original launch titles for the VCS and consisted of 27 game variants on one cartridge – including anti-aircraft, torpedo, shooting gallery, polaris, bomber and polaris vs. bomber games. The most popular with gamers was the torpedo series of games (games 7–12), and the call to create *Captain Seahawk* was a result of that.

Assigned as developer to the project was Mike Albaugh, a stalwart within Atari's coin-op division and fresh from completing the well-received *Atari Football* arcade machine. When asked to convert the title, Mike had his reservations and warned management that, although the game was fun to play at home, it would likely never work in the arcade environment. It was decided to proceed anyway, regardless of concerns, and Mike (perhaps reluctantly) got to work on converting a title which he felt was doomed from the start.

Mike wasn't completely alone working on the game and had a team (managed by Dave Stubben) around him to help with particular aspects of development. "Core electronic teams consisted of an engineer, developer and technician, with typically either the engineer or developer as 'game designer'," explained Mike. "In this case, not a lot of game design was actually done. Dave Stubben would have been the engineer, but I don't recall if Joe Coddington or Steve Ehret was the technician. Since Steve was more familiar with the hardware, I'd guess him but not wager a lot on it."

Unfortunately, Dave could no longer remember specifics about the development, but he gave an insight into his role at the time. "I was involved in game ideas, hardware development and subsequently teaching the developer how to program the hardware, besides personnel management, reviews, etc.," he explained. "Many games were based on my hardware, even on games developed by other teams."

It wasn't initially clear if there was to be anything new added to the game or for it to be just a straight conversion. Surely there had to be something more substantial compared with the original game to gain interest? "My recollection was that I was supposed to do an exact port," Mike told us. "The graphics were certainly minimal, although we 'may' have taken advantage of the slightly higher horizontal resolution available."

"My recollection was that I was supposed to do an exact port."

Bizarrely, *Captain Seahawk* ended up becoming a development that went full circle. The hardware used was lifted straight from *Destroyer*, which was the original part inspiration for *Air-Sea Battle* in the first place. There were some modifications, with Mike asking Dave Stubben to remove expensive RAM chips that were handling the large motion objects, as well as increasing the non-maskable interrupt frequency. "Doing it in software was less of a pain in the arse than the 'helpful' hardware that *Destroyer* had!" Mike explained.

As a result of sharing the same hardware, the game ended up using the same 2-bit (four shades) colour system from black to white, which was common for most Atari arcade games of that time. Graphics were quickly interpreted by Mike and enhanced from the VCS version of the game by hand and were likely not too dissimilar to the style of those actually found in *Destroyer*. The background was likely kept relatively simple as well, not deviating much at all from the original game.

Sound for the game was somewhat 'custom', as it was for most Atari arcades of the time. Each game essentially had its own bespoke sound hardware developed, rather than a shared generic sound chip. The hardware would be built in a very specific way to achieve the exact sounds required for the game as a whole, which resulted in very high-quality output.

"Before the days of large, cheap ROMs and/or a tolerance for distorted, compressed sound, we made our very own sounds," Mike explained. "*Captain Seahawk* inherited the sound circuitry of the *Destroyer* board it was based on. The centrepiece of that was the ping-boom-bang circuit, which 'may' have been designed by Rich Patak or one of the Dave's (Stubben or Sherman)." Rich was later confirmed by Dave as having left before *Captain Seahawk* was started, which narrowed it down to either of the two Daves.

Within just six weeks, and thanks to being a simple port using pre-existing hardware, the game was ready for full-blown testing by the general public. Everything was also completed whilst juggling other new projects at the same time. "As I was finishing up, releasing one game, I'd be in mid-development on another, and maybe even doing some exploratory coding on a possibly modified existing board for a third," Mike recalled of their busy schedule.

When it came to field testing, it didn't take rocket science to go ahead and make use of an existing and modified *Destroyer* cabinet to save time. "The game was always intended to go in a *Destroyer* cabinet with a modified bezel," Mike recalled. "We drew cabinet design and panel art from George Opperman's group. I don't recall who, or if they'd like to be named if I did recall." Surprisingly though, the cabinet art produced was never actually used on the test cabinet, which could have helped to draw more players in perhaps.

As Mike had predicted from the very start, the game would fail spectacularly during testing. When pitted against the general public, the results were damning. "If I recall correctly, it collected something like $25 (100 plays) over the week it was out," Mike told us. "I don't know of anyone other than the original 'Marketroid' who didn't expect it to fail, but maybe I am biased."

Not only was the concept felt to be unremarkable to gain the interest of players, the lack of a computer-controlled opponent also limited it. Was this something that could have later been added? "A computer opponent was never asked for, and the schedule was very tight," Mike responded. "Maybe if it had got through testing, I'd have been asked to add AI."

The poor test results were enough to put *Captain Seahawk* out to sea and never be seen again. Due to the time period when the game was being built and how it was built, the likelihood of anything surviving is very slim. Did anything at all survive of the development that could be shown today?

"Doing it in software was less of a pain in the arse than the 'helpful' hardware that *Destroyer* had!"

"Not that I recall," Mike responded. "I may have a diazo print of the top of the bezel art, which might have been used on the test unit, but I haven't seen it in years. I also haven't run across any code, graphics or source." Although searches have proved fruitless so far, it is still plausible that something could surface someday, though not in time for this publication, unfortunately.

"It was basically just a quick project we all mostly wanted to forget!" concluded Mike. It does seem that, in this particular case, gamers didn't miss out on much, but, as with anything with the history of video games, it's a curiosity that many would like to see regardless of whether it was actually any good or not.

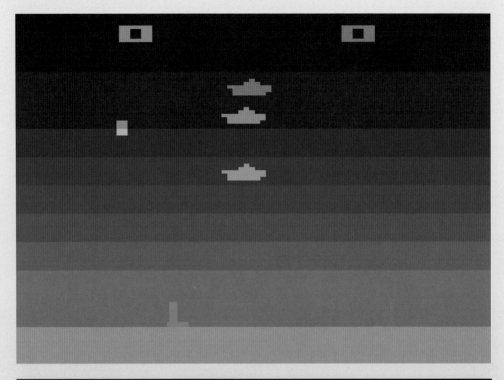

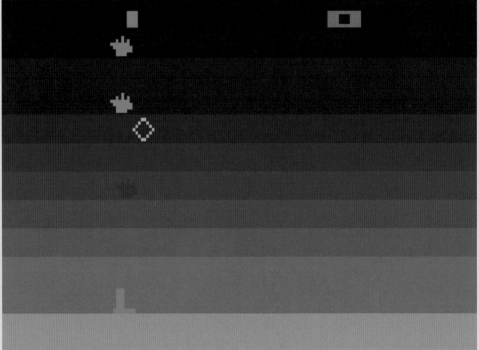

Above: Game 7 on *Air-Sea Battle* (Atari 2600) used as the template for *Captain Seahawk*.

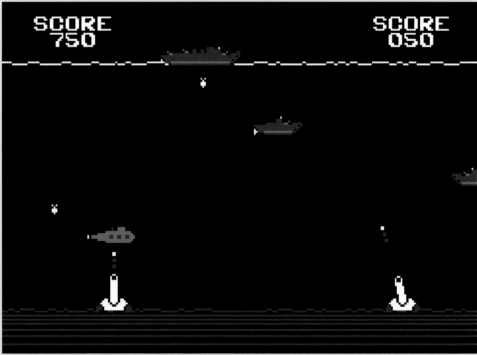

Above: Artist's impressions of how *Captain Seahawk* (arcade) may have looked based on developer recollections; essentially, a 2-bit high-resolution version of *Air-Sea Battle*.

Mini Golf Atari cancelled

Year: 1978
Developer: Atari
Platform: Arcade

Available to play
 Yes ◯ No

It wasn't just about shooting invaders from other galaxies when it came to early games. Atari's initial output didn't actually feature a huge amount of space-themed titles but did feature a plethora of sport/leisure themes, such as football and baseball. Even miniature golf could not escape Atari's runaway arcade train and was next in line for the company.

Compared with other unreleased Atari arcade games, there is very little documented about *Mini Golf*. It was not known exactly who was involved with the game, and there was hardly any recollection or memory of it by those who worked at Atari at the time. After some lengthy detective work, the developer was established to be a young engineer called Dan Moss. "I can't believe that anyone remembers *Mini Golf*!" exclaimed Dan, taken aback by the sudden interest in his game out of the blue.

Dan isn't an instantly recognisable name from the Atari stable, and this could well be due to the rather short period that he was present at the company. "I was there from mid-1977 to October 1979," he explained. "Noah Anglin was in charge of engineering; Lyle Rains managed coin-op, which had five teams, each with its own sub-manager and three to five game developers. I started out on Shalom Kass's team, then got sucked over to David Stubben's team."

Mini Golf was not Dan's first assignment at Atari either, an accolade that belonged to *Starship X*, sporting an ambitious free-standing design with a six-foot black fibreglass and hemispherical dome supported at a 45-degree angle above the player. "The player sat in a swivel 'space' chair with a 'laser' to shoot at enemy space crafts projected onto an expanding star field," Dan recollected. "I did the electronics, including detecting which spacecraft was hit, and all of the sounds."

The project was cancelled due to taking up too much floor space to be realistically marketable. Shortly afterwards, the teams were relocated to new premises. "We moved into a new engineering building (with the hot tub) in the spring of 1978 I believe. Coin-op engineering had a common cube space plus a lab area for each of the teams, and each developer had his own bench in the lab," Dan recalled. The hot tub was a 'pool of inspiration' for Atari, where the idea of *Mini Golf* first received its water birth. "Two or three times a year, Nolan Bushnell, Noah Anglin, Lyle Rains and a couple of other managers (plus a secretary who stayed sober) would soak in Nolan's hot tub and come up with game titles like *Buccaneer* and *Mini Golf*," Dan explained. "When a developer became available, he got the next title on the list. EVERYTHING else came from the creativity of the developer."

Following on from *Starship X*, Dan was now available, and *Mini Golf* was next on the list. There was no game design document to work from, and Dan would have full control over the direction. "Atari was the one and only time in my career that I was allowed to be creative. The rest of corporate America is 100-page design specifications that need to be approved by everyone and their dog. 'A camel is a horse designed by a committee'."

The game made use of the same hardware as *Sprint 2*, which came with a MOS 6502 processor (with two motion objects) and would share the same playfield code-base of the original racing game. The team had a black box development platform, which read from floppy disks and interacted with a *Sprint 2* motherboard hooked up to a black-and-white TV. Featuring a vertically orientated black-and-white CRT screen, the game utilised a 2-bit colour display with four shades from black to white and a resolution of 224×256 pixels overall. "I spent the first two weeks figuring out how the hardware worked and getting a ball with pointer to appear on the screen," Dan recalled. "Next, I had to figure out how to move the ball realistically, including through sand traps."

"I spent the first two weeks figuring out how the hardware worked and getting a ball with pointer to appear on the screen."

Dan had decided to go with an aerial-based viewpoint, including the option of one or two players, and covering a total of 16 holes. Each hole would consist of a single screen with a variety of obstacles, such as sand, water, walls (static and moving) and rough grass. Hills, sand and water were not depicted with any delicate shading to give a 3D effect. Due to the lack of colour available, it is spelled out to the player, with hills labelled with 'Uphill' or 'Downhill' (plus arrow icons), and appropriate friction applied to the ball as it moves over those areas.

"The gameplay (if you can call it that) was obvious," began Dan. "It was straightfoward to develop, but I had to remember my freshman physics to compute realistic ball action and deceleration. In case the player walked away from the game after ten seconds without making a stroke, a squirrel would appear on the edge of the screen. After another ten seconds without a stroke, the squirrel would run across the screen and grab your ball! This kept the game action moving along with the average, one-coin play time being less than four minutes overall."

Responsibility for all the graphics was another mystery. It was believed that Lyle Rains was the lead graphic artist, what with the lettuce-like bushes in *Mini Golf* being similar to Lyle's graphics in *Super Bug* (a top-down driving game designed and programmed by Howard Delman) that was developed for Kee Games the previous year. Almost every Atari Coin-op game at that time used the very same character set designed by Lyle, which was the case with *Mini Golf* too. However, Lyle had no recollection of the game at all. "He [Lyle] barely glanced at *Mini Golf*," Dan confirmed. "Roger [Hector] and one of his assistants actually did all of the main graphics for *Mini Golf*." Unfortunately, Roger had no recollection of the work at all, now clearly a memory completely lost to time.

Sound, on the other hand, was confirmed to have been handled by Dan himself, using a General Instruments sound chip to produce decent quality sounds. "I seem to remember that the sound chip would play a little tune in attract mode, a respectable 'thunk' when the ball hit, a scratchy sound when the ball rolled through a sand trap, and a squeak when the squirrel ran across – but that's all."

Thinking ahead for the final cabinet design, controls proved a challenge. "A standard trackball worked to set the direction for the ball, but how to 'hit' the ball?" Dan had initially pondered. "In the end, I used a pinball plunger with a magnet and a Hall effect sensor that would indicate how far back the plunger was pulled." This gave a satisfying way of applying power to strokes, without any clunky visual power gauge controlled with a single button.

Development was swift, taking just 3–4 months before the game was ready for field testing. "We were all turning out games at a fantastic rate – like throwing spit wads at the wall and seeing which ones stuck," Dan colourfully described. "The cabinetry was to be standardised: either a two-player stand-up or a two-player/four-player cocktail table."

A complete prototype cabinet was produced by the industrial designers upstairs at Atari, and a rare photo located at The Strong Museum shows that it was a stand-up cabinet, with a type of trackball moulded to look like a golf ball.

The marquee and cabinet artwork was produced by George Opperman's design team, believed to be mostly the work of Bob Flemate in the case of *Mini Golf*. The marquee was set up with blinking lights behind it to light up key parts of the image and logo. "The cabinet with graphics and the plex for *Mini Golf* showed up by magic, and I kept the plex," added Dan – referring to the marquee artwork, which you can see within these pages.

"After another ten seconds without a stroke, the squirrel would run across the screen and grab your ball!"

One coin would give you approximately 30 strokes to carry out in the game, an amount that could be adjusted by the coin operator in increments of five strokes. You would be placed on one of the 16 holes and would proceed to work your way through each of them. Strokes available only increased when you added more coins, and you were prompted to add more when you got low. Once you played all the holes, the game would simply loop around.

Testing had gone well – very well for couples playing the game. "I received a report from the field test that, during attract mode, the guys would roll the trackball while the girls flipped the plunger – you don't have to be [Federico] Fellini to figure that one out." (Referring to Italian film director Federico Fellini - well-known for his sexual innuendos.)

There were no fixes or changes requested at all. "At this point, Dave Stubben took *Mini Golf* away from me, and I was assigned a menial and dangerous task of etching printed circuit boards, so I received no more information." So why then was a fun, playable and complete interpretation of miniature golf never let out of the door in the end?

It is believed that, although the game was solid enough and fun, players just didn't take to it compared with other titles being tested at the time. Dan personally feels that the game was simply not appealing enough. "Our target player at the time was a 13-year-old, illiterate, male gorilla. We let him act out his fantasy to be totally destructive and anti-social without consequences. *Mini Golf* was not sufficiently anti-social and destructive."

It was a sad outcome for what was a good, solid game. Eventually, hearing that it would not be fully released was a contributing factor towards Dan leaving Atari. "At this point in time, I was burned out by the Silicon Gulch fast lane and I decided to move back to Indiana."

Mini Golf would make an appearance on the Atari 2600 the very same year (under the full name of *Miniature Golf*) as the arcade development. Developed by Tom Reuterdahl, it bears little resemblance to the arcade, with simplistic level designs and limited features. Although from the early days of VCS development, it wasn't greatly received, with Atari withdrawing the game from sale not too long after its release.

"We were all turning out games at a fantastic rate – like throwing spit wads at the wall and seeing which ones stuck."

In 1985, Bally Sente released their own *Mini Golf* game, sharing the same name as Atari's unreleased title. Comparing the two, the design similarly includes a trackball to control stroke direction but minus a plunger for stroke power. Considering that Bally Sente was set up by a number of ex-Atari employees (including Dennis Koble, Roger Hector, Ed Rotberg and Owen Rubin), you would think they were inspired by Dan's game. Dennis (the main designer on the Bally Sente game) confirmed that similarities were merely coincidental and he was not aware of the Atari arcade game at the time, though it's plausible that Roger Hector suggested the idea from his involvement on the original Atari game.

Shortly after leaving Atari, Dan heard rumours that a limited production run had actually taken place, but believes that only a few field test prototypes ever got produced. The game was soon forgotten, then appeared out of nowhere when it was made available in MAME around 2004, thanks to the efforts of Stefan Jokisch. Although playable, it currently lacks sound support, and, without a plunger or trackball available, it is difficult to aim or gauge power.

Either one or two players can play (represented at the top of the screen as 'White' and 'Black' for shots) by pressing the start button once or twice. The four-player cocktail edition is still at large, and it seems never made it to the prototype stage. A photo of a stand-up prototype PCB board (labelled A033252 and believed to be where the preserved ROM came from) can be found online, but just who owns it or how it came to surface is a mystery. It is hoped that, someday, a better emulated version will be made available, complete with the original sounds.

Dan reflects on his happy but brief time at Atari: "Every once in a while the stars and planets align – a magical place appears, such as Disney with *Snow White* and Pixar with *Toy Story*. Atari, during this all too brief period, was such a place. Nolan created an environment where we could try different things, limited only by our own creativity. When Nolan left, so did the magical environment."

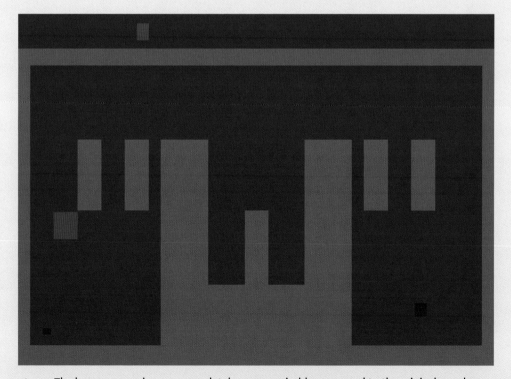

Above: The home conversion was completely unrecognisable compared to the original arcade game with many features missing – *Miniature Golf* (Atari 2600).

Above: An official Atari photo of the *Mini Golf* prototype cabinet, showing the golf ball-shaped controller and shot plunger.

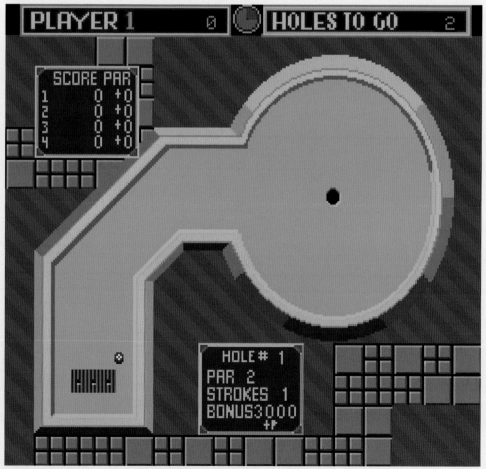

Top: The full-colour arcade marquee artwork for *Mini Golf* by Atari, courtesy of Dan Moss.
Bottom: Inspired by the Atari prototype? – *Mini Golf* (arcade) by Bally Sente.

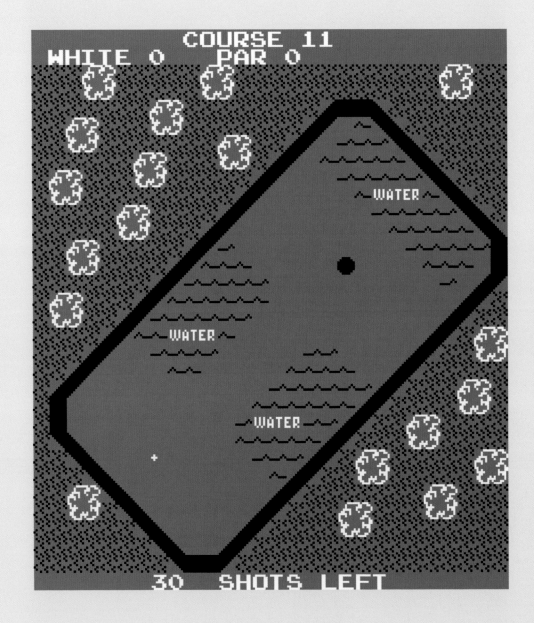

Above: *Mini Golf* (arcade). Course 11 from the recovered Atari arcade ROM showing the water obstacles in your path. Clearly labelled too to compensate for the limited shading available.

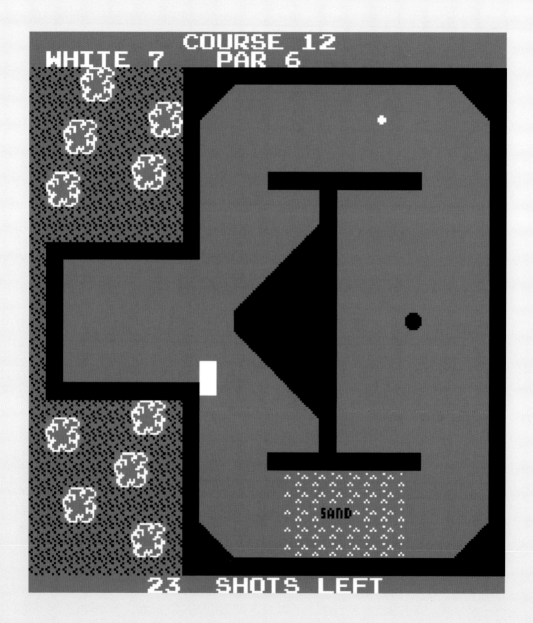

Above: *Mini Golf* (arcade). Course 12 has a slightly more complex layout, including a sand bunker to avoid (again clearly labelled for the uncertain players).

Discussing 'Wolf Pack' No fun factor

Year: 1978
Developer: Atari
Platform: Arcade

Sea-based games were popular back in the late 1970s, what with the release of Midway's arcade *Sea Wolf* in 1976 and *Air-Sea Battle* on the Atari 2600 in 1977. In 1978, Atari was about to add to the genre with a new arcade game with a twist – literally.

Wolf Pack gave the opportunity to take out ships using a realistic periscope embedded within a complex cabinet design. After production of a few field test prototypes, the game was cancelled. Members of Atari's coin-op division, Dennis Koble (DK), Dave Sherman (DS), Mike Albaugh (MA) and Dan Moss (DM) talk about the project and what happened.

How did the idea for *Wolf Pack* first come about?
DK: Midway's *Sea Wolf* was the catalyst. At that time, Atari did not have any products that involved an ocean environment, so, consequently, it seemed like a good idea, and many of Atari's employees played and liked *Sea Wolf* too.

As well as Dennis, there seem to be links with Steve Calfee, Dave Sherman, Mike Albaugh and Jerry Lichac. Did they all work on the game?
DS: Yes, I worked on *Wolf Pack*. I was a very junior engineer when I worked on the game (working title was *U-Boat* for a while). I had just been hired by Atari less than a year out of Berkeley as my first job, so I got put on as 'help' for a few projects to get me up to speed. I joined *Wolf Pack* in the middle when it was slightly in trouble from delays and mechanical frailty.

Available to play
◉ Yes ◯ No

DK: I don't remember Jerry Lichac at all. Nor do I believe Steve Calfee or Mike Albaugh (both good friends) ever worked on the game, although it is possible all three worked on it after I left the group. I do remember that (I think) Ed Logg took over for a short while after I left, but my memory could be faulty here.

MA: I recall Calfee having something to do with it and almost certainly Jerry. It was in the next lab over from our (Dave Stubben's) team, so I was aware of it but not really involved. Possibly some of my code for the position sensor was in there if it was a typical quadrature encoder as used for steering wheels (and, later, trackballs and the like), but *Sprint* used a steering wheel of that sort, so maybe Dennis had his own code.

"Lipkin definitely 'hated boat games'. And yes, he was capricious."

There was impressive sprite-scaling from Dave Sherman's 'growth-motion circuit', but also voice synthesis – possibly the first arcade to feature it?
DK: While it may have been the first, I can't say for sure. I saw and heard it in the online video of the gameplay, but we didn't have any at the beginning.

DM: Well, it was our first use of a voice synthesiser (probably the TI chipset used in the *See 'n Say*). When we were developing the speech synthesis, Mike quipped about an arcade full of games in attract mode arguing with each other: "Play me", "No, play me, I'm more fun", "Don't play him, he's no fun at all".

How was the impressive missile wake effect achieved?
MA: Dave Sherman designed the *Wolf Pack* wake, modulating a hardware-generated triangle with pseudo-random 'sparkle'. He later adapted it to use a bitmap, instead of the triangle generator, to allow arbitrary wake shapes for *HydroPlane* (another cancelled game). That version required software to draw into the bitmap, so 'weird programmer' (me) was enlisted.

DS: As I recall, the wake circuit was the same basic idea adapted from the patent, just from a different viewpoint. Expanding circles with stationary centres launched along the trajectory of the torpedo with white noise imposed as I recall.

The cabinet had an authentic submarine periscope and metal plating, with liquid producing a realistic waterline effect. Who came up with the design?
DK: Memory fails me here. It was an innovative design but, as with most things in life, innovation and originality usually come at a cost. The periscope tower made you want to try it out but also caused many problems to make it fully arcade proof. The viewing port between the player and the monitor also caused no end of problems for the mechanical aspect of the game. The project was also very long-lasting and troubled, primarily due to that design.

MA: The initial idea of the complex mechanical environment 'may' have come from a mechanical engineer whose name I do not recall but was possibly a guy called Phil. Not Phil Hash, whose was at Atari then, but he was a sparky or coder.

"It was also a long and troubled development."

How far could you rotate the periscope to locate ships?
DK: I believe it could only rotate 180 degrees or so – maybe less. I do believe, if memory serves me, that the periscope had a mechanical set of sensors that delivered the details of the position to the software.

I don't remember the exact details, though. I know that was another area of redesign at some point, when it was discovered early on that the sensors weren't accurate enough to deliver a real-time position to the software. That involved putting more sensors in, I believe.

DM: The periscope could rotate by at least 270 degrees and not all the way around. The periscope rotation used the standard steering wheel mechanism (a disc with notches around the perimeter and a pair of led sensors).

How long would a game like *Wolf Pack* have taken to develop?
DK: I really can't say, except to note it was a long time due to the technical issues. I was on the game for only a few short months (at most) and was also working on one or two other games which occupied most of my attention. I would say it was certainly more than a year though, and that was a long time for a game development cycle in those days.

"Sometimes, you have to acknowledge that you are just not the right person for a particular project."

Eventually, the game was cancelled, with only a handful of cabinets made. Was it true that Gene Lipkin cancelled *Wolf Pack* as he "hated boat games"?

DK: [Laughs] Well, that may well have been true as Gene was capricious at times. He had the ultimate power to cancel any game at any time, and he used that power often. I remember feeling a little fear of him as he was also loud and commanding. I do believe though that, ultimately, what caused him to cancel the game was simply that it wasn't fun.

MA: Lipkin definitely "hated boat games". And yes, he was capricious. Many games, by 1978 at least, had a 'Lipkin Switch' that could be thrown on, upon hearing him approach, and fake a hardware malfunction: "Sorry, Gene, have a little problem and can't show it today".

DK: It was also a long and troubled development. Back in those days, many of us felt you could 'save' a game by just tweaking it ad infinitum, but, later, I came to believe that it was generally not worth spending the extra resources and time to try to fix a broken concept. It didn't develop in a very satisfactory way, for me at least. *Wolf Pack* was a small part of my whole experience at Atari and was indeed a disappointment of mine, for which I take responsibility. It caught me at a transition time in my career at Atari, but I don't believe that was the reason for the game's lack of fun. Sometimes, you have to acknowledge that you are just not the right person for a particular project.

DS: I think big pieces like *Wolf Pack* were pretty self-limiting for the market they could get into, and I was actually glad when it got killed. I had already done interesting electrical design for it, and, when it got canned, I got to work on other projects like the '*Sprint on Water*' (*HydroPlane*) game that the patented wake circuit went into; it never made into production, again probably because "Gene hated boat games" [laughs]. And there was *Meteor Storm* which also never saw daylight, which was actually fun. After that, I got to do my own game design on *Missile Command* with Dave Theurer, which was the first electronics I was totally responsible for, so that was much more fun.

Oops! Failed field test

Year: 1979
Developer: Larry Rosenthal
Platform: Arcade

Available to play

 Yes No

When the topic of controversial games is broached, we often think of titles like *Mortal Kombat* and *Grand Theft Auto* – but such controversy existed at the beginning of the industry too. Exidy's *Death Race* and Atari's *Gotcha* are two prime examples of titles which ended up causing offence in one way or another.

Often, the controversy was deliberate as it would help to get the game into the media spotlight and more people wanting to experience it. Vectorbeam seemingly wanted a piece of the action too, with what was actually to be one of its last productions.

Vectorbeam was founded by Larry Rosenthal and Bill Cravens in 1978, after breaking away from Cinematronics. Bill was Larry's first sales manager and someone who had encouraged him to start his own company. They were well-known for producing a Transistor-Transistor Logic (TTL)-based Vectorbeam board for vector graphics-based games, which was then licensed to Cinematronics as well as being used for their own games. It was just a year into Vectorbeam's existence when Larry decided to sell the company to Cinematronics. Following the sale, Larry began working on his own game during his personal time, using his own personal development tools. The game would become *Oops!*

Dan Sunday was working alongside Larry as his main programmer and, at the time, was working on a game that would become *Tail Gunner*. "In all game development, Larry was in charge," explained Dan. "He did all the hardware, and I did all the software development. We collaborated on developing ideas for game enhancements." However, in the case of *Oops!*, this was just Larry's own project, including all of the programming duties.

Oops! was pretty wild as a concept; even in this modern era, it would still probably cause offence. Larry's prototype kicked things off with a human egg situated at the centre of the screen, with sperm swimming onto the screen from various directions to try and fertilise the egg. Beginning life as just a two-player game, one player would control the large group of sperm; the other player would control a syringe which fired sperm-killing foam to try and protect the egg from being fertilised.

"I have a vague recollection of Larry showing me his first prototype of the game, where the syringe could be flown around the screen, much like a spaceship. An important aspect was the control of the attacking sperm," Dan recalled. "They would always move in random directions, but the directions could be rotated either clockwise or counter-clockwise by the player. When the player used this control, all sperm on the screen would change direction simultaneously."

This meant that the controlling player knew which individual sperm they were trying to direct in the attack. The other defending player would not and only saw the whole group rotating together, providing an element of uncertainty. "As time progressed in the game, the rate of sperm entering the screen would increase, eventually overwhelming the defender. There was no time-out to end the game," Dan explained. A percentage of fertilisation was also displayed on the screen, where the game would end if it ever reached 100%, with the words 'OOPS!' plastered across the screen to signify that it was game over.

Dan suggested that part of the inspiration behind *Oops!* was down to a young lady that Larry was infatuated with at the time. Larry didn't agree with Dan's recollection when talking about the game at the California Extreme show in July 2014, so we got in touch and asked what really inspired its creation. "I, unfortunately, don't remember my exact thinking from almost 40 years ago," Larry began. "I had just built *Oops!* with the hope that it would be a popular game and make lots of money. I probably did hope that the theme would get me some publicity as well."

With a playable build eventually complete, Larry was keen to see how the game would fare with the public. He brought the game temporarily out of the research and development lab with a few basic additions, including a newly added coin-controlled timer. "The game was tested in a *Scramble* (people have heard about, but never seen one – the 50 or so *Scramble* games that were built shipped out in a single container to somewhere in Africa) cabinet which was tested in an arcade in Berkeley," recalled Larry. "I also gave a cabinet to my wife, who was working in a small town in Washington at the time. She set it up there, so I could get a federal registration on the name *Oops!*"

"I probably did hope that the theme would get me some publicity."

The *Scramble* cabinet (not to be confused with the Konami 1981 game) used had originally featured dial knobs, like those used with Atari *Pong*. These were replaced with a series of push buttons that *Oops!* would use for its own control system. Larry believed that push buttons were a far more responsive control method overall.

Whilst the game tested in Berkeley, Larry kept a close eye on proceedings. "I remember watching people play. I set it up so you would get infinite play based on how many quarters you would put in," he recalled. "The first person I watched play put several quarters in – then walked away with three minutes of time remaining on the game! I then knew there was nothing in it. It took a few quarters overall, but it was just not exciting enough."

The game was playable to a degree, with some innovative ideas for the time, but flaws badly hindered it. For instance, there was the lack of a single-player mode, the syringe almost always won due to its free movement, the game concept was confusing to some users, and others were just put off by the content. Larry got to work on trying to fix some of the issues found, dropping the time concept and attempting to shape things into a more accessible game. "I think there was a small time-lapse added for the syringe to recharge, but this didn't help," Dan recalled. "So the syringe was moved to the screen's centre, where it could only rotate/pivot about that point. This worked somewhat better, but the rapidly increasing sperm now had a large advantage."

Just before *Oops!* had been started, Vectorbeam had been really struggling financially, only a year into its founding. Cinematronics was offered the vector system patents and Vectorbeam in exchange for an undisclosed sum and taking over the Vectorbeam debt. It jumped at the opportunity. "Jim Pierce and 'Papa' Tom Stroud were set to gain plenty – Larry Rosenthal's patents," explained Tim Skelly in a 1999 interview (www.dadgum.com/giantlist/archive/cinematronics). "They had been paying (or were supposed to pay) a licensing fee to Larry for every game sold. Now they wouldn't have to."

"The defending space station player could only see the whole hoard of ships, all rotating at once."

Tommy Stroud (son of 'Papa' Tom Stroud) would take charge and set up in Vectorbeam's front office at its Bay Area location. Production would continue on existing products, some released under the Vectorbeam label and others under Cinematronics. With *Oops!* under development in the R&D lab as a non-Vectorbeam development, two new secretaries (employed as part of the Cinematronics takeover) caught a glimpse of the game. They ran out, exclaiming to everyone that "They've got sperm on the TV monitor!"

It was pretty amusing to the team at least, though concerns over the content material had been a cloud hanging over the project for a while now. This incident had seemingly helped Larry to see that this was a game that was not going to be marketable to arcades, which included mostly young children.

Since Cinematronic's acquisition, Larry began to really cut back on his involvement at Vectorbeam. He stayed on for a little while longer but would eventually leave just before Cinematronics closed the doors on the company in late 1979. Larry had originally considered taking the *Oops!* concept with him and selling to another company, but there were contractual non-compete issues with the game. Also, using the Vectorbeam technology would mean having to license it from the new owners, Cinematronics, so Larry decided to call time on the game. *Oops!* was left in a state of limbo in the R&D lab.

After pretty much completing *Tail Gunner*, Dan decided to rework Larry's *Oops!* concept as a new project. A major overhaul would result, seeing the original theme dropped (including the name) and new ideas brought in to salvage the project, which would remain as a two-player only game for now. Originally, Dan suggested that he had jumped on board to help Larry rework the game, but Larry could not recall the transformations and felt that it must have been after he had left Vectorbeam.

"The egg and syringe were changed into a space station ship, and the sperm became attacking spaceships," explained Dan. "There were still many of these attacking ships entering the screen as a hoard, and only the attacking player knew which ship was turning in to attack. The defending space station player could only see the whole hoard of ships, all rotating at once."

The issue still remained with the disadvantaged central piece (now the space station) being rooted to the centre of the screen. As a result, three layers of shields were added around the space station, which rotated in alternating directions when the player rotated. "These were originally displayed as bricks and not just line segments," recalled Dan. "The attacker would now have to break through all three layers of shields to destroy the space station." The game was practically unrecognisable from the original concept that Larry had produced and was now finally becoming something playable and, crucially, marketable to arcade distributors.

"It took a few quarters overall, but it was just not exciting enough."

Not long after the takeover, Tim Skelly (at the time, recently employed as a designer and programmer at Cinematronics) paid a visit to evaluate what software assets Vectorbeam had, and he met with Dan. After the completed *Tail Gunner* was demoed to him, Tim asked what else was being worked on, and it was then that the newly reworked *Oops!* concept was demonstrated to Cinematronics for the first time. At this stage, no new name had yet been given.

"On the screen was a *Space War*-type ship surrounded by a couple of rotating rings of rectangular blocks," recalled Tim back in 1999. "The player controlled this ship, and the rings moved as the ship moved. What I saw, in addition to that, was a flock of what looked like giant snowflakes. These moved towards the player's ship with increasing speed. When a 'snowflake' collided with a brick, the brick disappeared. Eventually, enough bricks were knocked out, and enough snowflakes got through to destroy the player's ship. The End. Game Over."

The revolving rings idea caught Tim's attention, but he didn't feel the game was that playable. "The demo wasn't very good since, eventually, the player would be overwhelmed by sheer numbers – no real defence strategy except rotate and shoot like hell," he remembered. "Worse, because of the size of the rings, if the player moved the ship to attack or dodge, it was likely that they would move the shield blocks right into the attacking snowflakes."

Development paused whilst *Tail Gunner* was polished up for release by Cinematronics, but this was to be Dan's last game for the company after deciding to move back to the East coast 2–3 months after the acquisition.

All was not lost. The initial embryo of *Oops!* would live on, thanks to Tim Skelly. Not too long after his visit to Vectorbeam, Tim began working on a new game called *Rip-Off*. However, newly recruited Scott Boden needed a new project to work on, so Tim would arrange a design for him as a result. Inspired by the rotating shield rings from Dan's modifications, Tim devised a new game with that concept and started a basic design for Scott to work with.

"I put the enemy inside of the rings and anchored it to the centre. The player would have a free-moving ship, much like those in *Space War*," explained Tim in 1999. "The player's goal was to shoot through the rings and hit the enemy. This was made more interesting by the fact that the enemy's shots, very accurate and deadly, could not pass existing ring segments. This meant that, by shooting out the shield, the player was shooting away the one thing that was protecting them from that nasty gun in the centre. I cut the shield segments down to lines instead of blocks (fewer unnecessary lines) and added more rings."

Star Castle was born. A brand-new game, taking just the rotating rings and centred player as inspiration from the original demo that Tim had seen back at Vectorbeam. It has been suggested that the original code from the *Oops!* prototype lived on in the game, but that wasn't the case.

"All of the code was written from scratch, some of it lifted from *Clown Skeet*, a practice game I was working on," recalled Scott Boden. "Tim's instruction to me was, essentially, to shoot through rings to hit the centre ship, the centre ship shoots back. The number of rings, the number of segments, gnats, etc. were all a function of the hardware limitations."

"I had no idea that *Oops!* had anything to do with the creation of *Star Castle!*" exclaimed a surprised Larry when informed of how his game had gone on to inspire the title. *Star Castle* went on to do particularly well indeed and is still fondly remembered today. Just to think, if it wasn't for Larry's prototype (and Dan's modifications), it may never have existed – or could have at least been very different.

After over 40 years, you'd be forgiven to think that the original *Oops!* game is now long gone. However, Larry offered hope. "I saved all my electronics. I also saved all my development notes – both hardware and software," he told us. "However, I left the prototype cabinet outside next to the garage for several years, and the particle board started to rot. Unfortunately, I didn't realise at the time that the *Scramble* cabinet would be a collector's item. I finally put it in the garbage about ten years ago."

But, of course, there were two field test prototypes built, and it was just the Berkeley one which had succumbed to time. "I actually pulled out a logic board that was shipped back from Washington," Larry continued. "The box had been sitting there, sealed for 25 years. I opened it for the first time three months ago! The phosphor on the inside of the CRT had numerous burn marks (if something goes wrong with the electronics, the electron beam inside the CRT can burn the phosphor coating), but the board was intact. I unplugged the board from the *Space War* game I had, plugged it in... Sperm appeared on the screen! Unfortunately, I couldn't play the game as I couldn't get it to recognise the switch in the coin mechanism and enter play mode."

Promising news, but, unfortunately, the game was only to run for a short time before halting completely. Luckily, not before Larry had taken a video of the game attract mode at the time on his phone, which helped to create the artist's impressions. The short video clip is available on the Games That Weren't website.

There could be more to come soon too, as Larry concludes: "At the California Extreme game convention, I gave my *Oops!* board to a friend from Texas a few years ago, who has repaired many Cinematronics and Vectorbeam boards. He is going to try and get the game running again for me." Therefore, someday soon, we could all be seeing flying sperm on our screens – perish the thought!

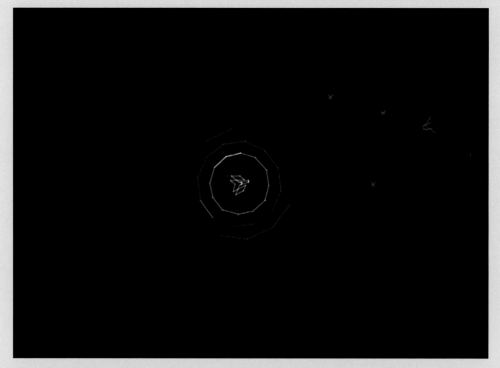

Above: Star Castle (arcade), the game *Oops!* had indirectly inspired and showing the rotating walls around the player, which had sort of originated from Dan's update of Larry's game.

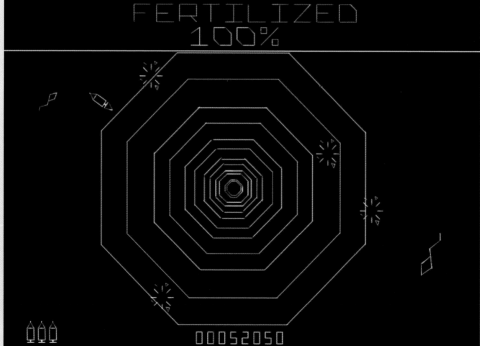

Above: An artist's impression of how *Oops!* (arcade) may have looked, based on Larry's descriptions and rare video footage.

Sebring Cabinet production too costly

Year: 1979
Developer: Atari
Platform: Arcade

Available to play
 Yes No

During the influx of *Pong*-themed games throughout the 1970s, early arcade gamers were also treated to a healthy dose of car games too. By 1979, Atari had already released such games in the shape of *Gran Trak 10/20*, *Le Mans*, the *Sprint* series and *Night Driver* amongst others. Most of the microprocessor-based games were designed from an overhead viewpoint with single colour graphics, *Night Driver* being the exception at the time, consisting of a more realistic first-person perspective.

In 1976, Atari licensed a mechanical-based racing game developed by Namco called *F-1*. The game used an electromechanical projection technique, with a rear-lit projector and a track made from a circle of plastic and transparent track graphics overlaid. Light would shine through the plastic and project the track onto a large piece of frosted plastic. The cars (coloured transparent plastic pieces) were projected in the same way and would move up and down the track. Your own car would feature at the bottom and could move left or right to avoid other cars and keep within the track. An accelerator allowed you to change the speed of the spinning disk that gave the illusion of the track moving. It was a simple but effective and fun game for the time.

That game would inspire a brand-new racing title from Atari's own stable called *Sebring*, a microprocessor-based development by Owen Rubin (game design and programming), Jed Margolin (hardware engineering) and Karen Bjorkquist (assembler assistance) – created at 1272 Borregas in Sunnyvale. "We originally had an *F-1* cabinet at Atari, and I liked the feeling of driving it," recalled Owen. "We thought we could do this as a real video game so took the hardware of another Atari title called *Sky Raider* and modified it to do a track effect."

Sky Raider (thought to be one of the first vertically scrolling shooting games) had just been released the previous year by Atari, featuring an impressive smooth scaling effect which Owen and Jed felt was ideal for their new game. Although *Night Driver* was also a microprocessor-based first-person driving game, the technology used from *Sky Raider* meant that *Sebring* would look and feel more realistic. "Unlike *Night Driver*, where the car was still and the track moved left and right, with *Sebring*, the track moved and you had to steer to stay on the track," explained Owen. "If I recall, the bonnet of the car was displayed at the bottom of the screen and also shook as you drove."

The aim of the game was to drive around Florida's Sebring International Raceway track, avoiding collision with other cars and obstacles thrown in front of you. "I think we added oil/water patches which could cause you to lose control for a moment, but mostly it was about going as far and as fast as you can whilst avoiding cars," recalled Owen. "There were signs and billboards that went by on the side of the track, but they were only there to give the feeling of motion. We did not have fuel or extra time from what I recall. The game score was based strictly on distance, so I suspect there was a high-score table involved."

Compared with the black-and-white *Sky Raider*, *Sebring* featured colour graphics and made use of 'stamp hardware' to create a playfield displaying game objects, scores and times.

"Almost all Atari games of the era used stamp hardware for playfield and text," Owen began. "All the scores, text, and much of the playfield graphics would be done with that hardware. A stamp playfield is made up of a number of stamps that 'tile' the playfield. Each stamp may be one of, say, 256, 8×8 or 16×16 bit graphics item that are displayed from a ROM. In a colour stamp system, the bits in the stamp were typically 4-bits deep, or one of 16 colours. But each bit could be its own colour, so you could create 'stamps' with multiple colours, and multiple stamps could be put side by side to make larger graphics."

"The graphics were designed to 'loop' on themselves so that the track would seem infinite."

The track drawing routine would use a special memory-mapped scrolling playfield, where the hardware would do all the scaling and morphing grunt work for the curved track. "A memory location's value would tell the hardware where to start, in another graphics ROM, displaying the graphics in the scrolling area," explained Owen. "By changing the value of the memory location, the track would appear to move down the screen by simply starting later and later in the memory. The graphics were designed to 'loop' on themselves so that the track would seem infinite."

"The playfield memory used a Variable Frequency Oscillator (VFO) for its clock," added Jed. "This was clocked out faster at the top of the screen and slowed down as it went down the screen. It gave the illusion of perspective. The frequency control came from a ROM connected to the vertical line counter, so no programming was required. I think that had come from *Sky Raider*."

Objects, such as cars and roadside objects, were rendered over the top using sprites or motion objects, which could be moved arbitrarily around on the screen. The stamp hardware allowed the team to set different scale levels on the objects and give the illusion of them appearing from a distance.

To increase the realism, it was decided to make *Sebring*'s cabinet sit-down-based, featuring a steering wheel, pedals and brakes. The display consisted of a large 25-inch colour monitor seated above the player, which was a cunning way to use up surplus monitors, according to Jed. "The display was very cool as the monitor was reflected in a curved mirror, so it made the image VERY large, and gave a real 3D effect as well," recalled Owen. "So now you had a first-person driving game with an optical '3D' illusion system to make it feel more realistic. And, of course, the giant speaker under the seat not only made very low rumbling sounds but also vibrated the seat as well."

Due to a bug with the sound hardware, the speaker under the seat would additionally make a large bang sound when the engine first started. This actually worked out to be quite effective, leading to Owen and Jed keeping it within the game as a 'feature'.

It was suggested that Paul Mancuso had done a lot of the technical work on the game. Although Paul had initially confirmed his involvement, he later retracted, feeling that he had got mixed up with another project. "I had nothing to do with *Sebring*," he concluded. "I saw it in a lab though, and the cabinet is familiar, but I never worked on it. I don't know who the tech was on that project." This surprised both Jed and Owen, who could not think who else it may have otherwise been.

After approximately six months of development work, *Sebring* was ready to be unleashed for some early testing. "We did field tests fairly early on to get feedback," recalled Owen. "It did great as a 50-cents game. New for that age. It was practically complete, but there was a lot more that I wanted to add, including bonus times, other obstacles, and maybe even things you had to pick up to get extra points."

Owen would hope to get these additional features squeezed in along with any final bug fixes reported from the field testing. However, the project would surprisingly hit a brick wall, followed by the abrupt cancellation of the game. The reasons why this occurred exactly are slightly hazy, with Jed initially suggesting that the cabinet vendor just didn't want to make the game. Owen felt that there were other reasons. "I'm not sure what is correct, but I can tell you what I believe," Owen began. "There were several issues. The 25-inch colour monitor and cabinet were expensive and quite top-heavy. The idea of hanging a 25-inch colour monitor above the head of the player worried some people. But, there was also another driving game being done by my boss at the time (Steve Calfee), and, even though *Sebring* earned more money, it was a LOT more expensive to make, so got cancelled in favour of the other game."

"The display was very cool as the monitor was reflected in a curved mirror, so it made the image VERY large."

Jed also felt that the cheap solution to the curved mirror might have been a contributing factor too. "Since the curve was set by stuffing a flat (plexiglass) mirror into wooden guides, it was optically rather poor and gave the player a headache – this was the Mechanical Group's idea of how to make a cheap mirror." he explained.

Whatever the reason, in the end, this was the loss of an exciting and technically advanced title, which could have blown everyone away. Though maybe the fear of players being blown away by a 25-inch monitor falling onto them was too great? With much time and effort put into the title, it's easy to imagine how the developers must have felt about the outcome. "We used to call this the 'ugly baby syndrome'. It didn't matter if the game was great or not; it was your baby, and you do not want anyone telling you it is awful or ugly," Owen reflected. "For sure, I was quite upset about it. At the time, I felt it was a conflict of interest that my boss got to choose, and, of course, he would choose his own game. In reality and hindsight, there was a lot more to it. But it was sad nonetheless to see a lot of work just get tossed away."

"The idea of hanging a 25-inch colour monitor above the head of the player worried some people."

The big question was whether Atari missed an opportunity with the game, considering the innovations within it. "Who really knows?" Owen pondered. "There is no way to know how well a game will do in the field. That is why we field test and all. But, looking back now, if this game had been built, it probably would not have done as well as other games just because of the size of the large cabinet. That would have seriously limited who could have bought it or put it in many locations."

Jed believes that many innovations from *Sebring* would later turn up in other games, much to his and Owen's annoyance. So, which game would it have been most comparable with in time? "*Pole Position*," stated Owen. "The main difference was that *Sebring* only went around in a circle. Otherwise, it is VERY similar."

With *Sebring* permanently parked and titles such as *Pole Position* later taking the plaudits, Jed and Owen moved on to new projects, and the title was long forgotten. It was not until the dawn of the Internet that sketchy details of the game began to surface. Compared with other unreleased Atari arcade titles, *Sebring* is yet to surface in any physical shape or form to be preserved. Unfortunately, both Jed and Owen confirmed that they no longer had anything of the game to help change that situation.

Jed suggested that Paul Mancuso was likely the last person to have seen a prototype of the game and could still have something. Though with Paul confirming no involvement on the project, and it not being known exactly who the technician was, the game is still no closer to being found. As the game's 40th anniversary passes, will *Sebring* ever make it to the races?

Intriguingly, Paul originally suggested that he once had the prototype and passed it over to Atari Museum's Curt Vendel for safekeeping. It would be quite something if Curt did indeed have the game, but surely a big reveal would have happened by now if that was the case? The search goes on in the hope that another piece of Atari history can finally be restored.

Above: An official Atari photo of the *Sebring* prototype cabinet. The search goes on in the hope it will surface someday.

Above: *Sky Raider* (arcade), released in 1978 by Atari and featuring the same scaling technology which *Sebring* used for its track display and scaling.

Above: *Pole Position* (arcade) – the 1982 classic racer released a few years after *Sebring*, but which the team felt shared similarities.

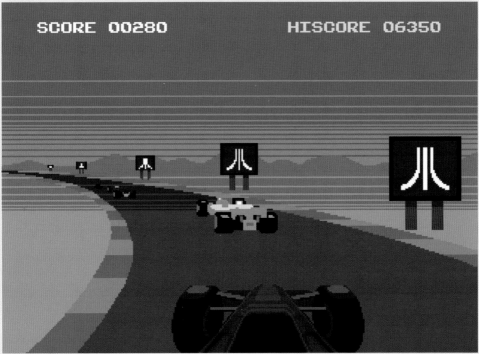

Above: Artist's impressions of how *Sebring* (arcade) may have looked, based on developer recollections. Featuring a standard score panel and prominent car front.

Nineteen Eighty — Nineteen Eighty Nine

The decade where the industry really went into overdrive. Games were becoming more readily available in shops, and there was a massive choice too. It wasn't just the question of what game to play or purchase, but also which platform – with a flood of consoles and home computers produced. The choice was almost to the point of madness, and many failed and became lost in a jungle of hardware releases.

Overexpansion and saturation contributed towards the US video game crash of 1983, causing the collapse of not only games but companies too. Elsewhere, it wasn't as noticeable, though many hardware and software companies would still fall by the wayside, losing out to certain key players in the industry as the years progressed. Even so early in the timeline, the 1980s had many gaming casualties – so many, you could probably write an entire book just on this decade.

Conquest
Put on hold and never resumed

Year: 1982
Developer: Vid Kidz
Platform: Arcade

Available to play
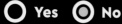 Yes No

When *Defender* first blasted into arcades in 1980, game players were mesmerised by the wonderfully energetic graphics, sound and gameplay. The success of the title led to the formation of Vid Kidz by Eugene Jarvis and Larry DeMar in 1981, a venture that may have only lasted a few years but resulted in three further amazing arcade titles with *Stargate*, *Robotron: 2084* and *Blaster*. Unbeknown to many, there was one other title that showed initial promise but was eventually superseded by a title with far more promise.

Stargate, a follow-up to *Defender*, had just been finished and handed over to Williams for release towards the end of 1981. It was now time to strike whilst the iron was still hot and produce the next big hit. With two great minds on hand, both Larry and Eugene set off on their own separate pathways, each starting new projects. Eugene got stuck into a vibrant and wild shooter that would go on to become *Robotron: 2084*, while Larry decided to go down a multidirectional scrolling space shooter route with *Conquest*.

Development had originally been slow going at Vid Kidz, using just a single 1MHz 6809 Motorola EXORciser development system that resulted in Larry developing during the night and Eugene during the day. Following on from *Stargate*, Larry and Eugene rented an office together and brought in two development systems, where they would create a brand-new development environment and be able to turn their games around in quicker fashion.

Conquest was a raster-based game set in an *Asteroids*-like environment. "Rather than fighting just rocks, it was a battle to dominate the universe with other players and AI," recalled Eugene of Larry's new development. "You were a ship, roughly in the centre of a 2D universe that, like *Defender*, was much larger than the visible screen," added Larry. "It played with controls like Midway's *Omega Race*, where you had a wheel for rotation (like in Atari's *Tempest*) and two buttons for thrust and fire. *Defender*'s ship would slide around in one dimension, but the *Conquest* ship would slide around in two dimensions to keep you away from what you were flying at."

Played out on a vertical display, the play area was set in open space, where you fly around freely in multiple directions. For each level, the aim was to destroy a set of planets before you could move on to the next level. It came with a scanner that would indicate what planets were left to destroy, sharing much in common with the previous *Defender*/*Stargate* developments.

During its early prototype stage, the target hardware had not been fully decided upon, with *Stargate*'s hardware used as a starting point. The game also started off with simplistic placeholder graphics, focusing fully on getting the game's core engine up and running first. "The ship that we created (which would have been replaced) was initially an homage to the ship from Nutting Associates' *Computer Space*," explained Larry.

The *Computer Space*-like ship was a rotatable white rocket that could fire multi-coloured fireballs. Planets were initially represented by circular pods that colour-cycle and launch slow-moving missiles at your ship (looking similar to the Space Hums from *Stargate*). Missiles could be destroyed, just like the planets themselves, and destroying a planet would result in a satisfying circular ringed explosion, which would be later reused as a special effect in *Blaster* and its time tunnel level.

After a short while, the scanner and score panel areas were fully functional, with lives simply represented as dots. The top-right panel was not being used for anything just yet. Placeholder sounds were included for now, borrowed from *Defender* to set up a decent enough showcase for the project and give a good indication of what was to come.

It is likely that the eventual hardware used for *Robotron: 2084* would have also been used for *Conquest*. "*Robotron*'s hardware didn't exist at the time, but it would have been a good match for *Conquest* with the pioneering *Robotron* graphics coprocessor," suggested Eugene. Regardless of the limited hardware initially available, both developments were shaping up nicely and were becoming more playable by the day.

However, there was still plenty of work to be done to get near to a field testing phase. "There was very little game there at the time," explained Larry. "I had only created the 2D scrolling world, the ship control, the scanner, the ship's fireball shots, the collision detection and explosions, and enemy tracking for the end of a wave." There were many notable gaps to fill overall, with a lack of player explosion when you died, and just a simple blank attract screen that slowly cycled through colours."

"At the same time, the team also learnt that Stern was working on a sequel to *Berzerk*."

More enemies, levels and better graphics and sounds were all required; not to mention planned multiplayer and enhanced AI features within the game. "The broad plan was to have planets around the universe, with you doing battle in the greater universe or coming into range of a planet where you could possibly zoom in and battle in a macroscopic view of the planet," explained Larry. "This would provide a much richer environment for cooperative or player-vs.-player multiplayer experiences. Those aspects were not at all developed, though."

Around two months into both of their developments, the Vid Kidz team learnt of a new project underway at Williams called *Sinistar*, which was surprisingly similar to their *Conquest* prototype. Larry and Eugene were immediately concerned that Williams would never consider publishing such a similar game at the same time, especially from an outside group.

"At the same time, the team also learnt that Stern was working on a sequel to *Berzerk*," added Larry. "We decided to, therefore, double the effort to get *Robotron* out ahead of the new Stern game."

"There was very little game there at the time."

Eugene and Larry felt there was something special taking shape with *Robotron: 2084*, and it was a title that could blow the previous success of *Defender* out of the water. Therefore, they didn't want to miss the opportunity and lose out to Stern. With *Sinistar* already well in development at Williams, Vid Kidz decided to shelve *Conquest* and decide later if they would resume the project.

Comparing *Sinistar* with Larry's early prototype, there are clear resemblances, with a ship in the centre of the screen and a scanner to show the location of enemies. "The concept was a very logical extension of the *Asteroids/Space War* world to multiscreen 2D – so developers could easily and independently come to the same idea," Eugene explained.

However, Vid Kidz felt that they had instantly missed the boat when they postponed the game. "If we'd concentrated on it, we probably would've beaten *Sinistar* to market by a year," Larry suggested. Thankfully, *Robotron: 2084* went on to become the major success anticipated, so it wasn't so bad in the end for the duo. But was *Sinistar* inspired by the original Vid Kidz game in any way?

Sinistar was originally born as a simple demo written by Sam Dicker and Lou Harp. "Long before it was named, it started out as a test for a new game engine. I wanted to test collisions and different types of 2D 'physics'," explained Sam. "There was a scrolling field of asteroids that I think were inspired by Atari *Asteroids*, but raster instead of vector. A sort of 'rasteroids'." Williams loved it, setting up a team including John Newcomer, Noah Falstein, Jack Haeger, Python Anghelo, Rich Witt and RJ Mical to help finish the game.

Interestingly, Sam had worked with Eugene and Larry on *Defender*, and so was close to the team, but he confirmed that there was no link. "I never heard of or saw *Conquest*," he began. "I think I only visited Vid Kidz once briefly after they completed *Stargate* and were developing *Robotron 2084* at that point." Larry also suggested that Vid Kidz were reasonably secretive, so any similarities were merely coincidental.

In a bizarre twist, around the same time as *Conquest*'s development, a game show called *Starcade* in the United States featured a star prize that looked familiar. A title called *Journey* (not to be confused with the 1983 Bally Midway arcade game of the music group) had been built by Stern. It had decided not to release the game, and the game show was provided with two prototypes as unique prizes for the winners.

Tago Electronics then later licensed the game from Stern and renamed it *Conquest* of all names (and is also currently unpreserved today). Yet again, it was a mere coincidence, with Vid Kidz's *Conquest* and Stern/Tago's game being very separate developments, as with *Sinistar*. Eugene felt that the idea of a ship in expanded space with a scanner was a concept that was clearly popular at that time.

Vid Kidz's own development would never be resumed, with the development team disbanding in 1984. Left to gather dust for many decades, freelance writer Paul Drury ran a *Desert Island Discs* article for *Retro Gamer* magazine in 2010 that focused on Larry's past work. Resulting from this was the mention of *Conquest*. No prototype cabinet had been created of the game, though Larry disclosed that he had kept all of his source code as both he and Eugene were meticulous at archiving their work – and *Conquest* still existed.

"The concept was a very logical extension of the *Asteroids/ Space War* world to multiscreen 2D."

Digital Eclipse and Jeff Vavasour had worked with Larry back in 1996 to produce the *Williams Arcade's Greatest Hits* compilation for multiple platforms. For the project, Jeff was given sources for most of the games, which included remains of the *Conquest* prototype. It was from this that a PC executable was first produced. Larry more recently dug up planning and internal workings for *Conquest*, depicted on graph paper, which you can see within these pages.

"In the picture showing the ship on graph paper, you can see how it matches the 'diode memory' image of the *Computer Space* ship, literally drawn on the circuit board using diodes for pixels," explained Larry. "The little red '+' in each image is the coordinates where bullets first appear. The number table and starburst mathematically show the components for thrust and bullet trajectories based on the orientation of the nose of the ship (24 positions around the compass). The red lines are the 24 positions to show the ship's image. With the blue lines, the game actually plays at twice this resolution in rotation. Turning the tempest wheel provides 48 steps of rotation, with each step causing thrusting and firing 7.5 degrees beyond the previous stop. However, the image is rotated every other step, thus rotates 15 degrees for every two steps."

As for the game itself, it is yet to be made available for emulators such as MAME, but that may well happen someday soon. Larry gave his blessing for the game to be made available when asked, so Jeff has been duly notified. There isn't much to see, mind you, but it is nonetheless a piece of Vid Kidz history that will certainly be worth playing someday. Just watch this space!

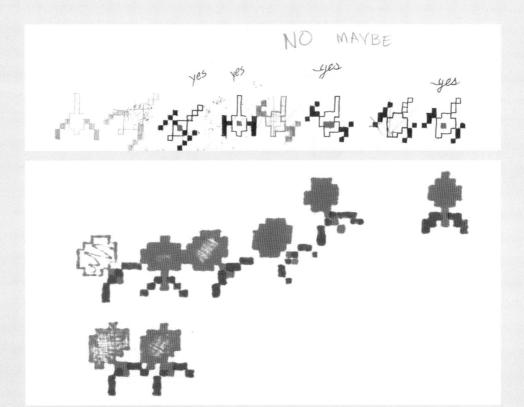

Above: Unused ship designs for the game created by Larry, done on grid paper to later be translated across.

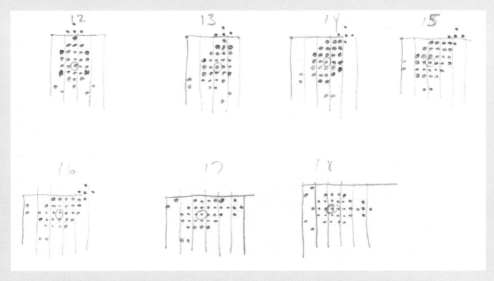

Above: Diode memory-mapped image of the main ship that Larry refers to in the piece.

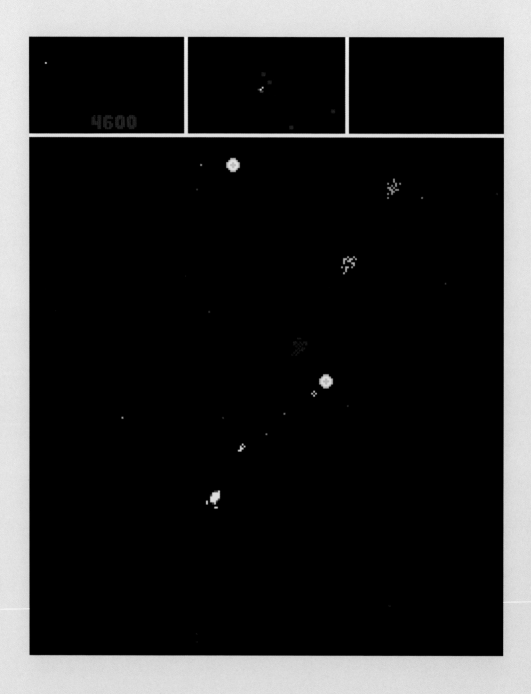

Above: About to engage with some pods – *Conquest* (arcade). The multicoloured fireballs are the ship's bullets. The graphics would have been heavily spruced up for the final release.

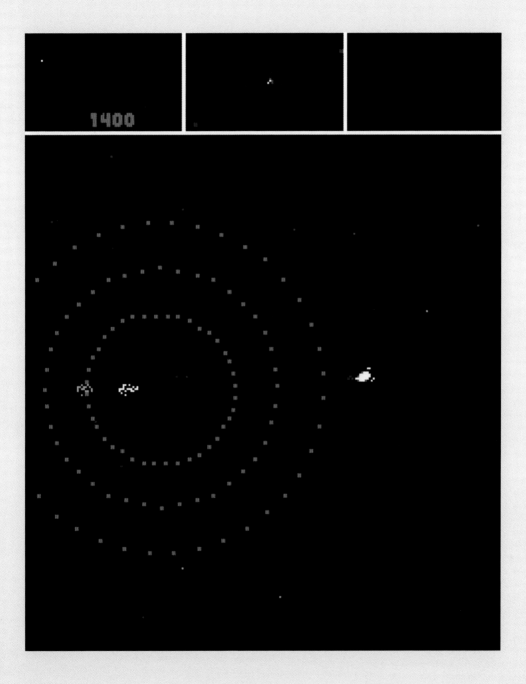

Above: Pod destroyed sequence – *Conquest* (arcade). This effect would eventually be used in *Blaster* for one of its levels.

Akka Arrh Crushed by Robotron

Year: 1982
Developer: Atari
Platform: Arcade

A mysterious and intriguing 'Tempest meets Missile Command' shooter by John Salwitz (of Paperboy fame) where you must use trackball controls to defend your star cannon. If enemies get too close, the action zooms in for you to pick off enemies at close range. Missing for many years, the game was recently preserved, but through somewhat controversial circumstances.

"I joined Atari in the fall of 1981, assigned to work with designer David Ralston on a game later named *Akka Arrh*. Dave and I made games together at Atari for the next ten years. 'Akka' was originally a hybrid pinball/video game, designed with loops, where you shot the ball to destroy incoming alien invaders in corresponding rings on the screen. But, after a time, we found the pinball action wasn't adding much (other than cost), so we switched to traditional video gameplay.

We worked on it for around six months before field testing. Unfortunately, *Akka Arrh* was tested against this little-known game called *Robotron*, which absolutely crushed us. And so it was never manufactured. By the way, the name *Akka Arrh* was 'borrowed' from our friend (and fellow game maker) Rich Adam. Rich had signed a brainstorming document with a fictitious name and then added 'Also Known as Rich Adam' – AKA R."

John Salwitz, developer

Available to play

 **Yes** ○ **No**

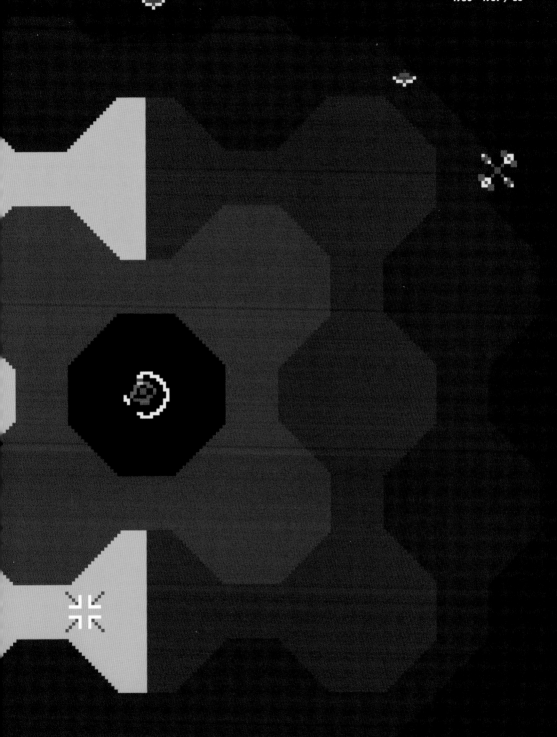

Dark Tower
Video game crash

Year: 1983
Developer: General Consumer Electronics
Platform: Vectrex

Available to play

 Yes  No

During the early part of the decade, we were surrounded by home computers and consoles, each with their own different range of capabilities. The Vectrex was a particularly unique and stand-out home console, coming with an integral vector-based display and not the raster display you would find in a television. Experiences of vector-based graphics for many would have been through arcade games, such as *Asteroids*. The Vectrex was a bold innovation that led to home gaming with a major difference: visuals that always felt like they were popping out of the screen with their bright phosphorescent glow.

The story of the console itself is well told, with unfortunate events seeing the console caught up in the video game crash that started back in 1983, resulting in the console being discontinued as early as 1984. Tragedy didn't just strike the console itself but also a number of games that were so desperately close to release – titles such as *Mail Plane*, *Tour de France* and a game based on Milton Bradley (MB) Company's recent board game of the time, *Dark Tower*.

Dark Tower was a microprocessor-driven fantasy board game produced in 1981, released at a time when role-playing games were at their height of popularity. The game was very well received but was caught up in litigation, where it was claimed that the idea was stolen from a prototype board game shown to MB just a year before (read more on *Triumph* at www.well-of-souls.com/tower). Eventually, the game would disappear from shelves completely by the end of the 1980s (due in part to the court case) and ended up with cult status and a following in subsequent years as a result.

In March 1983, MB acquired General Consumer Electronics (GCE) and, with it, the Vectrex. With the acquisition and *Dark Tower* enjoying commercial success, GCE's vice president, Lee Chaden, saw a great opportunity for a Vectrex adaptation of the game and assigned developer John Hall the task of turning MB's board game into a Vectrex-based title.

John's journey began when he was hired by Jay Smith at Western Technologies (the company that developed the Vectrex console) in late 1981. A project called *Breaker* had been started a few months previously with Mark Indictor and Paul Allen Newell. John was brought in to help the team. The outside company interested in *Breaker* had second thoughts and cancelled the project. With the development of the Vectrex showing more promise at the time, the team was reassigned to develop new games ready for the launch of the console in November 1982.

After finishing *Mine Storm* as a built-in game for the Vectrex, John resigned from WT, and, a couple of weeks later, he was hired by GCE after it made him an offer. Mark also went over to GCE, while Paul would part ways by leaving for a start-up company called Simutrek. John's first assignment at GCE was the development of *Fortress of Narzod* for the Vectrex.

A few weeks before completing *Fortress of Narzod*, John was preparing for his next assignment. "Lee Chaden told me that my next project would be based on the *Dark Tower* board game and gave me one that was unopened," John recalled. "When I got home, I opened it and thought, 'What the hell am I going to do with this?' It seemed like a forced effort to make the board game into something electronic, and I never felt that I understood how to play the game. I spent less than an hour or two with it, and I remember thinking that it was really confusing."

After an initial struggle, John soon began to formulate ideas. He began by sketching out some graphics and detailing some basic game logic. This was gradually fleshed out into a document which would fully propose and describe a game with a third-person warrior in a 3D world. The main warrior character would remain centred on the screen, and the world would move around you as you moved. It would feature elements of the board game but was basically a completely different game.

"I would work longer and longer hours until the game was done."

The ambitious design was submitted to Lee Chaden on the 22nd July, 1983, and was quickly approved. "The contract with GCE had a provision that I would receive a bonus if I designed a game, and it was accepted for development. There was another bonus if I finished the game on time. I received both bonuses, so I can probably claim to be the game designer," John smiled.

John wasn't completely alone working on the game, and he got input from others at GCE. "I remember discussing various aspects about the game with Mark Indictor, Jeff Corsiglia and, a couple of times, with Richard Moszkowski," explained John. "During development, Jeff helped me with a couple of graphics problems, Mark did my sounds for me (I had no talent when it came to sound) and Richard had some ideas on my game logic. They certainly deserve credit on the game as well."

Development was carried out on a Z-80-based system by Ithaca Intersystems, with 64K of memory and two 8-inch floppy disks, running Digital Research DOS. John wrote his code with the *WordStar* text editor and assembled it using a 6809 cross-assembler. When code was ready for testing, the generated hex data was either downloaded into 'The ROM-ulator' or burned onto an EPROM. "The ROM-ulator (or ROM Emulator) was a tool that took the place of an EPROM. It contained RAM, allowing our code to be loaded to the development Vectrex. This made it easy for us to write code, assemble it and then download it to the ROM-ulator. Once in the ROM-ulator, we would reset our Vectrex, and it acted like a regular game," John explained.

John worked from home in the San Bernardino mountains, overlooking Lake Gregory, a couple of hours from the GCE office in Santa Monica. John would start as early as 4am in the morning and work almost solidly (apart from stopping for lunch and dinner) until around 9pm. Work would continue like this for three to four months solidly until completion. "As I went along, I would work longer and longer hours until the game was done. The game would consume all, and it was fortunate that I was single and didn't mind the long hours," John recalled.

The eventual result of John's hard work was a single-player game where you control a warrior that must locate four different keys (gold, silver, bronze and brass) scattered across a large game world. Once found, you must then unlock the door of the Dark Tower by solving the 'Riddle of the Keys' – where you must list the keys in the correct sequence (determined randomly for every game). You have six warriors in total at your disposal for each game, but, if you find things particularly hard, then you have four difficulty settings to choose from. The easiest setting starts you off with three of the keys already in your possession, the hardest with nothing but two bags of gold to your name.

When starting the game, you are placed randomly in a benign setting in the game to give the warrior a chance of a safe start. The game map was split into four quadrants, each containing a 32×32 grid of positions (or what John calls 'nodes'). The quadrants contained forests containing pine trees, dead trees, elm trees and maple trees – all graphically different so that you could determine where you were. Boundary fog exists on the outer edges of the map, preventing you from breaking out of the map and which teleport you to a random place in the game. To help players navigate and map their progress, John implemented a basic pedometer at the top of the screen. As your warrior rotates in eight directions, the direction is represented as a compass direction – the number of steps in the current direction is also displayed.

At the centre of the game was the Dark Forest, a mostly clear area surrounded by an outer area of all four tree types together. It is here that, once you have all four keys in your possession, the Dark Tower then appears for you to be able to attempt to enter and complete the game. Many parts of the map contain various game objects to help create the 3D environment for the player. Objects include trees, bags of gold, chests or simply a trigger for a particular event.

The chests play a crucial role in the game. "It was intended that opening a chest would be an angst-filled experience," John explained. "To suit my sense of humour, sometimes opening a chest did nothing at all. The player would anticipate the opening of a chest, preparing for what might happen. The box would creak open, pause a moment, and then close again. The first time they encountered the Do-Nothing Box, it was very much a 'WTF' moment!"

When the game wasn't being so cruel to you, there was the potential of finding bags of gold, one of the keys, or a wizard to buy items from. But you could also unleash a 'fog' (teleporting you to a random location), a 'deadly plague' (losing you a life if you were without sufficient protection), or be sucked into the chest to fight with a group of Brigands. Fighting the Brigands is a scenario you cannot escape without either winning the encounter or losing a life. From the base of the screen, you move from left to right to avoid shots (flamoids) from the Brigands, who appear from behind a set of pillars. At the same time, you can use three of the Vectrex controller buttons to fire back flamoids left, right or centrally towards the enemy. If you survive the fight, you might find some gold, one of the keys – or you might simply find nothing at all.

Losing the fight puts you back into the forest with a life lost but with the chance of re-entering again if you wished. If you chanced upon a wizard instead, they would steal money from you, tell you to go away, or offer you the chance to buy an item. With enough bags of gold, you could buy a key, an extra life, a healer, a scout, or the Crystal Crown. A healer in your possession would protect you from the plague. A scout would prevent you from being randomly placed on the map by fog (though not including the boundary fog). The Crystal Crown would give a bonus of 1,500 points if it were in your possession upon finishing the game.

Although development of the game was relatively smooth, there were challenges to overcome. "Development of the Vectrex was very stressful for everybody involved," John recalled. "From having to develop new hardware and the programming techniques to go along with it, we had to share equipment and frequently conflicted on access – all to a schedule that permitted no delay. We also only had 1K of RAM to keep track of everything (drawing, game logic and sound generation)." Due to the game's complexity, *Dark Tower* required a cartridge size of 12K, when other games were 8K maximum.

During development, John was unaware that MB had taken over GCE due to his living distance and being focused on the game. "I didn't hear anything about MB until I was nearly done with *Dark Tower*," John revealed. "That's not much of a surprise – after all, I was living a couple of hours away from the GCE office, phone conversations with anybody were weeks apart, and I had only a couple of visitors during the whole time I was at the cabin. Calling myself a recluse is truly an understatement."

With a lack of knowledge of what was going on in the outside world, the ongoing lawsuit over the board game had no effect at all on the Vectrex development. "The lawsuit is interesting, but I realised that there was very little similarity between their board game and what I designed," John states. "Even if the plaintive won the claim against MB about the board game, they would have needed to start another lawsuit against the Vectrex version."

John worked hard to get the game done in time for the assigned Hong Kong manufacturing slot so that the game would be in stores in time for crucial

Christmas sales. This meant that the 12K EPROM, manuals and packaging preparations had to be ready. Everything was just about completed on time, with some sacrifices made just to make sure. "The animation and game action for the solving the 'Riddle of the Keys' was weak, and I wasn't happy about it. Truth is, my deadline was approaching, and, if I had missed the deadline, I would miss the manufacturing cycle," John reflected.

Regardless of John's efforts (and for reasons unknown to him) – the manufacturing slot was abruptly cancelled and pushed back to the next, which was never to happen in the end. "I'm not sure that there was a deliberate decision to skip the manufacture of *Dark Tower*. I think it was just a victim of circumstances," John suggested. "I'm somewhat surprised that *Dark Tower* wasn't released – I do remember seeing a final product." The reason for *Dark Tower* seeing its production slot cancelled would not become clear until years later.

On the 22nd October, 1983, George R. Ditomassi (executive vice president at MB) was quoted in the Boston Globe saying, "We were badly hurt by Vectrex." A statement that Gary Bergmann was in agreement with. Gary was senior electronic project engineer for MB at the time and saw first-hand a sequence of events which culminated in the death of *Dark Tower* on the Vectrex. It had nothing to do at all with the litigation case against the board game but the demise of the very hardware it required to run on.

The video game crash was now underway, taking no prisoners, and with many companies becoming casualties. No matter how great it was, the Vectrex was not immune to the situation. "Summer CES in June of 1983 was not kind to the Vectrex as there were perhaps too many accessories (an attempt at a computer add-on, 3D glasses, etc.), and buyers started to stay away in droves. George Ditomassi's comment was a true reflection of the situation," Gary explained.

"I don't think that it was generally known, but my intention was to make *Dark Tower* into a two-cartridge game."

"All products in development and testing were put on production-hold, allowing them to complete coding and testing, but not releasing code to build chips (a very expensive milestone at that time for any electronic product)," Gary continued. "If Vectrex had any hope of resuscitation, it would have been at Winter CES (January 1984) and Toy-fair (February 1984), but, again, there were no takers. They pulled the plug and closed it out. The likes of *Dark Tower*, *Mail Plane*, *Tour de France* and probably a few more titles were ultimately canned before full-fledged production runs."

Although attempts were made to relaunch the Vectrex as a colour handheld device in later years, the console was fully discontinued by the end of 1984 and was never to be seen again. However, the system kept a very loyal and dedicated following over the years, which would not only result in the release of some stunning new homebrew developments but the recovery of long-lost titles that got caught up in the crash. *Dark Tower* was one of those which would be lucky enough to relinquish its 'lost' status.

It all began with Mike Hoffberg posting on a Vectrex newsgroup in late 1994 regarding a prototype cartridge of *Dark Tower* that he had. At this stage, the game was merely a rumour mill title, with only brief mentions of 'coming soon' in adverts. Many rightly assumed that it was based on the board game of the same name, but that was all that was known. Mike had an opportunistic link to MB through his brother, Robert Hoffberg, who had produced a number of titles for the MicroVision handheld device.

Mike was put in touch with Gary Bergmann via his brother to do a short interview about the Vectrex, when the vital discovery was made. "I had known Gary from the days I worked at MB (1978–1981) in East Longmeadow, MA," Robert recalled. "When my brother told me Gary had a prototype of the *Dark Tower* game, we went to visit Gary, where he gave my brother one of the prototypes."

"Development of the Vectrex was very stressful for everybody."

Mike managed successfully to extract the code from the cartridge. However, he had something owed to him and wanted to trade before fully sharing his recovery. "My brother had ordered a multicart from someone, but the person was not delivering it," Robert explained. "So he posted the code for half the game and said he would post the rest when he received it. He quickly received the multicart and posted the rest of the code." Arguably, not a bad deal at all for the community.

Gary was a major advocate of the Vectrex. So much so that he kept a lot of memorabilia from that era. "I have a console still sitting in my office, proudly displayed on an in-store kiosk. It's a little worse for wear but still functions, sitting atop about 25 games, mostly in their original packaging. I got married in 1984 and gave my best man and ushers Vectrexes as gifts," Gary smiled. He also managed to keep hold of prototype cartridges of *Mail Plane*, *Tour de France*, *Pitchers Duel* and *Dark Tower*. There wasn't just one copy of *Dark Tower* in his possession, but several in prototype form, which came with a fully produced colour overlay design by Miva Filoseta and a Xerox copy of a professionally produced manual for the game (sadly, the original is now completely lost).

In later years, enthusiasts would make reproduction copies of *Dark Tower* on real cartridges. At the time of writing, there have been efforts to do a commercial quality release, complete with restored manuals and proper overlay. Amazingly, it seems that *Dark Tower* is finally going to see a physical release.

We end with a final revelation about the game from John: "I don't think that it was generally known, but my intention was to make *Dark Tower* into a two-cartridge game. Successfully answering the 'Riddle of the Keys' would enable additional play in Volume II," he explained. "I didn't have any definitive plans about what would be in Volume II. This was around the time MB had bought GCE and everything pretty much went to hell." Although there is, sadly, no sequel to find, we are grateful to at least be able to play the original game as intended – thanks to all of those involved in its preservation.

Above: An accurate recreation of the *Dark Tower* overlay for the Vectrex, based on a photo of the real thing from Gary's personal collection.

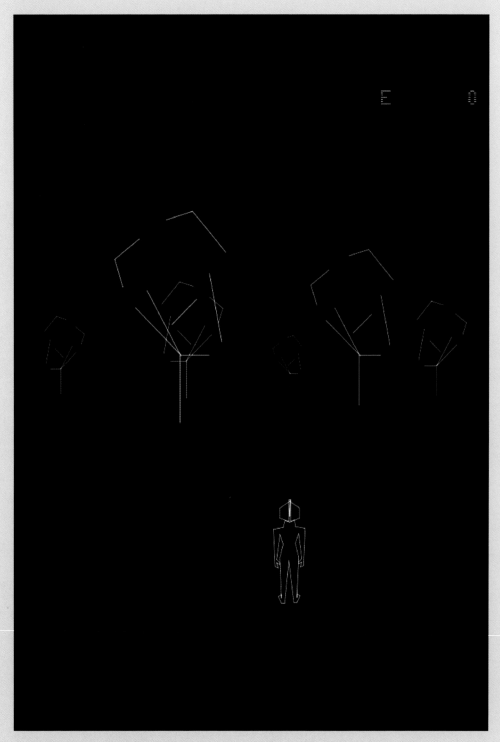

Above: The start of *Dark Tower* (Vectrex), within a forest and ready to begin your quest. The 'E' refers to the compass direction, and the '0' is how many steps you have taken.

Above: Fighting a group of Brigands to try and escape – *Dark Tower* (Vectrex). You must fire flamoids at them and avoid their return fire.

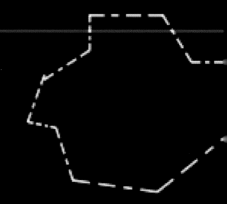

Mail Plane Vectrex failure

**Year: 1983
Developer: General
Consumer Electronics
Platform: Vectrex**

A once 'Holy Grail' Vectrex title, putting you in control of a plane travelling around the United States, delivering mail to state capitals and helping children learn state and city names. Making use of the light-pen peripheral, the game got caught up in the collapse of the Vectrex and was hunted for years until its eventual preservation in 2013.

"I recall there wasn't much commitment when we developed it overall – I had very little direction except for a few drawings and a terse storyboard. My wife helped me encode the map of the US that was complete with state lines. She also typed the coordinates of the vertices into a text file, which I then adapted to 6809 assembly language. We are still married, by the way!

The gameplay itself was pretty shallow, and the difficulty was minimal, involving some very rudimentary eye-hand coordination to 'fly' your plane from one state capital to the next. It was more of a learning game, teaching the player the names of the American state capitals. I remember that I didn't know many of them when I programmed it. The light-pen was problematic, but I thought it was fun and had a good time with that part of the development."

Mark Indictor, developer

Available to play

◉ Yes ◯ No

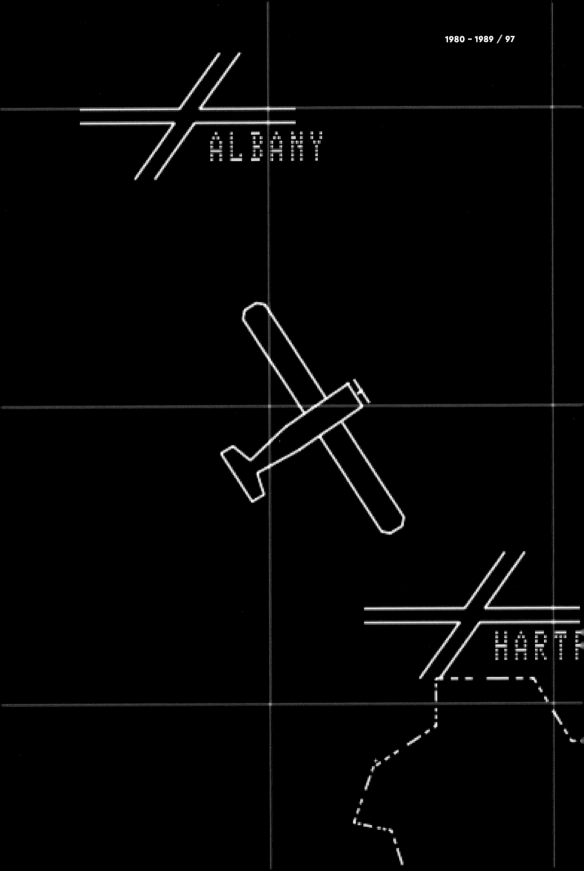

ALBANY

HARTF

Keystone Kannonball
Video game crash

Year: 1983
Developer: Activision
Platform: Atari 2600

Available to play

 Yes No

Often, with early gaming technology, you would have to let your imagination fill in the gaps where the visuals were somewhat less than to be desired. If you weren't controlling a square block protagonist in Warren Robinett's *Adventure*, then it was a limited animation framed *Pac-Man* on the Atari 2600 collecting rectangular 'wafers' instead of circular power pills. Essentially, it didn't always matter, so long as the game was fun to play.

We are honestly not picking on the Atari 2600 – it is a machine which brings us warm and fuzzy memories, with its blocky visuals adding to its charm. The point is, the graphical limitations of the Atari 2600 didn't stop pioneers from pushing the boundaries and creating titles which looked the part too. Activision, in particular, were the kings of just that, with games that not only played brilliantly, but looked superb too. One such title from the Activision stable was Garry Kitchen's *Keystone Kapers*, released back in 1983. Using all manner of tricks, the game presented you with a very cartoon-looking title on 1970s hardware.

The game had you controlling officer Keystone Kelly, who must chase criminal Harry Hooligan across a three-storey shopping store and roof. You would start at the bottom and work your way across, climbing each floor via escalators at the ends, or via an elevator in the middle with careful timing. You would need to catch up with Harry before he escapes via the roof or the timer runs out. Trying to stop you are obstacles such as runaway shopping trolleys, toy planes, beach balls and radios, all of which cause a time penalty if touched.

Everything was so clearly defined that you knew exactly what everything was, whereas, when playing titles such as *Raiders of the Lost Ark,* knowing what each object was could be a challenge without a manual. The game was released and received a great following over the years, featuring in many 'Top Atari 2600 game' lists. What wasn't known was that a sequel was on the cards almost immediately after, not by Garry, but by his brother, Dan Kitchen.

Dan had just finished work on his first Atari 2600 title, *Crackpots*, and was now hungry to move on to his next game. This time he wanted to try and do something that pushed the boundaries of the hardware even further than before and create yet another fun and visual treat for the eyes. He began by focusing on a subject close to his heart.

"Since I've always liked trains, it seemed natural that my next game should take place on a railroad," explained Dan. "So, after I finished *Crackpots*, I started working on a display with railroad cars and a character that would jump on top of a train from screen to screen. After I had the boxcar kernel on the screen, I needed a character to put on top of the train. Garry had recently finished *Keystone Kapers,* and I thought Keystone Kelly would be a perfect choice, possibly appearing as a lawman on an old-time Western train."

Rather than just calling the game *Keystone Kapers 2*, Dan came up with the new title of *Keystone Kannonball*. Garry, however, was already 'cooking on gas' by this point and was pushing on with his new development of *Pressure Cooker* (assembling hamburgers to customer specifications with the ingredients that fly at you), so wouldn't have any involvement with the game. It was up to Dan to create the entire premise for his new title.

The basic story sees Keystone Kelly moving to the West and living out his days as a conductor on the Gold Rush Railroad. All set out in the desert, with lots of cacti, mountains and wonderful sunsets. The game planned to follow on from his shopping mall days, with Harry Hooligan reappearing as a Western 'varmint' in a ten-gallon hat and carrying a six-shooter. Keystone Kelly's aim was to chase him across the top of a number of train carriages from left to right and catch him before reaching the main caboose or before the timer runs out.

"The background parallax scrolling worked out well!"

"I had planned to have 25 gameplay levels, with each level having the train increase in length and different enemies/obstacles appearing on the train cars," recalled Dan. "The colours of the boxcars would also change as well. I was planning on also having a few train-related obstacles hanging from fast-moving trackside poles. A tunnel was also in the works, as long as it appeared instantly as I didn't have the display cycles to make it scroll onto the screen."

The game would only ever feature scenes outside and on top of the train, with cartridge space availability dictating features. "To fit everything in a 4K ROM configuration, I didn't plan on having inside gameplay, although I would have loved to have added it," explained Dan. So, to compromise, there would be a good solid variety of obstacles instead, such as tumbleweeds, crawling tarantulas, snakes and vultures. As it was designed as a sequel to *Keystone Kapers*, the plan was to have the objects/enemies moving in familiar ways. So bouncing beach balls were replaced by bouncing tumbleweeds, flying toy planes by low-flying vultures and wiggling snakes replacing radios. There would be similar bonus collectables, with money bags to collect alongside the addition of gold bars.

Most carriages also featured ladders which you could climb up or down, replacing the escalators and giving a new element compared with the original game. "The ladders were designed as a way to avoid fast-moving obstacles flying above the train," explained Dan. "Also, some of the train cars were going to have platforms near the base of the ladders that players could jump onto to get to hard-to-reach pick-ups."

Apart from the original game characters, there was no inspiration taken from any other games at the time. Instead, Dan would see other games later looking much like his original plan. "I recall, shortly after shelving the game, reading about an unreleased version of a James Bond game by Parker Brothers that had the Bond character on top of the *Octopussy* Circus Train," he recalled. "Also, a few years later, I saw an arcade game called *Express Raider,* which had a cowboy character fighting villains on top of an old Western train."

Before his ideas would come to fruition, Dan set to work on producing a highly impressive set of visuals for the game. After a month or so, the results were technically stunning for a game from 1983, featuring clearly detailed carriages that bounced on the tracks and impressive smooth parallax scrolling. "The background parallax scrolling worked out well!" beamed Dan. "I used bands of different-sized players to create that effect. I was really proud of the eight non-flickering animated train wheels below the train cars. We could easily get six non-flickering players on a line and sometimes trick the hardware to display an extra one or two on the same line. I worked really hard to get all eight wheels positioned perfectly. Those were the days when we would do tricks on the 2600, not only to make our games look better but to impress other 2600 programmers as well!"

"I was really proud of the eight non-flickering animated train wheels below the train cars."

Unfortunately, the game wouldn't progress any further than its initial prototype stage. "The game was eventually shelved along with other 2600 games Activision had in development due to the fact that the market had changed radically and consumers were no longer buying premium-priced games," confirmed Dan. Caught up in the crash of 1983, only a prototype demonstrating the main parallax and carriages would be done, with no gameplay yet implemented. It was, at most, around 40% complete, and Dan still had to implement a considerable amount more of the game to make it playable.

Dan moved on to new projects and away from the Atari 2600 for a while, leaving the game to gather dust. He later returned and produced ambitious conversions of *Double Dragon* and *Ghostbusters* on the platform. Gamers were none the wiser until the final prototype of the game was suddenly found by Dan in June 2018 in an off-site storage facility. He donated the game to the National Videogame Museum US, which would preserve it and now has it kept in its archives. The prototype hasn't yet been made available, though a video can be found online of the game running, showing just how good it looked.

The excitement of seeing his game running again after all these years and the popularity of producing new games on the Atari 2600 prompted Dan to resurrect and continue the development under a new name. "I have changed the name, rewrote it all from scratch, and changed the characters because I don't have the rights to the *Keystone Kapers* brand," confirmed Dan. "Based upon the player rushing to find gold bars on the train, the name *Gold Rush* worked fine though. I'm planning to launch a Kickstarter soon, primarily to raise the funds to manufacture the game as a cartridge-in-box product," he continued. "Instead of *Keystone Kannonball* being a 4K game, *Gold Rush* will be a 32K game with many different train cars, enemies and obstacles. Additionally, there will be gameplay both on top of the train cars and inside them. Since the game is no longer *Keystone Kapers 2*, Keystone Kelly has been replaced by Kasey O'Kelly, his cousin from the Old Country. And while Harry Hooligan is no longer the villain, he and a few of the other Activision characters may be found riding the rails of the Gold Rush Gulch Railroad."

As well as rewriting all of the code, many other elements are changing, including new graphics and more variety between coaches and with the enemies/ obstacles. "Now that the ROM size is no longer an issue, I've updated the parallax scrolling and added many more types of train cars," explained Dan. "Some of the enemies and obstacles from the original concept will make their way into the game, along with a number of new ones."

It is, for once, a development that could result in a happy ending. It is hoped that Dan's campaign is the success that it deserves to be, with all of us eventually being able to play *Gold Rush* on our Atari 2600s.

Above: Dan's brother, Garry, created a fun and original title with the release of *Keystone Kapers* (Atari 2600) in 1983.

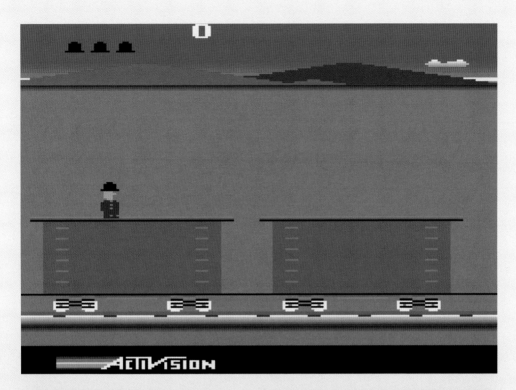

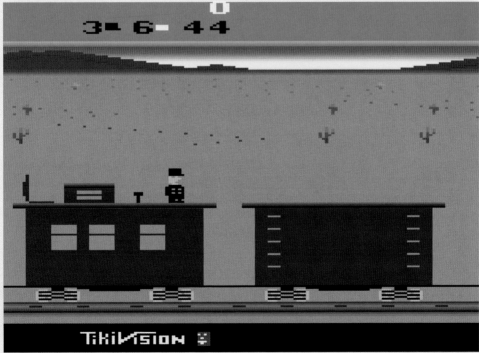

Top: Dan's original incarnation of *Keystone Kannonball* (Atari 2600). **Bottom:** Dan's new development – *Gold Rush* (Atari 2600) – due to go to a Kickstarter fundraiser at the time of writing.

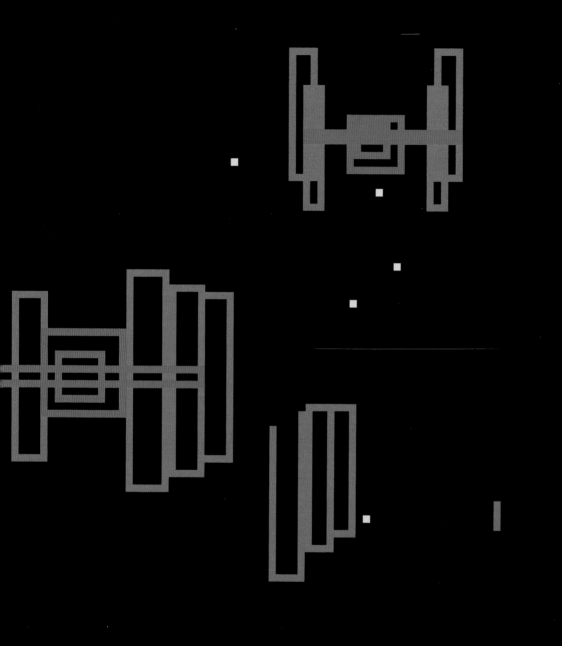

Blaster
Poor 5200
sales

Year: 1984
Developer: Vid Kidz
Platform: Atari 5200

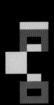

**An unofficial sequel to *Robotron: 2084*
tragically not experienced by many in arcades
due to a limited production run. Surprisingly,
the arcade was a conversion of this planned Atari
5200 release, started after seeing promise in the
platform. Instructed to focus on an arcade version
first, by the time they came back, the market
was collapsing, and the boat was missed.**

"I love coming in low for a strafing run on the
Robot Grid, ducking under the arches and point-
blank blasting the gigantic Robotrons into chunks
of roboflesh, then refuelling with the Energiser
to make my escape to space! It's a long way
to Paradise without Elon Musk!"

Eugene Jarvis, developer

"It was exciting to make what would be the
only Vid Kidz console game as an early entry
to the 'certain to soar' 5200 console. It's sad
that the game didn't run early and the platform
didn't soar. We love that players are, however,
able to experience the game on emulators."

Larry DeMar, developer

Available to play
◉ Yes ○ No

Safire
Development
put on hold

Year: 1984
Developer: Scott Adams
Platform: Atari 400/800

Available to play

 Yes ● No

The late 1970s and early 1980s are often fondly remembered for the popularity of the text adventure genre – one which has struggled for survival in the modern gaming era. As a child, the author often spent hours trying to escape capture from deadly goblins in *The Hobbit* and trying to get used to the various different parsers that were used by different developers. Like when reading a book, you have to use your imagination a bit to fill in the gaps where there are no visuals to see, but a good text adventure would usually have you absorbed and feeling as if you were in the game in no time.

Scott Adams is best described as the grandfather of home computer-based text adventures, having been one of (if not) the first to develop one for a home computer. Co-founder of Adventure International with his ex-wife, Alexis, back in 1978 with their first release, *Adventureland*, Scott produced many famous adventures from the late 1970s and into the early 1980s, including *Pirate Adventure*, the *Questprobe* (Marvel Comics) series and more. Showing that text adventures still had a place in the gaming world, Scott made a comeback in 2013 with the release of *The Inheritance*, his first game in over ten years.

Looking through Scott's softography, there is one notable title missing from the list, but one that is far from the game genre that you might expect. A major (but brief) departure was looming from a world of text parsers and story dialogue, all of which would begin in 1984.

Scott wanted to have a go at doing something different, something to prove to himself that he could do other games as well as text adventures. "I also wanted to see if Forth as a language was useful and then discovered its many problems," explained Scott. "But, mainly, I wanted to program a game that took full advantage of the Atari 400/800 graphical sprites."

Safire (pronounced 'sapphire') was to be a top-down scrolling game with no parser in sight. Scott started off by producing a proof of concept to see if he could achieve his goal, and one which could offer something new to his current audience at the time. The game would put you in the control of a fireman who must go into a blazing building to put all of the fire out and save what you can. Each level was represented by a floor of the building, each the same size but with different layouts. To complete a level, you had to successfully put all of the fire out to be able to move on to the next floor.

With Scott wanting to try and push the boat out as much as possible, he explored the Atari's various strengths and moved away from a static screen approach for the game. "I had the screen scroll so it wasn't all visible at one point if I remember correctly," Scott recalled. "It was about four times the size of the screen (i.e. four quadrants, so it was as if you had four television screens' worth). I don't remember how many rooms were shown."

Graphically, the game was functional in its early stages, with a bitmapped main display and text for status panels. Walls were represented by thicker lines compared with the doors that you could go through, and colour was used to the fullest to make use of the Atari's vibrant palette.

Carrying just a hose, you would need to hook this up at various water points scattered around parts of each floor. You could then proceed to put out the surrounding fire and prevent it from spreading to other rooms or areas. If you got caught by the fire, then you could heal yourself with first aid kits that you found along the way.

"You could also find fire extinguishers that worked short term."

As you moved around each floor, your hose would leave a trail behind, with a limit to how long the trail could be. "If the fire burned behind the firefighter, it could burn through the hose, and he would need to find a new connection," Scott explained. "You could also find fire extinguishers that worked short term. Doors and weakened walls in areas were also kicked down to be able to progress." If you couldn't find a hose connection, then fire extinguishers were just a temporary relief to your situation.

On your travels, you would also find sapphire gems strangely scattered around, which you could collect for bonus points. It was a rather small part of the game, but there were added connotations in relation to the clever naming of the game. "The spelling 'Scott Adams' was for the 'SA' part, and it was a FIREfighting game. The tie was with the sapphires you were to collect," Scott explained of the bizarre sub-task.

So far, there has been no mention of saving people in the burning building; surely something that was to be added later in the development? "No, it was just going to be fighting the fires and collecting the gems," responded Scott. During its early stages though, the game was just organically grown as it went along, and it's likely that more features would have been added as time went on. The task of saving people could well have been considered later as a result.

Each of the game's levels were to be generated through a clever engine that Scott had developed early on, which would randomly generate layout and placements of objects. This meant that every game played would be fresh and unique, adding to the potential longevity of the title. However, only one level would ever make use of the engine.

The game was looking good early on, and Scott was keen to test it out on people to see how it fared. "Safire had taken me approximately a month to write and was really just a concept game on the Atari 400/800," he explained. "I showed to a number of folks locally though, and they enjoyed it."

Although the reception was promising, the development ground to a sudden halt shortly afterwards due to other development commitments. "There were pressures to get other projects done, which had me shelve it," explained Scott. "I was doing games based on the Marvel Comic universe. That had me tied up."

Scott would only temporarily shelve the game and had planned to come back to it once the Marvel games were completed and out the way. However, one project after another would continually pop up and keep *Safire* in a shelved status until, eventually, the Atari platform became obsolete and rendered the project officially dead. The potential of a completely different gaming direction for Scott was never fully explored as a result.

When asked if anything of *Safire* still remained today, Scott responded with the dreaded "I wish there was!" Several searches over the years by Scott for something of the game have so far proved fruitless. Although there is always a possibility of *Safire* being found in some shape or form, Scott personally feels it is unlikely that it will ever surface again, especially with now over 30 years passing since the original development.

"There were pressures to get other projects done, which had me shelve it."

Was *Safire* the only time that Scott had diverted away from the text adventure genre? "For home computer games development, yes," he confirmed. "I had a cash register inventory system (CHRIS) that I created for my chain of computer stores and was also selling it. Before I had started my company or even done the first adventure, I had a *Star Trek* game conversion at a radar station that took over the video monitor of the radar to allow the game to be played. I have a sample of what I believe is the first 16-bit home computer video game ever written on my website. I also did a tank war game and designed the controllers for my Sphere computer."

Scott's hidden talents were indeed very widely spread, though sadly, for *Safire*, it was to be an example of something very different from him that would never be experienced by his fans. However, with a new software development team in the form of Clopas, could Scott be tempted once more to divert away from the world of adventures? Maybe even decide to come back to *Safire* for a new audience today? Only time will tell.

Above: Two of Scott's adventure games – *Questprobe 1: The Incredible Hulk* (Commodore 64) and *Adventureland* (Commodore 64).

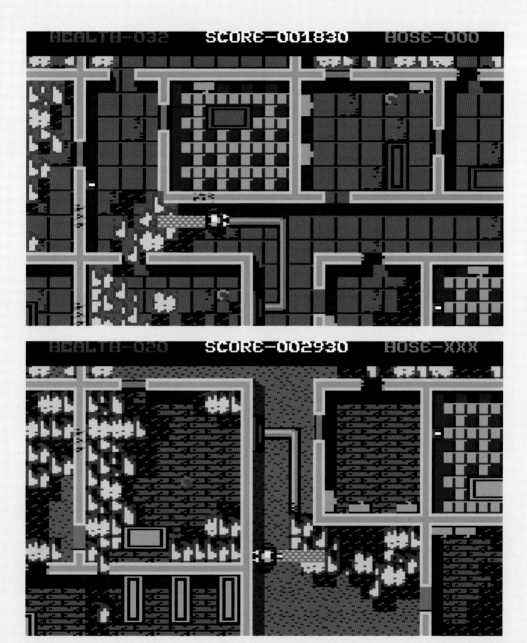

Above: An artist's impression of how *Safire* may have looked, based on concepts recalled by Scott, including the hose and connection points.

Bandersnatch Bankruptcy

Year: 1984
Developer: Imagine Software
Platform: ZX Spectrum

Image: Artist's recreation of a scene from
Bandersnatch (ZX Spectrum), based
on grainy video footage from the BBC
Commercial Breaks documentary.

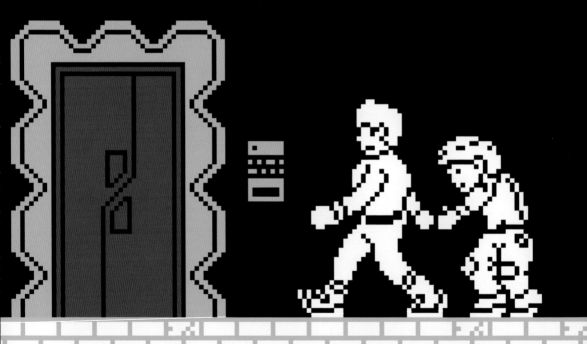

The most famous of the "Mega Games" series, which contributed towards Imagine Software's collapse back in 1984, *Bandersnatch* was an arcade adventure featuring large characters interacting with each other via a speech bubble system. The sophisticated graphics and animations were made extra-special thanks to the RAM expansion add-on as part of the overall package.

"Both *Bandersnatch* (and *Psyclapse*) were developed in an area of Imagine's vast open-plan office, completely cut off from everyone else. Secrecy was the key, so only people working on the 'Mega Games' were allowed in that particular area. The late Ian Wetherburn and I were *Bandersnatch*'s programmers. Ally Noble and the late Steven Cain were its artists. Fred Gray was the musician.

I worked on the game's engine whilst Ian worked on the speech bubble system, which was to be a key feature of the game overall. By the time Imagine went completely tits up, the engine was virtually complete, but, by then, it was based on the engine I used for all of my Imagine games, so there wasn't much development work actually needed. Ian's speech bubbles were hardly out of the design stage at all when it all fell apart."

John Gibson, developer

Available to play

◯ Yes ◉ No

Millipede
Internal
politics

Year: 1984
Developer: General Computer Corporation
Platform: Atari 2600

Available to play

 Yes ◯ No

One of the great aspects of 1980s arcade games were the vibrant colours, wide variety and crazy but innovative ideas that convinced us to part with our coins. *Centipede* (developed by Ed Logg and Dona Bailey) was one such title where the slightly odd choice of colours made everything just 'pop out' of the screen at you. With the mesmerising centipede weaving its way down, you would frantically have to try and pick off parts of it with your laser shots, whilst avoiding or destroying other creepy crawlies in the process.

The game felt alive with the variety of creatures buzzing and crawling around. There was always something going on, meaning that you couldn't let your guard down for a second. Much of this was the reason why the game became such a massive hit for Atari, so much so that a sequel was never really in doubt. *Millipede* would follow swiftly and build upon the success, keeping things close to the original's winning formula. What made it stand out more than its predecessor was the inclusion of more creatures, swarm waves and DDT bombs that created large explosions when shot – hopefully catching the millipede in mid-flow.

Being an Atari game meant that it was inevitable that it would soon appear on the Atari 2600, especially after already seeing a successful conversion of *Centipede* on its ageing hardware. That first development had been handled by General Computer Corporation (GCC), a company set up by Doug Macrae, Kevin Curran and John Tylko in 1981. Originally, they created modification kits for existing arcade games; such as *Crazy Otto* (which built upon *Pac-Man*).

GCC began getting involved in doing conversions on the Atari 2600 not too long after being sued by Atari for doing an unofficial modification kit for *Missile Command*. In a rather shrewd move, and dropping the suit in the process, Atari arranged with GCC to produce games for its 2600 console. GCC created high-quality conversions quickly, thanks to having several people working on a game at a single time, compared with usually just the one at Atari.

One of GCC's most triumphant conversions was *Centipede* in 1983. It had raised the bar for future 2600 games. GCC knew that *Millipede* was likely next on the list and naturally felt that it would get the contract after its superb work on the prequel. "With 2600 *Centipede* being successful, we assumed that we would be assigned to modify its code to create *Millipede*," Doug Macrae recalled. "While management was trying to decide, we started programming, knowing that there would be a very quick deadline once the decision was made. Yes, it was 'on spec' but a risk worth taking."

Atari was more than happy for GCC to go ahead and develop a conversion, but it also wanted to put more faith in its own developers and would do so with Dave Staugas. "From the very beginning, I was aware that GCC wanted to do the port as well," Dave remembered. "They had developed 2600 *Centipede* (brilliantly done, I might add) and *Millipede* was just the sequel. My managers at

Atari wanted to give me a chance to make a better game than GCC, but, since they were developing *Millipede* anyway (without any specific contractual arrangements), it was left as a competition. So, may the better game win!"

Thanks to unearthed communications from the Atari VAXMail vaults (VAXMail being the internal mail system used at Atari), Ed Logg was not happy at the time with the competition. "I was told that GCC were instructed NOT to do this cart, but they went ahead and did it anyway," he wrote. "I guess they felt that, if they finished first, Atari marketing would use theirs." Doug however says that Atari management was fully aware that GCC was developing *Millipede*, and Atari engineering knew it too and GCC was not instructed to stop.

So the race was on to see who could produce the better conversion, a scenario that Atari management felt it couldn't lose. GCC's team consisted of Doug (graphics), Betty Ryan Tylko (programming), Dave Payne (programming) and Patty Goodson (sound). They got to work quickly during the fall of 1983, with approximately 50% of the codebase taken from *Centipede* as a starting point, making perfect sense, given the shared core mechanics.

The engine was tweaked to become more in-line with *Millipede*, with the new additions and waves that were an integral part of the sequel. An attractive title screen was then constructed to add some final polish to what was a solid-feeling sequel and conversion. The production was swift and smooth throughout, apart from just a few minor niggles. "The trickiest part was producing the large number of moving objects with as little flicker as possible," confirmed Doug. After just a few months, GCC was done, bar some final bug fixes and polishing.

At the same time, Atari's own team of Dave Staugas (programming), Jerome Domurat (graphics), Robert Viera (sound) and Andrew Fuchs (sound) had their heads down and were working hard. With the known competition of GCC, it was a pretty stressful time for the team. "This would be one of the most intense periods of work in my life. It was three months of round-the-clock programming, stopping only for eating and sleeping," Dave recalled.

"I reverse-engineered *Centipede* (with no help from GCC), and came up with ways to get more processing power," he continued. "I worked out a scheme to process sound events during the on-screen 'kernel', rather than during the v-blank time. I timed each branch of every scanline in the kernel to execute in sync with the horizontal retrace so as to eliminate the need for 'STA WSYNC'. This bought me extra processing time. I also changed the method used to query the expiration of the v-blank timer from a two-instruction loop with BNE (branch non-zero) to BPL (branch on positive). This made the occasional overrun of game logic processing more graceful, with just a minor screen 'twitch' rather than a full screen roll. These three innovations had never been used by any other 2600 game to my knowledge, and I got more processing power as a result."

"During this period of 2600 development, both Atari and GCC were squeezing the hardware further and further, porting arcade games to the 2600 that were originally not thought possible," added Doug. "In many cases, each scanline's 76 machine cycles were carefully counted, such that even the 'STA WSYNC' could be removed. This let us get full use of the 6507's measly processing power. Dave switching how the v-blank timer worked was quite innovative in that, should the program miss on timing, it would do so more gracefully. With each cartridge came new techniques to get more and more out of the hardware."

Atari's own team was certainly not going to let GCC walk away without a fight. However, its development fell slightly behind schedule according to Ed Logg. Their worst possible nightmare also occurred at the same time, when an essentially complete conversion turned up from GCC. Dave Staugas got to see exactly what his team were up against and how they fared in comparison.

"We were told that our game was better, but management went with Atari's internal version for political reasons."

The internal team were stunned, with a more colourful approach to the graphics done by GCC. They were determined to work out how they did it and would pick apart and analyse GCC's prototype as a result. However, nothing would be utilised from the GCC edition in Atari's own internal development; it was more just to figure out how GCC had achieved everything.

According to the VAXMail communications, the remainder of the Sunnyvale edition of *Millipede* was produced in the final few weeks before the meeting to decide on which version to go with. Ed had talked Atari into waiting a bit longer on their own internal version as it needed just a bit more time to be fine-tuned. Eventually, that meeting resulted in Atari going with their own home-grown version, much to the dismay of GCC.

"We were told that our game was better, but management went with Atari's internal version for political reasons. That didn't sit well with us as we knew we had produced the better game," Doug laments. "I flew out to make our case to Skip Paul and Ray Kassar, but they asked me to back down on the issue. There were so many irons in the fire at that time that we accepted the decision, though we were not happy with it. In the end, Atari got two great *Millipedes*, and both were probably better than if either group had just worked on it alone."

Atari's version went on to become one of the best arcade conversions to grace the hardware. Meanwhile, GCC moved on to new projects, and its conversion was long forgotten until an Atari historian made a chance discovery in 2003. Curt Vendel recovered GCC's prototype and helped preserve it. "I don't recall having an actual cartridge, so it could have been from a mainframe recovery," he explained. "But I didn't start doing those until 2003 once I finally freighted in two 20'x20' storage lockers of items I'd recovered from Atari, so it must have been on some ROMs I'd found during my travels."

No matter how, it is thanks to Curt's preservation that users can play and compare two great conversions. You can decide which is the better game, just like the Atari management did over 35 years ago. So, were there many differences in comparison to the released version? Pretty significant ones, which Atari Protos (www.atariprotos.com/2600/software/millipede/gccproto) goes through in great detail. Although the core game was very similar, the GCC version has better titles and main character, compared with the square block of the released edition. The rest of the positives and negatives of each are down to personal opinion, though many will likely side with the released edition, as that's what they grew up with and know best.

"The trickiest part was producing the large number of moving objects with as little flicker as possible."

We conclude the 'battle of the conversions' by asking Doug if they faced similar issues with Atari. "Not that I recall. I do remember doing some early storyboarding on *E.T.*, but, fortunately, that got assigned to internal Atari development with a very unrealistic schedule," Doug responded, possibly with a sly smile.

Above: GCC's research area, including a *Millipede* arcade cabinet that was most likely used to help create its conversion at the time.

Top: GCC team members, including Doug (third from left). Bottom: The GCC offices where, somewhere, *Millipede* was developed.

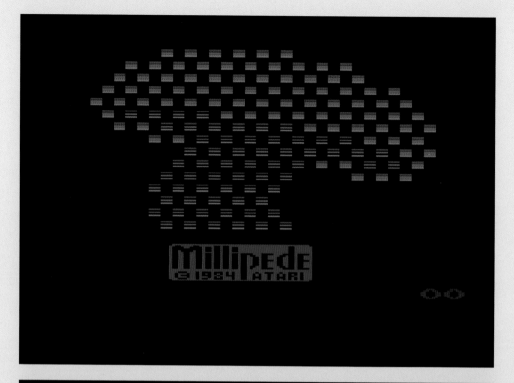

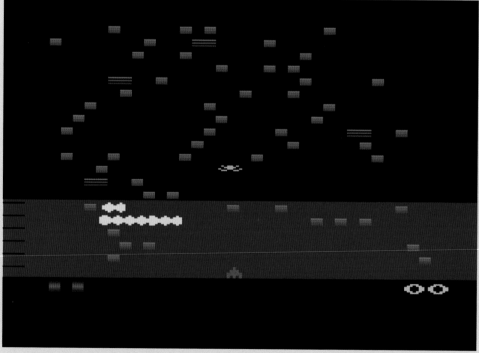

Above: GCC's *Millipede* (Atari 2600) title screen and main game, with a lot more detail and colour compared with the published conversion.

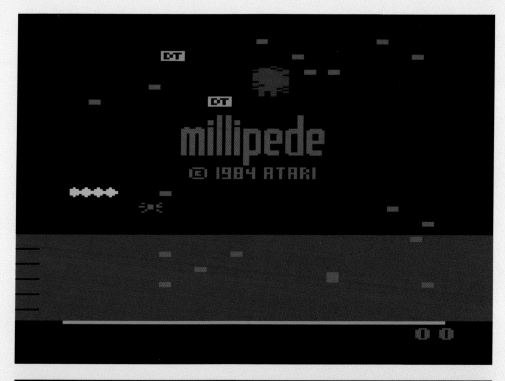

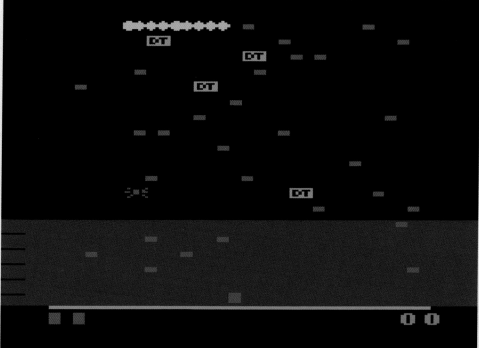

Above: Atari's own internal *Millipede* (Atari 2600) to compare, with title screen and main game. Featuring a plain square main character compared with the GCC version.

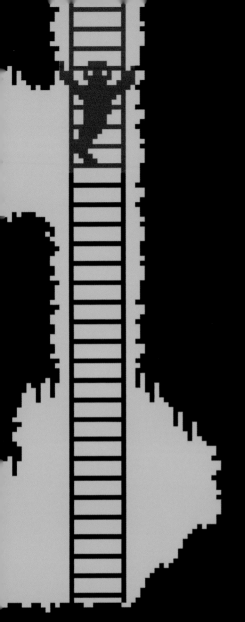

Death Pit
Quality
issues

Year: 1984
Developer: Durell Software
Platform: ZX Spectrum 48K

Sometimes, things don't quite work
out as planned. Although advertised
fairly heavily, *Death Pit* was canned
for simply not being up to scratch.
All was not lost for developer Clive
Townsend, who reused routines for
his hit release *Saboteur* that followed.
However, many were left curious
about Clive's abandoned development,
until it was finally recovered from his
decaying development microdrives
in later years.

Available to play

◉ **Yes**   ◯ **No**

Attack of the Mutant Zombie Flesh Eating Chickens from Mars

Progress slow

Year: 1987
Developer: Software Projects
Platform: ZX Spectrum 48K

Available to play

 Yes ⦿ No

The rise of the games industry saw many stories of teenage programming prodigies driving in sports cars and having more money than they possibly had sense at the time. It was all mostly made up by the press to generate publicity for the companies involved, Imagine Software being a prime example of this. Caught up in all of the hype and hysteria at the time was the enigmatic Matthew Smith, who hit dizzying heights with the wonderful *Manic Miner*.

Although that only took around six weeks to create, its sequel, *Jet Set Willy*, took considerably longer. It was not a fully enjoyable project for Matthew, what with the newly added 'pressure cooker' environment from within his own company to produce the next bestselling game. The urgency to get the game released would be at the cost of various game-breaking bugs. As Matthew once described in an interview with Paul Drury, "*Jet Set Willy* wasn't released, it escaped!" The game still did very well regardless and added to the status of its creator.

Even after *Jet Set Willy*, the pressure was on once more to produce another bestseller, but the cracks were now growing at Software Projects. The games *Mega Tree* and *Miner Willy Meets the Taxman* both befell the same fate. *Jet Set Willy 2* was merely an opportunist sequel, an expanded version of the original game with no direct involvement by Matthew himself, who felt a sequel should be a completely unique experience.

By 1987, it had been three years since the release of *Jet Set Willy*, and it was looking unlikely that another Matthew Smith game would ever surface. There would be one last roll of the dice, kick-started through another development and new idea from Commodore 64 developer John Darnell. Already successfully developing titles for Software Projects such as *Jet Set Willy 2*, *Dragons Lair* and *Dragon's Lair 2*, John was now keen to develop his own unique creation. Just by chance, his sights fixed on a game based on a famous Warner Bros. classic.

"I had been watching Wile E. Coyote and Road Runner cartoons with my daughter at home and saw ideas for a game based on what we were watching," John recalled. "I suggested to Alan Maton ideas for a *Road Runner* game, and he told me to go ahead while he chased down the licence. I never saw the arcade game at the time. Whilst Alan sorted out licensing, myself and the artists (Martin McDonald and Nicole Baikaloff) got two working levels going."

At a loose end and needing a new project, Matthew was assigned the task of creating a Spectrum version of John's new idea and was set up in an office directly next door to John. "We were all assured we had it [the licence] in the bag, paid for, done and dusted. I spent ages getting 'That's all folks' displayed on the Spectrum!" he recalled back in 2005.

Progress was slow in comparison with John's Commodore 64 edition, which was shaping up quicker thanks to the larger team and slight head start. There are rumours that Matthew attempted to claw back time by reusing code from the unfinished *Miner Willy Meets the Taxman* development, though he confirmed that everything was done from scratch. Even though just next door from each other, both John and Matthew worked separately in their own directions, with two different games gradually taking shape.

John remembers the work produced by Matthew and recalls seeing a brilliant replication of the Warner Bros. intro. There was also a basic prototype of Road Runner running within a canyon scenario, featuring very large and fast-moving characters. Road Runner would, at this early stage, just need to avoid large trucks and various traps set by Wile E. Coyote.

It wasn't long though until the pre-existing Atari arcade became a stumbling block when it was discovered that U.S. Gold already had the licence. "We were in a dilemma!" John exclaimed. "We already had two great levels for a game, so we just changed the graphics to outer space. Wile E. Coyote became Captain Rover Pawstrong, Road Runner became Tasty Space Griffin, and we carried on developing under the (later established) name of *Star Paws*."

Continuing to work independently, Matthew had no involvement in John's new direction. With the *Road Runner* licence tied up, John recalled that Matthew came into the office less and less. It is believed that Alan attempted to resurrect Matthew's interest and worked with him to come up with a new title called *Attack of the Mutant Zombie Flesh Eating Chickens from Mars* (AOTMZFECFM from now on, for the sanity of the author) to repurpose his Spectrum *Road Runner* work done so far.

"It was just a re-title of what we were doing. I just put a space helmet on the coyote, and he became Zappo the Dog!" Matthew giggled. "Actually, a friend of mine's dog was called Zaphod Beeblebrox... and, instead of *Road Runner*, he was going to be chasing alien chickens down the road. Now it wasn't *Road Runner* anymore, and I was going to have more than one of them – and flying saucers!"

"There wasn't much gameplay to it. I had a horizontal smooth-scrolling road with a parallax backdrop."

"It was a brilliant idea!" added John. "It was based on the hope that *Star Paws* (which didn't have a title at that point) might inspire or pressure Matthew to lay another golden egg." Matthew, though, saw it rather differently: "The title came from desperation... the mother of invention," he suggests. "Fortunately, the title gets you halfway down the page! I mean, there were some '50s B-movies that did the same kind of thing, piling it on."

Alan and Matthew created an elaborate and inventive backstory with the newly created protagonist. The story described how Zappo decides to take on a group of mutant flesh-eating chickens that have arrived in the heart of Arizona in their silver Martian ship after hearing of their evil plans for dogs and beasts. There was very little given away about the gameplay, but the *Road Runner* concept would essentially be role-reversed in terms of who you controlled, like with *Star Paws*. There would be a graphical overhaul and more 'Road Runners' added, reskinned as mutant chicken enemies who had to be destroyed or captured.

Software Projects had perhaps started to get too excited, and, without the game anywhere near completion, adverts were printed in major Spectrum magazines in June 1987. The advert came with the words 'A new game from MATTHEW SMITH, author of *MANIC MINER* and *JET SET WILLY*' blazoned across the top. Though this was a bizarre decision, to produce an entire palette of empty cassette inlays without a finished game was even more bizarre.

"That was done, in defiance of my instructions, by Tommy Barton," Matthew responded. "The company was basically down to him, me, and his accountants. The cover was done by Roger Tissyman. We just let him get on with all that. It wasn't under my direction. He just winged it. And, anyway, the words filled up most of the cover! I remember once being locked in the warehouse with a palette of them. The factory was locked up at night, and I had to get the night watchman to let me out in the end."

It was confirmed later by Alan Maton on Facebook that Roger wasn't behind the artwork. It wasn't disclosed who created it but was likely either another design agency or Martin McDonald. Neither Alan nor Martin responded to contact attempts to clarify this. "I don't remember who I was talking to, probably Alan or Tommy, but it was explained to me that the cassette inserts were just a way of pressuring Matthew to finish the game," John explained about the production of the inlays. "The magazine adverts would have been partly to achieve the same goal, as well as building interest in his next game too."

Interestingly, the inlay suggests that, at some stage, the space-suited Zappo would travel to Mars to finish off the zombie chickens. Matthew confirmed that the game was only ever going to be situated in Arizona on Route 66 within a canyon environment. The graphic style inspired by the 1950s American sci-fi B-movies of the time.

Regardless of the change of direction, progress was still slow and the enthusiasm was still draining from Matthew due to personal issues and ongoing fallout at Software Projects. John recalls very little of a game ever being created, only recalling an impressive animated introduction screen and a short demo of *Road Runner* running through a canyon. There was no recollection of ever seeing the game with its new branding applied.

Sinclair User magazine would see it, though, and reported so in its June 1987 news section. It described Matthew's game as having "Speedy scrolling roads with some trucks and some birds and a dog." They felt the game was technically impressive, with enormous graphics and everything moving around at an impressive speed. However, they felt the gameplay was shallow, with only the ability to run left and right, trying not to get run over or blown up.

Matthew's reflection on what he developed fitted much in line with what *Sinclair User* had seen at the time. "There wasn't much gameplay to it. I had a horizontal smooth-scrolling road with a parallax backdrop. A Greyhound bus 16 chars wide, a big truck, and Zappo all properly layered. You were going along this road and there was a bit of depth/3D to it. Scroll left and right and avoid the traffic – the tracks [of the traffic] overlapped each other, and it looked very nice for the Spectrum," he recalled.

"It would probably have played somewhat like *Defender* unless I'd thought of something better. I don't think I ever drew the chickens, but their sound was made from a chunk of the ROM used as a rapid note table. I forget which part of the Speccy ROM sounded most like an alien chicken. Technically, it was in the bag though. It had very impressive animation and was very impressive visually. I even had the characters going across the screen without colour clash. It was also playable; I just needed to balance the gameplay and make it something people really wanted to play."

Just two months later, in August 1987, *Sinclair User* reported that Software Projects were not going to release the game and that Matthew had been instructed to rework it. It was the very same month that *Star Paws'* adverts began to surface, including a note to say that Spectrum and Amstrad versions were coming soon. This was no coincidence, as John reveals. "When it was realised that Matthew was not going to produce a game, Software Projects had to have a Spectrum version of *Star Paws* instead," he explained. "The whole idea of *AOTMZFECFM* was an elaborate attempt to get Matthew to work, but there never was any game, nor anything like a game."

Matthew gives a different account of what happened. "*AOTMZFECFM* could have been a good game," he insisted. "When you've written two number-one games, you don't want to do something that is barely charting. I would've finished it, but I was just getting so much stress at the time. It was my decision to stop it. The Spectrum market was dying by then."

Regardless of the reason, the last news snippet from *Sinclair User* was a clever way of retiring Matthew's game. It looked like a positive move by Software Projects, demonstrating that quality was paramount to them. But, in combination with the new adverts, it indirectly suggested that *Star Paws* was the reworked game from the brain of Matthew Smith, which wasn't the case at all.

For years, it has since been claimed that *Star Paws* started out as *AOTMZFECFM*, though, actually, the only relation was that they both started off as a *Road Runner* game. "People want Matthew to be the underlying inspiration for *Star Paws*, but it's not true," confirmed John. *Star Paws'* protagonist was never called Zappo at any stage, and *AOTMZFECFM* certainly never became *Star Paws*.

What didn't help rumours was that the protagonists for both games were strikingly similar. John believes that both cover designs were created by the same artist, Martin McDonald, which would explain the similarities. Had *AOTMZFECFM* not been cancelled, then Captain Pawstrong may have been given a very different look to differentiate.

It was crazy that Software Projects was going to allow two very similar titles to be released with different titles/story/packaging. It's possible, though, that management came to its senses, and *Sinclair User's* last news snippet was an indication of this. It is plausible that Matthew was instructed to scrap his development and start a conversion of *Star Paws* on the Spectrum instead, but perhaps refused to do so. Unfortunately, no one was able to confirm or deny.

John's *Star Paws* eventually saw its release in September 1987, with high praise from the press and even from Matthew himself. "At the very end of developing *Star Paws*, I was playing the game through. Matthew came in, watched for a few minutes and gave me an unforgettable compliment – 'Fucking well done John!!' Coming from the legend that Matthew was, I consider that to be quite a compliment," smiled John. The Spectrum conversion of *Star Paws* was arranged with Software Creations straight after. Developed by Ste Cork, the conversion took approximately 4–5 months to complete – released in April 1988.

"When I picked it up, I was astonished."

Overall, events would result in yet another Matthew Smith game never seeing the light of day. It was feeling increasingly likely that it was never going to happen for Matthew and Software Projects. "Matthew was just a kid when he first wrote *Manic Miner*, and he wrote that for his own satisfaction," John explains. "He was under enormous pressure getting *Jet Set Willy* to production, and it was an incredibly stressful experience for him. I don't think he ever got over it – the trauma took all of the motivation out of writing computer games."

After completing *Star Paws*, John decided to venture down the freelance route, briefly returning to Software Projects in 1988 to discuss his new *Kane 2* game with Tommy Barton. At the time, Matthew was still at Software Projects and even had a copy of *Manic Miner* running on an Atari ST. According to John, it looked beautiful but was yet another game that failed to see completion. Not long afterwards, things broke down completely at Software Projects, with the company eventually closing its doors as time went on.

After going off the radar for many years (at one stage relocating to The Netherlands) and attracting much speculation and rumour, Matthew resurfaced in 1999 at Runecraft Studios. It was here that he was involved with a conversion of *Scrabble* for the Game Boy Color, and he has since appeared at retro events – most recently for the 35th anniversary of *Jet Set Willy* at PLAY Manchester.

AOTMZFECFM would become as much of a mystery as its creator once was. It became news once more though during the late 1990s when retro historian Keith Ainsworth made an amazing discovery by locating one of the infamously printed inlays. "I found it in a charity shop in Liscard in the Wirral," Keith recalled. "A box of tapes caught my eye because of all the Bug-Byte games (who were a local company). After pulling out the tapes, I noticed a game inlay not in a cassette box lying on the bottom. When I picked it up, I was astonished to see which game it was for. I checked all the other tapes in the box, but there was no matching tape. I asked the assistant if there were any other tapes in the shop or in the back, but she said there weren't. I left my number with her and asked to be phoned if anything similar turned up."

Keith was never called back but was happy with his unique find. "I put it in a frame many years ago, so it's in perfect condition. Despite several offers to buy it over the years, I have never been tempted to sell. There are very few items like this that are truly unique." John had also kept a copy of the inlay to this day and kindly provided scans and photos which will be available on the Games That Weren't website.

Around the same time as Keith's discovery, the game's loading screen surfaced thanks to Steve Leyland back in 2000, who digitally recovered it from an old tape of his. Steve had created the loading screen as a favour for Matthew but never got to finish it when the game was cancelled. The screen would actually feature Zappo in likeness to his original inspiration, Zaphod.

"Matthew is a personal friend and used to visit frequently back then," said Steve. "Zaphod was a cross-breed between a German Shepherd and a Doberman, a friendly dog and always made a big fuss of Matthew whenever he arrived. So, when he showed me the plan for his new game featuring my pooch, I volunteered to make a screen for it, even though I was a novice at computers. I used *Art Studio* on my Speccy to create it. I was unemployed at the time so had plenty of spare time to dedicate to it. It was still pretty much a work in progress when the game was sadly cancelled."

Steve also suggested that Matthew had kept a copy of the game on tape, which was indeed the case until the early 2000s, when (typically) it was lost. "There may possibly be something left of it somewhere," Matthew suggested. "But I've had to move with the world in a suitcase on several occasions, and most of it has probably been binned now, to be honest."

Of course, miracles do happen occasionally, and recovering something of the prototype is not outside the realms of possibility. At the time of writing, there is indeed a faint hope. Steve revealed that he had saved some of Matthew's old Spectrum tapes and kit, kept in his attic, and is in the process of digging them out to let Matthew sift through and see what gems can be uncovered.

So, remains of Matthew's prototype could finally surface for fans to get a glimpse of what could have been. Though, to be fair, you have a better chance of finding one of the printed inlays. *AOTMZFECFM* may likely just remain a daydream for those who grew up seeing the adverts.

"I was coding *AOTMZFECFM* in the offices of Software Projects, and I couldn't go home to eat because I couldn't afford it."

We conclude by asking Matthew if he had any other memories about the development that he wanted to share. "Nah. Except, I never want to smell another microwaved potato!" he responded. "That's what I was living on at the time. I was coding *AOTMZFECFM* in the offices of Software Projects, and I couldn't go home to eat because I couldn't afford it. It was just me working on the game. There wasn't anyone left by then. Tommy got rid of everyone, but I was tenacious. Yeah... it wasn't too much later after that when I gave up."

Was that perhaps the moment that Matthew finally felt he was never going to reach the dizzying heights of *Manic Miner* and *Jet Set Willy* ever again? Perhaps, someday, that will change. Considering the rumours that Matthew is to start game development once again, we really hope it happens someday.

 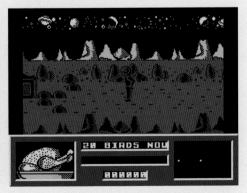

Left: Star Paws *(Commodore 64). An original development that didn't start out as* AOTMZFECFM *like many believe.* Right: Star Paws *(ZX Spectrum) that likely resulted from* AOTMZFECFM's *cancellation.*

Above: Advert shown in various magazines of the time, featuring a rather wild logo containing a variety of styles and part of the game's story. Matthew Smith is clearly spotlighted too.

Top: ZX Spectrum loading screen by Steve, featuring his dog Zappo. **Bottom:** Artist's impression of how *AOTMZFECFM* (ZX Spectrum) may have looked, based on recollections and press details.

Rescue on Fractalus!
Cost cutting

Year: 1984
Developer: General Computer Corporation
Platform: Atari 7800

A rumour-mill conversion for years of a classic that had you flying over a fast fractal-based landscape rescuing pilots. Recovered from the developers in 2004, the early prototype showcases the 7800's power with its impressive frame rate. Tragically believed to be cancelled due to extra RAM requirements and Atari cost-cutting.

Rescue on Fractalus! and *Ballblazer* caused a sensation at GCC. We never imagined 8-bit hardware rendering first-person action of that complexity and smoothness. Dave Krall and I flew cross-country to meet the developers and get a crash course in fractals. While Dave worked on the out-the-window fractal view, I put together the ship's interior. We needed 4K of extra RAM but couldn't afford it; intern Jeff Bell devised a PC board hack to fill the view with 2K worth of double-height pixels.

Artist Paul Moody created a spectacular interior for the 7800's higher resolution. This got a cool reception at Lucasfilm, who wanted to reproduce the 5200 visuals for backstory reasons. We settled on simply adding detail to the original layout. It was a highlight of my young career. The project was cancelled before we got to see higher-resolution ships, pilots, bases and scary aliens, which was a darn shame."

Lars Jensen, developer

Available to play

◉ Yes ○ No

Starring Charlie Chaplin

Developer financial woes

Year: 1988
Developer: Canvas Software
Platforms: Atari ST and Commodore 64

Available to play
 Yes No

British actor Charlie Chaplin is one of the most iconic figures of the film world, rising to fame in America during the silent film era. It was his character 'The Tramp' that would propel him to megastardom and forever etch Chaplin into the status of comedy film legend. Starring in groundbreaking films such as *The Tramp* and *The Bank*, Chaplin would entertain many for years, even long after his passing at the age of 88 in 1977.

With computer games decades away at the time of Chaplin's active period, it came as a surprise that a game based on the actor was announced so long afterwards. Seeing the potential and knowing the value of a licensed game was U.S. Gold, who announced *Starring Charlie Chaplin* to the world in late 1987. Canvas Software, fresh from its developments of *Road Runner* and *Wizard Warz*, was approached by U.S. Gold yet again to carry out the work for its new project. Roy Gibson would head up the initial design and contract negotiations but would leave the company before the game got seriously underway.

A full design plan was then implemented by the late Gary Bolton (who passed away in 2000). Paul Clansey, a good friend of Gary who worked at Canvas, described his role: "Gary was overall manager at Canvas, coming up with some of the high-level designs (for example, *Chaplin*, *Wizard Warz* and *Iron Hand*), and probably did project-manage some of the work too. Gary was a close friend of mine since the mid-'70s, and he was only involved with computer games for a couple of years – ending up in IT in the Civil Service."

Gary's design would put you in the control of a silent film director, who is required to produce slapstick films starring Charlie Chaplin. With a tight budget, you can produce films such as 'The Immigrant', 'Modern Times', 'The Drunk', and many others. Each film comes with a set number of scenes, and you must control and get Chaplin to interact with other characters and scenery within each. One of the key actions would be to knock down characters or get knocked down yourself for comedic effect.

At the end of each scene, you would then get the chance to replay and tweak your recordings in the editing suite and decide if it is good enough for inclusion in the film. A reshoot will cost more of your budget, with it being game over if you run out of funds. Once a film is complete, you are whisked off to the box office, where an audience and a 'Variety magazine' review will decide if you will earn enough to produce your next film. End with a flop and your time as a director is brought to an abrupt halt.

The very first issue of *The Games Machine* magazine (a multi-format publication) released by Newsfield Publications) in October/November 1987 dedicated a half-page news spread to the new development, showing an early screenshot of the lead Atari ST edition and also listing conversions for the Amstrad CPC, Commodore 64. IBM PC and ZX Spectrum platforms.

Adverts began to show from December that year, with a more advanced Atari ST screen featuring characters on a film set. *Atari ST User* magazine's Robin Nixon visited U.S. Gold to see its new titles, where marketing manager Richard Tidsall gave a tour and showed what seemed to be stills of *Charlie Chaplin* – the magazine printing the same screen as shown in the advert.

Early news reports and magazine adverts were slightly misleading as they suggested that you would be able to 'choose scripts, cast characters, select scenery, props and backdrops'. One magazine even suggested that you could save your films and play them back at a later date, and there was mention of a bad guy to avoid that grabs you and wastes valuable production time. Many of these suggestions would be thrown by the wayside, with a simpler approach taken for the final release due to growing issues occurring at Canvas.

"Although reviews noted the excellent presentation, the gameplay was too shallow and devoid of much playability."

After some delay, the game was eventually released in June 1988 for the ZX Spectrum, Amstrad CPC, and IBM PC platforms. The Commodore 64 and Atari ST editions were notably absent, listed as 'coming soon'.

Although reviews noted the excellent presentation, the gameplay was too shallow and devoid of much playability. There was just not enough to do. All you really needed was to keep punching the cast to earn enough money to progress. Other actions in the game just included twirling your cane, kissing and shrugging shoulders as you wandered around each set, but none of them seemed to have much effect. It was a case of 'rinse and repeat' across different films and scenes until you likely switched off in boredom. Although the PC edition had better detail and presentation, it wasn't enough to bring it out of mediocrity. It felt like a missed opportunity, and it was.

Computer and Video Games magazine's Matt Biebly suggested in his review that the Commodore and Atari versions would likely be as bad as the ZX Spectrum edition. When we asked if he had seen either of the unreleased versions at the time, Matt could no longer recall. Unbeknown to anyone at the time, Canvas was in dire financial trouble, and *Starring Charlie Chaplin* had been caught right in the middle. Simplifications to the original design were made in an attempt to get the game to U.S. Gold quicker and to receive payment in a bid keep the company afloat. Though, when things began to go pear-shaped, alarm bells rang for U.S. Gold, and it decided to step in.

"The game was almost finished on all systems until U.S. Gold pulled the plug and had us ship all data to Tiertex," recalled Amstrad CPC graphic artist Martin Holland back in 2000. Dawn Hollywood (née Drake), graphic artist on the ZX Spectrum version, had actually already left Canvas some months earlier due to lack of payment and through what she quoted as being "the obvious closing stages of Canvas". Others involved on *Chaplin* followed a similar route, and many had also lost motivation with the inevitable expected.

Only the Spectrum and Amstrad versions were to be handed over due to being the furthest behind of all the versions. Tiertex's Donald Campbell confirmed that he personally developed the ZX Spectrum version in 2–3 weeks, after being asked to take on the project by Geoff Brown and Tim Chaney at U.S. Gold as a rescue job. The Amstrad CPC version was based off the Spectrum code, also done by Donald and likely with some assistance. It was decided that it would be easier to start from scratch rather than try and interpret someone else's code, but they used the already completed and supplied art assets.

Donald had no recollection of the Atari ST or Commodore 64 editions, never being asked to take them on. With the Atari ST and PC editions felt to be in better shape compared with the other conversions, U.S. Gold kept faith with Canvas to get those versions completed. U.S. Gold's other go-to team, Probe, were already booked up with other developments anyway, so the options available were limited. The Commodore 64 version would be quietly dropped from the line-up, due to difficulties in obtaining the assets to pass on to another programmer, details of which we will come to.

Although the PC version was just completed by Canvas, the Atari ST version failed to appear at all. Canvas had struggled on for a few more months since the initial *Chaplin* releases but ran out of money and closed its doors before the end of 1988.

With key members of Canvas – such as Gary Bolton, Ian Weatherburn and Steve Cain – no longer with us, it was difficult to establish what happened exactly to the two unreleased editions. Investigations began by contacting as many as possible who worked at Canvas, many of whom did not know or had forgotten after all the time that had passed. For many, Canvas was not a pleasant time in its final darker months. Even members from U.S. Gold couldn't recall what happened, with Tim Chaney, Charles Cecil, Richard Tidsall and Danielle Woodyatt all giving a collective shrug of the shoulders when asked.

"It felt like a missed opportunity, and it was."

With the Atari ST as the lead platform, it was perhaps a surprise that no one could recall who was developing it compared with the other versions. "Canvas had a number of people that worked from home, any of which could have done the Atari ST version," explained Stephen Ward, developer of the PC edition. "It's possible it was never finished as I remember *Chaplin* was very late in the life of Canvas, so it may have gone pear-shaped before it could be released."

Working through potential developer candidates, *Wizard Warz* Atari ST developer Phil Blackburn was a possibility, who only had the credit of Psygnosis's *Brattacus* to his name otherwise. Paul Hobart and John Smith were two others. Attempts to track down John, Phil and Paul were unsuccessful at the time of writing. Another possibility was Ian Weatherburn, the head of Canvas himself, who sadly passed away a few years after the closure of the company.

"It could well have been Ian [Weatherburn] and Scott Johnston who did *Chaplin*," Paul Clansey suggested. "Strangely, though, I worked for Ian and spent quite a bit of time socially with him. We rarely talked about our own projects, but *Chaplin* rings a faint bell from our conversations." Scott initially responded to enquiries, indicating some involvement, but the line went dead with no further replies. Thanks though to graphic artist Jon Grimshaw, he suggests that Scott may have done the sprite and animation work on the Atari ST.

Jon himself was employed by Canvas as a game designer and became more of an art team leader as time went on. Memories of the Canvas years had faded badly, and Jon had forgotten completely about his role as graphic artist on the PC edition. Luckily, synapses were sparked to life when he was provided with the Atari ST screenshots to evaluate. "Looking at them, I feel strongly that I actually did them," he said. "I remember researching US brownstone buildings and fire escapes, etc. I also remember how tricky it was trying to represent the angles of a cogwheel within the limitations of the screen resolution and of the art software. I'm really surprised at how much game design I must have done!"

With Jon's details about the background research, it seems more than likely that he was the lead graphic artist on the Atari ST edition, even though he couldn't recall anything more specific about the development. It was becoming clear that the Atari ST screens were produced first and then passed on to other teams to convert to their respective platforms. "I have a vague memory that I didn't do all the versions of the games – I remember feeling a bit odd that others were reproducing what I'd come up with," Jon added. He would only end up converting his own work down to 2-bit monochrome for the PC edition it seemed.

"The record/playback functionality was even more of a headache."

For years, it was suggested that the Atari ST screenshots from the press and adverts may have just been mock-ups and were only ever so. Although some were indeed early static screens, they did accurately form how the game was going to look. With the game development closing to completion and still expected to be released, the Atari ST version was fully documented in the released multi-format instructions (including specific loading and keyboard commands). In comparison, the Commodore 64 edition was not included at all. With Ian as the likely Atari ST developer, delays were probably incurred due to coding and simultaneously trying to run the company and keep it afloat.

Therefore, two scenarios seem likely for its non-release. Firstly, Canvas may have completely run out of money and closed its doors before the delayed Atari ST version could be fully finished off. The second scenario is that, when the released versions bombed as badly as they did, U.S. Gold decided not to proceed with the delayed Atari ST version. Tim Chaney could not recall and was not able to confirm the exact reason, so it may always remain a mystery. Following the collapse, Ian went on to work at a new software house called New Frontier Productions, working on a new Activision game called *Exodus* for the Atari ST.

The reasons for the non-release of the Commodore 64 edition was simpler to solve, thanks to its developer coming forward. Sean Townsend contacted Games That Weren't back in 2015 to confirm involvement and share the story on what happened. "I had recently finished the C64 version of *Road Runner* and was just starting to put together the basics of an in-house game called *Rolling Thunder* (later called *Iron Hand*)," he explained. "This was a side-scrolling jet fighter-style game which was suddenly put on hold to work on *Chaplin*. I don't recall having any start-up meetings or anything, but there must have been some kind of design brief, otherwise, I couldn't have really started on the development."

"The game was almost finished on all systems until U.S. Gold pulled the plug and had us ship all data to Tiertex."

Sean worked from home and had to travel to Crosby every 3–4 weeks to demonstrate progress on his version of the game. "It was probably a 100-mile round trip," he recalled. "On one occasion, I arrived at Canvas only to find I had the wrong disks with me. I then had to travel home, get the correct disks and travel back to Crosby. This only happened once!"

Sean suggests that Martin Calvert was the man behind the Commodore 64 graphics, though Martin couldn't be 100% certain if it was him or not. It is plausible that Jon Grimshaw instead handled the C64 graphics, but he also couldn't recall. No others from Canvas at the time would lay credit to the work, so the strongest bet so far was that it was one of those two graphic artists. However, the music was confirmed as being composed by Mark Cooksey, on freelance duty away from Elite Software.

Development began well for Sean and was on schedule, but there were issues with receiving the artwork early on. "Looking back at my notes, there are a few frustrated scribbles where I have been waiting for graphics. When they finally do arrive, they are wrong," recalled Sean. "There's nothing quite like working in the same development studio as the graphic artists. You can quite clearly discuss your requirements and verify that they are progressing as expected during the development life cycle, rather than getting a disk through the post only to find the graphics aren't quite what you were expecting."

Once the correct graphics had finally been sorted out, there were still major challenges to overcome. Sean would struggle at first getting all of the sprites working, going in front or behind scenery. As the Commodore 64 only had eight hardware sprites, and with limitations of how many per line you could have, Sean opted to do all the characters as software sprites. This worked well enough, given that the background images were being stored as bitmaps.

The record/playback functionality was even more of a headache. "I never got this fully working," Sean confessed. "The basics are in there as it does record and playback, but, occasionally, it would be slightly out of sync, which resulted in Chaplin doing something different. For example, if he walked up to the woman and kissed her, during playback, he occasionally wouldn't be close enough to kiss her and would raise his hat instead. Issues like this could take a long time to resolve as we didn't have the debugging utilities like we have now. The only solution was to print out the source code and spend a good few hours trying to figure out what was going wrong."

Ultimately, though, it was the implementation of each scene as a bitmap image that would cause the biggest woes. With no compression techniques used, loading was horrendous, even on disk. For tape users, it was going to be a complete nightmare. "If I was to redo it now, though, I'm sure I'd be using some kind of LZW compression and it would be possible, but, back then, I hadn't even heard of LZW compression," lamented Sean.

But, perhaps thankfully, the nightmare would never be experienced. With plenty still to do, Sean started to notice problems at Canvas when payment was becoming more and more inconsistent. Frustrated and fed up with the lack of financial stability, Sean handed in his notice around February/March 1988 and got a job working at Barcrest. He was never asked for anything of his work.

No one could recall what happened next or if there was any attempt to allocate to someone else to complete. Canvas probably didn't have the resources to restart the development itself with its financial woes. Tiertex was also a very small team at the time and probably didn't have the capacity to take on the additional conversion work either. We may never know if anyone else was ever approached to re-develop the conversion.

Luckily, Sean's unfinished Chaplin work was miraculously recovered from decaying disks sent through to the Games That Weren't archive in 2015. The game was released in its final state in late 2016. The recovery shows that key parts of the game were not finished, including the ability to select your starting scene and the replay/editing components. There are heavy bugs present, and it's clear that the game would not have worked at all on tape. At the very least, it is now a great curiosity to experience.

What though of the Atari ST edition? With Ian sadly no longer with us, it would rely on someone else having a copy of the game or assets. Simon Butler suggested that Ian was very careful with his code and would not have given copies out to anyone. Jon also confirmed not having anything at all from his brief time in the gaming industry, and Scott hasn't responded to any enquiries. Therefore, it is likely that the Atari ST version is now gone forever. Strange things can happen, but, at the time of writing, nothing has been forthcoming. Parts of the mystery have been solved for now, though Atari ST fans will feel that, for them, it's a chapter yet to be properly closed.

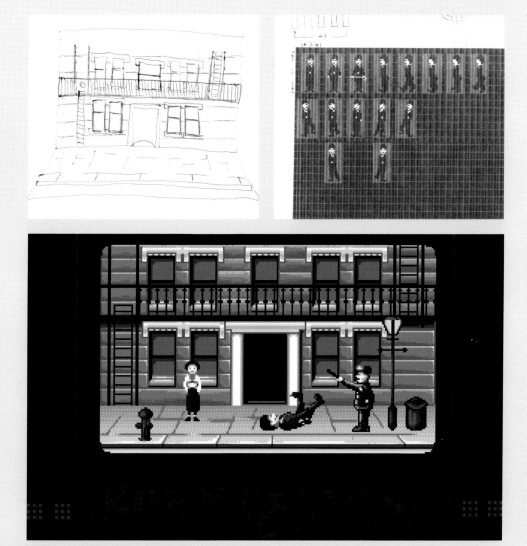

Top: Sean Townsend's sketch of the street scene and development notes. Bottom: An artist's pixel interpretation of *Starring Charlie Chaplin* (Atari ST) based on the advert screenshot.

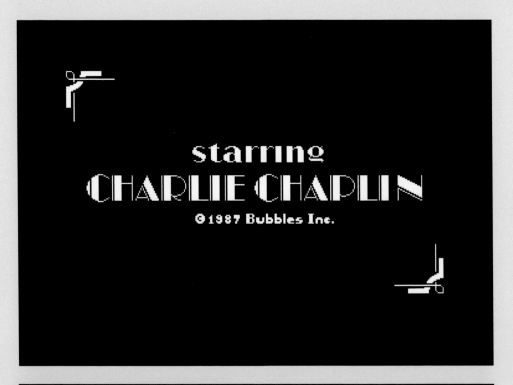

Above: Various screens from the recovered *Starring Charlie Chaplin* (Commodore 64), including the introduction screen and the boat scene.

Above: U.S. Gold advert for the game, advertising all formats and including an Atari ST screenshot. It even encouraged you to create your own flip book.

Discussing 'Black Hawk' Limited hardware

Year: 1987
Developer: Lucasfilm
Platform: Commodore 64

As much as we love the Commodore 64, it was admittedly not the best equipped to handle fast 3D simulators, where some games felt like you were wading through treacle. However, this didn't stop many from persevering to squeeze something decent out of the beige 8-bit wonder.

Black Hawk was one such attempt from Lucasfilm during 1987, aiming to build upon the success of *Koronis Rift* and *The Eidolon*, utilising the same fractal approach. The game was actually closer to *Rescue on Fractalus!* with the concept of rescuing people, but it came with the plotline of thwarting terrorist attacks. Noah Falstein (NF), Aric Wilmunder (AW) and Charlie Kellner (CK) talk about their ambitious simulator.

How did the concept for *Black Hawk* first come about?
AW: I don't recall having any real involvement with the concept. I remember Noah coming back from the company library with books on helicopters and having them around his office. The *Black Hawk* helicopter got a lot of attention since it was taking on a variety of roles in the military. There were variants being used for navy, search and rescue, moving combat troops, etc., so it was a great candidate for an aircraft to build a design around.

NF: After *Koronis Rift* and *The Eidolon* came out, Steve Arnold (our boss at the time) asked me to focus on making a game that could be a sales hit, and I thought that military vehicle simulations might be a good direction. MicroProse, in particular, had started to do well in that line. I did some research in the wonderful library we had at Skywalker Ranch, found a book on hovercrafts and hydrofoils, and that inspired *PHM Pegasus*. We had begun a sequel called *Task Force 1990* which eventually became *Strike Fleet*, but we also were hoping to use the fractal technology that had served us well before and thought perhaps it could work to do a flight simulator.

Available to play Yes No

Above: An artist's pixel recreation of *Black Hawk* (Commodore 64), showing the loading screen. Based on a screen shown in the Lucasfilm promotional video.

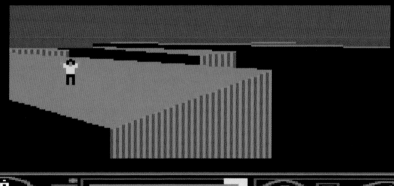

Above: An artist's pixel interpretation of *Black Hawk* (Commodore 64), showing the main game. Based on a screen shown in the Lucasfilm promotional video.

CR: One of our best assets during those years was Loren Carpenter's fractal engine. When Loren went back to making movies with the film division (the group that eventually became Pixar), I did most of the maintenance work on the fractal code. Some new ideas came along for how to use it, including shaded mountain ranges (*Koronis Rift*) and turning the mountains upside down to make caves (*The Eidolon*). Although it may not look like it, the cityscape is being generated by the same fractal engine. At first, there was no game as such associated with the simulation, other than flying around a city. I suppose the idea of rescuing people was natural after *Rescue on Fractalus!*, but I think it was Noah who suggested the terrorist threat scenario.

NF: What I recall is that we had a meeting after an early 'Helicopter Simulation' document I wrote, and then I went off and refined ideas into a *Black Hawk* design document. I remember, for me, the key idea was from a mention somewhere in a book that I also found in the Skywalker library. I learned there was a team called NEST, Nuclear Emergency Search Team. Combined with my enjoyment of an early Apple II game called *Choplifter!*, it occurred to me that we might be able to make a sort of first-person version and perhaps combine it with a storyline that I believe I was inspired to create from reading early Tom Clancy novels at the time.

It was pretty hard to fly, though, especially given the low frame rate and the early input devices."

Was it planned for linear progression in the game, from mission to mission, or to fly around different cities and respond to nearby alerts in an open world?
NF: I had in mind that there would be a sort of sequential story through a series of missions, but we never got to implement it. The team also never even got to flesh out the first city, so there was no design on multiple levels or even a decision on whether to do more than one location.

The Lucasfilm preview video online mentions a city where you rescue people and defuse bombs. The game seemed to be fairly advanced at that point.
NF: The video was a very early prototype with non-functional dials and was just for our annual company meeting. Our group had a bit of an inferiority complex at those meetings, the video you found would be projected on a tiny portion of a movie screen with those quaint 8-bit graphics, and then ILM would show the most exciting ten minutes of movie special effects they'd done in the last year.

Aric, what were you working on at this point?
AW: Around this time, I was working multiple projects, including the graphics engine for *Habitat* and preparing for *Maniac Mansion* on the PC. Most of my recollections were meeting with Charlie to see how the city renderer was coming and offering technical suggestions for ways to improve the frame rate since that was also a focus – maybe including *Koronis Rift*

NF: Never implemented. My thought was the helicopter could shoot at terroris eams but primarily be both rescuing civilians and dropping off NEST commandos vho would seek and destroy the terrorists. Since the terrorists were proceeding nostly on foot or in the buildings, it would be rare that the player would eve ctually see them.

Were there plans to allow helicopter customisations or upgrades?

NF: Again, never implemented. I was inspired, in part, by MicroProse's *Gunship* game and thought you could reconfigure the helicopter between flights dropping off rescued civilians, loading missiles or gun ammo, picking up troops We didn't even begin to detail that though.

How was the fractal engine utilised to create the environments?

CK: The Mountain drawing code was driving the simulation but with the nountains rendered as buildings and city streets. There were a limited numbe of block layouts that could be chosen, selected by building height. Each block had streets that connected with the other blocks to make it look like a city The shading on the sides of the buildings was then a further extension of the *Koronis Rift* idea – consistent with compass direction, to give a better sense o prientation as you flew around. Since the screen had limited colours, we wen with vertical stripes of colour. It would have looked odd on mountains, but, or puildings, it suggested vertical architecture.

NF: As Charlie mentions, by turning the mountains into buildings, it allowed us to create a fairly realistic landscape with good fidelity but, unfortunately, with a low frame rate. With the early concept, Charlie went on to see if the frame ate could be increased to the point where a flying game was feasible.

CK: I remember also making a moving camera early on that could be 'flown through the city to debug the rendering engine. I suppose this suggested a helicopter, but developing the simulation really required all hands. I remembe we ended up with something like 50 variables to keep track of the fligh dynamics. It was probably the most intense physics simulation we did during those years. Ground effect was there, along with both ground and edge effec off the top of the buildings. It was pretty hard to fly, though, especially giver he low frame rate and the early input devices.

How hard was it to get the frame rate high enough to be considered playable

CK: One of the constant struggles back then was to keep a game idea from pecoming 'all things to all people'. We had very limited resources, a 1MHz, 8-bi processor, less than 64 kilobytes of memory, and no floating point or graphic hardware. Our ambition was to do what we could, given the constraints

AW: Maintaining a good frame rate was always critical to our efforts. TVs of the time would refresh the screen 30 times a second, and we had found that we could get away with 10–15 and maintain a pretty good illusion of real-time action. Every routine was examined with the goal to reduce the time required, but we were right up against the capabilities of the physical hardware. We had written our own assemblers and tools to aid our development, but there was still a hard limit to what the C64 could do.

CK: Our frame rate did slowly improve during the development process, and I believe it started rising into the double digits thanks to more advanced 3D clipping that would quickly discard whole buildings when they were hidden behind other buildings. The screen capture in the preview video was done early on, as demonstrated by the broken control panel.

Was frame rate the only problem facing *Black Hawk* overall?
AW: I remember that the core to moving objects inside the fractal universe was called PTOC, for Polar to Cartesian, though I believe we used a 256-degree world to map with an 8-bit value, rather than the 360 degrees we typically use. Charlie wrote this, and he can probably provide greater detail, but PTOC was crucial since the fractal world was mapped using one method, and objects in the world were mapped using another. If the two systems didn't provide nearly identical results, you would have objects that didn't move properly with the surrounding world. I remember that this was even more critical with *Black Hawk* since objects on top of the buildings needed to stay in place as you approached and moved around it. Another critical piece of the technology was the clipping of objects behind the buildings. Buildings were drawn with one approach and objects with another, but the objects needed to know about the buildings so they would clip, rotate, scale and render correctly.

Our ambition was to do what we could, given the constraints."

Electronic Arts seemed up for publishing, so what happened?
NF: EA was interested – *Pegasus* was published by them, and they were happy with it, but Stewart Bonn, our producer contact there, was not excited at all about *Black Hawk*. I remember he took me aside and asked if I was aware that it was sort of the helicopter equivalent of a 'bus', and he wanted a 'race car'. I had in mind a future proposed modification of the helicopter I'd read about, which was, to some extent, the US response to the Russian Hind helicopter, that could carry troops AND had some impressive armaments. But they were never very excited, and, as I recall, Charlie wanted to pitch them his own concept, and we decided that was a better path for him to do that, and me to switch to helping launch *Strike Fleet* and then *Indiana Jones and the Last Crusade*. So, the game basically was doomed because it was too ambitious for the computer of the time, with little support from EA (probably deservedly so)

AW. Although we also understood the power of illusion with techniques like shearing and mixing 3D renderers, we could also see the next generation of hardware was also on the horizon. These platforms included hardware blitters and scalers that we were having to write in software. Part of the decision to let the project go may have been based around our knowledge of what was coming.

Perhaps we'll see it again in a different light."

How far had the game got to before the cancellation?

NF: As I recall, it never got much further than the design doc and several impressive tech experiments by Charlie. I doubt the game ever got beyond what I'd consider 10–20% to actually being a playable game and was really just an advanced prototype, not even an alpha build of a game.

What were you all proudest of with the development?

CK: I'm proud of all the work we did back then, and I think, when people realise how much we did with how little we had to work with, they'll be impressed. The marvellous thing about the dancing bear is not how well it dances, but that it dances at all." – P.T. Barnum.

NF: The missile camera view was very exciting, I still remember us coming into Charlie's office to see it, but, as I recall, the small screen it had and the speed of the missile made it almost impossible to steer around buildings. I read later that the actual TV-guided missiles and bombs the military had developed had the same problem, and they mainly used them to guide them through clear terrain to hit open targets precisely, as we saw in the Gulf War a few years later. Given the 1MHz processor of the C64, it was very impressive. However, it wasn't until *Battlehawks 1942* running on faster computers with a purposefully simple background (sea and sky only) that we got decent frame rates for dogfighting.

What are possibilities of seeing remains of the game preserved?

CK: There seems to be efforts to reconstruct early game code. A mystery to me why people would suddenly get interested in that code after decades, but it's happening. Perhaps we'll see it again in a different light, as it might have been.

AW: Bits and pieces may be found. I'm a bit of a historian and kept a collection of many of the Lucasfilm design documents, both for games we shipped and many that we didn't. I visited the company when they were at the facility in Golden Gate Park and brought a bag of documents, hoping that they had a way to archive them. I learned that they didn't have an archivist, and I was told that it was best to hold on to them. After more than a decade, I began scanning them, first offering copies to the designers for their own records. My key interest is that these records are made public and historians will be able to get an understanding of the early days of computer game development – specifically

The Last Ninja Delays

Year: 1987–1989
Developer: System 3
Platforms: Atari 800/130XE, Amstrad CPC, Atari ST, Commodore Amiga, Tandy Colour Computer 3 and ZX Spectrum 48K

Available to play

 Yes ◯ No

Were you one of those kids during the 1980s who tried to replicate the crane kick from *The Karate Kid*, almost trashing the living room in the process – or was that just the author? The 1970s and 1980s were two decades obsessed with kung fu and ninja films, with the craze even swilling over into games too.

After causing controversy with half-naked models advertising their *Twister* game at the 1985 Olympia Show, System 3 caused a stir once more – but this time, in the shape of the stunning *The Last Ninja*. Gone were the half-naked women, replaced by a single masked ninja set in beautiful 8-bit isometric Japan. After numerous delays, the game eventually hit the Commodore 64 around June 1987 to critical acclaim and awards.

Sensing early on that the game was going to be a major success, System 3 had already set to work arranging conversions for all systems under the sun to milk the 'cash ninja'. BBC Micro, Apple II, PC and Acorn Archimedes owners were eventually lucky enough to sample the isometric delights, though Commodore Amiga, Atari ST, Amstrad CPC, Sinclair ZX Spectrum, Tandy CoCo3 and Atari 800/130XE owners (who were promised conversions at one stage or another) were not so lucky.

For the Atari ST, System 3 had a challenge finding a developer to take on the project. Showing how keen it was for the conversion, Hugh Riley had produced disks and disks of artwork before anyone had even been assigned to development. The problem was that the artwork consisted of individually hand-drawn pictures, with no map compression, paths or walkable areas defined. As a result, the prospect of trying to stitch them into a fully playable set of levels was a daunting task for whoever took the conversions on.

Eventually, Active Systems would answer the call. It was agreed that they would provide System 3 with conversions for not only the Atari ST but also the Commodore Amiga, which hadn't previously been included in advertisements. Active Systems would carry out the Amiga conversion itself and outsource the ST work to developer Marc Rosocha.

"That's how it ended up on my desk back in 1987," explained Marc. "It was just a huge set of floppy disks with all the raw graphics, without any chance to get the original artist to make changes. It presented a big challenge, and I was crazy enough to accept it. It looked pretty good but, from a programmer's standpoint, was quite useless and extremely memory-consuming. The solution to make this actually work was to personally edit every single screen, cut out overlays, define walkable areas, and write screen-specific code to work around remaining issues."

Marc was helped out by Klaus-Peter Plog on programming duties, with music duties handled by Jochen Hippel, who would create an interesting conversion of tunes from both *The Last Ninja* and *International Karate* for the game. After several months of painstaking work, the conversion took shape. It was faithful to the original C64 edition and looked very impressive, thanks to Hugh's artwork. However, there were a number of flaws that would cause problems and prevent an imminent release.

"Mark asked if I could complete the project as *Ninja Remix*."

As one of Marc and Klaus-Peter's first-ever 16-bit developments, they were still getting to grips with the ST infrastructure. Due to the technical stack, the game was relatively Atari TOS hard-coded by the duo, meaning that it couldn't easily become the basis for a quick Amiga port if ever required. Lack of proper map compression also left the game requiring 1MB of memory to run, with the majority of ST users only having 512K systems at the time. The game also spanned four disks in total, meaning higher production costs too.

Progression of the rather 'under the radar' Amiga conversion during this time had been a disaster in comparison. Members of Active Systems couldn't be tracked down at the time of writing to comment, but it is believed that the team struggled to get around the issue of the uncompressed maps, and development stalled as a result. The only evidence of the Amiga conversion seemed to be a screen printed in *Commodore User* magazine in April 1988; believed to be a static mock-up showing a fight against multiple enemies at one time. Interestingly, just a few months before, in *The One* magazine, Issue 3, Mark Cale had revealed that he felt an Amiga edition was out of the question. The main reason, in his opinion, was that it would take up to ten disks to release. So compression was clearly a major issue for that version too.

Communications between all parties for the Atari ST version had additionally been poor and gradually broke down. The development team had no direct communications with System 3 for instance, and its work eventually halted as a result, with the game in a final beta state. It was during this time when a leak of the ST beta occurred via an unknown source. This, coupled with the other issues and heavy delays, resulted in the 16-bit versions being written off by System 3, with the focus instead moved on to the sequel that was about to arrive.

Last Ninja 2 would grace both the ST and Amiga in 1990, handled by Activision and an external development team. The results were extremely disappointing though and, as a result, it was critically panned in magazines of the time. With a reputation of quality to keep up, System 3 responded by going back to the original ST team and the development that was so promising at the time.

"*Last Ninja 2* for ST/Amiga turned out to be less than stellar, and Mark Cale probably realised that what we did in 1988 was superior in comparison. So, he managed to track me down, and we finally talked directly, discussing what actually happened in 1988," Marc recalled of what was to be a moment of marketing genius from System 3. "Mark asked if I could complete the project as *Ninja Remix*. Since I was more experienced now, and because the original version wasn't portable to Amiga, I decided to rewrite the whole code and also reduce memory footprint as well."

Using the same original art assets with some tweaks and fresh tunes from Jochen Hippel (with his new and improved sound engine), the game was redeveloped to run on 512K ST's and now took up just three disks. More importantly, an Amiga version could also exist with a relatively quick port from the ST codebase. The conversions were both released in time for Christmas 1990 and were very well received, giving redemption for both System 3 and Marc. *The Last Ninja* would finally make it out – just in a slightly different guise, with a different name and much later than expected.

Bizarrely, a Tandy Colour Computer 3 conversion was also scheduled for release in late 1988 after Activision (working with System 3 at the time) agreed a deal with Tandy. System 3 had no real involvement with this particular arrangement. Tandy offered the conversion to various developers in mid-1988, where Rick Adams took on the challenge with a short deadline of 4–6 months to complete.

"Activision and I had a great relationship from my work on *Shanghai*. My project manager was super, sent flowers when my daughter was born," Rick recalled. "They offered *The Last Ninja* to Dale Lear first, who was one of my best friends and a carpool buddy at the time, and who worked at the same place as me. He said no. Dale was smart. So they offered it to me, and, like an idiot, I took it!"

"There were enemies, but no AI. So none of them did anything."

With Rick's development, there was no clear specification given to him for what was required exactly. Rick had only been provided with raw graphics from the C64 game, with no information whatsoever on the game at all. He was expected to play through the game to work out where everything was and what to do exactly, all of which took additional time within an already tight schedule. "I didn't get far with development. Just got all the screens working so you could walk around," recalled Rick. "There were enemies, but no AI. So none of them did anything but stay frozen in place. The Commodore 64 music was awesome, but I had to run under the OS9 operating system, and there was very little support for music, especially with movement on the screen. I did my best, but the music was pathetic."

The tight deadline took its toll on Rick, and it soon became clear that it was no longer an enjoyable time. "I stayed up until 2am for months working on it, then realised I wasn't going to make the deadline," Rick recalled. "My manager told me early on, 'If you think you can't finish it, PLEASE TELL US' – so I did. At that point, I just wanted to be rid of the project as it was burning me out badly. This was the project that broke me in the end. I got out of Colour Computer development afterwards. It just wasn't fun anymore."

Even after the major drain put on one of the machine's key developers, Tandy and Activision were still keen to see the project continue, so they passed the project (including Rick's code) to Steve Bjork. Steve was confident that he could get the game finished.

Over another month or so, Steve struggled to get the game to run in 128K and was hitting many problems. Things were progressing though, but, almost two months away from completion, Tandy abruptly decided to cancel the game with no given reason. Unfortunately, Steve didn't respond when asked about the development and why it was cancelled, but it is likely due to the dwindling market for the platform at the time.

For years, the conversion was forgotten about until Steve dug out two development disks and got an early build running to show people at the CoCoFest show in Chicago in 2007. It was found to be mostly playable, with enemies and a map that could be navigated, though there were elements still missing compared with the final game, and not all the levels were in place. At the time of writing, the game is yet to be made available to the public to play, and, sadly, Steve was subject to a robbery in recent years, where his full-blown CoCo development system was stolen. It is possible the development floppies have survived though, but otherwise, it is a curiosity that could be lost for good.

However, it is the ZX Spectrum, Amstrad CPC and Atari 800/130XE versions that have always posed the most questions from fans of the series. These were the ones advertised by System 3 from the very start. All versions were initially due for release by the end of January 1987, along with the C64 edition, but the Atari 800/130XE conversion was moved back to February. Whilst the C64 version saw its release in June of that year after delays, the other versions were nowhere to be seen. System 3 informed the press of further delays.

"They asked me to rescue the project, but I did not like the idea of struggling with someone else's code."

It is around the time of the C64 release that the first signs of the Spectrum version surfaced. News snippets and preview screenshots teasingly showed the game in action for the first time, looking promising and comparable with the C64 edition. News on the Amstrad version was radio silent in comparison. By this stage, the Atari 800/130XE edition had completely slipped off the schedule list, with System 3 feeling that there was not enough of a market to warrant doing a conversion.

Due to the close release date originally stated in the adverts, many believe a conversion was actually started on the Atari, but it was confirmed by System 3 that it only ever reached planning stages and it never found a suitable developer to make a start. Even a brief development of the sequel in later years by Harlequin Software would fail to see the light of day on the platform.

"So they offered it to me, and, like an idiot, I took it!"

Unbeknown to the public, both the Amstrad and Spectrum editions were causing headaches for System 3 behind the scenes. The ZX Spectrum edition was being developed by Phil Churchyard, who previously brought an impressive conversion of *Spindizzy* to the platform. The graphics were being translated by Nick Cook, who had himself just come off from working on *Xarq* for Electric Dreams. Phil would work in-house at System 3, whilst Nick worked off-site.

"*The Last Ninja* showed such promise and looked great on the Spectrum. It really was one of those titles that should have been released. I'm certain, if it had, it would have been a massive hit," reflected Nick. "*The Last Ninja* project was actually the last-ever Spectrum game project I worked on," added Phil. "I was employed by System 3 to hopefully write the game in two months. Most of the levels were written in the time allowed, but the specification for the game changed multiple times. System 3 paid me an advance for completing most of the work and, as far as I was concerned, the project would be completed."

"The setup with the house in Watford was an interesting one, which game developers probably take for granted nowadays," he continued. "The basement in the house had an arcade setup with *Defender*, *Nemesis* and *R-Type* machines, where I spent many an hour playing. Downstairs, we had a living room and shared kitchen where we would sometimes meet to discuss the priorities for the projects we were working on. My bedroom was a fairly small one, with just a bed and the desk where I coded *The Last Ninja*. So, every day, I would wake up with the prospect of having to get down to the coding of the day."

Phil revealed that the Amstrad CPC version was just supposed to be a straight port of his Spectrum edition and would have been an additional task for him once the initial Spectrum work was complete. This explained why nothing was ever shown of the CPC edition.

Although the game was also intended to be as close to the C64 edition as possible, Phil felt, originally, there were also opportunities to make improvements. "I did once change the viewing angle to make the game look more realistic," he revealed. "This had allowed the player to move in more directions than was previously possible, though I don't think this went down very well." As a result, the design was brought back to be more in line with the C64 version.

The coding of the conversion was made much easier with a custom setup used by Phil. Using a CP/M rig to assemble the code, specialist hardware would then load it up directly onto a ZX Spectrum for testing. It meant that any crashes would be easy to recover from, and compiling was much quicker as a result.

"I didn't get far with development. Just got all the screens working so you could walk around."

A key tool used in the C64 development was *The Integrator*, which allowed graphic artists to rapidly construct maps for the game. However, this was lacking for the other machines, with Phil left to produce his own tools to help Nick out. "I wrote a nifty editor for the maps that worked really well, allowing Nick to build by dragging collections of game objects around," he recalled. Development had gone well overall, and the somewhat daunting two-month deadline hadn't seemed to faze Phil at all.

"The puzzles were working well, and the fighting logic was in the process of being written. The graphics were ported from the C64 version, and obviously modified to be monochrome," he confirmed. The graphics certainly looked the part, as made evident in the press screenshots that would surface.

With the help of the straight porting and tidy-ups, plus the addition of Phil's map tool, Nick was able to fully complete all of the levels to insert into the game relatively quickly. It had easily gone past two months at this point, and the game was still needing plenty of work to complete it, but a solid conversion was finally taking shape. It seemed that Spectrum and Amstrad owners were perhaps not too far away from getting their conversion.

By November 1987, *Sinclair User* printed a large preview piece dedicated to the game. They played a preview showing a faithful conversion that had much of the level content in place, and a main character that had all the moves. At this stage, there were no enemies at all, or, at least, moving ones. The magazine suggested that one reason for the delays was due to trouble getting the main character moving authentically, but which was now working fine.

Phil suggested that change requests to the specification caused the project to overrun further than anticipated. "We had regular meetings to discuss extra content to incorporate into the game; this made completing the coding for levels very time-consuming as I constantly had to add new features while under huge pressure to complete working levels as fast as possible," Phil recalled. "The project took a lot longer than the two months expected and, as I was, by then, heavily in debt, I could not support myself on only the advance I was given. In the end, the stress of the situation got the better of me, and I decided to leave the project to continue my career elsewhere."

At this point in time, the Spectrum edition was approximately 60–70% complete with no sound, lacking enemy AI, and was now suddenly without a developer. All of this was unbeknown to the press, but the delay couldn't be covered up any longer, and System 3 had to respond. However, help was about to arrive in the shape of Mevlut Dinc at the end of 1987.

"I had just finished a very successful conversion of *Enduro Racer* from Speccy to Amstrad for Activision," Mevlut explained. "As the publishers for the game, Activision asked me to help out with the development of *Last Ninja* on the Speccy. I remember the demo they showed being very slow and not very playable. I remember it looking far away from completion, and it would have taken me months to do anything with it. They asked me to rescue the project, but I did not like the idea of struggling with someone else's code."

It was clear that System 3 must have only had an early build of the game as Phil's conversion was far more advanced. "When my involvement in the project ended, I did ask System 3 if they would like the source files back," Phil explained. "They said that I could do whatever I wanted with them as they were rewriting the game from scratch and did not want to have somebody go through my code for anything useful."

With users still anticipating a conversion and it now creeping into 1988, C64 users were already looking forward to the sequel. System 3 was still hopeful though that the Spectrum and Amstrad editions could surface via Mevlut, and it was advertised once more in February 1988. But, with the amount of work felt to be involved in taking over someone else's incomplete code, Mevlut saw an opportunity. He convinced Activision and System 3 to cancel the two conversions and tell users that it was canned due to not being up to standard, saying that the sequel would be concentrated on instead. System 3 and Activision agreed, and it was hoped that the decision would gain them some respect from punters and leave Mevlut free to concentrate on helping to create the sequel.

"The graphics were ported from the C64 version and, obviously, modified to be monochrome."

"It took John Twiddy (C64 code), Hugh Riley and me around eight months to develop *Last Ninja 2*. I believe it is regarded as the best Ninja game in the series! To be honest, I am glad they agreed with me on my proposal," Mevlut reflected. "I really enjoyed working with John and Hugh, which, in fact, resulted in us three forming Vivid Image!" Strange to think that, if the development woes with the Spectrum version of *Last Ninja* never happened, then we may never have got to see *First Samurai*, and *Last Ninja 2* could have been very different too.

Eventually, Spectrum and Amstrad users were satisfied with a sequel at least, and ST and Amiga owners eventually got *Last Ninja Remix*. The CoCo 3 version is still, unfortunately, at large, and Atari 8-bit owners were not so lucky to see anything developed at all. However, there is the curiosity of seeing the ZX Spectrum edition of the first game. When Phil was asked whether anything of his conversion had survived, the answer was surprising: "I have some 5.25-inch disks with source files for *The Last Ninja*, and I'm in the process of building a PC capable of reading them. I will let you know how I get on." Could *The Last Ninja* finally surface on the Spectrum?

"I have some 5.25-inch disks with source files for *The Last Ninja*, and I'm in the process of building a PC capable of reading them."

Phil concludes on what was a tough time personally, but one that ended positively. "Interestingly, the failure of the project is what launched my career into IT management, which I have been doing for the last 20 years or so," he told us. "This chapter of my life was definitely my lowest point, but it has, since then, made me a hugely stronger personality as a result. Whenever I get bogged down with any situation and stressed about it, I think back to my *Last Ninja* days and remember that it could never get worse than the stress I felt at that time."

Above: The original and where it all began for many. *The Last Ninja* (Commodore 64), developed by System 3.

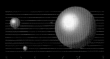

Above: February 1988 advert of *The Last Ninja* for the ZX Spectrum, showing off screenshots for that format.

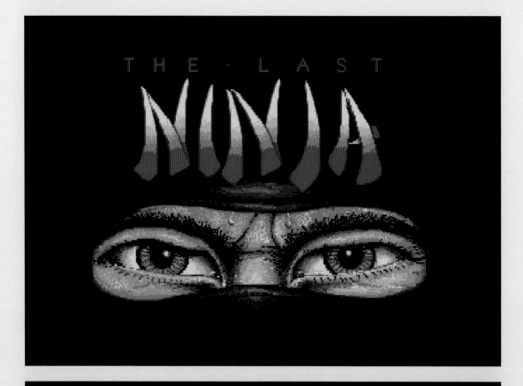

Above: Loading screen and part of level 1 from the leaked Atari ST version of *The Last Ninja* – about to have a battle with one of the game's enemies.

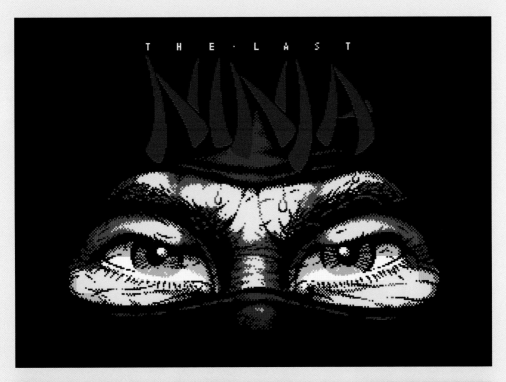

Above: An artist's impression of how the loading screen could have looked on the ZX Spectrum, followed by how the game looked based on preview screenshots seen in magazines at the time.

USSA
Focus shifted to new game

Year: 1988
Developer: Williams Electronic Games, Inc.
Platform: Arcade

Available to play
 Yes No

Due to the latter part of the Cold War and continued deteriorating relations between the West and the Soviet Union, a major fear for many during the early part of the 1980s was the potential threat of nuclear war. Although the subject of nightmares for many who grew up during that time, it was ideal material for many games that popped up during this era; the most well-known being *Missile Command* (released in 1980 and developed by Dave Theurer).

Williams was about to add to the list with a brand-new game, but not after surviving a particularly tough period following the industry crash a few years earlier. "Williams exited developing video games internally after the video game industry fell apart in the early '80s, and concentrated just on developing pinball games in order to survive up until then," began Williams' then VP of engineering, Ken Fedesna. "With the success that Williams had experienced with its pinball games in the latter part of the '80s, and with the purchase of Bally/Midway in 1988, it was decided that it was time for Williams to get back into video game development internally."

Helping to build towards this exciting new era, hardware designer Mark Loffredo began work on a new 256-colour graphical display that would take arcade games to whole new levels in terms of visuals. In anticipation that this new generation of hardware would support 256 colours, developer Warren Davis (creator of *Q*Bert* and various other titles at Williams and Gottlieb) began creating some advanced software tools. "I'd been experimenting with video digitisation and seeing the potential for photo-realistic graphics using 256 colours. I wrote some software to grab images off a videotape and condense the palette down to 256 colours," he explained. The results were stunning and impressed everyone at Williams.

Around the same time, Eugene Jarvis (creator of hits such as *Defender* and *Robotron: 2084* for Williams) returned back to the fold after a few years away studying at Stanford University. "Eugene had his own ideas about how a 256-colour system should be designed," recalled Warren. "So we went with his ideas in the end, and that became based on the Texas Instruments 34010 Graphics CPU, which was pretty new. Eugene wrote the operating system, I wrote the display system, and Mark did the hardware design."

Once their work was complete, thoughts moved to building something playable with this new visual triumph, which was unlike anything else around. Both Warren and Eugene separately set to work on two new games which would make specific use of the new video digitisation system and display hardware. Suggestions of a football and a fighting game were put on the table, but neither were popular with management. Going back to the drawing board, a new title called *USSA* (an odd amalgamation of 'USA' and 'USSR') was first born thanks to the creative mind of John Newcomer (who worked on classics such as *Joust* and *Sinistar*), taking inspiration from a classic film and a cult comedy show.

"Inspirations were *Red Dawn* (1984) and a Michael Nesmith (of The Monkees) TV show called *Elephant Parts*," confirmed John. "It had a sketch called *Neighbourhood Nuclear Superiority*. I thought defending your home soil would also make a good game." Warren also liked the idea and felt that it could be fun, so both joined forces to make the game a reality. Meanwhile, Eugene separately worked on his own game, which would become known to many as *NARC*.

"The enemy tanks were Soviet, and the players controlled a 4×4 flatbed truck with a missile launcher on the back."

Was *USSA* a game in a similar vein to *Missile Command*, defending against waves of nuclear missiles? Or was it perhaps based on the infamous Ronald Reagan 'Star Wars' project theme? Although not directly inspiring the new game, the design would be comparable to the classic Atari/Kee Games *Tank* game (converted in combination with other titles to the Atari 2600 later as *Combat*) and Bally Midway's *Sarge*, with controllable vehicles and an overhead view – but with various modern twists and using real digitised objects.

"The backstory of the game was that there was a Soviet invasion of the US. The enemy tanks were Soviet, and the players controlled a 4×4 flatbed truck with a missile launcher on the back," Warren explained. "It was set in suburbia, with battles in shopping malls, fast food joints, strip centres, high schools, cul-de-sacs, etc.," added Eugene, who gave his own brief recollections of the development.

Warren and John wasted no time getting started, with the first step being for John to digitise images of objects for the game from a 'directly above' but slightly angled perspective – so you could see sides of a building to identify them better. "The plan was to build 'Hometown USA' to defend rather than a big city," he recalled. "Hometown was more personal and would give a better emotional connection for the player if they saw their neighbour's house and local convenience store blown up."

John went to town producing a realistic environment, buying in and assembling model kits of various buildings, houses, a 7-11 supermarket and even a McDonald's restaurant. Additionally, John scanned and digitised vehicles, such as tanks, flatbed trucks and various other cars, to use as enemies or civilian vehicles. However, human beings would not make an appearance at all in the game, at least, not in the early design stages.

After a while, and with plenty of digitised assets now available, Warren and John started putting some of the objects within a quick prototype. They were not disappointed with the results. "The realism was truly amazing and unlike anything else from that time!" enthused Warren. Seeing a realistic flatbed truck player moving around a realistic scanned environment proved to John and Warren that they were on to something special.

Although both *Tank* and *Sarge* were static-screen affairs, *USSA* would be no such thing, with a split-screen display with separate views for both players and a map that scrolled in multiple directions. "The monitor was mounted horizontally, and the screen was split, so the left and right sides had independent views of the landscape centred on that player's truck. This allowed our playfield (the suburban cityscape) to be larger and more complex," explained Warren.

It was originally attempted to have a single large display when both players were in the same area, which then split off into separate views when not. However, the switching between split and merged views became disorientating, so it was dropped and kept permanently split. Additionally, it was decided that both player trucks could only be an allied team and had to work together against the Soviet enemy within the game. There was only a slight element of competition when you would each try to compete for performance bonuses throughout the game.

"One player truck was red, the other blue. In the truck bed, they both had a large white missile propped up at an angle ready to launch," recalled John. Controls were carefully considered, with each truck rotated using a steering wheel, pedals to accelerate and brake and a button to fire missiles. "When you launched a missile, the steering wheel was then used to guide it. This, I thought, was a pretty cool and unusual feature," Warren recalled.

"When you fired, the missile wobbled/rumbled then shot off. I don't think we had the VFX in yet for the missile launch, trail or hit – definitely would have made a difference if we had," added John. "Warren really made the controls work for guiding the missile off the pickup truck, and that's when it started to properly click. The guy is a genius and really grasped how things should work in a game and pushed it further. That was the point where I was able to envision what the finished product would look like once we added special effects, more buildings, sounds and narrative."

Not only could your missiles be used against enemy artillery, but you could also cause damage to surrounding scenery and buildings, which could have tempted some players to go rogue and cause carnage of their own. It added an extra element of fun to a game which was certainly on the right tracks, with Warren and John growing in confidence as everything continued to evolve. Their confidence was rewarded when colleagues within the offices were impressed by the game and would keep stopping by to witness the progress being made.

After a few months of development, *USSA* was still some way from completion due to the digitisation process taking a good chunk of the development time early on. By this stage, though, the game was fully playable. It had a single map, controllable vehicle and missiles, enemies that could be destroyed, and could be played with both players. There were also basic sounds in place too.

According to Warren, a computerised second player was to be added at a later date for single players without a friend to play with. However, the development was about to come crashing to an abrupt halt. Only one of the two games in development was ever going to see the light of day; sadly, it wasn't going to be USSA. "I think it's likely that they didn't want to release two games at once because they didn't want USSA and NARC competing against each other for quarters in the arcades." suggested Warren. "Still, in my opinion, they could have held one back until the other had run its course, but they didn't."

"It appeared that NARC's development was moving forwards faster than USSA at the time," explained Ken. "Because of the cost of developing the games simultaneously and the amount of development time it was taking, the decision was to go forwards with NARC first. So both groups were combined and instructed to work on NARC together." John then added, "Williams had wanted one game to come to market faster. They needed to see some revenue – that eliminated USSA. If I was in management's shoes, that would be the one I would have chosen as well! I wasn't happy about it, though, because I could visualise the potential. It was becoming a baby, and no one wants their baby cancelled."

Although it was looking like the team could later go back to the project after NARC was finished, there was another problem that quashed any possibility of this happening. A member of upper management had not taken to the game during office testing and campaigned against it, which was felt to be the final nail in the coffin. "We got hit hard by this," began John. "Williams' management were also unsure about doing a driving game because they felt it would be competing against state-of-the-art Japanese hardware. I thought there was room for both since ours was story-driven and digitised and not a driving simulator." Cancellations are part and parcel of companies, and, with little time to reflect, Warren and John were swiftly moved on to other projects, with John moving on to NARC to help finish it off.

"The realism was truly amazing and unlike anything else."

Unfortunately, USSA was to be Warren's last piece of development work at Williams for a little while. After being initially assigned to High Impact Football, a subject area that Warren had no interest in, Warren decided to move on to pastures new. A few years later, he returned to join the Terminator 2: Judgement Day development team after they lost a developer mid-stream. By this time, USSA was a distant memory, with no chance of being picked up and continued.

Now over 30 years since the cancellation, the critical question is whether anything ever survived of the prototype. Warren and John first confirmed that no field test cabinet or artwork was ever produced as the game was never officially scheduled for manufacturing. Things also looked bleak regarding the game code itself. "Unfortunately, there is nothing," John confirmed. "There was only one prototype cabinet, which is what Warren used for development. I am positive that the development game was a cut-up *Super Sprint* cabinet as it already had the wheels, foot pedals and horizontal monitor."

No one knows for sure what happened to that prototype, though it is believed to have been scrapped at Williams shortly after cancellation. The models and scenery used in the game were disposed of. "The problem with games that get cancelled is that no one wants to remember these failures," John explained.

Warren's concluding words were slightly more upbeat. "I don't think I have anything relating to this game unless there's something that's been buried in a box in my attic. Someday, I'll go up there and look." A glimmer of hope perhaps, or just hopeless optimism by the archivists in us that *USSA* could miraculously have survived after all this time?

Above: *NARC* (arcade). Utilising the same vibrant display technology that *USSA* would also eventually have used.

Above: Artist's impression of how *USSA* (arcade) may have looked, based on a mock-up created by Warren and recollections about the game's features. This side showing the left-hand player's view.

Above: Artist's impression of how the second player's screen for *USSA* (arcade) may have looked, and how a fired missile could have been guided completely away from your player vehicle.

The Konix Multi-System Ran out of funds

Year: 1989
Developer: Konix

A missed opportunity that could have changed the landscape of gaming as we know it. Starting life as a reconfigurable controller called the Slipstream, Konix saw an opportunity to integrate a console within it too. An article on the powerful new Flair One system ignited a journey alongside Flare Technologies to produce a console with a performance and appearance like no other.

The system could be configured into a steering wheel, motorbike handle and flight yoke modes, as well as allowing connections of joysticks and a light gun. Other peripherals also planned incredibly included a motorised Power Chair. Although well-supported by software houses and anticipated by many, numerous delays resulted in Konix running out of funding before the system could ever see the light of day.

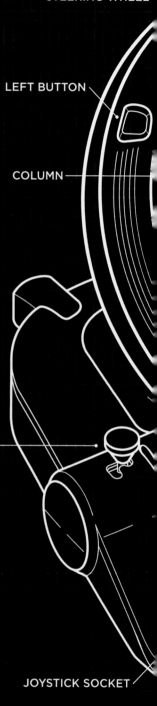

STEERING WHEEL

LEFT BUTTON

COLUMN

CLUTCH RELEASE KNOB & GAME SELECT MECHANISM

JOYSTICK SOCKET

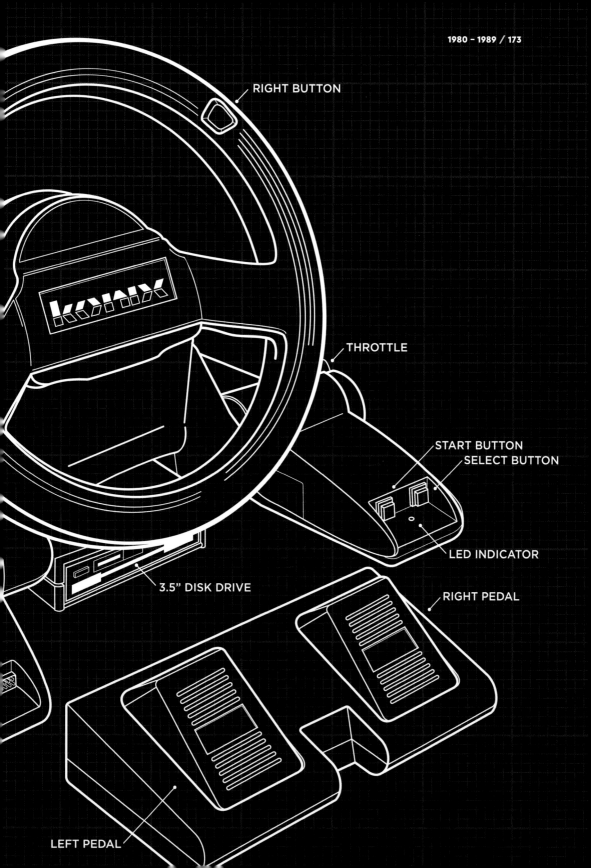

RIGHT BUTTON

THROTTLE

START BUTTON
SELECT BUTTON

LED INDICATOR

3.5" DISK DRIVE

RIGHT PEDAL

LEFT PEDAL

Heart of Yesod Licensing

Year: 1989
Developer: Eldritch the Cat
Platforms: Atari ST, Commodore Amiga and PC (DOS)

Available to play

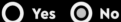 Yes No

"The right honourable Charlemagne Fotheringham-Grunes sat on a deck chair on the patio of his mansion, 'Asgard House'. He was sipping his third piña colada, which had been brought to him by his trusty manservant, Hilda, when it happened: Hilda, who had been walking back up to the house, stopped in his tracks, paused, then burst into flames, a human fireball, incandescent with a million different colours," began the imaginative introduction to the new and third game of a popular 8-bit series.

Heart of Yesod was a proposed follow-up to *Nodes of Yesod* and *The Arc of Yesod*, both released by Odin Computer Graphics in 1985. The games were similar in style to Ultimate Play The Game's *Underwurlde* and were very well received by gamers. There was quite a gap with the newly proposed game coming a good four years after the last game and two years after Odin Computer Graphics had fully closed its doors. The game's proposal would be put together by both Steve Wetherill and Colin Grunes, who then attempted to pitch it to various different publishers.

"This was in the era of Eldritch the Cat," Steve began. "After leaving Denton Designs (which is where Colin and I ended up after Odin), I formed Eldritch the Cat with Marc Wilding. Although we hung out from time to time, Colin wasn't really involved with Eldritch, so we didn't work together for a year or so."

So what had inspired Steve and Colin to resurrect the Yesod name and theme after all that time? "I really wanted to do something on the 16-bit platforms to showcase Colin's art, and that's how the idea for *Heart of Yesod* came about," Steve explained. Steve began by creating a storyline document (which you can see parts of here), and the plan would be to produce a small demo on the Atari ST as a showcase. A design document was also created, detailing and showing the themes for each of the levels and what creatures/objects would be present.

The story was cleverly thought out and detailed, set to draw potential publishers in. Astro Charlie (the lead character, known in full as Charlemagne Fotheringham-Grunes – named after both Stuart Fotheringham and Colin Grunes, who worked at Odin Computer Graphics at the time) has inherited a mysterious old oak wardrobe from his late Uncle Willy, which is subsequently squirrelled away in his attic. Upon further inspection of the wardrobe, Charlie notices shards of colourful light coming from beyond the door, as well as some odd noises being emitted.

Venturing forwards, the wardrobe doors fling open, and Charlie is stunned by a brilliant white beam of light. He notices figures of an astronaut, a knight, a man in a top hat, and other indistinguishable figures within. With an irresistible urge, Charlie enters to investigate further. As he does, he disappears from sight, along with the wardrobe itself.

We learn at this point, that Charlie's manservant, Hilda, is not quite what he seems. It is discovered that Hilda was sent from a parallel plane of existence ten years before, on a mission to find the gateway that takes you into the land of Yesod. The human form is a disguise, and his real form takes the shape of a two-headed winged arch-demon. Hilda was told to look for the 'War Drobe' and searched in vain. When he realised that this meant Uncle Willy's wardrobe, it was too late – Astro Charlie had just beaten him to it and had now disappeared with the gateway. Hilda vows revenge as he tries to recapture the wardrobe, and sends a series of demons in to try and destroy Astro Charlie, as well as probably appearing himself towards the end of the game to thwart you.

It's suggested to Steve that perhaps the design may have been heavily influenced by the likes of *Mr Benn* and *The Lion, the Witch and the Wardrobe*. "Yes, 52 Festive Road and all that," he confirmed. In particular, the *Mr Benn* influences would become more apparent once Charlie re-emerges from his disappearing act and pops up in what appears to be a costume shop. This is, in fact, the inside of the Tardis-like wardrobe, with all kinds of outfits hanging up. Whilst looking around the shop, a wizard would appear and warn your character about the perils that now lay ahead. You are made to choose from four outfits: a spacesuit, a suit with top hat, armour and an unknown costume which Steve could not recall.

"It was more of a tech demo showing smooth scrolling and sprites."

Upon first jumping into the spacesuit, you would head out of twin doors at the end of the room to begin your journey in a part of the Yesod world – the first of the four levels. Each level would tie into the theme of the four costumes worn in some way, and the idea would be to locate the wardrobe at the end of the level, changing into the next outfit and moving on to the next area. The last level would be the very 'Heart of Yesod', offering a gateway back to your own world if you succeed in getting to the end.

The style of the game across the levels was to be a vertical push-scrolling platformer, each level consisting of a variety of platform types (solid, moving, dissolvable) and a large array of enemies to avoid/destroy. "I wanted to tie in the Yesod world with the *Heartland* world, so the enemies would have been 16-bit evolutions of things seen in those games," confirmed Steve.

If you went off the left or right of the screen, you would appear on the other side automatically, very similar to *Kid Icarus* on the Nintendo Entertainment System. "I think *Nebulus* was doing well at the time, though our game did not play similarly. In fact, the current-day *Doodle Jump* game would probably be closer in style," Steve explained about possible influences. Once you got to the top of the level in one piece, you would then find the wardrobe, ready to transport you on to the next level by getting into your next costume.

The game would feature references throughout to the previous *Yesod* games, but also *Manic Miner* and *Heartland*. "Only in the sense of a nod and a wink," smiled Steve. "Maybe some sly references here and there, perhaps to the Starship Enterprise in *Jet Set Willy 2*, and some of the other real-life-based locations that were added to that game, such as Holt Road, that sort of thing."

For each of the four levels, the different costumes would also give you different capabilities within the level you were put into. So, for instance, the spacesuit would allow for lighter jumps, whereas the armour would result in jumps being tougher to achieve.

Aiding the pitching process was a prototype that was rapidly developed in just a few weeks or so on the Atari ST. Steve was on coding duties for this, with Colin on artistic duty for what was just a very brief development. Marc Wilding possibly helped out in places, though there was no response when questioned about the game and his exact involvement.

There was a working and playable vertically scrolling level produced, but not much in the way of interactivity at this early stage. "As I recall, it was more of a tech demo showing smooth scrolling and sprites. I think I was working on *Projectyle* at the time and had done a bunch of scrolling tech for the Atari ST."

It was enough to show off to potential publishers. Along with the plans, everything was pitched to a number of publishers, which included Gremlin, Millennium, Mirrorsoft and Electronic Arts. But no one was biting. "There was little interest because of the connections to 'Yesod', for which Colin and I did not have any real right to," Steve explained. The 'Yesod' rights actually still belonged to Odin's director, Paul McKenna. Eldritch the Cat would either have to gain a licence first or redesign the game to move away from the Odin prequels so that publishers were more willing to take it on.

The lack of a publisher meant that Steve and Colin were forced to put the game to rest and move quickly on to other projects to bring money in for the newly set up company. No consideration was even given to separate the concept from the Yesod series. "We felt that the *Heartland/Yesod* ties were an important aspect to the game, and we never talked about rewriting the backstory," confirmed Steve. "With 20/20 hindsight, that would have been easy. But, for whatever reason, we just dropped it."

With thoughts of a trilogy now lost, it wasn't until *Edge* magazine's 'Making of' article on *Nodes of Yesod* that the lost third part was first publicly heard about. A few years later, in 2010, a 25th-anniversary edition of *Nodes of Yesod* was produced and released on iOS, and a 30th-anniversary edition followed by Steve himself in 2016 on the same infrastructure. Could there be consideration about finally developing *Heart of Yesod* as well? "You never know!" Steve teased.

"I have various ideas, too many to tackle. I'd been prototyping something using the old-school, high-contrast and pixelly art from games like *Nodes of Yesod*, with smooth movement, scrolling and physics." Referring to the engine eventually used for the 30th-anniversary release: "It has a very unique look, but not something I've had time to work on."

As for the original development, only the storyline pitch document seems to have survived, with the design document and ST prototype currently at large. Steve believed that it is probably lost for good, with neither him nor Colin finding anything after initial searches. But there is perhaps hope that the missing third part will someday make its way onto modern-day platforms, what with Steve's recent iOS and new ZX Spectrum Next developments. So, maybe we will all get to experience *Heart of Yesod* in some shape or form.

Below: An excerpt from the outline document for *Heart of Yesod*, courtesy of Steve Wetherill.

```
An outline for a video game, tentatively entitled 'Heart of Yesod', for
the Commodore Amiga, Atari ST and IBM PC and compatibles. The text and
graphics contained herein are copyright (c) 1989 Eldritch The Cat.

Produced by:    ELDRITCH THE CAT
                4 CROMPTON DRIVE
                LIVERPOOL
                ENGLAND

Text:           Steve Wetherill

All Eldritch The Cat games are dedicated to the Eldritch the cat: gone but
not forgotten.


All rights reserved. No part of this publication may be reproduced, stored
in a retrieval system, or transmitted, in any form, or by any means,
electronic, mechanical, photocopying, recording or otherwise, without the
express permission of Eldritch The Cat.

                       Heart of Yesod

The right honourable Charlemagne Fotheringham-Grunes sat in a deck chair
on the patio of his mansion, 'Asgard House'. He was sipping his third pina
colada, which had been brought to him by his trusty man-servant, Hilda,
when it happened: Hilda, who had been walking back up to the house,
stopped in his tracks, paused, then burst into flames, a human fireball
incandescing with a million different colours. Then, equally as suddenly,
the fireball extinguished itself and there stood the most beautiful woman
'Astro' (as Charles was known to his friends) had ever seen, on this
planet or any other.
  The beautiful creature surveyed Charlie, her icey blue eyes burning into
him as he sat there, flabberghasted. Then she spoke:
  'Hello Earthling!'
  Now Charles was even more amazed, for far from the silken voice which he
might have expected to utter from that perfectly formed mouth, this
creature spoke in the manner of a Yorkshire miner in deep, gutteral tones.
  'Eeh, dun't jus' sit theer, tha's got wuk t'do, tha knows,' quoth she.

  Luckily for Charlie, this was only a dream, of the kind one has after
eating blue cheese for supper. Had it not been a dream, the consequences
for Mankind could have been drastic: it is almost unthinkable that such a
beautiful name as Hilda could be applied to a person as drab as Charlie's
man-servant; war would have been a certainty.

  Astro did have work to do, however. He was an adventurer by trade, and
his job took him to many exotic locations. This tale concerns the sequence
of events which occured after Charlie inherited an old oaken wardrobe,
left to him by his old uncle Willy, who had himself been a bit of an
adventurer in his day. Uncle Willy had been killed by a cave-in in the
vast subterranean 'key' mines beneath Surbiton. Charles was at a loss as
to what to do with the old wardrobe, and had decided to store it in the
roomy attic of his mansion.
```

Above: Artist's impressions of how *Heart of Yesod* may have looked, based on recollections of plans for the game and featuring familiar characters from previous games the team worked on.

Attack of the Mutant Camels '89 Console unreleased

Year: 1989
Developer: Llamasoft
Platform: Konix Multi-System

Available to play

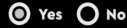 **Yes** ○ **No**

If you were ever bored of the same generic platformers and space shooters, you might have been tempted by the more abstract titles that adorned our screens during the 1980s. Strange and wonderful concepts exist where you manoeuvre birds that build nests and crap on cars, or even where you control a rich miner who must tidy up his mansion before being allowed to go to bed. There seemed to be no limit to the imagination.

Jeff Minter is well known for his surreal and psychedelically rich games released under his own Llamasoft label, featuring mammals such as sheep, goats, llamas and even camels. A fan of arcade shoot-em-ups and inspired by the Atari 2600 version of *The Empire Strikes Back*, Jeff created *Attack of the Mutant Camels* (AMC) for the Commodore 64, where you must destroy giant camels to progress. Sequels followed, with the camel becoming the main protagonist.

When a new and exciting console was about to emerge from the depths of Wales in 1989, Jeff had the opportunity to resurrect his camel-themed game for a fifth title in the series and go back to the roots of the original 1983 title. "I was invited to view a new prototype console which was planned to be released, called the Konix Multi-System, and it was based on chips from a Cambridge outfit called Flare," began Jeff. "I ended up getting one of the first dev kits. It sounded like an interesting prospect, and this new console was very promising and ambitious."

Built upon the impressive Flare One system, the Multi-System was a console unlike anything seen before. Jeff would become almost a 'poster developer' for the console, featuring in press photos demonstrating hardware and talking up the console regularly in interviews. It was felt by Konix that Jeff's high-profile character and personality was the perfect 'loudspeaker' for promoting the console to the gaming community and press.

Jeff took a gamble by investing his own money in a development kit in early 1989 but was convinced that he was backing a strong horse. "I've always liked working on new stuff," he explained. "There was an opportunity to do that with the Konix, which could work out well by having a launch title on the machine. So, I thought, 'yeah, let's go for it!'." With 128K of RAM (later 256K), fast blitter, a 256-colour bitmapped screen display and a Digital Signal Processor (DSP), Jeff knew he could produce something special.

Jon Dean (setting up the Software Development Kit and support for the system) worked with Jeff to establish a title to develop. "I had known Jeff since my days at Atari, and I thought that he could provide us with a compelling title that would demonstrate the speed and overall power the system could offer," began Jon. "As I recall, Jeff was quite keen on making a light synthesiser for it, but I wanted a version of *AMC*, and he concurred."

The decision was made to revamp one of his most famous titles with the creation of *Attack of the Mutant Camels '89* (*AMC '89*). "I thought it would be a nice update as the game hadn't really been updated at that point, and the Multi-System seemed a good platform to do it on!" Jeff explained. The game could be played with the Slipstream controls, but you could also use a standard joystick as well. Jeff was once pictured playing his game sitting in a Konix Power Chair and holding a light gun; only the chair would fully work with the game if detected. The gun was likely just being used as a temporary fire button.

"Whilst loading, the game displayed concentric rings that would form a tunnel and give an impressive depth effect."

Work began around May 1989, with development carried out on *AMC '89* during the morning, before switching over to *Gridrunner* on the Atari ST in the afternoon. Development was carried out on a 12MHz 286 VGA PC, with PDS, where code would be compiled and sent down a cable to the black box containing the prototype Multi-System board for testing.

Jeff wasn't alone on development, enlisting the help of artist friend Beatrix Grimbly to produce bold and vibrant graphics throughout. Jeff and Beatrix would make full use of the available 256-colour mode (one of the only games to do so) and a 256×200 resolution. The Multi-System included a fast bitmap display that Jeff would utilise to give a wide variety of impressive visual effects throughout the game.

After just a few months, Jeff had produced a demo that would excite everyone, including Jon, who visited Jeff regularly for progress updates. "After shipping the first dev kits, it took a while before we saw much playable content; Jeff was the exception and probably had the first playable game proto, so *AMC '89* was a natural to showcase at press events," Jon explained. "*Mutant Camels* would really have been a killer app because it was so fast, so colourful and so loud."

The game mechanics were fairly similar to the original, where you had to prevent the camels from reaching your base at the end of a horizontally scrolling playfield. Expanding the concept was the addition of enemies supporting the camels, such as rockets and flying saucers trying to bring you down. The familiar 'camel scanner' was kept at the top of the screen, showing the progression of the camels and placement of other enemies. It also wasn't just a case of destroying a fixed amount of camels to progress, but you now had to also destroy their base to prevent further camels from materialising.

Destroying camels and enemies would result in large, colourful explosions, showcasing the arcade qualities of the hardware to great effect. Upon destruction of a camel, 16 pieces of neutronium would be released. If you manage to collect all of them, you are awarded a 'neutronium pellet' to fly back to your home base. Repeating this process five times would then provide you with a large 'neutronium bomb' on a winch to fly into the camel's base to destroy and subsequently complete the level. After a short hyperspace sequence, you would resume on a new world with even more enemies.

Overall, there were nine types of weapons to aid progress, ranging from a basic 'cannon' to 'wide beam asskickers'. Some of the weapons could fill the entire screen with their large bullets, with up to 16 bullets on screen at any time. The 'smart lasers' weapon would latch onto a target automatically, making life easier whilst flying around at speed. In early builds, all the weapons were active, but it was likely that you would have to unlock them over time in the final game.

Thanks, in part, to Beatrix's visuals, the game was a visual spectacular. Jeff complimented things with a colourful background raster horizon that transformed from day to night, complete with a sun and moon orbiting in synchronisation. As the game scrolled from left to right, you were also treated to effective parallel scrolling and lightning strikes on some worlds. Typically of Jeff, the game displayed colourful captions to accompany actions in the game, including 'My nipples explode with delight' at every opportunity.

One of the stand-out features was also the sound. Jeff squeezed ten channels from the DSP hardware and produced an impressive fractal-generated music system to accompany powerful shot and explosion sounds. "It was something I dabbled in very briefly before with some of the music for *Iridis Alpha*, which was generated procedurally," he explained. "There was an opportunity to try it out again and produce fractal music for *AMC '89* which changed its tone according to how well you were doing. So, when you were doing well, it would go major key, and when you died, it would go minor key. It wasn't perfect, but it was quite nice."

"It was still shaping up nicely, but needed optimisation."

Presentation was also kept to a high standard. Whilst loading, the game displayed concentric rings that would form a tunnel and give an impressive depth effect. You would then be presented with a sequence of enemies flying from the top of the screen to the bottom, before being hit by a vibrant title screen with a colourful Llamasoft logo and the abbreviated title of *Mutant Camels '89* overlaid. Information screens and high-score tables were included (with up to 44 entries, savable to disk), with what Jeff described as having an "exceedingly groovy" variety of purple-and-black colour flows behind them.

Jeff even had time to add three special pause modes to continue a trend that many Llamasoft fans were well accustomed to. First was your classic pause mode; second was a demo showing various beautiful fractal Mandelbrots gradually drawn onto the screen.

However, the third mode was an impressive mini-lightsynth called *Laserium*, featuring sub-modes where you could control different vector shapes. All modes included six-channel sound effects, possibly based on the fractal generator that Jeff had constructed. *Laserium* would actually inspire artist Steinar Lund (designer of many previous Llamasoft game covers) for the cover design for *AMC '89*.

"Steinar came down to visit me in Wales to see the game, as he usually did whenever he was doing artwork for me," Jeff recalled. "There was this little thing (a lightsynthy kind of toy) that I'd built into the game, which created patterns of spinning vectors you could mess around with using the joystick. It was really rather good fun, and me and Steinar zoned away an afternoon playing with it and listening to music. That little pattern around the sun [within the artwork] echoes the memory of that happy little session."

After approximately seven months of work, the game was now around 70% complete. "Basic mechanics were there, a lot of power-ups were in there – but only with about two levels with the 'Egypt' and 'Stonehenge' themes," recalled Jeff. "It was still shaping up nicely but needed optimisation. The frame rate could get a little bit low when there was a lot of stuff on the screen."

More content was required to finish everything off, with plans for at least another 3–4 major themes, including 'Volcanic', 'City' and 'Strange' themes (the latter Jeff couldn't recall anything about). Those themes would have been recycled and stretched the game to 20–30 levels in total, though, in an interview with the French *Joystick* magazine, Jeff suggests there could even be up to 200 levels in total. "There was also going to be a much greater variety of enemies," added Jeff. "There were only a couple enemy types really; the camels and the saucers that flew around, but not a lot more than that. It needed a lot more than that. We probably would have added warp levels as well."

"It was supposed to be the first time they were showing the release version of the machine."

Jeff was additionally waiting on the 'final' release of the Konix development kit (featuring an 8086 processor) to overcome the remaining frame rate issues and provide a triple-speed increase. According to his October 1989 *Nature of the Beast* newsletter, Jeff hoped *AMC '89* would be finished by November that year, but the final version of the development kits was constantly delayed and prevented it from happening.

Cracks had already started to appear, though, when Konix was scheduled to demonstrate a final build of the console at the Personal Computer Show in September 1989. "It was supposed to be the first time they were showing the release version of the machine," Jeff explained. "We showed up hoping to demonstrate, but they just weren't there! Literally, the stand was empty!"

Konix eventually showed up after apparent traffic delays and customs issues, but this was towards the end of the event. The latest build of *AMC '89* (complete with titles and high-score presentation) was finally put on show and enjoyed by the public, but the initial no-show was damaging. In the background, there were major issues with funding the console, which threatened to derail the entire development. Scheduled December/New Year release dates were subsequently missed after much-needed cash injections just didn't happen.

"Jeff could always write very playable and great-looking games."

Computer Trade Weekly additionally reported that software developments had halted in October when it was felt that development for titles could not continue until the hardware was fully finalised. "I stopped finding new developers sometime before the show," explained Jon. "I recall now that dev kits that had been paid for weren't being delivered, so I refused to continue my developer tour. I wasn't getting paid either, but I was still talking up the product."

Although Jeff felt that Konix had missed the boat by not launching that Christmas (with a launch date now pushed back as far as autumn 1990), he continued development of *AMC '89* into the new year; this was, however, at a much slower pace, and focus was put more onto other developments that would bring in money. He did what optimisations he could though and added a third (believed to be 'Volcanic') level theme. Interviewed by French *Joystick* magazine in early 1990, Jeff was still optimistic and still believed in the platform.

Unfortunately, his faith was not to be repaid in the end. Konix would continue its decline into 1990, starting with Jon Dean officially severing his ties with the company. Konix would never obtain the investment needed to properly complete development, and debts became too much to bear. It would finally close its doors in September 1990, and, with that, the Konix Multi-System was no more.

Months of work and investment had fallen through, much to Jeff's dismay. Due to the architecture, Jeff couldn't easily move the game to a new platform to continue. "It was all written in assembler, and it wasn't particularly portable, so I just moved on," he lamented.

Not all was wasted, with some ideas and features being later reused in *Llamazap* on the Atari Falcon a few years later. There were subsequent requests for Jeff to revive *AMC '89* on a new machine based on the Multi-System that used a new 386-based architecture, though, by this point, Jeff was working on the Atari Jaguar and so declined the chance to go back to the game.

It wasn't until 2005 that the game was back in the public eye once more, with *Retro Gamer* magazine running an extensive feature on the Konix Multi-System (written by Craig Vaughan). It was here that Jon Dean revealed he had kept video footage showcasing various parts of the Multi-System's progress. Some of the footage included *AMC '89* in action, recorded in July 1989. "I can show that video of the game even today, and people want to play it." suggests Jon. "Jeff could always write very playable and great-looking games."

The footage only made people hungry once more to play the game, and efforts were subsequently made to see if it could be recovered. Although Jeff rarely threw anything away, he was unsure of what had become of his Konix development kit and disks. "I think I just gave it all up and probably trashed it. It could still be in the loft at my mum's old house for all I know. I don't know where the hell it is," he responded. However, searches proved fruitless, and Jeff was becoming resigned to the fact that *AMC '89* was probably lost for good.

Elsewhere, as the years progressed, a more ambitious search bubbled away, one which would result in one of the most staggering recoveries in preservation history. Mark Campbell had grown up like many of us, reading about the Konix Multi-System and dreaming of being able to pop into the likes of Dixons to pick one up. As well as building an impressive archive of research and interviews around the console (www.konixmultisystem.co.uk), Mark wanted an actual emulator built and set about finding a programmer who fancied the perhaps crazy challenge.

Lee Hammerton would answer the call and would go on to have a daunting reverse engineering task to achieve. "The initial set of emulation work was based on material Mark had procured relating to the MSU (386) era port of *Robocod*," recalled Lee. "It was my day job that led to the second discovery, a set of discs (mostly IBM PC format) containing sources/binaries for some of the earlier era Flare One/Konix systems."

Lee and Mark had hit the jackpot, with demo code recovered that had been seen running on the Multi-System at various shows and pictured in the press at the time. "The source code helped immensely in discovering things about the Konix hardware, many of our 8088-era ROMs had to be built from source because the binaries were never archived – which is a shame," Lee explained. "The ROM format used was based on the 2–3 images I had (MSU era). I actually had to build an assembler from scratch to build all of them as well, as the original toolchain has never been recovered."

What they hadn't quite bargained for was what they found next. "There was an archive labelled 'Jeff'. I didn't even realise what it was for a few days," recalled Lee. "*AMC '89* (or, at least, an early demo build) happened to be on one of the PC disks – which I read in via a USB floppy disk drive plugged into the PC." Attention now focused on getting the Multi-System's most famous game up and running on an emulator still in its early stages.

Lee spent just nine days from the discovery of the sources to having a playable build of *AMC '89* up and running on his new emulator. It was no simple feat as the code introduced features that were not yet even properly implemented in his emulator. "I had to implement Blitter Line Drawing (it was the first ROM I encountered that used it). Also, the ROM taught me quite a bit about how the 4-bit blitter modes worked – or, at least, my first stab at them," Lee explained. "Perhaps surprisingly, though, the music and sound effects pretty much worked the first time I hooked them up."

"We showed up hoping to demonstrate, but they just weren't there! Literally, the stand was empty!"

Recovered and now running was an early build of the game, believed to be around 40% complete and featuring a significant chunk of the game engine. Although playable, only the 'Egypt' level was present, with no trace of the 'Stonehenge' or 'Volcanic' themes at all. The titles and presentation are also all missing, and destroying the camel base results in the demo crashing, just as it did in the video clips. Jeff was understandably blown away by the work achieved.

"It was amazing! I never thought I'd see it again," beamed Jeff. "I know there were some little videos of it, but I never thought I'd actually see and play it again!" With Jeff's blessing, both the binary and source code remains were later released to the world to check out and hopefully be inspired to finish. "In my long career as a developer, seeing Jeff tweet a picture of *AMC '89* running under emulation is one of the highlights," Lee concluded.

A happy ending of sorts, but there is still a twinge of sadness amongst Llamasoft fans that *AMC '89* was never fully completed and released. There is still potential that the very last build of the game could be found, but, for now, we can at least see and play something of the game. Considering that it's for hardware that never got released itself, this is somewhat phenomenal.

We concluded by asking Jeff for his reflection on what was a significant amount of time wasted on the Konix. "I don't think any development is ever a waste," Jeff quickly corrected us. "You always learn something from it, even if it doesn't get a release. Every development experience is a good experience. Even if you can't release, you always learn from the code you have done, and, quite often, you have stuff that you can carry forwards on to another project."

Above: Emulated screens from the recovered build of *AMC '89* (Konix Multi-System), showing the Egyptian-themed level and its armoured camels. The 'day to night' system is also in full flow.

Above: Jeff at home working on the game, showing the Konix development kit in the background and a rare glimpse of the title screen on display.

Left: Jeff in the Konix Power Chair, playing AMC '89 with a strange combo of peripherals. Right: Steinar Lund's unused art for AMC '89, inspired by Jeff's mini-light synthesiser built into the game.

The Terminator Licence dropped

Year: 1989
Developer: Sunsoft
Platform: Nintendo Entertainment System

Arnie should have made his NES *Terminator* debut in 1989, but, although complete and promising film-like cutscenes, the licence was revoked. The game was later reworked and released as *Journey to Silius* (*Rough World* in Japan). Why? The game didn't follow the film plot due to cultural differences between Sunsoft Japan and the US.

"*The Terminator* was in development whilst Jay Moon was US product development director. His job was to help/assist Sunsoft Japan's R&D in producing authentic games of various licences obtained. When prototype builds were sent to the US office, Jay was often frustrated as Japan always took great poetic licence; the games being very different from what the licensor believed possible.

Licensed games are often difficult, and having a Western culture licence developed in a Japanese culture was often very difficult too. Japan wanted great gameplay, but licensees are often blinded by their own agenda. Finally, the push came to shove, and the licensee would no longer approve of the builds. Sunsoft had, unfortunately, already paid a guarantee upfront, so they lost that non-refundable money. The title *Journey to Silius* was actually a rather loose dig at the US office, interpreted as 'Journey to Silliness'!"

David Siller, producer at Sunsoft USA

Available to play

 Yes No

Image: Artist's recreation of *The Terminator* (NES) title screen, based on a screenshot shown in *Nintendo Power* magazine

Bubble Bobble Expired licence

Year: 1989
Developers: Peter Gillett and Martin Kelsey
Platform: BBC Micro

Available to play
 Yes ◯ No

With the many platforms around at the time, it was possible to feel that you backed the wrong horse – especially when it came to the one with the most games. Don't get us wrong, the BBC Micro was no lightweight, and there are plenty of fantastic and unique games to check out. In comparison, though, to some of its 8-bit counterparts, there was a clear difference. When it came to conversions of popular arcade titles, many BBC Micro users were left wanting; not always getting the conversions so desperately needed or deserved.

Bubble Bobble has been a major success for Taito since its arcade release back in 1986. Since then, there have been numerous sequels and spin-offs for over the past three decades. The original game is arguably the best though, where you take control of brothers Bub and Bob, traversing through 100 unique levels to defeat the Super Drunk, save their girlfriends and ultimately lift a curse which has seen the inconvenience of them being turned into dragons.

On the surface, the concept is simple but deviously addictive, with ingenious and complex layers to it. Each level is represented by a single screen consisting of an arrangement of platforms. The aim is to simply clear all of the enemies on every screen by firing bubbles to temporarily contain and then pop them. If you don't pop an enemy in time, they will break free – angrier and faster than before. Take too long on a level, and Baron Von Blubba will chase you until it's cleared.

Masses of bonuses are available to pick up throughout, as well as there being power-ups and secret rooms to discover. The bubble system in the game was very clever too. You could jump on them to help reach high-up platforms or hard-to-reach enemies, and some levels featured custom air flows to move bubbles around in different ways. The attention to detail set a standard at the time, and many who tried to imitate it often failed.

It was inevitable that home conversions would happen for the 8-bit and 16-bit platforms of the time. There were no complex graphics or scrolling to be concerned about, making the 8-bit versions, in particular, a far more attractive proposition compared with other complex arcade conversions of that era. Although Firebird was seemingly the lucky publisher to 'win' the licence, Richard Hewison (once a games tester at TelecomSoft) revealed that it wasn't their original intention to convert the game. "TelecomSoft got more than they originally bargained for when the deal to sign *Flying Shark* had to include a little-known coin-op called *Bubble Bobble* as part of the overall package," he revealed.

It was an amazing slice of luck for the company, and superb conversions would appear for the Amstrad CPC, Atari ST, Commodore 64, Commodore Amiga and ZX Spectrum platforms in 1987 and 1988. The success would, however, leave a bitter taste in the mouths of BBC Micro owners, with *Bubble Bobble* yet another conversion opportunity missed. Peter Gillett was one such disgruntled BBC Micro user, who felt it was time to readdress the balance. "*Bubble Bobble* was one of the great games from the 1980s that ported very well to home computers. We spent a lot of time playing the C64 version, as well as the arcade when we had the chance," he recalled. "As with many conversions, the BBC was left out again." A conversion was certainly doable on the BBC Micro, and so Peter decided to embark on what was to be his first commercial gaming venture (not *3D Tank Zone* as incorrectly credited online).

Joining him was school friend Martin Kelsey, who recalls how the two became friends. "I vividly remember meeting one day on the way back from school," he began. "Peter asked whether I'd got a computer. We established that, as he'd got a BBC, and I'd got a C64, we should get together and check out some games! Pete's house swiftly became my second home – a dream house for a teenage lad, stuffed with gadgets and two really welcoming parents only too willing to have a house stuffed with rowdy teenagers and supply them with endless quantities of tea and cake!"

Martin described how, even at the age of 14, Peter was clearly a prodigious talent in computing, maths and logic. Completely self-taught, Peter was programming impressive smooth-scrolling routines described as "perfect" by Martin. By mid-to-late 1988, confidence was there to tackle a full game, such as a conversion of *Bubble Bobble*. "I'm not sure that, when we started it, we had in mind to produce something marketable – it was more a case of 'is it possible? Let's see!'," Martin explained.

"As there was only the one BBC Micro available to work on, the machine had to be carefully time-shared."

The majority of the graphics and level design work would be handled by Martin, a role encouraged by Peter to help reduce boredom levels of Martin just watching him code. A third team member also shared the role in the form of Tim D'Aubney, who, although not quite as involved, chipped in with graphics and moral support throughout. "Tim, like me, was another hanger-on at Pete's house – of which there were many in those days!" Martin explained. "Tim did a bit of work at the beginning but then just kind of lost interest and drifted away." Peter then chips in: "Towards the end of the project, Tim used to sit in while I programmed, mainly to give a shove if I started getting distracted."

The conversion was based on the Commodore 64 version, with Martin's own machine and copy being the only real access they had to the game. The development epitomised the whole cliché of the 'bedroom programmer', with everything done from within the confinement of Peter's bedroom. "The BBC was set up on my desk, but I think we had the C64 and portable TV just sat on a chair, with us on the floor," Peter recalled. "We'd just started sixth form, so we fitted development in between school and homework, grabbing as many hours as we could."

Nothing was converted from raw source materials, with everything painstakingly analysed and replicated by playing and pausing the C64 version. "It took serious repeat-playing to access all levels, not helped by having to avoid level skips and keeping enough credits to complete it," Peter explained. "Certain things only appeared under certain conditions, so we had to find these too – though many didn't make it to our conversion."

Martin carefully translated the graphics and maps by hand, using level and sprite designer tools written by Peter. Everything was as faithfully copied as the BBC Micro would allow. The screen was a little bit shorter in comparison, which affected some layouts and dynamics, but was otherwise accurate. However, not all of the features could be included from the C64 edition, which was, in part, due to limitations on sprite numbers and how the game was being translated.

Even halfway into the development, Martin and Peter hadn't seen all of the C64 version in its entirety. "We had no idea how it ended and certainly had quite limited knowledge about the game's mechanics, e.g. activation of rewards, secret rooms, and so on," Martin explained. "My main achievement, in the end, was completing it and mapping out all the levels."

As there was only the one BBC Micro available to work on, the machine had to be carefully time-shared. Whilst Peter was coding, Martin played through C64 *Bubble Bobble* on the small portable telly and made careful notes. As Martin then started to recreate the graphics on the BBC Micro, Peter took care of playing the game and pausing at certain points to help Martin to replicate what he needed.

Along with the graphical challenges, memory restrictions were a major issue, with the graphics mode eating up most of the memory and leaving very little else for the actual game. "We couldn't compromise as we needed the colour range," Peter explained. "We ended up loading level designs from disk just to give ourselves a bit more room, and blacked out a couple of lines from the top and bottom of the screen so that we could store program code in the memory allocated to graphics. This gave us a bit more memory but resulted in the screen being slightly squished compared with the 64 version, which, if I recall correctly, was slightly shorter than the arcade version already."

Without source code to reference, working out the game logic and all the features was difficult. Many were ditched or missed out, including some bubble path routines, the 'EXTEND' bonus bubbles and having popped monsters bounce around. "On the C64 and arcade versions, enemies bounce around the screen before landing on a platform and turning into pick-ups. This was too much for the BBC, so they just sort of drop vertically," Martin explained.

The lack of hardware sprites on the BBC Micro also didn't help matters, especially when there was a need for lots of movable items on the screen. There was a struggle to get all of the sprites moving and interacting in the correct ways, and Peter spent a lot of time on the movement of the bubbles to get them working in an acceptable way. Regardless, challenges were overcome and development neared conclusion by early 1989. The two-player mode was retained, music and sound implemented and all 100 levels were present and playable. Thoughts now turned to seeing if an official release might be plausible. An obvious first choice was to submit it to Firebird/TelecomSoft, though this wasn't a smooth process.

"Oddly, every time Pete sent them disks, their contact claimed they didn't work," Martin recalled. "We thought this was bullshit at the time. In fact, they never showed the remotest bit of interest, which we thought kind of strange as they'd already got the licence, and we'd delivered the finished product." Even attempts to catch Firebird at one of the computer shows that year proved unsuccessful for the two.

Unfortunately, Firebird was going through a state of flux as TelecomSoft had been put up for sale around February 1989. Richard Hewison suggested a few reasons for the game not being taken on. Firstly, the BBC Micro wasn't as commercially viable as it once was, and uncertainty at the company was likely why there was also a lack of interest. Also, with a sale underway, no titles could be signed up until the conclusion of the deal.

Crucially, though, too much time had also passed since the original release. *Rainbow Islands* was now due for release by Firebird, and *Bubble Bobble* was being scheduled for a budget re-release on the Silverbird label. Shortly after MicroProse had taken over in May 1989, there were no longer publishing rights for *Bubble Bobble*. Undeterred, Peter and Martin approached other publishers, including Superior Software. "They weren't interested in a licensed product, although they released a game soon after that had remarkably similar characters," Peter revealed. "I couldn't tell you the title, but there was a sprite that was very like the 'Blubba' character!" added Martin.

One final attempt for publication saw the developers send a copy to a company called 4th Dimension, which was a relatively new outlet for new BBC Micro games. Though, with the licence costs and the amount of time since the original release, it too was not interested. There was no choice but to retire the game. "With hindsight, we probably should have approached companies earlier and checked whether there was any potential interest beforehand!" admitted Peter. "Naive in the extreme, but there you go – we were only 16 or whatever," added Martin. "It was good for us, though, to take something from concept right through to completion – we even did the cover art for the game box!" Peter concluded.

It wasn't all doom and gloom – the duo's conversion efforts impressed 4th Dimension. This led to the development of a game called *Arcade Soccer* on BBC Micro and Archimedes. "I spent the next year or so working with them on side projects. I developed a music/sound module that worked in a similar way to *SoundTracker* but specifically for use in games – low CPU, auto-background and fading, sound effect overlays, etc. – wrote music for a number of their other games, and was responsible for their copy protection," Peter explained.

"We thought it was probably the best BBC Micro game never to see the light of day – in a commercial sense."

Martin also worked on *Arcade Soccer* but then decided to move off in a new direction. "After *Arcade Soccer*, I think 4th Dimension wanted us to make an *Operation Wolf*-like game. At this point, my artistic limitations were cruelly exposed. My efforts looked like something akin to a primary school child's attempts to draw a war scene! By this point, our sixth-form years were drawing to a close, and my energies became focused on applying for university."

Neither Peter or Martin would pursue a career in the games industry. Peter later went down a different IT career path and is now a partner in a software business. He is also a guitarist and songwriter for a band called *Eight Deadly Words* (www.eightdeadlywords.com). Martin became a business analyst for many years, before becoming a secondary school teacher and part-time karate instructor.

Martin concludes about how, ironically, he almost got hold of an original *Bubble Bobble* arcade some years later. "In 1995, I spent the summer doing my master's thesis in South Wales. I lived for a few months in a flat close to the local amusement park," he recalled. "I noticed that they were selling machines off – *Bubble Bobble* was up for sale for about £100! But I was brassic and had no way of getting the machine back to Sheffield. Would have loved to have seen Pete's face, rocking up with the actual bloody arcade machine after all that time!"

As for the unreleased conversion, there would be a huge surprise for BBC Micro users, who never knew that one existed. Peter released the game into the public domain in January 1998, sending it to the 8-bit Software Public Domain library after rediscovering the disks during a sort out. "At least, we thought some niche enthusiasts would get to see it," smiled Martin. "We thought it was probably the best BBC Micro game never to see the light of day – in a commercial sense."

Although not without its flaws, it is a solid conversion which clearly shows that it was possible. An incredible achievement, considering the development restrictions and how the game was translated. Thanks to the generosity of its authors, it is a curiosity that you can fully experience for yourself.

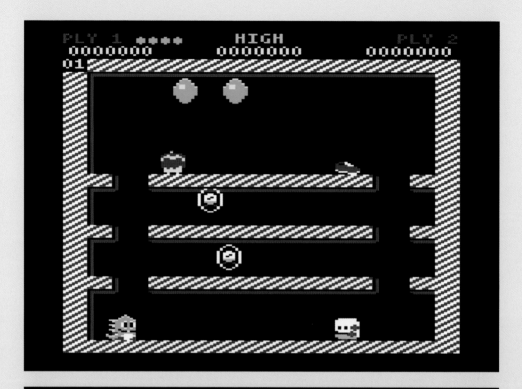

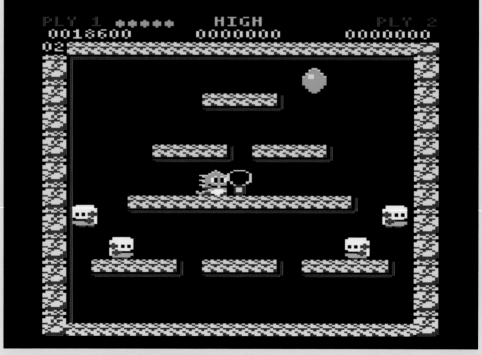

Above: Levels 1 and 2 from *Bubble Bobble* (BBC Micro), looking very comparable with the arcade, let alone the Commodore 64 edition.

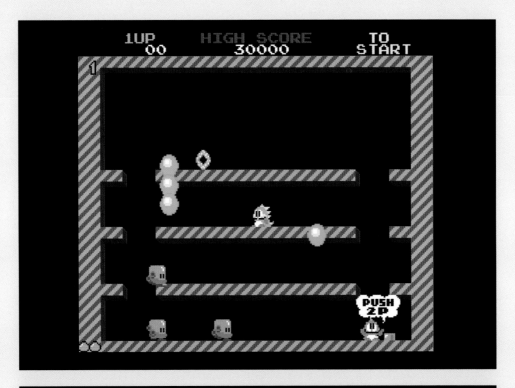

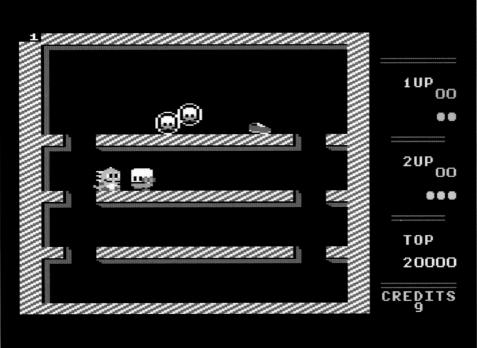

Top: Bubble Bobble (arcade). Showing off level 1 and where it all began. *Bottom:* The Commodore 64 conversion which was used as the basis for the BBC Micro port.

Nineteen Ninety — Nineteen Ninety Nine

As the industry grew during the 1990s, the platforms to play games began to settle. Eventually, it boiled down to just a few key players, with the home computer wars eventually won by IBM PC and Apple Mac standards as the decade concluded. Consoles would flourish from companies including Nintendo, SEGA and Sony, with Atari forced into an early grave as time went on. Handhelds showed that you could also take console gaming outside – as long as you had plenty of batteries.

With the improved hardware capabilities, the complexity of games also increased. The losses for a cancelled game became greater, sometimes taking companies down as a result. Getting your game onto the likes of the Super Nintendo or SEGA Mega Drive now required more hoops to jump through, pushing out many smaller companies. The industry was becoming big business and far from the bedroom industry that had helped kick-start everything in the beginning.

Dick Special Dissolution with the industry

Year: 1987–1992
Developers: Sandy White,
Activision and Miracle Games
Platforms: Atari ST, Commodore Amiga,
PC (DOS) and SEGA Mega Drive

Available to play
○ Yes ◉ No

Our next title, and first of this chapter, aptly bleeds between the previous and current decades of this book. A concept that stretched beyond its original and well-documented status, flirting with dognapping and murder mysteries across various missed opportunities over the space of approximately five years. A title that gamers who grew up during the 1980/90s will no doubt remember during the advance of 16-bit-powered platforms.

Dick Special – The Search for Spook was the tongue-in-cheek title that captured imaginations back in 1987 with its large and lovable cartoon character set in a striking isometric world. There was an unsubtle nod to the third Star Trek film title *The Search for Spock*, but why the odd name Dick Special for the main protagonist himself?

"Willy had done well, so why not Dick?" responded developer Sandy White. "I oft had lamented (still do) that *Ant Attack* had missed a trick with its nameless characters, with respect to marketing, sequels, etc. So, I vowed to make something with a named leading character. The joke (fnar fnar) was that he would be called Dick, in homage to *Jet Set Willy*. The other famous Dick was *Dick Barton, Special Agent* – and voilà, Dick Special (aka Special Dick) was born."

Long before *Dick Special* had existed, the basis of the character had been bubbling right back to Sandy's ZX Spectrum programming days. He always wanted to have a go at creating fully 3D characters and populate them within a complex isometric environment, and it would be a chance viewing of a television program that would plant the initial seeds of inspiration.

"I saw an archive documentary on the creation of Mickey Mouse, where the animators demonstrated how Mickey's features are based on circles, drawn around US coins of varying sizes," he recalled. "Mickey's ears always appear circular to the viewer, no matter what way he's facing. In computer terms, less storage! I immediately started sketching out what a character based only on circles and capsules (again useful symmetry) might look like. I created an impression, from memory, of Mickey Mouse, and I also worked out how many rotations might need to be stored of the capsule shapes, which would make up the nose, limbs, body, etc."

The basic appearance took into consideration the technical constraints that were expected to be encountered, with visual inspirations from characters such as Mickey Mouse, Tintin and Oor Wullie also thrown in. The initial thoughts and sketches are believed to have been created sometime around 1984–5 but were taken no further by Sandy. Storage was extremely limited on the Spectrum, and the ability to render something that looked as good as Sandy wanted was tricky with the limited resolution and colours available at the time.

It wasn't until the arrival and purchase of a Commodore Amiga that the dream became technically feasible. Dick would begin simply as a circle for a head in *Deluxe Paint*, and then he grew from there, building on the original concept sketches. There was even a nod to the *Beano* and its character Plug, with the inclusion of a bright-red jumper. "Notice Dick's rather fat neck, which is almost as wide as his head," Sandy keenly pointed out. "I was thinking ahead at this point with regard to how collision detection and masking was going to work. It was technicalities dictating the look."

Spook (Dick's dog that you were searching for) began similarly, starting as a basic triangular shape and eventually morphing into the character. "I always imagined Dick Special to be pretty much like Tintin, with a 'Snowy' little sidekick, to boot. My interest in him extended to how he was going to look, move and express himself," recalled Sandy.

In a development partnership with Angela Sutherland at the time, both saw the potential to create a new game around the two newly formed characters. The lead character was initially named 'Special Dick', but the rude connotations were felt unwise, so it was changed quickly to 'Dick Special'. 'Spook' had also been called 'Spik' but was renamed due to its offensive meaning to the Spanish.

Angela would help to manage and create a design for the game, forming a backstory where Dick is trying to find the dognapped Spook, who has been locked away in a large dingy mansion. The idea was for Dick to explore the mansion, collecting objects and solving puzzles to find Spook and his captor. Along the way, there would be nasties and various booby traps to avoid.

Angela's inspiration for the story and character profiles came from a comic strip created whilst at art college some years before, featuring a detective character called Eppington Bongo. Eppington was meant to be the lead detective, though it was actually his dog, Spik, who was the real detective, earning money and solving cases whilst his owner was more interested in metaphysics and philosophy. No visual cues were taken from the comic for Dick Special, but Angela suggested that her own personal vision for his 'personality' was heavily inspired by a combination of both Eppington and Spik.

Not only was it also going to be the first 16-bit game created by Sandy and Angela, but it was also to utilise the Hold and Modify (HAM) display mode on the Commodore Amiga. This allowed for a staggering 4,096 colours in resolutions between 320×200 and 360×576 at the time – great for displaying photo-realistic images but not felt to be practical for utilisation in an actual game. Sandy felt differently and wanted to create an experience unlike anything before. A game that felt like a cartoon but with more interactivity compared with the likes of the LaserDisc-based *Dragon's Lair* in the arcades.

Sandy started exploring the Amiga's architecture and began developing an engine with an isometric viewpoint that would scroll in eight fixed directions as you moved around. Characters would take up about a third of the screen overall. As you went through a door, the game would switch to a completely new location. The main character was taken and animated by Sandy using careful precision for all the directions that he could move in.

Initially, Sandy designed his own placeholder graphics due to initial technical complexities of being able to easily add new artwork at the very start. The animations, in particular, were tightly coupled with the driving software. An old ghostly room was produced, including a trap door scene that became iconic thanks to screenshots that featured in the press at the time.

"I was never very happy with my own graphical efforts that appeared in those tech demos," reflected Sandy. "I certainly would have asked Angela to try to improve on them later on. Plenty of other versions of Dick appeared in storyboards and mood panels done by her and by others, and, to be honest, I was never very happy with them either. I kind of wanted him to have that beautiful quality that Hergé put into Tintin. But, really, I felt that this would be solvable, and, in many respects at the time, it was the very least of my worries compared with the technical challenge of getting it all working on the Amiga."

Efforts soon began to pay off, and, after a while, Dick was interacting with environments, complete with accompanying digitised sound effects, such as creaking floorboards. But there was nothing much else at this stage, apart from triggering a monster to jump out of a trap door as you approached. However, the early build was enough to gain the attention of TelecomSoft, which signed up the game for publication on its prestigious Rainbird label in 1987.

Meanwhile, Angela had started creating a number of drawings for projected cover artwork, storyboards and cartoon strips. She also recalls using *Deluxe Paint* to create a series of scene mock-ups and ideas. As time went on and Rainbird became involved, the original storyline evolved and switched to a new environment. Dick now had to solve a murder mystery within a hotel environment, as well as find his dog, Spook.

"The redevelopment made little reference to anything which went before, beyond the central character, Dick."

Details of the game began to surface in the press. Although intended for release only on the Amiga due to its chosen display mode, the game was also advertised for the Atari ST in early 1988 as well. Rainbird had jumped the gun because any potential conversion had to first be evaluated. James Hutchby, a friend of Sandy, was tasked with seeing if a conversion could really work on the platform.

"My role was to produce a proof-of-concept to see if the ST could scroll the background fast enough entirely in software as it didn't have any of the flexibility of the Amiga's video sub-system," explained James, who attempted to replicate Sandy's first prototype. "It could just about manage, a little jerkily, but that took the processor working flat out. So there wouldn't have been anything left over to animate the sprites or run the game logic. At that point, it was basically abandoned as a result."

The Amiga version would press on, but, after several months, there hadn't been much progress since that first working prototype. However, Sandy had been working hard on a new groundbreaking skeletal animation system, so Dick could be made to walk, run and jump around his world more realistically. "The big animated characters were later motion-captured using puppets. I built what you'd now call a 'waldo' in film terms, which let you capture the motion," he explained. Waldo puppetry was a way of controlling a digital puppet using a telemetric input device known as a 'waldo', pioneered by Jim Henson. The input device allowed for X-Y-Z-axis movement of the digital puppet on screen.

Once this background work was completed, a few more scenarios were added, which had, by now, completely moved away from the original haunted mansion theme and over to the hotel theme instead. This included a scene with Dick walking along a building ledge, which was shown and demonstrated at a computer show in 1988 on the Rainbird stand, where the game attracted a lot of attention according to Sandy.

Behind the scenes, there were ongoing memory issues due to the chosen HAM display mode. A rethink was now required on the whole approach for development. Ultimately, though, cracks were forming in the creative partnership which drained the enthusiasm for the project. In particular, there was a major disagreement over the artistic direction and design of the game as a whole.

Eventually, Angela would move on for a new life in London in early 1988, starting with a PA job at TelecomSoft and, shortly afterwards, promoted to Head of Development at the company. Sandy was given the rights to complete *Dick Special* for Rainbird, with Angela able to use the characters at a later date if she so wished. Although no longer directly involved on the game, Angela would, for a short period, continue to provide design ideas for Sandy to use, up until artist Alastair Hearsum was brought on board to help fill the void.

"Sandy and I met at art college – me painting, him sculpture. We were good friends and shared an interest in making music using multi-track recording and synthesisers," began Alastair. "Sandy had been unconventional at college, eschewing the traditional sculptural materials in favour of electronics and computer-controlled movement. His creations were innovative and exciting and often amusing. He introduced me to computers, and I got an Amiga around the time Angela moved on. I was looking around for a direction for my life, having languished as a lifeguard for a few years, unable to capitalise on my art skills. *Dick Special* seemed a very exciting opportunity." In unison with the change of team, the direction of the game also changed as the memory issues came to a head. Significantly, it was decided to drop the HAM display mode which had been causing all sorts of headaches early on for the project.

"The first engine looked really human and quite compelling – not something you'd really see on a computer back then. But it wasn't very useful for gameplay. The previous version demoed at trade shows, etc. and was entirely unplayable," confirmed Sandy. "Our ideas of what it would become were way ahead of what we could achieve. The engine was good for a cutscene, but I needed something the player could drive. So, I made a new engine which was isometric but with a higher resolution than anything on the Spectrum [for instance]. The redevelopment made little reference to anything which went before, beyond the central character, Dick."

For the new build, Alastair designed a number of impressive hotel-themed rooms and locations in *Deluxe Paint*, with everything now neatly broken up into tiles to save on memory. Set piece animations were also created and were to feature throughout the environments in various parts. Apart from working from a basic template that Sandy provided, Alastair had a relatively free visual reign, with just a few technical restrictions imposed.

"The challenge I most remember was having to conjure up an interesting environment with very few colours. As Sandy tweaked code, he may have spared more," Alastair recalled. "A solution was to make up a palette of patterns with various densities of coloured dots, much like you can make interesting pictures with black-and-white halftoning as newspapers used to/still do. The resolution was so small that it was manageable making up these patches. I would then paint/fill shapes with them."

Sandy was very impressed with Alastair's first-ever computer-generated artwork, which had really come together quickly. "One problem he managed to overcome somehow, was making things look rounded, when, in fact, everything was built just with cubes," he remarked. "You can see an incongruous difference in style between my character animation and his backgrounds. That would have been unified, and, I think, in favour of his aesthetic."

Using the new artwork, Sandy built up various parts of the hotel, adding creatures and objects, such as wardrobes, fireplaces, statues and paintings. There was also a basement-like environment, full of water and pipes that dripped or leaked gas, and holes in the ground to avoid. Sandy also arranged a set of tunes and bouncy sound effects to accompany each location and action to bring things further to life. Although the new redevelopment was progressing, the game drifted along at a slow pace, which may have been due to the project no longer having a project manager to help push things along.

Regardless, Sandy and Alastair completed a demo of the engine by October 1988, but, by now, Sandy was running out of steam. "I had found a lot of pleasure in doing everything – design, coding, graphics and music – but was increasingly finding that I couldn't cope," he admitted. "There were also probably half a dozen people at TelecomSoft trying to manage *Dick Special,* and I got fed up with the games business. Out went the nice friendly bods from the cottage industry I knew, and in came money, politics and people in suits."

TelecomSoft had also had enough too. The new engine looked good, but there still wasn't much to do in the game, with months of work still required to finish it. Now more than a year since Rainbird announced the game, it felt that it was now unlikely to get the invested money back. "They pulled the plug, with me owing them quite a lot of money," Sandy confessed. "It was just too big a project for me to complete single-handed." A year or so later, TelecomSoft was taken over by MicroProse, but the game had long been cancelled to have ever continued under the new ownership.

"I was never very happy with my own graphical efforts that appeared in those tech demos."

Dick Special would become a legendary 'Whatever happened to...' article piece rather than the classic anticipated by many. Built up a little in our minds perhaps, but there is no doubt that it could have been amazing, had the direction and engine been finalised earlier. "It went through so many iterations. I think it would've eventually ended up as a point-and-click detective story," suggested Sandy on how things could have been.

This was not the end of Dick by any means. The character was still felt to have potential by those who had some involvement with the Rainbird title. A year or so after being put to rest, TelecomSoft's Colin Fuidge took up a new role as producer at Activision. Although Colin didn't respond to enquiries, it is believed that he turned to Delvin Sorrell (now Patricia Curtis) to create a new title for the company in the shape of *Dick Special: The Captain is Dead* in 1990.

"I signed a contract with Activision for £30k to write the game, which was just a straight contract programming job. I was doing a lot of that in the '80s and '90s," began Patricia, who got Nick Pelling involved to help. Patricia suggested it was Angela that she dealt with for the project, though Angela responded that she never had any role at Activision. At the time, Colin and Angela were married, and Colin was also good friends with Patricia – so it's likely that any involvement was indirect due to holding rights to the character and name.

As the new title suggests, the storyline changed once more. Dick was now to be situated on a large cruise ship but with a murder-solving theme retained. "The plot was that the purser of the ship was smuggling stolen art. The captain had found out about it and got himself murdered," explained Patricia. Dick would take up the role of detective to try and solve who did it by gathering evidence and solving puzzles.

"I signed a contract with Activision for £30k to write the game."

Angela suggests that the story idea may have slightly evolved from an experience shared with both Colin and Patricia in general conversation. Recalling an aeroplane journey, where a champagne cork had popped out suddenly and startled everyone, she joked how bad it would be if the cork had killed the captain. This brief recollection likely planted the initial seed for the captain-based storyline. She also vaguely recalls speaking to Nick Pelling about how the rooms in the game could work, but she couldn't recall why.

Making a start on the project, Patricia recalled that art assets were obtained from the very first Rainbird prototype as a starting point. Patricia concentrated solely on programming, whilst Nick (who, unfortunately, didn't respond to enquiries) provided technical assistance on the game's engine. One key decision would be to side-step the memory-hungry HAM mode but retain the isometric viewpoint and large characters. As a result, plans for an Atari ST version were now back on.

After a few months, an efficient game engine was constructed that allowed for large locations to be implemented within a very small memory footprint. "The game was written to have locations generated procedurally from a very simple data set, wallpaper textures, room size and shape, door positions, etc.," explained Patricia. "It was still isometric with flip screens between rooms. There was also a part of the game that was going to be set on deck, but it was not otherwise based outside."

Unfortunately, development began to flounder quite early on due to a lack of resources allocated. "I made a great start on the Amiga and Atari ST versions, but I was constantly asking for art and design documents," confirmed Patricia. "Most of the code was created; it was just lacking art and the story. I remember the last code I worked on was an isometric sort for complex table arrangements, which was originally a fair way down the schedule."

Patricia revealed that Angela was behind the artwork and design for the new game. However, Angela says that she was not involved at all, not wanting to have any involvement with new projects featuring the character. Although Patricia is still adamant that Angela was involved in the game in that way, a cohesive agreement couldn't be made to the fact.

Although development was stalling, there were bigger issues about to hit. "A few months in, I was ready to give up, when I was told I should hang on a few weeks as something may be going down at Activision," recalled Patricia. "A few weeks later, I get a call saying that the project was cancelled as Activision UK was being closed, with everyone being moved to Germany." It left Patricia without payment to continue development. After contacting her lawyers, all of Activision's UK assets were frozen, including bank accounts. They were now in a predicament where they had to phone Patricia to get permission to pay employee wages. "Over the next few weeks, Activision negotiated with my lawyer, and I got a settlement, and Activision left the UK," she confirmed.

Due to the short lifespan of the project, only a basic engine ever existed, with some test graphics. It never got to a stage where it could be properly presented to the press. Yet again, Dick Special would fail to see the light of day, but the character and concept had now found a new admirer in Patricia, who felt that there was still a game there desperate to break out.

"They pulled the plug, with me owing them quite a lot of money."

A few years later, Patricia founded a new company called Miracle Games along with Graeme Ashton in 1992. Still fond of the Dick Special character during her brief time on the Activision project, she suggested a new development with the character. Now with the simple title of *Dick Special*, could it be third time lucky? "What I liked about *Dick Special* was the name and look of the character, the whole idea of this large cartoon character in his red jumper and blue trousers. Back in the early '90s, that was amazing for me; it's just something that I really liked," explained Patricia on the decision to resurrect the character once again.

However, Miracle Games needed the rights before being able to proceed. It is believed that this was arranged with Colin and possibly signed by Angela – something she has a vague recollection of but nothing more. "I believe I purchased everything. Character, name, artwork concepts – everything – as my lawyers at the time were pretty damn good," recalled Patricia. "They took the piss out of the contract because my lawyers had bound it with ribbon!"

The game was started from scratch with a brand-new direction. "Patricia already had something working on the Amiga, where you could walk out of one room, and it flipped into the next room with this cartoony character and cartoony feel. It was very cartoony and more than just little sprites. But we didn't use any of the graphics from it at all," recalled Graeme Ashton, who would take on the role of lead developer for the new game. No Atari ST version was considered this time; instead, the SEGA Mega Drive was brought into play along with the Commodore Amiga. Graeme's brother, Jeremy, would handle all of the graphics, and designing the game and its puzzles was newly employed Gordon Leggatt – with help from Debbie Sorrell (Patricia's wife at the time) and Patricia herself.

"I came into the industry, knowing virtually nothing about gaming," explained Gordon. "Somebody said to me, 'There's a place down the road that makes computer games'. I wanted to do commercial art as I had just left school and didn't really know what I wanted to do. Miracle Games let me have a go at doing some little 16-pixel three-cell animations that were absolutely appalling. But they thought I had a good imagination and that I was quite funny. So they asked if I wanted to have a go at developing some games with them."

Given his first break, Gordon was now tasked with creating game designs and ideas for the team, with *Dick Special* as his first assignment. "*Dick Special* was always sitting there in the background. So, in between projects that were going on, we'd fall back onto that and do a bit more work," recalled Gordon. "I concentrated on writing stories for it, developing characters and plotting it out because a lot of it was puzzle-based."

Amiga Power magazine got an early exclusive whilst doing a feature on Miracle Games in late 1992. In its October issue, it seemed to show early screens from the Activision edition of the game, before, in the next issue, showing the new version that Graeme was working on. It described the game as being a fully interactive animated cartoon, with a main character of 108 pixels high. It was to combine elements of arcade adventure, slapstick and situation comedy with cartoon and comic book quirks, with Dick conversing with the player via speech bubbles. Each scenario played out with a number of puzzles to solve and strange collectable objects, such as 'strings of sausages' and 'inflatable people'.

A storyline given in the magazine described Dick as a private detective who must recover and reassemble his mutilated teddy bear and bring the culprits to justice. "It's all a bit twee, isn't it? From my point of view, I'd have almost certainly said 'I don't like that'." laughed Graeme when shown the story. "I think that was Patricia who came up with that," added Gordon. "I can almost see her face cracking up at the idea and us saying, 'Yeah, let's go with that!'."

Patricia often had a bit of fun with the press, but these were genuine ideas batted about. Patricia, Gordon and Debbie were constantly coming up with crazy ideas for their games, and with *Dick Special,* there was no exception. "There were times where it was like a writer's room, so much so that you came up with something and went 'Look, I've got this idea'," explained Gordon. "Debbie would also often come up with something and just chuck it out there, but almost as if it was someone else's idea."

With Gordon just arriving out of school, ideas and scripts would go through Debbie, who would help tidy and put things together. "I would have loads of scattergun ideas with little sketches and whatnot. She would put it into something cohesive," he confirmed. "So, as much as I might be credited, it was as much Debbie making it into something presentable."

The teddy bear story wasn't quite accurate; the plan was actually to have Dick solve a number of crimes. Compared with the previous games, the team had an established game plan. Linking up all of the individual stories/puzzles, Dick was to have a suitcase that opened and revealed a Tardis-like pop-up office. This would act as an interactive area to select a crime by choosing a wanted poster on the wall. Once a villain was captured, the relevant poster would curl up and fall. Unfortunately, none of the team could recall any of the stories/puzzles.

Before any of the storyline/puzzles were implemented, Graeme needed to create a new game engine. "I eventually developed an engine which actually worked on both the Amiga and the SEGA Mega Drive combined. It was isometric scrolling with a pretty funky physics engine!" he exclaimed.

Using Gordon's concept sketches and old character graphics for reference, Jeremy started off by producing a tweaked version of Dick (now featuring hair!) and a set of office-like rooms with tables, chairs and objects, such as crates and books; enough to put together a good solid proof of concept. After a few months, Graeme had a fully working demo where you could move from room to room with object interaction. As with earlier iterations, the rooms were larger than the visible window and would scroll as you moved around. Moving to a new room would result in the screen flipping to the new location. However, it was the physics within the game that would really stand out.

"The physics engine received most of my attention. It was a fully functional virtual 3D physics engine. In reality, complete overkill for *Dick Special*'s isometric layout," explained Graeme. "At the time, we did toy with the idea of making *Dick Special* a first- or third-person 3D-rendered game. However, it wasn't possible, given the hardware constraints of the Amiga and Mega Drive, combined with the required gameplay. So, isometric it was, and most objects were restricted to 90-degree rotations."

The demo was enough to tout to potential publishers, with Virgin Games showing brief interest at one stage. But progress was slow on further developing the title to incorporate the game design. Graeme was managing people as well as code, and this meant that *Dick Special* was not a key focus. Priority was also given on other titles, such as *Apocalypse*, which were closer to completion and already tied up in publication deals. *Dick Special* remained a back-burner title and resulted in storyline and designs only existing on paper.

Intriguingly, whilst Gordon's game was in development, yet another *Dick Special* title was started after it was felt by the team that it could become a series of games. The tongue-in-cheek aspect was pushed to the max, with a working title of *Dick Special: The Mystery of Phucton Island* given to a whole new development.

Programming duties on this particular title were handled by Philip Sharpe (who remained elusive during research) on both PC and Amiga platforms. A Mega Drive version was to be potentially considered for a later date. Once more, Jeremy Ashton handled the graphics, as well as the design for the game as a whole. "*Phucton Island* had far more work done on it," recalled Graeme. "It had loads of graphics and code produced. How long was it in development for? I don't know, but many months at least. It kind of worked on the same principle as *Dick Special*, but more inspired by *Another World* in terms of game design."

"I eventually developed an engine which actually worked on both the Amiga and the SEGA Mega Drive combined."

With a dedicated programmer, the game progressed much faster compared with Graeme's game. With its complex sequences, each scenario took a long time to build. "Every level involved a hell of a lot of work and choreography with the graphics and even the code," explained Graeme. "So, to actually finish, it probably needed another 12 months at least. It was quite a big effort and a lot just to get it to where it was."

The basic story of the game had you situated on an island after escaping a shipwreck. You would have to solve puzzles and mysteries to survive and eventually escape. Graeme couldn't recall much specific content from the game, but he did recall individual features, such as bridges, that would start to fall as you walked on them, and where you would have to grab a rope at the opportune moment to prevent yourself from falling to your doom.

Like *Another World*, everything in the game was carefully choreographed, with actions and events triggered as you moved through the game. "You could walk along and jump, so the user thought they had full control. You thought you had some kind of freedom, but a lot of the choices had already been made for you. Like tax returns, really you have no choice!" Graeme laughed.

Luckily, *Phucton Island* never featured the horror of tax returns and was progressing well. However, Graeme's own earlier development had, by now, completely stagnated. After a year or so, Patricia and Graeme also decided to go their own separate ways. "Patricia and I broke the company up, and the original *Dick Special* fell by the wayside," Graeme confirmed.

Patricia kept the rights to *Dick Special*, meaning the end of Graeme's work on the game, and *Phucton Island* now needing a new lead character. Required changes would never be made in the end. Not long after Patricia left, Miracle Games had come to its natural end, with all funded projects being completed. Graeme felt it was time to move on. Staggeringly, the third and fourth attempts of *Dick Special* would also fail to see fruition, but there were now no more twists left. *Dick Special* was just never going to be.

With the number of iterations undertaken, the chances of seeing something related to the character preserved are plausible. Although Angela and Alastair no longer have their original artwork, Sandy, on the other hand, still has materials. "I'm a great hoarder, and I'm sure bits of it will surface eventually. I'll steel myself and put the demo disk into an Amiga one day," Sandy concluded. However, recent new development ventures on the likes of *No Man's Sky* have heavily limited his time. Perhaps once things quieten down?

Alastair did, however, keep hold of some amazing video footage of the version of *Dick Special* that he worked on with Sandy, and he kindly shared it. Watch out for the full video on the Games That Weren't website. Patricia wasn't one to keep hold of past work, and so the brief Activision development is now long gone. Gordon also no longer had anything, just fond memories of his first break. "It was a really exciting and vibrant environment to work within. To leave school and to have that experience really spoilt me," he concluded.

"Every level involved a hell of a lot of work and choreography with the graphics and even the code."

Graeme, instead, gave hope and is convinced that he still has everything for both Miracle Games incarnations, and he plans to resurrect it all someday. If this happens, there will be an interesting tech demo to behold, and *Phucton Island* will, no doubt, be of great interest to see, with its vastly different design direction. Interestingly, though, Graeme's physics engine lives on to this day.

"I converted the *Dick Special* physics engine into 'C' towards the end of 1995. It was going to be used in a space simulation game I was working on called *Empire*," recalled Graeme. "It was eventually deployed in a suite of space management applications used by most international retailers to layout their stores, aisles and products. Eventually, it was purchased by Oracle (circa 2008). So, *Dick Special* lives on – sort of. In some small way, he has affected the lives of every single person who has ever, at some point, visited a supermarket and wondered, frustratingly, where they have moved the coffee aisle this week!"

Still owning the rights to the character, we conclude by asking Patricia if there could ever be a fifth time lucky for the *Dick Special* character. "I bought the rights with the intention to make a game; however, I have just not found the time yet. Maybe that's something I should consider soon," she responded. "The trouble is that so much time has passed and, even though it would be truly retro, would the game players know the mighty *Dick Special*? So, maybe I have left it too late? Maybe, I don't know!"

Above: Quickly mocked-up scene idea by Angela, found by Sandy and tidied up for print here by our artist.

Above: The infamous trapdoor scene printed in the press at the time, tidied up for print here by our artist. Very much still in development, as seen within the art package, *Deluxe Paint*.

Above: Static screenshots taken from a rare video, showing the last iteration of *Dick Special* at Rainbird. Here you can see the loading/title screen and two different scenes. This also shows the new background artwork by Alastair Hearsum. Bottom Right: Sandy at a 1988 computer show, standing by the Rainbird stand showing off *Dick Special* (Amiga).

Above: Screenshot of an early concept by Graeme, complete with object interactions (Amiga). Image has been tidied up by our artist for this publication.

Above: Early screens likely from the cancelled Activision development (Amiga), tidied up by our artist for this publication.

Hard Drivin'
Publisher cancelled

Year: 1990
Developer: Tengen
Platform: Nintendo Entertainment System

Many may argue that this was a conversion too far for 8-bit platforms. That didn't stop an ambitious NES conversion, which got around complex 3D hurdles by translating key parts into animated scenes played back to the user. Unfortunately, the quality wasn't there, so Tengen rejected it. Thankfully, the Lost Levels website would preserve the early prototype to show the world.

"Working on the conversion of *Hard Drivin'* was a very special time for me overall. I had the privilege of working with arcade veterans who were a great inspiration to me growing up, and who made me want to become a video game developer in the first place.

The technical challenges with the conversion were immense, and it was Jurgen Friedrich's incredible work on the Atari ST version that provided a solid foundation for us to build on with the Nintendo Entertainment System. It just simply would not have been possible without him."

Mark Morris, developer

Available to play

◉ **Yes**   ○ **No**

1

MPH

60

20 100

HIGH SCORE

000768

BEAT TO CHALLENGE

Gazza 2
Poor sales
of GX4000

Year: 1990
Developer: Active Minds
Platform: Amstrad GX4000

Available to play

 Yes ◉ No

Gazza's 'Tears in Turin' in 1990 epitomised the so-called 'years of hurt' for England football fans. Thirty to be precise, according to David Baddiel, Frank Skinner and The Lightning Seeds in 1996, with fans still counting to this day.

During the late 1980s and early 1990s, fans were optimistic at the prospect of footballing genius, Paul (Gazza) Gascoigne. England's national team, in the doldrums for decades, finally had hope once more for success. With football games becoming ridiculously popular, Empire Software jumped on the bandwagon and secured a licence to create games with the midfielder's name.

Unfortunately, things went rather pear-shaped with the release of *Gazza's Super Soccer* in 1989. The game sported an odd side-on perspective of the pitch, switching frequently to a vertical perspective when heading towards the goal. It was dire and universally panned across all formats. "Well, it wasn't too hot, was it?" Empire's production manager, Rik Yapp, told *Your Sinclair* magazine back in Issue 61. "I did the game design on that one, but the finished thing turned out to be nothing like it."

Regardless, it sold by the bucketload on name alone; enough for Empire to commission a sequel to ride the wave of England's successful 1990 World Cup run. Hoping to produce something a little better for even more sales, Empire turned to newly formed Manchester development studio, Active Minds, founded by David Colley and Alison Kelly.

David had attempted a football game just a year earlier with a Liverpool-licensed title. Planned for release under his short-lived budget label, Impact, it never got past the planning stage. Grandslam would eventually jump in instead and take over the licence. *Gazza 2* was perhaps an opportunity for David to make amends. He began by constructing a development team consisting of Mike Hiddleston (ZX Spectrum and Amstrad CPC), Paul Clansey (Commodore 64) and Chris Pink (Commodore Amiga, Atari ST and PC). Handling graphics across all platforms were ex-Ocean stalwarts Simon Butler and Mark R. Jones. Music would be handled by the prolific David Whittaker.

Empire requested the game around July 1990, with the aim to release it in time for Christmas. Things didn't get off to the best of starts, with Mike abruptly disappearing, leaving the ZX Spectrum and Amstrad CPC versions without a developer and very little actually started. ZX Spectrum legend, John Pickford (creator of classics such as *Zub*, *Amaurote* and *Feud*), was swiftly employed to fill the void and start development from scratch.

The concept design for the game was created by David and inspired primarily by Dino Dini's *Kick Off*, with added input from producer Rik Yapp. One early decision was to make the game play from left to right and vice versa, with a top-down perspective, instead of top-to-bottom scrolling, as it was felt to be a disadvantage for the person at the bottom half of the pitch. The game would feature multidirectional scrolling to enable a large play area, as well as a scanner showing all players across the entire pitch.

Although the general look and feel remained similar across all versions, due to time constraints, the programmers were given carte blanche to make their own design interpretations and tweaks. "I've been working on console games lately, and they've influenced me quite a lot," John told *Your Sinclair* in Issue 61. "I've taken the same approach as the Japanese really – I've just made it playable and fast and more or less forgotten that it's actually about football."

John cites *Game Boy Soccer* (referring to *Soccer Mania*, released as *Soccer Boy* in Japan in 1990) as his basic inspiration for development. The game wasn't particularly outstanding, lacking a lot of the basic rules, but it was simple, pure and fun to play. "I always think that, if the basic game plays well, then you can add anything else you want to it afterwards," John continued. "The advantage for me is that I don't like football very much, so I just tried to make it fun." The influence explains why John's developments excluded fouls, penalties, offsides, free kicks or any player management compared with other editions. Empire didn't care as long as it got a reasonable game to put in a box.

Only the 16-bit editions would feature full managerial options, which Chris Pink had himself decided to build. "They only wanted a *Kick Off*-like game. I added the management side because I wanted it there," he recalled. "We got into a little trouble actually with Dino Dini because a magazine posted a screenshot showing an 'import *Kick Off*' button on the editor. I'd written code to load his AI data to compare with what we were doing. I guess he thought it was more than that. Don't know what happened, but it all went away pretty quickly."

The majority of the graphical work was handled by Simon Butler, who worked simultaneously on a *Total Recall* film licence that Active Minds had been assigned by Ocean Software. Mark R. Jones confirmed having no involvement at all on the 8-bit editions. "I started *Gazza 2* first but mainly because the lead artist/designer (sic) on *Total Recall* was absent on the day I started," recalled Simon. "I had no input whatsoever on the design; I was on the project purely as an artist. I was told what was needed, the sizes, the number of frames, and I then got on with creating those graphics. I doubt I would have been of any use if design were required because it was a football title, and I could not have been any less interested in the subject matter if I had tried."

"Day-to-day work on *Gazza 2* was very easy," continued Simon. "There was a graphics list of moves and frame numbers that I needed to create, a list of additional screens and other assets. That's all there was to it. I don't remember having any great problems with the development of the graphics for the title other than the viewpoint. Top-down is not a very attractive angle, and some of the sprites you create don't look like much on their own but do work in an animation cycle. So it's always a challenge trying to find that odd visual 'something' that looks right when you're animating a running man seen from directly above."

Compared with *Total Recall*, Simon suggests that *Gazza 2*'s team had a lot more experience and just got on with it, working individually and effectively. Apart from the usual bugs during development, nothing problematic occurred, and everything was on schedule. Rik would travel every two weeks or so to see how everything was going, and he was happy with the progress being made.

Whilst the developments were underway, the new Amstrad GX4000 console was separately building up steam for release in September 1990. With the console urgently needing games, Empire would answer Amstrad's call. "A decision to create a GX4000 version was very last-minute," explained David. "John had already worked wonders getting the game up and running on the Spectrum and Amstrad, but, unfortunately, there was little time to add his usual touches to the console version."

"A decision to create a GX4000 version was very last-minute."

To support the extra platform, John simply ported his existing Amstrad CPC code over and built on top of it, taking advantage of the GX4000's extra capabilities where possible in the time remaining. In particular, the game utilised the console's ultra-smooth scrolling capabilities at a decent speed. As with the other Z80 versions, an arrow above the player indicated who you controlled. The graphics were more colourful compared with the CPC edition, with players given proper flesh-coloured skin and a larger variety of shirt colours. The score panel was given a little extra with some chunky scrolling colour bars, and vertical space was allocated for the game's shot power bar. That was it though, and the rush meant never taking full advantage of the console's capabilities.

Simon no longer recalled anything specific about his GX4000 work. "Most days, I can barely remember what colour socks I'm wearing, so, sadly, details regarding specific machines have been lost in the mists of time," he explained. "The entire period seems to have been overpowered by the fiasco that was *Total Recall*, so the ordinary trouble-free side of my duties involving *Gazza 2* has been pushed to some dark corner."

Finishing off the game's polish was a title screen with an impressive greyscale digitised picture of Gazza, making great use of the extended palette. This was created by Chris, who created similar loading screens for the other conversions. From here, you could 'Kick off' a new game or make adjustments under the 'Options' area. The options were sparse, with just the ability to change controls, teams, length of a game, select one or two players, or enter a sound test demo.

By late November, the game was practically finished across all of John's three platforms. John's brother, Ste, had jumped in to help finish it off, sneakily skiving off work at Rare Manchester for a day to draw the game's logo and provide a font borrowed from *Solar Jetman* (though, oddly, not used in the GX4000 edition). David Whittaker's music and SFX were swiftly bolted into the console game using the same Amstrad CPC tunes, which shared the same AY-3-8912 sound chip.

Unfortunately, there were some frustrating bugs missed, which also featured in the ZX Spectrum and Amstrad CPC editions. At kick-off, the ball always went straight to the opposition, and goalkeepers performed terribly, only ever tracking up and down. Regardless of that, the game was far superior to the first game in every way. Empire had the game they were hoping for.

The game was sent off for review by Empire Software by the end of 1990. The GX4000 edition was reviewed between January and February 1991 in *Amstrad Action*, *Computer and Video Games*, *Mean Machines* and also French magazines *Amstrad Cent Pour Cent* and *Player One*, receiving above-average to good reviews. It was certainly no *Kick Off 2* but felt worthy enough of the £24.99 asking price. "The action is fast, and the graphics are very smooth! However, start playing, and some major shortfalls become apparent. The goalies are hopeless – shoot diagonally, and a goal is guaranteed, and the way the players patrol the pitch is completely unintelligent. Football-starved GX4000 owners might like to give this a go – but don't expect the world," Julian Rignall told *Mean Machines* readers in Issue 4. The French press was slightly more critical, with particular focus on the bugs present.

More approving was *Amstrad Action*, giving the game a 'Stunner' status with an impressive score of 88% and, seemingly, getting what John had set out to achieve. "Your team plays like a meandering rabble, and any pre-match tactics the team may have gone through are out the window the instant the kick-off whistle is blown," Adam Waring reported. "Perhaps that's why it's such a darned good game! It's not bogged down with all the tedious offside rules and is more like playground football than anything. Niggles aside, though, the speed and superb playability makes up for it all."

"I've just made it playable and fast and more or less forgotten that it's actually about football."

Adam couldn't recall anything about the game today, apart from the painful screenshot process. "The terrible moiré patterns on the screenshots bring back memories," he shuddered. "We photographed the screen via a camera inside a box to block out the light and played the game peering through the viewfinder, one hand, one joypad, the other on shutter release. On CPC we just pressed a button on a dongle to take a screenshot."

Although not much else was included in the console edition, the French publications did reveal a cheat mode where you could start with a zoomed-in camera view. This was achieved by pressing 'up' on the D-pad several times on the title screen, resulting in the *Gazza 2* logo shrinking to signify activation. It gave the game a neat twist and a very different feel.

Intriguingly, the reviews also revealed that the ball never left the ground, even though it does on the other Z80 editions. With text also rendered in a low-res font and not utilising Ste's *Solar Jetman* font, it is likely that the review copies sent out were actually not 100% final.

The game was nowhere to be found once reviewed. It seemed to be missing from mail order lists, and the GX4000 was completely absent from released instructions for the game. There was just nothing to say what happened. *Gazza 2* became a mystery for years, with the question of whether it ever made it to stores going unanswered. Unbeknown to all, a decision had been made by Empire to cancel it due to the market changing. "My recollection was that production delays caused the decision as there were not sufficient numbers of the console sold to justify release," explained David.

Although cheap at £99, the GX4000 bombed spectacularly. It all had been too little and too late from Amstrad, which was trying to compete not only against the SEGA Master System and Nintendo Entertainment System but also against the growing 16-bit market. A severe lack of software further condemned proceedings, with companies such as Empire dropping their support as soon as they saw the poor sales figures. Although there were rumours of seeing copies for sale on the shelves back in the day, David confirmed that it never got to a manufacturing stage at all.

All other editions were released, however, receiving average to good reviews. It sold very well, before swiftly disappearing from consciousness when *Sensible Soccer* was unleashed. The initially pleasing outcome was not enough to save Active Minds, which closed its doors not long afterwards. The fallout from *Total Recall,* no doubt, had taken its toll.

Some 25 years or so later, whatever happened to those few builds made of the mysterious GX4000 game? Could Amstrad fanatics ever get to play the game as intended? Unfortunately, no one directly involved on the development has anything of the game today, not even source code. David also gave the same conclusion but suggested that at least three copies should be out there somewhere, referring to the review copies sent out. There is a remote chance that those copies were returned to Empire Software, though the company had regular clearouts and was known to not keep hold of historical materials.

"All review copies were property of either the supplier or EMAP, the magazine publisher. I definitely don't have a copy and never did," confirmed *Mean Machines* reviewer Matthew Regan. "The cartridge we were sent is long gone and probably ended up getting thrown away in an office clearout, which we'd have every so often. Shame, really. Had I any inkling that there would be a collector's/preservation market, I'd have kept a lot that we were sent over the years," added Julian Rignall. Richard Leadbetter also confirmed the same.

Things didn't fare better with *Amstrad Action*. "Generally, we kept review copies and put them in a cupboard, though it may have been different with pre-production console cartridges," Adam confirmed. "But, in any case, as the mag closed around 25 years ago, I would suspect they long ago ended up in a skip. I suppose there is a very slim chance it's still in someone's attic!" At the time of publication, there was no reply back from the French reviewers.

Adam's attic prospect is indeed the best and only hope now of finding and preserving the game unless John happens to chance across his source disks. Could one of the review copies ever be found? Never say never, but perhaps it's too slim a hope to cling on to after so long. With the so-called 'Holy Grail' of *Chase HQ 2* seeming more likely to be preserved, things look bleak for Gazza's long-awaited debut on Amstrad's forgotten and underrated console.

Above: Artist's pixel recreation of the *Gazza 2* (GX4000) title screen shown in the press at the time, boasting an impressive greyscale digitised picture of the famous footballer.

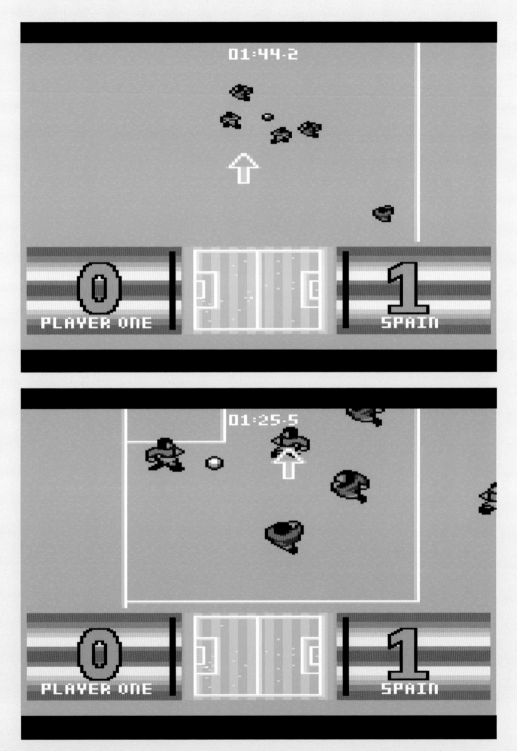

Above: Artist's pixel recreations of *Gazza 2* (GX4000) based on press screenshots. The bottom image shows off the special zoom mode.

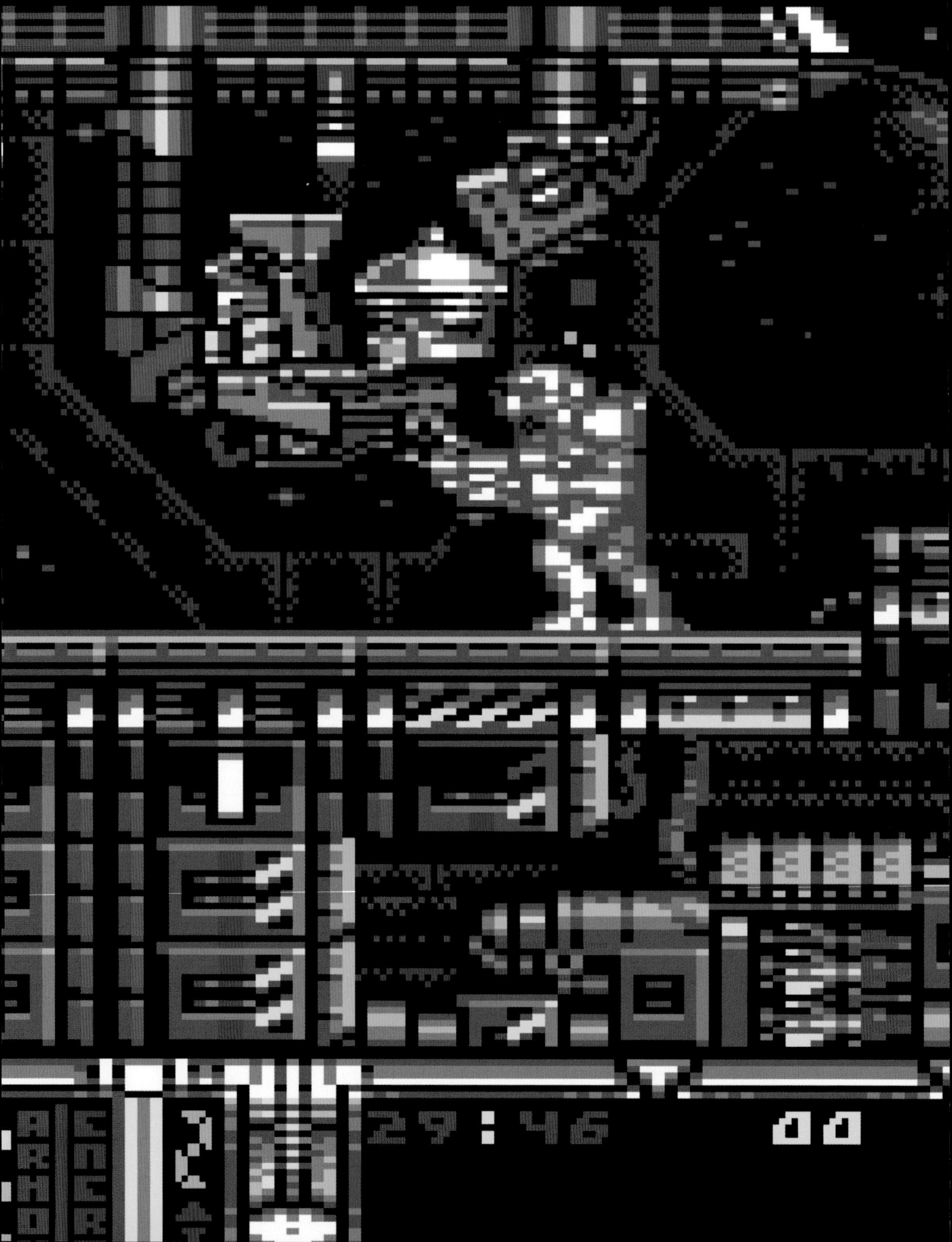
29:46

Deadlock
Style over substance

**Year: 1990
Developer:
Cyberdyne Systems
Platform: Commodore 64**

"Games should be fun or a fair challenge. About a year in, we realised *Deadlock* was neither, yet were locked into a contract. When System 3 called, desperate for a *Last Ninja 3* artist, I saw an opportunity. I spoke to the rest of Cyberdyne, and we agreed to make a counter-offer: I'll move to London and do *Ninja 3*, but the *Deadlock* contract must be destroyed.

Desperate times, desperate measures. Making games is all about balance, every feature added subtracts from another. We had loads of original ideas, but the project was too far off balance for us to glue everything together in a fun way. I'm glad we did *Armalyte* first, but I'm possibly gladder I got my huge failure as a designer out the way early in my games career. I've spent a while regretting the 18 months wasted on *Deadlock*, but, in the end, it was a valuable learning experience."

Robin Levy, graphic artist

Available to play

◉ Yes ○ No

Chip's Challenge Licence expired

Year: 1991
Developer: Images Software
Platform: Nintendo Entertainment System

Winning the affection of that someone special may be considered more terrifying than hard work. Spare a thought then for poor Chip McCallahan, who would have to navigate through Melinda the Mental Marvel's 'Clubhouse' to gain membership to the Bit Buster Club in an attempt to win her heart.

The 'Clubhouse' consists of 148 levels of brain-teasing 2D puzzles, where you must collect a specific number of chips to progress past a level. Levels scroll in four directions, with elements such as doors that must be unlocked, movable blocks, door switches, fire/ice/escalator tiles, various enemies and much more. Maybe a poem and some flowers could have been a less daunting alternative?

Developed by Chuck Sommerville for the Atari Lynx as one of its original launch titles, *Chip's Challenge* was a concept that Chuck wanted to bring to life for a long time. The pending launch of the Lynx was the ideal opportunity to see it finally happen, resulting in a classic and essential title for the handheld.

With its resounding success, it wasn't long until the game was licensed and ported to all the platforms under the sun, including the Commodore 64, ZX Spectrum, Amstrad CPC, Commodore Amiga, Atari ST and PC. UK-based Images Software was entrusted by U.S. Gold (which had licensed the game from Epyx) to convert the brunt of the home computer conversions (except for the PC edition) with great outcome and positive reviews across the board. Therefore, it was little surprise when Bullet-Proof Software would eventually contract them to do the Nintendo Entertainment System (NES) edition.

Our story begins with Images Software in late 1990. Fresh from completing *The Amazing Spider-Man* on the Commodore 64, developer Jim Smart was keen to get his teeth into the NES and its architecture, which was fast becoming a lucrative platform to develop for. "I was between projects as we had recently put in a feasibility study for *G-LOC R360* and were awaiting U.S. Gold's nod to start," Jim recalled. "I'd been tinkering with a homebrew NES development system, which consisted of a hacked cartridge with a piggy-backed EPROM emulator. I'd also been learning about its hardware from a blurry photocopy of some very unofficial documentation, and by reverse-engineering *Super Mario Bros.* I'd worked out how to do scrolling, sprites, get player input, and learn how memory was laid out."

Jim didn't mess around, and his impressive dissection of the NES meant that he could soon begin developing an actual game. "My buddy, Tom [Pinnock], was just completing the C64 version of *Chip's Challenge* and had ported/kinda cross-assembled most of the core game code from the Atari Lynx source provided by Epyx. As a bit of an experiment, I suggested to Karl [Jeffery] about getting *Chip's Challenge* running on the NES. Karl was keen for Images to develop NES titles, so I bounced a few ideas around with both Tom and Karl and started coding."

Chip's Challenge was a perfect candidate, still very fresh within Images Software minds. It wasn't long until Jim had made significant progress. "I just hacked the core of the Lynx code. It had a very similar processor to the NES, so it was mostly just translating non-existent 6502 op-codes into something that would assemble on the NES's RP2A03 processor — an almost identical process to that which Tom Pinnock had completed on the C64," he explained. "I had a playable demo up and running pretty quickly, after just a couple of weeks or so (a month max). Once Karl saw that I'd broken the back of the work, discussions with Epyx began regarding the possibility of publishing."

"Nintendo was very controlling in those days about who got to work on its platform, and we were a tiny company, so no chance of breaking in whatsoever. When I first saw the early demos [of *Chip's Challenge*] working, I was blown away and incredibly excited," recalled Karl Jeffery (founder of Images Software). "We felt we could finally break into the emerging console games world. We were just a home computer game developer until that point."

Due to their previous involvement, the communications process was smooth. "I had a couple of contacts at Epyx in San Francisco – I had been travelling there to try and drum up business for a couple of years. I flew out to Epyx to meet Matt Householder (who went on to be one of the co-founders of Blizzard North) and the Epyx president (John Brazier)," confirmed Karl.

Epyx was very enthusiastic and supportive towards a NES conversion, but it had the problem of not being an official Nintendo publisher/licensee. Bullet-Proof Software (BPS) was, though, and so Images Software was put in touch. "The coolest thing I remember about BPS was that they were based in Hawaii and had this office (large house really) that had a pool in the centre. When work got too much, they all dived in and had a swim," Karl warmly recalled. "The other thing was that they got into work fairly late and were nine hours behind the UK, which meant waiting around till eight or nine at night to call them on the phone."

Impressed with how Images Software had managed to both reverse-engineer the NES and get a conversion up and running so quickly, BPS signed them up. A sliding scale of royalties vs. cartridge size was arranged within the contract, giving an incentive to squeeze the game into a smaller cartridge capacity if possible. David Nolte (main producer) from BPS would regularly communicate with Karl (project manager) to periodically monitor how progress was going. Occasionally, Henk Rogers got involved too, assumably when David was in the pool. The game was announced at the January Winter CES show in Chicago in 1991.

Things almost crashed into the ground when Images Software's NES-hacking escapades caught up with them. "When Nintendo in Japan heard that a small dev team in England had cracked the NES, they were concerned and wanted to find out what we were up to. In those days, Rare was effectively Nintendo's rep in the UK, and so I was summoned up to their farmhouse offices in Ashby-de-la-Zouch to explain myself," Karl explained. "Putting on my best smile, I managed to convince them that we meant no harm and just wanted to make games. They decided to bring us inside the tent and granted us one of the first Nintendo developer licences in the UK. I framed it and had it on my wall for several years."

Breathing a huge sigh of relief, development began building upon the initial prototype. However, Jim now had his hands full after U.S. Gold gave the go-ahead to start work on G-LOC. "Not long after getting the basics up and running, we started work on G-LOC. So, during the latter period of Chip's development, I was effectively working on two projects — a fact we never let on to either publisher concerned," smiled Jim. "After the initial development period on Chip's, i.e. getting the basic game mechanics running, there wasn't much code to write, so I was primarily spending most of my time on G-LOC."

Jim was joined on the Chip's Challenge project by graphic artist Stephen Bedser, who was also working with Jim on G-LOC at the time. "As far as graphics go, it was by no means challenging (pardon the slight pun), and little or no alterations were needed to create the different versions," recalled Stephen. "I did the graphics on the Atari ST in Degas Elite, which was then passed over to Jim." Stephen picked and chose elements from the C64, Amiga/ST and Amstrad conversions that worked best with the NES palette and resolution.

With mostly just colour changes and adjustments to suit the higher resolution required, it made for a relatively quick and painless conversion job. The map data was also pulled straight across from the Atari Lynx. Stephen's work mainly focused on getting Chip's walk to look good, before then going to town on the title screen and presentation polish, with a neat Nintendo monitor design to display cutscenes. The results were possibly the strongest of the 8-bits – comparable with the 16-bit editions.

"It was like trying to get an elephant into a matchbox."

Development wasn't without its problems, and, on older hardware compared with the Lynx, the limitations of the NES bit hard in certain places during development. "The Lynx had really awesome sprite capabilities, and there was no way the NES version could really contend with hardware that awesome overall," Jim conceded. "Although Chip's looks a very simple game at first glance, the biggest complexity/challenge for the game (on more lowly platforms) was the amount of mobs on some levels — literally, all of the empty tiles were filled with moving baddies on some of the levels!"

With only a basic sprite system in place initially and contending with sprite limitations, several of the levels would need to be adjusted before the publication of the game. "I had not yet tackled the many-sprites-in-a-line issues, which always needed some kind of flickering/alternating," Jim explained. "On some levels, you couldn't see all of the baddies that you had to avoid. We'd have to address levels which featured a lot of mobs, either cut them out entirely or get them redesigned. We hadn't been provided with any runnable level designing/editing tools, and the level data we had was compressed, so not easy to modify."

An intriguing design decision was also made to increase the size of the playfield to a 16×13 visible grid, rather than 9×9 like the original and other conversions. Jim could not recall why exactly, but it is believed that there were technical issues masking off the 9×9 area, so it was kept pretty much full screen. It gave players an advantage, being able to see more of what was ahead and making the game slightly easier as a result.

After a short time, 135 levels were converted, along with an extra level created especially for the game (see further on). However, 14 were missing, to be either added in later or replaced. All levels could be accessed via a password system (as with the original). There were titles and cutscene presentations; all the game mechanics and logic were present and working 100%. No sound had yet been created, and the ending was missing, but, crucially, the game was almost complete. The sprite problems present needed to be overcome to finish the game, but they were solvable issues. It would be the initial choice of cartridge used that would become a 'thorn in the side' for the project.

"There was great incentive from BPS to have the game in a smaller cartridge. For them, this would be a reduction in production costs, and, for us, it meant a higher royalty. They had no problem with the amount of ROM we wanted, but our chosen *Mario 2* (or *3*) cartridge had the max amount of RAM, which cost a lot more than any amount of extra ROM," explained Jim. "I needed this RAM because the level maps needed unpacking (the maps got changed at runtime, so storing them in ROM wasn't an option), and we needed various arrays to hold the data for the levels' mobs. Sure, we'd love to have twice the royalty (and this certainly did motivate us to try and achieve the necessary RAM savings), but, if it just wasn't possible, then both Karl and I were fine with a lesser amount."

"I did the graphics on the Atari ST in *Degas Elite*."

Many weeks were spent trying to reduce the RAM required, with ideas 'chipped' in by colleague Tom Pinnock. Source code was sent off to a consultancy company in San Francisco, and even a last-ditch conference call with Rare's Chris Stamper was made to try and help.

"They all thought it wasn't doable, and offered half-baked suggestions to save a bit of RAM (but not nearly enough to go down a cartridge size), most of which, if done, would've increased the code complexity no end (and likely affected performance)," Jim reflected. "There was just no way the game could run in the standard 2K of onboard RAM without a complete redesign of the game and the maps. We needed an extra 8K in the cartridge. It was like trying to get an elephant into a matchbox."

Images Software eventually went back to BPS and expressed that the full amount of RAM had to be added to allow development to conclude. But, after just over a year passing, BPS's licensing contract with Epyx had now expired. Karl suggested that BPS could have easily renewed it, but now felt it was no longer financial viable for them with the new larger cartridge cost requirement. This ultimately ended their interest in publishing the game. When Henk Rogers was approached for recollection on the project, he couldn't recall them ever having the licence to the game. Sadly, Henk also informed us that David Nolte had passed away, meaning that we may never know the full details from a BPS point of view.

"There was no way the NES version could really contend with hardware that awesome."

With *Chip's Challenge* now without a certified publisher, Images Software removed references to BPS from the game and attempted to pitch to other companies with ties to Nintendo. Sadly, there were to be no takers, and the conversion was permanently shelved as a result. There was almost a reprieve when Images Software was approached to finish the game as a budget title some years later. "An offer was eventually made to fix up the code and publish, but Karl and I decided it probably wasn't really worth it," confirmed Jim. By this point, the NES was practically dead, and Images Software was already busy at this point, working on the new Sony PlayStation. "Images was renamed Climax, and we used the experience gleaned from the NES and SEGA Master System consoles to break into console development; something we still do to this day," Karl concluded.

Chip's Challenge (NES) became a long-running mystery over the years, thanks to the press coverage received. Frustrated by the lack of a conversion, an unofficial homebrew development was started in 2010 but also never completed. Then suddenly, whilst interviewing Jim for this write-up, an eBay auction appeared in December 2014 for a prototype cartridge, believed to have been produced for the 1992 Consumer Electronics Show in Chicago. The cartridge sold for a staggering $4,123.99.

Sourced from a now-defunct publisher's licensing and purchasing department in Germany (possibly Rushware, who had Epyx links), it is believed that a manager visited the May 1992 Summer CES trade show and obtained it for evaluation. Appended was an Images Software sticker, with a date of 1992/05/18. The prototype still worked perfectly. "I thought there wasn't anything out there!" exclaimed Jim. "I half suspected I (might) have enough code to (perhaps) get something running again (one day) perhaps (are there enough disclaimers in there?). But, now you've gone and surprised me with that cartridge!"

Remarkably, Jim and many of those following the auction got their wish. The game was preserved in late 2015 by auction winner Steve Lin and made available via the Lost Levels (www.lostlevels.org) in a generous gift to the unreleased games community. Preserved was the very final build, with 136 levels (four, for some reason, only accessible through codes) and a skip mode for testing. Oddly, the order of the levels was not quite the same as the original.

"Nintendo asked me to design a level that would be exclusive to that platform."

The pleasant surprise was the discovery of level 132 – an exclusive contribution from the game's original creator, Chuck Sommervile. "Nintendo asked me to design a level that would be exclusive to that platform. I designed the level and lost my copy over the years," Chuck responded. "I think they softened the level up a bit though. Part of this level is a torturous pushing of a single block all over the place to get it back to a spot very near where it started. It looks like they edited it to remove some of the long path. I was very proud of how I integrated the long push within the other puzzles." Jim couldn't recall changing the level, which suggests that it was most likely an unfortunate glitch in the map data.

With the recovery of the game, it has been suggested that the conversion could be actually finished off and given a full physical release in the future (if legal issues can be overcome). It would be a wonderful outcome to see a gap filled for many NES owners at long last. In the meantime, though, if you are a fan of the series, we highly recommend checking out the prototype for its curiosity value and, of course, Chuck's new and previously unseen level.

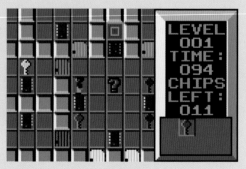

Above: Photo of James around the time of the NES *Chip's Challenge* development, alongside a screenshot of the Lynx original.

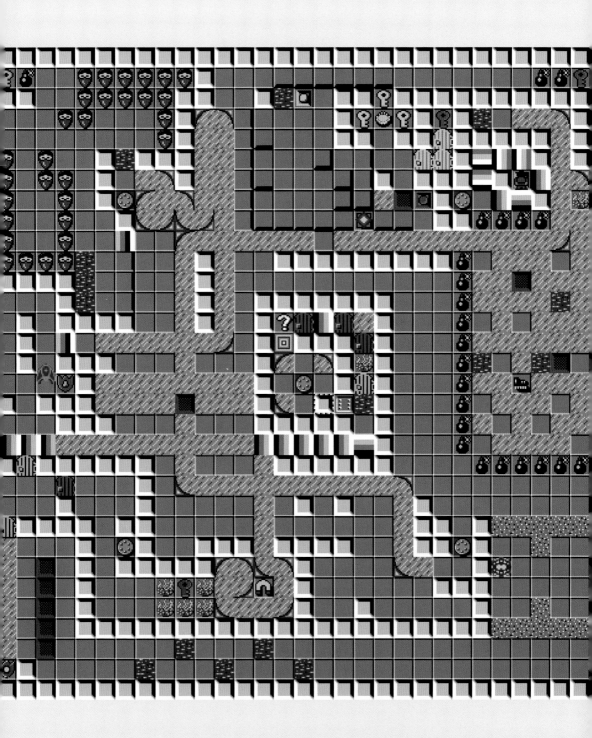

Above: Chuck's specially created level 132 for the NES version in its entirety.

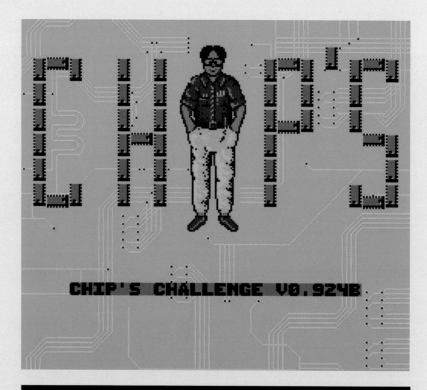

Above: *Chip's Challenge* (Nintendo Entertainment System), showing title and presentation screens, with a cool Nintendo-themed monitor.

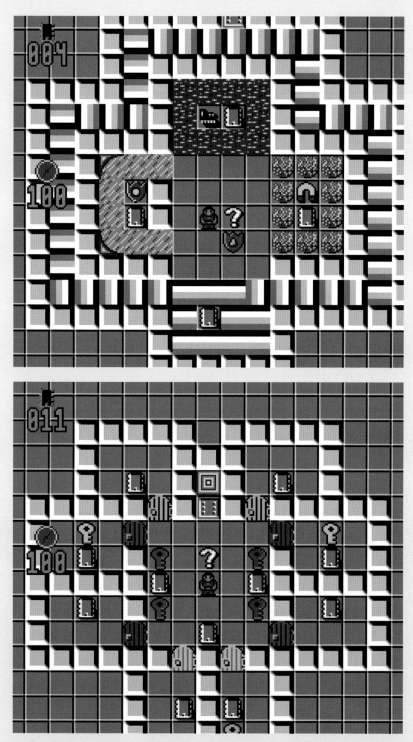

Above: *Chip's Challenge* (Nintendo Entertainment System), showing two levels from the game. Notice how the play area is much larger than other conversions.

Space Fantasy Zone
Legal dispute?

Year: 1991
Developer: NEC Avenue
Platform: PC Engine

A strange but curious hybrid of *Space Harrier* and *Fantasy Zone* – the main protagonist taking the form of Opa Opa. It is rumoured that a legal dispute with SEGA caused its cancellation, though other sources suggest that it was a quality issue – the game admittedly isn't great. A prototype exists so you can, at least, judge for yourself.

Available to play

 Yes ○ No

The Commodore 65 Production issues

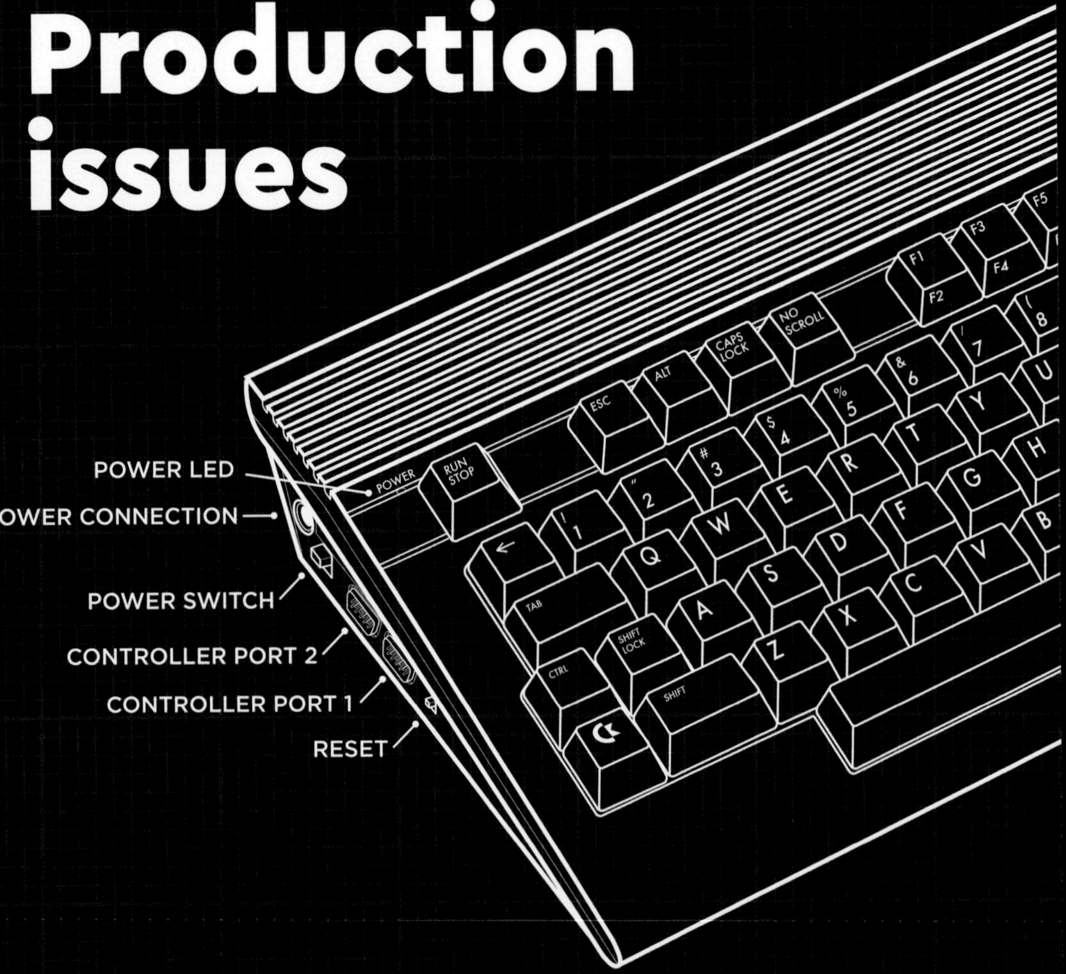

POWER LED

OWER CONNECTION

POWER SWITCH

CONTROLLER PORT 2

CONTROLLER PORT 1

RESET

POWER

RUN STOP

ESC

ALT

CAPS LOCK

NO SCROLL

F1

F2

F3

F4

F5

TAB

CTRL

SHIFT LOCK

SHIFT

Year: 1991
Developer: Commodore

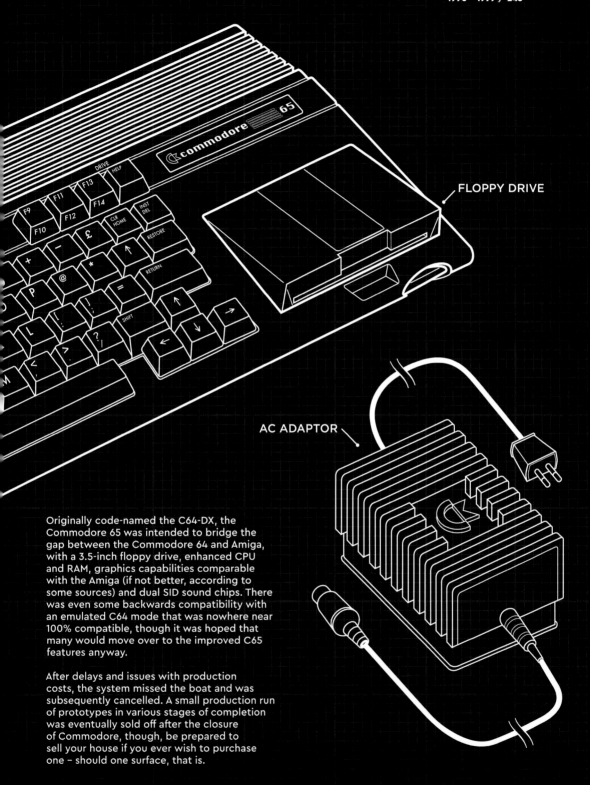

FLOPPY DRIVE

AC ADAPTOR

Originally code-named the C64-DX, the Commodore 65 was intended to bridge the gap between the Commodore 64 and Amiga, with a 3.5-inch floppy drive, enhanced CPU and RAM, graphics capabilities comparable with the Amiga (if not better, according to some sources) and dual SID sound chips. There was even some backwards compatibility with an emulated C64 mode that was nowhere near 100% compatible, though it was hoped that many would move over to the improved C65 features anyway.

After delays and issues with production costs, the system missed the boat and was subsequently cancelled. A small production run of prototypes in various stages of completion was eventually sold off after the closure of Commodore, though, be prepared to sell your house if you ever wish to purchase one – should one surface, that is.

Solar Jetman
Publisher's cold feet

Year: 1991
Developer: Software Creations
Platforms: Amstrad CPC,
Atari ST, Commodore 64,
Commodore Amiga 500
and ZX Spectrum 128K

Available to play
◉ Yes ○ No

For many during the early 1990s, the dream was to get a Nintendo Entertainment System (NES) and enjoy the delights of the *Super Mario Bros.* series or newly released *Teenage Mutant Ninja Turtles*. Many weekends were spent by the author playing the display NES set up in a local Dixons electronics store, hoping that the parents would take notice and pick one up for Christmas. When not being wowed by *Super Mario Bros.*, the author was being mesmerised by the wonderful *Solar Jetman* instead.

Created by Zippo Games for Rare back in 1990 and published by Tradewest, *Solar Jetman* began life as a game called *Iota*, inspired by titles such as *Oids* (Atari ST), *Gravitar* (arcade) and *Thrust* (BBC Micro and various other platforms). After a while, it was found that the game wasn't quite working out, so the team sat down together and reworked it into something more fun. Shortly after seeing their progress, Rare made the request for the team to transform the game into the third and final instalment of the Jetman series.

The final result was a 2D multidirectional scroller where you control Jetman, who must gather all pieces of the Golden Warpship across 12 large levels. You would fly around using your jet pod (which could later be upgraded) to explore large cavernous levels, having to find each piece of the warpship but also collect enough fuel so that you could take off and escape. Collecting enough points along the way would also allow you to buy upgrades to aid your progression. If you took too much damage to your pod, it would explode and leave Jetman fully exposed. If you then don't get him back safely to the mothership for a new pod, you could easily get taken out and lose a life.

In a familiar fashion to *Thrust/Gravitar*, you rotated your pod using left and right on the controller and had to use your thrusters to move forwards in the direction you faced. Items were hooked with a tow cable, which then had to be dragged carefully back to your mothership. As well as trying to contend with a range of enemies, you also had differing gravity levels on each planet, causing a whole manner of problems if you were not suitably equipped.

Apart from criticism for its high difficulty curve, the release was met with decent reviews across the board. Around the time of its release, The Sales Curve (referred to as just Sales Curve from this point on) started speaking to Rare in 1990, with a view to bringing some of its titles to home computer platforms and publish on its Storm label. One title of particular interest was the newly released *Solar Jetman*, swiftly signed up by the publisher/developer.

However, its own internal development team was already busy doing arcade conversions and original developments, so it was decided to contract out the work to Software Creations. The plan was for them to produce all of the conversions for the Commodore 64 (C64), ZX Spectrum, Amstrad CPC, Atari ST and Commodore Amiga platforms.

Leading the way were both the C64 and Atari ST developments, kicked off together around July/August 1990. Tasked with cramming the game onto the C64 was veteran programmer John Buckley, fresh from working on *Sly Spy: Secret Agent*. Atari ST coding duties were handled by Pete Andrew in his first full production after recently being employed by Software Creations. The Amiga conversion was then started a few weeks later by David Broadhurst, making use of Pete's initial start on the ST. Graphics were handled by freelance graphic artist Haydn Dalton and internal graphic artist Andrew Threlfall, with Andrew concentrating purely on the 16-bits and Haydn on all versions.

There was little/no reference to the *Solar Jetman* source code or assets, just a direct translation by playing the NES game. "I'm pretty sure we had all the maps for each level, and I could physically see them so that I could make the C64 ones as close as possible, but just a bit smaller. The Pickfords did later join Creations, but that was after this, and I can't remember having any input directly from Zippo Games," recalled John. "The conversions were rather heroically done totally in the dark," added NES *Solar Jetman* programmer Steve Hughes. "I wasn't even aware they were taking place until they were more or less complete – although, I would have been delighted to help."

John and Pete first kicked everything off by trying to get the physics working on both of their conversions, with Pete admittedly following John's lead at the start. "I struggled with the maths/physics and leaned on John a lot – which was nothing new – he was a top programmer, and I'd be a fool not to learn what I could from him," confirmed Pete.

Controls were also nailed down early on, which was crucial after losing the luxury of the extra buttons of the NES control pad. In the end, it was settled on using the fire button to fire, down button for shields and up on the joystick to thrust, which was slightly clunky but better than assigning key game actions to the keyboard; only pause and map modes would be restricted to that.

Specifically for the C64 edition, John had to decide early on what was going to be kept and what would be 'jettisoned' from his conversion. "I had originally wanted the whole thing in one load," he explained. "So everything that wasn't part of the main play, I dumped. I think some bonus gem levels may have survived. I was also using the sprite multiplexer that Creations had but still ended up moving the odd turret and things to avoid more than eight sprites on a line. And, of course, the in-between scenes got cut."

As John mentioned earlier, the maps had to be shrunk and modified, and the final golden warship scrolling level also dropped. Even in its reduced form, the plan for a single load was far too ambitious, and everything quickly switched over to multi-load early on. "I remember going through each level and 'condensing' it whilst keeping the same overall shape. Also, a couple of homing missiles had to go. Otherwise, it was as close as we could get to the NES version," John recalled. "I had forgotten about the map sizes," added Haydn. "That was a big problem. They ate character graphics because of the slope angles more than anything. The 8-bit versions were always going to be very tight, memory-wise. I remember having to be very careful about how I made the level building blocks. The 16-bit versions felt like a breeze in contrast."

Even with the cuts, the conversion was looking impressive after just a few months, but John still wasn't 100% satisfied with how it was turning out. "Even at the time, there were things I would have liked to have changed," he explained. "For instance, it gets a bit frustrating at times as various gravity pulls thrust you into the background, just like the NES version. But, with the music, it would have been nice to have had a piece of subtle music running on each level, rather than just SFX only, like we eventually had."

Tasked with the music composition work was Geoff Follin. Possibly due to budget, time or memory limits, he would compose just the one tune. The game otherwise featured just sound effects and missed out on the wide range of compositions that featured in the NES edition. His composition was also original and not a direct translation of any of David Wise's NES music.

"My brother, Tim, gave me a few tips at the start, and then I just tried to come up with something that made use of the nice synth sounds," recalled Geoff. "Listening back to the C64 music, I can certainly hear a Vangelis influence! It was also VERY free reign. I think I probably saw a few screens of the early game, what it looked like, how it played, etc., then just went off and did what I wanted! I seem to remember one of the main issues was getting the music to loop perfectly in sync after a few minutes, which was always a good challenge."

"The conversions were rather heroically done totally in the dark."

In comparison, Pete's Atari ST edition wouldn't suffer from such cutbacks like on the C64 but still had its own sets of challenges to overcome, especially with establishing multidirectional smooth scrolling on hardware where it could often be a struggle. "It wasn't quite full-screen, but it was smooth scrolling in the end," recalled Pete. "Funny (to me) story, I remember this as one of my most stupid bugs. I had it all working, but it wasn't as optimal as I had hoped. I spent a couple of days doing what I could to improve it – only to realise that I was calling the draw function twice in my main loop. Dumb, but the best optimisation I've ever gotten from a bug fix!"

Unfortunately, Pete's memories had otherwise faded about the conversion, believing that it didn't get very far at all. David Broadhurst's memories about the subsequent Amiga conversion had also completely gone too. John's synapses were luckily still firing well enough for that era to help fill in some gaps.

"As I remember, Pete did most of the engine code for both versions as Dave was doing project management at the same time, so Dave would later port Pete's code," he recalled. "Pete ran parallel to my C64 version, and the Amiga was about a week behind. I'm almost sure both were finished just like the C64 version. Graphics for the 16-bit versions surpassed the original by far, and, as I remember, they both played just as good."

The majority of artwork on the 16-bit conversions was handled by Andrew Threlfall (who, sadly, couldn't be reached at the time of writing), with Haydn helping out. Both spruced up the graphics to make full use of the enhanced 16-bit palette available, also making improved animations for the main character and enemies. It is very likely all the cutscenes were included this time too. Maps were direct copies from the NES, with no reductions in scale or features, and included added flourishes to try and make it feel like a 16-bit title and not just a straight 8-bit port. It couldn't be recalled if the bonus scenes or final scrolling Golden Warpship level were included, but, again, it was probable that they were all there.

"Graphics for the 16-bit versions surpassed the original by far, and, as I remember, they both played just as good."

Geoff's memories had also faded with regard to the two 16-bit conversions, but it is almost certain he was involved on their audio in some capacity. It is likely that his brother, Tim Follin, assisted him with the work, though nothing was heard back from Tim when questioned. It's also uncertain if there was more than one composition made in comparison with the C64 edition.

A few months after the three conversions were fully underway, the ZX Spectrum conversion was finally started. The reason for the delay wasn't known, but it is plausible that Software Creations just didn't have anyone available at the start to work on it. Eventually, development duties would fall to Tony Williams, who was asked as a result of previous work for the developer. The focus would be to complete the ZX Spectrum conversion first, then later port it to the Amstrad CPC in its monochrome glory.

"It was quite a compliment to be asked to develop such a challenging and high-profile game," began Tony. "I was working from a rented office in Prestwich, North Manchester, a few miles from Software Creations. Paul Tonge and I had started Sound Images by that point as well. For development, I used an assembler and editor running on a Tatung Einstein computer. This was more a consequence of using the same setup at Icon Design and Software Creations."

Although juggling two roles with game development and music compositions, Tony had a bit more in the way of materials to work with from the start, compared with the other conversions. "If I remember correctly, I got access to John's C64 source code," he confirmed. "There were some technical discussions, particularly about the 'physics' effects. As was always the case in those days, I also played the game a lot in order to be able to reproduce the 'feel' as well as the appearance of the game."

For the graphics, Haydn used his mostly complete C64 artwork as a starting point, going the full monochrome route to avoid colour-clash issues. The maps were essentially going to be the same as the C64 versions, converting the very same map data that John was using. Assisting Haydn briefly with the graphics was Simon Street, who was waiting for Haydn to finish, so they could both begin working on a SEGA Mega Drive conversion of *Double Dragon*.

"I was just given a picture of the *Solar Jetman* character and asked to make a loading screen and a front-end screen, but no in-game stuff," Simon confirmed. "There was no need for lots of colour on the loading screen as Jetman was a cartoon character, in black and white, with a passing similarity to Ash from *The Evil Dead*. He was very central to the image, with a *Solar Jetman* logo in yellow, and the standard 'Ultimate' *Jetpac* font with colour banding. The front end was an animated Jetman floating across the screen with little smoke rings off the back of his jetpack. All with no colour because of attribute crawl, so it was black and white. Well, actually, the background was blue, if memory serves. As far as I know, the pictures no longer exist as I don't think they ever got implemented into the game."

It couldn't be recalled if the ZX Spectrum edition would include the NES cutscenes either. "I do vaguely remember discussing cutscenes, and it was probably going to be down to memory being available at the end," recalled Tony. "I do remember though that all of the graphics that were done were really good (within the Spectrum's limitations of course). I remember liking Haydn and his work – he was always smiling as well, if I remember correctly. Simon (and his brief work) I don't remember too well, so my apologies to Simon!"

"It wasn't quite full screen, but it was smooth scrolling in the end."

To try and match the smoothness of the C64 edition, Tony opted to go for an approach which would result in 48K owners missing out. "The scrolling was, if I remember, looking quite impressive. It was fast and smooth because it used the 128K Spectrum's multiple-screen addressing to do double buffering," he explained. "In simple terms, the next frame required for display is created in memory, and, once complete, it is displayed by setting the display to show it using the hardware. This was so much faster than copying screen data, which was a common technique on the Speccy."

Trying to keep the game moving smoothly and keep track of all of the key game elements was a huge challenge overall for Tony, but it was taken on with gusto.

Multi-load was unavoidable, like with the C64 edition, and the physics had proved problematic to port from the 6502 to the Z80 – initially, not working as expected. However, after a few weeks of probable swearing, testing and correcting, the conversion and engine hit its stride. The ZX Spectrum was well on its way to getting the perfect farewell from one of its most famous mascots.

"It was a month or so behind the C64 version, but it was going to make an excellent ZX Spectrum game."

Again, although he couldn't recall for certain (and neither could Tony), it was likely that Geoff was the composer for any music on the Spectrum. "I can't remember doing the other versions, but I might have!" Geoff tried to recall. "If so, I would think I'd have just rewritten the C64 music on an appropriate music driver from scratch as I don't think there was any capability for even 'copying and pasting' note information across."

By late 1990/early 1991, the Commodore 64, Amiga and Atari ST conversions were all complete and ready to go. However, it was decided to hold back their release until the ZX Spectrum and Amstrad conversions had caught up – they were still a few months behind. The other programmers subsequently moved on to other projects (John, in particular, preparing to work on the SNES conversion of *Super Off Road Racer*) whilst Tony pushed on.

During early 1991, *Crash* magazine caught up with Tony and reported on the new *Solar Jetman* conversion that was about to surface, showing impressive screenshots of level 1 and declaring the game's planned release date as April 1991. At the time, Tony had more than half of the levels left to implement as well as the final presentation, so April was a bit too optimistic as he was still juggling the development with day-to-day audio work for Sound Images.

Progress was still going well though, with the buffering solution providing the basis of a conversion that was very faithful to the NES game. "I glimpsed the Spectrum version a few times, and it was looking very good indeed," recalled John. "Tony was working off-site, and he would appear every couple of weeks with updates. It was a month or so behind the C64 version, but it was going to make an excellent ZX Spectrum game."

By April, there was still a bit left to do on the game, and it was now time for the yearly European Computer Trade Show (ECTS) on April 14–16th. At the event, *Zzap!64* magazine caught up with Sales Curve, who reported that *Solar Jetman* was due for release in September 1991. Oddly, though, there were no advertisements ever shown, and, from this point on, everything went completely dead. There was not even notification of a cancellation, causing ZX Spectrum and C64 fans (the only ones really aware of a conversion) to question what had happened.

Unbeknown to the public and shortly after the ECTS show, Sales Curve got cold feet when news started to arrive about how the NES game had been performing in the US. The sales had been a complete disaster, with Tradewest reportedly ordering too many cartridges, leaving many to gather dust unsold in a warehouse. It was enough to spook Sales Curve, who quietly made the decision to cancel all of the conversions and not take the risk.

"It was frustrating because we thought we were doing a good job and doing justice to the original version. In those days, though, canned games happened a lot due to the low cost in making them," lamented Haydn. "It was a phone call out of the blue – a complete shock at the time," added Tony. John also added, "It was frustrating when you found out it's NOT going into the shops, and that was, of course, the buzz for programmers back then."

It was perhaps a strange decision as the game would have far fewer production costs involved. European sales also fared much better when released in September 1991, suggesting that the game could have done just fine had Sales Curve kept faith. "I don't think it's strange for a publisher to pull a game based on forecasting," responded Haydn. "At the time, they [Sales Curve] were doing very action-orientated titles, whereas *Solar Jetman* was just a thrust-like title which focused on inertia movement with light action."

Rob Henderson (working at Sales Curve at the time) speculated that another reason could have been Sales Curve's Jane Cavanagh and Software Creation's Richard Kay falling out over budget or schedule, causing the cancellation. Unfortunately, both Jane and Richard didn't respond to enquiries about the game. Regardless of the reason, it left three complete conversions and a Spectrum conversion two-thirds complete to gather dust. "We were at the point where I was about to add the remaining C64-based level data, integrate presentation screens and make sure everything worked," confirmed Tony. "No doubt, there were areas in later levels which still needed work though as well."

Before the dawn of the Internet and wider knowledge of *Crash* magazine's preview, it was believed that *Solar Jetman* on home computers was nothing but a myth. It was in 2000 when Games That Weren't established from ex-Software Creations staff that the game actually existed. The late Martin Holland was influential in helping to work out who was involved with the C64 version of the game and putting those involved in touch to reveal more.

No one had a copy of the game; but then, suddenly, in 2003, whilst preparing for relocation to the US, Haydn found two C64-formatted disks in a briefcase shoved behind a radiator of all places. Thankfully, the disks still read perfectly, and the complete C64 game was preserved and shared with the community, from possibly the last remaining copy in existence. It was a conversion that no one ever expected to see or even dreamt was actually completed.

John believes that it probably wasn't the very final version (probably lacking some final polish/playtesting), but all the key levels and the end sequence were present to mark it as a 'complete' game. Interestingly, on the second C64 disk, a bonus-level character set and map data were found that couldn't be located within the game – a clear casualty of John's early culling work. However, the shop and map screens were present, as was the ability to change ships and most of the other key features that made the NES version so good.

"It played just as good as the NES version."

Overall, it was a very solid conversion, and it was staggering that it never got released in any shape or form. "I really enjoyed working on it," concluded John. "Haydn working off-site was a bit of a drag as I tended to get graphics in batches rather than constantly, but it was the best C64 game I ever worked on. It played just as good as the NES version."

The news was not so good for the ZX Spectrum edition, with nothing surfacing many years after the success of the Commodore 64 recovery. Tony has attempted multiple times to find something of the game but to no avail. "I was using 5¼ and 3½ Tatung Einstein disks to store the game and have moved house a few times since then. I am pretty sure I no longer have them and definitely don't have an Einstein anymore," he confirmed.

It was a similar story too for the Atari ST and Amiga editions. After multiple house moves by the programmers and artists, disks were mislaid and are now seemingly lost or binned long ago. "To my eternal regret, I didn't keep any code or assets from those days," confirmed Pete, with David giving a similar response. But Haydn concluded with a glimmer of hope once more. "I had a bunch of disks with Amiga/ST graphics on them, but they were lost in my move to the USA," he began. "I do believe that, somewhere, I have one Amiga-formatted disk with *Solar Jetman* written on it, but I haven't searched its contents. I'll search again though to see if I can find it."

Therefore, the 'Hunt for the Golden Warpship', goes on for three more platforms (not including the Amstrad conversion that wasn't started), the likelihood of recovery growing weaker by the year. But, when you consider how the C64 edition was found, anything is possible. Sooner than later for the Amiga version?

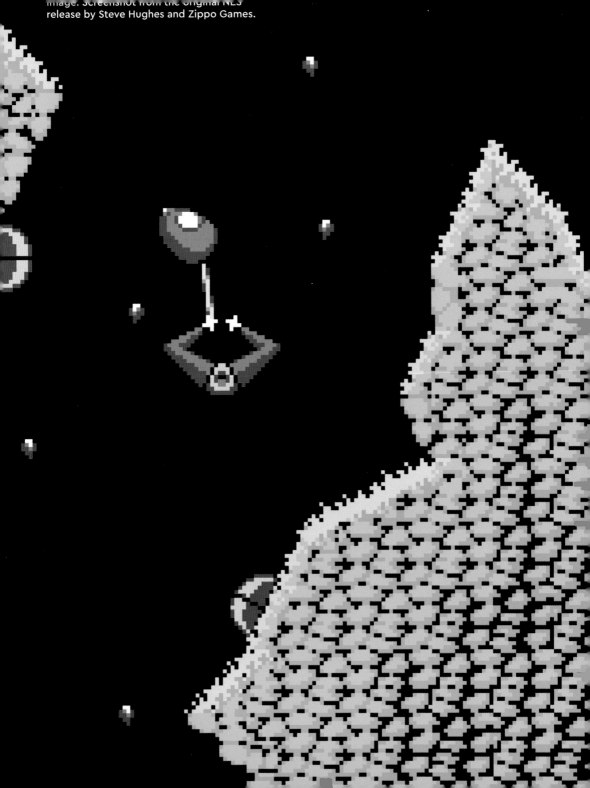

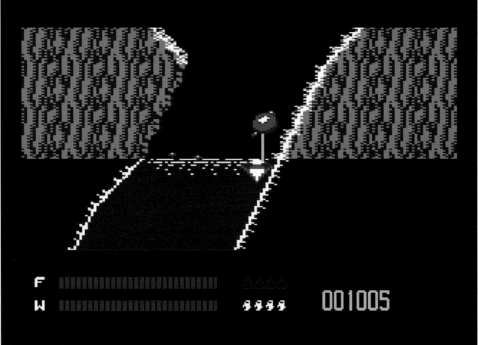

Above: Various screenshots from *Solar Jetman* (Commodore 64). Miraculously saved from obscurity from possibly the last remaining copy – found in a briefcase shoved behind a radiator.

Mega Twins Rise of consoles

Year: 1991
Developer: Tiertex
Platforms: Amstrad CPC
(pictured), Commodore
64 and ZX Spectrum

"Over 25 years, and there is still interest in this cute multiplayer conversion that never was. After finishing *Alien Storm*, *Mega Twins* (*Chiki Chiki Boys* in Japan) arrived for conversion. It followed many Capcom games at the time – same art style, scrolling tiled screen, familiar gameplay, and was generally ideal for 8-bits. Usually, we videoed a playthrough and captured to Amiga, but I remember drawing this game directly on C64/Amiga, remaking levels using in-house tools.

Whilst the coders worked on their respective versions, the artists worked across multiple platforms. I worked on C64 and Amstrad (largely the same backgrounds with additional shades). Spectrum art was by David Bland, who likely helped with the Amstrad conversion. From what I recall, I finished the backgrounds, sprites and much of the other artwork before leaving Tiertex. Unfortunately, home computer sales declined, 8/16-bit consoles were on the rise, and, ultimately, it didn't seem worth finishing, hence its cancellation."

Wayne Billingham, graphic artist

Available to play
◉ Yes ○ No

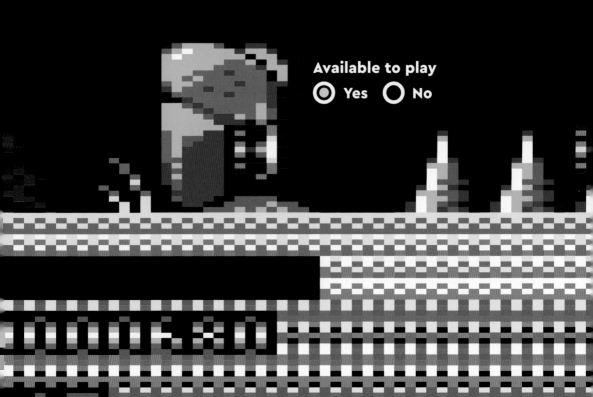

Note: We've deliberately left the corrupted score panel as per the prototype.

Green Lantern Commercial viability

Year: 1991–1995
Developer: Ocean Software
Platforms: Atari ST, Commodore Amiga,
SEGA Mega Drive and Super Nintendo

Available to play

 Yes ⦿ No

The last few decades have seen us spoilt for choice with a plethora of superhero films and games, especially with the major resurgence of Marvel in recent years. DC Comics has seen major success with adaptations of _Batman_ and _Superman_. _Green Lantern_ wasn't quite as popular compared with its more heavyweight counterparts, but it still has a very healthy fan base.

The role of _Green Lantern_ has been played by a number of fictional characters since its first publication back in 1940. Starting out with Alan Scott, the role was then played by Hal Jordan, Kyle Rayner and many others. All carried a special 'Power Ring' that grants incredible power to help them get out of tight situations.

Ocean Software always kept its finger on the pulse when it came to licensing deals. Following the success of the licensed _Batman the Movie_, it was no surprise when other characters from the same stable were evaluated. _Green Lantern_, in particular, caught the eye of the head of development, Gary Bracey, during the early 1990s. "I was really into comic books and established a good working relationship with DC Comics as we had already been thriving on movie licences from their parent company, Warner Bros.," Gary explained. "It started with _Watchmen_, then we looked at _Lobo_ and, finally, _Green Lantern_."

With a licence deal swiftly arranged, production was planned for the Atari ST and Commodore Amiga platforms, with others potentially to follow. Tasked with overseeing and creating an initial design was Ocean stalwart, Steve Wahid. Working under Steve was John Tatlock, assigned as an artist for the project. John had been working at Ocean for just a few months, but his time on the new development would be brief. "My involvement was so minimal; I can't even remember who else was on the project," he reflected. "I was, in theory, drawing backgrounds, but there was no design to speak of and no real plan. After twiddling my thumbs for a while, I figured it would be wise to get away from what seemed to be becoming a doomed project, so I left to work at Software Creations. I think _Green Lantern_ got mothballed more or less at that time."

John did recall that the programmer was someone named Allan (believed to be Allan Shortt), who worked at Ocean at that time. Sadly, Allan Shortt passed away in 2012, and, with others unable to clarify his involvement, details remain sketchy of whether he was involved and what exactly was started. The only person likely to know would be Steve, who didn't respond to requests to discuss past work. If any code was started, then there likely wasn't much – if any. "_Green Lantern_ never got any further than the drawing board," confirmed Gary. "It was so difficult then to create enough varied ring effects for the game. So it was canned very early on." With other projects now underway, such as _The Addams Family_, plans for _Green Lantern_ went dormant, but only for a brief period.

Months later, a new artist named Mike Marshall came knocking at Ocean. "I was a wannabe graphic designer/illustrator and approached local companies to get my foot in the door," he began. "One of the companies was Ocean, who'd just moved into new offices at Castlefield, Manchester. They had no positions available, but Steve Wahid gave me loads of comics on *Green Lantern* and *Lobo* and told me to come up with character designs and animations."

"Ray, for instance, created most of the artwork and animation for the main character."

Mike worked voluntarily from home for some much-needed experience, returning to Ocean a few weeks later to demonstrate his creations in the hope that it would land a paid job. Although impressed with his work, Ocean still had no roles, marking the end of Mike's brief involvement. Put back on the shelf, it would be just over a year until the licence's dormancy was finally brought to an end – now at a time when consoles were the dominant force.

Andrew Deakin and Ivan Horn were friends since school and found themselves later working together at Ocean. Often, they were paired up, with Andrew on code, and Ivan on art. We did track down Andrew, though, sadly, he did not want to talk about his past work. Fresh from completing *Dennis the Menace* (Super Nintendo) at the end of 1993, they were next assigned to *Green Lantern* on the same platform, with no plans for other ports. "To some extent, the game was based on *Dennis*," Ivan explained. "That was our first game on the platform, and Andrew worked on it for about three months before I started, then I worked on it for about six months before both of us moved on to *Green Lantern*."

Joining them were graphic artists Ray Coffey and John Lomax. "Myself, Andrew and Ivan all shared the same small office, so it made sense that we would roll on to the next project together," John reflected. "We didn't know much about the licence at all, to be honest, and, at that time, I wasn't massively into comics."

All four (overseen by Gary Bracey) began to create a rough game design with the Hal Jordan character. A story was established with Hal hunting down the Queen of Xaos, who seeks a set of powerful crystals. If successful, the crystals would render her army of alien soldiers invincible and enable her to take over the universe. The queen herself was inspired by the alien queen from the 1986 *Aliens* film, complete with eggs and egg sac. Hal would first have to battle through five different alien worlds, each ending with an arch-rival boss battle, before concluding events on the planet Xaos to seek the alien queen.

There was no design document being followed, with inspiration just taken from various issues of the comic – mostly characters and locations. "It was the good old days of making it up as you went along. All I did were a few highly detailed concepts, but we didn't use them in the end," recalled Ray. "I created the main character animations, some backgrounds and bad guys, and I also did the main title screen."

Intriguingly, the main Xaos storyline wasn't from the *Green Lantern* universe at all; it was concocted by Ocean. "The planet [Xaos] was only shown once (*Green Lantern* #23 from 1963!), and there was no mention of a queen," clarified *Green Lantern* expert Myron Rumsey. "I imagine Ocean were sent source materials and may have found the Xax character interesting, coming up with an original idea that played off of the popularity of the *Alien* franchise. All conjecture on my part, to be sure!" It was a risky move; one which DC could easily reject.

With the project now fully underway, the team would lose one of its designers early on. "I was moved off the project to work on *Lobo* with Warren Lancashire," confirmed John. "I must have spent about a month on the project, just doing prototype art and maps in *tUME* for Andrew to test out. I had a good working relationship with Andy and Ivan so would still pop into their office from time to time and get a look at the game."

Over the course of the project, other graphic artists would fill the void, including Adrian Page, Colin Rushby and John Farmer (all three, sadly, were unavailable to talk about their time on the project). Steve Wahid also had a brief involvement, producing 3D renders of a rotating green ring and of Hal for cutscene sequences. John Reitze would also finally join the group a few months later to help out. "We worked on all aspects of the game art. Each graphic artist had their own set of levels and created artwork for them – background and character sprite work," explained John [Reitze] on how design work was split up. "Ray, for instance, created most of the artwork and animation for the main character, whilst we created additional 'hero' sprites when needed."

"It was the good old days of making it up as you went along."

Whilst the game rapidly took shape, DC Comics had a major shake-up with their comic book hero that would cause delays. Readership figures were falling, and a change was needed to reverse the fortunes of the comic. This resulted in a controversial 'Emerald Twilight' story in early 1994, with lead character Hal Jordan turning bad after seeing his home city destroyed. Destroying the Green Lantern Corps and stealing their power rings, Hal emerged as a bad guy named 'Parallax'. In the aftermath, the last remaining guardian, Ganthet, travels to Earth and finds an illustrator named Kyle Rayner, giving him the last remaining ring and making him the only remaining *Green Lantern*.

"Over the years, they had mishandled the character [Hal], and his popularity waned, and, coupled with a badly dysfunctional relationship between the writer and editor, DC decided that it was easier to try and replace the character rather than put any more energy into fixing things," explained Myron of the change. "DC were really trying to sell the Kyle Rayner character, and they would not have wanted any representation that didn't fit that agenda." The dramatic overhaul by DC would mean the team having to hastily replace Hal with Kyle, redressing

Hal as a villain to use later on. Characters specific to Hal's era were also reworked, but no levels were modified. The Xaos storyline was kept intact, perhaps surprisingly, considering Kyle never had any interaction with the planet, and there was no relation to the *Green Lantern* universe.

By now, news had already filtered through to the press about the game's development. Three early mock-up screens produced by Ray and John Reitze were printed in the May 1994 edition of *Edge* magazine, showing the Kyle Rayner character in action. Around this time, it was decided to also kick off a SEGA Mega Drive conversion, with Mike Delves on coding duties and Adrian Page as the lead platform graphic artist. The project would share art assets and most of the design from the leading SNES development.

The levels forming the worlds would consist mostly of platform-based action, but other genres would break things up a little. The exact sequence of the levels for the game has been forgotten, partly due to the lack of communication between the team at the time and lack of a game design document. Each person mostly worked in isolation on their designated levels.

It is known, at least, that the platform-themed levels would feature scenarios, such as a street scene, a mercenary planet and the planet Xaos. The rest could not be recalled. Across the game, you would have access to up to approximately 30 items that you could call from your ring and use to defeat enemies or aid progression throughout the game.

"The green projected objects were sprites," recalled Ivan. "I remember Andrew having discussions with James Higgins (programmer of *The Addams Family* on the SNES) about an idea for drawing a green line or trapezium shape connecting the hand of the sprite to the object to give the impression of projecting it. I can't remember if that was implemented or not."

Other genres included an *R-Type*-inspired level with a flying Green Lantern, shooting enemies and finishing with a large boss encounter. The ring was used in a similar fashion to the beam charge mechanic in *R-Type*, creating a large, powerful blast that would kill all enemies in its path. Andrew created a fast-paced SEU level, which featured large sprites and fast-moving backgrounds. There was also a top-down shooter level, following the same theme, but vertically scrolling instead.

Then there was a third-person flying level, utilising Mode 7 to great effect. Briefly previewed in *Super Gamer* magazine in July 1994, you flew across a moonscape environment, collecting pick-ups, killing enemies and avoiding various hazards. The level concluded with a deadly showdown against Hal's new dark persona, Parallax. Some graphic artists suggest that this level was recycled in the game, with different objectives and enemies applied.

A final platform action-based showdown on the planet Xaos set you in an insect world, fighting against insect-like enemies whilst trying to hunt down the alien queen. A key item to generate on the level would be an anvil object, used to crush insect enemies in seconds. "That level had predominantly orange/brown colouring, with a hexagonal cell structure to the backgrounds," recalled Ivan. "The player started on the top level, worked their way sideways through it until reaching a gap in the floor where they could drop down to the level below. Then they would work their way back in the opposite direction, before dropping down another floor. Eventually, they would find their way to the Xaos queen, at which point, the final battle began."

"Some characters went from being good to bad and vice versa."

Although early character changes had caused significant delays, it was the continued lack of communication across the team that would cause the game to go on much longer than anticipated. With so many graphic artists working separately, the game became disjointed in its application. "Back in those days, the artists were also the game and level designers; that's the reason why the gameplay and level style jumped around so much," remarked John [Reitze]. The game was otherwise looking and playing rather well, all things considered. Andrew was pushing the SNES hard, getting the game running at full speed with lots of sprites on the screen and no visible slowdown. It was shaping up to be a solid new release on the platform.

With the game nearing completion, and after completing work on *Jurassic Park 2*, Dean Evans was brought in for the remaining musical and sound effect duties. "It must have been right near the end of the project when Andrew and Ivan were still working on it. I recall being asked to write the music after working with them both in the past," Dean recalled.

Dean had free reign on the tunes produced; the only requests being that they had to feature guitars, and all of them had to be done quickly. "The music had to be written fairly quickly because the project had been in development for some time," explained Dean. "The title music was originally for *Lobo*, which was being developed in the States. That never happened, so it ended up in *Green Lantern*, where I wrote another six pieces. Two tunes were eventually used in *Waterworld*, (map and shop), but they were originally intended as interlude pieces between levels. I think there were just a couple of level tunes left to write, along with spot jingles and extra SFX."

A near-complete build would also make a surprise appearance at the Las Vegas Winter CES event in January 1995. It resulted in publications showing new screenshots and detailing the planet Xaos story in the months that followed. The press, though, was blissfully unaware as to what had been happening behind the scenes at Ocean.

With the games industry landscape changing rapidly, Ocean was undergoing changes of its own. Gary Bracey, who had been at Ocean for almost a decade, decided to leave for a new challenge towards the end of 1994, with Ian Turnbull taking over his role. With the rise of the 32-bit consoles, Ocean also wanted to focus more on 3D-based titles to keep up with the competition.

"The game had been in test for just a few weeks when it was announced that, after the current crop of titles were completed, all staff would be moving over to true 3D projects for PC," recalled Ivan. "Both Andrew and myself voiced our concern that the decision was not a wise one as, essentially, no one had real experience of 3D in any form. Obviously, 3D was the future, but we were concerned why this wasn't being fed into games development more gradually."

Although it would affect developments after the likes of *Green Lantern*, it was yet another major change at DC that would now put the project into complete turmoil. "They reset all of their Universe!" recalled Ian Turnbull. "From memory, some characters went from being good to bad and vice versa." DC had kicked off what was known as the 'Zero Hour' crossover event, where it was hoped to fix many of the issues from past events and storylines. DC wanted the new outcomes represented in the game, as well as accurate ties with the new comic stories released. It effectively meant having to redesign the entire game.

By now, the SNES was fading fast against the new 32-bit competition. With a shrinking market, high upfront costs for cartridge manufacturing and ongoing costs to DC, it was no longer becoming commercially viable to continue. Ian decided to call time on the project as a result. Although Mike Delves moved straight on to firefighting another project, Andrew and Ivan's fate was more of a shock. Both were let go as part of a major restructuring at the company shortly after the cancellation, with both moving rather abruptly on to pastures new.

"The artwork was nice, but the gameplay just wasn't up to it yet."

Astonishingly, just weeks later, Ocean had a change of heart when programmer Bobby Earl sought extra out-of-hours work to help fund a mortgage deposit. It gave a perfect opportunity to give *Green Lantern* one last roll of the dice, with a quick new build of the game as a background project, with a lower financial risk involved. The arrangement would have Bobby working during the day at Ocean on a PC project called *Silver* (an action RPG eventually released in 1999 by Infogrames) and working on *Green Lantern* outside of usual hours.

"I was coming off the back of *Jurassic Park 2: The Chaos Continues* on the SNES. I heard DC were not keen on the direction that *Green Lantern* was going in," recalled Bobby. "I began a complete rewrite based on our *JP2* engine, with Ray Coffey and John Reitze creating new sprites, but using a lot of the backgrounds already created for the old game. A new GUI and other characters were created."

The new compact team would be joined once more by Dean Evans, rolling over his musical talents from the previous iteration. "I had already written a couple of pieces when the project was taken over by members of the *Jurassic Park 2* team," recalled Dean. "I am pretty sure that the majority of the music was written after they joined." Work was carried out over weekends and evenings by the team, with much of the artwork repurposed from the old game. "We wanted to tie the game more closely to the comics; hence the start-up sequence contained an accurate story from the comic about how Kyle became the *Green Lantern*," explained Bobby. "We planned on doing this at the start and end of every level, but it was quite intense at the time to do sequences like this."

"Andrew created a fast-paced SEU level which featured large sprites."

Although the old storyline had now been forgotten, John Reitze recalled that they took inspiration for the new development from current issues of the comic at that time, including the new 'Zero Hour' series. The Xaos, scrolling shooter and Mode 7 level themes from the previous game were dropped, though Bobby confirmed that the game would still eventually feature different genres intertwined in every other level or so to break up the structure of the game. Also, instead of objects being projected at a large scale from the ring, like in the first game, things were simplified as you now collected ring power-ups to upgrade your ring shot power (which acted like a gun). So, your initial puny green laser would turn into larger and more powerful shot shapes, such as rockets that would kill enemies in a flash.

A couple of months in and two platform levels were mostly ready. Ray used his pre-existing street assets to produce the first level, where you shot various enemies and just had to get to the end of the map. The segment that followed featured a large robot (not yet active), suggesting a boss battle segment to be completed. The second level was designed by John. "My level was a side-scrolling platformer on a mercenary planet," he recalled. "I seem to remember an issue of the comic that was an alien planet full of vicious aliens. There was a real mixed bag of characters in the issue that I got to use." However, none of the levels would ever be fully completed.

If the SNES was creaking by the end of Andrew Deakin's development, it was certainly now at death's door compared with the flourishing Sony PlayStation and SEGA Saturn platforms. Although coming together quickly, the new game wasn't yet blowing anyone away and was lacking early on. "I don't think the game was as good as it could've been. The artwork was nice, but the gameplay just wasn't up to it yet," admitted John [Reitze].

It was, to be fair, very early on in the project, and these were issues that could be fixed. But time was against them, and the market had suddenly deteriorated even more, making the financial risk too high to be confident of making back any money. With still plenty of work to go and a platform about to become obsolete, Ocean quietly decided to drop the title for good. It is plausible that the game could have later been picked up again for 32-bit development, though it would have been under new management. Ocean lasted one more year, before being absorbed by French company Infogrames in 1996, eventually disappearing for good when the well-loved name was retired.

In the years that have since passed, many of those involved in the various developments no longer have anything. Andrew Deakin's development, which is the most desirable to try and locate due to the content, is still at large, with a CES prototype potentially still out there, waiting to be discovered.

"Eventually, they would find their way to the Xaos queen, at which point, the final battle began."

Artists Ray Coffey and John Reitze were more conscious about keeping their old work and dug out various art and animation assets to show here for the first time as well as on the Games That Weren't website. Mike Marshall recovered his early concept sketches that he produced way back in the early 1990s, though his Amiga work is yet to be found.

The most significant recovery was made in 2016 whilst writing this book when ex-Ocean graphic artist and tester Roy Fielding approached Games That Weren't to preserve a prototype SNES cartridge containing the final build of the final iteration. The prototype PCB was produced after the cancellation by Bobby and handed to all of those involved on the project. Luckily, John Reitze had kept his copy and passed it on to Roy to arrange preservation. There is some corruption with the title panel and with some colours, and there are only two unfinished levels in total (including an incomplete boss battle). It even has some *Jurassic Park 2* assets still present. Some of Dean's music and SFX were added into the game, and more could yet be discovered tucked away in the code. Overall, this was as far as Bobby Earl's development had ever got.

Due to licence issues around the character, it has not been possible to put the prototype into the wild just yet. By the time you read this, a full video of the prototype running should be available in collaboration with the Unseen 64 website at www.unseen64.net, and it is hoped that Dean's music will be ripped and made fully available too.

With Andrew and Ivan's development containing many more layers of gameplay and variation between levels in comparison, we are left to wonder what may have been, had their version been finished off. Maybe, someday, we will find out and judge for ourselves whether we missed out on something special.

Above: Artist's tidy-ups of early *Green Lantern* mock-up images shown in *Edge* magazine. The bottom image demonstrates one of the proposed projectable objects available.

Top: Cutscene image courtesy of Ray Coffey, showing the main character. Bottom: Various map and character asset test mock-ups (SNES), provided by John Reitze.

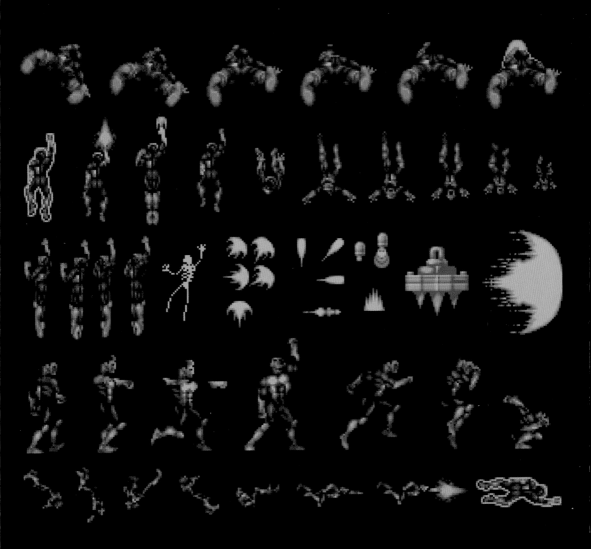

Above: *Green Lantern* (SNES) character sprites that were originally created for Andrew and Ivan's development. Some of the main sprites are from the Mode 7 and *R-Type*-like levels.

Above/Opposite: Screenshots from Bobby Earl's recovered SNES development, showing level 1 and part of an end-of-level guardian encounter with some panel glitches.

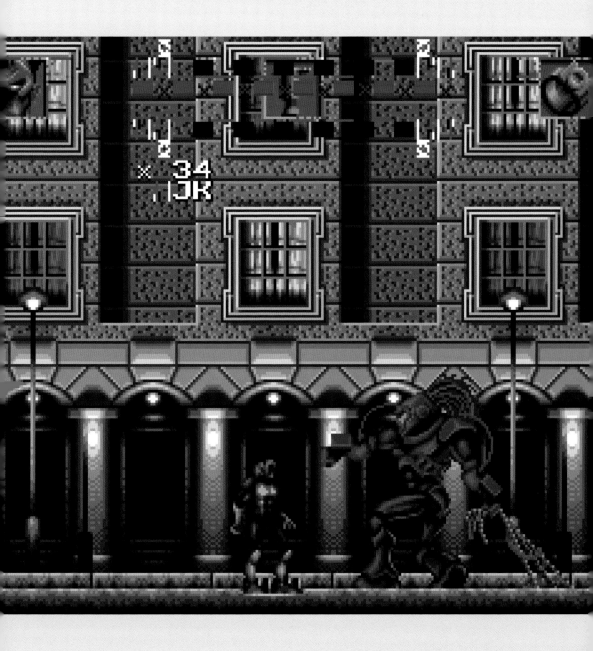

Snow Bros. Licensing

Year: 1991
Developer: Ocean France
Platforms: Atari ST
and Commodore Amiga
(pictured)

A lovingly crafted conversion of the Toaplan arcade, a sort of 'Bubble Bobble on ice', sadly lacking a simultaneous two-player mode and unreleased due to Ocean apparently not fully securing the licence. Along with *Putty Squad*, this was one of the so-called 'Holy Grail' titles for the Amiga, thankfully preserved in 2006. The Atari ST edition is tragically still at large, but it's hoped that it too will surface someday.

Available to play

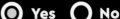 Yes No

Daffy Duck
Publisher demise

Year: 1992
Developers: Digital Design,
Maximum Effect and PAL Developments
Platforms: Amstrad CPC, Atari ST,
Commodore 64, Commodore Amiga
and ZX Spectrum 48/128K

Available to play
 Yes ◯ No

Growing up, many of us had a soft spot for games featuring our favourite film or cartoon characters. As we moved into the 1990s, publishers were by now well aware of how lucrative licences could be for generating sales, especially with younger audiences. Very savvy in this respect was Hi-Tec Software, run by David A. Palmer and best known for its Hanna-Barbera-licensed titles, such as *Scooby Doo and Scrappy Doo*, *Yogi Bear* and *Atom Ant*. Focusing on budget-based releases, Hi-Tec Software hit a sweet spot with kids and parents alike through its combination of licences, fun games and low price point.

Building upon Hi-Tec's early success, David pulled a major coup in the form of a licensing deal with Warner Bros. "A licence agreement was signed with them in 1989, and I had worked and knew the Warner executives and studio for quite a while before then," David explained. "This covered all 103 characters in Looney Tunes, including educational and PC CD-ROM rights." The deal began with the release of *Road Runner and Wile E. Coyote* in 1991, marking the start of what was hoped to be a promising future for the company.

Daffy Duck: Starring in the Great Paint Caper was the second game to result from the deal. Planned for release on a new mid-priced range called 'The Premier Series', this was a larger game compared with budget offerings, breaking away from the usual single load and presented in larger and more stylish packaging. *Alien World*, *The Jetsons* and *Potsworth and Co.* would be the first releases to greet the label, of which initial sales were strong according to David.

As with most Hi-Tec titles, *Daffy Duck* was to be released on all major home computer formats of the time – including the Commodore Amiga, Atari ST, Amstrad CPC, Commodore 64 and ZX Spectrum. Press announcements of the game began to surface from mid-1991, giving little away apart from news of the new Warner Bros. games coming soon.

The brains behind the initial storyboard for the new game was a newly created team called Maximum Effect, run by Alastair Dukes, who had previously done development work for David. The development itself of all versions would be handled by a mixture of PAL (Palmer Acoustics Limited) Developments and various contracted developers, graphic artists and musicians. Alastair often worked in-house at PAL Developments and, in combination with Gary Antcliffe and David Palmer, would help to allocate resources to each of the conversions as required. Maximum Effect would themselves develop *Bugs Bunny: Private Eye* (also unreleased) on the Amiga, whilst Daffy was brought to life by others. Unfortunately, Alastair was unavailable to share his memories due to his current role at Rockstar Games, Leeds.

Richard Morton, a well-established graphic artist at PAL Developments, took on the role of designer for the game across all the formats and created all of the level designs. A Game Design Doc (GDD) was a collaboration between Richard and Maximum Effect – detailing levels, puzzles and storyline throughout and building upon an early storyboard. This was then provided to each of the development teams, with only minor adjustments and compromises made between the 8- and 16-bit platforms.

The game's story consisted of Marvin the Martian hatching a plot to destroy Earth with his deadly 'Illudium Q-36 Explosive Space Modulator' device. For this, he needs all of the colour from Looney Toon town to fully activate the weapon – though, without colour, Looney Toon town cannot survive. Determined to stop his arch-nemesis, Daffy sets off in pursuit to restore the colour by collecting paint pots that Marvin has dropped whilst escaping. The story concludes with a final confrontation on Mars to put a stop to Marvin and his destructive machine.

Daffy must navigate through seven semi-scrolling/flip-screen levels, in a typical kids arcade adventure game. A number of puzzles and tasks must be completed to progress, but everything is kept simple to make for a fun and achievable experience for younger gamers. Dotted throughout the game world were many well-loved characters from the Warner Bros. stable, including Bugs Bunny, Foghorn Leghorn, Sylvester, Tweety Pie, Road Runner and many others. Each character offers something different, some giving or requiring items or providing hints, others offering no help at all. Communicating with them involved using a simple joystick-based menu system to select pre-determined phrases.

Daffy could collect bonus items for points throughout, though the focus was on finding objects that were crucial to solving a particular task or puzzle. A key side task involved Daffy having to fill a quota of a particular colour per level to progress by collecting the paint pots strewn around. On the 8-bit editions, this may have been removed and simplified by having the colour retrieved by just finishing the level.

Every level had its own distinctive theme, starting with 'The Film Studio', where Daffy would need to find a key to escape. Next, it was on to 'The Sewers', avoiding spiders and piranhas whilst flicking switches to turn off electrical barriers and find a key to exit. 'The Desert' had Daffy locating various rocket pieces scattered across the land for Speedy Gonzales.

On the 'The Farm Yard', Daffy had to collect eggs for Foghorn Leghorn, avoiding angry squirrels and using frogs to travel over large areas of water. 'The City' placed you in more suburban settings, exchanging items in various shops to obtain a key item for Sylvester the Cat. An odd diversion to 'The Forest' then saw Daffy helping a Pygmy bake a cake, before finally travelling to Mars with Porky Pig to defeat Marvin the Martian and disable the generator powering the 'Illudium Q-36 Explosive Space Modulator'.

Although lacking some cohesion, the levels were imaginative and well thought out. A lovely additional touch was Daffy sporting a different costume for each level (except for the ZX Spectrum version it seems), such as an Indiana Jones outfit for the desert, a space outfit for Mars, and a miner's cap for the sewers. He would also have a small weapon to accompany his outfit on each level, such as a whip, yo-yo or a laser gun that could temporarily stun enemies (though weapons were seemingly omitted from the 8-bit versions).

Leading the developments was the Commodore Amiga edition, programmed by Anthony Lloyd at PAL Developments, in one of his first commercial ventures. Anthony would also handle the Atari ST conversion, which was to be converted mostly from the Amiga code where possible. Due to legal commitments in his current employment, Anthony was unable to talk with us.

Richard Morton would stretch his game design role to being the graphic artist on both versions. Unsurprisingly, his 16-bit work took good advantage of the extra colours and memory available, with plenty of animation frames allocated to Daffy and the other characters. "The graphics were created in eight colours per tile to take advantage of the hardware playfields on the Amiga, allowing us to create parallax scrolling between the game playfield and the background playfield," Richard described of the graphical techniques implemented. "We also used scroll splits to give even more parallax depth and could even interrupt the priorities of the playfield store to allow for a foreground layer. If you look at *Scooby and Scrappy Doo* on the Amiga, you'll get a good idea of the same effects used."

"Neither had any knowledge of the previous development, but, by the time they started, there was catching up to do. Work began for them in late 1991, where little time was wasted."

The decision to design with eight colours per tile would unintentionally help to smooth the process of conversion to the Atari ST afterwards. "We didn't use the limited palette purely for the ST, but it was a happy side effect that the graphics were already colour-reduced," clarified Richard. "It wouldn't have looked as good though because the ST didn't have hardware playfields, so the parallax effects had to go."

Wizball was also an inspiration for Richard, with collecting colour paint pots intended to have a visible effect in the game. "We intended to replace the palette with greyscale tones; then, as each colour was found, the tones got replaced with the colour," he recalled. "I remember it being possible on Amiga and ST because you could affect the palette in nice ways, using colour-cycling effects, water, lightning, etc. I might have even developed greyscale versions of the tilesets so the coder could get the palette information required."

Music was handled by Paul Tankard (with sound effects/samples handled by the developer), who had just completed work on two other Premier titles – *Alien World* (Amiga/ST) and *Potsworth and Co.* (Amiga/ST). Gary Antcliffe arranged the work with Paul after a positive experience of working with him on *Alien World*. In a letter from Gary to Paul, five tunes were requested – including title, in-game, game over, game complete, and a Looney Tunes theme tune to be used on Daffy and other titles. There was an 80K limit for the four main tunes, and 50K for the Looney Tunes theme tune, where Paul would create a fully digitised sample.

Apart from a slight change request for the intro tune, Paul met the brief and produced tunes that accompanied the game perfectly. Paul didn't compose directly for the Atari ST; his Amiga work was instead sampled and reused. The in-game tune was replaced by just sound effects (as done for *Alien World* and *Potsworth and Co.*).

"The graphics were created in eight colours per tile to take advantage of the hardware playfields on the Amiga."

David and Richard recall the development going well overall, without too many complications – the only issues being some minor change requests by Warner Bros. The Atari ST conversion was soon put into motion once the Amiga edition was close to being complete, and it was relatively painless to convert across, thanks to Richard's attention to the graphics.

The 8-bit conversions had already been underway at this stage, aiming to follow the exact same design specification. Changes would mostly be cosmetic due to memory/storage issues, including removal of some cutscenes. Some level adjustments were made, and it is believed that underwater sewer segments and an underground train sequence with Marvin the Martian driving were dropped in particular. No one could recall exactly, though this was certainly the case for the Commodore 64 edition, but for other reasons covered later on.

Both Spectrum and Amstrad conversion duties were put in the capable hands of developer Nigel Speight. Fresh from working on *Chevy Chase* on the Amstrad CPC, Commodore 64 (C64) and ZX Spectrum, Nigel had just been promoted to studio manager at PAL Developments, a role which would be balanced with his development work.

Graphics would be handled once more by Richard, and were converted down and tidied up from the 16-bit tile and sprite sets. The Spectrum edition would feature monochrome graphics throughout (apart from colour changes in the score panel), but Amstrad CPC users would have been thrilled to learn that their version would make full use of its vibrant palette, with no lazy Spectrum porting to be seen.

Nigel could not recall much about the project, though he remembered that it was relatively straightforward, with just minor compromises throughout. "If I remember correctly, the multilayered graphical parallax effects and animations took up nearly all processing time, so we opted for just sound effects in-game," he recalled. "I can't remember who did the menu page music though." After some investigation, the ZX Spectrum and Amstrad CPC music and sound effects were found to be composed by C64 musician regular Mark Cooksey, who had recently composed the Spectrum and CPC tunes for *Potsworth and Co.* around the same time. Mark would compose the intro and title tunes for the game, and he also produced all of the sound effects to be included.

Commodore 64 development was handled by David Saunders and Ashley Routledge (better known at the time as 'Ash and Dave'). They were, however, not the first-choice development team, with freelance duo Alan Benson and Craig Wight originally subcontracted by Maximum Effect. "Alan did some great graphics for the main character with hi-res sprite overlays, and I did a multiplexor, as I recall, to get more than the good old eight sprites on screen," Craig explained. "We got as far as the scroller and some sprite routines. I forget why we stopped working on it. I do, though, recall going to Gainsborough to see the Amiga version being worked on – I just wish my memory wasn't so hazy on it!"

Alan added that they had done some of the presentation work too for the game and also set up a new SFX editor and map-building tool for the development. He recalled ruffling a few feathers right from the start. "I thought the Amiga animations were not fluid enough, so I added extra animation frames to a few of the better-known characters (especially Daffy)," recalled Alan. "I remember it not going down too well with the Amiga lads (who had subcontracted us) as Warner Bros. (they had to approve all animations) asked why an inferior machine was better animated than the current gen. This meant a lot more work for their poor animator.

He wasn't 100% certain if this was the genesis of the fallout, but, after coming back from a short break, Alan and Craig were suddenly told that they were off the project. They had spent approximately three weeks or so on the project, and the C64 edition now had no team on it. It wasn't long, however, until that was rectified with the introduction of Ash and Dave. Neither had any knowledge of the previous development, but, by the time they started, there was catching up to do. Work began for them in late 1991, where little time was wasted.

"By this time, we had moved from an office above my dad's antiques shop (where we were very lax with working hours, often taking days in a row off just to play games up the pier arcade) into our own office and our set-up was a whole lot more professional," began Dave. "Working for Activision on *Hot Rod* and *Dragon Breed* had allowed us to buy the Programmers Development System (PDS) which streamlined our whole work environment, so working on *Daffy*

Duck and the other licences from Dave Palmer was a breeze. I could pull in trusted routines from other platform games we had made and quickly get the basics of the game up and running in no time. I had a great sprite multiplexor with a demon-fast bucket sort, a full screen-scrolling routine and a sprite character animation routine, including all the collision detection needed for such a platform game."

This time, Richard Morton was not directly involved, with Ash handling most of the graphic work himself, using Richard's 16-bit assets and Maximum Effect's storyboard as reference. Most of Alan's sprites would, however, be utilised to save time, passed over to Ash, with just minor adjustments made. "Ash would be working on the graphics using various editors we had, which I would slot into the game. Before long, we were working on the gameplay elements and sending versions back to David Palmer for testing," recalled Dave.

"The C64 version was the most memorable of all the conversions."

The C64 music was composed by Gerald Gourley, who also had previous Hi-Tec credits composing for *Potsworth and Co.* and *Turbo the Tortoise*. Gerald's contribution was very solid, with some great-sounding tunes, even if they didn't really fit in with the theme of the game.

As with most of Ash and Dave's C64 work, *Daffy* evolved into a game with plenty of polish and was arguably one of their best titles. Likely due to delays from the first aborted development though, they would have to drop a number of key gameplay elements, including the concept of collecting paint to colourise Looney Toon Town (with no paint indicators in the status panel).

Daffy would also lose his weapons (as believed to have happened with the other 8-bit editions) and would only be able to jump on enemies to stun them. It seems though that the intentions were there to be feature-complete, with the last level still containing a Ray Gun that you could collect but was completely useless. The ending would also still make reference to Daffy making Looney Toon Town colourful again. Ash and Dave's conversion was handed over to Hi-Tec and, in almost a blink of an eye, focus switched to finishing off yet another title for Hi-Tec in the form of *Yogi's Big Clean Up* (which would become yet another unreleased title), a brand-new development started towards the end of *Daffy Duck*'s development.

Towards the middle of 1992, all of the conversions were completed and underwent a phase of internal testing. The game was at a stage ready to be sent out to magazines for review, and the mastering process was about to be kicked off. Packaging artwork was produced by Julie Hebdon, who created artwork for most (if not all) of Hi-Tec's releases at the time. Possibly Hi-Tec's best release yet was about to be unleashed.

The C64 version was the most memorable of all the conversions. Reviewed in Issue 87 of *Zzap!64* magazine and gaining a 94% rating (the highest grade for a C64 Hi-Tec release), it was the only version to see a full review. Only the ZX Spectrum edition came as close, with a preview spread and screenshots in Issue 97 of *Crash* magazine. Nothing of the Commodore Amiga, Amstrad CPC or Atari ST versions were to be seen in the press, the reasons why soon becoming clear.

Hi-Tec had started to hit financial issues around July 1992 due to a recent recession. "Our biggest problem was financial structuring," David Palmer stated in an interview with *Computer Trading Weekly* at the time. Although everything was done to keep the company afloat, no financial backing could be found to replace the bankers who had pulled out their support. Hi-Tec went into receivership the same year.

Daffy Duck ended up being the largest casualty as it was just about to go to the duplicators when everything fell through. Although *Turbo the Tortoise* would be bought by Codemasters and had a continued release, the Warner Bros. and Hanna-Barbera licences were still owned separately by PAL Developments. This meant that there was still hope of a release.

Publishing rights for the licensed titles were later handed over to a new company set up by David called Citizen Software (Citizen Electronics Ltd.). The plan was for *Daffy Duck* and other titles to be rebranded and published under this new label, but David suddenly decided to pull out from publishing, focusing just on development instead.

By now, sales for the 8-bit home platforms were starting to dry up and would see David move his focus to the consoles of the time instead. This resulted in game developments featuring Speedy Gonzalez, Tasmanian Devil and Dennis the Menace in the years that followed, but *Daffy Duck* (along with other Hi-Tec games) would never see the light of day.

Over the years, the C64 edition gained attention and notoriety due to its glowing *Zzap!64* review. It became the most wanted of unreleased C64 games, and a large focus for the Games That Weren't website for many years. Eighteen years, to be precise, and a long search occurred that exhausted most avenues. Thankfully, it paid off and resulted in the game miraculously being fully recovered.

Ashley Routledge had kept all of his C64 disks, including the gold dust that was David Saunders' PC backups. On the backups were the full source code to the game and the keys to the entire castle. After careful reconstruction, the full game was finally released to the world in September 2015. Although it wasn't quite the game that people expected, it was a major recovery and release.

Unfortunately, the news was not so good for the other versions. "I haven't kept any of the old Spectrum/Amstrad stuff," Nigel confirmed when asked about his conversions. A similar story was to be said for the Amiga/ST editions, though with slightly more promise on the horizon. Richard Morton firstly managed to recover graphical assets for the Amiga version, including rare snippets of graphics from the Amstrad CPC edition. It is speculated that magazine review copies could also still exist. "Pete Frith handled sending out demo copies of games. He copied them and mailed them," David confirmed. Pete was asked whether he may have kept anything and responded that the only thing he had was an almost complete set of the games that were released, but that was it.

David believes that he still has master copies of all versions somewhere in storage, but he has been yet to locate them. A 3.5-inch demo disk did once surface with a label of 'Daffy Duck – Amiga Demo' written on it, but it subsequently disappeared after various office and house moves over the years. David still remains the best hope for any of the remaining versions to be found someday. However, he did recover a rare video showing a preview of the Amiga version in action. The video should be available on the Games That Weren't website at the time of publication.

The video demonstrates the first three levels from the game, including the intro, title and cutscenes, and shows what seems like a mostly complete game. As a bonus, the video also includes a preview of *Bugs Bunny: Private Eye* on the Amiga and a recording of the ZX Spectrum intro to *Daffy Duck* with a sample of Mark's music – though, sadly, with nothing of that version in action.

C64 historian and journalist Mat Allen also preserved a rare copy of the game's artwork that came on a large A2 poster within his copy of *Alien World*. This is the closest indication of how the packaging would have looked, had the game been released. Some enthusiasts have since used the artwork to produce packaging for their own homebrew copies of the C64 edition.

"I haven't kept any of the old Spectrum/Amstrad stuff."

With such a positive outcome for the C64 edition, it leaves hope and inspiration that the very same result could happen for the other systems. Although one chapter has closed for one platform, the rest are yet to be written and concluded, and the search goes on to find them. Hopefully, it will just be a matter of time and not a case of 'That's all, folks'.

Above: Rare poster art of the game that managed to sneak out in a copy of *Alien World*. This would have been the game's box art.

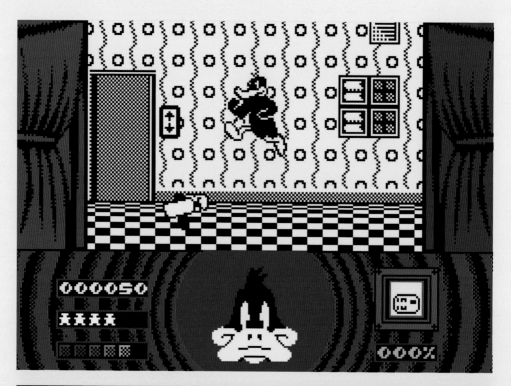

Top: Artist's pixel recreation of *Daffy Duck* on the ZX Spectrum, based on a magazine screenshot.
Bottom: A rare recovered Amstrad CPC screen showing the end sequence.

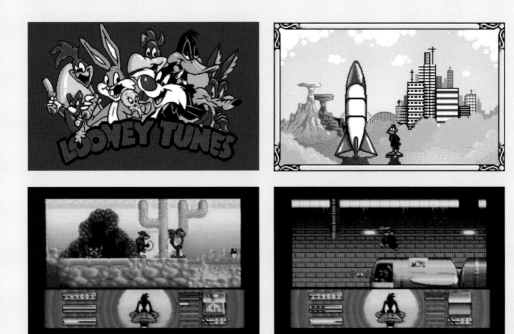

Above: Various Commodore Amiga/Atari ST presentation screens and cutscenes, as well as two actual gameplay shots from the grainy Amiga video obtained from David.

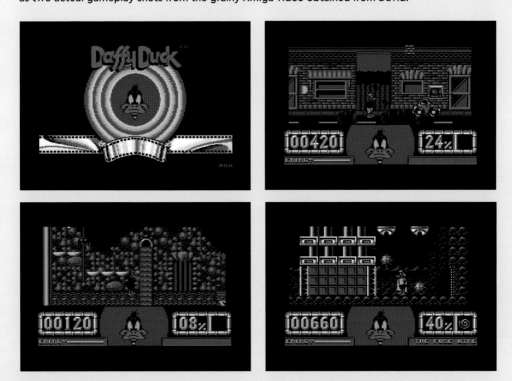

Above: Various screenshots showing the title screen and different levels from the recovered Commodore 64 edition.

Available to play

◯ Yes ◯ No

It's startling to imagine a Super Mario game on anything other than a Nintendo platform, but that was the case when a deal was made with Philips. Set on Earth, across locations including Egypt and the Arctic, the game lacked the imaginative design of *Super Mario World*. Poor sales of the CD-i saw it cancelled early – leaving us to wonder what could have been.

"All of the artwork was done in *Photoshop 2*, and it was also the first time I was able to use a Mac to create everything. All the tiles (8×8 characters) had to be cut out by hand and very clumsily coded through a primitive DOS program to get them integrated into the game. I thought I did some pretty awesome art though, especially since my only other experience was with bootleg NES games!

I particularly loved the pirate ship. I think the real reason that *Super Mario's Wacky Worlds* was cancelled was due to changes in personnel. The lead (and only) engineer on the project decided to leave and work for EA. When a replacement programmer wasn't found to continue the project, I also left and went to EA, and the game was ultimately cancelled."

Nina Stanley, graphic artist

Super Mario's Wacky Worlds
Poor CD-i sales

Year: 1993
Developer: NovaLogic
Platform: Philips CD-i

Vindicators
Publisher
cancelled

Year: 1992
Developer: Atari Games
Platform: Atari Lynx

Available to play

 Yes ◉ No

It's fair to say that the Atari Lynx was a slightly underappreciated handheld, which is odd, considering the vast power it had over its rivals. Unfortunately, the battery life wasn't great, and marketing could have maybe taken a leaf from Nintendo with its handling of the commercially dominant Game Boy. That said, the Lynx is still home to a number of groundbreaking and wonderful titles: though, sadly, many would never be experienced.

Software for the Lynx comprised of a number of arcade conversions, with Atari Corporation utilising its rich back catalogue to great effect. *Hard Drivin'* and *Stun Runner* were two particularly notable conversions putting other conversions to shame. Adding to its conversion list next was a far simpler game in comparison: the 2D tank arcade *Vindicators*.

Released in 1988, the arcade featured a futuristic tank-themed cabinet design, complete with tank tracks at the base. The game took place in the year 2525, where the mission was to destroy invading forces from the 'Tangent Empire', battling through 14 stations with an 'SR-88 Strategic Battle Tank'. With constantly draining fuel supplies, you had to regularly replenish the tank by collecting fuel canisters, as well as collecting 'battle stars' to later enhance your tank with new weapons and armoury to help progress.

You could play with one or two players simultaneously, each using a double-stick controller that reflected almost real tank-like controls. Pushing both sticks in opposite directions would steer the tank in a clockwise or anti-clockwise direction and pushing both forwards/backwards would move you in those particular directions. There were also buttons for primary fire, special weapons, and for rotating your gun turret. It was fiddly at first, but a lot of fun if you were willing to persevere.

The arcade was popular enough to see a conversion to a host of platforms during 1990, including the NES (not officially by Tengen), Commodore Amiga and ZX Spectrum, among many others. Shortly after, Atari would add the game to its own rapidly growing Lynx line-up. Assigned the task of converting the monstrously sized arcade to the tiny handheld was David Kurensky, in his first assignment at the company. "It was the only title I ever worked on for Atari," he began. "Before then, Chuck Ernst and I both got started in games around 1987, working for a small company doing conversions. Chuck jumped to Atari first and then dragged me along a bit later."

David was based at Atari's Lombard office at Illinois in the United States, where most of Atari's internal Lynx and 7800 programmers were situated. When assigned to the game, David was already quite familiar and taken in by it. "Ironically, it was one of my favourite games, and I still remember when I first saw it on the west side of Milwaukee," he recalled. "It was huge, and I was like 'What is that?' when I first saw it. I ended up playing the game for hours!"

Being a fan would, of course, prove useful, but development was hard to get going with David's first experience of the Lynx architecture. With a lack of documentation, tools and help available, David had to work out as much as possible for himself. "It was tough. There was no collaboration across projects or with others," he explained. "Every game was a different world. Information and tricks held on to closely. Nowadays, you can do a search and come up with code and examples, but that wasn't possible then. There was no standard platform or engine; everyone mostly started from scratch for every game."

Development was carried out using Amiga-based technology, much to the annoyance of Atari's upper management. A developer from California was even tasked with porting all the technology over to Atari ST hardware, but, half of the time, it never fully worked. "We just kept using the Amiga setup in the end. People would come through on office tours for whatever reason, and we'd have to drape things over the machines to show we were 100% Atari!"

Supplied with printed source code from the arcade, David carefully pored over it all, making notes and trying to understand how everything worked. "It was all assembly language and was cool to read through and decipher what they were doing in the game. It was cool to see how the arcade was designed as a pure quarter-sucker. The longer you played, it would just get more difficult, the AI would increase, and the collision detection would become more finely tuned."

Atari also supplied an arcade machine as a reference. "I had it at my house! It was huge, with two large tank controls and a huge monitor. All press board/ particle board and weighing a fucking tonne!" laughed David. "At some point, they took the arcade back from me, and I remember the mover trying to take it. I had a pretty wide staircase, but it was just so heavy and needed two guys to negotiate the stairwell. In the end, one of the guys goes to the other, 'Just go away! I'm gonna coffin-lift it!'."

Although comparatively not breaking his back converting the game, David's task became a lot tougher once learning early on that there would be no dedicated graphic artist assigned to help. Artwork assets from the arcade were instead supplied by Susan McBride, who worked with Kris Moser on the original arcade.

"Susan shared lots of artwork, but it was difficult to use. There were huge sprites and sections of background elements with no reference to where things went. Levels were not laid out, and maps had to be built from scratch. It was a starting point, though," recalled David. "I used *Deluxe Paint* to rework sprites and draw levels and wrote tools to extract tiles to make tiled-based maps. It was difficult to make everything line up, with things often being out by one pixel. I wrote tools as much as I wrote actual game code, such as tools to strip/scale down graphics so I could use them in the game, or place enemies and that kind of thing. Overall, it was tough and all very time-consuming."

Although music wouldn't be thought about until nearer the end of development, colleague Joel Seider would early on provide sound effects ported across from the arcade. The early inclusion within the game would give it an extra boost and feeling of progression.

David was mostly left to his own devices throughout development, with management only occasionally checking in on progress. Combined with the lack of documentation, tools and dedicated graphic artist, he was fairly isolated and responsible for most aspects of the project. Not only that, both David and Chuck were often pulled in to help with testing or fixing problems on other projects when they should have been just working on their own. It meant that progress was slow on *Vindicators*, with development stretching well into 1992.

The progress was still positive, though, and David took everything in his stride, finding enjoyment in the face of the challenges and getting around hardware limitations. "Part of the fun was trying to squeeze as much out of the Lynx, doing tricks to make levels overwrite what used to be code and reuse areas of memory," he explained. "Doing all these kinds of crazy things to squeeze as much as you can into a game. To save space, *Vindicators* used the same tileset for all levels, just with different palettes applied."

"Part of the fun was trying to squeeze as much out of the Lynx."

Another challenge tackled early on was with controls. The complex arcade controls were neatly adapted to the Lynx, with directional control via the D-pad, 'A' for regular firing and 'B' for special weapons. Press 'Option 1' and the joy-pad would rotate the tank turret, and 'Option 2' would swap between special weapons. In many ways, the Lynx version was more accessible.

The two-player mode was also preserved and made possible thanks to the ComLynx system. "Eventually, I had the network and two-player link-up all working, which was a lot of fun," David smiled. "The arcade had both tanks in one display. But, on the Lynx, I was playing around with allowing players to be in different areas of the map at the same time, as they each had their very own screen display."

Sliding gradually into 1992, the game was shaping up and, crucially, was playable. Levels came together thanks to David's initial groundwork and tools, and, thanks to the supply of the original arcade assets, it was looking and feeling just like the arcade in miniature form. There were gameplay elements still left to complete, bugs to fix and levels to design, but completion was certainly now on the horizon at last.

Packaging artwork was also commissioned and completed by local commercial artist Mark Wickart. When asked about the work, Mark responded that he had been involved in thousands of pieces over 25 years. Although he recognised his illustration, he couldn't recall any other specifics, apart from that he was given a loose marker layout for a final illustration to be rendered from.

As the months edged into summer, David and Chuck began to feel that the Lynx was struggling commercially and wasn't being properly marketed by Atari. Although *Vindicators* was mentioned in some Atari catalogues and press at the time (including due dates) and the box artwork had been designed, there were still concerns that soon became justified.

"Up until now, we had a lot of fun. We worked and played hard," David began. "I remember being told about the Atari Jaguar and how our office was going to be the development centre for it all. At least, that is how I remember it. They sent guys down from corporate that were meant to be bringing us Jaguar development kits and doing a demo. I happened to oversleep that day as my alarm didn't go off, so I bust my ass to get to work, showing up late for this really important meeting. I'm met at the door and told that I may as well go home as they had decided to close the office!"

Atari's decision to close the Lombard offices in the summer of 1992 was part of a cost-saving exercise. Those not moving to Sunnyvale to continue at Atari and whose Lynx projects were closest to completion were asked to 'work for hire' to finish them. David, needing the money, signed an agreement to complete *Vindicators* in just four weeks during mid-September. Those weeks would rapidly turn into months.

"Up until now, we had a lot of fun. We worked and played hard."

In hindsight, David agreed that he should have walked away at the time. Enthusiasm had waned as a result of the Lombard closure, but he was keen to finish the nearly completed game, as well as put food on the table. "It was kind of hard. I really wasn't motivated at all by that point, but I was motivated to get paid," recalled David.

David kept in regular phone contact and would send Atari a build of the game to show progress before the initially agreed four weeks were up. He provided a list of what was broken and still outstanding. There were collision bugs, missing sounds and link-up play had broken at some stage, but the major issue was with RAM, which David had completely used up.

At this point, the music had been supplied, but there was no space to integrate it. As a result, David supplied a separate ROM image with just the tunes, so management could at least hear what had been supplied. It couldn't be recalled exactly who did the music, but it is likely to have been either Comp Inc. (who supplied music for Joel's *Elvira Pinball Jam* game) or prolific Lynx musician

Matthew Scott. By late December, many of the issues were resolved, crucially including the RAM issues for the music to be bolted in. The finish line was in sight. The titles were all in place, and most options were implemented; it was now just the final polish, level finishing, and a few niggling bugs to zap.

Working on a project for over two years, doing mostly everything, seeing your workplace close down, and lacking regular income security can take its toll on the best of us. Coming into 1993, enthusiasm and drive had practically disappeared, with development dragging on long enough to cause concern. Atari demanded that the game had to be fully completed by the end of April otherwise it would be cancelled.

David attempted one final push to complete and be rid of the project once and for all, but, by this point, the market had declined badly for the Lynx – the platform having taken a battering by the Nintendo Game Boy. Not long after their final demand on *Vindicators*, Atari re-evaluated and decided to cancel titles that were felt wouldn't recoup any money. "They just pulled the plug on everything! I think they may have killed the Lynx not long after," David confirmed.

Ted Tahquechi (a senior producer at the time at Atari) informed us that most Lynx titles were shelved around this time due to Atari focusing funds and resources towards projects such as the Jaguar, saying that it made more sense to cancel titles than complete them in order to support future products. *Vindicators*, although practically complete, was by now an almost five-year-old arcade that had been forgotten, so it made sense to drop it. The game disappeared from release schedules along with many others. Perhaps a relief for David, who was now finally able to move on to pastures new. Although, for the most part, he enjoyed working on the game, it was no doubt a development hell during those last six or so months. The Lynx would continue for a few more years yet, though the releases would drastically dry up over time.

David continued as a software engineer for a number of years, even showcasing his *Vindicators* development to get further work. "I would carry the development kit around to show people as we couldn't make demo tapes or anything. I'd set it up in some shed/office and show off the work," he confirmed. David still works in software development today, even dabbling again with game development recently, working on a 2D top-down, tile-based, arcade-like tank game. Sound familiar?

As for *Vindicators* on the Lynx, almost 30 years on, the game became a mystery for Atari Lynx fans, with the rumour mill going into overdrive ever since the advent of the Internet. Carl Forhan from Songbird Productions originally found hints of the development when he came across backups of the arcade source code on an Amiga development system. This was very likely what was extracted for David, though there was no sign of any Lynx work.

Around the turn of the millennium, a bunch of *Vindicators* Lynx screens were then preserved by Harry Dodgson, which have since resided on AtariAge for many years. When questioned about them, Harry explained that he had found the artwork on an Amiga development kit, consisting of just a few mocked-up screens.

Then, in 2011, a YouTube video surfaced showing a bizarre home-made promotional display for the game, with a customised *Action Joe* Stratos moon buggy. Reportedly found in the US, the demo shown on the Lynx included three rolling demos and a time-limited playable demo. Playable in the loosest sense as it had very basic movement and no actual gameplay elements. When it was shown to David, he confirmed that this was nothing to do with him. Was it, therefore, an elaborate fake, or perhaps a special promotional demo mocked up by another developer? The prototype has yet to be dumped for analysis, but comparing it with Harry's screenshots, the graphics look to be the same.

The recovered art and video clips were also similar to what was shown of the game in the press, rumoured to be mock-ups, suggesting that someone may have obtained graphics from David for the 'promotional demo', but it couldn't be verified. Score panels are present in the press screenshots but seem to be static and inactive. An almost identical score panel can be found in *Zero* magazine Issue 20 (June 1991), looking as if it was taken from an actual Lynx, but with a solid background and smaller/less detailed tank sprites, likely depicting an early build. David is certain that the press shots were from his game and not mock-ups.

Finding a playable copy of the game has eluded all so far, but the exciting news was that David kept all of his *Vindicators* work and development machines, quashing rumours of code being destroyed after payment disputes. Although Atari would have asked David to hand everything back – for one reason or another, that never happened.

"They just pulled the plug on everything! I think they may have killed the Lynx not long after."

"I gave my dev kits and other materials to Chuck when I moved to the Netherlands. He's still got them and plans on booting things up for a laugh," he confirmed. Even printouts that David was given of the arcade source code are present, complete with comments, such as "What the fuck does this do??", included at various points and indicating the fun that David was clearly having at the time.

Sadly, the machines didn't boot at the time of publication, so work is still required to try and get them running once more for something to be shown. David didn't promise anything, but our discussions may have given him new enthusiasm to get *Vindicators* up and running once more. Could we someday see this solid conversion after all?

Above: Unused box artwork by Mark Wickart for the Atari Lynx edition of *Vindicators*, shown in press previews for the game. This is a blown-up scan from a small sized print, hence the unfortunate moiré pattern.

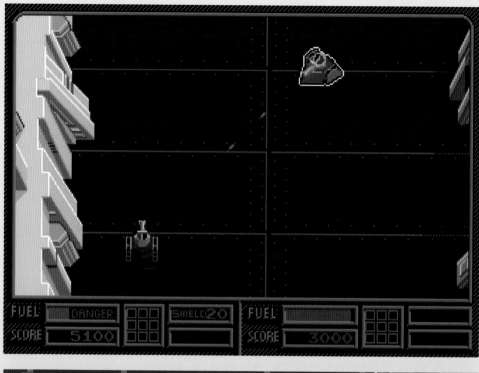

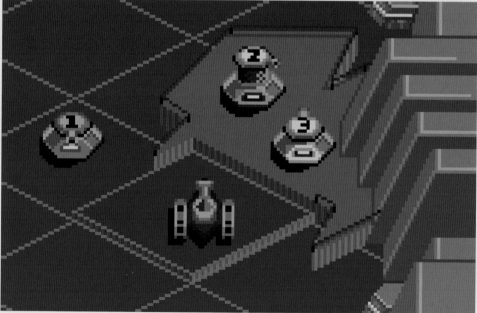

Top: *Vindicators* (arcade) showing part of the main game. Bottom: Lynx artwork mock-up recovered by Harry Dodgson from an Amiga that was used for Lynx development.

Above: Artist's impressions of how *Vindicators* (Atari Lynx) may have looked, based on screenshots from *Atari Log* magazine and *Grey Matters* magazine.

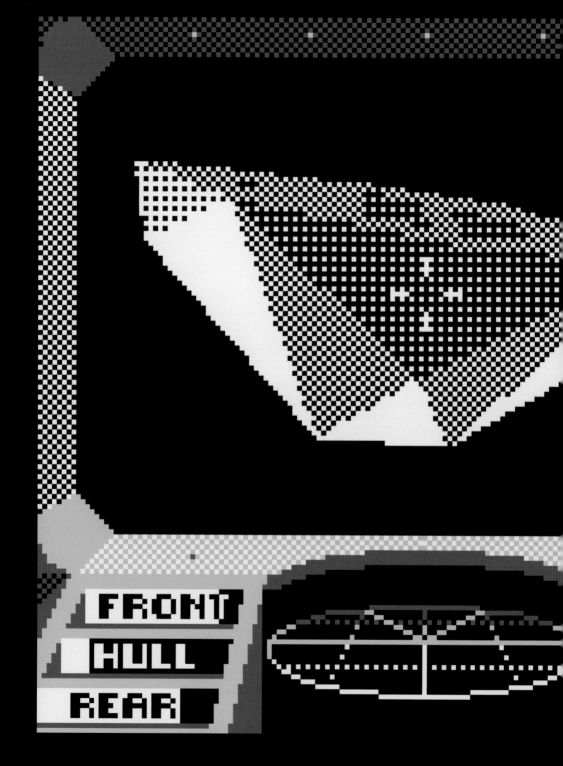

Elite
Deal fell through

**Year: 1993–1994
Developer: Hybrid
Platforms: Nintendo
Game Boy (pictured),
SEGA Mega Drive
and Super Nintendo**

Hybrid once attempted to bring the classic
3D space trading game to a new console-
based audience. The Super Nintendo edition
came first, apparently progressing quite far.
Later, Game Boy and Mega Drive versions
followed, reaching early prototype stages.
Signed up by Ocean Software, everything
fell through, denying a new generation from
getting their Elite combat status.

Available to play

◉ Yes ○ No

Spitfire Fury
Publisher cancelled

Year: 1992
Developer: Andrew Hutchings
Platform: Acorn Archimedes
(A3000, A310 and A400)

Available to play
 Yes No

When it came to games, the Acorn Archimedes may have taken a bashing from the likes of the Commodore Amiga in terms of support, but it was certainly no failure. Released as the 300 and 400 series back in 1987, it was the first computer to house a RISC CPU with a 32-bit ARM processor. May 1989 saw the A3000 model launched, following a similar design to the Amiga 500.

The machine would steadily build a solid support base during the early 1990s. As with the BBC Micro, the Archimedes was very much seen as an educational machine, popular for schools and not so much for games. However, it got to experience its fair share, including unique titles that showcased the underlying raw power of the machine.

Spitfire Fury was hoping to add to the slowly growing list, a game born from another Archimedes title named *Chocks Away*, an impressive flight simulator released by The Fourth Dimension (4D) in 1990. Both titles shared the same creator, Andrew Hutchings.

Andrew had dabbled with programming using a Commodore PET at school and a ZX Spectrum at home. He was fascinated with 3D-based titles ever since playing *Star Wars* in the arcades. After leaving school and starting a full-time engineering role, Andrew felt an urge to get into programming again during the evenings. He was blown away after seeing an Archimedes for the first time in his local computer store, running titles such as *Zarch*.

Obtaining a loan, Andrew bought one and began playing with BASIC to create simple wireframe demos, before progressing to assembly language. After almost two years of self-teaching, Andrew felt confident enough to put a game together and began working on a flight simulator. When submitting a demo to 4D in 1990, they were blown away and hastily arranged a contract and £1,000 advance for him to complete what would become *Chocks Away*. Andrew quit his full-time job and became a full-time games developer.

Everyone was bowled over by the game, becoming a success story for both 4D and Andrew. An expansion pack was swiftly released the following year. However, the company couldn't just keep releasing expansion packs, so it arranged a sequel of sorts with the development of *Spitfire Fury*.

4D asked Andrew for a brand-new flight simulator, so he suggested a game with Spitfires as the main subject matter. "Both *Chocks Away* and *Extra Missions* had been critically well-received, so another flight combat simulator in the WWII era seemed an obvious progression," explained Andrew. "At the time, I worked closely with Mark Botterill, and he came up with the title *Spitfire Fury* and was a big influence in the development of the game. Development started immediately after completing *Chocks Away: Extra Missions* in mid-1991."

During the development of *Chocks Away*, there had been a number of improvements and refinements to the graphics engine, allowing the game to run faster and with more detail. With a working engine already in place, it made sense for *Spitfire Fury* to build upon it. As a result, the focus was on building new 3D models and game logic to take it to the next level but also to improve the game's artificial intelligence.

"The game was developed to have smarter AI, with enemy planes taking off and landing, fighters flying in formation, and bombers dropping bombs on cities and targets," recalled Andrew. "There would be more tactics involved, with multiple targets to defend or attack. There were also plans to have allies fighting alongside your plane, as well as higher quality and realistic graphics for planes such as the *Messerschmitt*, *Stuka*, *Junkers Bomber*, *Flying Fortress*, *Lancaster Bomber* and *Spitfire*. Destroyable tanks and trains featured, all with realistic explosions of objects, deconstructing them from their original polygon mesh."

As with his previous game, Andrew had help from others, including developer and graphic artist Gordon Key. "Gordon created the internal cockpit artwork and would produce some highly optimised code to render the cockpit with minimal CPU impact," confirmed Andrew. He would have also contributed more help towards the end of the project as and when needed.

Also involved was Mark Ferguson, who helped to map the geometry of World War II planes from plans obtained from his local library. "I helped Andrew back in 1991," began Mark. "He was a good friend of mine and was starting to make his name in writing and designing games. My role was simply to help with the vector/wireframe graphics for the planes. I spent time looking at schematics of World War II planes and converting them to wireframe diagrams with coordinates that could then be input and rendered in the game environment."

It was a one-off job for Mark, taking 2–3 weeks to produce 4–5 planes, drawing from his educational experience. "I had done something similar for my degree, in terms of coordinates for statistical analysis for ecology, when it was necessary to relate this to aspect/topography. But I had no experience of doing this in a game context," explained Mark. "It was a case of learning by trial and error and coming up with a system that worked. The major achievement that sticks in my mind was the production of the *B-52 bomber*, which took the greatest time to convert into a wireframe and render correctly."

Early on, Andrew was struggling for enthusiasm on the project compared with *Chocks Away*. At that time, he was doing something completely new, but *Spitfire Fury* was just more of the same and felt too similar to his previous work. The interest just wasn't there. Andrew also felt a need to catch up on a lost social life. "During the development of *Chocks Away*, I had been very focused and was quite a recluse," explained Andrew. "With the money from the game,

I started to go out to pubs and nightclubs and enjoy myself. I also bought a car and would leap at any chance to go on holiday or to festivals. My commitment to programming changed whilst I took time out to enjoy myself."

Perhaps unaware of the scale of Andrew's 'slacking off', 4D began to advertise the game with a series of early development screenshots and a large list of features. Amongst the usual promotional blurb, the specifications were similar to *Chocks Away*, as you might expect. Details of a 12–18-frames-per-second screen update, a two-player split-screen/serial link, AI-controlled enemies, save/load options, 256-colour graphics, and digitised sound effects were some of the standard features mentioned.

The key selling points were a large variety of missions, over 100 enemy targets and open-world maps with roads, hills, railways, buildings and other common landscape features. Missions included bombing raids, torpedo attacks on gunboats, escorting *B-52 bombers* on a bombing raid – all with the ability to practise beforehand. As well as destroying planes coming into your path, you could seek cover from them between hills and buildings.

Accompanying Mark's realistic *Spitfire* mapping, the handling of the plane was set up to be highly realistic, taking into account gravity, drag and lift across different surfaces. There would be the ability to perform realistic stunts and spins, which, apparently, had not been seen on any other Archimedes flight simulations at the time. You would also be able to select from a range of different camera angles and viewpoints, as well as record all of the action and play it back.

"Development might have continued with less ambitious features, better time management and a longer timescale."

Acorn User magazine additionally revealed details about the game, though had clearly not seen anything of the game in action. Following obvious comparisons to *Chocks Away*, the magazine explained how the missions were to be structured differently and increase in size and difficulty as you progress, with elements of teamwork occasionally required for some.

The teamwork referred to a planned ability to play missions with a second player, as well as looking after computer-controlled planes as part of a mission. There were also to be multiplayer options of setting up two teams of ten planes; one or two of those planes being controlled by yourself and possibly a second player, with the players either on the same or different sides, ready to battle against each other.

Many features would never see fruition. A few months into 1992, 4D became concerned when progress started to stall. "4D planned the release of the game, anticipating a high level of productivity. "During the development of *Chocks*

Away, I had been very focused and was quite a recluse," recalled Andrew. "Although many features were in development, such as graphics and smarter AI, these were not coherently put together as missions or gameplay structure, and remained only in a prototype stage. 3D models for the planes and AI and logic to control their flight were present. There were also features to set camera focus on the enemy planes, where it was fun to watch the AI battles."

"All development was stored on floppy disks, with many versions and backups ending up on lots of disks that were thrown away at some point."

In early 1992, Stephen Scott became briefly involved, producing some artwork for the game. Andrew felt this might have been an attempt to help the stagnating development along, but it was Stephen who had himself approached 4D to do the work whilst still undertaking his A-levels.

"It was a fun thing to do at the time. 4D were happy for me to do an initial loading screen upon asking them, but I had no idea of any problems," began Steve. "I happened to have built and painted an Airfix kit model of a *Spitfire*, and it sat on a shelf behind where my Acorn A3000 and monitor was stationed. I used *ProArtisan 2* to create the screen and performed some touch-ups in *Paint*. I did draw the plane first and then added scenery later."

"It took a few days to finish; bear in mind, that I used the mouse to draw, no tablets used. Drawing with a mouse is hard, thank goodness for the 'Undo' button! I sent it to 4D, and, for some reason, one thing led to another, and I ended up getting a free copy of *Birds of War* as payment." It had now been approximately eight months since the start, and things hadn't progressed any further. 4D had by now lost patience and decided to cancel and cut its losses.

"The 4th Dimension had an invested interest in the progression of the game's development. During development, I was advanced royalties (I seem to remember figures of about £500-£1,000 every month or deadline). Development might have continued with less ambitious features, better time management and a longer timescale," reflected Andrew. "During mid-1992, I started to work in partnership with another developer (Tim Parry – an old school friend) on a new Archimedes game called *Stunt Racer 2000*."

Ironically, their new game was taken on and published by 4D in 1993, before they then embarked on their final Archimedes development *Star Fighter 3000*. This resulted in full-time employment at Krisalis, converting *Star Fighter* to the 3DO before going their separate ways. Andrew later went on to work at Eurocom and Disney and now works at Microsoft as an audio programmer. *Spitfire Fury* was quickly forgotten and has since become a mystery for many Archimedes fans who remember the adverts.

Could the game ever be found? Some years ago, a copy of Andrew's development system passed into the hands of Jon Abbott, who runs the Archimedes Software Preservation project. He confirmed that there was nothing of the game present when he looked through the archives. The Archimedes Public Domain Library then released a *Flight Simulators* collection containing a title named *Spitfire Fury*. Initially thought to be Andrew's game, it was disappointingly found to be nothing more than a game created in a flight simulator kit.

Superior Software's Richard Hanson informed us that Mark Botterill sadly passed away some years ago. Unfortunately, Steve was also not available to talk about copies of the game. Andrew also had bad news: "All traces have been lost. At the time, I had an Archimedes A310 without a hard drive," he confirmed. "All development was stored on floppy disks, with many versions and backups ending up on lots of disks that were thrown away at some point. It was only in 1994 that I eventually upgraded to an Archimedes A4000, with a hard drive."

It is still possible that Gordon (who we were unable to get a response from) has remnants of his old work, which could be something for the future, but it is unlikely. So far, the only remains of *Spitfire Fury* are Stephen's unused and recovered loading screen. Sadly, this is one *Spitfire* where you may never get to hear its engine roar.

Above: The box inlay for *Chocks Away* (Archimedes), the game that started it all, and which would lead to *Spitfire Fury*.

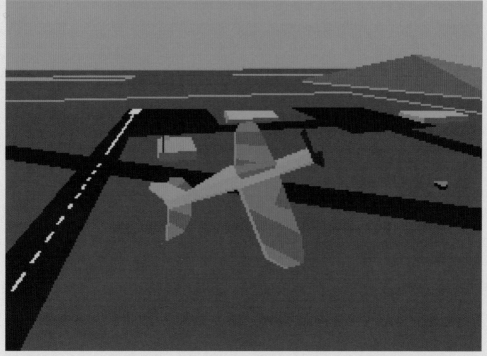

Top: Unused loading screen (Archimedes) that Stephen Scott keenly made to help out production of the game.

Above/Opposite: Artist's recreated screens from grainy magazine screenshots of *Spitfire Fury* (Archimedes), which Andrew confirmed were from the actual development.

Akira
Company merger

Year: 1994
Developer:
Black Pearl Software
Platforms: Nintendo
Game Boy, SEGA Mega
Drive (Pictured) and CD,
SEGA Game Gear and
Super Nintendo

After witnessing the incredible Japanese anime film of the same name, Black Pearl's CEO, Lawrence Siegel, saw something special. Created with passion, the team was set on developing a game with a variety of different stage types, including third-person motorcycle scenes and platform levels. It was cancelled not long after a merger with THQ – the parent company was seemingly not interested. Other conversions befell a similar fate, but Hidden Palace recovered an early SEGA Mega Drive prototype in late 2019.

Available to play
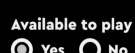
Yes   No

Lethal Weapon

Contractual obligations

Year: 1992
Developer: Ocean Software
**Platforms: SEGA Master System
and Game Gear**

Available to play
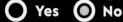 Yes No

Ocean Software has always been synonymous with producing either arcade conversions or film-licensed titles. Licences for titles such as *Robocop*, *Batman* and *The Addams Family* were very successful for the Manchester-based company, so it was no surprise when *Lethal Weapon* was to be added to that long list. Although just called *Lethal Weapon*, the game was to coincide with the release of the third film and would feature elements from the entire film series.

While Eurocom Entertainment Software developed the Nintendo versions of the game for Ocean, others handled the likes of the Commodore Amiga, Atari ST, Commodore 64 and PC editions of the game. But, in addition to this, there was also a SEGA Master System and Game Gear version on the list that wasn't known about, at least not that well known anyway.

The first suggestion of a conversion for SEGA's 8-bit console and handheld was thanks to the recovery of some impressive music demos from Jeroen Tel's collection, which were made available online around 2010. However, the project was something of a blur to Jeroen.

"I don't know much about the game itself. I composed the music whilst at Probe Software," Jeroen recalled. "It was an 'urgent project' issued by Ocean. I just had game design documents but not the game itself and a list of the tunes/sound effects required. So I couldn't tell you anything about the game really." The tune set was not fully complete, with many level tunes missing, and was likely to be an early demonstration of progress from Jeroen to Ocean. Some of the tunes were based on those produced for the Amiga and SNES editions.

It seemed plausible that it could have been Probe (which had been involved on a lot of Master System games) that was the main development team. However, after 'probing' most of its ex-developers, it was discovered that the conversion was actually done in-house at Ocean. The music was likely a paid favour from Probe due to a shortage of available musicians at Ocean. Jeroen had already done a number of tunes for Ocean before and was well known.

Although Ocean's Gary Bracey had zero recollection about the SEGA conversion, QA lead Tim Welch recalled that the team was, in fact, made up of Andrew Deakin (programming) and Ivan Horn (graphics and design). "I can confirm that Andrew and myself did work on *Lethal Weapon*," Ivan confirmed, once finally tracked down. Unfortunately, Andrew declined to talk about his past work.

Main development started on the SEGA Master System edition, which would later be ported over to the Game Gear with minor graphical enhancements and screen adjustments. According to Ivan, Gary Bracey would oversee development and would check on progress every now and then. "Development of the game straddled a move from the old Central Street office to the new one in Castlefield.

I remember that the project was quite a rush job," explained Ivan about the development. "Apparently, Ocean had some kind of agreement with Nintendo at the time about not putting anything out on SEGA platforms."

Intriguingly, this was also one of the first SEGA games that Ocean was attempting to produce. Ocean was potentially about to break that agreement now, though, in later years, there would be Ocean games appearing on the likes of the SEGA Mega Drive.

Both the Eurocom and other Ocean versions of the game were quite different in style from one another. Ivan informed us that their SEGA version was also quite different, featuring yet another design, compared with the other versions that Ocean produced and released. However, it was closer to the Amiga/SNES version in style than the very different NES and GB editions. Mick West later confirmed that Andrew and Ivan's development was very much a separate development and that he had no involvement, even though he revealed working on an unreleased Mega Drive conversion of the SNES game, showing how much Ocean was pushing to release on SEGA platforms.

"My memory of the game was that it was similar to most of the Ocean action games of the time (scrolling, action shooters)," reflected Ivan. "One level was set on top of a moving train, possibly also inside of it, that included moving obstacle avoidance gameplay." Other levels were of a similar theme to the internal Ocean versions – including docks, sewers, building site themes. The range of enemies would also be similar, with dynamite-loving criminals and your usual baddies with guns and knives.

The game also shared the mechanic of being able to choose between Murtaugh and Riggs. In the case of Ivan and Andrew's version, though, you could switch as many times as you liked between both characters at particular points in play. Each character had varying strengths and weaknesses, which would be crucial to completing specific parts of the game.

"One level was set on top of a moving train, possibly also inside of it, that included moving obstacle avoidance gameplay."

Compared with the Amiga version, where both characters could shoot, Murtaugh would be the only character able to do so and would also be able to push large objects (such as barrels/crates). Riggs, on the other hand, would only be able to punch/kick and not push items, but he was far more agile in comparison to Murtaugh. This allowed for a slight puzzle element to the gameplay to be established in places, echoing slightly from the *Head over Heels'* team mechanic that worked so well previously for Ocean (minus maybe Riggs jumping on Murtaugh's head!).

Games based on films were often subject to changes requested from the studios, and *Lethal Weapon* was no exception to this. "I remember having to change the Murtaugh sprites after some feedback from Danny Glover's agent saying they were too caricatured," confirmed Ivan. "Also, in the original game proposed to the IP holder, there were some guard dogs to shoot, but that was knocked away due to Riggs being an animal lover." Apart from that, things would otherwise run smoothly for the rest of the design, with very little in the way of changes requested.

After a few quick months of intense work, the game was fully completed for both SEGA platforms and within a tight deadline set by management. "As I remember, the game was complete and had gone through QA," Ivan confirmed. "We had the game fully working on the Game Gear, and it had at least some testing carried out on the platform." Only minor additions were made to get it working on the Game Gear by adjusting the head-up display to fit with the lower resolution, as well as adding colours from the extended palette.

The game was very playable and was reported to have done well during testing, which was overseen by Tim Welch (who didn't respond to requests to talk). However, Ocean had a sudden change of heart and decided not to release the game, much to Ivan's surprise. "I've no idea what the actual reason was," he began. "I'd left Ocean for a few months on completion of that project (returning a few months later to work on *Dennis* on the SNES), so it's possible the decision to scrap it could have been taken after. I would imagine that, as the company had several big-name titles coming out on the SNES, the decision was made to keep to the agreement with Nintendo rather than 'upset the apple cart'."

Although no one could recall exactly why the game was cancelled, it is strongly believed to be a result of a possible agreement that Ocean had with Nintendo. Ocean may have tried to negotiate out of its agreement at that point in time and failed, which left the completed conversion in limbo. It would be another year before Ocean would finally see games released on the SEGA platforms.

A cancelled project is always frustrating, but, for Ivan, it was just a case of moving swiftly on to other projects. The game was archived and forgotten about within the Ocean vaults, its whereabouts now completely unknown. Sadly, Ivan had kept nothing from the game, apart from a film script containing scenes that never made it to the final film.

Andrew may have something of the game, but, by not wanting to look back on past work, it is very unlikely we will ever find out if he has. The best option may now lie with someone with ties to Ocean who may have kept hold of a prototype cartridge or a disk backup – the search is now very much on to save what could have been a solid film tie-in on the SEGA platforms.

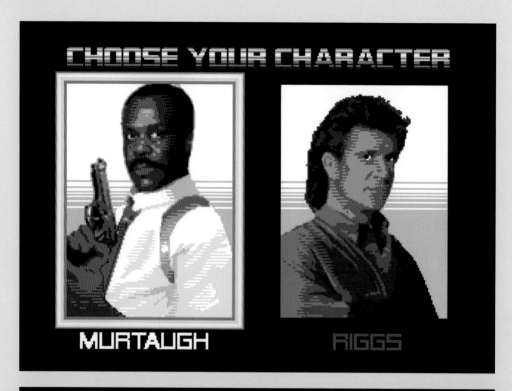

Above: Artist's impressions of how *Lethal Weapon* (Master System) may have looked, based on developer recollections, including a character selection screen and train-themed level.

Top: Jeroen Tel's music player for *Lethal Weapon* (Master System). Bottom: Artist's impression of *Lethal Weapon's* (Master System) sewer level, based on developer recollections.

Rolling Thunder
Declining Lynx sales

Year: 1992
Developer: Atari Games
Platform: Atari Lynx

Available to play

◯ Yes ◉ No

The intention was just to cover a single Lynx title with *Vindicators*, but, like buses, two always seem to come along at once when you least expect it. That was indeed the case when the opportunity arose to shed light on yet another Lynx title at the same time and also solve the mystery of another title that still haunts Lynx fans today.

Following its launch, Atari Corporation was steadily building a solid line-up for its new handheld, using its back catalogue for inspiration as well as licensing titles from others. Namco arcade classic *Rolling Thunder* was chosen as part of that line-up, which was perhaps risky, considering the arcade was released way back in 1986. It was also a title that had already seen home conversions a few years previously.

Rolling Thunder was a scrolling platform shooter, which arcade classics *Shinobi* and *Shadow Dancer* no doubt took notes from, sharing the ability to perform impressive jumps between platforms. Perhaps itself inspired by *James Bond*, you control a secret agent named Albatross, who must save a missing female agent named Leila, kidnapped by the Geldra group.

Throughout the game, you mostly dispose of various hooded bad guys with your pistol, who appear from doors and from the sides. The aim was simply to survive and get to the end of each level, with level environments ranging from warehouses, apartments and underground caves. You had limited ammo throughout and had to conserve and replenish it by entering doors with an ammo sign. On later levels, you would encounter enemies, such as bats, panthers, ninjas and even lava men, who try to thwart your rescue effort at every opportunity. A total of ten levels concluded with a final battle against the head of Geldra, Maboo.

It was very tough to play, but a title perfectly suited to the Lynx, where there was an opportunity to make a decent stab at an accurate conversion. Assigned to the task was Matt Markwalder, who, at the age of just 15, had previously started his very own software company called Banana Development, specialising in converting games for the PC market. A few years on, Matt was bought out of the company and would take up a developer role at Atari's Lombard Offices during the fall of 1990.

Based on recovered documents, it's believed that Matt signed up to an agreement where he would get $25,000 on completion of the project with royalties of $1.06 per unit sold from the first 60,000 sales and then $1.25 thereafter. A decent deal with plenty of incentive to produce a decent conversion.

The game's graphic artist (who we have been asked not to name) was the only dedicated artist at Lombard at the time. The artist couldn't recall much on the game as they were thinly spread across multiple projects and also handling box artwork on top of that. Unfortunately, *Rolling Thunder*'s game art would suffer as a result, where the levels and sprites produced were not of great quality and didn't work well on actual Lynx hardware. Matt would call upon newly employed graphic artist Robb Mariani (who is today a TV host) to help improve the quality where possible.

Robb previously had worked for Matt's Banana Development company, which helped lead to his role at Atari. "I received a call from Matt from his desk at the Lombard offices. He asked if I wanted to interview for an artist role," Robb recalled. "By that time, I had put together a small body of work in the pixel art side, so I aced the interview and got the job. Matt was complaining that the previous artist's work sucked and was not compatible, so I was assigned to be Matt's 'horsepower' artist for speed reasons, and off I went."

Matt initially was going to share memories of his time on the game, but no more was heard after that. Joel Seider filled in and suggested that Matt had struggled overall, with development stalling after several months of work. Everything that was produced would equate to a rolling (no pun intended) demo with little or no playability at all. "Much of the quality control was lost. It took a skilled developer to go through Matt's code (or any developer's code) and verify what he was doing. Progress for *Rolling Thunder* was the equivalent of a train with wheels welded to the tracks," Robb described of that first iteration.

"Rolling Thunder was pretty much a one-man show."

When Atari realised that *Rolling Thunder* was going nowhere but off a cliff, Matt was let go from Atari, and the project was temporarily paused. Development would eventually be reassigned to a new recruit called Chuck Ernst, in his first and only game development at Atari. Chuck had also worked at Banana Development and had known Robb since college, both studying graphic design together. A talented developer who was self-taught in C/C++ and assembly language whilst at high school, Chuck originally helped Robb to get a graphic artist position at Banana, so Robb returned the favour for Chuck whilst at Atari.

"*Rolling Thunder* was pretty much a one-man show. A game that probably took eight people to make initially, then you have to make it fit on a new platform with less resource," Chuck began. "After about six months or more of absolutely no progress with Matt's version, they decided to have someone else come in and finish it. It meant starting over as everything in there was a bit of a mess."

During the moment of purgatory for the project and after assigning Chuck, the original graphic artist was hijacked onto other projects, so Joel Seider would step in to help get the project back on track. "At the time, when Chuck took over, I think I might have been between projects, so I agreed to help out on art. The artwork from the original artist was not the best, and I spent a bunch of time cleaning up sprites," Joel recalled. Everything, including the background art, was started again, except for Robb's early work. Robb stayed on the project with a particular focus on sprite and animation work, which was starting to look great within the Lynx constraints. He also assisted with constructing the maps from his and Joel's artwork.

Joel worked mostly on background art, trying to be resourceful with tiles and make as much as possible reusable for other levels, with palette shifts to save space. There was a major problem with the arcade provided, though, which made it impossible to complete all of the artwork required. "The arcade we had only had eight of the ten levels as the machine was an early prototype *Rolling Thunder*. It was all set up for success really!" Chuck laughed.

Adding to the woes, obtaining artwork directly from the arcade was not easy either. "We should have been able to rip artwork directly from the ROMs, but our chip reader was broken," Chuck explained. "Atari wouldn't buy a new one as they were 1,200 bucks or something like that. They felt it was cheaper to have an artist recreate the artwork from scratch, which then ended up taking more time to recreate!"

"In theory, you could take that artwork and scale it down, but, because you were dealing with such a primitive palette, it usually didn't turn out very well," added Joel. "If you wanted quality, you were better off redrawing everything by hand using the original as reference. So, the process for transferring the artwork was completely manual anyway for *Rolling Thunder*. We would look at the game, then redraw each level and each frame of animation by hand."

Luckily, a pause mode installed by Ed Schneider would help with capturing key parts of the game and give some relief to the art team. "Part of my job was to play the coin-op and study the animation and graphics, including mapping out the entire game – level by level. It was a long and daunting process, with each of us having to play the game to death. I was able to play and stop-frame much of the action and then go back to my desk and draw what I saw," Robb recalled.

"Robb did animations where he would animate a character, and we'd reuse that animation to create the other characters, just with different colours applied," added Chuck. "So, for the hooded dudes, some would have a yellow mask on their face or a purple hood. There were probably 16 bad guys that all used the same art, and it was really efficient. Then a monkey wrench was thrown in when we discovered we had to put a panther in there that couldn't share the same animation frames."

Robb recalled that his style was simple, but he obsessed with every detail and sharpened contrast with darker tones, making the artwork look superb on a real Lynx screen. The process was still very difficult and was a major challenge for both himself and Joel. "What few people realise is that you had an 8–16 colour palette and a colour 0 for transparency," explained Robb. "Each colour palette was locked in after a calculation/consensus as to what tones the game had (*Rolling Thunder* had blue, purple, green primary tones, etc.). Palettes were also separated; one for backgrounds, and one for sprites. Each level could alternate a background palette, but the sprite palette was locked in. That meant I had to try to make the main character, all the enemies and animations from the same eight shades – seven, counting a neutral colour, 0."

"Progress for Rolling Thunder was the equivalent of a train with wheels welded to the tracks."

With the artwork progressing steadily, Chuck was regularly getting pulled onto other projects and testing, meaning that development time on *Rolling Thunder* often took a back seat. One particular distraction would see Chuck temporarily moved on to a major new hardware project bubbling away at Atari.

"For around three months, I was tasked with getting up to speed on the Atari Panther, doing debugging," explained Chuck. "I was given a development kit, essentially an Atari 7800 with a couple more K of RAM and slightly faster CPU. It was supposed to be their next Bleeding Edge console (before the Jaguar), but it was a mess and pretty much didn't do anything it was supposed to do. I was totally frustrated. Eventually, Atari went, 'We're going to get our asses kicked by the Super Nintendo!', which had scaling and other crazy technology. So they killed the Panther, but didn't tell me! A month later, I get a call saying, 'Oh, we killed the Panther, so go back to work on *Rolling Thunder*'."

After perhaps a lucky 'Panther' escape, *Rolling Thunder* was by now looking great, with all levels (except the final two) complete. Chuck managed to catch up and start rapidly piecing everything together that Joel and Robb had provided so far. "It started to all look dead on," recalled Chuck. "All the play mechanics were there, and it was actually fun to play. It just had a couple of bugs that I was still working on, mostly with the transition from horizontal to vertical scrolling. I think it would have done and sold well on release."

No music had yet been arranged for the game, with Chuck just creating basic sound effects from the arcade himself, after working on a sound compression routine with Joel. "We had 16-bit audio that you had to crunch down to 4-bit. Both I and Joel worked initially on audio compression that ended up in *Elvira*. I needed to figure compression out too, so we just combined some research on it together," Chuck confirmed.

As development swerved well into 1992, the team was still getting regularly pulled onto other tasks, and development could not be completed until those final levels were accounted for. Atari had still not replaced the prototype arcade with a complete board, and catalogues were now even advertising the game with screenshots from Tengen's Nintendo conversion sneakily depicted as Lynx screens. Things felt haphazard and disorganised, with no real push to get the game finished, contributing towards ever-ebbing morale.

"It was really a struggle," Joel summarised. "Matt was not a very good programmer, and the original artist wasn't the greatest hand-pixel artist, so, in many ways, it was kind of doomed from the start. Chuck, Robb and I were definitely more skilled in our respective areas, but, by then, Atari were struggling."

"It was disappointing that, with the Lynx, the hardware was so advance, but marketing didn't keep up with it and made the dumbest decisions," added Chuck. "I remember going to an arcade and watching a kid play *Mortal Kombat*, tearing someone's head off and blood going everywhere. I went back to work and said we should definitely convert this game to the Lynx as it was going to be big. Management went, 'Nah!! We've already got *Pit Fighter*! Same thing!' If we had done it, the game would probably have helped save the company!"

Morale hit the floor when the Lombard staff was shocked by the closure of the office during the summer of 1992. Employees were given a choice to either move to other premises (including Sunnyvale, California) or find new employment. Some developers were additionally offered contracts to finish off their nearly completed Lynx developments from home. As with *Vindicators*, Chuck would continue to work on the *Rolling Thunder* project under a work-for-hire agreement for Atari.

Joel had decided to move on, next working on the Super Nintendo version of *Bubsy*. However, Robb would hang around to help Chuck with missing artwork, as well as implement the intro, end and status screens. However, to be able to finish, Chuck had to get details of those two missing levels for the remaining artwork to be completed and implemented into the game.

"All the play mechanics were there, and it was actually fun to play."

"We ended up going to this arcade, called Dennis' Place for Games, with a camcorder and videotaped the gameplay," recalled Chuck. "I think I spent $40-worth of quarters to film the rest of it. The owner was asking, 'What are you doing?' and I responded, 'You don't mind if I videotape this?' and then was asked, 'What for??'. Halfway through, the joysticks then stopped going left, which made the game even harder to finish with no movement in that direction. At that point, I was so angry, and I was throwing things. It was 12 o'clock in the afternoon, there was no one in there, and you just felt like a degenerate."

Although Robb had now finally been able to start creating and mapping out the last two levels, Atari had begun to get impatient with the progress, desperate to get more titles out to buoy the struggling Lynx. They requested that *Rolling Thunder* was completed by mid-December 1992. However, Chuck had decided that things couldn't carry on the way they were, with the financial situation and arrangement not exactly stable. Feeling Atari was hitting the rocks financially, both he and Robb found more stable roles at SEGA, resulting in a complete walkaway from the development.

The game was left with no music, two levels outstanding, a missing final boss battle, and some bug fixing and polish needed. It was tantalisingly close to completion, and, had the Panther distraction not got in the way for those three months for Chuck, it may well have snuck out before the Lombard closure. Perhaps then we'd be talking about a classic arcade conversion instead.

Atari's final deadline subsequently passed, and the contract was cancelled, with Chuck having to return all hardware and software. Atari would then try one last attempt to salvage the project in late December 1992 by calling on external developer Al Baker to finish off Chuck's work. John Skruch would send over all of the development work to try and get a review and quote on how much it would take to finish the game, stating that, "The game was apparently just two weeks away from completion."

Al had no recollection of ever working on the conversion, with no personal correspondence or notes to jog any memories. It seems plausible that Al gave a quote that was more than Atari were willing to wait or pay for. If the work was taken on by someone else, then it likely got caught up in the culling that Atari did for many of its planned releases, which had also ended the *Vindicators* conversion. Additionally, the licence could simply have expired with Namco to convert the game, and Atari decided not to renew. Unfortunately, John Skruch didn't respond to contact attempts to confirm what exactly happened, but the game would disappear from release schedules not long afterwards.

"Atari knew the Lynx was done at the time, and there was not even any real life support," suggested Chuck. "It was just a case of getting those last games done, and that would be the end of the system. It was kind of depressing and really hard to get motivated when people didn't care and just wanted the game to be done and know when. It was a shame as, when I was growing up, I was really into Atari. It ended up though being a case of 'never meet your heroes'."

"It was 12 o'clock in the afternoon, there was no one in there, and you just felt like a degenerate."

Even almost 30 years on, the experience is still slightly raw for those involved, with chances of the game surviving expected to be low. Matt Markwalder's original development with the original graphic artist's artwork may never be found unless someone happens to uncover any prototype cartridges in the future. But miraculously, Robb did keep some of his sprite work, which will be added to the Games That Weren't website.

Joel also suggested that he may have artwork somewhere, but he couldn't find anything in time for publication. "It would be on 3.5-inch floppy disks for the Commodore Amiga. Good luck finding any of those still working, especially in the US!" he said. There were recent rumours that Telegames had a complete version of the game (unpublished due to not being able to get the licence), which was never the case as the game never saw completion.

More crucially, though, Chuck still has all of his Lynx development work backed up, which he hopes to get running in the future. The development systems still need attention to get going again, but it is promising to hear that something of the game is at least safe. With just two levels missing and a practically complete Lynx game to be recovered, was *Rolling Thunder* really the masterful arcade conversion wished for by Lynx fans? Hopefully, someday, we may all finally get the chance to judge for ourselves.

Above: *Rolling Thunder* (arcade) showing the first level from the game.

Above: Atari's own catalogue (Italian edition), advertising *Rolling Thunder* for the Lynx as 'coming soon' but, oddly, using screenshots from the Nintendo Entertainment System version.

Above: Artist's recreation of *Rolling Thunder* (Atari Lynx) title screen, based on a grainy screenshot from *Grey Matters* magazine, which Chuck believes is from his development.

Above: Artist's impressions of *Rolling Thunder* (Atari Lynx), based on a rare (but low-quality) screenshot of the Lynx version from *GamePro* magazine, showing two different scenes.

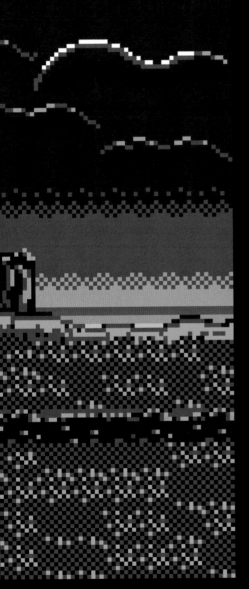

Lemmings 2
Dying
market

Year: 1994
Developer: Spidersoft
Platforms: SEGA Master
System (pictured)
and Game Gear

Sadly, it was too late in the day for this SEGA 8-bit bound sequel, with Psygnosis cancelling due to the dying market and infeasible cartridge production costs. Almost 20 years later, developer Matt Taylor recovered both conversions for all to enjoy. Although the amount of lemmings on screen is limited, it's a fantastic conversion.

"To this day, *Lemmings 2* is one of the most enjoyable projects I have ever worked on. It had everything an 8-bit console developer could want: a fantastic game to port, tricky technical challenges to overcome, and a great publisher to work with. My biggest challenge was developing a solution to enable lemmings to modify large swathes of the landscape at any pixel position – something 8-bit consoles were never designed to do.

Once that had been achieved, only a handful of skills and levels were impossible to implement, so it remains a faithful port of the original. It was disappointing to learn that the SEGA Master System and Game Gear versions would not be released – especially as I felt the Game Gear version was the best, with better colours and sampled sounds. But, now they can be enjoyed by everyone, everywhere, thanks to emulation."

Matt Taylor, developer

Available to play
◉ Yes ◯ No

Waterworld
Flawed game design

Year: 1995
Developer: Software Creations
Platforms: 3DO and Sony PlayStation

Available to play

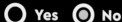 Yes No

Post-apocalyptic themes have always been very popular, not only with films, such as *Mad Max*, but in games too. Back in 1995, the budget-busting film *Waterworld* was released to the world, and you could say that it was a sort of *Mad Max* on water. It's most famous though for being the most expensive film ever made at the time.

The story of *Waterworld* is set hundreds of years from now, following on from the melting of the polar ice caps. The sea level has risen over 7,600m and now covers practically all of the land, meaning that everyone is probably seasick. Kevin Costner leads the way as 'the Mariner', who gets caught up in a war between sea pirates and an Atoll (a floating human community), with the pirates searching for a girl who supposedly has coordinates to a rare area of land named 'Dryland'. The promise of the film was massive at the time, and video game developments were on the cards way before the film had been set for release. Both Interplay and Ocean Software would battle it out, securing differing rights across a number of platforms.

Ocean would end up handling console editions for the Nintendo Game Boy, Nintendo Virtual Boy, Super Nintendo, SEGA Saturn and SEGA Mega Drive, with a completely different design compared with Interplay. Interplay themselves would look to publish a real-time strategy for the PC (which was eventually released), developed by UK-based Intelligent Games. They also had rights to produce efforts for both the 3DO and Sony PlayStation platforms, both the focus for this write-up. Although not focusing on Ocean's unreleased SEGA Mega Drive and Saturn efforts, both titles are briefly covered towards the end for completeness.

Interplay's 3DO and PlayStation developments were action-based, rather than strategy like the PC edition, and would be separately handled by another UK-based development team, Software Creations (based in Manchester). Given the task of coming up with a design for the game was Ste Pickford, who, via his Zee-3 website, recalled how he first got involved.

"I had just completed a project at Creations, hanging around chatting early one evening before heading to the pub, when Richard Kay came upstairs to the office and said, 'Who wants to go to Hawaii?'," Ste recalled. "A week later, I was on the other side of the world, taking a tour of the *Waterworld* set at Interplay's expense to help me design a game based on the movie. I think me and the Interplay associate producer I was working with were the only game developers there – all the other people on the trip – from various video game companies (Ocean, Nintendo, and several others), staying in our 5-star hotel – were senior management. Funny that."

Although a fun and eventful trip, there were early warning signs when requirements for the game design were to prove frustrating from the off. "Interplay wanted a rendered video game with streamed FMV and sprites over the top – a copy of *Star Wars: Rebel Assault*. It was a truly terrible idea," lamented Ste. "I remember pointing out that the *Star Wars* game only (just about) worked because it was set in canyons that were visually interesting. We had an empty ocean with nothing but a horizon for *Waterworld*, so we weren't even going to be able to make the rendered video look that good. Making the background a pre-rendered movie of a flat ocean, with no ability to change direction, it was destined to result in a dull-looking, unplayable mess!"

"Musical duties would be handled by Manchester's Hallé Orchestra."

Ste pushed for something more akin to *Wave Race* on the Nintendo 64 (released a year later), with dynamic waves bobbing up and down and free movement to enable a larger variety of playability options. Interplay would not hear the concerns raised or Ste's better proposal. Resigned to defeat, the project would commence following Interplay's wishes in August 1994, over six months before the film was due for cinema release. Ste would put together the best design he could, creating an on-rails shooter.

"I produced a massive Game Design Document (GDD) that was probably way too long and detailed. This was at the height of the days when publishers weighed GDDs (as opposed to reading them – which nobody ever did) to decide how good they were!" smiled Ste. A team was quickly assembled to handle both conversions. Lorraine Star joined the project as the producer, though could no longer recall much about the development when questioned. However, she commented that it was a great team behind the game, just that the design itself was weak thanks to Interplay. She informed *PLAY* magazine back in December 1995 that the team felt they had actually improved upon the original specification they were given.

Carleton Handley was assigned lead developer for the Sony PlayStation edition, with Peter Scott separately developing the 3DO edition. "The PlayStation was an unknown quantity when I was hired; I don't think the console was even released in Japan at the time," Carleton recalled. "We used the very first development PlayStations, connected to a P90 PC running Windows 3.11 – the very first Pentium machines. Everybody else in the office was quite jealous!"

"I had a 3DO dev kit connected via the Nubus slot of a Mac Quadra 700," added Peter. "I was the first person in the company to get a modem, so I could email builds to Interplay each week. This often led to having many people around my computer at lunchtime looking at this new thing called the 'Internet'. Best memory of that time was talking to Americans and trying to freak them out with *Microsoft Comic Chat*, seeing how quickly you could get banned by being as offensive as possible. I held the record – one sentence – but I will not tell you what it was; just believe it was outrageous!"

When not insulting people across the globe, the team worked hard on trying to produce what they could. Completing the team and helping to polish up the proverbial 'turd' was lead graphic artist Andrew Pearce, with supporting graphic artists in the forms of Greg Holt, Ste Watson, Stephen Millership and Justin Eagleton (who were mostly unavailable or declined to give their recollections). A fairly sizeable team even back then, but a lot of 3D rendering work was required for all of the game's levels. In particular, Justin remembered them spending most of the time making the water look good, rather than the game.

Greg was the environment artist for the game, and recalled the following on his personal website: "I was part of a four-artist team who created, animated and rendered over an hour of cinematics and background stills. I was in charge of creating the 'sprites' for the player and the baddies." The pre-rendered artwork that the artists produced would stretch across 11 levels, created using a combination of *3DS Max* and *Deluxe Paint*. All of the levels were based on major scenes from the script that the team had seen, for example, focusing around the Atoll and the large oil tanker that featured towards the end of the film.

Musical duties would be handled by Manchester's Hallé Orchestra, who produced a wide range of dramatic orchestral backing tracks to each of the levels, cut sequences and titles. It couldn't be recalled who handled creating sound effects overall for the game.

Although there was a detailed outline to follow, with scenes and suggested enemies to shoot, the actual level design and gameplay elements were not all set in stone. "That was mostly left to me, and it wasn't a particularly strong point of mine," confessed Carleton. "The first level was a particularly dull one called 'Get the Limes'. I think it was just a rendered sea section, but there was the odd crate, around which you could shoot to collect limes. I think this seemed an important part of the script, showing how desperate the people were that they went to such lengths. So we added it to the game as a gentle introduction between the chaotic blasting action! In all levels, you just controlled a cursor to shoot mostly tiny sprites. About the only other bit of excitement were the pick-ups that were sometimes dropped. So you could have a machine gun for a little while, for example. Excited yet??"

With the game design dictated by the rails-based theme and set on water, there was little opportunity for much variation at all in the gameplay (as Ste had predicted), and there were going to be 11 levels that needed to be filled. Enemies would appear in the levels in a pretty bland way due to the uninspiring way that the camera would move around for the levels. "The main levels just had a camera stuck in the middle of the main scene, rotating slowly around. So the gameplay was closer to *Operation Wolf* than the more modern style of *Virtua Cop* at the time," explained Carleton.

"I remember there was also an underwater section where you swam through a water-covered city, but I cannot for the life of me remember why," added Peter. "We did also play with an open-water sequence, where you were attacked by Smokers, etc. between levels. I think this was dropped as the frame rate on the 3DO was terrible."

The open-water sequences were to occur as real-time 3D sections and represented moving between each level as a small respite from the dull main events. Although dropped from the 3DO edition, Carleton would keep it within the PlayStation edition due to the machine being more adept at handling real-time 3D.

After several months, the game was progressing as well as it could be, though it was a major learning curve for both developers, in particular for Peter with the rather hampered 3DO architecture. "One of the biggest issues was that we were forced to use their APIs for graphics rendering, but, unfortunately, they were terrible and extremely inefficient," Peter explained. "I remember doing a basic 'bob' test to see how many 'bobs' I could render in a frame, and it was around 70. I could do more on the Amiga! The API got better as they did future releases for it, but the 3D rendering was always terrible compared with the PlayStation."

As a result, the PlayStation edition mostly led the way, thanks to its vastly superior Software Development Kit (SDK). "I just used that standard SDK, which was being updated quite frequently back then. Peter could take most of the code (written in C) that I'd done and use it, and I took any relevant bits off him where I could," confirmed Carleton.

"We were firefighting the game from day one; the designs constantly changed, and the challenges of the new platforms kept forcing us to change things."

By now, there were working segments of the game that could be shown. Interplay decided to release a *3DO Buffet* CD, showing off demos of its upcoming games. It presented 3DO users with a non-playable and low-quality rolling demo of *Waterworld*, showing some of the rendered scenes that would have appeared in the game. Interestingly, there were no enemies shown or being shot, with just a basic score panel that didn't do anything. The trailer actually also gives away the ending of the game by showing one of the completion sequences where land is found.

The game was also shown at the European Computer Trade Show in September 1995, featuring in French magazine *CD Consoles*, and Carleton was interviewed by *PLAY* magazine in December 1995. The magazine reported that the game was around 70% complete at that time and was due for release in March 1996.

By now, most of the initial scenes were complete and slowly forming playable levels. There were around 100,000 frames of rendered animation included within the game, with heavy compression to get it working at 25 FPS on the 3DO and PlayStation platforms. Carleton told *PLAY* magazine back in late 1995 that it was a massive pain having to re-render everything if any problems were found, it was very time-consuming, and there were challenges trying to get the 2D sprites working over the top of the rendered 3D backgrounds without looking like they had just been pasted on.

Everything looked good, thanks to the excellent work of the artists, but it was still devoid of real playability and longevity. Whilst trying to struggle on with the hardware, there were always constant changes going on, either via the script or due to the hardware limitations. "We were firefighting the game from day one; the designs constantly changed, and the challenges of the new platforms kept forcing us to change things, so there were lots of late nights and weekends just to try and keep the project in some kind of workable shape," explained Peter.

Peter recalled some of the interesting script changes that occurred during the project. "Most of the time, it was just little things that changed. I remember one of the last updates where it went a little crazy," he recalled. "First was a sex scene addition after the Mariner's boat was burnt down – very sudden and completely out of context with what was going on. Then there was the crazy bungee jump from the air balloon at the end of the movie, which was just bizarre. We laughed and ridiculed it, expecting it to never go in... but it did!"

Seeing his predictions come true, Ste approached Interplay one last time to try and rescue the project, but it didn't work out. Perplexed, Ste decided to walk away from the project and move on to something else. His replacement was allocated in the form of Eitan Arrusi, who was hired by Interplay as an outside consultant to try and help things along to completion.

"Despite being competent, he, unfortunately, really clashed with our team," recalled Carleton. "He did a much more interesting render of a level through the existing models, but it didn't fit with the 2D sprites we had, and there was no chance we could change it all to full 3D that late on; the film had already been released and forgotten about! Also, the quality of the models used in the renders was far too high to be matched with the polygons the PS1 was able to draw."

Eitan had talent for sure, but he wanted to be a film director and tried to treat game development as a film production. However, the technology available at the time meant that his ideas couldn't quite translate across the way that he wanted. This caused friction with those in the team as it didn't fit in with their knowledge or way of working. "We probably treated him more harshly than he deserved. He was basically asking for the impossible though," Carleton explained. The team would end up spending several more months continuing to do battle with the game, but, even after all of this, Interplay frustratingly was not happy with the results and finally saw that the design was unworkable.

The film had, by now, been out for quite some time and hadn't done too great, and the games that saw release were also bombing too. It was too late to start things again for Software Creation's development, so the PS1 and 3DO editions were quietly dropped. The PS1 version ended up at around 80% complete. All the rendering, weapons and front-end screens were done, and you could shoot things. In comparison, the 3DO edition was a little bit further behind due to the platform struggles, with the mid-level open-water segment dropped due to frame rate issues. The team moved on to other projects and quickly tried to erase memories of what was a painful time for them.

"I remember there was also an underwater section where you swam through a water-covered city."

So, was it a case of 'I told you so'? "Oh god, yes!" Ste exclaimed. "Almost every cancelled game was obviously going to be crap right from the start, usually because of something dictated by the publisher that was obviously stupid. In this case, making a streaming rendered video-based game. So, while on one hand, it was disappointing to see the game cancelled, on the other hand, it proves you were right – it was a stupid idea!"

"It was a bad project from beginning to end," added Carleton. "I struggled getting to grips with the new hardware and 3D. Everything was a huge learning curve for us all, and two developers for two new formats just wasn't enough."

Ste just laughed when asked if there were any positives to be taken from the project. Carleton was more reflective: "Any experience in a job you're on is valuable, be it good or bad. I learnt C writing this project and got used to SDKs provided by the hardware manufacturers. There were lots of new things to learn coming straight from writing Game Gear projects – audio and video streaming, 3D model exporting, 3D rendering included." Peter colourfully concluded: "I learnt that I never want to do a game that is on rails with background video and sprites overlaid. Also, that the 3DO was a piece of crap!"

In comparison, Ocean's rather different design faired a bit differently for its games. They didn't have Interplay's very restrictive specification to work with, so they progressed much further, even though the games were decidedly average. However, neither the Mega Drive or Saturn versions would see the light of day due to a combination of platform demise and the poor outcome of the other released versions. Only the Super Nintendo, Game Boy and Virtual Boy developments by Ocean and Interplay's PC strategy would ever see a release.

Mega Drive users were lucky enough to see a pretty much complete version leaked that was very similar to the SNES edition. The Saturn edition was not so fortunate. Two sources, including the game's designer, Steve Woita, are said to have the complete game, though both are wary of releasing it due to legal issues. Universal Studios would very likely never allow anything of it to be released. "The Saturn version of *Waterworld* was a really fun game to play!" Steve told us. "It was completely finished, gold-mastered and ready for production. But a new company took over the USA part of Ocean of America at that time and cancelled it, and we were never really sure why."

The Saturn version currently only exists as a video of a cutscene online and as screenshots from the press, showing a large 3D open-world area to explore, with a reportedly stunning sea effect. It followed a similar direction to the Virtual Boy game (created by the same developers). Fans of the Saturn still hope that, someday, a leak will surface of what looks like a half-decent game, compared with the Interplay development.

With the 3DO and PlayStation editions, it looks bleak in terms of trying to find anything to show of the actual game. "The only thing I have is a 3DO magazine with a rolling demo of the game on it. I don't know why it's so jerky at the start; the game itself wasn't like that at all," confirmed Carleton. It was similar news from Pete, who, after looking through his backups, could not find anything of the game. Ste also no longer had any of his design documents relating to the game to give any further insight as much was left behind at Software Creations and likely binned.

"Perplexed, Ste decided to walk away from the project and move on to something else."

Out of all the artists, Greg did manage to recover some cutscene footage he had produced for the game. However, there has been nothing from an actual running version of the game itself to show for either platform, only magazine screenshots. Considering that there was not much of a game to play in the first place, are we really missing out on that much at all? It's merely a curiosity at best. Like many shipwrecks, perhaps this a game best left at the bottom of the ocean, and many of those involved would seem to agree.

Above: *Waterworld* (PlayStation). Two gameplay screenshots from Issue 2 of *PLAY* magazine, showing the overlaid sprites.

Above: Various screenshots from *CD Consoles* magazine – platform unknown. They accidentally show part of the end sequence rendering with the air-ship.

Above: Various cutscenes from a PC rendering recovered by artist Greg Holt and which he worked on directly. The bottom screen shows part of the end sequence from the game.

Above: *Waterworld* (3DO). Low-quality screens extracted from the *3DO Buffet* demo, showing title screen presentation, some gameplay scenes and cut sequences.

Dark Seed (aka Dragon's Heaven) Funding

Year: 1996
Developer: Kengo Asai
Platform: NEOGEO

A one-in-a-million finding, this early unnamed fighting game was established as being by Kengo Asai. Your player's characteristics would change based on the path you chose after each battle, affecting your strength during different time periods. The game was cancelled due to funding issues.

"Previous proto/dev carts I acquired contained revisions of an already released game, so I assumed this was no different. First dumping the EPROMS, the data was labelled *Voltage Fighter Gowkaizer*. The board had two SRAM memory cards with dead batteries that irrecoverably lost the text/overlay and sound data. Luckily, sprite data stored on flash memory was still intact.

Since the game looked to be *Gowkaizer*, I sat it to one side. After finally loading a new fix ROM to a SRAM card, I realised the two sprite flash cards were mislabelled and in the wrong slots. After switching them around, the game booted and wasn't at all what I expected. A weird experience seeing it for the first time, feeling almost guilty for having something like this. Didn't take the Internet long to find who worked on the game. An ambitious project I really wish had a chance to be completed."

Brian Hargrove, NEOGEO preservationist

Available to play

 Yes No

Virtual Tank
Poor console sales

Year: 1995
Developer: Boss Game Studios
Platform: Nintendo Virtual Boy

They helped rejuvenate the games industry after the 1983 crash with the Nintendo Entertainment System in the US, followed by blisteringly successful launches of the Game Boy and Super Nintendo. It seemed Nintendo could do no wrong at the time. So, when announcing that its next console was to be a portable virtual reality gaming device, there were one or two raised eyebrows. However, this was Nintendo, and 'failure' wasn't a familiar word to them.

To form a successful launch, it was crucial to gain the support of development studios to build up a solid pre- and post-launch portfolio. Also on the horizon was the new Nintendo 64 (N64) console (then under the early guises of Project Reality and Ultra 64), where a number of studios were keen to become officially licensed developers. One such studio was to be the newly launched Boss Game Studios (BGS) in 1994.

The studio was an offshoot of film company Boss Film Studios, seeing the potential that games were perhaps someday going to be as big or bigger than the film industry. "We were a small studio set up with the intention of making games using facilities of the special FX studio in Marina del Rey, California," Boss Game Studio's creative director at the time, Seth Mendelsohn, told us. "It was felt that we could use this facility to make content for games and also build a games development studio too. One of the managers had a connection with folks at Nintendo, so it was decided to open an office in Redmond, Washington – just down the street from them. We would start developing content for Nintendo from the start, prior to the launch of the N64."

With a working relationship firmly established early on with Nintendo, BGS would commence work on what would eventually become *Top Gear Rally*. Although not planning to develop anything for the upcoming Virtual Boy, Nintendo had a clever ploy, where some smaller studios had to agree to make a game for the platform in order to develop for the upcoming N64. The studio was hit with this requirement but didn't see it as a problem, rather more just another stream of income to help the fledgling company to get a foothold.

The Virtual Boy was an intriguing device, a 32-bit console built as a headset with two eyepieces to view games in stereoscopic red and black monochrome 3D. Part of the effect was achieved using parallax layers to give the illusion of depth. It was around the time that Virtual Reality was popular, thanks to the company Virtuality and its iconic arcade systems plus, of course, the film *Lawnmower Man* released a few years earlier. Thinking about what to produce for the unique hardware, it wouldn't take long until the perfect game hit the studio.

"Whilst having discussions with Nintendo, they showed us the development hardware. I saw the two separate joypads and immediately thought of *Battlezone*. I said to Colin Gordon [vice president of product development] that this thing is perfect for that kind of 3D game," recalled Seth. "Everyone said

'Yeah, you're right!' and then, on top of that, it was very much in line with the look and feel of those old vector games, so it made even more sense to make a *Battlezone* style game. The control system could be literally the same thing – pushing both sticks forwards to make the tank go forwards, both back to go back, and opposite directions controlling the directional movement. It could follow the exact style and learnings of *Battlezone*. We asked Nintendo 'Is anyone doing such a game?', and they responded 'Nope!', and so off we went to create a pitch."

In the original arcade, the task was simple: track down tanks and UFOs on your scanner and shoot them before they shoot you. You could hide behind rocks from enemy fire, but, most often, you had to quickly navigate your tank out of the firing line. The arcade controls were not everyone's cup of tea, so replicating on the Virtual Boy could risk alienating some games players.

Seth maintained that this would have been compensated for accordingly. "I imagine that, if you had never played *Battlezone*, the concept of two sticks forwards and two sticks back, especially the turning, would seem very odd," he admitted. "I imagine too that we probably would have looked into simpler control systems as an option anyway."

From the initial idea, Seth fleshed out a short brief with more detailed suggestions and ideas. Back at the studio, the concept was then assigned to artist Todd Downing to spend a few weeks producing visual sketches and further ideas that would go into pitching documents to present to Nintendo. Seth would continue to oversee the evolving of his 'baby' with great interest, seeing as it was one of the studio's first productions.

"It was never intended to be a full or hardcore simulation but just an action arcade game. We were aware that the style of the system wouldn't suit people playing for five and six hours at a time, so it made sense to have things broken down into smaller doses," explained Seth. "The flip side was that it still had to have more depth than the original *Battlezone* to take it forwards. Unlike the arcade that just really had the one button that fired, one intent was to have different types of firing missiles and shots and a larger variety of enemies with differing capabilities, giving much more depth than just straight driving and shooting."

In many ways, it was becoming comparable with Realtime Game's *Battle Command*, with the similarity of having missions and destroying certain targets or a number of different enemies. However, *Virtual Tank* would have landscapes with terrain that you could climb and descend and various obstacles to navigate past to hunt down enemies. Some of those enemies would be harder to kill than others, requiring particular weapons to destroy them effectively. Tracking enemies was also a very familiar affair, using the same style of enemy scanner as found in *Battlezone*.

Following from Todd's sketches, 3D artist Hans Piwenitzky soon became involved, spending a month visualising the concept in 3D for a moving demonstration to present to Nintendo. "At the time, I was employed as a 3D modeller and texture artist," began Hans. "Colin and Seth tasked me with creating a 3D demo movie of the concept. We were all excited about developing for the new platform, and I liked the concept as a whole as real 3D games were just in the embryonic stages."

"It was never intended to be a full or hardcore simulation but just an action arcade game."

"The environment was created out of a red-lined grid, lines defining the edges of the polygons," he continued. "I created the look of the environment, as well as simple polygonal shapes representing enemy units and projectiles. I used *Autodesk 3D Studio* as a modeller/UV mapper, *Deluxe Paint* to create textures and head-up display (HUD), and *Autodesk Animator* to assemble the different elements together to form a short demo. I had to teach myself how to properly apply a grid texture so the models looked lined in with the red vectors, as well as how to plot several series of complex animations as the tank moved through the environment and destroyed various enemies. It was also the first time I had really started to delve into Autodesk Animator. Very rewarding work, all in all."

The effort from the trio paid off, and Nintendo was impressed with the pitch, giving the thumbs up to proceed with the development of a game that the hardware seemed destined for. By early 1995, *Virtual Tank* was fully born – at this stage, known simply as *3D Tank*. Todd and Hans's involvement on the project had, by now, come to an end, with both having moved on to other projects. "By the time the game was to start active development, I was already working on *Spider: The Video Game* for the PlayStation and was doing concept art for other titles. I did later check in once in a while and got to see the game take shape," recalled Todd. It was now all about getting a playable game put together and completed.

According to the website Planet Virtual Boy, the May 1995 E3 event in Chicago revealed that the title was coming soon. Known only as *3D Tank* at the time, very little was given away, but many would guess what the general premise would be. Shortly after the event, a final name was settled on which, seemingly all too obvious, was set in stone as *Virtual Tank* to fit in with the console moniker.

BGS's technical director Rob Povey was assigned to oversee the development of the project. "I remember making the decision to make *Virtual Tank* a real 3D game instead of one with sprites. I also remember hating the VB development kit," recalled Rob. "We were short of engineers at the time, so the original idea was to have Brian Soderberg (a friend of our then-CEO) provide the rendering code. Because of a non-disclosure agreement, he didn't have access to the actual platform." Brian would end up writing the engine on a PC as a result, which would then later require porting across to the Virtual Boy by the studio. Working with Rob as lead engineer would be newly employed Warrick Holfeld, who first had to get familiar with the sparsely documented Virtual Boy architecture before he could make any start.

"There just wasn't anyone to ask to get assistance with the development system. Unlike the other hardware over the years that I have worked with, there just weren't enough other people to reach out to at Nintendo," explained Seth. "It was a lot of work to get the initial development hardware working and get anything on the screen, so it was not as simple as knocking out a flash mock-up. We were also very early on getting the development kit."

Warrick couldn't recall very much about the development due to how brief his time was on the project, but he did recall his first task of working with Brian's code. "The engine was written in C on a PC, where I spent some time porting the code over to the Virtual Boy," he explained. "I got the new code working, and, right after that, Rob came along and gave me the 3D engine he had written to use within the game instead."

"There was generally a feeling that this was something neat."

In the end, the solution provided by Brian hadn't been quite fast enough, not helped by his lack of access to the real hardware. Therefore, Rob decided to rewrite and produce a much faster 3D rending engine, working directly to the strengths of the hardware. Warrick began working with Rob's engine to construct something playable, as well as implement the HUD elements detailed in the specification demo.

Rob would now mostly oversee Warrick's development work but kept a hand in the project, assisting with bits and pieces of code when required to help out. Unfortunately, Warrick's recollections ended there. "All I remember is that you could move around the 3D environment. I don't remember if there were any characters, or if there was a UI or sound effects," he concluded.

Luckily, Seth and Rob would be on hand to fill in the memory gaps, though no one could recall who handled the non-3D artwork for the game. It is believed that Hans' 3D demo artwork was just translated and used as placeholder graphics, with additional bits and pieces probably added in by Warrick as required. Everything would likely have been tidied up towards the end of development, so the main focus, for now, was just on the 3D rendering and getting something playable put together.

Nintendo regularly saw the progress made by the team, giving input and any suggestions along the way to help ensure the game was on track. "One of the nice things of being in the area and knowing folks at Nintendo was that we could easily share what we were doing and get good feedback from them as to what to do and things to stay away from," Seth confirmed. "A lot of it was not wanting to end up making a game that someone else had already made as well."

As with Han's demo, the landscape was implemented using plain vector lines, with undulating hills. The distant horizon was kept blank for now, but there were plans to include detailed artwork later to add more depth and make it even less visually like *Battlezone*. One major difference to the arcade was that enemies would be rendered as filled/shaded vectors, with the hardware and Rob's engine more than capable at handling them at a decent speed.

After approximately 3–4 months of hard work, the game was fully playable, with a variety of ground, air enemies and targets that you could destroy. There was also a working HUD panel, complete with the familiar-looking enemy scanner. Just a handful of levels were present at this stage, enough to get a good feel for the game. During the development, the studio employed Barry Leitch as its audio director, with one of his very first assignments to produce sound effects and music for *Virtual Tank*. Barry briefly recalled the game but could not remember anything at all about doing work for it, being very surprised to learn that he was involved.

Everything was looking perfectly on track, with the studio now about to start looking for a publisher. It was now the summer of 1995, and the Virtual Boy was about to launch in July and August in Japan and the US respectively. Unfortunately, there was about to be a rather unexpected turn for the worse. Felt to be rushed to market with a number of critical flaws, poor visual effects, high price and weak initial titles, the launch ended up a disaster for Nintendo. The monochrome display, impracticality of the console, and rumours of it being 'seizure-inducing' meant that it was heavily discounted by stores early on. After just a few months, Nintendo waved the white flag and put the console to bed, swiftly moving on and putting all focus into the imminent N64 launch.

"We had all gone and bought ourselves Virtual Boys when it first launched and were really surprised at the speed that the platform died in the end. There was generally a feeling that this was something neat, and it was cool and definitely different to the Game Boy and any of the TV consoles," remembered Seth. "I didn't get any headaches from it, but part of the problem was your neck hurting after a while. It was hard to find the perfect table and chair for the thing to stand on, so I think that is probably more likely why it failed."

BGS saw the writing on the wall early on, and associates at Nintendo just down the road would admit that they should probably just move their focus to the N64 developments instead. *Virtual Tank* was swiftly dropped, no longer required in order to produce *Top Gear Rally*. "The game ended up getting to something that I wouldn't even call an alpha. It was probably between a first playable and alpha, where there was a tank that was rolling around and shooting. It wasn't close to being finished," explained Seth. Though far from being a finished product, with a just couple of levels, it actually had full presentation and options screens present. But, most surprising, was the early music and sound effects being included, something usually done nearer the end of a project's life cycle.

"Sadly, a *Battlezone*-like experience was just never to be for the platform. *Virtual Tank* now remains a curiosity."

Overall, a significant and impressive amount of work was put in within a very short space of time, and it was a shame that it would ultimately all go to waste. As the game was designed around the Virtual Boy's hardware, there was nothing on the cards for transferring the idea to other consoles, so it was shelved indefinitely. The studio would focus on *Spider* (which Warrick also moved on to) and *Top Gear Rally*, before later creating games such as *Stunt Racer 64* and *Twisted Edge Snowboarding*.

Thanks to the reveal of the game (under the name of *3D Tank*) during the Internet era, Virtual Boy fans would be left wondering what it would have been like to play a *Battlezone*-like game on the hardware. Even mock-up screenshots surfaced of a potential arcade conversion at the start of the new millennium, with others clearly sharing the same vision as Seth once did back in 1994. The question now was whether anything of *Virtual Tank* could be found and shown after just over 25 years of being in the shadows. Both Todd and Hans confirmed that they no longer had anything relating to the game as everything was kept at the studio at the time. Warrick and Rob concluded the same, but there was better news to come.

Seth miraculously kept a final build of the game, digging it out to get it up and running so we could show it here for the very first time. On these pages, you can see tidied up screenshots, interpreted from photos of the game taken through the console's lens. The screenshots show just how much the game was inspired by *Battlezone* and was comparable to the original arcade. No doubt, it could have been a showcase game for the platform. Unfortunately, Nintendo will not allow the release of the prototype as it is copyright protected, something that Seth cannot break. The only way it may ever surface is if another prototype somehow turns up by other means. For now, check out screenshots from the game and photos of the prototype. It is hoped that video and audio recordings will someday be available on the Games That Weren't website.

Sadly, a *Battlezone*-like experience was just never to be for the platform. *Virtual Tank* now remains a curiosity that we hope surfaces someday to give a taste of what could have been. Hopefully, in time, a homebrew conversion of Atari's arcade will give the platform the game it sorely deserves.

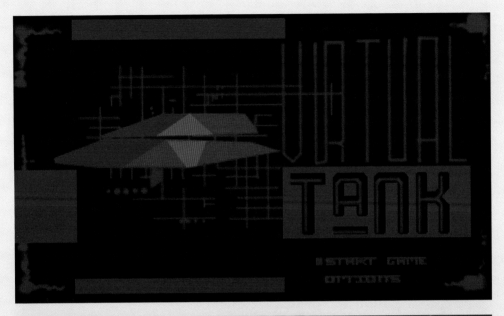

Above: Artist's recreation of *Virtual Tank* (Virtual Boy), based on photos taken by Seth of a final build of the game. Showing title screen and an in-game screen of an enemy encounter.

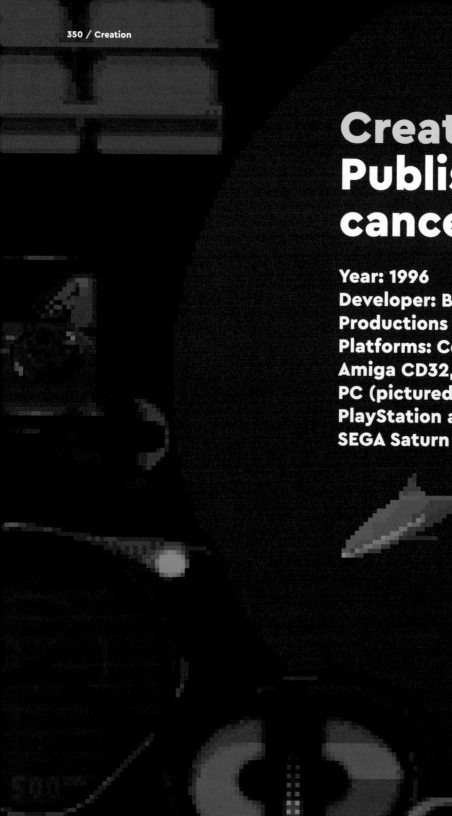

Creation
Publisher cancelled

Year: 1996
Developer: Bullfrog Productions
Platforms: Commodore Amiga CD32, PC (pictured), Sony PlayStation and SEGA Saturn

An ambitious game set within the *Syndicate Wars* time frame in an underwater world, where marine life has been saved from the Earth's destroyed oceans. A first-person-based submarine game, where you explore the ocean and marine life and carry out different missions, it was eventually cancelled after feeling that it wouldn't sell compared with other titles.

"An underwater game bouncing around for years. Moving from Amiga to PC around 1991, I started writing polygon routines. Texture mapping and Gouraud shading hadn't really been used in a game, so my experiments ended up as flat, shaded polygons (like a higher polygon/more colourful *Midwinter*).

One day, I focused more on lighting, replacing the palette with a black/blue/cyan/white fade to get better lighting, then worked on Gouraud shading, making it smooth rather than faceted.

Peter Molyneux suggested, 'That game should be underwater', so I pushed on. Seeing screenshots of *Ultima Underworld*, I realised simple texture mapping was similar to Gouraud shading so added that to my engine. The underwater theme got boring though, changing to above ground and becoming *Magic Carpet*. A few years later, Paul McLaughlin and Guy Simmons took up the project, and my involvement was indirect from that point. It used a version of my *Dungeon Keeper/Hi-Octane* engine."

Glenn Corpes, developer

Available to play
 Yes No

Virtua Hamster Poor 32X sales

Year: 1995
Developer: Peakstar Software
Platforms: SEGA 32X and Saturn

Available to play
 Yes No

Coming up with something unique for a gaming concept can be a tough ask, especially when it comes to a new game for a brand-new console. Eric Quakenbush was tasked with just that by SEGA in 1994 when he was asked to design and produce a new style of puzzler for the upcoming SEGA 32X platform (an add-on for the SEGA Mega Drive with two 32-bit processors and dedicated 3D graphics processor).

"I could not come up with anything," Eric told Ken Horowitz back in 2009. "I had hamsters as a kid, and I really liked the habitrail cages with the tubes, and the idea of a race/fighting type game inside a habitrail tube maze came to me. I pitched it as a puzzle/action game to shoehorn it into the puzzle category. I figured the maze could be very puzzle-like if it were changeable by the player."

Eric devised a plot with 'Chip the Hamster', a test pilot who has been stolen from a rival laboratory. His owner/professor had created gadgets for hamster-sized creatures to allow them to go places where humans couldn't. "Chip was originally named Buzz, after Buzz Aldrin, and renamed after the upcoming *Toy Story* was found to have a main character by the same name," Eric explained on his website. "I thought he should have a test pilot name that led to nicknames since all the famous test pilots seemed to have nicknames."

The highly desired gadgets would become the target of an evil scientist, who steals Chip and the gadget blueprints so that he can create a mechanism to steal without being detected. Chip would need to escape using his rocket-powered skateboard through a large habitrail-style maze that has been devised to test the evil scientist's rodent experiments. Whilst escaping, Chip must also retrieve stolen blueprints spread around the habitrail.

Unsurprisingly, the main focal point of the game would be within the habitrail. Throughout the tunnels, you would be placed within a first-person viewpoint, seeing through Chip's eyes and his head-up display. Whenever leaving the maze briefly (through a gap or other means), you would switch to a third-person view to make it easier to see where you were going. Eric suggested that you would have been able to select between the two viewpoints. The habitrail would branch off into different routes at certain points, where Chip would need to lean to the sides to travel down a particular route.

Whilst navigating the maze, Chip must defend himself from other rodents trying to prevent his escape by smashing him into the sides of the tunnel, kicking out, or shooting various items at him. Rival characters included imaginative names, such as 'Thorn the Black Rat', 'Stockpile the Pack Rat', 'Gizzard the Desert Rat', 'Maximilian the Mole', 'Sherman the Armoured Armadillo' and 'Outback the Kangaroo Rat'. Each would offer different strengths and weaknesses, with Gizzard, for instance, being the fastest-moving character. Sherman was slower in comparison but could smash you into oblivion with his sheer strength.

To top it all off, Chip must also beware of a mechanical snake that tracks through the habitrail, attacking from the front and behind in the tunnels. He is difficult to avoid, but you would be able to slow him down by using various weapons or tricking him into falling out of the maze. Counteracting attacks and helping you along the way though is an 'Oldster' hamster, who, on his own steam-powered rocket vehicle, travels in the maze and helps you out from time to time by giving various levels of assistance.

Weapons were also key, which you could pick up and select from an inventory system. These included 'seeds' (to shoot at opponents), 'bubble gum' (to blow bubbles and get opponents stuck), 'elastic bands' (for greater hits compared with seeds), 'water jet' (to slow down/disable opponents), 'oil' (to make characters skid/slide), 'glue' (to slow down characters), 'popcorn' (to create an obstruction that opponents would need to eat through), 'bedding bomb' (to obscure a player's vision), and a 'super squeal' (to stun your opponents).

It was also planned for Chip to be able to use his front paw to swipe, as well as produce a 'Mule kick' or 'Tail swipe' to keep enemies at bay. A number of supporting power-ups were also planned, including 'speed up', 'slow down', 'reverse rockets' to go backwards temporarily, 'pixie sticks' to make you invisible, and finally an 'energy sap' to drain energy from your opponents.

There was plenty going on within the habitrail itself to make life generally difficult and hinder your progress, including snake oil dropped by the mechanical snake to make you skid around and slow you down. Your opponents could also make use of the same power-ups and pick-ups to use against you or just try and collide with you and get in your way. As your damage increased, Chip's control was planned to degrade over time, shuddering and stuttering around in the habitrail to add further problems to an already tricky task.

To aid your next moves, the habitrail was to be translucent so that you could see outside of the maze and other parts to determine where enemies were and upcoming pathways. In addition to this, there would be multiple intersections and twists within the habitrail and large gaps that you would have to jump across. Missing a jump would mean having to get back into the maze quickly before the laboratory cat (who patrols the laboratory) eats you.

Extending the game past the main story, Eric proposed a two-player mode, where you and a friend could race against each other within the tunnels. You would have the use of all of the main game's pick-ups, which could make a difference as to who would finish first. Where the tunnel would get narrower, Eric even described to Ken Horowitz how players could get trapped and 'wedged' together. The 'Wedgey' in Eric's full design document had the idea of a stalemate where you could drop out of the maze (in a 'Wedgey Meltdown') or get caught by the snake if one of you didn't break free in time.

Helping to visualise all of Eric's proposals was concept artist Matt Crane, who produced detailed sketches depicting characters and viewpoints of the game in action. Matt's wonderful artwork would breathe life into the characters, who each had their own individual characteristics to differentiate between them. Eric would design the mechanical snake himself, going for a chrome-like finish in an almost *Terminator*-inspired design.

"Matt's wonderful artwork would breathe life into the characters."

Visually, Eric wanted the game to have the same hard-edged polygon feel that *Virtua Racing* and *Virtua Fighter* had. With that in mind, the name of the game was settled on with the name of *Virtua Hamster*, which Eric felt was a fun twist for the Virtua series. With SEGA of America on board with Eric's warm and amusing idea, it was now time to find a development studio to make it all happen.

David Palmer (of David Palmer Productions) was good friends with SEGA of America's Stewart Kosoy at the time, which one day resulted in a discussion about the *Virtua Hamster* project. "We often talked about different bits of work, then, when Stewart started working for SEGA America, he said that he had got this project and asked if I was interested," recalled David. "I said yes, so went up to see him and talk about the game. We sat down, worked out a costing and budget, then put a bid in based around what we had roughly agreed. Stewart said, 'OK, great – go ahead and get on with it'. Contracts were drawn up, and away we went."

Luckily, David had a team on hand to make a start right away back in the UK in Sheffield, thanks to unfortunate but timely circumstances. "A lot of the development staff assigned were the old Peakstar Software team that I had bought out at the time. Bill Caunt and some of his guys formed the basis of that team," he confirmed. "I'd been originally working out of my own premises, but we moved to the Science Park in Sheffield and took offices there. That seemed to work pretty well; we got a nice room and sub-offices to use. The first part of the project was to look at the design proposals by Eric."

Roddy McMillan and associate producer Ben Palmer (no relation to David) started putting together a 3D animation to visualise the proposals digitally. "I had worked at 21st Century Entertainment, working on *Pinball Magic*, *Illusions*, etc., via Spidersoft. I got a job with David as he knew me from the PD animations I had done," explained Roddy. "We created an impressive 3D animation (over 100MB in size) rendered out from *3D Studio Max* and saved onto nearly 100 floppy disks. This was sent via modem as a multi-part zip file over to SEGA of America to check out."

A game design document was simultaneously created to flesh out Eric's concept and start putting together detailed plans for the game. Development initially focused on just a 32X edition and then later develop the game for the SEGA Saturn. Work properly commenced in March 1995, with industry veteran Bill Caunt overseeing the project as well as giving technical direction and support. Nick Kimberley was assigned as lead developer, with Andrew Slater and Paul Tankard available as additional support programmers. Phil Riley would later join Roddy on art duties.

Sound duties fell to Paul Tankard, who, according to his work colleagues, was a mean office chair racer. "Often, we spontaneously took part in an office chair derby, navigating the Science Park on our chairs across two floors. I think it was only Andy, Roddy, Ben and myself that took part; the rest were far more mature," confessed Paul. "We used the lift or stairs to get around. The lift only fit two people on chairs, so there were many times where others in the building (usually professionals in suits) would see four of us going mental along the corridors. I'm sure, when I was in the lift once, Roddy took the stairs, and I just heard an almighty set of crashes!"

To complete the office chair racing-obsessed team, David had made an extra addition to help inspire everyone on the project. "We got in Chip as a real Hamster," he revealed. "I got him when we first started the project, and he was brought into work quite often." Roddy would subsequently use the team's new member as a reference for art produced for the game.

Early on, Roddy and Phil kept throwing artwork over for the developers to test out and see what worked within the 32X infrastructure. "We were doing all 3D work on *3DS Max* (DOS) on a 286 machine. There were limitations because 3D hadn't really kicked off at that point, and we were under the restrictions of the 32X. We had to work within the boundaries of what we had, so there was a lot of trial and error to see what we could get away with," Roddy confirmed.

Along with Roddy, Ben would handle some of the art production using *Deluxe Paint*, but he mostly liaised between the team and Eric regarding the visual aspects of the game. He would also produce content for the game, level designs and also the HUD map for each level. Although the artwork was progressing well, things weren't so smooth at the start of actual development.

"The Cross Products PsyQ dev system didn't work," explained David. "We had a meeting at SEGA HQ in Redwood City, San Francisco. Present were SEGA Execs and a senior tech guy, Cross/PsyQ, and me. The PsyQ dev guys swore blind there was nothing wrong with their kit. However, I had prepared well and had their code printed out and error-trapped the bad bits. The team in Sheffield did all of this, and Bill fed-exed it out to me in time for the meeting. So I had copies and handed them around, and 'red-faced' wasn't the word! We had to rewrite the dev kit code, reverse-engineer it with two developers working full-time on it for weeks as we couldn't compile anything."

"I think the bad dev kit was something else from Cross Products, and the PsyQ kit was from another company in Leeds and was superior," added Nick. "The Cross Products kit was terrible and would crash for no reason at all and refuse to work for hours afterwards. This was early GNU C (Compiler) things, so everything was a bit rubbish back then, but the problems caused a lot of wasted time."

Once the issues were finally resolved, development started to catch up, and monthly milestones were regularly met, though some of Eric's original proposal had to be simplified. A number of the ideas were found to be too difficult to implement – the 32X not quite as powerful as first hoped.

"The 32X was basically a new platform for us, and a bit of an odd system, being just an add-on for the Mega Drive," Ben explained. "This meant we had a hard time predicting performance capabilities, where a few bottlenecks jumped up and bit us. Much of the project was spent trying to overcome these limitations. Sadly, the scope and ambition of the project had to be scaled back in order to fit within performance limitations. The limited number of polygons we could push was an issue, becoming more acute in split-screen mode."

"One additional big problem was where the original design envisaged hamster tubes as semi-transparent, allowing the player to look ahead down the track and plan accordingly," he continued. "Unfortunately, technical constraints prevented the tubes from being transparent at all, meaning the main view gave players little information about the upcoming track. It shifted focus to the small radar/map, much like how experienced *Defender* players would play via the scanner."

David explained that the 32X version was always intended to be a much simpler edition, but the later planned Saturn edition would be closer to Eric's original design. All changes and cuts were regularly discussed and communicated with Eric throughout the duration of the project. "Eric was a great guy, and I loved working with him," recalled David. "He had really got his finger on the pulse and knew what he wanted to do and how to do it. We were in contact all the time on the phone and occasionally met up."

"There would be multiple intersections and twists within the habitrail and large gaps that you would have to jump across. Missing a jump would mean having to get back into the maze quickly before the laboratory cat eats you."

For now, on the 32X, the eventual habitrail effect was created using a clever pseudo-3D solution, with a tunnel that smoothly came towards you and featured bends and intersections. It would end up looking visually similar to Atari's *S.T.U.N. Runner* (an impressive 1989 Atari arcade).

"I mainly worked on the pseudo-3D tube-rendering and map-generation side," recalled Nick. "The maths behind the pseudo-3D generation wasn't true 3D (like matrix stuff is now), so it limited what could be drawn. This was mainly down to CPU power and fixed-point maths. Each section of the tube was 'flown' through by moving the Z forwards and generating the XY coordinates from it. The models used a similar trick. It was good getting to grips with writing software polygon renderers in SH-2 using the hardware accelerator in the 32X hardware, which was little more than horizontal line filler."

"The 32X was basically a new platform for us."

Over time, more was cut from the development, and it is likely that the ability for Chip to exit the maze (resulting in a third-person lab floor chase with the laboratory cat) was dropped. The team couldn't remember and did not recall any such sequences being developed. The idea of collecting blueprints across one continuous game was certainly scrapped due to technical issues, with the game instead broken down into levels and different habitrail maps. Chip's aim would now be to capture a Skuttle droid to open each level exit and move on to a further part of the habitrail. The Skuttle could also be knocked out of Chip's possession by his opponents if you were not careful.

Levels were eventually reduced to a total of eight, each with its own palette of 256 colours and with new features introduced to keep up interest across the game as a whole. Each was built using a specially developed editor created internally, allowing defined tube sections to be linked together to form a tunnel and allowing the placement of pick-ups at certain key points. Levels were colour-coded to help distinguish different areas of the habitrail and included markings to show any oncoming hazards.

Overall, a single level would take approximately 15 minutes to finish, with the first level acting as a training level. Difficulty would increase via the introduction of more complex mazes on later levels, more splits and junctions to give more decisions to make, harder rodent opposition and faster-moving Skuttles. The game would essentially boil down to *S.T.U.N. Runner* with hamsters. The only difference was that you had many more path choices within the maze, so it wasn't as simple to get to the finish. It still had the elements of escaping a maze, enough to still be classified as an action puzzle game and meet SEGA's original request. Setbacks with the original plan aside, the team was determined to make the best possible game they could within the constraints.

The two-player mode of the game was left relatively intact from Eric's original proposal, allowing you to play as the other characters within the game, and race each other from start to finish, using the game's collectables to try and thwart each other. It was planned to be able to also set either or both players to be CPU-based, though it could not be recalled if this was implemented or not. Plans to enable a dual-player game, where you could team up with another player to complete the main single-player story was dropped early on.

The simplification of the original concept and fast pseudo-3D method helped to ensure that the speed of a split-screen view was not affected much. The team had even considered utilising a diagonal split-screen approach, something that hadn't really been done before. "Splitting this way maximised the screen space for both player's tubes, and the idea was toyed with and would have certainly looked unique, although, in the end, a simpler side-by-side approach was chosen," confirmed Ben.

"Over time, more was cut from the development."

Paul was also making progress on the music and sound effects. The intention was to use the original Mega Drive sound hardware for the music but utilise the 32X PWM hardware for samples. "Most of the time early on was spent writing a pro-tracker-type application for DOS which hooked up to the SNASM interface that connected to a SEGA Mega Drive," recalled Paul. "It utilised instruments that came on the GEMS diskette, but we didn't use GEMS itself for the music. I can't remember why that was – cost maybe. There were even tracks written that used some proper drums samples, just before we were informed of the project's cancellation. I didn't have a 32X development kit at the time, so Bill wrote the sample playing routines, and I hooked up to them."

Music included tunes for the intro, titles, demo mode, options screen, in game, results, end sequence, and a number of jingles for the SEGA logo, failure and success. There were a number of digitised voices in the game for battle cries and when you got hurt. Then, finally, there were many different sound effects for rocket engines, weapon firing and collision noises, as well as R2D2-like noises for the Skuttle droid.

It wasn't long also until the artwork was near completion, and it seemed everything was coming together. "The creatures, animations for the rats, etc., were pretty much done, very polygonal-looking and not smooth like today. The skateboards and animations were done for all the characters and were implemented into the game and tested. The developers got them flying around on the screen with the interactions with the characters," confirmed Roddy. "We thought it was fun, but it was nothing groundbreaking yet, apart from the pseudo-3D effect, which was really good."

Even disaster of the offices being broken into and machines being stolen would not cause too much of a setback for the team. Luckily, everything was backed up, though there were inevitable delays waiting for new hardware to arrive. By September, most of the game was ready and at an alpha stage for playtesting. Nick had decided to move on to pastures new, but the engine was already complete, and the two-player mode was mostly operational, so the other team members could continue the polishing up. Options screens, animated sequences, music and sound effects were practically done.

Titles were also complete, showing the different characters and statistics, and animated sequences for the intro, between levels and end sequence were complete (where Chip is reunited with the friendly professor). It's believed that a password system was also in place, and recording features were present to allow you to record levels and play them back afterwards. It was mostly a case of tidying up and getting the rest of the levels fully finished and integrated.

"The creatures, animations for the rats, etc., were pretty much done, very polygonal-looking and not smooth like today."

"I would have said another few months, and it would have been ready for release," confirmed Roddy. "The game just did not really get to the final polish stage, so the look and feel didn't get the sun needed to blossom," Ben added. David was also excited overall, feeling that there was real potential in the title and that the complete suite of characters could later be used to produce a cartoon animation series, more video games and peripheral products. Unfortunately, this would require a successful launch for the game, but the SEGA's 32X was far from the success that SEGA had hoped for and would dash David's hopes.

The 32X had launched around the world between November 1994 and January 1995, but, although initial sales were promising, the lack of software support was telling. By mid-to-late 1995, the *Virtua Hamster* team started to sense that something wasn't right when milestone payments began to slow. With the 32X launch fast becoming a disaster, SEGA dropped titles felt to be the least profitable, which, unfortunately, included *Virtua Hamster*.

The team received a sudden visit from Eric around December 1995, bearing the news they were all dreading. "He met with everybody at the office, took us all out for a meal and, the next day, delivered the news that the game was going to get canned," recalled Roddy. "It was horrible because we knew something was up as we hadn't been paid for a few months. We had carried on developing in the hope that things would rectify themselves."

It was also rumoured that SEGA of Japan was not keen on the Virtua name being used anyway, though David wasn't aware of any problems at the time. Eric had also heard of the concerns but didn't know why it was a problem. Even so, the game would never reach a stage of being renamed.

"To put it bluntly, SEGA of America just simply ran out of money and were in a mess financially and had to be bailed out," David explained. "It was literally 'Night of the Long Knives' as the Japanese just went in and fired everybody.

Many people I knew very well lost their jobs overnight. They knew *Virtua Hamster* was close to completion, so they had to cancel straight away otherwise they were due another invoice from us. This went on for a few months and was a horrendous finish for the project. I still had to pay my staff, but I was getting no cash in, and we had completed the milestones as per the timeline. In the end, there was a $275,000 loss from the cancellation, although I did get a paltry $44,000 settlement on a 90%+ completed project!"

To act as a form of compensation, David was given complete ownership of all of the game design and code as part of the settlement. However, nothing more would happen with the idea, and it was completely shelved. "The game was 95–99% there at the time and was a perfect game for 8–13-year-old kids," David reflects. "It was mostly a simple and straightforward project. It had its hiccups and problems in creating a pseudo-3D game on a very chugging piece of hardware, but it was done, and we got around any problems. We'd have liked it to have been better, but hardware limitations were there, and we did the best that we could."

It brings us neatly on to what happened to the planned SEGA Saturn version of the game. Although rumoured to have been in development, David confirmed that nothing was started. The intention was to only start on the Saturn once the 32X version had shipped. A shame because it would have been interesting to see more of Eric's original vision as intended on the beefed-up hardware.

According to one online source (www.bit.ly/virtuahamster), a British company had picked up the title for a potential PC release after the SEGA cancellation, which also never made it to market. "This was nothing to do with me," David confirmed. "No one ever approached us. If one had been underway, I'd be tapping on their door due to the amount of money it cost us doing the 32X version. If anyone wanted to do a PC version, it would have been a case of 'show us the money' first before letting them proceed."

Over the years, the 32X game became an intriguing mystery, with it appearing in magazines, showing some of the concept sketches and cover artwork, but there was never any reason given as to why the game was cancelled. To many, it had just disappeared, like the 32X itself. Luckily, over the years, various prototypes have been spotted of the game, but it wasn't until 2009 that a pre-alpha version was bought and made available online by the SEGA Saturn website.

"We thought it was fun, but it was nothing groundbreaking yet."

The prototype shows a semi-playable game, where you can move through the maze and join different parts of the habitrail. No collisions are present, and, at different points, you can see some of the other characters in the game – currently static. You can collect a few items, but nothing does anything at present. It is a good indicator of how everything was going, and, clearly, you can see and feel the *S.T.U.N. Runner* influences. "The music that features wasn't what we ended up with," explained Paul. "These were just tracks experimenting with the tracker program. We also hadn't got far enough in development for any SFX. Bill may have added some plinks and plonks when doing the sample player though."

Could a more complete version ever be found? Eric does have a later edition of the game, of which he posted screenshots on his website showing a different split-screen approach for the two-player mode, with the screens stacked on top of each other. This version is believed to have collisions in place and is more playable than the version currently out there. There are currently no plans to preserve this version of the game and release it to the community, though it could well happen someday soon.

"It was horrible because we knew something was up as we hadn't been paid for a few months."

None of the development team could find anything themselves. Nick suggests he may have something, though nothing was found by the time of publication. David offered greater hope as he had kept all of his files from the project, including concept artwork, developer and artist notes. David kindly provided a temporary loan so that a number of new scans and information could be presented here for the first time and shared on the Games That Weren't website.

David has also suggested that he has the final copy of the source code and assets, and, if someone is able to compile everything together, then he would be happy to see its release into the community. This is currently being discussed, and it is hoped that it will eventually become a reality to see the game in its final form.

Intriguingly, David mentioned in Ken Horowitz's article that he had toyed with bringing back the game for modern-day platforms, but nothing more was heard. "I had thought it would make a nice game, given the technical capability of hardware today," explained David when asked about this. "Especially when you look at Xbox and PlayStation, you could quite easily make a game like that. It really just needed really decent graphics, and you could have had something that almost looked like a real hamster through 3D space. I think it would have been such a hoot for kids."

It never progressed past those initial thoughts, with David having no further plans to re-explore the game at present. But, with ownership of the concept still with David today, there is always the chance that *Virtua Hamster* could make its long-awaited debut on modern platforms. Perhaps even a VR edition to really make you feel that you're controlling Chip in that habitrail. Nothing sounds more terrifying, but why not?

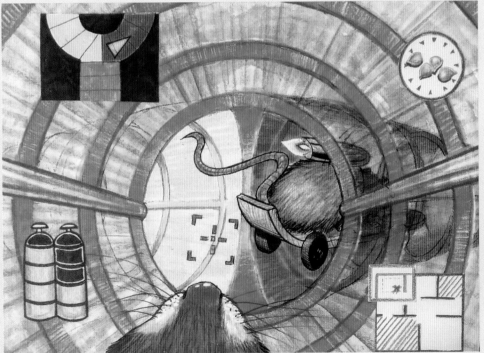

Above: Concept drawings, showing how the game would look and feel within the habitrail.

Top: Concept drawing for the main character, Chip. Bottom: Concept drawing showing the Habitrail tunnel system within the lab environment.

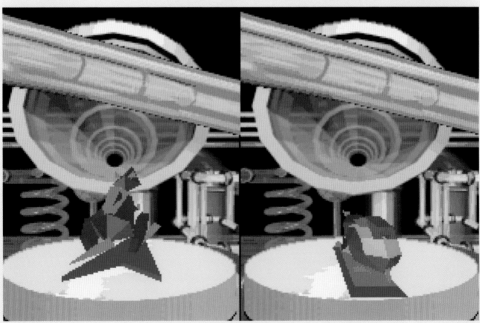

Above: Screenshots from the leaked early prototype of *Virtua Hamster* (SEGA 32X), showing the title screen and cut sequence for the split-screen mode.

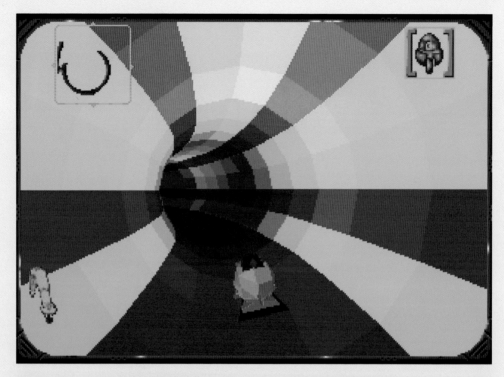

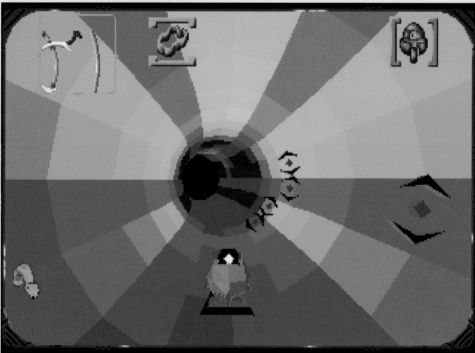

Above: Screenshots from the leaked early prototype of *Virtua Hamster* (SEGA 32X), showing the main game.

Above: Original artwork that was to be eventually used on the final packaging, featuring Chip the hamster with part of the blueprints.

Primal Rage 2
Financial troubles

Year: 1996
Developer: Atari Games
Platform: Arcade

The game featured innovations, such as dynamically streaming animation frames from a hard drive for smooth animation, morphing between beast and humanoid titan forms, and self-induced finishing moves. Once regarded a myth, the game eventually received praise from fans who played the prototype at the Galloping Ghost Arcade in 2014, and when it was made playable via emulation in 2017. As a developer, I was happiest that the sequel had significantly improved controls and gameplay over the original."

Chris Tang, game designer

The franchise was built on stop-motion animation technology. Stop-motion animator Pete Kleinow was involved with both games, with experience on the *Gumby* series, and other film and television special effects including the *Terminator* movies. Animator Jon Berg joined us for *PR2* and is best known for his work on the AT-AT walker sequence in *The Empire Strikes Back*. Working alongside these two seasoned veterans was my favourite memory of *Primal Rage II*."

Steve Riesenberger, production coordinator

Available to play

 Yes ◯ No

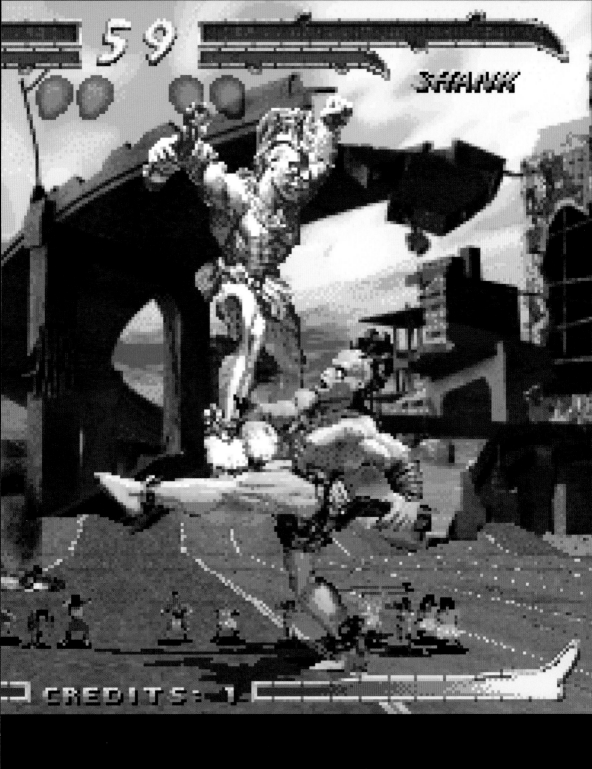

Deathwatch
Move away
from 2D

Year: 1995
Developer: Data Design Interactive
Platform: Atari Jaguar

Available to play

 Yes ◉ No

The Atari Jaguar is a somewhat undervalued console, completely destroyed by the SEGA Saturn and Sony PlayStation in terms of sales and support. Atari didn't particularly help themselves, with poor marketing of the machine and a shortage of killer games. The complex architecture made it difficult to develop for as well, which meant that it was harder to make the hardware sing, especially with shaded texture 3D titles (*Alien vs. Predator* being an exception of course).

Where it really excelled though was with its 2D capabilities, with higher resolution graphics and a higher colour palette which would set it well apart from the likes of the SEGA Mega Drive and Super Nintendo at the time. Data Design Interactive's Stewart Green took a particular shine to the console very early on, and it would be a concept sketch which would give birth to their first planned title for the console.

Artist John Court had just completed another project and was waiting for a new assignment. "After a modicum of success working on *Pinkie*, we moved on to a slew of high-profile conversions on the SNES, Mega Drive and PC that I helped with. However, our little team downstairs mainly were working on a number of original projects heading for a new breed of consoles," John recalled. "The idea for *Deathwatch* came from a sketch I did of a beetle character, where I went on and produced some run-and-shooting animations based on games I loved at the time – *Midnight Resistance* and *Super Contra*. Stewart Green seemed to like these and wanted to make it into something for the new Atari Jaguar – a console of the moment that had very few games, certainly no decent 2D platform/shooters as everyone was going 3D."

The idea was christened *Bug* as a working title, with John asked to flesh out a story and more ideas to form the basis of an actual game. The beetle character became known as Rem, featuring characteristically large boots and wielding a massive gun to blast enemies with. John created a story that described Rem's planet as being on the brink of extinction, with many of his kind already having died. This was due to the shutdown of the planet's 'purifying system', a large mechanism hidden below the planet's surface that keeps the planet alive. The ancient device operates via five golden discs, each with a crystal in its centre. The discs were stolen many moons ago by Celtic Space Pirates and sold to all sorts of villains and dodgy guys. Your job would be to get them back by all means necessary to save your planet from extinction.

Rem would have to locate the discs by negotiating a number of different themed levels, destroying a large bad guy on each to then retrieve one of the discs. John initially sketched out ideas, including a forest-themed level named 'The Forest Moon', which was described as having "an overgrown feel about it, with lots of wooden-type stanchions and rocky platforms."

Other ideas included a tech industrial/war-torn theme and a *Waterworld*-like level split into two parts – the first featuring standard platform action, the second where you control an underwater vehicle. There were also plans for Dead Sea, Underground Cave and Sandworm-themed levels, with the latter having you ride on the back of a large sandworm. "It was mostly an A-to-B affair, working through levels of shooter mayhem, platforms, insectoid enemies, death pits, and bosses aplenty," John confirmed.

"Instead of pixel work, I painted a platform, ground or a bunch of spikes using acrylics, then scanned them in and used them as the base of the sprite sheet."

Some of John's early imaginative sketchbook ideas would also include mouths within the walls, which would have tongues popping out to form platforms, crumbling and moving platforms, firepits that you must jump over to avoid, and spikes that could kill Rem instantly. There were also 'Krusher blox' which constantly rose and fell, attempting to crush Rem.

Enemies would consist of almost anything from the insect/larvae world, including mosquitoes, flies and beetles to name but a few – warped and mutated with armour plating and guns attached in most cases. Many of those initial ideas would be dropped or adapted as the project evolved. A large number of weapons were also initially suggested by John, which included grapple claws, rockets, handguns, machine guns and pulse laser weaponry. Other additions and power-ups suggested were homing rockets, three or five-way shots, shields, smart bombs, timed nukes (to remove obstructions on levels) and a freeze ray.

Stewart was happy for the project to progress after seeing John's proposals, and he requested a working prototype to present to Atari. Assigned to oversee production was Eamonn Barr, who recently came across from Arc Developments. "I was the project manager and became the main point of contact between our company and Atari," he began. "When we first had the concept, Atari was really interested in it. John was a very talented artist as well. Often, he'd go off on some tangents that wouldn't necessarily always be practical, but that same creativity was great as it generated things that were a little bit off the wall and that hadn't been done before, which *Deathwatch* massively benefited from."

Lead development was assigned to Richard Hackett, with early assistance from Dale Johnstone. "I was initially assigned to work on the project to help us get to grips with the new hardware, going with Richard to a technical talk about the Jaguar at Atari," explained Dale. "Previously, I'd figured out (what later became known as) Mode X and hardware scrolling on the PC, so I was assigned to help Richard figure the Jaguar out. I recall Eamonn being blown away by the lack of colour palette limitations as it was 16-bits per pixel and a brave new world! In the end, Richard didn't need my help, so I quickly moved to other projects."

With John already the lead graphic artist, Andrew Shepherd joined him as a supporting graphic artist. The focus would initially be on the forest and tech industrial-themed level ideas, where all graphics were drawn in *Deluxe Paint*, with the extra colours available making everything look vibrant and bold. However, partway through the project, John would decide to switch to a new artistic technique that was becoming popular, giving the game a rather unique look and feel, and taking the visuals to a whole new level.

"Instead of pixel work, I painted a platform, ground or a bunch of spikes using acrylics, then scanned them in and used them as the base of the sprite sheet," recalled John. "The original idea came from me using a scanned picture of coffee beans in the very first pass of the game. These new ideas had been creeping in elsewhere via *Earthworm Jim*, *Clay Fighter*, *Rise of the Robots*, etc., where scanned images or 3D-generated images were being used as there was no 32-colour limit on textures anymore."

Although Richard Hackett didn't respond regarding the project's development, Dale recalls early concerns from Richard over the JPEG decompression speed of the hardware. Atari had said it was as optimised as best it could be, but it would cause a few headaches early on for the large detailed graphics. "I think the dev kits were also buggy, and the documentation was poor," added Eamonn. "Richard definitely had a bit of a challenge, but he was a great guy and did extremely well. He had to figure most of it out himself." Therefore, it wasn't long until Richard formulated a smooth basic working game engine with a fully controllable main character.

The Jaguar's pure grunt in terms of ability to throw around sprites would benefit the game massively too, with 'swarms' of creatures possible within the game. Perfect considering the premise of insects as enemies. The game would also implement well-weighted physics throughout, with a tiny bit of inertia also put into each main movement to make for more satisfying controls. As soon as you would start to walk, there was a small bit of acceleration and plenty of animation frames included, making it feel almost like an interactive cartoon with the combined addition of high-quality artwork.

To help show progress to Atari, Eamonn would work with John to put together some basic level maps, utilising the available platforms, obstacles and enemies created so far to demonstrate the engine. "The maps were put together from a single screen of blocks, as games at that time always had been, just in a bigger way with more blocks. No more 16×16 for us," John smiled.

According to Eamonn, when shown a playable demo with some basic level maps, Atari was pleased and was keen to see it continue. Alistair Bodin was assigned as US producer for the game, and the new development was eventually given 'J9079' as its production code. Alistair was the main point of contact for

Eamonn, though Tom Gillen (who sadly passed away in 2017) was also listed as overseeing the game with Alistair. Eamonn only ever recalls directly talking to Alistair. Interestingly, early milestone feedback at Atari US doesn't quite add up, including question marks over a four-player adapter, which the DDI team had never heard of (and there was never a consideration for a four-player mode). It's plausible that there was a mix-up with another game in production at the time.

"The new Rayman games are just how I imagined *Deathwatch*."

With everything otherwise progressing steadily, in-house musician Darren Wood was now assigned to produce a few soundtracks and sound effects. "I don't remember too much about the game, but it looked great. I do, however, remember an underground level in a cave that looked really atmospheric," recalled Darren. "I had basically finished converting music for *Mickey Mania*, so I was inspired by orchestral soundtracks and put together a couple of atmospheric orchestral tracks for the cave level. Not sure if it ever got used though. I did random tunes for various game demos or pitches that were worked on at the time."

After a few months and many visual improvements, there was enough of a game forming to show it off. Coming up fast was the very first E3 gaming show at Los Angeles in May 1995. Ideal timing as Atari was about to showcase a lot of its new upcoming Jaguar titles at the event. The team was requested to make a video showing the game in action.

Due to negative connotations with the title *Bug*, the game was renamed to *Deathwatch*, named after the Deathwatch Beetle. However, it may have also been related to a Saturn game due out around the same time with the same name. The video would show someone playing through one of the tech industrial-themed mock-up levels. "The level on the E3 video was from the second iteration of the game, with the newly painted and scanned artwork. It was a big level you could jump around on but had no real focus, apart from the enemies, spikes and moving platforms," explained John.

The demo had Rem wandering around sloped platforms, jumping on moving platforms and shooting mosquitoes with his blaster gun, whilst collecting little orbs. In addition to the wonderful animation, there were vibrant and colourful backgrounds with bits of metal junk and broken ships that smoothly parallax-scrolled as you moved around. Visually, the game looked like a spruced-up mixture of *Plok* (Super Nintendo) and *Metal Slug* (NEOGEO), but also felt a bit like the new upcoming *Rayman* game – ironically, about to be released for the Jaguar. At no point, though, did it inspire *Deathwatch* in any way. "It was just coming out at the time and pipped us to the post. Funnily enough, though, the new *Rayman* games now are just how I imagined *Deathwatch* would have been," John confirmed.

Visitors were reportedly impressed, feeling that it was a very fresh-looking game compared with other 2D platformers of the time. The positive reception was enough for Data Design Interactive to push on, though a growing lack of engagement coming from Atari was starting to cause concern.

"After a while, the momentum and excitement died down quite a bit," Eamonn began to explain. "Of course, the time for things to be painted was an extra step in the process; to get it in *Deluxe Paint* and ready to use to build a map and tiles was also time-consuming. But it was Atari constantly dragging their feet that heavily delayed our progress. We'd develop each agreed milestone, hand it in, and the approval would be something like up to six weeks. What would happen if they came back and said there was something they don't like? During that time, Richard [Hackett] and John Court ended up jumping temporarily onto other projects. It was a business reality that we had to focus on the projects that were bringing in money and could pay us on time."

"I remember speaking to Atari and saying that we need to keep the guys motivated and on track," Eamonn continued. "That meant we needed to be paid on time, and approval should be a 3–4-day turnaround as that was what we were used to. We were really starting to wonder how much time we should be putting into the project due to how long everything was taking. There was real concern that we'd put all our time into the game, and then Atari would go bust or something. We just started to get a bad feeling that *Deathwatch* was never going to get finished, and we were never going to get paid."

Work continued regardless, and, in fleeting moments, the team would briefly come back and add further features to the game, as well as further improve the artwork. Eamonn recalls that, during the whole period, Atari would comically ask how the game was coming on, with him retorting that DDI had sent them a milestone for approval weeks previously without a reply.

"Once, I even phoned Atari chasing a milestone payment and stated that we required payment as they had previously approved the milestone, and payment was well overdue," he added. "Amazingly, they said something like, 'We are feeling concerned that you are chasing this payment so much, and we want to be assured of your stability as a company'. I replied with almost laughter with something like, 'You must be joking. You are the company that is long overdue on your payment, and yet you are questioning our financial stability!'."

To further complicate things, there were also suggestions from Atari about changing to 3D, no doubt in response to pressure from the 3D successes on the SEGA Saturn and Sony PlayStation platforms. Eamonn explained that going 3D would require starting from scratch, stating that there just wasn't a magic '3D button' that could be pressed to make it all happen quickly. Wisely, the 2D approach was retained.

Regardless of the frustrations and challenges arising, the game began to preview in magazines, such as *GameFan* and *CD Consoles*, with a projected release date of late 1995. It wasn't too long after the E3 show that an exodus slowly began, with Andrew first deciding to move on, leaving John alone on artistic duties. With the vast amount of artwork required, fellow graphic artist Richard Priest was brought on board to fill the gap, producing a number of animated sprites, including some boss characters and some superb explosion sprites, according to John.

"I was working previously on *Waterworld* for the SEGA Mega Drive. At the same time, John was working on *Deathwatch* and had been for a while," recalled Richard. "I remember him designing the main character and the graphics for level one, and that was it. John had already set the style of the game that I tried to follow. I drew inspiration from other platform shooters around at the time. There was a game on the Amiga called *Ruff 'n' Tumble* that had particularly nice graphics. I remember looking at that and thinking that's the quality I should aim for. I always looked up to great artists in the industry at that time, including Dan Malone (who worked for the Bitmap Brothers), an amazing pixel artist who inspired me greatly, and probably a lot of other game artists."

Not long after Richard had jumped onto the project, John decided it was time for a fresh challenge and took up a new role at Rage Software, leaving *Deathwatch* completely light on resources. Simeon Hankins and another graphic artist called Nik (whose surname couldn't be recalled) were called up to fill in the gap. This would be Simeon's first role in the games industry, where he was hired to help paint the backgrounds in the game along with Nik.

With the team stabilised, for now, a game design document was then fleshed out, detailing the level themes and content for the game. A recovered copy of the document reveals that the game was boiled down to five distinctively themed levels. These included 'Forest', 'Water', 'Industrial', 'Underground' and 'Ant's Nest' levels. Rather than play sequentially through the game, Deathwatch would allow the player to choose a region to start via a 3D globe that you could rotate. Before selecting a region, you would be given statistics on the area and a scaled preview before making a choice.

The 'Forest' level included your typical branches, rocks and root-style elements. It was planned to feature enemies, such as large spikey caterpillars with armour plating, dragonflies that drop bombs onto platforms, mosquitoes that swarm and fly at you, woodlice that roll into balls and jump at you (jumping on them made you bounce higher onto unreachable platforms), and a fungus that explodes into tiny spores if touched. Reaching the end would treat you to a large spider boss that tries to grab you from above and drag you off-screen, where you must shoot off all the spider's legs.

The 'Water' level changed the style of the game, with an auto-scrolling, one-screen-deep underwater section. Compared with the other levels, this was far simpler in design but featured a water wave effect applied over the top of the main character and enemies. Rem's only weapon is a torpedo-like device that leaves bubble trails as it shoots. Enemies would include larvae worm creatures, water beetles, pond skaters that swim along the surface and dive down at you, and mud worms that jump out at you. The level then concludes with a large unknown underwater creature to defeat.

"I don't think all the planned weapons were implemented."

'Industrial' (as shown in the online videos) takes you back to the usual platform action, with sloped platforms and ones which float and allow you to reach higher places. The backgrounds would look almost like a massive car scrapyard, with discarded jets and other metal junk. Enemies would include woodlice, attacking wasps that generate from a hive (which you can destroy to stop spawns), and, finally, scorpions that shoot laser beams at you or catch you with their pincers. Concluding the level is an encounter with a large caterpillar boss, where you must shoot out each of its segments to defeat it.

'Underground' sets you in a dark cave environment, full of shadows and flickering flames, and resumes the platform action once more. Enemies/obstacles included worms that pop out from holes in the ground, fireflies that launch jets of fire and dive-bomb at you, ants that fire guns, and lava spouts that you must avoid when jumping over pits. A unique element to the level were the wormholes that were actually the mouths of creatures (described as a type of 'lion ant') that snap shut and eat you if you walk over them. If this happens, you would switch to a scene inside the creature's stomach, where you must escape from green bubbling bile that rises steadily. The level concludes with a large soldier ant boss to defeat.

Finally, 'Ant's Nest' concludes with a claustrophobic level of narrow tunnels, underground roots and larvae chambers. Not much detail was given for this level, which may well have required more fleshing out. There were to be three types of ants with different weapons and armoury, and a maggot pit which Rem can sink into if he doesn't jump out in time. Unsurprisingly, the boss was to be a large Queen ant, which shoots eggs that hatch into smaller ants. Rem would need to destroy the egg generator to stop the small ants from spawning, before then destroying the Queen herself. Upon completion of all the regions, the globe was to explode, and Rem would emerge in a victory stance end sequence, complete with final game credits.

Rem's character himself would be tweaked and improved as time went on and would be given additional weapons, including a 'power sword' and a 'spiked mallet' to bash enemies with. Rem also collected special abilities, which were charged up and enabled by collecting elemental points for 'Fire', 'Ice', 'Air', 'Earth' and 'Water'. Abilities would include higher jumps, being able to flutter or fly like Mario, and being able to produce acid vomit from his mouth to kill enemies. He would be only able to carry a fixed number of elements, so you would have to carefully choose what to collect to get the abilities you wanted. It could not be recalled by the team if any of those features were implemented in the end.

Presentation was to include a title screen set at Rem's home with a fireplace setting. There were plans for an options screen for player settings, sound/music selection, music and FX tests, difficulty level (easy, hard, MANIC), and a password entry system. To encourage replay, each level was to show the percentage of completion, points gained, and hidden areas discovered. In addition to this, a high-score table with up to ten entries was also planned, which would come with a clever character entry element where Rem would run on a cylinder of letters to select and enter a name.

After each level, a sequence was to show Rem returning to his home with a log fire, which shelved trophies (insect heads from each defeated boss) displayed on the wall above the fire. This segment was designed by Richard, who afterwards moved on to more of the sprite work side of the game. "It was a case of being told, 'I need a woodlouse that can transform into a ball and roll down slopes', and I would then go away, draw and animate just that," he confirmed. "In total, I completed seven fully animated bug enemies: a caterpillar, a dragonfly, a deadly fungus, a louse, a scorpion, a wasp, and a water beetle. I also started work on an end-of-level boss – a giant spider that never got finished in the end."

Unfortunately, not long after the design had been fleshed out, Richard also felt that it was time to move on. "I didn't work on *Deathwatch* for long, maybe 2–3 months. At the time, I think the company was going through a bit of a bad patch; people were leaving, and projects were drying up. I eventually decided to leave later that year," he confirmed.

Richard Hackett was next to leave, potentially disillusioned with the project dragging on like it did. Eamonn tried to convince Richard to stay, but it was to no avail. With all seemingly lost, a fresh graduate straight out of university was about to become an unlikely saviour for the game. "I was looking for something to do during the summer, so I had an interview with Eamonn, who needed a new Jaguar developer," recalled Ben Whitlock. "I convinced him that I knew a bit of 8-bit coding and that I'd be fine at picking up stuff, but I was secretly a bit nervous as it was a big challenge to take on."

However, Eamonn recalls Ben having a good attitude and thought he would do what it took to get the job done. Giving Ben his first break, the immediate intention was to take over from Richard Hackett on the project. Both would spend a few weeks working together as part of a handover. "Richard basically took me through all the code and what was going on," recalled Ben. "It wasn't too difficult to pick up, in the end, to be honest, but what they really needed was just to get it all working. What we had was a pretty good demo, but it didn't work in places and had a number of bugs, where things would crash at different points. Eamonn wanted me to try and get the current game ready for a video to show off as a near-finished game. By that point, it had a few levels already and a lot of gameplay elements. Initially, I just had to fix the bugs and get it working."

"I convinced him that I knew a bit of 8-bit coding and that I'd be fine at picking up stuff."

Compared with the original E3 video, the game had come on quite a bit visually by this stage. Ben recalled artwork for all five different themes being available, but not all the levels were yet fully mapped out and complete. "I remember almost an entire first level with different creatures and large dragonflies with an organic feel to them. Then there was another level with flies/bees that would come and buzz around you," remembered Ben. "I also remember Richard explaining how he came up with the motion for the flies from walking through a field, seeing a swarm and how they behaved, moving from one point to the next. He wrote the logic where a fly went from point A to point B, and, when it reached point B, there would be a random model to move to a new point. It was a great effect to feel like you were surrounded by an actual swarm."

Many creatures had been added to the game by this stage, including large end-of-level baddies. One in particular was the huge crawling caterpillar made up of many sprites that would appear at the end of the industrial level. "It was a very large composite sprite made up of lots of different sections, and there were some logic errors where it kept crashing," confirmed Ben. "I pretty much bug-fixed the entire game for three weeks. A quite lengthy effort that went through a number of different bits of software to compile and run on a Jaguar development unit. After a 36-hour last-ditch effort, we managed to get a video done of the game being played. I recall it showing a lot of the impressive forest level as well as other levels available."

The game was shown at the first-ever European Computer Trade Show at Olympia, London in September 1995. Just before the show, *Ultimate Future Games* magazine would feature the game within a special Jaguar supplement, with press shots provided by Atari. Writer Andy Dyer was full of praise with the visuals at the time, saying: "Another platformer, and one with loads of shooty action, but more importantly, one that has graphics the like of which you've never seen. Just get a load of this beautiful artwork. Thrill to the subtle colours, gasp at the gorgeous textures, go a bit funny in the head at the beautifully designed characters."

What the magazine didn't know was that *Deathwatch* was about to be shelved. Atari was still stalling on feedback and payments, and DDI had decided enough was enough. Stewart told us that Atari was feeling the crunch and decided that it now just wanted 3D titles to fight back against the SEGA Saturn and Sony PlayStation. Rather than redevelop the game in 3D, DDI opted to cancel and swiftly move on to other productions that were paying on time.

Deathwatch would become one of many casualties of the Atari Jaguar, with both Atari and its console in a dire commercial state by the end of the year. Hasbro would eventually buy out much of Atari's property and later make the Jaguar an open platform. This led to some unreleased titles being picked up by companies, such as Telegames and Songbird Productions, as well as producing brand-new titles. It gave the Jaguar an extended life and helped to establish a community that still sees games produced and released today. *Deathwatch* wasn't so lucky, perhaps because it wasn't as high-profile compared with other titles at the time. It would instead become the subject of forum posts and websites, asking about what happened to the game once seen in magazines.

"Engine-wise it was probably about 80% complete. We had enemies, collisions, the main character moving, jumping, and gravity all working."

In 2011, Urs Koenig preserved a video that he had in his possession, produced by *Atari Explorer Online* (a regular newsletter from 1992) and showing Atari Jaguar content from the E3 event. At one point, there is a short clip of *Deathwatch* with a backing track. It gave most people a glimpse of the game in action for the first time and demonstrated just how wonderful it looked and moved, even though it was an early build. The ECTS video produced by Ben and Eamonn has yet to be found, which showed a far more advanced game, in terms of both visuals and content throughout.

It was rumoured for years that the game was finished, but this wasn't the case at all. "I think we did between 3–5 levels in the end. At the time, we had a few level designs ready, and for one of the milestones we had to show workable levels," Eamonn responded. "Engine-wise, it was probably about 80% complete. We had enemies, collisions, the main character moving, jumping, and gravity all working. I don't think all the planned weapons were implemented, just basic shots. I'm also sure we didn't get to do any presentation, menu or options either. Graphics were around 60% complete, with a lot remaining in John's sketchbook. If I remember correctly, there was meant to be some kind of flying machine and a submarine-type thing that never got painted up or implemented. I feel like I am correct, and these were actual ideas at the time, but whether they were suggested/rejected or whatever – I really can't be sure after all the time that has passed."

It could not be recalled if Darren's music or sound effects had been integrated. Ben recalls that a simultaneous two-player mode was implemented and working at the time he took over. No doubt, recovery of the game or the ECTS video would clear up many of the unknowns as to what did and did not feature towards the end of development. So what are the chances of finding something of the game?

Eamonn revealed that much was lost just after cancellation. "The company was burgled, and we had our PCs stolen," he explained. "This was a massive loss, but, when we went to retrieve all the backups, we found that the guy doing them had been doing so without selecting the right checkboxes. So it was backed up as one single continuous stream of data and was literally useless." Both Eamonn and Stewart also mentioned that the Jaguar development kits just disappeared as well, with their final resting places unknown to this day.

Therefore, hope remains with those who worked directly on the game, though Richard Hackett, Nik and Andrew couldn't be reached. However, John, Ben, Simeon and Richard Priest did have some artwork and sprite work, which you can see some of here. The Games That Weren't website will feature animated versions of Richard's work. Darren feels that he may still have recordings of the orchestral tracks he produced, but he hadn't found them at the time of publication. If anything turns up, Darren has offered to make MP3 recordings available at a later date.

We conclude with John and Eamonn reflecting on what could have been, all starting from a simple sketch of a beetle with big shoes and a gun. "The game could have been very special as we were making original breakthroughs. Alas, the industry had its sights firmly focused on the world of 3D," John reflected. "I've always felt it was 'the one that got away'," added Eamonn. "Had Atari given milestone approvals quicker and paid on time, we could have been done and dusted with *Deathwatch* in only around six months, and it would have done well because it was different. If Atari pushed out more games quicker and encouraged more developers to the Jaguar, things could have been very different indeed."

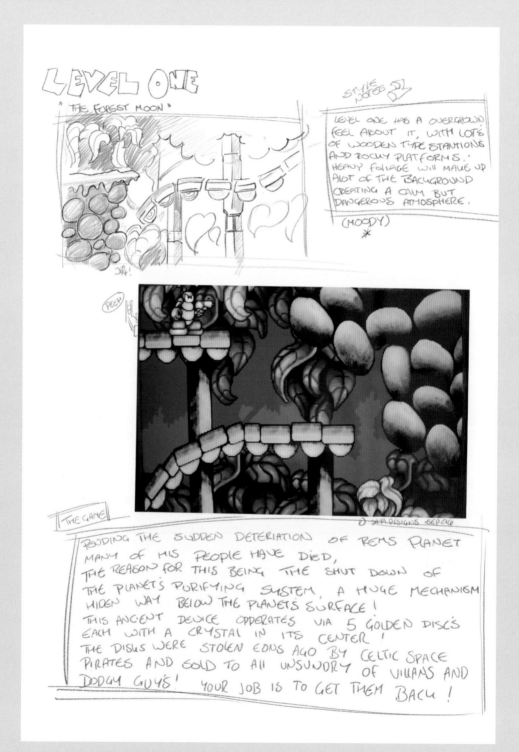

Above: Level 1 – The Forest Moon proposal by John, complete with a pixel mock-up to visualise the colours and theme as a whole.

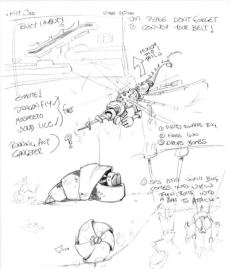

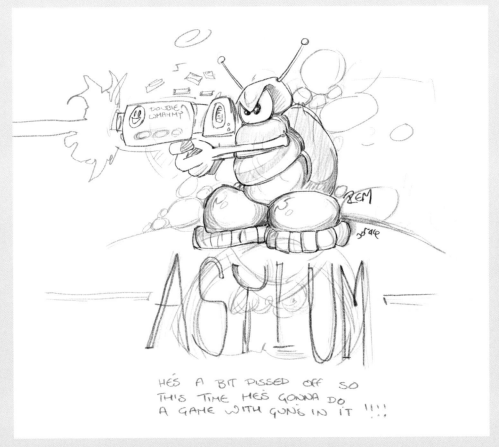

Above: Various early sketches of Rem and enemies from John's sketchbook, showing the very large boots and weaponry that make up the key characteristics.

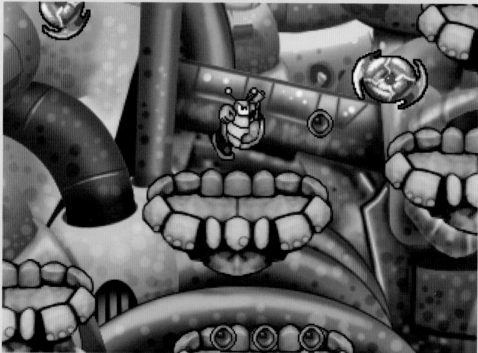

Above: Artist's interpretations of *Deathwatch*'s 'Industrial' level, based on stills from the E3 demo and some of the recovered sprites.

Above: Sprites by Richard of the caterpillar boss, scorpion, lice, wasp and water beetle creatures.

Above: Artist's interpretation of *Deathwatch*, based on a rare screenshot from *Ultimate Future Games Jaguar* supplement, showing a much later build with vastly improved visuals.

Bound High! Delays

**Year: 1996
Developer: Japan
System Supply
Platform: Nintendo
Virtual Boy**

Control Chalvo the robot, transformed into a ball to bounce and destroy alien invaders across a number of levels. A fast-paced and promising title that was delayed so much that the Virtual Boy had been discontinued by Nintendo before it could be released. However, Chalvo later surfaced on the Game Boy classic in *Chalvo 55*.

Available to play

 Yes  No

Discussing 'Star Fox 2'
Focus on N64 instead

Year: 1996
Developers: Nintendo and Argonaut Software
Platform: Super Nintendo

The superb Super FX chip debut of *Star Fox* (renamed to *Starwing* in Europe) gave the Super Nintendo a huge shot of adrenalin back in 1993. Following the adventures of Fox McCloud and his team, you had to defend your homeland of Corneria from the onslaught of Andross in a wonderfully frantic polygonal on-rails shooter. Although a major success, it wasn't going to be until 1996 that a sequel would be released to the world, rather late in the Super Nintendo's life.

Too late in fact, as the game was cancelled to switch focus towards the imminent Nintendo 64 launch. The game would eventually see an official release in 2017 through the Super Nintendo Classic Edition. Dylan Cuthbert answers questions regarding his time on the sequel.

Although due as a late Super Nintendo release, it seems that *Star Fox 2* was started as soon as the original game had been published. Is that correct?
I had made the *Star Fox* competition cartridge, but, apart from that – yes, it was a straight transition to a sequel. Shigeru Miyamoto had also already decided, at that point, that we should not make it 'on-rails' based as now we had the FX chip v2 which would have more than twice the performance of the original.

Available to play
 Yes No

Image: Part of the animated intro sequence (Super Nintendo),
showing off in all its Super FX glory.

Was the new Super FX chip built around the needs of *Star Fox 2*?
No, we had all already decided what would be added to the chip a long time in advance, even before *Star Fox*'s release.

What advantages did the new chipset give you for *Star Fox 2* in particular?
The main thing we got from the new chipset was the ability to draw into mapped sprites, so 3D could be drawn into the hardware sprites. *Yoshi's Island* used this to full effect.

A non-linear approach was taken with the sequel to set it apart from the original game. Were titles such as *Star Raiders* an inspiration?
[Katsuya] Eguchi was a big fan of *Star Raiders* at the time, and the *Rogue*-like style of play was definitely an inspiration for the game. But we took it all a lot further, of course.

What do you feel were the stand-out features of the sequel overall?
The 3D clipping we used to allow you to submerge in lava, and also the much faster particle/sprite system that let us have denser asteroid fields and similar effects were particularly impressive. Also, all the 3D platform elements were very fresh and new at the time.

Can you tell us more about the 3D platform elements; was there any inspiration from *Mario 64*, which I guess you may have all seen early previews of?
Within the 3D platform segments, the player could run up slopes and jump onto rotating platforms, and this hadn't really been done back then. A lot of the basics of *Mario 64* were played around with when we were developing this part

Was there anything that you were not happy with or felt did not work?
Probably the lack of some of those epic on-rails sections like we had in the original game.

'I still enjoyed the time on the game – so it wasn't that bad."

At one point, you had an ambitious split-screen battle mode working. Can you tell us why this was eventually dropped from the final version of the game?
It was pretty tough to develop and ultimately was dropped because we couldn't get it to be enough fun at a decent frame rate. In the end, we decided to concentrate on just the single-player part of the game.

A reason *Star Fox 2* was not released was Nintendo wanting a clean break between 3D games on the SNES and Nintendo 64. Seems a strange decision?
I feel they should probably have released *Star Fox 2*, especially as the N64 was very late in the end. However, Nintendo was not very friendly with Sony at the time and couldn't even consider being compared with the newly released PlayStation. So, it couldn't be helped.

Still, it must have been frustrating with the amount of time spent on it?
Even though it 'wasted' two years of my life, I still enjoyed the time on the game –
so it wasn't that bad. Plus, I was still only 22 at the end of the project, with
plenty of things to be getting on with.

"I feel they should probably have released *Star Fox 2*, especially as the N64 was very late in the end."

Star Fox 2 **eventually saw an official release in 2017 on the Super NES Mini. However, prototypes have already been around for some time. Any idea how?**
No, but I have a fully complete version as part of my own personal collection,
although the ROM doesn't boot anymore, unfortunately (UV rays slowly wipe
those old EPROMs). All my old data files were in storage at Argonaut Software
though, so perhaps something went walkabout when that company closed
down. I do seem to recall a very early version of the ROM leaking from the USA
too. People just go to extreme lengths to play *Star Fox* it seems.

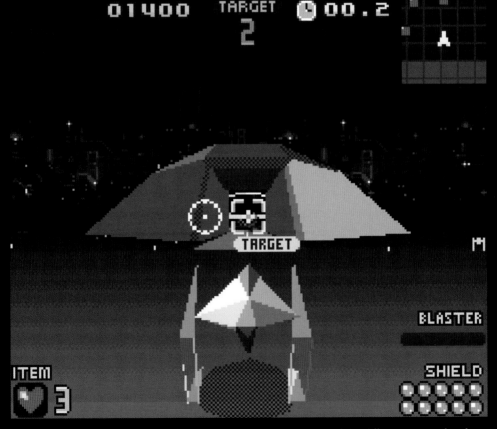

Above: Screenshot from *Star Fox 2* (Super Nintendo) showing one of the different types of craft
you could control.

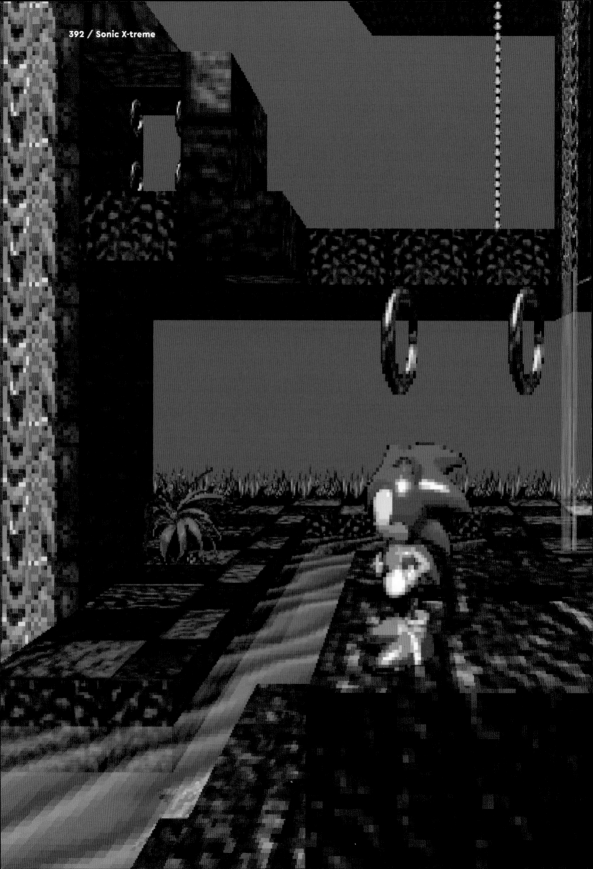

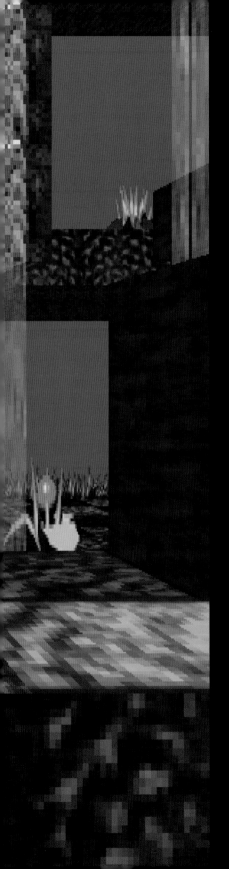

Sonic X-treme Developer illness

Year: 1997
Developer: SEGA Technical Institute
Platform: SEGA Saturn

It should have been the first proper foray into 3D for Sonic. In development hell for some years, with versions dropped and use of the *NiGHTS into Dreams* engine denied. After the lead developer fell ill, the game was eventually scrapped, denying the Saturn a title it so desperately needed. Years later, leaked prototypes and levels showed what could have been.

"It was an honour and a privilege to work on *Sonic X-treme*. The many challenges and ultimate cancellation of the game led to exponential personal and professional growth. I'm very grateful for the relationships that were developed directly and indirectly during and in subsequent years. Definitely a life-changing experience for me!

A lot of people worked hard on *Sonic X-treme*, and it is a shame it was never finished. However, amidst that disappointment, I have many fond memories. The many hours spent every day discussing the development of the world-building editor with Ofer Alon, brainstorming new ideas with Richard Wheeler, composing conceptual music that inspired character designs for countless enemy and boss characters, witnessing these characters come to life through the talent of Ross Harris, getting to a point where we could really build the core of what could have been an exciting game and a pivotal product for SEGA."

Christian Senn, co-director, project leader & art director

Available to play
 Yes   No

Ridge Racer Required PS1 exclusivity

Year: 1996
Developer: Psygnosis
Platform: PC

Available to play

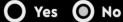 Yes No

Although we already had driving simulators, such as *Hard Drivin'*, with 3D polygons to try and create a sense of realism, 1993 marked the arrival of racing games that actually felt and looked real. Namco's *Ridge Racer* blew arcade gamers away on arrival due to its groundbreaking use of texture-mapped polygon graphics and shading, which contributed in spades to a fast and exhilarating racing experience.

The game was lined up as one of the major launch titles for the new Sony PlayStation console in 1994, developed by Namco itself to help ensure a solid conversion. Although the PlayStation was nowhere near as powerful as Namco's System 22 arcade hardware, the conversion was stunning, to say the least, and helped to firmly establish the PlayStation as the must-have console.

Before its bold entrance into the console market, Sony was already getting its teeth into games, working with Psygnosis on a number of Super Nintendo titles, such as *Last Action Hero* and *Mickey Mania*. At the time, Psygnosis was also experimenting with CD-based technology, knowing that the format was going to be big with its large and cheap storage. These factors ultimately culminated in Sony purchasing the company in 1993 to help produce new games for its upcoming console. Eventually, Psygnosis saw itself renamed to Sony Studio Liverpool in 2000.

Psygnosis became a major developer for the PlayStation, delivering great titles such as *Wipeout*, *Destruction Derby* and many more over the coming years. Interestingly, its work was not fully exclusive to the PlayStation to start with, retaining a level of independence to develop for the PC, Nintendo and SEGA. This independence resulted in conversions of its early PlayStation titles to the PC and Saturn, with dedicated teams assigned to each conversion. What may surprise many is that *Ridge Racer* was part of the schedule. No licence had yet been fully agreed with Namco, and, in a somewhat risky move, it would be negotiated whilst the game was in development. It was expected that *Ridge Racer* would form a new wave of conversions from the PlayStation to PC, which resulted in relatively successful translations of *Wipeout* and *Destruction Derby*.

Overseeing production was studio manager Morgan O'Rahilly. Andy Yelland was assigned as lead developer and also acted as producer – both commonly shared roles at the time. Unfortunately, Morgan did not respond, and Andy declined to discuss his time on the project, as did a few others who were also involved.

This has meant difficulty in getting a complete credit list for the development, but what we have established is that developing alongside Andy was Jed Adams, Chris Eden, Dave Smith and a recently employed Andy Satterthwaite. "This was very early in my career, back when I was still a newbie junior programmer," recalled Andy. "Psygnosis were looking to put *Wipeout* and *Krazy Ivan* (two of their internal PS1 games) onto PC. Someone somewhere signed up *Ridge Racer* as part of the package." It is believed that Ian Grieve may have arranged the conversion with Namco, but we heard nothing back from our enquiries.

All of Psygnosis's conversions of the PlayStation games developed were translated from well-documented C code and were generally not too painful to convert over as a result. In comparison, the PlayStation *Ridge Racer* code was fairly incomprehensible, not helped by the fact that all of the comments were written in Japanese. Without a translator to hand, it required clever thinking by the team to find an effective way to port the game. "We decided just to rewrite the PlayStation library functions for PC so that we could effectively recompile each game against our library, and so it 'should' just work," revealed Andy.

Jed Adams's main focus was developing the graphics-rendering engine and ensuring that different PCs were able to handle the game at a decent speed. "It was a lot of fun working on the project, and I loved working with the guys. I think we'd started work on *Wipeout* PC when we got the source for *Ridge Racer*," recalled Jed. "Since our chosen port method was to basically convert the PlayStation SDK, we shared the core code between the two projects. I worked mostly on the graphics and rendering side, also decoding the PlayStation data – converting it to PC-usable format. We used Watcom C (I think) and a lot of homegrown tools we created ourselves internally at Psygnosis/Sony."

Working on graphics were Gary Burley and John Dwyer, both long-time friends who had studied at university together. "It was a 'simple' up-resolution job of the polygons and texture size," explained Gary. "All of it was part of a two-game deal where we went and did the same for *Wipeout 2097* with existing polys and textures too. We were a closed team and were pretty experienced. We had about 30–40 games under our belt by then and knew exactly what to do."

The development team had full access to everything from the PlayStation version but not the arcade, causing problems when trying to improve the visuals for more graphically capable PC owners. Much of the artwork would be mostly identical to the PlayStation edition, but upscaling was a difficult and frustrating task for the team. "The problem is that, if you are scaling something down, then that is easy. If you're scaling assets up, then you have to improvise and make sure the new and higher resolution artwork holds up in the game for speed, and the details don't flicker going into the distance," explained Gary. "We just used *Photoshop* and Silicon Graphics machines for the polys."

John agreed with Gary's assessment and remembered spending a lot of time on the high-powered PCs to upscale all the textures. It was one of his first conversion projects, and he recalled it being very exciting to work on due to being such a well-known title. Although John couldn't recall too much else about the project, he remembered that particular attention was paid to the livery and banners, where input came in from marketing on what to include.

Menus and titles would remain very similar to the PlayStation edition, with minor improvements and options relevant to PC users, such as controls and resolution. Audio was ripped straight from the PlayStation as well, with very little work done to it at all, apart from some minor optimisations to help with the game's running speed. Content-wise, the game was just a port of the PlayStation game.

Once the core libraries were written and in place, it only took approximately six months or so to get the game fully up and running. With the PlayStation version already out there for a while, it was easy to keep playtesting and ensure that the conversion was accurate in comparison. The only struggles were with the teams trying to do several titles at once and jumping between projects, but also with essential optimisation work required to cover the range of PC specifications that existed at the time.

Although it ran very well on Pentium PCs of the time, it wasn't great on lesser specifications. "We were told it had to work on 486 PCs (without graphics acceleration)," recalled Andy. "Turning off all the Pentium optimisations meant that the game only ran in a postage stamp-sized window; so not great."

"The conversion was such a good clone of the PS1 original."

Jed remembered the performance differently. "I wrote a few versions of the rendering for different spec hardware, but we never ran in a postage stamp, always full screen," he recalled. "One of the things I remember was writing a screen doubler so, whilst the game was rendering to half resolution, it was displayed full screen with double pixels, but the UI was just normally rendered, so it didn't look too awful. I remember we didn't have access to 3D accelerator cards until way late in the project, but we did make prototype versions for the early Nvidia and Rendition cards. The software-rendered version was quite a decent port."

It was felt that the conversion was comparable with the PlayStation edition, with vastly improved graphics when running at higher resolution options. To get everything running on lower spec machines, the team worked hard to optimise what they could to make things more universally available to owners not yet able to get hold of a 3D accelerator card. Work was going well overall, and the team was confident that it was onto another solid conversion. "The conversion was such a good clone of the PS1 original that it looked the same. Thanks to the programmers, it was also smoother and faster around the track – without too much distant digital noise," confirmed Gary.

Whilst development was underway, there had oddly been a distinct lack of press coverage on the conversion compared with *Wipeout* and *Destruction Derby*. Everything was at a 'blink and you'll miss it' level. *Computer and Video Games* magazine first briefly mentioned the conversion as late as March 1996 within its editorial pages, talking about how the likes of Namco were now open to seeing their titles converted to the PC. *Ridge Racer* was mentioned and was suggested to be in development for some time and close to arcade perfect.

The very same month, *PC Gamer* listed the game under a 'Where are they now?' boxout, suggesting that it was behind schedule. A release date of April/May was slated. In the same magazine, another article talked to Psygnosis, where it was stated that its next wave of PC conversions was held back to improve on the graphics and gameplay. *Computer and Video Games*'s 'Checkpoint' scheduled release dates (apparently obtained from HMV) showed the game for just one month in June 1996, with a projected release date of May 1996.

"Ridge Racer was basically refused a release."

After that point, the conversion completely disappeared and was never mentioned again. Behind the scenes, and although practically complete, it had been decided not to release the conversion. Jed felt that it might have been due to negotiations falling through between Sony and Namco over the conversion underway whilst the game was in development. Intriguingly, Namco was also involved in a project at the time which could have had implications for Psygnosis's conversion being continued.

In late 1995, a PowerVR graphics chipset was making waves in the PC world, with impressive specifications that threatened to outclass the likes of the PlayStation and Saturn. There were boasts that it could handle four times the graphical work of the PlayStation version of *Ridge Racer* with the new *Rave Racer*. Namco was involved directly and pledged support through arcade ports of *Air Combat 22*, *Rave Racer* and *Tekken*. Even Psygnosis was looking at the technology, according to Dominic Mallinson in the press at the time. *Rave Racer* was the only title to be seen in any visible form, with an impressive demo produced to showcase the chipset's capabilities.

Namco's involvement with the PowerVR chipset may have been a factor in the cancellation of Psygnosis's *Ridge Racer* conversion. However, once the chipset eventually saw a release around late 1996, there was nothing of the promised Namco conversions. This may have been due to the result of a deal struck with Sony, and likely the real reason why the Psygnosis conversion was canned. An agreement was reportedly made between Sony and Namco to ensure that arcade conversions of their popular titles would feature only on the PlayStation console.

"*Ridge Racer* was basically refused a release as it became a flagship title at the time," confirmed Psygnosis's musician, Mike Clarke. Although Sony owned Psygnosis and had games like *Wipeout* converted over to other platforms, it seemingly wanted to hold some titles back as exclusives to encourage people to buy its console. It would be a number of years until users saw the likes of

Ridge Racer 64 appear on the Nintendo 64, once the exclusivity deal had no doubt expired. Although it meant throwing away a practically complete conversion, Psygnosis had learnt plenty from the experience and had better tools available as a result to help convert future PlayStation work to the PC and possibly other platforms. In Psygnosis's eyes, it was time well spent. The teams would move on to projects such as *Wipeout 2097*, with *Ridge Racer* shelved without too many tears being shed.

But how would a *Ridge Racer* conversion on the PC have really shaped up? Although those involved suggest that it was close to the PlayStation edition (if not better), we may never know fully for ourselves, unless a build is leaked someday. No one involved on the project was able to keep anything of the game or would be allowed to show anything anyway. It would have been interesting to see how the PC edition would have fared, but some things are just not meant to be.

In the end, PC owners longing for a *Ridge Racer* conversion would be left with a game called *Screamer*, a blatant clone of the arcade game which had appeared in 1995, released by Virgin Interactive. It was something at least, but not the conversion fans of the arcade had craved.

May (no set release date)

		•	•
A-10 Silent Thunder	Sierra	PC CD	
Alone in the Dark	Infogrames	PlayStation	
Baku Baku Animal	Sega	Saturn	
Bioforge Gold	EA	PC CD	
Blam! Machinehead	Core	PlayStation/ Saturn	
Championship Manager All Stars	Domark	PC CD	
Deadline	Psygnosis	PC CD	
Earthseige 2: Skyforce	Sierra	PC CD	
In the Hunt	THQ	PlayStation	
Loaded	Gremlin	Saturn	
Primal Rage	Time Warner	PlayStation	
Return to Zork	Activision	PlayStation/Saturn	
Quake	GT	PC CD	
Ridge Racer	Psygnosis	PC CD	

Top: Screenshots from left to right of *Screamer* (PC) and *Ridge Racer* (PlayStation).
Bottom: It seems the press (*C&VG* at least) knew of a PC conversion – somehow.

Thrill Kill was an unreleased fighter billed as a new *Mortal Kombat*, impressively featuring four players fighting simultaneously. Controversy around the game's violence and sexual content had raised eyebrows. When Electronic Arts took over publishing, it felt the game was too violent and canned it. The game snuck out from former employees, showing at least what all the fuss was about.

"The Paradox team's effort to make a cohesive and competitive 3D four-player fighting game (not to mention the first of its kind) was overshadowed by the controversies *Thrill Kill*'s subject matter created. The hype came on so fast that it was impossible for Virgin Interactive's PR team to not capitalise on the violence and adult themes. Unfortunately, at the time we were wrapping up the game for release, Virgin sold their entire library to Electronic Arts, a publisher that was not willing or wanting to take on the polarising press.

It was hard on myself and the whole team to see years of hard work instantly gone. Fortunately, the engine we created and the lessons we learned on creating *Thrill Kill*, helped us quickly improve upon our eventual release of *Wu-Tang Clan: Shaolin Style*. The content in *Thrill Kill* would not have been as controversial if it were released today."

Kevin Mulhall, producer

Thrill Kill
Controversial
content

Year: 1998
Developer: Paradox Development
Platform: Sony PlayStation

Available to play
Yes   No

Is it right that *SDRR* was inspired by a pre-Sensible Software game idea called *Drugged-out Hippy* from the mid-'80s? What did that particular game involve?

JH: That was one of the oldest game ideas in the company and was actually discussed before we even made *Twister* (our very first game). It was just a fun idea about a guy who was a singer in a band, with seven different drug habits and who had to pay some money back to some Hell's Angels before they kicked his face in.

Available to play

 Yes ● No

Top: Cutscenes produced for the game, showing the main protagonist passed out, singing in the studio and then playing with the band. Bottom: Various gameplay screenshots.

H: The band and lead character Nigel Staniforth-Smythe came across from tha original idea. It just evolved, and we kept on shaping it to make it more acceptable commercially. We firstly got rid of the seven different habits, all o which had different effects on the way the game would run, and made drugs more occasional and the character less dependent on them. We also focused more on a band that becomes famous and goes to the US quickly, rather than ust bumping along the bottom in seedy British gig venues.

At one time, we also considered him grabbing girls off the street to take into hi van and pimp them out. This was in 1994 (three years before the first *GTA* came out). In any case, we decided to ditch this as it might have been too dodgy. The concept was miles ahead of its time, we always saw it as '*Leisure Suit Larry* with Balls'. It was not practical to pitch or sell to anyone until we moved beyond the 6-bit era, where suddenly we saw an opportunity and took it.

Would it be fair to say the game's controversial subject matter was designed to deliberately catch people's attention, including the mainstream press?

H: No, not really; we were just having a laugh. It was classic British humour more like *Derek and Clive*, *Spinal Tap* or *Viz* magazine than *GTA*. Chris [Yates and I had played in bands for a long time together, so we knew the life; it was ust meant to be fun. However, as we were about to discover, not everyone has the same sense of humour. Things like *Viz* magazine, *Oasis*, *Max Headroom* and *Pulp Fiction* would have encouraged us, along with older stuff like *Leisure Sui Larry* and *The Young Ones*. This was all just before the boring PC brigade kicked n and fucked our humour up forever.

Were you envisioning a point-and-click-like design for the gameplay?

H: Yes, *Leisure Suit Larry* was an early inspiration, as was *Monkey Island*. It was ntended to be the world's first truly multimedia project. In our minds, it was an adventure game with full music videos from a cartoon band, a cartoon series and an album.

Game-wise it would have been a progression in the point-and-click adventure game world, and *SDRR* would have been a natural progression from SCUMM. I would have always looked like a cartoon on-screen at all times, just one you could interact with. I even studied *EastEnders* to work out camera angles needed for conversations.

Were you going to develop your own engine or use something like SCUMM?

H: Yes, as the design was very advanced at the time compared with anything else. I am really sad that we never got to prove that engine, which is something blame almost entirely on incompetent programming at the start. It would have been the first adventure game with no HUD, just a transparent context-sensitive ursor that you controlled, as well as adventurous pencil-drawing, black-and-white flat backgrounds with colour *3D characters*, like the *Paddington* cartoon. So the game was always going to look and play more like a film and sometimes slip into music videos in the same cartoon world. For controls, think *Heavy Rain* about 18 years earlier.

We signed the game in a three-game deal with Warner."

Once the concept came together, did it take long to find a publisher?
JH: Two parties were interested: Warner (formerly Renegade – *Sensible Soccer* publishers) and Virgin (*Cannon Fodder* and *Sensible Golf* publishers). We signed the game in a three-game deal with Warner, including *Sensible Soccer 3D* and *Have a Nice Day*. We did actually want to split the products between the two companies as we liked both of them, but neither Warner nor Virgin would agree to that, so we had to choose and signed with Warner for around £1 million per game, which was a lot of money back then.

Apart from the visual look, what was planned to make it a blockbuster game?
JH: Our game would have been massively groundbreaking in terms of control system, conversation system, presentation style, and being a true multimedia phenomenon. This was the devastating thing to lose when game development stopped as, to me, it mattered far more than the actual subject matter.

Controversial elements were going to feature heavily within *SDRR*; can you give some examples of what you could have expected to find in the game?
JH: There were some stupid childish crass bits like wanking at a girl spinning around on a wheel and trying to hit targets on her breasts and pussy, or drawing a big knob on a poster of Jesus. It was meant to be funny though, and, at Sensible, we had an office full of very dark, male, British humour. Those days are now long gone. We also had to change a bit where Nigel was nailed to a cross and being shagged by a girl with colossal pneumatic tits. We had to change the cross to a star – so as not to offend Christians.

Did the changes happen when Warner sold its games publishing arm to GT?
JH: GT was a Bible belt US company that was backed by the Walmart group, and they really didn't like the content. I kept on batting them back on requested changes, but, in retrospect, I should have listened to 'Uncle' Frank Herman, who was chairman of GT at the time in Europe. He asked me could we change the 'coke' to 'space dust', and I said, "No, Frank, the coke is the whole point of it." He warned me that I would be "hoisted by my own petard", and he was right. Frank had previously distributed *Texas Chainsaw Massacre* in the UK and knew a thing or two about how to handle controversial products.

The game pushed on regardless, with tension building with the publisher. The storyline, graphics and sound were happening fast, but the engine wasn't?
JH: Yes, it was the biggest showstopper of all. Loads of graphics, music, script

FX and speech samples, but no working code to show it off. The lead developer had about 18 months, and he was clueless; what I would class as a 'coding bullshitter'. He was a weak lead programmer giving his designer boss (me) free rein to go overboard with design, because he wanted to get on my good side and get paid in the short term, rather than acting like a responsible coder and reeling me in earlier. I shudder to think how much work the art team and I wasted because of this.

With too much content, was it going to take up too much disk space?

JH: We had to reduce the game from 100 to around 60 locations and ramped up compression to get our disk count down. Every night, our office turned into a giant rendering farm to process all of the graphics. By the time we sorted out the problem, the code was at least a year behind, and GT was already breathing down our necks.

Robert, you were brought in during late 1996 to replace the lead programmer and salvage things. Did you have much to work with from when you started?

RT: Jon had already written a large number of 'scripts', which described various scenes of the game and the gameplay in a kind of informal programming language. The previous programmer had built some tools but had no knowledge of compiler technology, which was required to turn the scripts into a game.

So, you had to essentially start building from scratch?

RT: Yes. Based on what I knew of compiler technology, I figured a way to formalise the language and translate the scripts into something that could be consumed by a game engine. I set to work building a script compiler and game engine and also specified a bunch of tools and technologies to manage and process the enormous volume of rendered cartoon-style animations – turning them into backgrounds and interactive elements of the game. The other programmer worked diligently on those tools, and, between us, we moved the project towards something that could have actually been fun and entertaining.

Who was now working on the game along with yourselves at this stage?

JH: A guy called Graham King did all the drumming on the soundtrack, as well as helping to turn my scripting into more accurate code data for Rob's program to read, but, by this stage, it was all too little too late. I also wrote nearly all of the songs together with Richard Joseph; we recorded some great sound for this game, not only music but a lot of recording actors as well in his Pinewood studio.

Programming was our Achilles' heel with this game. Chris Yates was working on *Have a Nice Day,* and Chris Chapman was busy with *Sensible Soccer 3D,* while Tools was setting up on his own after *Sensible Golf.* So we had to hire a lot of new coders, some of whom were not so great initially. We did get there eventually on the code side, but, by then, time was running out.

RT: I remember another programmer called Neil – but I forget his last name and a whole stable of other artists working on building all the rendered content.

H: He was called Neil Duffin. We also had ten artists on it by the end, led by Johnny Watts and John Laws, who are now both senior employees at Frontier.

Eventually, the game was cancelled, but is it true that there was still a final opportunity to see the game finished and released? What happened next?

H: The game left GT, and we needed to find another publisher because our publisher had been taken over by fundamentalist Christians. Sean Brennan (a great supporter of ours at Virgin) was the only person to make an offer to continue, but such was the market at the time, he could only guarantee sales in the UK. Because of this, the advance wasn't big enough to finish the game without losing money. So we thanked Sean and reluctantly called time.

RT: As I see it, there were two main barriers to getting the game published. First, it was very adult content – exactly what you'd expect from the title, so publishers were scared. Second, all the pre-rendered content was going to fill a lot of CDs so manufacturing costs would have been very high compared with most games.

We needed to find another publisher because our publisher had been taken over by fundamentalist Christians."

How much was left to finish at the time?

RT: The technology was coming along nicely, maybe 50% or better, but only a very small section of the game was actually playable. I remember having one complete playable scene up and running, effectively a proof of concept that could be shown to potential publishers, with every reason to think that the rest of the game could be built. The huge unknown in terms of time to completion was going to be debugging the scripts, so it's almost impossible to estimate how far we were from being done.

H: Art was 75% complete, music was 90% complete, script (coded version) was 80% complete, videos were 50% complete, speech/sound was 40% complete, game engine was about 50% complete (but non-functioning).

If you had the chance to start over again, what would you do differently?

H: Very simple: we would not have made *Have a Nice Day* (which also got canned) and would have had Chris Yates as lead developer on *SDRR*. Also, we'd have spent a bit more time hiring a couple of shit-hot 3D programmers, a couple of great 3D animators and modellers, and a middle manager who could work with our team. We would have also insisted on signing *SDRR* with Virgin and *Sensible Soccer 3D* with Warner. I wouldn't change anything else.

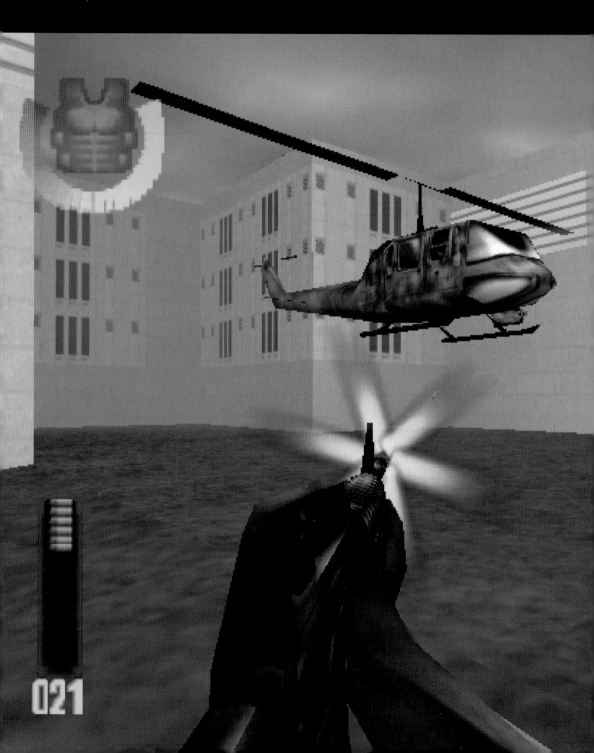

021

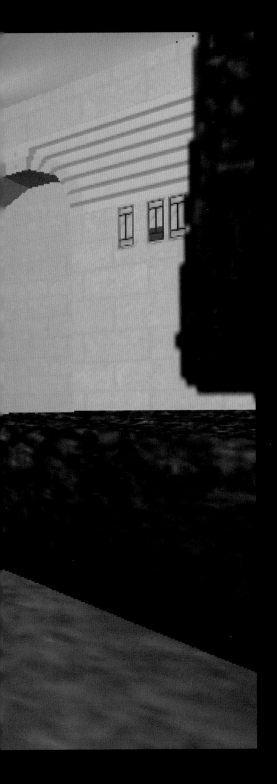

Die Hard 64
Decreasing N64 sales

Year: 1999
Developer: Bits Studios
Platform: Nintendo 64

Only mentioned briefly in the press, it came as a surprise when prototypes surfaced in 2017. A first-person shooter featuring impressive large maps, there was still plenty of work to be done before its eventual cancellation due to the dying N64 market. The game was eventually reworked and released as *Die Hard Vendetta* on other platforms in 2002.

Available to play

 Yes ◯ No

Two Thousand — Two Thousand and Nine

A now vastly different scene compared with the previous three decades, with innovations and evolution that many probably never imagined back at the start. As the dust began to settle on just a handful of platforms, mobile gaming via phones and tablets would start to appear – creating a whole new gaming arena. There were a few surprises too, with SEGA eventually limping away from the console race to focus on games, never recovering from failures such as the SEGA 32X.

By now, the complexity and size of the games would require teams of hundreds. If it didn't before, then getting a development wrong now could result in catastrophic losses financially. The risks often meant that companies were less willing to take risks on unproven titles and would stick to knocking out sequels to well-established franchises. Creativity would suffer; though, thankfully, the likes of the new emerging mobile gaming market would ensure that there was still a chance for smaller teams to keep on innovating.

Putty Squad
Commercial viability

Year: 1994–2013
Developer: System 3
Platforms: Apple iOS, Commodore Amiga 1200,
Nintendo Game Boy Color, Nintendo DS,
Nintendo Wii U, PC (DOS + Windows),
SEGA Mega Drive, Sony PlayStation 2
and Sony PlayStation Portable

Available to play
◉ Yes ◯ No

***Putty Squad* on the Amiga 1200 is probably one of the most famous unreleased games of all time on the platform. It wasn't just Amiga fans that were feeling left out though, with a number of other conversions for later platforms also falling by the wayside. To mark the start of a new decade, we cover a game crossing over three decades and covering an almost 20-year period.**

Putty first started life within System 3's *Silly Putty* (later shortened to just *Putty*) back in 1992, as a blue blob that could mould and stretch into various different shapes and sizes to move around platforms and obstacles with ease. The aim was simply to save a number of robots and get them to safety on each vertically scrolling level. Everything was great to look at and listen to when first hitting Amiga screens, with wonderful animations, speech samples and crazy characters throughout. The positive reception was deemed successful enough for System 3 to consider a sequel in the form of *Putty Squad*.

"Almost right after *Putty*, I felt the character deserved a bigger game, something as large as *Super Mario World*," explained designer Phil Thornton. "It all got a bit out of control during the design stage (the original level layout was epic), so I was reigned in a bit by the programmers. I had wanted *Putty* in an *Apocalypse Now* scenario. The original *Putty* developer Dan Phillips and I used to discuss the Vietnam War, and I had a comedy routine I used in the pub where I pretended I was in Nam during the 1970s on special operations before joining the games business, but I couldn't talk about it."

"We came up with very silly ideas regarding special forces, including an Origami Unit, a secret program by the CIA that involved using sarcasm to wind up the enemy, and many other daft concepts," he continued. "These were not related to any game but lingered in my mind. Eventually, the thought came to me to apply the 'Nam' nonsense from the pub to the new Putty game – so *Putty Squad* was born. He would be part of a Special Forces operation behind enemy lines. *The Terminator* movies were very inspirational as well in both games; Dan Phillips was a huge fan of Arnold, hence the Terminator Carrots."

The general idea of the game would remain similar to the original, with the aim now to rescue other putties. However, the game now would have multidirectional scrolling to completely open up Putty's world. There would be further inventive characters added, including chattering teeth and robots and also the ability to call a flying machine to help you navigate around levels. Phil would construct most of the background and general artwork for the game, with artist Nick Lee carrying out the sprite work.

"This was my first job within the games industry, having bumped into the System 3 folks down the pub," began Nick. "I felt the design was pretty much open – Phil and I just kind of made things up as we went along, and there was no schedule or game design document. Phil drew the map tiles and put the maps together along with me. I think Phil might have led the sprite design, and I took a single image and animated them – some were refugees from the original *Super Putty* game. When we started the project, it was all 2D sprites drawn in *Deluxe Paint*, but, by the end, Robin Levy was on board, where we started to use *3D Studio Max* on PCs to create animated intro scenes and the box art."

Nick and Phil would take inspiration from the *Sonic the Hedgehog* titles and *Super Mario World*, but the Bitmap Brothers were also a major influence for Nick. "I thought their games looked amazing," he confirmed. "Dan Malone eventually came to work with us and taught me a great deal. We're still good friends 20 years later, and, every time I go back to London, I'll meet up with him."

Bringing all of the design to life was John Twiddy, who would lead development on the primary Amiga 1200 platform. Richard Joseph and Jason Page would round things off by producing a variety of lively music tracks and sound effects to accompany all of the action. The game would see a release eventually in 1994, but only as a European release on the Super Nintendo platform. The planned releases for the Amiga, Mega Drive and PC would never see the light of day.

The Amiga version, in particular, would rapidly become one of the 'Holy Grail' unreleased games, thanks to being complete and fully reviewed by the press at the time. However, the bottom had fallen out of the market for the Amiga, so it was decided not to release the game, with Mark Cale suggesting that they also had trouble finding stores that would stock the game. "That was the worst experience – I wouldn't wish it on any developer," reflected Phil. "So much hard work thrown away; it was a bad call. I am sure we would have made a good profit on the Amiga version, especially after the rave reviews."

The Mega Drive edition befell a similar fate, completed by 1995 and reviewed in a number of magazines. By mid-1995, the Mega Drive was declining, and many planned releases (including *Putty Squad*) were no longer financially viable for Ocean. The conversion is believed to have been commissioned for development to Miles Barry under the name of 'Dynamic Interactive Computer Entertainment', with music conversion work by Gerard Gourley. Clues to this would be found within the high-score table featuring names that Miles knew, including famous C64 developers Ashley Routledge and Dave Saunders, and Ash's brother, Olly, who Miles shared a flat with briefly at the time. Phil revealed that Miles did the voice of the Scouse Sausage in the original game.

Nick recalls handling the graphics porting for the development and the struggles of trying to choose the right palettes. "The Mega Drive conversion work was complex," recalled Nick. "I know it didn't look as good colour-wise, but I can't remember the limitations imposed. I can't recall if I ported these from the SNES or Amiga versions, although, bizarrely, I do remember staring at the screen, dealing with the palettes! Kinda burnt into the retinas."

With the PC edition, a four-level demo was eventually created and distributed, including new CGI cutscenes between each level. With no publisher interest, another conversion was cancelled. Compared with the Amiga and Mega Drive versions, though, the development never progressed much further than the preview. It is unknown who the programmer was, though the musician was confirmed to be Martin Oliver, who could not recall anything about the project.

"I was convinced it'd be impossible, and Jon proved me totally wrong and really impressed me with his technical skills."

The game would lay dormant for many years, with Amiga and Mega Drive users questioning what had happened, with the arrival of the Internet further fuelling rumours over both. Meanwhile, as a new millennium dawned, Thalamus Interactive was starting to get involved with the Game Boy Color platform, which had started to rejuvenate 8-bit development once more. As one of their first pitches to get a paying contract with System 3, they decided to come up with a prototype of *Putty Squad* in 2000. Heading up Thalamus Interactive was Andy Roberts, who would oversee the 2–3-week development phase, with veteran C64 developer Jon Wells handling all of the coding. Michael Smith would handle a brilliant conversion of some of the level artwork assets.

"Jon and I went way back from high school," began Michael. "He asked if I'd be interested in doing some graphics for a game called *Space Invasion* on the new Game Boy Color (GBC). After that, we started some prototypes including *Putty Squad*. Since we were doing just a technical demo, I only ported a minimal selection of tiles from the original game. I used *Photoshop* to resize the tiles down, where I think I grabbed them from the SNES version. I then brought them into my favourite bitmap editor, Cosmigo *Pro Motion*, to clean them up and finally laid the tiles out in a map editor for Jon to construct a level."

Utilising Michael's work, Jon created a wonderfully fast and efficient scroll routine to show everything off, with a basic Putty sprite that moved and jumped around at speed. Most of Putty's moves were not implemented at this stage due to the fact that it was just a simple prototype, but it was enough to demonstrate the potential. "It was all produced pretty much off his own back," explained Andy. "I was convinced it'd be impossible, and Jon proved me totally wrong and really impressed me with his technical skills."

"I did all the coding in Z80, which was real fun as I had to learn from scratch while trying to code an audio player, *Space Invasion*, and demos, as well as other useful routines as I went. I'd pretty much only coded in 6502/10 before that, but it wasn't too difficult to pick up," recalled Jon. "The GBC had sprites so was similar to the C64 and Amiga, so, although there would be challenges in developing it, I could see there was the potential to produce a really good conversion. With this in mind, the aim was to create a demo to impress so much that it would increase the chances of being accepted. If not, it would be a really good demo to show off our skills to any publishers when pitching for other conversion work. It took roughly three weeks to do overall."

Accompanying the game were basic sound effects and a conversion of Rob Hubbard's *I-Ball* title tune, with a demonstration of *I-Ball* samples included that could be activated with a button press. "I looked into Rob Hubbard's *I-Ball* source code (oo-er!) and figured out how his music routine worked," recalled Jon. "I jotted down all the channel track sequences and notation on paper. Next, I recreated the music on the Dutch USA *Music Assembler* and ported all the track and note info over to my GBC music player."

This would demonstrate Jon's additional ability to work with the GBC's sound chip and produce decent music, taking all the experiences from his C64 SID composing days. It was a solid start, and System 3 was very impressed with the work carried out by the new team. However, a tentative budget and a rather short deadline were all that was given for completing the conversion. Andy felt that there was no way the game could be properly constructed given the time and monetary constraints, so it was decided to pass on taking it any further.

"I think the reason there wasn't a bigger budget was that there was so much fierce competition on the GBC at the time," reflected Andy. "The market had just become flooded with licences. Even though the Putty brand was a strong one, it probably wasn't strong enough." Not all was lost, and the prototype would lead to Thalamus Interactive being given further work, including the job of creating *International Karate Advance* on the Game Boy Advance a year later.

Andy would remain involved with System 3 over the years following, including involvement in another title in the form of *Last Ninja: The Return* during 2003 (which also was unreleased in the end). Whilst that title was underway, System 3 had decided to launch a budget PlayStation 2 label called Play-It. Andy would propose developments of both *International Karate* and *Putty Squad* for the label, with System 3 particularly keen on the idea for *Putty Squad*.

Given the green light, Andy would start the developments under his Thalamus Interactive label. The plan wasn't to do anything vastly different from the original game, keeping close to the original, with just enhanced graphics and audio to modernise the title for a new audience. It meant that the development should be relatively straightforward and quick – perfect for a low-cost budget title. The team was even supplied with a complete copy of the Amiga source code from John Twiddy to use as a reference point for the conversion, a fact that would have caused shock waves in the Amiga community at the time had it been known.

The development was going to be a near-perfect replication of the A1200 game from John's code, though the team would refer to the SNES edition as a running benchmark due to difficulties with compiling the Amiga code into a runnable state. Nick Lee, who worked on the original, was drafted in to do revamped versions of the sprites. "I had remained in contact with the guys at System 3 long after leaving," recalled Nick. "I did a ten-year stint freelancing and was contacted regarding going over all the sprites and upping the resolution. I just did it as a contract job and never saw the game running. It was just a case of manually scaling up all the sprites and going over the frames cleaning them up. I think I might have just used a generic 256-colour palette for the job."

"I did all the coding in Z80, which was real fun."

Graphic artist Gary Tonge would also be called upon to scale up the old backgrounds and tidy them up in a similar fashion. With the many levels and all the enemies, it would result in a few months of work for the two artists. Luckily, Nick and Gary had access to the original artwork to use as the basis for the new artwork to save some time at least. Early on, System 3 had even suggested extending the maps and adding further abilities for the main character, but there just wasn't time within the financial constraints. With the limited time, budget and small team, Andy would also have to step in to help.

Updates to the original music and sound effects would be carried out by Octagon Music's Jon Colling, who reworked all of Richard Joseph and Jason Page's original Amiga modules note by note. For the game's iconic character voices, Andy enlisted the services of voice artist Marc Silk, who had previously worked on films, such as *Star Wars: The Phantom Menace* and *Chicken Run*, as well as children's TV shows, such as *Bob the Builder* and *Johnny Bravo*.

Although the artwork and sound conversion were coming on well, things were not going so smoothly with the development work to bring it all together. Andy began to have major concerns when progress didn't seem too forthcoming. "I discovered the coder was taking the payments but not actually doing anything," he explained. "He had created a tool for me to view graphics on the PS2 and a very simple demo of a static putty blob scrolling around a level, but that is all I ever saw in terms of a game."

Eventually, the lack of progress with the programming side would catch up and result in key milestones being missed, resulting in payments subsequently not being given. It would eventually lead to Andy reluctantly having no choice but to put Thalamus Interactive into liquidation in 2004, which sadly led to his biggest regret of colleagues losing money, including close friends. Andy not only lost the company but a roof over his head too, rounding off a chastening experience for all.

Was there ever anything fully playable of the game, and how much actually existed in the end by the time of cancellation? "It's hard to tell," Andy reflected. "Although the programmer basically did not deliver on his milestones, certainly the background graphics, presentation screens, sprites, animation, music, and SFX were all complete."

The prospect of a new *Putty Squad* launch would go dormant, but only for a few years, with Mark Cale announcing to *Retro Gamer* magazine in 2008 about remakes being in the pipeline for both the Sony PSP and Nintendo DS platforms. This moment would trigger an unexpected timeline of events for a game release over the years that would follow.

Everything went quiet for a few years after Mark's first announcement, but System 3 would then, out of nowhere, suddenly announce new developments for the Sony PS3, PSP and iOS platforms in Autumn 2010. The planned release date for later that year would come and go, though dedicated Twitter and YouTube pages would launch early the following year, showing early mock-up screens of how the game was going to look. The Twitter account gave hints that a Nintendo 3DS edition was also on the cards, with the Nintendo DS edition now seemingly dropped to make way for it.

Although there were suggestions that a PSP edition was close to completion just a few months later, everything would fall silent once more. Behind the scenes, the release of a PSP edition was under scrutiny as the PS Vita successor was about to launch in late 2011. "We had been working on producing it as a PSP Mini title," recalled lead developer John Twiddy. "But then, as time went by, it was expanded to be a full PSP product by early 2011. This then eventually turned into the PS Vita edition." Joining John across most of the developments were John Jones-Steele (programmer), Steve Rose (programmer), Phil Thornton (artwork), Sound of Games (music), and X-Life Studios (sound effects).

"System 3 would finally answer fans' prayers."

At the start, the development was just going to use graphics from the abandoned PS2 version of the game, before it was decided to completely revamp all of the graphics once again. Phil Thornton would come home to work on the title once more, providing new background artwork and sprites. What began as a simple remake had additionally evolved into a huge new title, with new content planned throughout. John suggests that, as the game development expanded and the features of the Vita became more apparent, the Vita edition would become the primary focus for System 3.

To a point, it explained why the early release dates would come and go, with the game taking far longer than anticipated with the new content required. As well as vastly improved visuals and audio, the game would feature location-based services (on the portable editions) to collect *Putty Squad* stickers, have a touchscreen map (again on the portables), new levels, trophies, tutorial mode, time trial mode, and online leader boards. The conversion to the Vita was not straightforward either, with a number of "twists and turns" reported by System 3 that would cause further delays. They were not short delays either, and it wouldn't be until almost a year later that any further news would be heard.

"John Twiddy's insight was very helpful; the poor bloke having to try and recall what he programmed over 20 years ago."

March 2013 would see a press release almost repeating the last one – this time listing the expected platforms as Nintendo 3DS, PS Vita, PlayStation 3, Xbox 360, PC/Windows, iOS and Wii U. With the platforms growing, the development was becoming a lot more complex and stretched, rather like Putty himself.

Shortly afterwards, the platform support would grow even further, with Steam distribution and the Android platform bolted onto the list – it seemed that no one was safe from the extendable blue blob, if it was released that is. A few months later, there was yet another launch trailer, now promising the game for a summer 2013 launch. This time, there was a bit of a cull, with Steam, Android, PC/Windows, and iOS not making the cut. Phil could not recall ever seeing an Android or PC/Windows version in production but did confirm that the iOS version was at least partially developed, which he believes was created by Welsh-based West Coast Software. "There was a working app. I think I still have this on my PC in Cyprus," he confirmed.

Yet again, the projected release date would come and go, with no sight of the game on any platform. It was beginning to feel like déjà vu for those who had once anticipated the original 1994/1995 versions. System 3 would finally start to answer the growing doubters and surprised everyone by announcing the game as an imminent launch title for the European release of the Sony PlayStation 4. Perhaps ironically, towards the end of 2013, a near-complete prototype of the SEGA Mega Drive game also surfaced on eBay, eventually purchased by a collector named BeaglePuss. However, it would be the surprise scheduled with the release of a PlayStation 4 edition of the game in November (to coincide with the PAL console launch) that would spark pandemonium, in particular, within the Amiga community.

System 3 would finally answer fans' prayers in what was seen as a generous move. The plan was to release the Amiga edition of the game for free to coincide with the impending PS4 launch. Amiga cracker Galahad (Phill B-B) would offer his services for free to help out System 3, which eventually resulted in the release of the game for Christmas Eve of 2013. "The development team and management had a lot of telephone conversations beforehand," recalled Phil of the decision. "I was extremely in favour of the idea as I felt it would generate a lot of goodwill after all the nonsense regarding the non-existence of the game that had been circulating on the web. In the end, it was Mark's decision, and he went for it big time. It was a great Christmas Eve!"

"John Twiddy's insight was very helpful; the poor bloke having to try and recall what he programmed over 20 years ago. He was surprisingly quick with the answers, even with that handicap!" recalled Phill-B-B regarding his recovery work. "All of the work was done over the phone in the initial stages, but, once I got all of the relevant files, it was all done by email. I didn't do it for money, possibly a little bit of fame, but the PS4 that System 3 gave me finally got some proper use from my son, so everyone won I think."

With Amiga fans now in a jubilant mood, owners of the remaining modern platforms were still left wondering where their versions were. Did they also have to wait almost 20 years for their turn? By this stage, it had been decided to drop more planned conversions, with the PC/Windows and Wii U users losing out.

System 3 had decided to scrap the Wii U edition after being unable to get shelf space in retailers. Although rumoured that the Wii U game was close to completion, John confirmed otherwise. "We got hold of the Wii U dev systems with the intention of starting work on that version, but no real progress was ever made on it in the end," he explained. "I think there was an attempt to code it, but I didn't see any demos," added Phil.

Fans anticipating the release of the remaining versions didn't need to worry, with the PS Vita, 3DS, PS3 and Xbox 360 (Xbox Live only) editions finally seeing a release during 2014. Bizarrely, 2017 also saw the game picked up by the Virtual Programming development studio, with releases on Linux, Mac and Android. Generally, the game has seen mixed responses since its various releases, with some arguing that it was perhaps priced a little too high, and others feeling that the gameplay was now quite dated. But, if you are a fan of old-fashioned platform action, and the *Putty* series in particular, then there is plenty still to enjoy.

"We got hold of the Wii U dev systems with the intention of starting work on that version."

The SEGA Mega Drive prototype would be sold on by its owner in 2015 and was eventually dumped shortly afterwards. The game was found to be near completion and may have been a review copy. It was found to be a pretty much straight conversion of the Amiga edition, though missing sound effects, a game completion screen, and final bug fixes and optimisations. There is speculation that, as reviews talked of sound effects and showed some minor differences in the review screenshots, there could still be a later build out there yet to discover.

But, what about the other later editions and the chances of seeing something of them in action? The PlayStation 2 edition had practically nothing developed in the end, but, with the artwork all converted, Andy has very kindly provided some art assets from the title, which you can see here.

The various abandoned enhanced versions that followed for the PSP, iOS, PC, DS and Wii U are declined for release in any shape or form, though, due to the title still being sold today. It is possible something could be shown of all the versions in the future, but there is no reason or benefit for System 3 to do so. Videos of the Game Boy Color prototype can be found online, showing the mock-up first level that was produced. It is hoped that there will be an extra surprise for this version on the Games That Weren't website very soon.

Putty Squad is a title that has been on a massive journey for around 25 years and still continues to resurface on various platforms. It's very likely that it will continue to see updates and new iterations, with System 3 releasing *Super Putty Squad* for the Nintendo Switch in 2017. Thanks to System 3 and the efforts of the SEGA community, this is one of the rarer cases where you can finally play the original title as intended – something that was once thought would never happen.

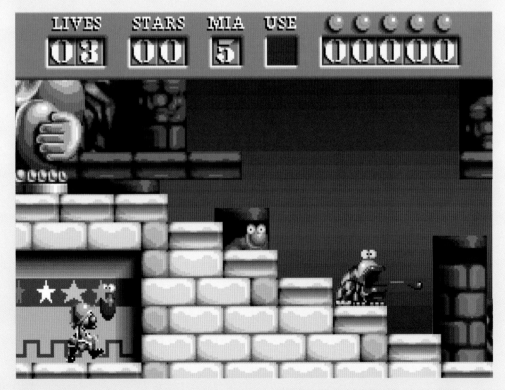

Above: The most famous of all the versions, the Amiga 1200 edition – finally released in 2013. The full story of its recovery can be found online and is certainly worth a read.

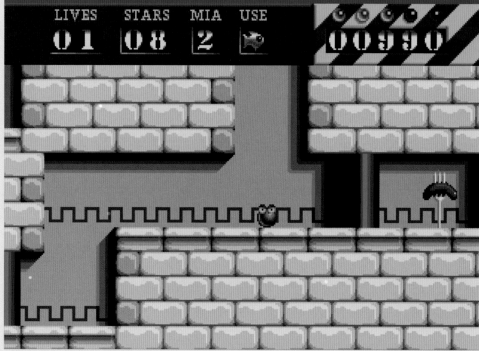

Above: Screenshots from the unreleased SEGA Mega Drive edition, showing title screen and part of the first level. The colour scheme felt a bit duller compared with other versions.

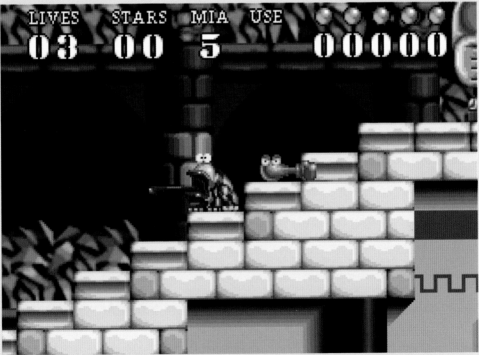

Above: Screenshots from the demo edition of *Putty Squad* (PC DOS), showing a 3D-rendered System 3 logo screen and part of the first level.

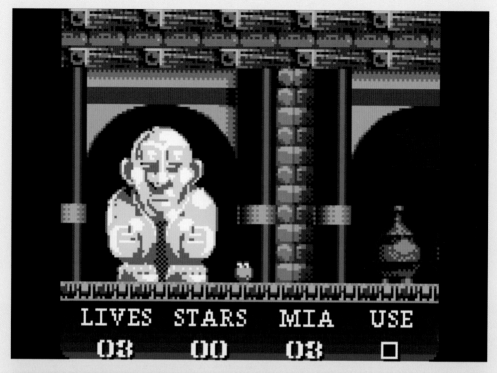

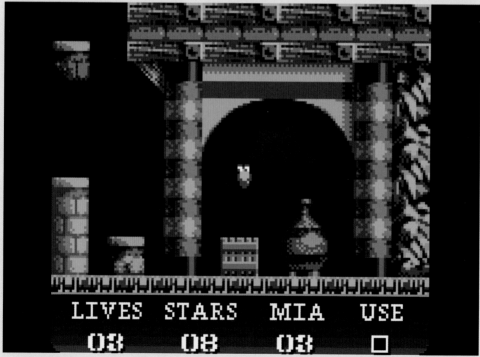

Above: Screenshots from the Game Boy Color prototype level produced by Thalamus Interactive, making great use of the limited screen display space. A shame that it never progressed further.

Above: Prepared screens for *Putty Squad* (PlayStation 2), showing the game map and game over screens and how they would have looked on the platform.

Resident Evil
Too ambitious

Year: 2000
Developer: HotGen
Platform: Nintendo Game Boy Color

An extremely ambitious port of the 1996 PlayStation original to the 8-bit handheld, featuring similar third-person perspectives. Perhaps too ambitious, with Capcom rejecting the game, lacking faith that gamers would enjoy it. Prototypes have since surfaced of the game, with a complete and finished build confirmed to exist but yet to be preserved.

"I was called upon to design and create all the sprites. Great fun until being told they could only be two sprites tall and one wide, with nothing protruding far from the characters, i.e. weaponry. My characters were animated from front, side and rear views. We discussed putting a slight 'tilt' into the graphics but decided on a full-face view – for the most part, it seemed to work. Colour limitations brought their own challenges, but I rose reasonably admirably to said thrown gauntlet.

I remember harsh words spoken towards the end when asked to redraw the entire set from a different viewpoint. When the topic of further payment was broached, I was informed none would be forthcoming. Time to down tools and look elsewhere. It was too adventurous, and a direct conversion was not what Capcom were after apparently. It was fun and productive while it lasted, and I'm happy people still remember our efforts fondly."

Simon Butler, graphic artist

Available to play

 Yes No

SimMars Shelved to focus on The Sims

Year: 2000
Developer: Maxis
Platforms: Apple Macintosh and PC

"The planet Earth has been our home for thousands of years... We have walked upon the surface of the Moon... Now, prepare yourself for mankind's next giant step into space..." Maxis was seeking to hook in fans with an introduction to its next big simulation. Moving on from building vast cityscapes and city life in *SimCity* or running a safari in *SimSafari*, its latest title would put you in control of directing mankind's first colonising mission to the mysterious red planet. All in the hope of creating a viable alternative to planet Earth.

"*SimMars* was an idea I began working on back in 1994, right around the time I joined Maxis," confirmed lead gameplay engineer Jason Shankel. "It was a game that Mike Perry and I had been pitching for a few years, and I'd been working on my own Mars projects for a few years before that. *Mars Direct*, *Red Mars* and the terraforming papers were key sources of inspiration, along with Martyn Fogg's book on terraforming."

"Mars is a topic always close to my heart," he continued. "It's the closest planet to our own in terms of habitability, yet still a barren, nearly airless, radioactive, toxic rock. The challenges of colonising Mars force us to really think about how we want to go about populating a new world. Will we continue with capitalism, or will we have new models of ownership? Will we terraform, or will we preserve the natural state of the planet? Will separate nations emerge, or will everyone there live under a unified government? These are the kinds of questions that were ideal for a Sim game."

Initial designs were enthusiastically weaved together, proposing an agent-based, multi-colony simulator, with a planetary globe containing multiple colonies upon it. The early idea was that clicking each colony would take you to a separate management screen, not looking too dissimilar to a modern-day real-time strategy game. Over the years and following multiple pitches, the design changed to focus on making a more accurate simulator, paving the first steps of mankind going to the planet and trying to inhabit it. Pre-production was finally green-lighted in 1997, shortly after *Streets of SimCity* had shipped, with plans for a release on the Windows PC and with an Apple Macintosh version to follow.

Joining the team of Jason and Mike were Jeff Charvat (director of development), Luc Barthelet (general manager), Matthew Thornton (project manager), Kevin Hogan (designer and producer), and Dan Brazelton (associate producer). "I came on board to help get the project finished. It was already designed, and the tech was in place," recalled Dan of embarking on his first production role. "The design had got bogged down, so the producer [Kevin] and I spent a lot of time with the designer, but it still wasn't gelling. If I remember correctly, the design was more philosophically designed than having the mechanics worked out. I ended up saying some indelicate and insensitive things that I still regret today."

Thankfully, there were no fallouts, and Dan and Kevin got themselves stuck into the design for the game, fixing the early issues, with Kevin taking a leading role. Will Wright was not directly involved, only sitting in on some of the design meetings, where he would ask questions and give feedback.

"I went to Maxis specifically to work on *SimMars*. It was exactly the kind of game I'd always wanted to play, so I was deeply invested in being a part of the group."

At the time, Will was busy himself working on his own new title, named *The Sims*, where there were concerns internally that the game may not catch on. "It was interesting; not a game, not finished, revolutionary to the point of not understandable," recalled Dan. "We spent a lot of time talking with Will – both about *SimMars* and about his game. We took some of his ideas and incorporated them, but I made the mistake of mentioning this."

Surprisingly, EA was not convinced at all by *The Sims* at the start, feeling that it wouldn't sell. When executives heard that *SimMars* would incorporate ideas from the title, they felt that it was a terrible idea. The design team would still press on though and kept the faith, gaining additional inspiration and ideas from Sid Meier's *Alpha Centauri* game, particularly regarding the management of materials and resources.

Over time, the designs and concepts formed became so realistic that they could have been mistaken for actual NASA plans. This was no accident and was thanks to the involvement of the space agency, whom most of the team would spend a lot of time with over the course of the project.

"We wanted to have the game based on real science, and we frequently talked about science, literature and possibilities for the game," recalled systems engineer Alex Zvenigorodsky. "NASA had a program to support any space-related entertainment or journalism. They provided access to facilities and personnel, so we got to spend time there. We attended site selection committee meetings for what would be the Spirit rover, as well as colloquia on planetary science. At that time, Robert Zubrin was just putting together the Mars Society and promoting *Mars Direct*. Stan Robinson and Chris McKay helped Dr Zubrin start up the society, and several of us on the team were founding members."

"It was kind of like an Algonquin Round Table for space exploration – it was a bit intimidating," added Jason. "Here are all these PhDs, including literal rocket scientists, and me with my humble little Bachelor's degree in computer science and electrical engineering. But, the thing is, while all these guys were deep geniuses in their fields, they didn't know each other's very well, and so they communicated at an undergraduate level. It was really exhilarating."

NASA's link-up with Maxis gave the opportunity of seeing a model of what could happen based on some of their own research and projections. It was a vision of events and technology that was felt could be a reality in just 10–15 years. As a result, the outcome of the game was of great interest to them, giving some kind of interactive and visual indicator of whether their ideas could work. It was a win-win situation for both parties.

With a game design close to finalisation, a development team was assembled with Alex Bilyk (lead platform engineer), Colin Andrews (lead graphics engineer), Heather Mace (gameplay engineer), and Alex Zvenigorodsky (systems engineer). Creating all of the artwork would be Bob King, Christian Stratton and B.J. West. Many others were also involved, too many to name here unfortunately.

"I'm a hardcore space geek and always have been," explained B.J. "I went to Maxis specifically to work on *SimMars*. It was exactly the kind of game I'd always wanted to play, so I was deeply invested in being a part of the group." Jason then added, "It was a great team, and everyone had tremendous passion for the subject. We were all big fans of *Apollo 13*, *The Right Stuff* and *From the Earth to the Moon*. The more we learned about the reality of NASA's mission profiles, the more fascinating we found it as a game topic."

Early concept work was by artist Ron Cobb (some shown on www.roncobb.net), who had previously done concept art for movies such as *Alien*. Ron's work assisted the team through a number of produced models of robots, habitats and ships, which the game's artists then used as inspiration. "He was meticulous about things that could actually exist," Dan recalled of his impressive work.

The team would take its lead from an eventually finalised design that depicted a real-time survival strategy game with open-ended gameplay and featuring a number of surprises along the way. You began by sending robot rover probes to explore the surface of Mars at a chosen point on the planet, before then sending over human life forms. "Our gameplay cycle was based on Robert Zubrin's *Mars Direct* concept," explained Jason. "The player could launch several unmanned missions to establish habitats and produce fuel for human arrivals. Humans then arrived with payloads that allow them to expand." Once a colony was established, rovers were then used for planet exploration and prospecting.

"It was a great team, and everyone had tremendous passion."

Initial decision-making occurred from Cape Maxis, a central point on Earth where planning and launches would occur from. "Cape Maxis was largely my baby," recalled B.J. "I based it on NASA's Kennedy Space Centre, with a launch pad, vehicle assembly building, wind tunnel and spacecraft testing facilities, fuel storage, and astronaut training facilities. Starting on Earth, you sent the first missions from here, until the Mars colony became self-sufficient."

Within the game, there were to be over 60 technologies available to the player, which would mix "real-world science with cutting-edge scientific theory", according to Maxis. These were made up of different vehicles, robots, buildings and tools available to you (at a cost) to set up and deploy to Mars. All were based on actual NASA concepts.

With tight space available on any rocket journey to Mars, there was a limited amount of resources that could be taken each time. This was where scientists became very useful, helping with mining on Mars to discover materials and use them to build new resources and equipment to survive longer. "Eventually, mineral extraction and manufacturing allowed you to expand without further deliveries from Earth," explained Jason. "We also had a tech tree in the game that the player could unlock by discovering and researching mineral deposits."

"The first wave of mining consisted of small processing plants to harvest elements found in the Martian atmosphere and convert them to rocket fuel, water and oxygen," added B.J. "Later, you'd also be able to use the Martian soil to create 'marscrete' for buildings and other structures. Until then, you were mostly dependent on materials sent from Earth at a great cost." Before getting anywhere near self-sufficiency, you had to carefully choose what to send, ensuring enough basic supplies as the survival of your crew came first.

On top of resource management, there were disaster situations to contend with, such as spacesuit oxygen hoses accidentally being disconnected or storm damage occurring to vehicles and structures. Equipment could break down, so you had to send the crew to repair items when you could, or otherwise, you would have to send new resources by rocket.

With Arnold Schwarzenegger's 1990 film *Total Recall* still fresh in the mind of the embarrassingly non-scientific author, we ask whether the complex topic of terraforming would have featured at all. "It would indeed," confirmed Jason. "I was a big fan of Kim Stanley Robinson's *Mars* series, and I got serious about writing a terraforming simulator after reading Chris McKay and Robert Zubrin's paper *Technological Requirements for Terraforming Mars*."

"It was pretty clear that *The Sims* and *SimCity* were going to be our big titles, so I never held out much hope of a revival."

The player would have the choice to terraform small segments of the land, opening up gameplay and enabling players to grow plants if they managed to successfully alter areas of the planet's climate. After a while, it was hoped that you would create some kind of limited community/city in true *SimCity* style. However, the game would include no indigenous plant or animal life, with no plans for discovering Martians or any kind of alien life forms. Ideas regarding finding artefacts left behind by a dead Martian civilisation were considered but quickly brushed aside. Only bacteria were to be discoverable on the planet, which were at the top of the tech tree and would have unlocked options for genetically engineering Mars-friendly life forms.

Like with other Sim titles, thankfully, there was no dull task of waiting six months for a rocket delivery of supplies in real time. As the duration of a game could potentially span 100 years or more, games progressed at a steady pace to ensure plenty of action and real progress as you played over a number of hours.

"After a while, it was hoped that you would create some kind of limited community/city in true *SimCity* style."

Actual development of the game was initially delayed due to the design having to be reviewed and cleared. At the time, Dan felt that it was originally a six-month development job to complete. However, during the delays of firming up the design and getting the sign-off, the gaming landscape had changed, and now everything had to be done fully in 3D, with *SimMars* having to 'toe the line'. "Advanced 3D engines were becoming a thing, so most of our innovation was focused on that," explained Jason. "We did a lot of work with planetary-scale climate simulation. Between the advances in 3D tech and the climate and planetary science we were learning, we read a lot of scientific papers."

Maxis would develop its own 3D engine, where you could view the action from any position or angle. Inspiration was taken from the impressive *Populous: The Beginning* engine and was developed on the Windows PC, using *Microsoft Visual C++*. Prototypes would be developed as standard desktop applications, with the main game running in *DirectX*. No work was yet started on the Mac version, with focus on getting the PC version completed first.

Characters and vehicles were carefully constructed, making use of EA's impressive capture studio to ensure that the animations were realistic. The artists would use a mixture of *3D Studio Max* and *Maya* to help achieve the look and feel of the game. Small details would later be added, such as smoke effects to rocket animations and other special effects to bring the game further to life.

After several months of work, the team had created an engine far more advanced than anything previously used, helping to produce an impressive-looking game. There were plans to have the engine also perform an impressive continuous zoom from orbit to the ground, but this would never come to fruition. By this point, a dedicated website also appeared to engage with Maxis fans, showing CGI footage and an introduction to the game. Nothing was given away apart from brief descriptions of what to expect. You could sign up for news updates, where it was suggested that you were applying for "proper clearance and advanced notification of major mission updates".

However, stormy weather was coming for the title. With no solid deadline, the team had just concentrated on creating the best possible game they could. Although good for the gamer, development went on longer than anticipated. With many interesting ideas for the game, it was always tempting to jump between them without fully finishing what was being worked on at the time.

"Advanced 3D engines were becoming a thing."

Dan revealed that the "bar kept being moved" as well, and a request was made to add multiplayer at the last minute, meaning that a redesign was required. "A massive redesign," confirmed Dan. "Keep in mind – no one understood how to make a resource game like *FarmVille*. It would have been good to be multiplayer – but it was a huge leap." And the problems wouldn't end there.

"Another problem was that we only had a very compelling 15 minutes of gameplay. In games like *The Sims* or *SimCity*, the player is able to project stories and their own emotions into what they're seeing on screen," explained Alex. "In Jason's words, 'Mars is a frozen fucking desert'. There was not a lot of drama or emotional involvement to work with. What a great job Andy Weir did with *The Martian* by making it a survival story with a focus on a single protagonist. We did explore ideas of multiplayer vying for resources but flatly rejected science fiction ideas like aliens."

To make matters worse, part of the *SimMars* team was starting to be pulled onto other projects that were closer to completion. With the project needing a review and a bit of an overhaul, *SimMars* was put on hold until there was time to properly modify the design and finish off. What wasn't anticipated, though, was just how successful Will Wright's *The Sims* would become upon its release in early 2000. The title completely blew away EA's early concerns and would become one of their bestselling games of all time.

In May 2000, PR director of Maxis, Patrick Beuchner spoke to a *SimCity* fan site (www.simpage.net) and clarified the situation at the time. "We do not have staff at Maxis currently working on the game *[SimMars]*. With the phenomenal success of *The Sims*, we've decided to move resources to support that franchise as well as other titles that we haven't even announced yet."

It was the death knell for the title in the end, with temporary shelving turning permanent. The worldwide success of *The Sims* would dictate the development direction for Maxis for years to come. "Projects don't generally get uncancelled," explained Jason. "It was pretty clear that *The Sims* and *SimCity* were going to be our big titles, so I never held out much hope of a revival."

SimMars would live on but only via cameo appearances – in particular, within *The Sims: Vacation* in the form of a non-playable arcade game of the same name.

Elements of the game would also be repurposed in other games. "Shortly after *SimMars* was cancelled, Will showed me *Spore*," recalled Jason. "*SimMars* ended up providing the basis for the early prototype work on that project."

The closest thing to a Maxis 'Mars experience' was an unofficial *SimCity 4 SimMars* mod, created by the Simtropolis community back in 2004. No doubt inspired by the cancelled game, the modifications gave you the ability to create your own colony on Mars and even included a terraforming add-on at a later date. Some of the original Maxis *SimMars* team agreed that it was very much like the early concepts that they had developed.

Around 20 years on, working remains of the original Maxis game still exist. A playable demo disk prepared for the 2000 E3 show is still in the possession of one of the team, as well as other builds. Due to legalities, there is no chance of seeing anything in action anytime soon. If all goes to plan, then it's hoped that at least a video will be a possibility in the future.

"It was an amazing time. We'd do things like eat lunch in the conference room and watch the entire *Earth to the Moon* series together. It felt like school more than work."

We are, however, able to show some 3D models and renderings from the game, thanks to B.J., as well as screenshots from the released trailer video. One screen shows how the game was going to look, with views of the Cape Maxis launch complex. There are glimpses of the deployment sequence for the inflatable habitat building and an ISRU unit which would process the Martian atmosphere into usable materials. Most will be shown on the Games That Weren't website.

Even though *SimMars* didn't make it, it left fond and long-lasting memories for all involved. "We had great camaraderie and humour, and everyone was genuinely fascinated with the topic," reflected Jason. "I loved the ideas we explored, from the practical challenges of surviving on Mars to the ethics of terraforming. Intellectually, professionally and personally, it was one of the peak moments of my life. I'd jump right back on board today if I could, even if knowing it would be cancelled." Dan then added, "As Jason has said, it was an amazing time. We'd do things like eat lunch in the conference room and watch the entire *Earth to the Moon* series together. It felt like school more than work."

"I've been at EA for over 20 years now, and *SimMars* holds a special place in my memories," Alex added. "The team was a blast to work with. Every night at 6pm, someone would say 'Who's got a server up!?' And the rest of us would join and play *Quake 2* for a while. To this day, when NASA discovers something new on Mars, I'll fire an email to the old gang, and we'll reminisce about those days and marvel at NASA's accomplishments and dreams."

We conclude by asking if *SimMars* could ever see a modern-day revival, especially since the release of *Surviving Mars* by Paradox Interactive in recent years. "I think there's a much better opportunity to do *SimMars* today," Jason responded. "We were working with cutting-edge engine ideas that took a great deal of our energy. Today, you could do a much better job in *Unreal* or *Unity* engine without too much exotic coding.

"I think there's a much better opportunity to do *SimMars* today."

"Mars is also much more of a real place today. With everything we've seen from the rovers and the high-resolution orbiters, we have a much richer sense of what the Red Planet is really like. So I think there would be even more enthusiasm today from the public for a game that takes our real-world accomplishments and projects them into the next century. In the time since *SimMars'* cancellation, the grit got real!"

Above/Opposite: Various snapshots taken from the *SimMars* trailer video and showing a rocket probe leaving for Mars.

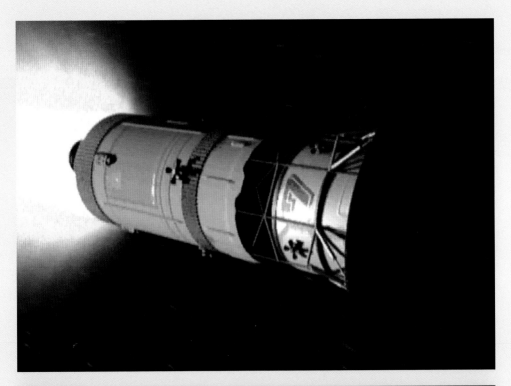

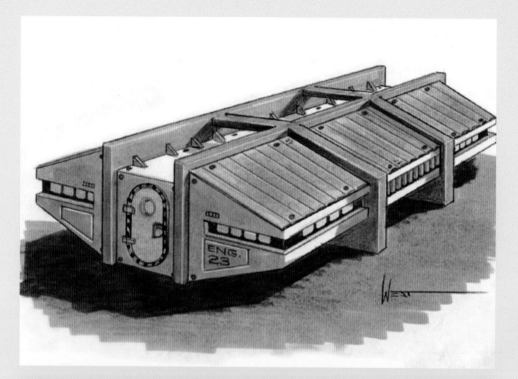

Top: Concept sketch for a Mars engineering building, created by B.J. West. Bottom: View of the Cape Maxis launch complex created by B.J. West, where all the decisions for your mission are made.

Top: Render by B.J. West of a Sample Return vehicle. Bottom: All of the key vehicles and buildings in place on Mars. A close indication of how the final game would likely have looked.

Frogger 2: Swampy's Revenge Cartridge costs

Year: 2000
Developer: Interactive Studios
Platform: Nintendo 64

Available to play
◉ Yes ○ No

There is something about *Frogger* that epitomises 1980s arcades, thanks to its vibrant colours, loud sound effects, and fast and furious gameplay. Its toe-tapping tunes are no doubt etched into the soundbanks of all who experienced the game. The aim simply was to guide your frogs to their home at the top of the screen, whilst avoiding road traffic and alligators, and navigating streams by hitching lifts on floating logs. A stand-out game from a golden era of arcade games, opening the floodgates to a multitude of home conversions.

Even if you never experienced it directly, you may have done later, through retrospective releases or perhaps Hasbro's remake in 1997 developed by Millennium Interactive. Hasbro looked to produce a sequel, but, with Millennium unavailable, Interactive Studios (run by Andrew and Philip Oliver) would step up to develop one for the PC, Sony PlayStation and Nintendo 64 (N64).

"Whilst the first *Frogger* was fairly poor, it was incredibly successful and in the US Christmas Top 10 a year after release," began Philip Oliver. "Hasbro had a lot of respect for the talented developers we had at Interactive Studios (because of the success of *Glover*) and offered us a development contract for *Frogger 2*. *Frogger* was a classic, like *Pac-Man*, so we felt it an honour to make the sequel. We felt we could easily make a better game, and it would sell even better. It would have been far more daunting and risky if the first game had been brilliant."

Kicking off development in 1998 was the fresh-faced Matt Cloy. "I went to college and didn't think I'd be good enough to become a games developer. But I had an interview with Philip and Andrew, and they pretty much said 'When can you start?'," he recalled. "It was my first break at the age of 20, first working on *Glover*. The possibility to do *Frogger 2* came up, and the Oliver Twins asked if I could make a start and build a team. I ended up becoming technical manager for pretty much all of the project, right up until the end."

Managing the project across all platforms, Matt also led development for the PC edition under the newly formed Team Spirit, which started small and grew as the project wore on. Game design would eventually be handled by Alex Rigby and Joff Scarcliffe. Concept art and illustration were handled by Richard Whale, with level design and testing by Lauren Grindrod, Simon Little, Bruce Millar and Joff. Animation and 3D modelling work would be carried out by Simon, Bruce and Joff, along with Sandro Da Cruz focusing on the characters.

Joining Matt and developing the N64 edition was the even fresher-faced Andy Eder in his first development role. "The Olivers very much inspired me to take up game development. Their passion for work and the larger industry was infectious, and I wanted to become a part of that," recalled Andy. "The Olivers asked me to help Matt out as and when needed. So, whilst I was busy working on the N64 edition, Matt was busy putting together the PC version. The rest of the programmers focused on general components that weren't platform-specific, such as game mechanics, NPC AI, camera movement, and so forth."

N64 was the primary focus early on, leading the way for the other editions. Development was carried out on PCs with *Visual Studio*, connected directly to development consoles; the N64, in particular, using the SN64 development kit by SN Systems. The majority of the C-based code was fully cross-platform, with common game code shared and platform-specific code (such as controller code) either created from scratch or borrowed from titles such as *Glover*.

"My very first task was getting familiar with the dev kit and working on a core 3D graphics viewer/engine," Andy recalled. "The aim was to combine newly written technology with tech already available from other N64 titles (such as *Glover*), so we could quickly get a 3D world realised with a controllable *Frogger* character. The N64 didn't have the grunt of the PlayStation, in terms of pumping out polygons, but offered nicer visuals (in my opinion) thanks to more advanced graphics capabilities (such as perspective correct and filtered texturing)."

"Hasbro's *Frogger* stuck closely to the arcade and just made it 3D. We tried to take things another step forwards."

Art assets were produced using *3D Studio Max*, with other image tools for texture drawing. A useful internally developed tool called *JOBE* (John's OBject Editor) allowed the team to texture low polygon models with a lot more ease compared with the unnecessarily complex tools available within *3D Studio Max*. Assets were intentionally kept simple and cross-platform friendly in design to ensure that the game looked and felt the same across all platforms.

Early designs suggested basic modes and mechanics, though it was difficult putting it down on paper and not visualising it beforehand. "Hasbro's *Frogger* stuck closely to the arcade and just made it 3D. We tried to take things another step forwards," explained Matt. "The whole team helped design the game, so we gave level designers tools, and they would ask if we could add new features. I remember myself and Andy building a PC 2D experimental tool where we could try out different mechanics on a 2D grid, so we could see what worked – it was the very first thing we wrote. Andy and I then started to port some of the *Glover* 3D and animation code to a fresh N64 codebase, ready for artists to join in."

After a few months and whilst a proper 3D engine was being developed, the team had various puzzles and ideas working within the 2D tool. One stand-out prototype was clearly inspired by the SEGA arcade classic *Flicky*. Within the prototype, you could run around levels collecting frogs, but, rather than them just disappearing, they would follow you around the map. The further you got, the more difficult it was to keep them all safe.

Nothing was set in stone, and the team was just testing out ideas. The project took on a very agile style of approach, with regular development and client feedback cycles. Hasbro and the development team would organically evolve the design of the game over its lifetime. "The structure was a quote based on man-months, predicted people required each month for every month of development," explained Philip. "We produced a schedule of monthly milestones, showing costs and what would be produced. We delivered builds at the end of each month to the schedule. Hasbro would approve it, and we'd raise an invoice for that month's work."

The process would lead to the *Flicky*-inspired design being ditched early on, and progression to a new design not too dissimilar to the style of *Super Mario Galaxy*, some years before it existed. "*Frogger 2* was very much grid-based, but we devised a way of mapping the grid to really interesting geometric shapes," explained Andy. "We had spheres, capsules, torus, cuboids (amongst other shapes), as well as the more traditional planar/flat levels." Steve Bond, who helped on the project towards the end, also recalls the pioneering idea: "Most of the levels were quite small planetoids – some spherical, some other shapes like cubes, and so on. One level I recall being Venice-themed and quite beautiful."

Hasbro was not keen, feeling that it wasn't really *Frogger* and wanting something more traditional. Taking it on the chin, the team reigned things in for the next build. The design was stripped back, starting with a more familiar distant perspective, almost completely top-down and with options to zoom in. "It was about providing evidence of simple gameplay mechanics and showing something playable rather than suggesting artistic direction," explained Andy. "One of our design briefs for that build was to show Hasbro the engine running in a more traditional 2D *Frogger* setting, which is why it was so flat and classical compared with both the sphere levels developed," added Matt.

The game was felt to be more on track, and the camera was tilted and brought closer by default. The grid-based movement was kept, but a double-jump mechanism was added. Now you could reach higher platforms and jump across larger gaps, making it closer to a 3D platformer. "As we developed the game, we realised that the essence of *Frogger* was about negotiating puzzles and obstacles in your immediate vicinity, rather than exploring vast levels. This resulted in tighter cameras, for the most part, and a mix of camera perspectives, depending on the situation," recalled Darren Wood, who joined the project towards the end.

A story was concocted as part of the main event, which became a slight bone of contention. "Originally, it wasn't supposed to have a story," revealed Matt. "Nobody on the team was very keen on adding a story, as we were like, 'This is *Frogger*; it's supposed to be just level after level!'. Hasbro were the publisher though and had the last word. But they were very good to work with and only occasionally came in and said, 'No, we don't want that'."

The eventual story described Swampy the Crocodile being jealous of Frogger's fame and fortune. He attempts to make himself the king of the swamp by kidnapping Lillie Frog's baby brothers and sisters. Along with Lillie Frog, you travel across ten varied levels to save the babies and foil Swampy's plans.

Levels followed a simple path, with the camera rotating around with you at various points. Between each level was a short cutscene, expanding upon the story. The levels included themes, such as gardens with lawnmowers and bees, and a boulder canyon with cannonballs, spikes and floating chests. There was even an infernal machine level, including a subtle nod towards Hewson's classic *Nebulus* and its tower-climbing theme. Ultimately, it was still the same core *Frogger* concept at heart, just with different costumes applied.

"We applied core mechanics in interesting ways to create something slightly different," explained Matt. "There is a level on a spaceship, flying through an asteroid field. You're just moving left and right, but the basic mechanic is still the same. You are just being moved, instead of moving. Instead of you hopping forwards, you hop left and right to avoid asteroids."

More seasoned gamers would probably complete the game with ease, but it was still perfect fun for families. If you did happen to get stuck, your croak helps to locate missing frogs on each level, who croak back to indicate roughly where they are (if close by). Eating various insects with your tongue also rewards you with power-ups, such as the 'Quick Hop' (which does as it suggests). As well as collecting baby frogs, you can also collect coins on each level, where finding all on each level would unlock bonus stages and characters.

Afterwards, you could replay levels within the game's arcade mode to attempt better completion times and select unlockable characters (different only in appearance). Special unlockable 'super retro' levels could also be experienced with the classic retro look of the original arcade but within the new engine and with interesting twists. This replaced the originally planned inclusion of the emulated arcade game. Multiplayer was also key, with up to four simultaneous players planned for the N64. Here you could select different characters and play a variety of different games, including 'Tron light-cycle', 'Rescue the most frogs' and 'Race each other' variants – keeping the game fresh beyond its main story.

Andy only had the first Garden level included for testing and tweaking. Occasionally, later levels would be pulled into the build to ensure that they worked on the original hardware. Although the base build lacked level content, the engine and mechanics were all present, and fine-tuning levels would be made within each build. "A very nice feature was the level editor built into the game, so designers could pause a level and edit enemy paths and so on. Then they could carry on from that point, which was a great system," recalled Steve.

As the project reached the alpha stage, it was suddenly decided to bring in Darren Wood to take over as project manager. "Darren had much more experience. I was only 21 at the time and didn't feel confident to take it through the final stages of beta and master," explained Matt. "Matt was an incredibly talented programmer but, like myself, was also inexperienced when it came to leading development. In fact, a large proportion of the team was quite green, with only a few key seasoned developers to steer and advise along the way," added Andy.

Matt and the team had done a great job so far, but now the project just needed a bit of extra experience to help bring it home. The N64 development was coming on well, with any issues encountered being swiftly overcome. With milestones all being met, all that was left was to get the remaining levels added, do a final polish, and stick in some proper sound. "The sound effects and music tracks had not been finalised and were still being debated and/or produced. As a lot of the N64 tech was shared between *Frogger 2*, *Glover*, and others, we had simply borrowed a soundbank of effects and used those!" explained Andy.

However, things were about to take a bad turn – the cost of producing cartridges proving problematic. It could make or break companies, and Hasbro was aware of an impending and increasing cost. "The cost and the long manufacturing time of 8–10 weeks from order (paid at the time of order) and delivery of finished goods was deemed too risky for potential profit," Philip explained. "Quite simply, it didn't make financial sense," added Andy. "Unsold stock resulted in significant financial loss. With PlayStation's popularity and CD-based production much cheaper in comparison, the writing was on the wall for the N64 edition."

"As we developed the game, we realised that the essence of Frogger was about negotiating puzzles and obstacles in your immediate vicinity, rather than exploring vast levels."

Therefore, Hasbro cancelled the N64 edition whilst it was at a 70%-completed state. "The only things remaining were finishing off platform-specific bits and pieces," recalled Darren of what remained. "Most features were actually there when they canned it, apart from the polish, video player, and the terrible story they decided to add. It was around the time we were finally starting to get some of the other levels added in," added Matt.

Focus switched to the PlayStation and PC editions, with a Dreamcast port added to the release schedule. All were completed and released, including a separate Game Boy Color edition created externally by industry legend David Lubar. Final music and sound effects were created by Andy Morris. By this point, Interactive Studios was renamed to Blitz Games, just as the game saw its release. Although reviewing well, it didn't hit the big sales figures as first hoped, but through no fault of Blitz Games or Hasbro. "It was doing really well for about one year before Konami asked for it to be removed from sale because the licence had expired," sighed Philip.

With well over a decade now passing, recent years have seen some of the milestone releases sneaking into collector's hands. An early prototype released in 2005 demonstrated two simple levels and selectable camera angles, with very little detail and no sound at all. "I noticed there were a lot of freezes and crashes!" responded Andy when seeing the prototype on YouTube. "Despite producing a stand-alone cart, there were certain aspects of the prototype that required it to be connected up to an N64 dev kit. The 'record keying' option allowed us to load a level and then record a playthrough of that level (i.e. recording user inputs). This recording could then be saved and played back later, effectively providing an attract mode that autonomously demonstrated the captured gameplay for that specific level."

A later build (Milestone 4) produced around 1999 surfaced more recently, with a number of videos showing something closer to the final release, but with major differences. Featuring an early version of the Garden level, the game has a closer camera point compared with the final release and is quite slow-moving – lacking a lot of polish. The game has you collecting frogspawn in an almost Pac-Man-like fashion for points, a concept that never made the final cut. It's lacking cutscenes and content, and contains sound borrowed from Glover.

The early prototype is unofficially available online, though Milestone 4 is yet to be at the time of publication. But, with multiple milestones created during the course of the project, is there any chance more could someday be found? "We kept a copy of every milestone produced," confirmed Philip. "I spent a few hours looking for them, but I have 30 years of game development for a studio that got to over 200 people. So that's a LOT of boxes, and they are not exactly neatly organised."

Although the Oliver Twins are very generous and open to showing and releasing some of their past unreleased developments (*Wonderland Dizzy* and *Mystery World Dizzy* on the Nintendo Entertainment System being two recent examples), there are licence issues with *Frogger 2,* which will likely prevent any release coming from them directly. Andy did, however, recently release a video showing early prototypes with the cylindrical-shaped worlds, of which you can see a screenshot within these pages. Philip also kindly dug out an unreleased advert to show here, as well as some photos of development kits and concepts which will be available on the Games That Weren't website.

"Working on a game that people genuinely enjoy is an awesome experience, so there was great energy on the team."

Compared with most titles covered so far, the lack of an N64 *Frogger 2* isn't perhaps too distressing. The game did at least see a release on other platforms, but it is the curiosity to see and play on the original platform that intrigues us more. The team members also have nothing but fond memories of their time on the game. "It was a lot of fun!" concludes Darren. "Working on a game that people genuinely enjoy is an awesome experience, so there was great energy on the team. The guys often played the multiplayer levels together after work just because it was so much fun to sit on your opponent. I also met my wife on this team as she was one of the level designers. We now live in Vancouver and have two kids."

"It was my first role and first game, hence a great feeling of satisfaction and being proud of my involvement," added Andy. "Then there were the people I worked with, an incredibly talented bunch of technical and creative people with a deep-rooted passion for game development. With them, I learned an awful lot about game development, yet was able (and encouraged) to share my own skills and experience too."

Why not see the passion for yourself, and pick up a copy of the game – if you can – on one of the other available platforms. All are a decent glimpse of what could have been on the N64. If only Nintendo offered a cheaper storage solution at the time, this could well have easily been a retrospective of yet another N64 classic instead.

Above: Photo of an unpublished advert for the game from the Oliver Twins' vault, showing the Nintendo 64 as a supported format at the top.

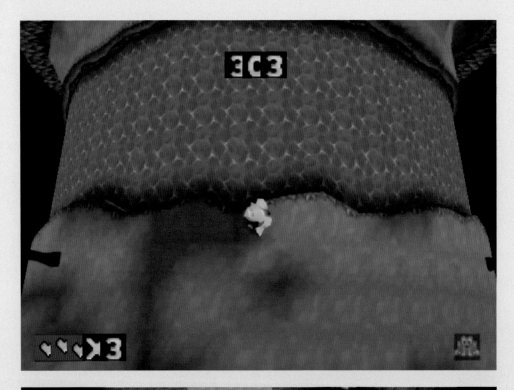

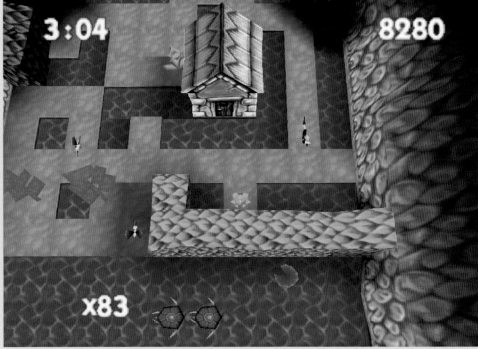

Top: Early prototype of *Frogger 2* (PC) recorded by Andy Eder, demonstrating the abandoned cylindrical design. Bottom: First level from the early leaked build of *Frogger 2* (N64).

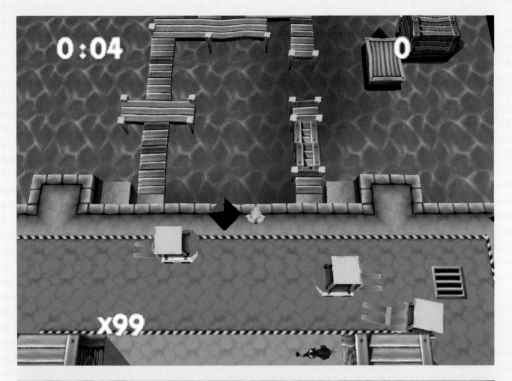

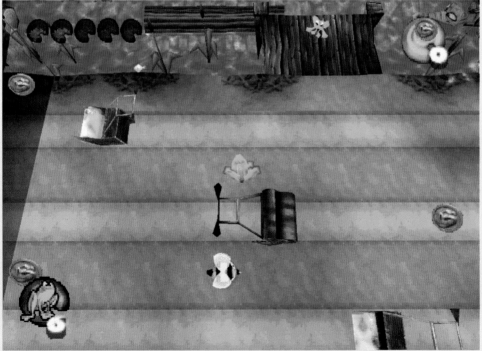

Top: Dockyard level from the early leaked build of *Frogger 2* (N64). Bottom: Screen from the released PlayStation 1 edition and the Garden level. The N64 edition looked practically the same.

Propeller Arena: Aviation Battle Championship
Real-world events

Year: 2001
Developer: SEGA AM2
Platform: SEGA Dreamcast

A fast and furious deathmatch in the air, featuring World War II-era planes battling across different environments. Play single-player, or multiplayer via split-screen or online. The dying Dreamcast platform was one factor for cancellation, but, crucially, the tragic events of September 11th, 2001, meant that a game with planes crashing could never be released at the time.

Available to play

◉ Yes ○ No

Half-Life Failure of the Dreamcast

Year: 2001
Developers: Captivation and Gearbox Software
Platforms: Nintendo GameCube
and SEGA Dreamcast

Available to play

 Yes ◯ No

As a new PC owner in 1996, it was hard to see how anything could top the phenomenal *Quake* at the time. Little did many of us know, this was a period where 3D titles were about to take major strides and feel more real in a very short space of time. When Valve's much anticipated (and delayed) *Half-Life* was released in November 1998, it sent shock waves throughout the games industry. With its seamless, well-structured narrative and impressive artificial intelligence, the game (quite rightly) won many awards and accolades.

During the very same month of its PC release, the SEGA Dreamcast had been released in Japan and was an impressive follow up from the disappointment of the SEGA Saturn. It included an optimised version of Windows CE as its operating system, which caught the eye of Sierra, who were curious as to whether some of their titles could be converted to run on the platform with little work required. With *Half-Life* their bestseller at the time, they requested their internal PyroTechnix studio to evaluate if such a port was plausible. Assigned to the task was software engineer Brian Kraack, who would spend a month playing the game and getting familiar with the Dreamcast development kit.

"I initially got the kit up and running and began learning about the toolchain and general DC code. I started looking at Dreamcast sample projects and doing some prototype work," recalled Brian. "Whilst I was waiting for the *Half-Life* code, I created a little radar app that would run on the DC Controller's VMU. I thought it would be neat if players could use that as a Head-crab detector whilst playing *Half-Life*, similar to the handheld alien tracker from the *Alien* movie. I had it working in a sample app but didn't get much further than that."

Unfortunately, Brian's time was cut short, with Sierra deciding to cut costs by shutting down PyroTechnix – subsequently killing the project. "As I remember, I received the *Half-Life* codebase late on a Thursday or Friday, and we were shut down the following Monday morning," Brian recalled. "Whatever work was done to get an initial build going done prior to the shutdown meeting was all the work I ever got to do on *Half-Life*."

Sierra was, however, still serious about bringing the game to consoles and began talking to Valve about the possibility. Valve was interested in seeing how this could work out, as it was also keen to explore the SEGA Dreamcast platform, thanks to the impressive design decisions made by SEGA with the console.

Jeff Pobst was Sierra's external producer at the time and recalled how things properly kicked off. "Some execs from SEGA flew up to Seattle, and all three companies met at Valve and talked about how each could support such a plan, what would be good for a conversion, and what the best way would be to get it developed," he explained. "My recollection is that SEGA recommended working with developer Captivation Digital Laboratories for the conversion as they had prior experience with the Dreamcast already."

Both Sierra and Valve felt there was a good opportunity to also have new content added, as well as give a visual upgrade to make use of the powerful graphical features of the Dreamcast. "We reached out to Gearbox to see if they'd like to make the new content, and, if I remember correctly, the work to upgrade the assets ended up being split between Captivation and Gearbox," explained Jeff. "Gearbox was excited to make new content, so the endeavour consisted of Sierra hiring both Captivation and Gearbox for the project, with technical support and promotion promises coming from SEGA and Microsoft to help bring the game to the console, and oversight and consulting on the game coming from Valve. I was the person at Sierra who ended up spending most of the time with Captivation and Gearbox on the game."

"The Dreamcast was a far better development experience."

Work commenced around late 1999, with Gearbox focusing on the design side and additional content work. "After finishing *Opposing Force*, we were invited to help bring the game to consoles," recalled Gearbox's CEO, Randy Pitchford. "Sierra asked if we would conceive another add-on for *Half-Life* as an exclusive for the Dreamcast, to which we agreed. We also wanted to help make the Dreamcast version sexier than prior versions because, if we were going to take the creative effort to create a new chapter for *Half-Life*, we wanted to encourage as many people as possible to play it. Sierra agreed and gave us enough wiggle room to do higher definition content and improve some areas of the game too."

Captivation simultaneously handled the technical conversion of the engine, optimising for the platform and also doing some artwork and content clean-up. "Our key programmers were myself, Russell Borogove (also known as Russell Bornschlegel), David Sanner, Bob Hardy and Dan Windrem. Our artists were Betty Cunningham, Brian Frederick, Bob Steele, Beckett Gladney, Arlin Robins and Dean Ruggles," recalled Captivation's founder, Robert Morgan. "Collaboration with Gearbox was great. I really liked them (and still do!). Communication was fluid, though, back then, it was mostly email, phone calls, and the occasional plane trip – about as smooth as you could expect for the era."

With Captivation and Gearbox working hard, the conversion was officially announced in February 2000 at the Milia trade show in Cannes, France. "*Half-Life* has become a big franchise with 1.5 million units sold worldwide. Its immersive environment, the depth of its story, and its unique action character lend well to creating a great console product that takes advantage of the high performance of the SEGA Dreamcast," said Hubert Joly, CEO of Havas Interactive at the time. "Valve's number-one objective is to deliver state-of-the-art entertainment experiences that push the envelope with every new release. By partnering with SEGA, our intention is to create an incredible new version of *Half-Life* that takes full advantage of SEGA Dreamcast's architecture," added co-founder and managing director of Valve, Gabe Newell.

The visuals were improved by doubling the polygons to make human models look more realistic and monsters more frightening. Some components were even separated out, so shirts and ties on the scientists, for instance, would have their own individual movements, free-flowing and flapping in the breeze. There were also improved lighting effects and adjustments made to better suit television screens, including changing parts of the colour palette as dark areas looked different on a TV compared with a PC monitor.

Compared with the Saturn, the Dreamcast was a far better development experience. It wasn't without its challenges, and getting *Half-Life* running well with all of the enhancements would require plenty of skill and competence. Unfortunately, we didn't get to hear back from Russell, but we learned that he was the technical lead and primary programmer on the conversion, converting the rendering code from OpenGL to the Dreamcast's Direct3D environment. Robert would also help out and play a key role in overcoming some of the issues encountered throughout the conversion.

"The Dreamcast rendering hardware was very capable, so that was pretty light. I remember rewriting a lot of the rendering systems because of performance, and to take advantage of *DirectX*," Robert recalled. "On the memory front, though, I remember that Windows CE dedicated a stupidly high amount of RAM to audio. I wanted to use it to store other data, but the OS didn't readily allow that, so I kept hacking until, eventually, I could load any data I wanted into it. It got slightly scrambled, but that was easy enough to fix. After that, I found I could hack the surrounding data structures to fake out the rest of the OS."

Although the visuals were undergoing major overhauls, the core game itself would be mostly left alone. Getting the actual basics of the engine conversion working wasn't too much of a problem overall; it was the optimisations and visual improvements that would take the majority of the work. It would be 6–8 months before the game was even close to being complete content-wise, including the planned extended content.

With *Half-Life* originally built for use with a keyboard and mouse, a lot of time also had to be spent getting the game working intuitively with the Dreamcast pad. The teams would make a point of testing the game only with the control pad to ensure that it was as usable as it could be. "At the time, there hadn't been many successful FPSs on a console, and a lot of people believed you needed a keyboard and mouse, but Russell really worked the controls and made it extremely playable on a game controller," explained Robert. "We also made it work with the Dreamcast keyboard and mouse anyway, and even the fishing controller (reel to move; cast to shoot)!"

It wasn't always smooth going, with some parts of the game map having to be adjusted slightly as the control pad just wasn't suitable enough to navigate in certain circumstances. It was taken into particular consideration when Gearbox started to build new content for the game. "One of the things you'll notice in the new content is that up and down movement was minimised since accurately aiming up and down tended to be more challenging on a controller than left and right could be," explained Jeff.

Gearbox's new content development was resulting in a side story called *Guard Duty*, designed and written by Rob Heironimus, David Mertz and Randy Pitchford. The game was approximately 30–40% the size of the main *Half-Life* story, where Gearbox cleverly came up with an idea of playing part of the main *Half-Life* story through the eyes of popular security guard character, Barney Calhoun. It was a story that Randy felt needed to be told as he was one of the popular characters in the original game. Marc Laidlaw's *Half-Life* storyline included a neat backstory to Barney and the *Half-Life* universe, which Gearbox was keen to see told. Many assets were already done too, saving on crucial development time.

As the main events from *Half-Life* occurred in the side story, you went through your everyday routine as Barney. When in the tram within the original game and seeing Barney banging on a door to get in, you played Barney in that situation and would be able to see Gordon Freeman from the opposite perspective. Eventually, the new side story was renamed to *Blue Shift*, cleverly referring to Barney's work shift, as well as the light phenomenon of the same name.

Carrying out work on the programming side was Sean Cavanaugh, Patrick Deupree and Steven Jones. Level design work was carried out by Matt Armstrong, Rob Heironimus, David Mertz, Randy Pitchford and Mike Wardwell. General sounds were handled by Rob Heironimus and Stephen Bahl, with voices carried out by Jon St. John, Kathy Levin, Harry S. Robins and Mike Shapiro. With the conversion and new content work coming together, Sierra and Valve were happy with the progress early on and would meet regularly with Captivation and Gearbox to discuss milestones. But, as with any conversion project to new hardware, there were still a number of issues that were unforeseen at the time and would considerably slow down production.

"We also made it work with the Dreamcast keyboard and mouse anyway, and even the fishing controller!"

At certain places within the game, the frame rates varied from good to poor. To work around most of the issues, some areas had to be adjusted or completely revamped to bring the rates back up, but they were mostly small changes that only the hardcore *Half-Life* fan would notice. "There were some usual idiosyncrasies to the Dreamcast platform that required some cleverness and some problem-solving," explained Randy. "Valve was extremely hands-off throughout and seemed to trust us to do what we do, so that made things somewhat easier."

Captivation also cleverly worked around many technical issues that arose, including repackaging content so that it could be linearly loaded in places. Elements, such as audio, also had to be streamed off the disk in real time along with the game data, so load times were slower compared with the PC version.

There were also issues with saving in the game, which Gearbox would help Captivation to solve. A PC save file was typically between 1–2MB in size, though the Dreamcast VMU only had 100K available overall (if you exclude the 28K reserved for system use). Although a password system was available to jump to particular points, saving was crucial, and certification on the Dreamcast wouldn't allow a single save file to take up the entire space of a VMU – it had to be fixed.

"*Half-Life* depended on autosaves as a backup for some level design flaws that could result in the player being permanently stuck," explained Randy. "So the reality was that as many as ten *Half-Life* saves were going to have to fit into less than half of the VMU. This is a professional software developer's nightmare and a hacker's dream. A quite elegant solution came from Steve Jones and Sean Reardon at Gearbox. They cleverly developed an indexing system where we generated prima facie save data for each level whenever the player wanted to save their game. The only thing stored on the VMU was a tiny little diff file that allowed the game to reconstruct an accurate save file from the disk-stored index and the VMU-stored diff."

With saving resolved, there was finally the question of whether the Dreamcast version would include multiplayer functionality. It seemed almost a given, considering that the console came with a built-in modem. Throughout various press releases, however, there was no full commitment for it to be present, with suggestions early on that the functionality would be later released separately as an expansion pack with *Team Fortress* and other sweeteners, such as *Opposing Force*, *Half-Life* multiplayer, and potentially *Counter-Strike* too.

"The networking ended up being rough, with modem-based networking always tough for latency," recalled Robert. "The Dreamcast modem did a lot of decoding in software which added to performance challenges, but these were all fun to have to solve." The team was confident that the speed issues could be overcome to make the crucial functionality later available, but part of the reason to delay was also to optimise the game as much as possible for its multiplayer functionality and later integration with SEGA's SEGANet service.

With most of the core game up and running, including extra content and visual enhancements, the game was now projected for an autumn 2000 release. As September edged forwards, adverts surfaced, and some shops opened pre-orders. Although everyone was geared up, unbeknown to gamers and the press, the development teams were still ironing out the remaining issues, in particular, with frame rate drops and loading times, which were not the best.

But there was also to be devastating news for Captivation. "We had a tragedy where our art director, Betty Cunningham, suddenly passed away," confirmed Robert. Betty's passing hit the team hard and was a massive shock to all.

The release was pushed back until Christmas with the hope that it could make the most crucial of sales windows. But, frustratingly, issues kept cropping up like a game of whack-a-mole, and Sierra conceded that the game would be pushed back into 2001. This was through no fault of the development team, which worked extremely hard to ensure the best possible conversion. Sierra was concerned about the constant delays, though, which was partly down to a limited understanding of the work involved. "One thing I personally learnt was that, because it was considered by executives at Sierra to be a pretty typical platform conversion, their intuition on how fast the team would make progress was much more accelerated than the reality turned out to be for the project," explained Jeff.

"The conversion was one of the most challenging projects I'd ever been part of. It wasn't that there were any team or planning problems, but rather the team faced huge emergent technical issues that kept appearing one after the other. Getting it to work at all on the console, at a high enough frame rate and with networking working, were all huge tasks that kept running into technical problems but kept being overcome. The solutions the team came up with were extremely impressive but took time to implement, and the folks at Sierra and Vivendi became impatient. While it was difficult with respect to internal politics during development, overall, the team made a ton of progress and overcame many huge challenges getting the game to work and be performant."

Even with the delays, a number of magazines actually reviewed the title and gave decent scores, including Paragon Publishing's *Dreamcast Magazine*, *Computer and Video Games* and *DC-UK* magazine. There were grumbles about frame rate, loading speed issues and the lack of a multiplayer option, but then they had surely reviewed a game not actually fit for release. Sierra's UK representative may have jumped the gun in some way, anticipating the pre-Christmas release would definitely happen. Content-wise, the game may well have been near complete, but the optimisation required, missing textures and other remaining issues meant that it was still not consumer-ready.

The loading issues were a problem that could only be resolved to a point anyway. "*Half-Life* was designed as a game where the large amounts of game data were stored on a hard drive. Small chunks needed for any particular segment of the game were also pulled from the hard drive and loaded into main system memory," Randy explained. "The Dreamcast did not have fixed storage like that, so all data that was run from main memory had to be pulled from CD, which had substantially slower seek-and-read times than a hard drive. *Half-Life* data was, by default, stored arbitrarily to reduce data redundancy and to increase convenience in development, but that is the worst possible way to store data when you're limited by seek times as it causes the disk read to have to constantly jump all over the disk to find the data it needs."

"Valve was extremely hands-off throughout."

A few months into 2001, the loading speeds were felt to be as best as they could be, and the majority of the remaining issues were now finally resolved. "Performance was pretty good in the end," recalled Robert. "There were still spots that chugged a little, but it looked good, and you could really, truly experience the full game on Dreamcast. We worked really hard on it, and I believe we pulled it off."

With the game now practically complete and ready to be certified, US Magazine *GamePro* would gain an exclusive final review copy in March 2001. "I reviewed a near-gold version of the game, but it was neither complete nor gold; the disk for my review was dated 13th March, 2001," recalled senior editor Dan Amrich. "Sierra wanted to get the game on the cover, so the deal we struck was a cover story on PS2 and Dreamcast previews, but with a verbal agreement that we would get the Dreamcast review as an exclusive when it became available. My PR contact at Sierra first informed me there were delays because Sierra were reconsidering publishing the Dreamcast edition, with signs the platform was in trouble. She stayed in touch and swore she would do everything she could to keep her promise. One day, she called and said, 'Would you be able to review a near-final build? It's about 90%, maybe 95% complete'."

Dan and his editor felt it was fine to proceed on what was a major scoop for them, even though 90% was right on the edge of what they would normally accept. With their good relationship with Sierra, they gave them the benefit of the doubt and would see what it was like. They were informed that the game was due for release in June 2001, so Dan wrote his review right away, meeting the June publication deadline to coincide with the projected release. It would score mostly straight 5s across the board, with some points lost on controls being fiddly compared with the PC.

Meanwhile, *Half-Life* was finally finished and passed its final testing phase – considered good enough to go 'gold'. However, SEGA was about to deliver a major bombshell, deciding to discontinue the Dreamcast in March 2001. This resulted in speculation and rumours that *Half-Life* would never see a release, especially when the *Blue Shift* pack then had a PC release announcement.

"When things went down the way it did with SEGA, with our game in between certification and shelf date, our revenue was basically shot in the head," explained Randy. "So, I appealed to Valve and Sierra to make a retail product out of *Blue Shift*. At first, there was a little fear since it was smaller than *Half-Life:*

Opposing Force in length and didn't add as much new content as far as monsters and weapons go, but the Valve guys really liked the story and content in *Blue Shift,* and Sierra was convinced it could bring in some revenue. So, by fluffing the package with the High Definition Pack and by including *Half-Life: Opposing Force* for free on disc, the deal happened."

"Half-Life depended on autosaves as a backup for some level design flaws that could result in the player being permanently stuck."

Sierra was now faced with a dilemma. It had a complete conversion of *Half-Life* ready to release but for a console no longer being produced. "The day SEGA made the announcement, Sierra had already contacted all the retailers to find out what they were going to do with respect to shelf space devoted to Dreamcast games," recalled Jeff. "All of the retailers reported that they'd be cutting the shelf space in half or even to a quarter. It became clear that it would be much more difficult to sell a game, even a game like *Half-Life*, in an environment where everyone perceived that the console was 'done'. And this was a pretty large decision point for Sierra as well."

At this stage, Sierra hadn't yet placed a disk order with SEGA (an expensive commitment), but manuals, cover art and disk art were already complete and ready to go into full printing. Prima publishing had even gone one step further, releasing a complete strategy guide to the game in anticipation of the expected release. Sierra was faced with a choice between getting a tax deduction against other profits for everything it had spent so far on development or ending up paying an additional amount in the hope that it could sell the game within a shrinking shelf and customer base.

In the end, it made practical and financial sense to just drop the title from the release schedule. Just a few months later, Sierra would issue a press release to confirm the cancellation, citing changing market conditions. "I understand the decision, though I clearly wish history had played out differently. I doubt *Half-Life* would have changed the outcome for Dreamcast, but maybe it would have given it a little longer for the killer app to show," reflected Robert.

As Randy had predicted that Sierra would cancel the release, he was already well on the way with the PC conversion of *Blue Shift* by this stage but had also already been working with his team on a PlayStation 2 conversion of the core *Half-Life* game. "We had been working on that for many months by this stage," recalled Randy. "We had other things going on, and revenue was still strong for *Opposing Force*, so we weathered the Dreamcast cancellation just fine. I then did another deal with Sierra to try to bring *Half-Life* to another platform (from a company that starts with N and rhymes with 'Wintendo'), but Sierra were going through some stuff of their own by that point and didn't have much confidence in the platform so decided to pull out of that deal before it really got started."

Referring to a planned conversion of *Half-Life* to the Nintendo GameCube, Randy was keen to see it happen, being a fan of the system at the time. In fact, Gearbox approached Russell Borogove, who was now working freelance, after Captivation didn't survive the aftermath of the Dreamcast cancellation. In a freelance role, Russell completed a feasibility analysis with a basic port of the engine to the Nintendo console to determine if it would be possible using the same techniques as employed by the Dreamcast edition. A very raw code compilation was rumoured to have been done before the plug was finally pulled.

The PS2 edition would eventually surface, where some Dreamcast art assets were used, but the development itself was all done from scratch. "The port was a completely separate project," explained Randy. "The PS2 was such a completely different beast from any other platform ever that it really required completely custom code. We really had to dig deep to get that one going, but, in the end, there were tons of valuable lessons, and I'm really proud of the result."

So, what are the chances of playing the Dreamcast conversion? Well, surprisingly good! Over the years, there have been various different builds surfacing, but many have not been preserved. Dan Amrich confirmed still having his review copy. However, a later build of the Dreamcast game would sneak into the wild in 2003, the build dated 23rd May, 2001 and including the *Blue Shift* episode. No one knew how it sneaked out, but, importantly, the build was made only weeks before the final cancellation, so it's believed to be almost a gold edition of the game.

The build includes occasional poor frame rates and loading times in places, but, crucially, a major bug with the VMU saving. "It's possible the leak doesn't quite match the final certification copy," suggested Randy. "Or some changes made by the leaker to make that version distributable without SEGA's specific copy protection messed with the indexing system relied upon for VMU saves. The load time situation was about as good as it could ever be and was the worst aspect of the game. The state it landed in, though, was a miracle compared with where it started, being upwards of five minutes in earlier builds. I think they landed at under a minute in all cases and under thirty seconds in most cases; but, when compared with the PC version, it felt like an eternity."

"So, what are the chances of playing the Dreamcast conversion? Well, surprisingly good!"

The final certified version of the game was put on display at Gearbox HQ. An indication of how proud Gearbox were to have worked on the game, regardless of the outcome. It may be slightly later than the build that leaked, though, any differences are likely to be very small indeed. Jeff very kindly provided some photos of his own personal copy, and Gearbox also provided photos, most of which can be seen on the Games That Weren't website.

Although the game was cancelled, Jeff was still positive. "As with everything in game development, the best memories are working with great people who solve tough problems, create cool artwork, and build great gameplay," he said. "I've always enjoyed working with Gearbox – a joy to collaborate with – and the team at Captivation put all their effort in and worked closely together in a family-like atmosphere. Valve were also super supportive throughout. As a producer, I learned a lot about success actually being a combination of setting expectations and accomplishing great things, and not just one or the other."

Fans of the Dreamcast may be left wondering whether *Half-Life* could have given the platform the shot of adrenalin it so desperately needed to carry on for longer. Had there not been all the technical issues, it could have been released in time for Christmas 2000, maybe helping to prolong life for SEGA's wonderful console. However, it's pure luck that we are able to experience the game for ourselves and witness just what a fine job Captivation and Gearbox achieved.

Above: Photo of the Dreamcast edition of *Half-Life* in CD casing and other related memorabilia – displayed proudly at Gearbox Software.

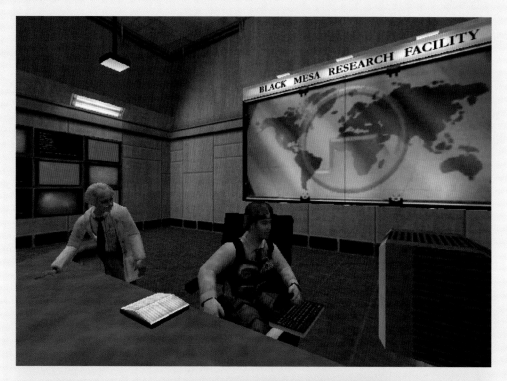

Top: Early on in *Half-Life* (Dreamcast), before all hell breaks loose. **Bottom:** A later scene in what was intended to be a SEGA exclusive with *Blue Shift* (Dreamcast).

Above: Title and option screens, followed by early scenes in the labs from the main game (Dreamcast).

Above: Later scenes in the main game as the action really starts to ramp up (Dreamcast).
Everything had translated very well across from the PC edition.

Flashback Legend Bankruptcy

Year: 2002
Developer: Adeline Software
Platform: Nintendo Game Boy Advance

The second sequel to the sublime *Flashback*, again taking control of Conrad to battle against the Morphs. Moving away from *Fade to Black's* 3D and back to classic 2D – it was a perfect match for Nintendo's handheld. Delphine's bankruptcy signalled its demise, potentially a saving grace for a game that many felt didn't live up to the original.

Available to play

 Yes ◯ No

8 Kings
Platform failure

Year: 2003
Developers: Argonaut Games
Platform: Nokia N-Gage

Available to play
 Yes ⦿ No

The US Prohibition during the 1920s and early 1930s was a dark time. With the sale of alcohol banned, organised crime blossomed, with bootlegging becoming very profitable for Mafia groups. The period has been an inspiration for many films and even video games.

Probably most famous was the 1987 film *The Untouchables*, where gangster Al Capone controls nearly the whole city of Chicago and has to be brought down by a group of police not influenced by the criminal boss. In 2003, the topic was broached yet again, this time for a game on a brand-new platform due from phone giant Nokia.

By the turn of the millennium, mobile phones and handheld consoles were extremely popular. Mobiles often came with built-in games but were not interchangeable like with a handheld console. Nokia saw an opportunity to create a single device that did this by announcing the N-Gage in 2002 – launching eventually in late 2003. After putting out a call to development studios for original titles, veteran games developer Argonaut Games responded.

Assigned to create a new design for the platform were Steven Grimley-Taylor and Craig Howard. It was decided to create a strategy game inspired primarily by *Advance Wars* on the Game Boy Advance, as well as *Command & Conquer: Generals* and *Army Men: RTS* on the PC. *Advance Wars* was a huge success, but the graphics were felt to be too cartoon-based and less appealing for the more mature gamers that the N-Gage was targeted for. The target audience for the new game was also casual and hardcore gamers, and it aimed to appeal to both sexes, with the ability to create a male or female protagonist game profile.

A Prohibition/Gangster theme was chosen to make the game more appealing, with inspiration taken from hard-hitting films, such as *The Untouchables*, mixed in with dark humour from *Goodfellas*. Similarly themed games of the time, such as *Gangsters 2* and *Mafia: The City of Lost Heaven,* also provided inspiration. All mixed in with an art deco-style brief, and *8 Kings* was born.

Steven and Craig set to work creating a story set in an alternative 1920s Prohibition Chicago, with you taking the role of an ambitious Mafia boss seeking to become the most powerful within the city. This must be achieved by taking down all of the 8 Kings, a group of hardcore opposing crime bosses that also want to be top dogs.

Each king had a unique personality, strengths and weaknesses, and consisted of characters named Yu Totsami, Mr K., Donovan Howard, Suzy Lee, Charles Nathan Smith, Hugh Anderson, Kurt Rollins and Lord Excelsior. Detailed profiles were constructed for each, helping you to decide the best strategy for defeating them.

With most of the game components and turn-based gameplay elements established, the project was given the green light. Craig would lead as the producer, with Martin Piper allocated as the lead developer. "It was after developing *Bionicle: Matoran Adventures* on the Game Boy Advance, so, around November 2002, we started," began Martin. "I had just written a 3D engine for the Game Boy Advance, and we were pondering doing a 3D racing game before *8 Kings* came along."

"Your progress is tracked on a 2D campaign map."

The audio composer could not be recalled, with Martin believing that it was possibly outsourced. However, voice acting was carried out by Martin Gwynn Jones. Completing the team were Douglas Hickmore and Oscar Ferrero on artistic duties. "I was given the chance to work on the project, and it sounded very interesting to me," began Oscar. "We were given 2D concepts and translated them into 3D. For artistic inspiration for the game as a whole, I was checking out *Mafia* screenshots."

Both Oscar and Douglas had worked together previously and shared a similar artistic style. Their brief was to take the game on an artistic direction that referenced the 1920s Art Deco movement and comic book-style artwork of *Batman* and *Dick Tracy*. The artists started implementing the design outlined, creating tiles, components, user interface and character profiles. The profiles would be used throughout the game to build up connections with the game's characters, conveyed through dialogue screens and different facial expressions to show emotion.

Within the game, the player would have two modes available to them in the form of Skirmish and Campaign. Skirmish would allow you to play with 1–4 players across single one-off battles, with a choice of game type and various options to tweak. The multiplayer options were particularly impressive, with the choice of having other players as CPU, Hot seat (sharing the handset) or Bluetooth-based – all of which could be combined in a manner of different ways.

A number of skirmish game modes were being developed and tested during the project, which would be finalised/tweaked as development progressed. The game modes would be implemented across a number of different maps. Initially planned were the following: 'Contract Killer' has you trying to find the 'grass' hiding on the map and teach them a lesson; 'Total War' has you completely destroying all of your opponents to win; 'Jailbreak' involves you being the first player to break five convicts out from jail and transport them back to base; 'King of the hill' required you to capture a designated building on the map and hold on to it for three turns.

For 'Bank Job', you must be the first to steal $10k from a bank. In 'Countdown' you must destroy as many rival units as possible within a limited amount of turns. 'Super power-up' involves war at full capacity, killing all enemies or taking over a rival base. 'Whack the boss' has you protecting your boss and having to kill all of the rival bosses. 'Gimme a dollar' sets you up in a cash-rich scenario, buildings loads of units and killing all enemies or defeating rivals.

Then, finally, 'Custom game' opens up the game by allowing you to change the win conditions. By default, you always win by capturing a rival base or destroying all of their units – but you can affect other conditions and criteria. So, you can set the maximum number of turns for the game, then how many captures, units, money or kills are required to win, and how much money each player gets per turn.

Campaign was the core single-player mode, where you must battle all of the 8 Kings across Chicago to become 'King of the City'. The mode consisted of a number of levels that gradually introduced all of the main concepts and features of the game.

Starting within your office, a sidekick character offers guidance, giving comments on your last battle and what is coming up. A telephone allows you to receive calls from your spy (if you have one) and will ring if there is something to report. The newspaper will detail the latest happenings going on in the city.

Your progress is tracked on a 2D campaign map showing a region of Chicago and giving options of where to move next. Areas held by any of the 8 Kings are labelled, as is the location of them. As you get closer to a king's position, they will move if they are feeling threatened.

"We were given 2D concepts and translated them into 3D."

Defeating a king will make all of their territory become neutral for yourself or others to take over. "When a map is won, you choose which area of the city to attack next," explained Martin. "Later maps would get progressively harder, with more opponents and units available. It wasn't quite a complete clone of *Advance Wars*, but it was building on ideas found in the genre at the time."

Initially, you are forced down a particular route whilst being trained on the game, before you can then later make your own choices. When choosing the next region, you first decide what units to use in battle. The designers wanted to give players freedom on how they could plan their attack. By removing linear progression and giving players the choice, you could strategically position resources, ambushes, or go straight into battle from the off. It was a complexity that Martin relished developing.

Battles themselves would switch proceedings to a more detailed 2D map, broken down into a tiled design with distinctive features making up the landscape. "Early versions did have a full 3D map. You could zoom in and see individual units, etc., but it was, unfortunately, a little bit too slow, so we moved over to 2D," confirmed Martin.

Units refer to the key battle pieces used in play, such as human objects and vehicles. They all had different move and attack distances, as well as defence and attack capabilities. Some of the key units consisted of soldiers, snipers, bikes, cars, trucks (including self-destructing bomb trucks), planes, boats and submarines. These were brought and used strategically to help you achieve your main goal of defeating an enemy or taking over resources.

"The N-Gage did not have 3D Hardware acceleration, so it had to be done all through software."

Human units could capture new buildings as well as defend them. Vehicles were effective for quickly getting defence to a location under attack, often giving the ability to carry multiple human units (depending on the vehicle type) and also came with good firepower qualities. Finally, transport units (not used in either attack or defence) were available in the form of trains and airships to help transport human units to a distant location within a single move.

Tiles making up each level map consisted of roads, paving, grass, mountains, water and various buildings. Each had a different effect on the units travelling across them, offered different amounts of defence, or could only be passed by particular units, such as boats across water. The design of the maps and careful placement of tiled elements would give different strategic challenges throughout the game, such as water being used to separate two islands, where marine vehicles would be needed to launch an attack on the other island.

Buildings also offered a source of income when they were taken over, but certain buildings additionally had extra functions. Factories and seaports allowed you to build new vehicles, and there were four resource buildings in the shape of banks, strip bars, casinos and jails. These allowed you to earn money or generate new human units (in the case of the jails). With the casino, you could also adjust your earnings. Setting low odds earned you more money per turn, but increasing the odds would result in a larger payout for waiting, as long as a rival didn't take it over in the meantime.

The base building was the most vital (and tallest) of all the buildings, as it housed either your own headquarters or one of the 8 Kings. This building had the highest level of defence, meaning that you'd need plenty of muscle to succeed. If a base was taken over, it is game over for either yourself or one of the big bosses. When attacking a rival king's base, the action would switch to inside the boss building. "It was a 3D boss battle room, which used detailed room models with animated characters," explained Martin. "This meant the player and the computer-controlled boss could fight it out visually. This was to be used at set points throughout the story's progression."

On each move, based on movement-distance ability, you could set a particular path for your unit to follow. When alongside another unit or building, you had the option to attack – taking up one turn. "Battles were 3D animated scenes. If the player was lucky with a bonus shot (controlled by clicking at the correct time), they would deal extra damage during the battle," explained Martin of a 'Sharpshooter' golf meter-style mechanism in the game. "The backgrounds would also change depending on the type of map tile the unit was on at the time. So we had lots of variation in the appearance of the battles."

When you completed a region/level, you were given a ranking based on the time taken and damage sustained on both sides. The ranking could be improved in future games, which added extra replay value to the game. There were also unlockable awards as you progressed, with new units, maps and resources rewarded based on certain achievements. You could also get profile upgrades for your appearance (such as hats or glasses), as well as unlocking new ringtones and phone wallpapers.

"We were very much into the game, and, after half a year working on it, I always thought it was going to be great."

Several months into development, everything was progressing well. However, the project wasn't without its issues, and the N-Gage had certainly been challenging, especially when it came to the 3D parts.

"It was tough as the N-Gage did not have 3D hardware acceleration, so it had to be done all through software," explained Oscar. "The specifications for the N-Gage didn't give us much room for adding lots of details into the geometry, but we tried as much as we could to mimic the 2D concepts. For environments, we tried to create a believable world but with hints of a cartoon style. We had a very good coder in Martin, and he did a great job. Thanks to him, we could create our cutscenes in 3D and export them into the N-Gage with ease."

Development also encountered a few issues with Symbian and its C++ platform along the way, but they were easily overcome. "Lucky that all technical issues were quite easy to solve," reflected Martin. "Nokia were tweaking the memory available to the system during hardware development, so we never really knew how much we had. Luckily, they kept on increasing it, so we kept on filling it with more graphics and sound!"

As the game neared completion, the team knew that they were onto a winner. "The game (and usually after a project, I never play it again) was fun, and we played it a lot whilst creating it. We were very much into the game, and, after half a year working on it, I always thought it was going to be great," reflected Oscar. Only polish, finishing maps and difficulty tweaks to gameplay remained, with the game more than 90% complete. However, Nokia wasn't to have the successful launch anticipated.

"When the N-Gage was released, it quickly became obvious it was a flop, and 8 Kings was cancelled as a result."

The N-Gage failed to make a major impact, being completely outsold by the Game Boy Advance, before eventually being retired by 2005. "When the N-Gage was released, it quickly became obvious it was a flop, and 8 Kings was cancelled as a result. Nothing was reused, and Argonaut concentrated on the bigger consoles afterwards," confirmed Martin. "We felt really down when it was canned as we thought the game was in good shape. Schedules were OK, and it was fun to play, so it was a real shame," added Oscar.

As found with many titles, the experience with 8 Kings was not wasted. "I had a really amazing time and felt great working with the team we had. Because of the constraints of the project, we had the chance to do it all (from modelling, texturing, rigging and animating)," Oscar reflected. "Soon after, we were moved to the Catwoman project. A completely different story with lots of people, levels of hierarchy, many departments, etc. So the comfy environment we lived during 8 Kings was kind of lost."

Unfortunately, Argonaut hit a troublesome period not long afterwards and folded by the end of 2004. Oscar would move back to Spain, setting up a games studio (www.elite3d.com) which he has been running for over a decade. Douglas now works as a UI/UX developer at a famous online poker website. Craig now runs a games studio in Liverpool. Steven manages a company selling modular synth DIY kits and supplies. Finally, Martin is now Head of QA Technology for a bank in Singapore. The team's time at Argonaut was now nothing but fond memories.

As for the game itself, it still exists and could easily be released to the world to play, what with N-Gage emulation sort of existing. But, in the days of strict NDAs and legal issues, it is likely never to happen, and certainly not from the developers. At the very least, check out screenshots here, a small glimpse for the first time showing the promise of what would have been a superb turn-based combat game on a portable platform.

If only 8 Kings had not just been limited to the N-Gage platform but also planned for other platforms, such as the Nintendo Game Boy Advance, then this could have been a title that had provided fond gaming memories for many instead.

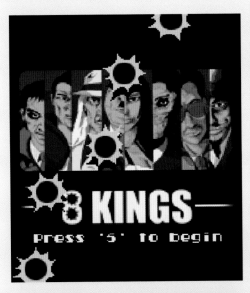

Above: Screenshots from the final build of *8 Kings* (Nokia N-Gage), showing the title screen, boss encounter scene, main game map and battle scene.

Top: Main game logo, showing all of the 8 Kings, which would have likely featured on the final packaging. **Bottom:** Various vehicles and character mock-up objects for the game.

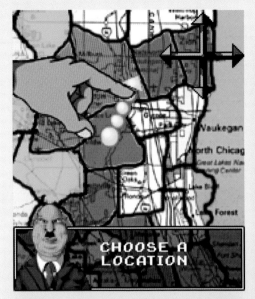

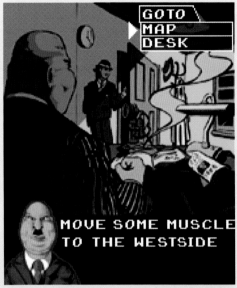

Above: Mock-up screens showing how the 'choose location' options and character profile areas may have looked.

Developed by the creators of the wonderful *Gunstar Heroes*, this was promised to be a frantic and fun expansion of Treasure's *Rakugaki Showtime* within the crazy *Tiny Toon Adventures* world. Up to four players would be able to unleash chaos, but it was never to be, and this promising-looking game would be cancelled for reasons that are still unknown.

Available to play

 Yes   No

Tiny Toon Adventures: Defenders of the Universe

Reason unknown

Year: 2002
Developer: Treasure
**Platforms: Nintendo GameCube
and Sony PlayStation 2 (pictured)**

Stunt Car Racer Pro Lack of publisher

Year: 2003
Developers: Simergy and Lost Toys
Platforms: Microsoft Xbox, PC and Sony PlayStation 2

Available to play
 Yes No

It was blind panic as an eight-year-old trying to escape the frightening gaze of *The Sentinel*. Many hours had been sunk into the addictive Firebird Software classic, trying to navigate through its 10,000 levels. Rapidly learning of the flawless reputation of author Geoff Crammond, it was a natural progression to the impressive and acclaimed *Formula One Grand Prix* and *Revs* games from the very same developer. If, like the author, you were not quite up to the task of driving an F1 car due to the highly accurate handling and controls, then *Stunt Car Racer* was a perfect alternative to experience Geoff's racing game wizardry in a pick-up-and-play form.

Released back in 1989 by MicroProse, and as with *The Sentinel*, there was nothing quite like *Stunt Car Racer* at the time. Unlike other first-person racing games, it was set on elevated racetracks that you could easily fall off if you went too perilously close to the edge. Tracks would raise and dip, resulting in something akin to a roller coaster ride, with plenty of thrills and spills.

The game consisted of a number of tracks across multiple divisions, where you have to beat a computer-based opponent over a number of laps. To assist, you are given a limited amount of turbo boost that must be sparingly used throughout the race – useful for playing catch-up or achieving decent track times. The higher the division, the harder and more daunting the tracks, with some terrifying high jumps. Speed must also be gauged carefully as going too fast can result in you flying off the track or damaging your car if hitting the ground too fast at a bad angle. Obtain too much damage, and it's game over.

Once you exhausted the single-player mode, the 16-bit editions allowed you to play against a friend – as long as you had two machines next to each other and a null modem cable to link them up with. For those lucky enough to have this setup, it was an experience unlike any other and one of the best multiplayer experiences you could have.

Reception of the game was fantastic, as you might expect. Impressive even today, and also fast on the 8-bit platforms, it created a stomach-twisting experience for many players across the world. Combined with its multiplayer mode, the game would have a long and loyal fan base for many years to come, frequently featuring on retrospective 'top game' lists.

So, it may come as a surprise that there was never a sequel. Geoff would spend many years preoccupied with Formula One-based games, except for a brief diversion with *Sentinel Returns* in 1998. But all of this was about to change in 2003 when Geoff finally got the chance to revisit his classic high-thrills racer.

"A sequel or upgrade to *Stunt Car Racer* has been suggested by various third parties over the years, but I could never agree to anything which didn't have my complete involvement at every level," explained Geoff in a *Eurogamer* news article in 2003. "My commitment to Formula 1 simulations over the past few years was very intensive and just didn't allow me to work on any other projects. Now, the time seems just about perfect to produce *Stunt Car Racer Pro*."

Confidence was high that this was a game that still had relevance in the modern-day market. Geoff would search for a team to help him tackle development alongside his Simergy company. The project was offered to Lost Toys, a development studio born from Bullfrog, founded by Jeremy Longley, Darran Thomas and Glenn Corpes. "Lost Toys will be key to making *Stunt Car Racer Pro* a success," Geoff told *GameSpot* in 2003. "I've chosen them because they have a proven track record of producing great multi-format titles on time and to budget. I also believe this team understands perfectly just how strong Simergy's commitment is to quality and playability."

Self-funded by both Geoff and John Cook (Geoff's business manager), the plan would be to produce as much of the game as possible so that a fully working prototype could be shown to publishers to help secure a deal. "John was our agent and also worked with Geoff, so it happened through him. All of us at Lost Toys were very keen to work on it," recalled Glenn Corpes. "We were looking for a second project to go alongside Darran's idea for a game called *Feral*, and Jeremy announced the *Stunt Car Racer Pro* plan shortly after that. I think Geoff had been looking for a team to do it for a while," added Alex Trowers.

Alex was assigned to the project as lead designer, focusing on making the iconic tracks that would make up the core of the game. Darran Thomas would act as art director, with most of the 3D modelling work carried out by Dave Cathro. Geoff himself would also be heavily involved, writing a lot of the physics for the game along with Jeremy Longley, getting the balance of the cars just right. Glenn would work on a track editor for the game, with John Treece-Birch developing the artificial intelligence (AI) for all the computer-controlled cars. Finally, Ben Carter would focus on writing the all-important core engine for the game.

"The engine was constantly worked on throughout."

The team was very excited about the project, with most having played the original to death. That is, apart from one member, who instead experienced another title heavily inspired by *Stunt Car Racer*. "I'd never actually played the original game prior to us starting on the reboot," confessed Ben Carter. "However, I was aware of it and was a massive fan of the Acorn Archimedes game *Stunt Racer 2000*. A wonderful expansion of the core idea, and, in particular, the two-player battle mode of that game was excellent."

The game was scheduled for release sometime in 2004, with the aim to modernise it but remain faithful to the original design. As a result, the game would feature classic tracks from the original game and retain the concept of progressing through different divisions. Like with the original, the tracks would be smooth and undulating but also could feature gaps, halfpipes, loop-the-loops and corkscrews. Any such additions had to be realistic, though. "Geoff was adamant that the game had to be an accurate simulation of a non-existent but physically possible motor sport," stated Glenn.

"The new mechanics ended up never getting past the design stage."

Perhaps surprisingly, the PC was not the primary launch target for the game like with Geoff's F1 titles. The focus would initially be on the Sony PlayStation 2 and Microsoft Xbox. A Sony PlayStation Portable (PSP) conversion was also discussed when early rumblings of a new Sony handheld were first heard. Ben suggested that conversations about a conversion were likely happening when the PSP was just a bunch of schematics deep in SCEI's R&D labs. Work would commence alongside another title called *Feral* (a werewolf game that was also never to be released), with most of the team working simultaneously on both games.

"*SCR Pro* was designed to be truly cross-platform. We weren't pitching a PC version at first as the publishers we were talking to weren't interested at the time," recalled Glenn. "We were keen to avoid the situation experienced on *Battle Engine*, where a chunk of the game had been developed on PC (prior to dev kits being available for the then 'next-gen' consoles)," added Ben. "We had a little bit of a nightmare cramming that game onto Xbox and getting it onto PS2. So, from day one, we were testing *SCR Pro* on all three platforms. I don't recall us ever having a concrete plan to ship the PC version, but it was useful for development purposes, and, like *Battle Engine,* I think it would have naturally followed, had the console release gone well."

Ben had already been working on a new engine for the *Feral* development, using a heavily cleaned up and stripped-down version of the *Battle Engine* codebase. However, the PS2 version had suffered as the underlying engine was too closely targeted towards the Xbox platform. The lack of RAM and multi-textures on the PS2 caused it to be significantly poorer visually, so Ben needed to make vital improvements for the codebase to work effectively across both platforms and appear visually consistent.

"The engine was constantly worked on throughout the entire development cycle. Used on both *SCR Pro* and *Feral*, it made life pretty interesting as they were radically different games in terms of gameplay and technical requirements," Ben explained. "But, with such a small team, we needed to keep as much of the fundamental code shared to avoid the workload becoming unmanageable."

Whilst developing the engine for *Feral* (which required complex lighting models), Ben implemented an impressive stencil-shadowing system inspired by John Carmack's *Doom 3* development notes. It used partially precalculated and real-time shadow volumes to build up realistic environment lighting. Although painful to get working well on the PS2, it was made possible thanks to the superb fill rate of that platform. Things were far more straightforward on the Xbox/PC, with less horsepower required to achieve the same effects.

"We were actually using what these days would probably be called a 'partially deferred' rendering model," recalled Ben. "Essentially, it did lighting accumulation in a separate buffer and then modulated it with the material data for the surfaces. In our worlds, every pixel was pitch-black until a light source illuminated it. This meant we could have multiple overlapping lights/shadows, self-shadowing objects, etc., and it all 'just worked'. In *SCR Pro*, this was particularly noticeable in the in-car view as you would see the shadow of trackside objects and the roll bars of the car cross the bonnet as you turned."

With two very different styles of games handled by one engine, Ben ended up having to include and develop two different rendering modes to cater for both games effectively. 'Full-fat mode' would be used by *Feral*, hitting 30 frames per second but including all the bells and whistles of the engine, such as large numbers of coloured light sources. 'Lite mode' would be used by *SCR Pro*, which trimmed out unnecessary features used in *Feral* and meant that the game could double up at an impressive 60 frames per second.

Working closely with Ben, Glenn constructed his track editor to build up the game and make the lives of the designers a lot easier but also more fun. "Glenn built a wonderful track editor," remembered Alex. "Seriously, I've used almost every editor Glenn has ever made, and this one was far and away the best. You could fly the track into place – a lot like *Mod Nation Racers* but whilst being suspended up in the air. You could tweak the banking and all sorts on the fly, as well as insert ramps, loops, halfpipes or any other object imported from *3D Studio Max* to form more technical areas of track."

Old and new tracks created in the game would be as narrow as in the original, with the same sloped sides as before. During very early playtesting, it was found to be impossible to stay on the tracks. Subtle steering assist routines were then translated across from the original game, which literally got everything 'back on track'.

"The game was scheduled for release sometime in 2004, with the aim to modernise it but remain faithful to the original design."

Another headache was with the big open spaces and huge tracks contained within. The problem was that you could see everything within the world, with no convenient blind corners to mask off the distance, as found with most racing games of the time. It meant that things could slow down heavily throughout a race. To get around the issue and also avoid having to use the dreaded 'obscuring distance fog', a solution was to 'load on demand' and render track components and other objects at differing levels of detail, based on position. Distant objects would have a lot less detail drawn in comparison to objects that were very close, which helped to ensure that the engine could achieve the essential fast speed.

"Seriously, I've used almost every editor Glenn has ever made, and this one was far and away the best. You could fly the track into place – a lot like *Mod Nation Racers* but whilst being suspended up in the air."

For the physics aspect of the game, Jeremy started by taking Geoff's implementation from the original and porting it from 68000 assembler to C. This initially caused problems as the physics system couldn't cope with the joints between the track polygons, so cars would just fly off the track. The issue was down to collisions in the original game being just against curved surfaces, and the new development's surfaces being a lot more complex. Glenn assisted Jeremy to fix the issue by writing an improved collision routine to handle the more flexible curved surfaces that were now possible.

"The physics system for the game was something we were very proud of and was quite ahead of its time, in my opinion," reflected Ben. "There were games doing car physics (i.e. what happens at the point where wheel meets tarmac) and generic rigid body physics (i.e. boxes interacting realistically) but very few games doing both at once like us. We had to cope with situations like cars flying over jumps and landing with just one wheel in contact with the track, or getting pushed up on two wheels by a collision. I remember coming in after lunch one day to find Jeremy showing a replay of a race he'd just had, where his car had come off a jump badly and managed to hit a flagpole at just the right angle to hook the pole into the front wheel arch. It span frantically atop the pole before finally settling down and dangling there like a bizarre ornament. That was pretty unique at the time."

John Treece-Birch's impressive AI system would round off the core game engine. His intelligent system would learn an entire game track by driving computer-controlled cars around them. The system would literally spawn hundreds of cars and force them to try out different approaches to each segment of a track until it found the best ones to use.

"You could watch it do all of this, which was great fun," recalled Ben. "There would be a stream of cars flying off a jump and missing the landing totally at first, but, over the course of a few seconds, it would home in on a working approach angle/speed, and more and more of the cars would land safely. Once it was happy it knew how to handle that part of the track safely/optimally, it would move on to the next one."

With a basic core game up and running, the team decided to go wild creating new cars to include within the game. The intention was to select and upgrade cars between races. "We had everything from a Toyota Supra to the General Lee from *Dukes of Hazzard*," recalled Alex. "Eventually, we pared it down to start making things that looked like they'd been designed to run on these tracks for a proper racing formula." Geoff Crammond added, "My focus was on making the cars in *SCR Pro* 'real' so, with big suspension and aero for flight stability rather than downforce, they could actually work in the real world – that is, if anyone was crazy enough to build and drive on the tracks! Making a game playable, but 100% realistic has always been the top priority for me."

Whereas the original just had the two cars battling it out within a race, in the new game, there could be anything up to a total of eight cars on the track at the same time. It meant that extra chaos would likely ensue along the already tight and treacherous tracks.

Finally, there were also new multiplayer features to be experienced. It was planned that not only could you play others across the other side of the world, you would have been able to play against a friend using a local split-screen mode. This would have been combinable with the online options too and had initially included a controversial added bonus. "It was all fully multi-platform – you could play a multiplayer game on any of the systems, and it would happily cross-play. Not that the platform holders would ever have actually let us release it like that!" Alex confirmed. It was somewhat symbolic, considering the original Amiga and Atari ST editions could be mixed up in multiplayer link-up play.

Alex also recalled an additional improvement which was set to fix a fault with the original game. "In the original, you'd fall off and (especially in multiplayer) that would be it – not a chance," he began. "Now I'm extremely averse to catch-up, but we needed something to keep the poor player in contention. We came up with a system whereby you'd be placed back on the track a proportional amount behind the leader and less a small penalty for falling off. This seemed like a really big deal at the time."

"Sadly, Lost Toys didn't last after that. Stunt Car Racer Pro was the last game Lost Toys was working on before they ran out of money and had to shut the studio down."

Many months of development would pass swiftly for the team, with a solid and exciting game rapidly taking shape. It was respectful to the original game but now smoother, realistic looking, and more responsive with the higher frame rate now available. It was already fully playable in both single and multiplayer modes, with the team often playing the game against each other and enjoying the fruits of their labour so far. All that remained was work on the presentation, tracks and the division system.

With the game in a presentable and solid state, they were ready to start properly pitching to secure a publishing deal. Although there was interest shown, none of the publishers would bite and sign a deal to publish the title. Tragically, it brought development crashing to an abrupt halt at around a 50%-completed state, with the funding completely running out. "The new mechanics ended up never getting past the design stage," admitted Glenn. "There were designs for all of the leagues, but we didn't get to implement any of it. We finished with just the core of a game, where you could select a level and race; nothing anywhere near ready for release."

"We'd created a multiplayer racer on roller coasters that was actually great fun to play, even including input from Geoff himself, but it's all for nowt if you can't source the funding," added Alex. "Sadly, Lost Toys didn't last after that. *Stunt Car Racer Pro* was the last game Lost Toys was working on before they ran out of money and had to shut the studio down."

"It was a real pity the game didn't get anywhere – it was a lot of fun to play."

"I remember discussions about writing an Amiga emulator so that we could include the original *SCR* as a bonus feature. Sadly, the project got canned before we could do anything concrete about that," recalled Ben. "It was a real pity the game didn't get anywhere – it was a lot of fun to play in its prototype form. If the experimental stuff we were doing with things like the track editor and online play had paid off, I think it would have been something quite special. Although, I fully admit that rose-tinted spectacles are probably in full effect here."

Speaking to *Retro Gamer* magazine in 2009, Geoff also reflected on the cancellation: "It's a real shame it never happened. It was a self-financed project that simply hit a patch where publishers just weren't signing on the dotted line. As it was self-financed, we had a limited timeline before it became impractical to continue with the team. My business manager [John Cook] calls it the best game he never sold."

Following on from the ashes of Lost Toys, most of the team went on to work for other development studios. At this point, Geoff would move out of the limelight to work on more personal programming projects. *Stunt Car Racer Pro* was put to rest, with no further attempts to try and resurrect the project. The wait for a long-awaited sequel would go on.

As with all titles covered in the book, the question was asked whether there was anything that could be shown of the game. No screenshots or video ever seemed to make it online, which is not surprising as no marketing had been started for the game before the plug was pulled. Sadly, when Lost Toys closed its doors, all of the development machines were wiped and sold off. Glenn suggested that backups and builds will likely still exist somewhere, where something playable could be obtained – but nothing was found at the time of publication, and it's unlikely that anything found could be released anyway.

However, the original trailer produced and shown to publishers at the time was found, showing actual parts of the game in action. It showcases an impressive-looking demo track and an indication of the fast-paced racing action that you could expect to see. You get a great sense of how fun it would have been to play against other players, and it does little to reduce the feeling that we have all missed out on something rather special. The next few pages show screenshots of the development for the first time, and we hope to add the video itself on the Games That Weren't website by the time of publication.

Many today will still likely hope for a sequel to someday surface on modern platforms, though the ex-Lost Toys team are doubtful it will ever happen and feel that maybe a spiritual successor is now the best and only hope. Of course, we hope they are wrong and that, someday, Geoff finds a way of resurrecting the concept for a whole new generation of hardware and gamers so that others can experience the fun that many of us once did. It feels as if *Stunt Car Racer* has unfinished business, with an audience still out there waiting to be thrilled.

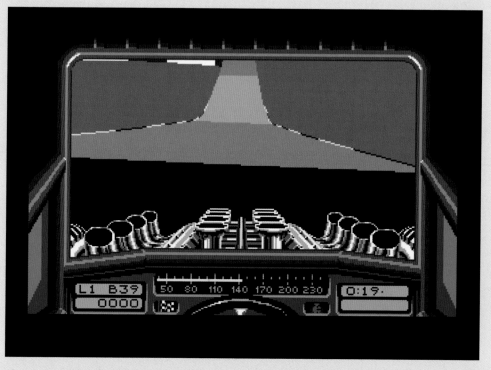

Above: Screenshot from the original *Stunt Car Racer* (Amiga), showing the front of the car where flames roar when using your speed boost.

Above: Title and a view of the game from the car, taken from a promotional video created to showcase the game to potential publishers, so the final look would likely have been heavily improved.

Above: More screens from the promotional video, showing what could well have been the car-selection screen, and then various different-angled shots of the cars racing around the track.

Above: There were going to be some death-defying jumps, as with the original game, but many more opponents to contend with. The original game just had the one opponent.

Fallout 3 Financial troubles

Year: 2003
Developer: Black Isle Studios
Platform: PC

Code-named *Van Buren*, this was to have been *Fallout 3*, created fully in 3D with a similar top-down/angled approach like the previous two games. This very promising title was cancelled when the development studio was closed due to financial troubles at parent company Interplay Entertainment. A leaked demo shows just how different the third main series game could have been.

"When I first started working at Black Isle Studios back in 1999, all I ever wanted to do was work on *Fallout 3*. A lot of the other people at the studio also felt the very same way. Chris Avellone had compiled hundreds of pages of notes that he was using as the basis for our designs, and we even did some playtesting in a tabletop RPG campaign.

Our engine tech was finally maturing (we had been using it at the time for another project, *The Black Hound*), and I think the team did great work in the limited time that we had available. Unfortunately, the circumstances that *Van Buren* started under were less than ideal, as Interplay was in terrible financial shape. Even though we put together a cool demo level, Interplay's upper management had decided to cancel it before they even saw it."

Josh Sawyer, lead designer

Available to play
◉ Yes   ○ No

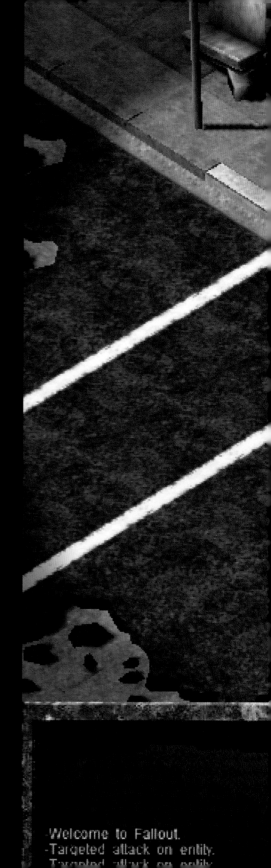

Welcome to Fallout.
-Targeted attack on entity.
Targeted attack on entity.

HEALTH
041

Frank

PUNCH

25 ACTION POINTS

FATIGUE
000

EVASION

AP3

Burnt Out Cop IP dramas

Year: 2003
Developer: Infinite Lives
Platforms: Microsoft Xbox,
Nintendo GameCube
and Sony PlayStation 2

Available to play

 Yes No

Ever dreamed as a kid of living out your favourite film and saving the world? Perhaps flying the X-Wing in *Star Wars* to destroy the Death Star or becoming Batman and battling crime in Gotham City? Games have allowed many to live those dreams to a certain extent, where many could finally fly down that Death Star trench and save the galaxy, thanks to Atari's 1983 arcade game.

Burnt Out Cop (*BOC* from this point on) was a development team's own dream to allow players to live out what felt like a fast-paced and violent action movie. It was inspired by films such as *Lethal Weapon*, *Die Hard* and, most crucially of all, John Woo's *Hard Boiled* (a cult classic film from 1992). The brief was simple: over-the-top carnage, stacks of weapons and kung fu aplenty, but with the added slapstick of Jackie Chan, Buster Keaton and the Laurel and Hardy films.

The brains behind the concept were Infinite Lives, a small development studio based in Clerkenwell, Islington – consisting of John and Steve Rowlands, Robin Ellis and Nick Lee, with industry legend Dan Malone later joining them on a freelance basis. *BOC* began life during a relaxing break away from games development during the summer of 2002. "Myself, John and a load of others went to Centre Parcs one weekend and were having this great time. We were watching TV one night, and *Hard Boiled* came on, which became the big inspiration and trigger for *BOC*," explained Robin.

Putting ideas quickly to paper, the guys wanted playable scenes reminiscent of their favourite violent action film scenes. Steve began researching other films for inspiration, creating small reference clips. "I can't remember what they were exactly, but I remember going through them and going to the guys, 'How about this one?', and so on," recalled Steve. "I know one scene was the start of *Hard Boiled,* where they were in the dim sum restaurant, with a gunfight across a small space, and the main character is leaping across booths. That's the kind of vibe that I wanted to have," added Robin. "Several characters and locations would come from that movie," added Nick. "The teashop that gets destroyed during a gunfight was eventually replicated in our demo. We also wanted everything highly destructible, where every tile could be destroyed."

A basic storyline was established where you controlled Harry Ran, a cop within the fictional Central City, based on Hong Kong in both climate and location and with levels of corruption as seen in Batman's Gotham City. Harry was a good cop, once respected by his peers, and wants to do things the right way.

However, corruption takes hold of the force, with influence and respect waning for Harry. Coupled with the tragic death of his wife, taking to drink and losing custody of his child, he hits rock bottom and burns out. Feeling that he must turn his life around, Harry begins a path of redemption, though what exactly that path was would be unknown.

Ultimately, there was a mission to the game, but you wouldn't know what it was until events played out. Starting off with a simple investigation, everything suddenly escalates as you delve deeper. "It was to be a page-turner, where you wanted to see what was on the next level – a cinematic romp with loads of mad gun battles too," explained Dan Malone. "There could have also been bonuses, where you get a particular high score or something on that path to redemption – all with a cut sequence that sets you up for the next level."

Each cutscene was to be cleverly rendered within comic book-like panels, with each part animating in turn before returning you to the action. Dialogues were even to be in Japanese, with a Western voice translation to give that 'imported movie' feel as a nice additional touch.

In addition to films, the team also drew on previous fighting game experience, having developed *IK+ Advance* and two unreleased beat-em-ups in the form of *Kung Fu Fighting* and *Bloodlust*. "A lot of our planned moves for Harry were heavily inspired by those games," Steve added. "It was all just kind of our mindset – the whole thing that we loved fighting games and martial arts films. Early Jet Li stuff was just brilliant too."

The main game itself would always be played from a third-person perspective so you could see all of Harry's actions and have a better viewpoint of everything around you. The story mode was to be single-player only, but there would likely be some kind of multiplayer party modes with up to four players (including CPU options), a *Power Stone*-like mode with selectable characters, as well as an open party mode with no rules.

With enough of an initial seed in place and ideas formulating daily, the team now needed a designer to visualise and ramp everything up into a full plan for the game. The team approached Dan Malone, who instantly fell in love with the idea that Infinite Lives presented. "It was more serious once Dan started doing some sketches, bringing it all to life and further fuelling our excitement for it," reflected Steve. "It was the peak of my time in the games industry," began Dan. "It was a great team, the best I've ever worked with. When I first joined, I started the main character, other characters and storyboarding. I was thinking of *Midnight Run* with Robert De Niro, where he's a kind of bounty hunter who just barges his way through. That was my visual reference for Harry."

Dan christened the game with a unique comic book artistic style, with beautifully hand-drawn characters and over-exaggerated movements. It wasn't meant to look realistic but feel more like a live-action comic book that you controlled. It was an almost ageless visual style that would still look fresh today, similar to *Jet Set Radio* and *Okami*. "BOC was not really based on technical realism, more just based on comic story and film-led. It didn't have to be realistic; it just had to look great, with beautiful lighting and simple textures," explained Dan.

With the theme and direction established, ideas continued to flow, and a start was made on nailing down the game's structure. This included working out the levels, spread across multiple themes including 'dockyard', 'bar', 'hospital', 'apartment', 'nightclub', 'warehouse', 'teahouse', 'peak' and concluding with an 'industrial construction site' area, complete with an epic Mr Big encounter.

Each level was broken up into a number of multi-route stages, for example, with the dockyard broken into segments, such as a yard, a container area and factory offices. Stages were mostly self-contained, forcing Harry into set pieces and large-scale fights. The primary aim would be for Harry to progress from A to B, disposing of enemies that get in his way and finding new evidence to open up the storyline. Dan sketched out the main game map, in a similar vein to *Final Fight/Ghosts 'n' Goblins*, showing the progression route ahead.

Distinctive characters for the game were also key, with plans for a female sidekick occasionally popping up in levels to help you out. Other characters would include innocent bystanders (used as human shields by enemies), bent cops, a city mayor, bodyguards, gangs, the femme fatale, and the gutter, whose kitchen you wouldn't dare enter. During early levels, villains started off as general thugs who would be simple to dispose of in order to ease the player into the game and allow familiarity with the controls.

Proceedings would soon be ramped up with large criminal gangs, henchmen and then later masterminds who control the city, complete with tough armoury and weapons. An enemy's health would be represented in a similar way to *Final Fight*, with an energy bar appearing when engaging in combat.

Events within the game would not often go to plan, ensuring chaotic and bungled situations, with a frenzy of fighting and having to get out of tight spots. One comical element was to be Harry's large brick phone, used to get information on stages. The phone would be heavy, making Harry's trousers frequently fall down, but it could also ring at the worst possible moment, making you swear and subsequently letting enemies know exactly where you were, spoiling your potential element of surprise.

To keep everything fresh, there were plans to move away from the standard game mechanics from time to time. As well as bonus interrogation scenes and drinking games, there were 'into the screen' chase scenes planned for specific stages. One particular chase was across a market and, overall, not too dissimilar to the infinite running games you see today. "It was based on a running foot chase scene in *French Connection*, where they are just slap bang running," recalled Dan. "All narrowed down into a mad sprint, where you'd have people getting in the way, stallholders and boxes of fruit flying everywhere. It was going to be fucking hilarious! If you caught the suspect, you'd get a bit of info and a cut sequence."

Steve then adds, "I remember borrowing a scene from the 1994 anime *Ghost in the Shell* where the protagonist looks down at a market. I took a screen grab, made it into a texture and just laid it out – it was totally the right feel."

"You'd get stronger and would be able to go longer and finish later levels, finally taking out the Brothers of the Leaf."

Dan focused on the dockyard area early on, storyboarding sections, for example, where you walk in on feuds between gangland workers and Russian crooks. He would also create visuals and storyboards for later levels, giving a flavour of the entire game. There were several possible routes to take in the dockyard, but, no matter which way you went, you'd soon end up in a final scene against the fish gutter boss. "The gutter would have helpers, and, as he turns around, he would grab his machine gun out his bag of fish guts and charge at you, shouting, 'Who are you?'," described Dan. "He was to be really strong but also one-directional, so you could really get him in the side and kidneys to defeat him!"

With core scenarios and characters being designed in great detail, Nick and Steve started creating the models for them. Steve also focused on the character animations. "I'd do hundreds of key frames, viewed from the angle you'd see them, and go, 'Are these alright for you Steve?', and he'd go, 'Yeah, that's fine', and he would just fucking nail it! He was just generating and animating – just churning out models," enthused Dan. All was in preparation not only for a playable prototype but also a pre-production film to accompany the design document and be presented to potential publishers.

Of course, Harry was the main focus to visualise and animate, with plenty of work going into his moves and armoury. By default, Harry would carry a chest-holstered pistol, with a plethora of other ammo-limited guns and weapons available to pick up, including shotguns and machine guns. These were picked up or stolen from enemies, even impressively caught in mid-air if the situation arose. If you were unsure which weapon to choose, then you could hold two simultaneously or use your spare hand to hold a shield of some kind. Using guns would be straightforward, with 'Line of sight' giving you a 20-degree shot arc, and 'Proximity target' allowing you to lock on to nearby enemies. Alternatively, you could use the manual override and have full control of your aim instead.

There were also melee weapons for Harry to pick up, from hammers and planks to fun objects like frying pans, prosthetic limbs and even fish. The size/weight of the object would be key to the damage that it would cause to an enemy or the surrounding environment. If there wasn't anything available, then you could revert to hand-to-hand combat and just use your kung fu skills. Then, if you didn't fancy killing everyone, you could alternatively arrest enemies, who may give up vital information or clues. The inventiveness of your actions were encouraged, with different levels of points available based on your creativity.

Controls were to be simple and intuitive, with action combinations established through simple button pressing rather than memorising combinations. Just as well, as Harry was to have a vast range of moves, being able to jump/dive over objects, crouch, strafe, push and pull objects, walk, run, throw, grab opponents as shields, edge along walls, shoot, and engage in combat. The team wanted you to feel like you were living out a film, with a wide range of spectacular actions that could be carried out in many sequences. Even spectators watching the game were expected to be engrossed from the sidelines.

With Harry on his path of redemption and with a poor mental and physical state from the start, he'd noticeably get sluggish and run out of energy faster at the beginning of the game. Carrying out the chase scene early on will almost kill him. "The mechanic was that you get improved movement, recoil and that kind of thing as you progress," explained Robin. "You'd get stronger and would be able to go longer and finish later levels, finally taking out the Brothers of the Leaf," added Dan. "There's a scene where he's tortured by them and had his teeth kicked in. You'd eventually meet again, but, when you do, you're prepared and now have a purpose, wanting to save the city and get your daughter back."

As well as that neat mechanic, there were a number of other touches planned, where you could use enemies as human shields, who become harder to move once they are dead. Enemies were also to react differently depending on the type of attack on them, spraying bullets as they fall as well. A gun hitting the ground or an object whilst fully loaded could also go off and shoot a random projectile and do harm. There were even plans for a developing love story between Harry and the Queen DJ, who runs the city radio station, which Dan described as trying to add a bit of softness to balance against the hard violence.

The entire development of the concept, design document and a pre-production film would take approximately four months, with inspiration aided by the 'playing hard and working hard' mentality within the team. The design document was very detailed, featuring Dan's concept sketches, and renders by Nick and Steve, giving a clear vision of the grand plan ahead. "That doc got pretty thick!" Dan reflected. "John and I spent one all-nighter doing the whole fucking thing in MS Word, which is completely ill-suited for moving type around with images. It's like trying to build a nuclear weapon!"

It could have been even thicker though, with many ideas not making the final cut. These were not to be wasted as thoughts moved beyond *BOC* early on. "We were already thinking ahead, saving certain things for a potential sequel," Dan explained. "A sequel could have had the girl detective as the protagonist, where it was her story," added Robin. "I also thought that we could do a cops and robbers variant as we were into *Medal of Honour* and *Spearhead* at the time. We could have done all kinds of crazy shit."

So far the team had invested around £80,000 between them to try and make *BOC* a reality, self-funding prototype animations and the game design document. Money was now starting to dry up, and the team ideally needed more time and money to next produce a playable prototype to help further sell the game to publishers. They started by uploading the game design proposal and pre-production film to their website to see who would bite first.

From previous experience of working with HotGen on games such as *Matt Hoffman 2* for the Game Boy Advance, they first approached them with the idea. HotGen loved the concept and decided to help bankroll the project, with the caveat that HotGen would own the Intellectual Property (IP) as a form of security if anything was to go wrong. It was additionally suggested that it would look better being sold as a concept from a large company, rather than a small, relatively unknown development studio.

"I was really excited about Rob's weapons work – they were recoiling out of control, and it was just chaos."

Feeling in good hands after past dealings, Infinite Lives agreed and would move from their small Clerkenwell office and into the HotGen offices based in Croydon. The reallocated *BOC* team would take up the 16th floor, which was mostly empty and a perfect large open space to stretch out. Dan's artwork was swiftly blown up to A2 to adorn the walls as you walked in. The team were joined by a number of HotGen staff, assisting with development, artwork modelling and animations. The offices had pro-development gear, so the team was able to create builds to the Xbox and PS2 and generate real disks to run on the platforms.

It was by now March/April 2003, and, with extra support in place, it was time to put together a playable prototype, making use of an off the shelf engine to kick things off. "We ended up using Criterion's *RenderWare*," confirmed Robin. "This was just before they were bought out by Electronic Arts, which would have scrubbed any potential use as an engine. But we didn't know that at the time!" Use of the engine meant easy deployment to the target platforms PlayStation 2 and Xbox. The earlier plans for a Nintendo GameCube edition were dropped after diminishing platform sales at the time.

Robin and Nick worked closely with Mitchell Goodwin, getting up to speed on *RenderWare* to create basic environments and other specifics. "We were just nailing it," reflected Robin. "I didn't have any experience of *RenderWare* before that. Mitch arranged a basic template, and we built on it. He taught us how to make the builds, and also did the physics, so that when you shot a box it would break into bits. He did all that kind of stuff. I was learning all this 3D shit and was in particular really interested in making the guns all work."

"I was really excited about Rob's weapons work – they were recoiling out of control, and it was just chaos. The independent tracking was really good too, and you could later handle two guns simultaneously," added Dan. "I did all that stoned," smiled Robin. "Getting it all working was an epic day. The lads were down the pub, I was really high in the office. I got it going and went, 'Mitch, Mitch come and have a look at this', and he was 'Wow!!! That's awesome!!'."

Whilst Robin worked on guns and main character development, Nick handled level environments and enemies. John may have also helped with development, though primarily he orchestrated the project, acting as the project manager and voice of the team to upper management. The team did have two producers, though one parted ways after differences of opinion, and another just left rather suddenly. It was felt that John filled the role perfectly anyway, so it didn't matter.

Although Steve and Nick started off doing all the modelling work, roles transformed at HotGen. Steve went into a pure animation role, with HotGen's art team stepping in to do the majority of the modelling work. Nick would take on an art director role, overseeing the art staff, as well as still getting his hands dirty on the texturing and modelling. Meanwhile, Dan would concept out all of the characters for the game, along with key frames for each, texture maps and model sheets, as well as designing the game's world and map elements.

Characters and backgrounds were textured and modelled in *Photoshop* and *3D Studio Max* from the model sheets Dan provided. "We were just putting stuff straight in. No deliberating, just 'Stick it in, stick it in!'," explained Dan. "In the meantime, the rest of the guys were building demos. I was like, 'let's just smack it all out!', so we could get everything in, see the game running, start building a big map and tweak it all later. There was no 'We'll have a meeting about this' or 'Oh yeah, marketing is involved' – none of that and that was the beauty of it all."

It was crucial to get the development of the controls right early on, therefore, plenty of time was spent on them. "The control method, in particular, the double-handed gun controls, was pretty special once we'd got it going. My most important contribution was coming up with the double guns control method, as well as making the 3D models look like the hand-drawn artwork of Dan's," explained Nick. Pulling off wonderful looking action sequences would be possible with little effort, and those with real skill would be able to achieve better scores and show off to friends as the team had envisioned early on.

As well as controls and visuals, sound was also extremely important for the game. Early on, the team would hear music on the radio that fitted the brief and put straight into the game temporarily. Sound effects were also borrowed from another game. "I got sounds (I think) from *Counter-Strike* and used them as placeholder sounds for the guns," Robin recalled. "We just threw stuff in, with real sounds to be added later. When listening to music at the time, we'd say things like 'this would be great music for the game!' and put it in. We were trying to get this particular feel, where we wanted music to suit the game."

Although thoughts on final compositions were a million miles away, the team already had someone in mind to do them. Ken Kambayashi was a good friend of Dan, sharing a studio with him, and he was thought to be an ideal candidate. "Ken was one of the most talented musicians I'd ever met, probably the most," began Dan. "A radical musician, jazz and bass player, he was very interested in what I was doing, and I was very interested in his talent. He was becoming more involved and was the closest I had to getting a working partner." Unfortunately, Ken would never get the chance to start anything as events unfolded.

After a short while, other members of HotGen became curious about *BOC*, often popping upstairs to take a look at what was going on. Some staff were busy working on a racing car game that was struggling. This created some tension for *BOC*, with a controversial suggestion of trying to merge with the racing car project. "*Grand Theft Auto 3* had come out, and everything now had to have free roaming – that's what people wanted. HotGen wanted a *GTA* clone and suggested *BOC* could be the indoor part of a new game, with the outdoor bit being the racing car game. We basically went, 'No, this isn't happening!', our game was always going to be roaming from A, B to C!" exclaimed Robin. "*BOC* was very much a story-based game – strong on story, characters and atmosphere," added Dan. "We stuck to our guns, until the end."

Luckily, the suggestion went away, and development resumed. With the dockyard levels well underway, Dan decided to switch focus and push ahead to level 5, where you could meet every single character within the game, all within a large nightclub environment. The idea was that it would allow for the design and development of all the main characters and bosses, giving an outlet to test them early on.

"The main aim was to just explore and feel all this vibe in a big industrial nightclub on a Saturday night, with all the gangs out to show, hang and represent. If you tried to take out a level-12 boss, you'd get your head kicked in and shoved into the alleyway," explained Dan. "We talked about having 3D bubbles of sound, so you would go into one area and get a particular sound for that, and then you'd wander off to another area and get another sound. Nightclub sequences were never done well in games, and they always looked half empty, so we talked about big meshes of crowds and keeping it dark, so it felt like it was rammed. It was exciting, and I thought that this was going to be the greatest level in any game ever made!"

Now, after around three exciting months, you could play most of the dockyards level with Harry running about, picking up and using different guns. There were basic drone characters for now, who simply walked about and who could easily be shot, then recoil and die. AI still needed plenty of work, but it was enough to get a feel of some of the game's characters. The title presentation was kept basic, and it was too early for any cutscenes just yet. The demo was fully playable on PC, PS2 and Xbox and was a clear demonstration of the title and team's potential.

It wasn't long until that very potential was shown off, with SEGA visiting the 16th floor and witnessing months of hard graft. SEGA was seriously impressed. "We didn't expect it at all when SEGA said they wanted to sign it up! You could see that one of the guys was quite high up, and there were all these smiles from everyone," recalled Steve. "The mix between slapstick comedy and violence seemed like something no one had seen before. Graphically, the game was looking unusual as well as we were able to make the 3D models keep the hand-drawn look of Dan's character art," added Nick.

"The control method was pretty special once we'd got it going."

However, the euphoria was to be extremely short-lived, with a rapidly following hammer blow that HotGen was in financial trouble. Not long after, HotGen would declare bankruptcy. Although resurfacing later on with the same name, *BOC* was stuck in complete limbo at the time. The IP was tied up in all of the mess, and £125,000 was the fee set by the liquidators to get it back. Desperate for the project to continue, the Infinite Lives group touted the game to other publishers to try and save it. There was interest from the likes of Bethesda, Kuju, Empire and even Rockstar Games. "We came out of Rockstar, and they really wanted it!" Dan confirmed. But, with the hefty price overhanging from the liquidators, no one would touch it. Infinite Lives lost its investment and beautiful concept, leading to the disbandment of the team and the end of *BOC*.

At best, the game was only around 10–20% complete at the time. The game hadn't properly entered full production, so there was still at least 1–2 years more work required. Most of the dockyard area was complete, but work was still required on the engine and AI, as well as level content. Thankfully, it wasn't long until further work was found by everyone, including a venture into mobile development for Steve and Robin, with the creation of *Mayhem's Magic Dust*. *BOC* wouldn't be forgotten, with later developments of *GTA 4* and *Hotline Miami* reminding the team of what could have been.

Over 15 years on, events are still raw. The design document, asset samples and pre-production video have remained online (www.infinitelives.tv/team) ever since. "We put it up there when trying to sell the game, and it's just sitting there, and, amazingly, no one has ripped it off!" laughed Robin. "I'm surprised also that no one else has been, 'Wow, this is a pretty decent game idea, let's use it!'."

Sadly, much of Dan's artwork has long been lost in a hard drive crash, including original model sheets. Luckily, he still has a number of concepts and pieces that were kindly shared and can be found further on. For those wanting to actually play the game, the good news is that remains of the development are believed to still exist, though they couldn't be found at the time of publication. Demo disks produced for the PS2 and Xbox, where you could play through most of the dockyard stages are also still out there. The Infinite Lives team has very kindly allowed us to make these demos available if ever found. It may see a partial release before then, though, with a collector on www.assembler-games.com obtaining a very early Xbox prototype copy, showing a build with basic scenery, and a demonstration of the dockyard characters can be found on YouTube (www.bit.ly/burntoutcop). You can shoot and run around, but there is no AI at all.

It doesn't end there, though. In an unexpected twist, the IP was sold back to the group in 2016 for just £1. Steve was already thinking of a revival. "I'd love to do a 3D development, but a 2D game would be the starting point. No solid plans at the moment though, just me playing around," he said. "Ideally, there needs to be funding to organise a team. Gameplay-wise, I'm thinking *Double Dragon*, and a few others, like *Strider*, which has a nice style to it – quick, with slopes and curves and things. These days, you could get a game like *BOC* to easily run on a mobile, which is probably more powerful than a PS2, to be honest." As the creative juices began to flow once more, Dan then added, "I keep picturing a scene from *Old Boy* with the fight scene in the corridor. A scene like that in *BOC* would be quite funny! Harry in a tight alleyway with 30 people all in 2D."

Dan also revealed that Harry was actually already living on in a Raspberry Pi beat-em-up, used for educating a new generation of developers. "It's just a little cameo appearance for him. The whole thing is just a simple street-level beat-em-up," he confirmed. With Kickstarter funding now a thing for game developments, there could be an opportunity for *BOC* to happen someday. Although textures and models need redoing, most of the design still exists.

Regardless of everything that has happened, Everyone (except John) are all still in the games industry, still great friends and still passionate – especially when it comes to *BOC*. "The last good game I worked on was *Chaos Engine*, and then it was *BOC* – an accumulation of experience, right time, right place and right people. It really would have been a beauty!" concluded Dan. "We had so much fun, with many an afternoon spent down many local bars. We worked hard though and had many all-nighters in the office," added Nick. "It's funny that, after all this time, we've got the rights back, are talking about the game and still laughing about it," concludes Robin. "It was a progression from nothing, leaving our office for Croydon and then having this team around us. It wasn't that long, just six months of rapid growth before complete catastrophe. But it was just fun, and *BOC* needs to be that fun thing if done again."

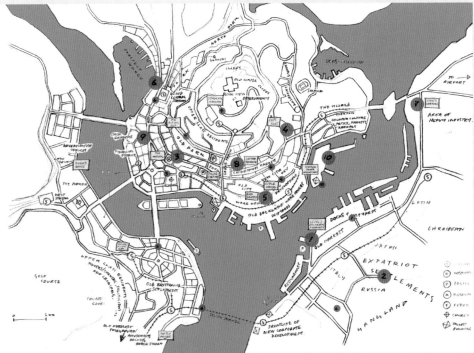

Top: Bar scene sketch, showing many key characters in one place, with Harry sitting in the bottom right corner. Bottom: Proposed map of the entire game by Dan, with key points highlighted.

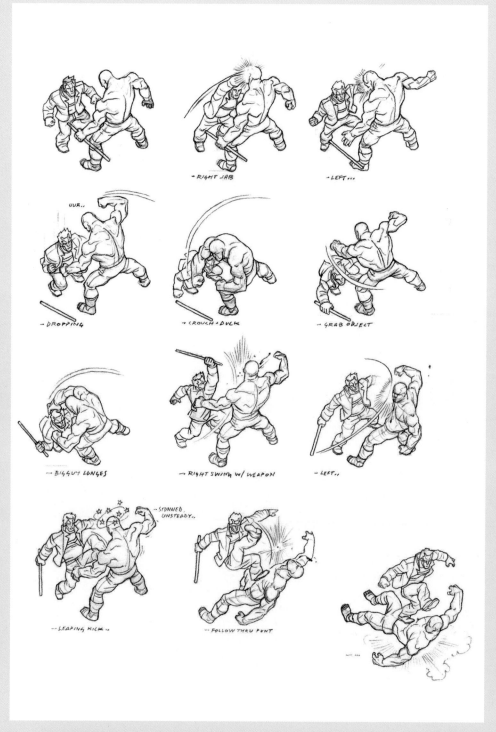

Above: Sketches by Dan, showing how Harry would have moved and interacted in a fight with enemies within the game.

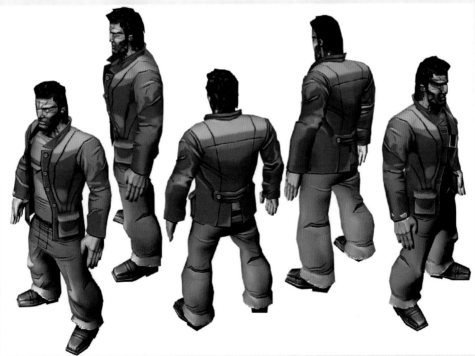

Top: Coloured drawings of Harry, created by Dan and ready to be rendered into 3D.
Bottom: Followed by the 3D-rendered outcome by Nick Lee.

Above: Two screens taken directly from the promotional video created by the team, showing part of the dockyard and a short cutscene from inside the fish packing factory.

Above: Two rendered mock-ups from the game design document (also shown in the promotional video) showing how stand-offs with enemies would have looked and felt.

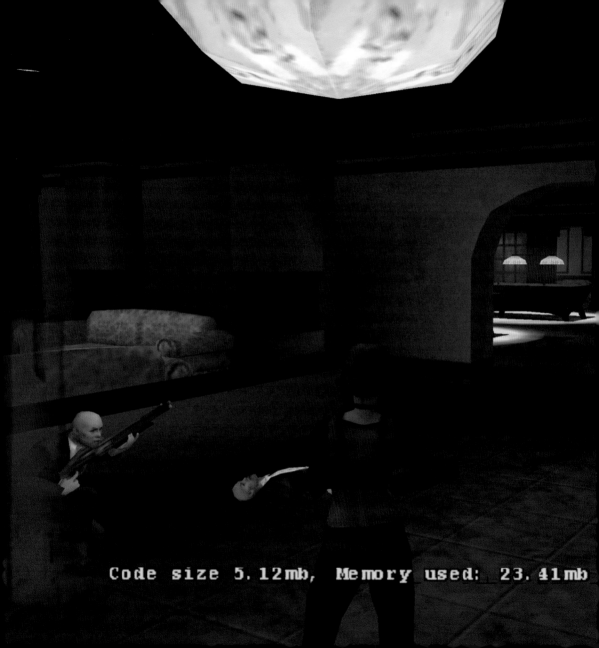

Code size 5.12mb, Memory used: 23.41mb

100 Bullets
Collapse
of Acclaim

Year: 2004
Developer: Acclaim
Studios Austin
Platforms: Microsoft Xbox
and Sony PlayStation 2
(pictured)

"If I remember correctly, the company involved in the design of the video game of *100 Bullets* asked me to develop two or three new characters that didn't exist in the ongoing series. They were going to interact with Cole. In fact, the only thing we got to see was a short introduction where the bullets came from everywhere, but that was it. Pity, as I had high expectations."

Eduardo Risso, comic artist

"I was excited about the *100 Bullets* project. We had a demo running, with you playing as Cole, along with two levels (casino and boxing gym) if I remember correctly. You could run through the levels in third-person view, kill enemies, use them as shields, wall cover, destroy gambling equipment, gym equipment, collect health, etc. We loosely based the fighting mechanics on the movie *Equilibrium* from 2002. We wanted the shooting to feel like you were doing kung fu-type moves. I loved the comic books and thought it would make for a great game. Too bad Acclaim filed for bankruptcy during the game's development."

Scott Brocker, graphic artist

Available to play

 Yes   No

Tork
Weak licence

Year: 2003
Developer: Realism Studios
Platform: Nintendo Game Boy Advance

Available to play

 Yes No

Experiencing the Nintendo Game Boy Advance (GBA) for the first time back in 2001 was mind-blowing. The unthinkable was possible, where you could play the equivalent of a Super Nintendo (with a bit more horsepower) in your hands.

The platform also gave many of us a respite from fully 3D games now flooding modern platforms, with a welcome return of 2D. There were attempts at doing 3D on the handheld – some were pretty abysmal, but others were beyond anything imaginable. *Super Monkey Ball Jr.* was one such title, converted by Andy Onions's Realism Studios. It was the fantastic outcome of that conversion which would land Andy's team a contract to do another conversion; this time of a new upcoming Xbox game called *Tork* (developed by Tiwak) on the GBA.

"How we got *Tork* is a bit convoluted," began Andy. "Software Creations went bankrupt in 2002, and several managers attempted to pick up various contracts for continuing development. *Super Monkey Ball Jr.* was one of them. I restarted Realism (a dormant company of mine at that time), and we finished *Super Monkey Ball Jr.* on time and budget, with a full-feature set and at high quality. It scored 9/10 in a Nintendo publication, which was unheard of for a non-Nintendo game at the time. We were duly offered a contract for conversion of *Tork* from THQ , and, obviously, we took it."

Tork tells the story of a 12-year-old prehistoric boy, whose town has been taken over by an evil wizard named Orgus, who has also kidnapped Tork's father and placed him in a different time period. With the help of a hermit called Yok, Tork must cross different time periods (each coming with their own distinctive visual style) to track down and defeat Orgus. You begin within a Prehistoric time zone, which is Tork's own time period.

It was hoped that the GBA game could be recognisable compared with the Xbox edition of the game, with obvious limitations. Assigned to make this happen as much as technically possible were developers Dave Reed, James Watson and Neil Millstone, with artwork handled by Michael Smith and Dave Worton. Music would be handled towards the end of the project, likely by an ex-Software Creations musician.

Andy would oversee and manage the project throughout. Development began in late 2002, with Andy and Dave Worton putting together a technical and game design document. These drew heavily from the Xbox design given to the team as a reference, with an entire storyline mapped out and ready to translate.

The game would begin with Tork carrying out an initial tutorial level to get you used to the controls, before arriving at Yok's hut to inform him of the events that have occurred. Going outside of the hut placed you within what was known as a 'Hub level', where you could wander around a small segment of the current world and select the level you'd like to play. From here, you would begin in your own current time zone, where you must complete a sequence of levels, involving escaping an erupting volcano, finding a mammoth tusk and a final boss battle before moving on to the next time zone.

Moving on to the Medieval time zone, you would need to infiltrate a castle, take part in a joust, hunt down a ferryman and scale Necromancer's Tower. Events would see your progression on to the 'Modern Times', set in the 1800s with a glimpse of an anticipated future. Here you'd navigate across a city-under-construction map to rescue a scientist, go underwater in a submarine, and chase and board a train to stop a fuel delivery to the 'Master of Machines' – ending with a battle against him.

The final phase concluded with you travelling to the Moon, flying Yok's hut through space. Upon arrival, you would need to infiltrate a lunar base, descend into a large moon crater, and explore a large abandoned temple to reach the 'Heart of the Citadel'. After defeating the age's boss, a battle ensues, with the pursuit of Orgus, and concludes with a final battle to try and free your village.

"From our perspective, there were always massive time constraints."

Realism had a job on its hands, having to complete the entire project within a very tight five months or so. "From our perspective, there were always massive time constraints," Andy explained. "We'd got a reasonable design outline of what we wanted to achieve, but there was just zero slack in the implementation schedule overall."

With a lack of dedicated 3D hardware built into the GBA, major compromises had to first be made with the translation. Yes, they had just done an impressive 3D engine for *Super Monkey Ball Jr.*, but that particular game design was far simpler in comparison. Although the easy option was to do a straightforward 2D platformer, Realism decided to go with a more complex isometric pseudo-3D approach. 2D platformers had been done to death, and the team felt that isometric games hadn't yet been fully explored on the platform, apart from *Spyro 2: Season of Flame* released a year or so earlier.

The added complexity was a good pay-off for not using real 3D, making it easier to translate models directly from the Xbox and add more detail into the worlds, as well as open up to extra gameplay elements. The vision was to create something that worked similar to *Sonic 3D Blast*, but with a lot more depth and greater detail in the artwork. Tork would move in 16 directions in total, most bad guys were restricted to eight, and other objects to four.

Using art assets from the Xbox edition, the artists were able to use parts as a template to create sets of isometric tiles, though the team could also improvise. "We were free to do whatever we wanted, as long as the look and feel matched the IP we were borrowing from. I can't remember whether we actually played the Xbox game, but we definitely saw videos of a beta version in action," recalled Neil. "We took Tork's trademark figure-8 melee attack and made something similar as Tork's primary attack for the levels, as well as making versions of the enemies and environments."

"Nobody cared very much about handheld versions of games."

Early on, a memory-friendly isometric engine was developed with high limits on characters that ensured detailed levels could be created, taking up to 50 screens in size and using approximately 30K overall. Sprite animations were mirrored where possible to give additional memory savings.

The engine would scroll at 60 FPS, with a very fast rate of 480 pixels per second, and could still include atmospheric special effects overlaid – such as mist, snow and rain. Although most levels had free movement, some parts of the game could force the scrolling, setting up various escape scenarios, such as avoiding a lava flow.

The game's levels would include a mixture of exploration, combat and fast-paced platform action in worlds featuring bridges, and collapsing and moving platforms. Wandering around the world, you could double-tap the jump button to do a double jump and reach higher platforms, with the other button deploying your primary melee attack. Ladders and ropes allowed you to climb, with some wall surfaces (such as foliage and rocks) being scalable too.

Certain objects could be pushed around and used to jump on to reach higher areas and platforms. Also dotted around the levels were statues that could be smashed to reveal extra lives, weapons, watermelons and energy pick-ups. Watermelon slices acted like coins in *Super Mario Bros.* or rings in *Sonic the Hedgehog*, where getting 100 slices will reward you with an extra life.

As you reached particular parts of a level, such as a tower entrance or a cave, the game would seamlessly change to a *Nebulus*-style section, where you would climb or descend a rotating display as you move left and right. Along the way, you would have to contend with enemies and collapsing platforms. The level style would feature in other stand-alone levels too.

"I worked on the rotating tower sections, doing gameplay code, collision and physics for those, with Dave [Worton] doing the rendering," confirmed Neil. "It supported switches which could turn moving platforms on and off, and you could enter the tower (which would transition to an isometric level) and come out somewhere else on the tower. In my fading memory, it was quite cool! I also did the front-end menus, using a cool Mode 7 effect to make a rotating slab of rock where the options were displayed!"

Accompanying the *Nebulus*-like mash-up was an impressive Mode 7 into the screen flight, underwater and space travel engine – the inspiration being *Space Harrier* mixed with a bit of *Star Fox*. Tork could race on the back of a baby T-Rex, fly a Pterodactyl or control the Minitilus (a flying/underwater vehicle found later in the game) in a variety of chasing and shooting-based levels.

"It was a great era to have worked in."

The Mode 7 and the *Nebulus* engine would both offer savings on memory, as well as break up the predominantly isometric-based levels. "Dave and Andy split the rendering code for the 3D sections between them. The floor was rendered using the hardware on the Game Boy Advance, whilst the walls were placed over the top, rendered on the CPU. This was very smart!" added Neil.

Dave Reed, James and Neil would separately develop the three-level engines between them. "Dave did a level design tool, as I remember, for the isometric parts of the game, as well as the core gameplay code for it," confirmed Neil. "I seem to remember me and James working on isometric gameplay code too and working on some bouncy physics for rope bridges!"

Progressing through the game, you additionally collected amulets, which would allow you to transform into three different characters. You obtained strength and power in the form of the Yeti, high speed and the armoured shell of the Armadillo as you rebound off your opponents, and, finally, flying abilities as the Flying Squirrel. Transforming into each allowed you to reach particular areas that might otherwise be too high or blocked off.

Enemies throughout the game depended on the type of level or world but could include dinosaurs, orcs, dragons, sharks, robots and more. There were also various cacti which you had to either avoid or destroy, sometimes revealing bonuses or access to hidden areas. Enemies would appear from set places or could spawn periodically to keep the action alive in the game.

The designing of the worlds and levels were split up equally, including the creation of small animated cutscenes to break up the game and let the story unfold as you progressed. "Both me and Dave [Worton] worked on different sections of the games," confirmed Michael. "What was strange was that we had all the assets in 3D, so I built my levels by rendering the 2D 'tiles' for the GBA using an isometric view in *3DS Max*, but Dave did all his from scratch."

Aiding with level construction was a level editor allowing the artists to add tiles onto an isometric grid, give different vertex elevations, and raise different levels to create walls, steps and cliffs. The monochrome-shaded result would then be extracted as an artist's template, with geometrical information kept to one side to be brought into the game engine for collisions and physics.

The surfaces were then painted over with characters to bring the world to life, with 3–4 extra layers available to give a perception of depth. "I remember writing a tool [with Dave Reed] which would consolidate unique 8×8 pixel tiles from a large *Photoshop* file which made up each level in the game, allowing us to fit it into the Game Boy Advance's tile-based hardware," explained Neil.

Andy recalls helping to optimise the tool after it was initially known as a 'lunchtime run' and took a few hours to complete. "I rewrote it with better algorithms, which optimised the comparisons and did things in a much more complex way but which would scale better. I implemented the optimised character mapper part of the tool based on an idea from Neil, which was about 50 lines of code," he confirmed. "We were taking bets on how long the improved character mapper tool would take. The lead programmer [Dave] reckoned I'd bring it down to about 15 minutes, but Neil and I were of the opinion that it would be seconds. He was gobsmacked that it could possibly be so fast."

One of the big technical challenges was also regarding memory and trying to squeeze everything onto an 8Mb cartridge. However, careful consideration and planning had been done very early on by setting limitations for character set and map sizes. The different level styles also offered a way to reduce the number of isometric maps required, so the challenge was very much with the artists to ensure that they could create something that looked superb within those particular restrictions overall.

After around three months of work and no development issues, the game was shaping up very well at around a 60%-completion state, and it was very playable. "Generally, it was going pretty well, but it was hard work," reflected Andy on the watertight schedule. "In terms of quality, we didn't really compromise. If you're up against a tight schedule, nowadays, you'd cut a feature list that you had ahead of time to create slack in the schedule. It was not really different back then. But, equally, you could cut quality to create slack. We just wouldn't go there and put in the hours to keep on top of the schedule."

"It was a let-down. We all wanted to finish the game, and there was this horrible feeling of emptiness when we found out."

Everyone seemed to be happy, including Tiwak, or so it seemed. "I imagine we must have shown what we were working on to the original game's team, but I don't remember them asking for any changes," recalled Neil. "Back then, nobody cared very much about handheld versions of games, so we were probably left to our own devices for the most part. Towards the end, we were really pulling it together, and it was looking good. I remember that I was still a little concerned that controls in the diagonal isometric sections would be a little difficult on a four-way D-pad, but it certainly looked the part, and there was plenty of variety."

By this point, the Xbox title was starting to slip, and the GBA edition was catching up. "They weren't exactly going fast, and our own tight scheduling meant we were overtaking them on development," confirmed Andy. "That seemed a bit daft, but, for us, it was a matter of getting on with it as best we could. I don't think it was going to have enough gameplay for a hardcore player (reckoned to be eight hours at the time)."

"They weren't exactly going fast, and our own tight scheduling meant we were overtaking them on development."

As with all titles covered in the book, tragedy was to strike when major overhauls took place at THQ. "The producer that I dealt with on *SMB* and *Tork* got his marching orders along with several of his staff one day," recalled Andy. "After the producer left, there was nothing for a week, then contact with his replacement, followed by canning of the GBA project a few days later. I am not party to their decision-making process, but it's conceivable that Tork was just not a strong enough licence for them. It didn't help that the original Xbox version that we were meant to be translating was also slipping due to not being driven with anything like the urgency that we were driving at."

Not long afterwards, Ed Fries would also leave Microsoft, which followed with the company deciding to drop Tiwak and the *Tork* development completely. Realism would never fully recover from the cancellation from THQ, with it feeling like the beginning of the end. The team was particularly unhappy with how things were unceremoniously dumped.

"It was a let-down. We all wanted to finish the game, and there was this horrible feeling of emptiness when we found out," began Neil. "I have no doubt that, if we had completed the game, then it would have been good. We were much more ambitious than most other teams working on the platform, who were mostly content to churn out endless 2D platformers. We all loved programming and were all very much into our games. I've been lucky enough not to have any other games cancelled in my career since then. I ended up moving back to London, where I grew up, and joined Sony Computer Entertainment. But that's another story!"

Realism marched on for a while, deciding to focus on next-generation 3D titles. "Development ceased immediately on *Tork*, and we began the technology development required for Xbox," confirmed Andy. "This, of course, was a very high-risk strategy." Work moved onto *Where Seagulls Dare* (an arcade flight simulator with birds), as well as a golf game on mobile platforms, but neither would see a release, with the first failing to find a publisher, and the other being cancelled by the publisher.

Surprisingly, Xbox *Tork* would eventually see a reprieve after Ubisoft purchased the rights from Microsoft and took over the Tiwak studio. The game saw a release in mid-2005 under the name of *Tork: Prehistoric Punk*. By this point, the GBA was practically dead, with the newly released Nintendo DS currently selling very well. Andy was never approached to continue the project, but, by this point, he was fed up of the industry anyway.

"Realism was essentially a work-for-hire software house. Without projects to work on that other people have the confidence to fund on an ongoing 'upfront' basis, any software house working on that business model cannot survive," explained Andy. "It was reckoned back then that 3% of games made a return on investment. So, you've got a 97% failure rate as a publisher. Obviously, they try to mitigate that risk with strong IP, but that is essentially a very expensive proposition. ROM production also had to be booked six months in advance, and you COULD NOT MISS the slot... It was all a big ask." Andy decided to move on to pastures new and wound up the company fully after things had been dormant for a while.

"We were free to do whatever we wanted, as long as the look and feel matched the IP we were borrowing from."

Although *Tork* never saw the light of day, the team has nothing but good memories of the project as a whole. "I remember Realism with real fondness. We were young, and there wasn't very much else in my life at the time but work and playing video games together!" reflected Neil. "I remember spending hours playing *Space Channel 5* and *Jet Set Radio* on Dave's Dreamcast. It was a great era to have worked in."

Although a prototype build does exist of the game, it has not been allowed for release due to legal issues with the licence being owned by Ubisoft. However, you can check out screenshots of the game running and its various stages, and, by the time of publication, there will be videos of the game running on the Games That Weren't website. A sad end to what could have been a fun title, but, at the very least, the Xbox version is out there to check out and enjoy.

Above: Various screens from the final *Tork* (Game Boy Advance) prototype, showing Yok's home area (top) and the *Nebulus*-style Necromancer's tower (bottom).

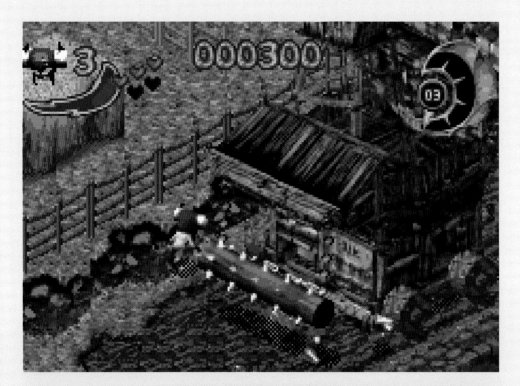

Above: More screens from the final *Tork* (Game Boy Advance) prototype, showing The Infernal Machine (top) and The Exodus (bottom) in all its 3D glory.

The Phantom Ran out of cash

Year: 2005
Developer: Infinium Labs

Believed by many to be vapourware, the Phantom console came as a shock when it was announced by the relatively unknown Infinium Labs in 2003. The console was intended to play high-end PC games through a standard TV set, with games downloaded through an Internet subscription rather than purchased on physical media; a risk, considering many still had slow connection speeds at the time.

A vast sum of money was pumped into the promotion and development of the console, with many release deadlines coming and going. Infinium Labs didn't have enough money to bring the system to market, and so the project was quietly cancelled. Bizarrely though, 2008 saw the release of a wireless PC keyboard/ mouse called the Lapboard, which had originally been intended as a Phantom peripheral.

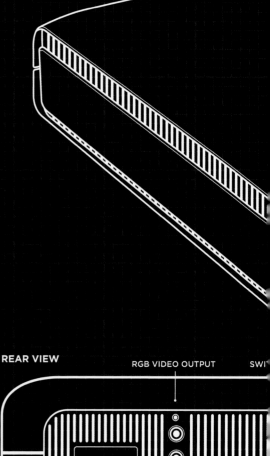

GAME CONSOLE

REAR VIEW

RGB VIDEO OUTPUT

SWI

POWER INPUT

DIGITAL AUDIO SIGNAL

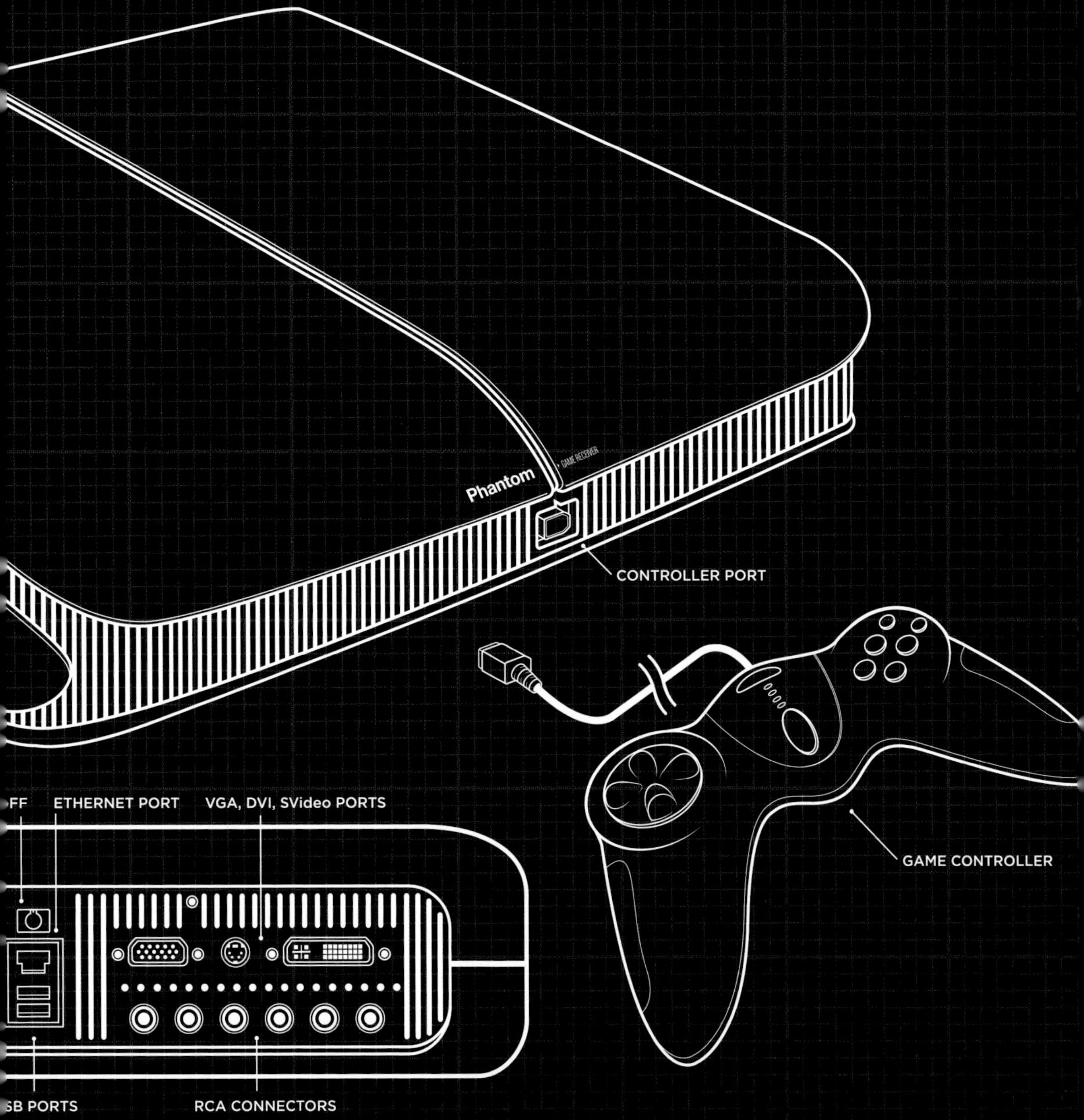

Phantom

GAME RECEIVER

CONTROLLER PORT

ETHERNET PORT

VGA, DVI, SVideo PORTS

FF

GAME CONTROLLER

SB PORTS

RCA CONNECTORS

Carmageddon TV
Development issues

Year: 2005
Developer: Visual Science
Platforms: Microsoft Xbox, PC and Sony PlayStation 2

Available to play

 Yes No

Our next investigation clears up what were, in fact, two completely separate _Carmageddon_ developments. Often, both are confused as being the same project by the same developer, mainly due to the slight overlap of their timelines. This misconception is corrected as we delve into what caused the popular series to go completely off the rails.

Carmageddon first crashed onto PC screens back in 1997, developed by Stainless Software (now Stainless Games) and inspired by the film _Death Race 2000_. You competed and raced against competitors across industrial and city-themed areas within a time limit, getting more time by damaging other cars or running over pedestrians. Alternatively, you could destroy all of the other cars to win a race outright. The pedestrian-killing element caused great controversy, and the game was censored (even banned) in some countries, with green-blooded zombies replacing red-blooded humans. However, it resulted in press coverage that pushed sales, immortalised the title and rapidly led to a sequel.

"We finished _Carmageddon II_ in Oct 1998, started immediately after _Carmageddon_ and _Splat-pack_, in a crazy 15-month period. This included a four-month burn at the end where we literally went home after dawn _every single night_," recalled Stainless Games' Patrick Buckland. "SCi then said to us, without us drawing breath, 'Right, off we go then – _Carmageddon 3_'. We said, 'Whoa there, hang on, give us a breather first!' We thought nothing more of it until we saw the announcement in _CTW_ (trade rag of the time) that a new _Carmageddon_ was being developed by an Australian company called Torus."

With relations soured between the publisher and development studio, the third game eventually surfaced in 2000, called _Carmageddon: TDR 2000_, which gained poor reviews. "It was a dog's testicle of a game," commented Patrick. "They also illegally used our code as an ex-programmer from Torus later told us. The fact that only we could make head or tail of our physics engine was partly what made the game so bad. _TDR2000_ basically killed the brand until they had the appetite to try and revive it."

It was a number of years before SCi decided to do just that, though Stainless Software was overlooked once again for the fourth game. Visual Science, fresh from completing _F1 Career Challenge_ for EA, competed against two other unknown development teams for the contract. Helping secure the project was creative director, Ken Fee, who put together an ingeniously gruesome pitch.

"It involved sending a container to SCi packed with dismembered limbs and a fake bloodstained letter," he explained. "The letter was addressed to the mother of a deceased contestant, who had lasted a record 40 seconds or so in the ring, but, as per the contract, she now had to take his place. While gore content was higher, such personalised pitches were nothing new. We had done a similar thing for _Medal of Honour_."

The pitch went down a storm, securing work on a new game targeting the Sony PlayStation 2 (lead platform), Microsoft Xbox and PC in 2003. Christened *Carmageddon TV* (*CTV* from now on), the game was to be set within a futuristic game show with a large flying stadium that travels the world at the whim of the corporations controlling it, landing in slums and ghettos in deprived city areas. Each level would take place within the ghettos under the stadium, racing against opponents, before ending up in the stadium for a final showdown. As with the original games, you could destroy opponents, and there were points for the most outrageous of stunts, styles of kills and amount of people/animals killed.

"Drivers could drive through the ghettos to cause mayhem and carnage before entering the stadium."

Inspiration was taken from both the film *The Running Man* and the game *Smash TV*, with Ken also suggesting that the later 2008 film *Death Race* had the actual visual feel of what they were looking to achieve at the time. Early on, the game also took inspiration from Mega-City One from 2000AD's *Judge Dredd*. The game would be gorier than previous outings, with improved hardware capabilities, meaning more severed limbs and colourful deaths.

To kick things off, a playable prototype was to be produced to showcase the direction and give SCi confidence, moving on from the *TDR2000* disaster and back towards the buzz of the original games. Leading the development was Grant Clarke, who, along with Pat McGovern leading the design, would spend 2–3 months putting a prototype together with a small team. Pat felt that the project didn't get off to the best of starts.

"My main gripe was that there was initially no design," Pat began. "There were four artists and myself working on the demo, two of which were juniors with no experience, and one an animator/rigger. There was lots of pressure (naturally) put on us as this project was very important to the future of the company, yet we got little support, and the demo wasn't going well. SCi's producers had suggested they wanted something different but were vague about it. When doing the demo, producers would say things like 'make it look like Mega-City (2000AD)' followed by 'don't make it look sci-fi'! I stepped down after the last poor milestone, and management realised they had to do something."

Ken Fee would step in to take over as the project manager to rescue and give the project some well-needed guidance, with Pat dropping back to a general artist role on the project. After a slight delay and a few more months granted by SCi, the prototype was rescued and impressively so. "It was eventually a fully playable version of a whole level," recalled Ken. "Drivers could drive through the ghettos to cause mayhem and carnage before entering the stadium. It had scripted sequence jumps and a full track layout. Grant is proud to this day that, at the time, SCi said it was the best demo they'd ever seen."

Now, after some finally promising progress, everything was about to fall apart once more. It was a time of change, with a new management structure coming into Visual Science that would slowly destroy both *CTV* and the studio over the next few years. "As the structure came in, I became more and more removed from the design," recalled Ken. "I'd clash with most decisions made, which included things like only management being able to talk to the client – an absolute nonsense. None of the original prototype staff were in charge of things any longer. It was like *Animal House*, without the keen sense of sobriety."

With new management came a change in direction: firstly, a modification of the originally pitched concept, with the large flying stadium theme dropped. Then, the game was switched to the United States, 20 years into the future. The story introduced an enterprising cable show host named Chester, who has started to pirate broadcast the gang's destruction on a show named *Carmageddon TV*, where you race others in suitably crowded public locations, set up by a crew overnight, with extra explosives and modifications to put on a show.

You would control John Damage (son of the series' legendary Max Damage), racing against his own team, who burst into public events to "whip the tar out of each other" and their surroundings, before taking off on to the next location. Each location was to consist of a number of events, such as killing a certain amount of pedestrians within a time limit. Overall, you're aiming to come away with the coveted 'Golden Chum Bucket' trophy to become a legend within your gang and your new viewing audience.

At this point, the project team began to grow, later expanding to close to 40 people, too many to speak to or mention in full. One of the first jobs was to expand on the original prototype and build it up into a fully fledged game engine: tightening up the AI, finalising game structure, audio specifications, vehicle customisation and characters. Opposition characters would be in a state of flux throughout the development, with early characters of 'Nutter', 'Babygro', 'Wrestler' and 'Racer' being dropped. Eventually, they became a mixture of male and female characters – competitive and masochistic in nature.

Level themes also switched from dark slum environments to more populated and public areas, with suggestions of a 'safari park', 'university', 'shopping mall' (inspired by *The Blues Brothers'* car chase scene), 'sports stadium', 'hospital', 'farmyard', 'film festival', 'cathedral', 'building site' and 'fairground' environments. Each environment would be fairly destructible, with smashable glass panes, shatter effects when colliding with walls or other large components, and certain props/small buildings that would fall apart when hit. The safari park theme was chosen as the initial focus to showcase developed events and represent all key gameplay elements. Early test levels were also generated to test the vehicle and character builds throughout development.

Compared with the previous games, a larger range of creatures and pedestrian styles were planned. There were to be generic pedestrians, but also ones themed on their environment, such as people dressed as cartoon characters at the funfair. Animations for all of them were carefully crafted and looked suitably impressive. "The animations were very nice, especially the zoo-level animals (done by Alan Redmond), and the gory splicing of pedestrians was cool for the time," recalled Pat McGovern. The pedestrians were, in fact, an integral part of the game, involved in a number of events and achievements, some particularly cruel.

"I remember that we were to put 100 pedestrians on each level, and you'd get a massive bonus if you killed them all," recalled level designer Jim Thompson. "I thought if I spawned one right on top of a building and gave him a patrol path that walks him off the building in the first few seconds of the level, it'd be like he's had enough of it all and committed suicide. Because he killed himself, he wouldn't count towards the goal of killing all 100, so the player had to race up to the rooftops and take him out before he walks off the roof. It created a secret and a difficult achievement at the same time."

For vehicles, well-known cars were taken and shifted 20 years into the future, modified into mobile killing machines. With inspiration from steampunk, comic books such as *Captain America*, and various post-apocalyptic-themed material, vehicles would include the likes of a 'Bandit', 'JCB-like heavy digger vehicles', 'large vans', 'Roadsters', 'Mustangs', 'trucks' and 'Humvees'. You'd start with just a Mustang, though a total of 14 additional cars would be unlockable over time. Cars were segmented so that the bonnet, rear and front bumpers, left and right wings, wheels and doors could come away with damage. Although, as with the original games, you could use credits/points to automatically repair on the go.

"Vehicles were all built from concept art," recalled lead vehicle artist Iain Anderson. "I built the early ones and worked closely with programmers to develop methods for export and damage allowance for customisation. They were created as polygon models in *Maya*, then split up into parts. Info was then added to the scenes alongside naming conventions to allow the models to be exported into the game engine and work as intended. Sculpted damage models were created, and things like swinging doors set up. The cars also came with named locators in a hierarchy to allow swapping of wheels and weapons, etc."

"My main gripe was that there was initially no design."

Vehicle customisations were actually to be a key feature, where you could attach spikes, lawnmower blades, scoops and saws to impale, dice or smash. Each vehicle came with mount points at the rear, top, side and front, inspired perhaps by Activision's 1984 release of *Ghostbusters*. Armour could also be applied, with the weight affecting car handling as well as the damage you could take. Titanium armour, for instance, was costly but very light and strong.

Temporary weapon pick-ups made a return, including 'guns', 'mine depositors' and 'flamethrowers' – some potentially controllable via a separate turret control. There were general power-ups planned including 'The Eviscerator' – where everything within a 10-foot radius of your car would explode – and 'The Nude Bomb', a fun but ultimately useless power-up which would make all pedestrians temporarily naked.

A potentially controversial idea that may well have caused a furore with fans of the series was to also have an out-of-the-car third-person scenario. The intention was for you to be able to get out of your car and hunt down hiding pedestrians on some levels, but also steal opponents' cars if yours was badly damaged. There was no doubt that *Grand Theft Auto 3* was clearly on everyone's minds, but it risked diluting the core of what *Carmageddon* was all about and trying to create something that was ultimately heading towards a *Grand Theft Auto* clone.

Controls are critical for the success of any game, and this was especially important to nail down very early on with *CTV*. Vehicle handling had to be easy and fun, but with the weighty, inertia-laden feel that you get with a proper vehicle physics simulation. One of the main physics programmers, David Guthrie, would act as the gel between designers and programmers, making use of the Havok engine to help achieve the goal.

"Probably most of my time was spent on vehicle behaviour, physics, handling, etc., and I worked with vehicle and character artists, designers and level designers," began David. "On their own, realistically simulated vehicle physics do not often equate to a fun experience, especially in a third-person arcade-style driving scenario, and the vehicles had to be able to do all sorts of stunts and cross different kinds of terrain/obstacles. So, on top of a realistic base handling model, I layered all sorts of subtle driving aids the player was never aware of to make things like drifting, doughnuts, jumps, driving on two wheels, etc. doable but, most importantly, fun and rewarding. My aim was to make you feel like a bad-ass wheelsmith without realising you were being helped."

The weighting of characters and animals were also to be as realistic as possible too, so hitting a rhino in the safari park would likely kill it but also do massive damage to yourself in the process. David recalls once struggling to reverse a car after being pinned down by a five-tonne elephant carcass, but it was the physics for the pedestrians that brought the game to life. "With hundreds of pedestrians running around the levels, it was immensely satisfying mowing through big crowds of them. It would be frowned upon now," confessed David. "I remember writing code that would cause the character ragdolls to be thrown, cartwheeling dramatically up in the air when you ploughed into crowds, instead of them just bunching up in front of the car if they were left to physics alone, all to make it look and feel more spectacular."

Audio was also vital to add humour and atmosphere to the game, with Mark Knight joining as the audio director whilst the project was already underway. We didn't hear back from Mark, but working with him among others was Andrew Parton. "I have very scant memory of the development itself," Andrew began. "CTV was in development when I started as a contract audio programmer. I did some work on the audio engine, placed some sounds around the levels, but very little else before the end."

There was to be your usual comic effects, death screams and squelches, as with the original games, along with full heavy metal soundtracks to accompany each level. Most interesting of all were plans for the audio to include a commentary system, giving feedback about events in the race and show dialogue between the characters, with voice actors to be brought in specially for each of them.

Finally, and often not appreciated, was the work going into the front-end and heads-up display, designed by lead front-end (UX/UI) designer Mark Traynor. "I worked closely with the lead game designers, detailing the flow, functionality and content of the menu screens within the game," he explained. "This was whilst working closely with the rest of the art team on the style and theme of the project to keep continuity throughout – from the GUI through to gameplay and HUDs." Mark ensured that the HUD was unobtrusive but informative enough of targets, map locations or current pick-ups.

Over the course of the development and several milestones, there were rather unhealthy amounts of change requests, sometimes with entire levels being thrown away. There seemed to be a lack of direction being taken by SCi and Visual Science. "I remember there were many requests for art changes," recalled Iain. "Not little but large changes in direction. So I guess that came from up-high not knowing what it should really be, feel or look like throughout."

This resulted in clashes between SCi and the new management, with some bewilderment at ideas that felt disconnected from the core *Carmageddon* concept. "One individual would humiliate people publicly and shout at staff when SCi didn't like the work presented," recalled Ken. "The team were busting a gut following the new direction (despite their own doubts) only to be constantly belittled. I tried to protect them as much as I could – they were my team, and I'd worked with them for years, but I was out of the client loop. Only upper management could speak with them."

The team members slowly lost faith in what they were doing, with internal fractures appearing, poor leadership, confusing development goals, and no decent communications with SCi any longer. After months of late nights and weekends, the team often didn't have a lot to show for their efforts, with long lists of changes required at the end of each 6–8-week milestone.

"The cohesive theme or style was missing for most of development. We had hired varying amounts of freelance artists on varying short contracts, which didn't help," explained Pat. "By the end of development, I think we were working on five levels with two artists each. I worked on around five different levels, most of which got trashed, including a canyon/desert-themed open area with some buildings, oil derricks and rock stacks dotted throughout. We'd do a level, SCi would go 'meh', we'd scrap it, change design lead, and start again."

"I remember that we were to put 100 pedestrians on each level, and you'd get a massive bonus if you killed them all."

"To me, it felt like management didn't know what *Carmageddon* was and were grasping at straws for a template to copy instead of doing a proper *Carmageddon* game. Every iteration was horrific from a gameplay point of view. The level of support to try and ameliorate the game in any way was also non-existent," reflected Jim. "I loved the original *Carmageddon* so tried to get much from the original into our game, but, due to how Visual Science wanted to make it, this was largely impossible. One iteration (the main one I remember) – it felt more like a skateboarding game but in a car. So, you'd have a level with jumps, ramps and halfpipes supposedly disguised into the theme of the level, and that was the gameplay, alongside murdering the pedestrians as you drove along."

Frustrated and fed up at one particularly depressing milestone review, Ken sat down with management and the team, going over work to be submitted for the next one. "One individual personally approved every bit of art, animation and design, said they loved it and that it was awesome, with slaps on the back all round," he recalled. "They then came back screaming at everyone two days later, saying it was all awful and not at all what SCi had wanted. It was ridiculous, and this went on for all but the prototype stage that was, in the end, the famous 'good' bit of the project. We were the ones skilled in client management and interpretation, not them, and that was really the beginning of the end."

Regardless of the ongoing issues, attempts were made to get things back on track, starting with locking down and creating a more focused design. Eventually, the game was boiled down to a total of 40 events, with five different event styles across eight different themed environments within the United States. The first five events could be played in any order of your choice, though opening up further areas would require at least three events to be completed within the first area. Characters were also trimmed down to around ten in total. The 'out-of-the-car' scenarios were seemingly kept (no one recalled them being dropped) but were possibly simplified to avoid detracting from the original too much.

Finalised areas now consisted of 'Mall Maul' in the world's largest shopping mall, smashing through shops, and ploughing into merchandise and shoppers. 'Amused to Death' was set in a Disneyland-like amusement park, ploughing into visitors and people dressed as characters. 'Open Season on Golfers' was set in a country club golf course, with opportunities to score a hole in one with golfers off the bonnet of your car. 'Safari Park' saw you within a wild animal park, rampaging into the various wildlife and visitors. 'Dead Dead Nude Nudes' has you smashing into a nudist colony in an Oregon forest.

'Run for their Lives' saw you enter the New York Marathon in slightly unfair conditions. 'One Wedding and a Hell of a lot of Funerals' was a wedding gatecrash at a large cathedral, with extra points for killing the bride and groom with a single strike. All concluded by 'Carmageddon TV: The Movie' – the final showdown within a fake *Carmageddon* set, smashing through celebrities and fleeing actors.

The five events spread across those areas consisted of 'Slaughter Circuit' in a race over three laps against three opponents, with no preset route but an optimum one existing. 'Dead Air' was a race to find a total of eight pick-ups scattered across the map in just three minutes, with some placed in precarious locations. 'Rubble Ain't No Trouble' had you trying to destroy eight static or moving targets across a level, such as people or a particular building, all whilst competing against three other opponents. 'Radical Rumble' was a three-minute deathmatch event, with you aiming to be the first to get ten opponent kills. Then, finally, 'Feeding Frenzy' had you trying to kill the most pedestrians within three minutes.

Completing events would award you with a 'Bronze', 'Silver' or 'Gold' rating, adding replay value to those wanting to achieve perfect scores and gain the ultimate 'Absolute Assassin' rating. Points could be scored in different ways, such as killing people/animals, but also by performing various stunts. New game modes would be unlockable, including new championship modes when achieving top ratings across a series of events. One particular mode was to be 'Carmageddon Classic' after getting Gold status across the entire game – a free-for-all race with the original series rules set.

Vehicle plans remained intact, though, due to the project falling behind, design studio Gameworld 7 was contracted in to help out. Assigned briefly to the task was Paul Walker. "It was just vehicles to start with, and landscapes to maybe follow later," he recalled. "The nature of the work was receiving a few sketches and making a full version with levels of detail, textures, etc. I didn't do the work for very long, maybe a six-week period. There was lots of promise at the start, then it all flatlined, so I assume I was brought in as a way of showing to the powers that be that things were still moving."

Multiplayer plans were additionally finalised, with up to seven competitors playing events from the main story and online-only modes. Those modes would include 'Slaughter Circuit', racing against other players, either to complete a certain amount of laps or become the last person standing. 'Righteous Rumble' was a free-for-all 'destroy all opponents within an arena' affair. 'Corpse 'n' Carry' would see you trying to carry a corpse on your car for the longest without it being stolen by another driver. 'Ped Hunt' would see pedestrians released one at a time, with players racing to their location to kill them first and be the one with the most kills. Finally, there was the imaginative 'Capture the Corpse' take on 'capture the flag', with teams of 2–4 trying to bring a corpse back to base, demonstrating an odd *Unreal Tournament* inspiration that perhaps had crept in.

Rounding everything off would be an online stats/hall of fame to increase the competition stakes, as well as integration of the EyeToy for the PS2 edition to allow you to add your own profile picture (Xbox users instead picking from predefined profile images). Unfortunately, there would be no local split-screen mode on any platform due to a lack of time.

Apart from ongoing internal management and direction issues, there were also the usual development problems, such as memory leaks, getting a decent draw distance, and ensuring that the physics were realistic enough – especially the ragdoll element of pedestrians and creatures within the game. They were all fixable problems, and things were generally now progressing better, with builds that could be generated for all systems.

Finally, after approximately two years of development, everything was getting back on track. Around 4–6 levels were now close to completion, with several cars available, and damage management implemented. Networking was working at least on PS2, showing basic link-up play between two players in the same environment. Although hardly any of the planned multiplayer elements were yet developed, a deathmatch mode was well underway by this point. There was still plenty of work to go into the structure of the gameplay, beyond driving around, crashing into other cars and mowing down people/animals, but, compared with before, it was in far better shape and was finally closing in towards an alpha status.

"With hundreds of pedestrians running around the levels, it was immensely satisfying mowing through big crowds of them."

However, the project was still heavily behind schedule, and there was now mistrust between the studio and publisher. Visual Science had started placing the blame on the producer from SCi for making unrealistic demands. "To be fair, we all felt that too," explained Ken. "But, in all likelihood, this was because we were completely outside of the loop with the client, so we only heard our own management's side. In the end, SCi were so furious that even we (now mere developers) heard about the arguments, and it was the case that their producer had been defending us to them for months, with no gratitude from our own senior staff."

Oddly, whilst Visual Science fell foul of SCi, Stainless Software was repairing relations with them. "I'm a 'life's too short' sort of person, so we arranged a conversion of *Carmageddon 1*," explained Patrick. "It came about after seeing Nintendo release a remastered version of *Zelda* on new hardware. So I thought, 'Why don't we do the same thing with *Carmageddon*', and contacted SCi about it. They liked the idea, and it morphed into a multi-game deal they'd arranged with Gizmondo. We were doing it as a sort of relationship-repairing exercise, with the plan that it would restart things and lead to a new *Carmageddon*."

The full story of the Gizmondo development is available on the Games That Weren't website. However, it is important to mention here as the Gizmondo development is often attributed to being a conversion of *Carmageddon TV*, which was never the case: the two were very separate developments overall.

"However, the project was still heavily behind schedule, and there was now mistrust between the studio and publisher."

Although relations improved between Stainless and SCi, they were coming to an end with Visual Science. The exact reasons couldn't be disclosed, but SCi decided enough was enough. There had been rumours of SCi wanting to cancel the game for some time, but this couldn't be confirmed. Postponement of the project was announced in 2005, ultimately resulting in its cancellation. The decision hit Visual Science hard, contributing towards the company going under in 2006.

"The madness of the previous year and a half had been forcibly addressed to a degree, but the game was now a pale and pitiful shadow of what it should have been," reflected Ken. "It was certainly not the feeling of anyone sensible that the game had been cruelly cut short in its prime. I have no memory of disappointment when it was cancelled – just annoyance at the wasted opportunity and effort."

"It's a long time ago now, but there was just huge pressure from the publisher," added Iain. "There was a very large amount of good-quality concept art in different styles that should have been locked down earlier in the project. From an art point of view, it was really like making several completely different games. Reflecting on it now, I don't think the game had the hook that SCi were looking for. I am not sure they even knew what they were looking for, either."

Lead developer Grant Clarke felt it was a project that had so much enthusiasm at the start, but, as the design got pulled in so many directions, it became hard to ever see how it would get finished. Maybe with a solid direction established early on, things could have been very different.

Years following the development, there has yet to be a leak of the game for people to play. No one we spoke to had anything in a playable state or that they were comfortable to see released. We were kindly provided with a few art assets and screens which you can see here, with more to be added on the Games That Weren't website. Pat McGovern also released a YouTube video in 2015 showing an early demo of the amusement park level and various assets.

In 2011, Stainless Games eventually gained the rights to the entire *Carmageddon* franchise – ironically including *CTV*, even though they never received any assets as part of the deal. So, after hiccups with the likes of *TDR2000* and *CTV*, the series is now very much home, with more developments planned in the future and with many of the original team members thankfully involved.

Above: A character that was proposed for the game, carrying weapons and add-ons to be used in the planned third-person out-of-vehicle segments.

Above: Early design concepts for the game, showing amusement park and hospital environments.

Above: Further early design concepts, showing farm and football stadium environments.

Above: A selection of vehicle renders from various stages during the game's development. Many vehicles were scrapped over the duration of the project.

Above: Various mock-ups created by Mark Traynor to demonstrate how the gameplay HUD and vehicle upgrading interface could have looked.

Above: Early snapshot renders of the funfair level and some of the rides that you could drive onto/into.

Above: Various screenshots taken from a recorded demo/promo of the funfair level that was dug out by Pat McGovern in 2015.

Tetris DS
Legal
dispute

Year: 2005
Developer: THQ
Platform: Nintendo DS

Yes, *Tetris* was indeed released on the DS, but not this version by THQ, which got held back due to a legal dispute with The Tetris Company. Preceding Nintendo's eventual release by a year, this was a promising version of *Tetris* and one that, luckily, you can experience for yourself – if you know where to look that is.

Available to play

◉ **Yes** ◯ **No**

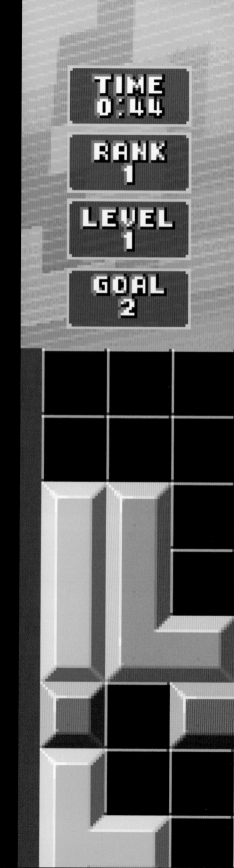

CCTV
No publisher

Year: 2007–2015
Developers: Jon Hare and Nikitova Games
Platforms: Apple iOS, Nintendo DS,
Nintendo Wii and PC

Available to play
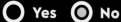 Yes No

"Big Brother is Watching You" George Orwell taunted in his famous novel *1984*, which would end up being a rather scarily accurate prediction of how things would become in the modern world. Jon Hare would take the concept of being watched and devise a novel and fun twist around the subject.

Following on from his Sensible Software days, designing and putting down pixels for the likes of *Wizball*, *Mega-Lo-Mania* and *Sensible Soccer* among many others, Jon began to project-manage development teams and come up with concepts for them to implement. His new Orwell-themed idea would emerge from a moment of inspiration whilst spending time with his daughter back in 2006.

"It all sparked from playing on the Nintendo DS and looking at some *Where's Wally* books with my youngest daughter," began Jon. "It was the first time I had really played touchscreen games, and I suddenly connected with the idea of picking out Wally from a moving crowd rather than a still one. That was the seed of the idea. The actual idea of making the guy you were picking out to be a criminal would come a few days later."

When thinking up a name, it didn't take long until the simple (and obvious) *CCTV* was picked, marking the arrival of a new development. Jon had just began working with Nikitova Games in Kyiv, Ukraine. It was from here that he began putting together a detailed initial design for what would be his first original title with the studio. Personally, it was the fourth unique concept in a row that Jon had designed, with the previous three never seeing completion, in the form of *Sex 'n' Drugs 'n' Rock 'n' Roll*, *Cannon Fodder 3D* and *Virtual TV*.

"All of those games were pretty unique for their time, but, unfortunately, unique wasn't 'en vogue' anymore. They all died after years of struggling to stay alive," Jon explained. However, the Nintendo DS, Nintendo Wii and Apple iOS platforms were ripe for ideas that were not considered 'mainstream', and *CCTV* was felt to be a perfect match.

With Jon's Commodore 64 background, you'd think that Activision's CCTV featuring *Hacker 2* may have been a source of inspiration, though this wasn't the case at all. "I have always been someone who has paid scant regard to what everyone else is doing and just do my own thing. In the days of Sensible, with *Wizball*, *Mega-Lo-Mania*, *Cannon Fodder* and *SWOS*, this method worked very well and was seen as being wonderful and unique." Instead, inspiration lay just with the likes of *Where's Wally*, *Mystery Case Files* and *Cluedo*, with no direct inspiration from any other particular games.

The aim was to create a criminal-catching game unlike any other, which could instantly be picked up and played by all age groups. With the title orientated towards families, crimes would not include anything too gruesome. There would be thefts, graffiti and minor assaults making up the types of crimes throughout.

The initial game design described you taking control of a security officer who is part of a city police force within a large city. Using CCTV, you would have to track down and arrest any petty criminals spotted committing a crime. Ultimately, the aim was to capture 100 of the most wanted criminals across a variety of scenarios.

Originally, the game was to be set across 20 cities in total, including New York, London, Paris, Moscow and many more. This would help contribute to a total of 100 levels in all (with a trimmed-down 50 on the Wii/DS), accessed across individual city maps with highlighted locations of where you can visit and play next at different times of the day (for outdoor scenarios at least). Early on, this was cut right back to focus the design around just one large city.

"I have always been someone who has paid scant regard to what everyone else is doing and just do my own thing."

Levels would be gradually unlocked as you progressed and gained promotion from capturing enough criminals. Starting as a shop security guard, you would only be able to monitor shopping malls, until gaining promotion to access scenarios such as car parks, subway stations, airports, art galleries, parks, colleges and stadiums. Each would feature different numbers of cameras (making different surveillance areas and viewpoints available), activity levels and allocations of criminals, with crimes relating to the scenario, such as art heists within a gallery.

The key route to promotion and accessing new scenarios would be by capturing those from the most wanted list. This was no easy feat and required building up their dossiers (viewed via the police department building), detailing appearances, activities, habits and, crucially, a photofit to help identify them. Details could be gathered from a variety of sources, including mini interrogation games of captured criminals, obtained evidence/items, or from deciphering of clues.

Once enough evidence was gathered, the idea would be to go to a particular scenario or level to try and capture them. This would offer a certain replay value to levels, where you might go back and play again to capture a big villain, as well as just trying to beat an old score. Ultimately, capturing the number-one most wanted will mean the completion of the entire game. However, the further up the 'wanted' tree, the sparser the dossier information becomes, and you would first need to do sufficient groundwork from the bottom up.

Within each level, there would be 4-9 separate camera feeds (to appear on the top screen of the DS version), which could be changed to different cameras dotted around the area. It is here that you must look for signs of suspicious activity and catch criminals in the act. In many ways, it was feeling more and more similar to *Night Trap* than *Hacker 2*, though perhaps that's stretching it.

Depending on the scenario, you have different types of objects to zoom in on and focus your attention. For the subway, this would be people travelling on the escalators or bags passing an X-ray screening process in the airports.

When spotting something awry, you must pause, rewind and freeze-frame a particular feed from one of the cameras and decide if you have caught a perpetrator red-handed. If you feel you have, then you must switch your attention to scanning over the area's exit (shown on a larger screen) and pick out that criminal from the mass exiting crowds in a *Where's Wally*-like hunt.

To help identification, clicking/touching the screen would provide a magnifying glass to zoom in on characters to help identify against the freeze-frame created. Picking the wrong person loses valuable time and potentially means letting the real criminal get away. If you also miss too many petty criminals, then the level would prematurely end in failure.

As well as just playing levels, you would be required to upgrade and repair camera equipment, using money received from role promotions. This would enable you to install improved night vision and X-ray cameras at strategic locations to help capture more villains. A cooperative mode was also suggested for the game, where you could play the same single-player campaign as a team. In addition, there were plans for competitive modes to see who could catch the most criminals within a set amount of time or be the first to get to a particular number of arrests.

Depending on the funding made available for the game from any publishing deal, there were plans additionally to have animations and profiles for all of the criminals, a wide range of civilian animations, full-motion video between levels, intros, and also the inclusion of speech where possible. Even on a small budget, there would be attempts to squeeze the maximum out of the concept regardless.

"Picking the wrong person loses valuable time and potentially means letting the real criminal get away."

Nikitova Games was excited with Jon's detailed and fun design, and so it kick-started the project with Jon in late 2007. With Jon as the director of development, he pulled together a small team onto the game for just a single month to get an initial running demo together for touting around for publisher interest, with the hope of getting full funding and more development time. The very short deadline was, in part, due to an upcoming game convention that Nikitova felt was crucial to show off the game.

"From recollection, there were two developers and between one and three artists at any time. There was also no sound but a lot of design input from me," Jon clarified. The team would consist of Sergey Ilushin as project manager,

Volodymyr Kyselov as lead developer, and Roman Matsybora as the second developer. Creating wonderful artwork to fit the brief would be Olesya Hryvenko in the role of lead graphic artist, helped by Polina Trofimova and Katie Watersell as additional artists (who couldn't recall much due to how brief the work was). No sound engineer was believed to have been allocated, with just placeholder sound effects and music temporarily added to the demo.

The primary platform of focus would be the Nintendo DS, with plans for development on the Wii, PC and iOS once a publisher had been found. "Our team worked on the Nintendo DS version only – as a proof of concept," confirmed Volodymyr. "The game mechanics were aimed at the Nintendo DS's dual-screen design from the very beginning. I don't think it would have suited the Wii without a major redesign of the gameplay. iOS, on the other hand, could have been a good choice, but, at that time, it was quite an immature platform, having its first-ever public SDK release for third-party developers right at the time we finished the *CCTV* game demo. iOS's market share as a gaming platform was quite insignificant, too."

"Game mechanics were aimed at the Nintendo DS's dual-screen."

Initially, the artistic style of the game would keep changing as the team tried to settle on a look and feel. "We went through many different art styles, from very cartoony to almost *The Sims*-like. At the time we were anticipating that, whichever publisher we signed, it with would probably assert its own preference, and we had a very big art team to call on at Nikitova," explained Jon. It was eventually finalised for the DS prototype, with a cartoon-based approach used due to memory limitations. Jon suggests that the other versions would likely follow something teetering between *The Sims* and an actual cartoon. The original design's complex nine camera options were simplified early on to work better on the DS and iOS's smaller screens, with a reduction to just four instead.

To bring the city alive, the team attempted to give the characters within the game different personalities, making them feel more real and have a real purpose. It was vitally important to have enough variety between characters (through clothes, hats, facial features, etc.), so criminals would be easier to identify. The intention also was to deceive, where normal everyday characters could turn and perform a criminal act, keeping you on your toes at all times.

Bringing it all together within a short space of time was hard work, and it was the first DS development the group had worked on. "None of us had previous experience with the Nintendo DS platform," confirmed Volodymyr. "We all had a good time though, with many fun moments parsing Nintendo's documentation and realising their revolutionary approach to handheld console design. Many tricks and workarounds were implemented to fit all the variety of required graphics and sound resources into the limited cartridge capacity as well."

"There were also not-so-fun moments with the toolchain officially recommended by Nintendo themselves," he continued. "Looking through a 'known issues' list accompanying an update patch for the C++ compiler, I remember having very mixed feelings stumbling upon a line saying something like, 'BUG#1234: wrong code generation in case [very common use case here]'. This was especially after I moved my glance from the compiler's 'known issues' list to the release schedule pinned to the wall."

Potential compilation issues aside, the team managed to pull off an impressive proof of concept – on time and showing all the basic elements. "The fully playable demo was produced in a single month, starting with Nintendo SDK's coding sample and resulting in a finished ROM image – successfully tested on a real Nintendo DS," confirmed Volodymyr. "If I remember correctly, in the game demo, you could play a few levels with gradually increasing complexity. All presentation parts were in place: splash screen, intro screen, main menu, player profile, level map stylised as the city map, game levels, achievement screens between levels (with some statistics), and background music."

Whilst the team moved on to other projects, the hunt was now on to find a suitable publisher to take the game on. "The general reception from our colleagues from Nikitova Games/Persha Studia was rather good," recalled Volodymyr. "Some were excited about the unusual game mechanics involving the touchscreen, and others had minor issues with controls at first as the DS was quite new, and the game exploited the console's dual-screen. I think it was the first dual-screen portable device we ever held in our hands. The most memorable side of the project was the surprisingly high quality of the demo, both technically and aesthetically, given such a tight schedule and absolutely unfamiliar development platform. I believe that's the achievement only very professional teams can reach."

The game would gain further positive feedback and attention at the game convention and beyond, but it would be an all-too-familiar scenario rearing its ugly head in the end for Jon. *CCTV* was felt by publishers to be too risky to take on, compared with licensed and already well-established titles. As a result, no one took on the game, resulting in the cancellation of the project at Nikitova.

"As the gaming world became more risk-averse in the mid-1990s, what was once unique was now thought of as a liability," reflected Jon. "By early 2008, we had frozen development, but I continued to work on the design and shape it for various platforms over the next coming years. We had approached quite a few publishers at the trade shows over the years and got some good interest from a few top companies, especially Eidos/Square Enix, with whom we eventually got on their shortlist of two games out of six that they intended to take on for the iOS in 2011. Unfortunately, we were one of the four that didn't make it."

The DS game was still far from completion, and, by now, the platform (along with the Wii) was less appealing financially. However, the design of the game continued to evolve. "As far as physical code is concerned, we never got further than the DS pitching demo. We never even started the Wii, iOS or PC versions. To be honest, people were asking for Wii, so we just said, 'OK, sure, we can do that'," Jon confirmed. "Later, that demand switched over to iOS. The design, however, was in great shape and perfectly aligned for iOS/PC as I fleshed it out a lot during the time we were talking closely with Eidos."

"As the gaming world became more risk-averse in the mid-1990s, what was once unique was now thought of as a liability."

The early prototype still exists, though it will not see release whilst the idea still has the potential for publication. Jon was unable to provide a new video of the prototype running, though clips can be found online from interviews with Jon on YouTube (www.bit.ly/cctv-jonhare). However, Jon did provide a number of screenshots and mock-ups from the game design document, which you can see on the following pages.

Even today, the design for *CCTV* is screaming out as a game perfect for iOS, Android or browser-based play. Jon also still strongly feels that this is a concept that has a chance, resurrecting the idea again in 2015 for a potential iOS-only release. "From my perspective, the game was probably better suited for touchscreen devices. I felt it would make a great iPad game or point-and-click mouse game on the PC or Mac, so I ended up working with Vivid Games on an art treatment for the game to make it more suitable for iOS," confirmed Jon. Again, no willing publisher could be found, though Jon is still optimistic today.

"I would still love the chance to make this game for the PC and tablets, especially as I own all of the rights to the game. It would also be great in VR. Not an intention at the moment but just more of 'it would be nice'," he enthused. "However, *CCTV* is a deceptively large game and would need some publishing backing from the off. If there is anyone out there that fancies making a go of it and marketing it properly, then let's do it!"

Publishers take note if you are reading this. *CCTV* could be the new innovative title you have been looking for and could give gamers something very fresh and new to play – so why not give Jon a call?

Top: Early mock-up screen showing a monitoring of suspects scenario, with a caught and missed counter. **Bottom:** Another early mock-up screen, depicting a more *Sims*-inspired design.

Above: Mock-up screens showing how various scenarios from *CCTV* could have looked on the Nintendo Wii platform, with the ability to select between different cameras.

Top: An early *CCTV* game logo concept. Bottom: An early mock-up of how *CCTV* (Nintendo DS) could look (left), followed by a real screenshot from the CCTV (Nintendo DS) prototype (right).

Discussing 'Gauntlet' Market decline

Year: 2008
Developer: Backbone Entertainment
Platform: Nintendo DS

It should have been the fresh launch of a classic and well-loved franchise on a modern-day platform, with *Gauntlet* about to entertain a new generation of dungeon explorers on the Nintendo DS in 2008. Although Nintendo had earlier decided to pull out of the project, publication duties switched to Eidos and resulted in the continuation of development. Completed and reviewed by the press, tragically, it wasn't enough to see the game reach the general public.

Creative director Micah Russo (MR), technical director David Sullivan (DS), sound designer and composer Yannis Brown (YB), original lead engineer Adam Rippon (AR), lead artist Tracey King (TK), and artist Gerald Broas (GB) give recollections of a project they were immensely proud of.

How did Backbone Entertainment get involved in a new *Gauntlet* game?
DS: It was our goal originally to pitch a *Gauntlet* game that was an update of the original arcade game. Mike Mika (studio head) had a lot to do with the initial game design and pitch to Nintendo. He is a classic game expert and was an awesome resource to the team. I have a classic background and was a fan of the original game, but most of the initial credit goes to Mike.

MR: I was also very active in the initial pitch and prototype development, and I worked on the creative brief for how to bring the essential *Gauntlet* ingredients to the Nintendo DS. At the time, the DS was a pretty innovative piece of gaming hardware – including the dual-screens, touchscreen, and ability to work in 2D or 3D. So we worked a lot on how to make the game experience walk the line between the DS's innovations and remain faithful to one of the best traditional video game franchises of all time.

Available to play

 Yes ○ No

Above: Gameplay screen from *Gauntlet* (Nintendo DS), showing a game faithful to the original but taking advantage of more powerful hardware.

the pitch resulted in a sign up by Nintendo, and development was swift from that point on. What did your roles entail, and when did you get involved?

AR: I was the first engineer and one of the first on the team. I was only on the project for the first nine months, though. It went really well at first, but there was a personality conflict between myself and a member of the team at the time (who I get on with fine these days). There were three eras on the project roughly from 2005–2008: mine at the beginning, then Brian Sawler and Anthony Vaughn in the middle, and then possibly Chris Larkin – who finished it off, I think.

TK: I was very excited to be assigned as lead artist on the project. This was my first opportunity as a lead to see a project through from start to finish, and the fact that Backbone had the confidence in my abilities to put this significant project in my hands was very important to me and highly motivating. I was very excited to both pay homage to the original game and bring in a level of graphics that next-gen gamers would enjoy.

GB: I was one of the artists on the project, and, during the concept phase, I was assisting with user interface and art concepts for the heads-up display. Additionally, I assisted with cleaning up the tapestries for the story mode and also did some clean-up attack animation for the 'warrior' and 'wizard' characters.

VB: I became the musician on the project whilst employed full-time in-house as a lead sound designer at Backbone. Being extremely passionate and pro-active about creating a demo track to try to give the game a feeling and direction musically, I started work on a demo in my own time (after hours, mind you!). When I surprised Sara Guinness (our producer) with the demo track, she cried hearing it. It really solidified the game, and we brought it to the attention of Mike Mika, our studio head and a huge retro gamer. He was equally blown away, and I was thus going to be composing all the scores from that point on.

We had big ambitions for telling a story via in-game events, cutscenes and video between levels."

What particular memories do you have of the development period?

MR: Our studio was set up with multiple projects running concurrently, and I oversaw design on all of them simultaneously. So, once the *Gauntlet* team was up and running, I stepped out of the day-to-day and tried to support the team with design guidance, critique, and staffing as much as possible. I did do bits of coding on the camera that handled the skewing of the two views to present a (mostly) seamless 3D perspective across the two DS screens. After the initial prototype phase, I helped set up the game structure and team and tried to give our design lead support to execute their vision for the project.

AR: I remember much time was spent getting the two DS screens displaying 3D at a reasonable speed. Luckily, as we were doing a top-down game design, we were able to do many enemies on just simple quads, which were not very expensive, compared with something like *Mario 64*. The world itself we made relatively low polygon but high-texture detail. As nothing was ever very far away and was always at a fixed distance, we could plan pretty well for our texture usage. I also remember that we had a design document to follow, but we just tried to make the game we wanted to make and didn't necessarily always keep to it. However, we were pretty close and were not going off in crazy directions.

When Nintendo declined to publish, they were extremely gracious in giving us the ability to find another publisher for the title."

TK: I remember creating a modular environment system, which allowed us to quickly iterate on the maps as design changes were made based on gameplay feedback. The modular system also enabled us to create rich and immersive environments, while staying within the texture limitations of the DS and also echoing the grid-like appearance of the original game. The level layouts were created by a design team, but every member of the team played the game and had input on the design through playtesting and feedback.

GB: It was a new adventure every day. Initially, it wasn't a large team; it was actually small/medium-sized. So I think it's fair to say that, in the early stages everyone needed to be able to carry their own weight. As time went on, team members were cycled out, and new members were cycled in. In some cases 'specialists', who were more adept at solving certain problems, were brought in as well. This is how so many hands were able to participate in the project.

Can you recall any features that were planned but were ditched?

MR: We had big ambitions for telling a story via in-game events, cutscenes and video between levels, but we quickly realised we were over-scope. The original *Gauntlet* games were light on story, so we figured we could simplify. We spent time figuring out how to preserve some of those storytelling experiences that modern gamers expect but in a scope-conscious way. I think it was our art lead who had the idea to create pictorial medieval tapestry scenes as a way to tell key story points. They looked great and fitted really well within the game.

DS: At some point, there was also a reality check to help get the game back on track, and several new design choices were made, but I can't remember specifics. I do remember we were pitching another idea of playing on the Wii and then seamlessly transferring an in-progress game to the DS to take it with you. It would have been great, but the idea didn't get traction.

One criticism was that the game lacked the role-playing mechanics of other *Gauntlet* titles. Was this deliberate to keep things closer to the arcade original?

MR: That was definitely a scope trade-off. We all enjoyed the light role-playing in more recent titles, so it was something discussed at length. We toyed with

You are now entering
ASCENDIA
Altine Mountains

more RPG mechanics, but we were concerned about the engineering and design impact in making those systems work in a fun and balanced way. Ultimately, we felt it was a reasonable trade-off to keep a very light levelling-up system and to put most of the RPG payoff in the form of each character's power moves. It also helped us simplify the work of balancing across multiplayer in both cooperative and competitive modes.

It's the best unreleased game I've ever played."

Were there any other difficulties during development?

MR: We were proud of how we managed to push so many enemy monsters on the DS in a 3D environment. The DS was an impressive machine, and 3D was a big feature, but 3D performance was underpowered when it came to rendering animated characters with high detail. Fighting swarms of creatures is one of the hallmarks of the franchise, so we had to figure out how to preserve that experience.

AR: Support for dual 3D on the DS was no small feat. Basically, we rendered 3D on the top screen that supported 3D rendering, then displayed it on the other screen (which didn't support 3D rendering) as a 2D texture. It effectively meant that the game ran at half the frame rate, 30 FPS max. It also had a fixed polygon pipeline of around 2,000 polygons per frame, so you didn't really have the option of optimising to get more, no matter what.

MR: We eventually wound up with a 2D-3D hybrid pipeline for the game. We built and rendered the environments and characters in 3D, but rendered out their animations to sprites, which was much more processor-efficient. What you see in the final game are 2D characters rendered in a 3D environment. It looked great, and we were able to have A LOT more enemies on-screen.

TK: Art-wise, the most difficult thing was just coming up with eight character colours. The first four were obvious: Red, Green, Blue, and Purple – but, after that, it got tricky. Teal wizard? Pink warrior? We had a lot of fun with this, but it was actually quite difficult to nail down. I actually referred to myself as 'Pink Warrior' (I had pink hair) and quoted "Pink Warrior needs food badly" for about two years after production ended.

YB: We also had to create a music system that was low in CPU since the game's engine was really pushing the DS's limits already. This influenced my decision to create a custom music engine. The DS had different limits and transfer speeds than that of the Game Boy Advance, which I had quite a bit of experience on.

And, on top of those challenges, you had multiplayer to get working as well?
MR: Multiplayer may have wound up being the Achilles' heel of the project. The original arcade was memorable for supporting four players, and the DS was one of the first handhelds to really embrace multiplayer, so we were pretty

determined to support it. Any technical developer can tell you that syncing four players AND a swarm of monsters is pretty tough. When you add the 2D-3D performance optimisation work on top of that, it was pretty thorny. So, a couple of our levels had some bugs, and we spent a lot of time trying to fix those.

AR: There was originally fighting about how the networking was going to work and whether or not it was possible. Nintendo had basically said that they wanted the game to be a showcase of all the different tech available, and my recollection is that we had planned to do a subset of what they asked for and not the rest.

The use of the shoulder buttons to rotate/turn was awesome."

Many new monsters were created for the game; what were their inspirations?
GB: I don't recall much about the inspiration, aside from going over reference material from the original and successor titles of *Gauntlet*. Although, I recall Tracy harnessing her medieval art knowledge during the concept phase.

TK: I knew that it was important to adhere to the iconic 'warrior', 'wizard' 'valkyrie' and 'elf', but I also wanted to bring the character designs into the present. When designing the characters, I embraced a diversity; something that would more accurately reflect the game community and draw players in with the appeal of diversity through representation. We did plenty of research on the original game and took note from visual cues, such as the stylised shapes of each character, which would be instantly recognised from a top-down camera, and the colour schemes of each level and the progression of those colour schemes as players get closer to the end battle.

Early on, Nintendo pulled out of publishing duties. Why was that?
MR: We created a prototype built on throw-away code, which was super fun and was a big part of the reason why Nintendo originally signed us. Once the project was signed, we spent a period refactoring into a proper engine. Unfortunately, it took us a while to refind the magic from the original prototype, and so the project kind of took a couple of steps back and to the side while the refactor was underway. I think that contributed to Nintendo pulling out. They were seeing the project taking longer and losing the gameplay that had excited them in the first place. I share that story as a word of caution to other developers who may go through something similar. Refactoring the engine was the right thing to do, but we fell down on maintaining the gameplay experience in the build and/or in communicating our plans to Nintendo.

Luckily, though, Eidos stepped in to take over the publishing.
MR: When Nintendo declined to publish, they were extremely gracious in giving us the ability to find another publisher for the title. But that meant we had to double-down to finish the game on our own while finding a new publishing

partner. I know that led to a lot of pressure and stress on the team, and I'm still impressed with the game they were able to make under those conditions.

Yannis, what are your recollections of creating the music and sound effects?
YB: After presenting the demo, I was given creative freedom to produce what I felt suited the levels. Of course, we had team reviews, but we seemed to hit the mark pretty well with the music created. I would play the level I was working on over and over, and being fully involved with the sound design and lore for each level really helped to provide ideas on what I wanted to hear in the game.

Working on the music was just an extension of what I did in my spare time - writing music. I would bring in 30 seconds or so of each new idea and present it to the team for feedback before continuing. Usually, there wasn't much change required, everyone was happy, and so I proceeded to complete the track and implement. I also worked with another composer, Scott Cairns, to help write music for a number of the levels.

It was a nice touch having newly recorded versions of the original's speech.
YB: This was our audio director Bob Baffy's idea to bring back the old speech. I was actually more partial to a non-retro voice-over, but I'm glad he pulled rank on that one! Bob came up with the processing method for the newly recorded voice-over, and it worked really well. Kevin James, also a huge fan of the original game and artist co-worker on the project, offered to do the VO. The story for the recording was quite amusing. Not having any recording room in the studio, I suggested using Sara's small car to get a clean recording. Sara, Kevin, Bob, and myself all crammed into her car on a hot summer day and did the deed. It was HOT, but we got what we needed. With Bob's processing magic, we had gold!

Any other recollections of parts of the game that really stood out?
GB: I would have to say that the use of the shoulder buttons to rotate/turn was awesome. Instead of turning by moving the D-pad left or right, you would hit the L or R shoulder buttons to turn left or right, while left and right on the D-pad gave you the ability to strafe.

TK: Some fun titbits to mention in particular: the FX animations, such as the Warriors' battleaxe throw, were animated using 8-bit animations, using approximately 3–6 still frames on a polygon that moved through space, and, to create transparency, most engines would use an alpha channel. We used the RGB value 255, 0, 255, and the engineers set the game engine to ignore this colour. Boom! > Alpha

YB: The theme music, in particular, was one of my favourites overall, as was one of the levels – I don't remember the name at the moment, but it was the 'Sky Palace' level. Those were the most fun to write and gave a big emotional boost to the game overall.

developed until 2008, and although completed and reviewed by the pres...
t was decided not to release due to the market drying up. That seems harsh

MR: It's the best unreleased game I've ever played, I think – better than a lot o
released games. To have it basically done but not released was really sou
crushing. As a developer, the payoff for all the blood, sweat and tears you pu
nto a game is seeing other people play it and have fun. Without that, what's
the point of making a game? To this day, I still don't quite understand how the
economics of publishing didn't work out, but the multiplayer issues were par
of the reason development dragged on longer than it should. The game may
have actually shipped if we had cut some of the multiplayer features and conten
out then, I'm not sure it would have been *Gauntlet* without those.

It was less frustrating and more heartbreaking. We were all ir
love with every aspect of the game"

Although frustrating, was it still a fulfilling experience?
MR: There were tough times, and having a publisher pull out is never fun. Bu
overall, I really enjoyed the experience. I thought the team did amazing worl
and I really enjoyed playing the game throughout development. It just kep
getting more and more fun. Plus it was one of my first titles as the studio'
creative director, so I was really proud of it.

DS: It had a tough start, but, once everything got going, it was something tha
all of us really believed in. Great team.

GB: Like many projects, it had its ups and downs. There were more enjoyable
moments of the project than others. But, I would say overall, it was an honou
to have participated in the project. Albeit difficult during some points o
production; many of us were most likely thinking to ourselves, "Who else car
say they played *Gauntlet* in the arcade as a kid and grew up to recreate it or
the DS?" So yes, of course, we poured our hearts into it. It's *Gauntlet*, after all.

YB: All of us at Backbone, having grown up on retro games such as *Gauntle*
made it a work of passion. We had such a great culture in the office, and I've
made lifelong friends working there. I remember the team really busting thei
guts to make deadlines to the quality bars they decided to hit. Hearing from
your future publisher that it had some of the best audio on DS they had hearc
was one of my personal career highlights. However, combined with the game
not shipping, that is one of the lowest points in my career. We all felt extremely
devastated that the game would never be enjoyed by the public.

TK: It was less frustrating and more heartbreaking. We were all in love with
every aspect of the game. Never have I worked on a product for 2+ years and
still enjoyed playing it every single day. I really wish this had made it out into
the world for others to enjoy as much as we had enjoyed making it

You have picked up a
Pile of Coins! Piles are
worth 10 coins!

x0 x1

Above: Navigating through mountainous areas in *Gauntlet* (Nintendo DS) and delving further into the level, collecting treasure along the way.

Two Thousand and Ten — Two Thousand and Fifteen

With an industry now bigger than the film and music industries combined, our last chapter is an era where titles can cost many millions to produce. With that, companies are far more protective of their work, with non-disclosure agreements preventing many from being able to talk about their time on certain projects.

Thanks to continually growing mobile gaming and emerging digital distribution channels such as Steam, there continues to be a great output of innovative and exciting titles. With better development tools available, it has never been easier for people to produce and sell their own games. With the multitude of games being produced by those in their bedrooms and the big player companies, the scale of potential cancellations is greater than ever before – many of which we may never know about.

MARSOC
No publisher

Year: 2010
Developer: Zombie Studios
Platforms: Microsoft Xbox 360, PC
and Sony PlayStation 3

Available to play

 Yes No

Zombie Studios was a successful development studio, one of the oldest in Seattle, USA, along with Nintendo and Microsoft. With a decent track record and high-profile developments, including *Shadow Ops: Red Mercury* and *Blacklight: Retribution*, it was decided to sell the company in 2015 – founders Mark Long and Joanna Alexander then moved on to pastures new.

As with most studios, Zombie Studios had one or two 'failed' projects that would never make it into living rooms during their day. *MARSOC: US Marine Corps Special Ops* (just *MARSOC* from this point on) was one such late title that the studio was particularly very proud of and which the studio had major ambition and aspirations for. It was never a failure, though – more an 'evolutionary' project that would live on in various ways.

Browse the history of the studio, and you'll notice a trend, with a particular focus on military first-person shooters, with it producing one of the first – *Spec Ops: Rangers Lead the Way* – back in 1998. It also worked uncredited on a lot of other franchises, such as some of the *Rainbow Six* series of games. *MARSOC* was to keep the trend alive by becoming its next military-based development.

The game began life as *CQB – Close Quarter Battle*, a class-based and team-orientated multiplayer game that focused on private military contractors (PMCs). The basic idea was that two PMCs would fight against each other within a dense war zone environment. The idea's existence was brief before it was swiftly decided to change it to a unit that not many people knew about.

Focus switched to the MARSOC – the United States Marine Corps Forces Special Operations Command, a unit of the United States Special Operations Command consisting of just a few thousand personnel. "They considered their entire branch to be like the Royal Marines, and the entire branch has that ethos," explained Zombie Studios founder Mark Long. "They were missing out on all the war dollars that were going to special operation commands, so they formed this unit. No one really knew much about them, and our new game would be the opportunity to create a whole new franchise based on them."

Mark began producing a full proposal for the game during 2008, which was gradually built up in the background whilst other projects were underway for publishers. "As soon as you close a title, it begins production, which, at the time, was 1–1 ½ years. So you'd immediately begin thinking about the next thing you want to design," explained Mark. "So, in between normal production activities, we'd start writing design documents and start peeling off a couple of people to test concepts, which is what happened with *MARSOC*."

An early story for the game emerged, where you controlled members of the US MARSOC, hunting down a dangerous warlord called Limbano in the lawless port town of Massawa, Eritrea – a haven for terrorists that has fallen into civil war and whose people are in desperate poverty. The Eritrean Defence Force (EDF) and proxy militias (who work under the command of Limbano) are fighting against the Eritrean Liberation Movement (ELM) for complete control of Massawa. Limbano is siphoning millions of dollars from UN food aid and medicine to fund his militias with weapons and vehicles – even selling vaccines and using the money to pay his soldiers. MARSOC is part of a Combined Joint Task Force called the Horn of Africa, which combats terrorism in the region, under the operational control of 42 Commando. Within the game, you played the team leader of a four-man MARSOC detachment, starting off by having to kill or capture Al Qaeda operatives wanted for the 1998 United States embassy bombings in East Africa. But, at the same time, you were tasked with taking out or capturing Limbano.

Your team consisted of four different characters, namely Captain Terry O'Connor, SSgt Ricardo (Gonzo) Gonzales, GgSgt Andrew Smith and Sgt Mark Collins. Each had their own roles assigned, including machine gunner, rifleman, radio operator, and sniper roles who can help in particular situations. You would have a choice of swapping between characters, or you could attempt to complete missions using just a single character, with AI controlling everyone else within the game.

"An additional element to the game was player progression, where you could develop your platoon and cross-train your operators."

The game was going to cover a significant chunk of Massawa. Mark was particularly interested in that part of Africa as it was originally an Italian colony that consisted of strange, dilapidated Italian art deco buildings, mixed with shanty town elements. The area was spread across three to five islands with bridges connecting them all, a perfect structure to construct a number of missions per island that must be completed before moving on to the next. Additionally, the location was carefully chosen so that a mixture of races could be used as enemies.

In previous developments, such as one of the *Spec Ops* games that Zombie had developed, the studio had the luxury of having access to the real units/teams for reference. They had even once invited the Ranger battalion up to Seattle, who allowed them to photograph every single one of them with full body gear, subsequently used to texture-map characters into the game. But, with the events of 9/11 and the war in Afghanistan, everything was locked down and it was suddenly impossible to get any further help.

As a result, the studio would mostly rely on themselves, especially with *MARSOC*. Luckily, its founder had prior experiences that would prove invaluable. "I was in the army for eight years and knew enough to ask the right questions or find the right support," Mark explained. "We also had an ex-Green Beret married to my business partner. He did a lot of motion capture work for us, weapons audio, and could get us access to any of that kind of stuff that we needed."

Zombie had good-sized staffing levels of around 40 people, and a small team was initially allocated to flesh out *MARSOC* into a form to be pitched to companies. John Williamson would take the role of producer, overseeing development of the idea and fleshing everything out into detailed game design documents. Helping to visualise everything was lead designer Jared Gerritzen, who had a pool of artists helping with modelling, mapping and texturing.

"It was our desire to do a more ambitious shooter," explained Mark. "*MARSOC* incorporated unique concepts; one of them was that it was going to be a sandbox shooter and a team tactical shooter. We had the idea that you'd have a mission in a North African village, for example, and there would be three to seven objectives where you could do them in any order that you wanted. But, to complete the level, you would have to 'pacify' the village by seizing entire objectives; otherwise, enemies would continue to spawn and would eventually retake objectives that you had taken. We wanted a really dynamic environment."

The aim was to get a high degree of veracity for the title to stand out from others, even without direct access to the MARSOC unit itself. Zombie Studios saw the likes of *Call of Duty 5*, *SOCOM* and *EndWar* as their competitors, who they needed to try and beat. The plan was to go for a third-person perspective for all of the action, with *Gears of War* being a clear inspiration. During the prototype development, a first-person perspective was tested, but the third-person view gave better visibility within the game, coupled with an uncluttered HUD.

"We wanted the idea of cinematics looking like they were shot by a combat cameraman," explained Mark. "So, we had a pink block of foam with a reticule on it that had markers so that we could track what we were looking at. We would direct two motion capture actors in the scene and get them to pretend they were shooting around a corner and moving forwards to suppress somebody. We'd then run by behind them and duck – an example of a proof of concept where we would output all that motion capture into the game engine and see what it looked like effectively."

The game would include a high degree of configurability for each of the four characters using a points system, where you could choose base layer uniforms, packs and body armour before each mission. What you chose for your team members would have an effect on your manoeuvrability or capabilities within a mission. "We wanted to integrate real brands into it," explained Mark. "One of the things we did was go to all these military and law enforcement brands, like Danner, CamelBak, Blackhawk, Garmin and Oakley. At the beginning of the Afghan war, they were just buying off-the-shelf high-tech camping gear basically and using their own camel patterns on them and stuff like that."

An additional element to the game was player progression, where you could develop your platoon and cross-train your operators. Between missions in the game, you would be able to spend points, not only to configure your team but also to send people off to airborne/medical school, demolitions or close-quarter battle training. Each would increase your capabilities going forwards in future missions and develop your platoon as a whole throughout the entire campaign.

However, one of the most innovative features to be implemented was the ability to jump from character to character, who could be situated in different areas of the map. "We had a trigger reserved on the controller that would pop up, and you would get a team wheel, so you could move the D-pad to the team member that you wanted," explained Mark. "You didn't even need to have to look at them; you could just jump to them. We got it working, and the AI when you jump out of a character would instantly take over and respond to what you were doing. It was fairly complex to do within a sandbox environment."

Changing between characters gave you access to different strengths and capabilities. For instance, a sniper team member would allow you to take sniper shots, and a machine gunner would be able to open suppressive fire on enemies, vehicles and particular constructions. "Basically, you could send a teammate to a better position of defence in the map and then 'hot swap' into that character," explained senior level designer Erik Bretz. "At the time, we referred to it as 'Man Jumping', which none of us could say without chuckling every single time. Nonetheless, it was pretty cool and fun to play." In addition to character swapping, you were also able to call in fire support, mortar artillery, rocket or air support.

"We wanted the idea of cinematics looking like they were shot by a combat cameraman."

Whilst juggling other projects, small pockets of Zombie Studios staff were allocated to create small prototypes of some of the ideas in the *Unreal* engine to test if certain concepts worked. As concepts were tested, the main structure of the game was being put to paper to flesh out a design document to show to publishers. Materials would be gradually added to the document, including test renders of buildings and areas, concept artwork and mock-ups, as well as character details. All of the planned missions, structure, scripted parts, and storyboards of the intro cinematic were detailed and broken down as well.

The missions were narrowed down to 14, spread across the four island areas of Massawa. You started off on an assault course, learning the basic mechanics of the game, shooting targets, jumping, climbing obstacles/ladders, and riding vehicles. The first proper mission would then have you raiding the Kikoni hotel to try and take out three targets, including the warlord Limbano, using skills obtained from the assault course. Here you would need to locate the hotel, then infiltrate the compound and clear any enemy resistance, before moving on to locate and kill/capture targets and move any live captures onto the roof (including a captured Limbano) to be picked up by air support.

However, Limbano would escape, and the only thing you could do is move on to the next mission, infiltrating and seizing the Massawa docks with the Royal Marines, before trying to find and rescue a downed Osprey helicopter and its crew. Further missions spread across the four islands included defending a UNME compound from attack, seizing a hospital to rescue abandoned patients, locating a stolen Cobalt 60, finding and disabling a dirty bomb, seizing control of port facilities on Dahlak Island and much more. Everything concludes with a return to the Kikoni hotel from a different perspective, where, this time, you must succeed in capturing the warlord.

Additionally, each mission would consist of a number of secondary objectives, such as locating stolen UN food aid or putting out looting fires to help with stability in the region. There would also be bonus objectives, such as seizing Limbano's laptop to find out additional intelligence, which added to your overall completion score for the game and helped to unlock achievements.

The sandbox selling point of the game was allowing you to decide how to carry out a particular mission, each one designed to be open-ended and not scripted. You could go it alone with one member of the team, or you could use all of your teammates and their particular skill sets in various ways to achieve your goal. Enemies would be tough to defeat, with a complex AI where only the really skilled players would be able to complete missions completely without the help of their teammates. To navigate your way around the map, you would use a virtual PDA device that guided you to particular points for mission objectives. You could also get into various vehicles within the game, such as ATVs, trucks and personnel carriers to get around quickly and obtain additional armoury or firepower in some cases.

After 6–12 months and now with a clear structure, location and direction, the team began designing and constructing artwork and 3D meshes for a 'vertical slice' prototype to show publishers. Satellite maps of Massawa would first be used to try and map out the locations as best as possible without the use of many real photos from the area as Massawa was far too dangerous to travel to for an asset photo shoot.

"We went instead to a town in Morocco where they shot *Black Hawk Down* [Rabat], sending Joanna [Alexander] and her husband," recalled Mark. "We had two people dressed like spies, with camera gear, backpacks and microphones. Everybody thought they were CIA, and the city didn't believe why they were really there! They took a binaural microphone, which is designed to capture sound in the same way your head hears sound. If you've ever listened to a virtual reality recording, they use a binaural microphone as the shape of your head and ears reflect audio in a really particular way. We used it to record street sounds primarily, e.g. ambient music from a block away or people chattering."

Along with reference images from Morocco, other imagery was used to aid the team to build meshes of Arab town buildings, hotels, docks, run-down/ destroyed buildings, and other relevant structures within a desert-like environment. The environment would be made to look war-torn, with blown-in doors, destroyed buildings and burnt-out cars, for example.

Highly detailed characters would be referenced from many different photos and materials that were gathered and scanned in by Zombie Studios. The *MARSOC* characters were rendered carrying backpacks, water bottles, first aid kits, ammunition, and wearing helmets with visors and radio communications. A high level of detail was aimed for on all of the human characters within the game to increase the overall realism.

When it came to the development of the prototype, Bill Wright led the way, with a number of developers working under him. Richard Starr would oversee the artists and animators working on the production, with Erik Bretz working as the senior level designer along with a few other level designers. As with all of their current projects of the time, development was carried out using the Unreal 3 engine, though Zombie Studios needed a large open environment for the missions to take place within, which the engine wasn't really cut out for.

Luckily, previous experience of developing simulation games for the military would help contribute towards making it possible. "The military once wanted to simulate and teach people how to respond when an IED went off whilst in a Humvee. So we took the Unreal engine and all off-the-shelf stuff, making a kit you could set up in a garage," recalled Mark. "You could drive, but Unreal wasn't designed for massive open worlds at the time. Its modularity and flexibility meant that each object you placed in the world would have a very large header file to describe and keep track of it. Because there were so many objects, there was a limit to how much of any kind of complexity there could be in a world. So, with Epic's help, we took that limit off and created simulation landscapes that were 50km by 50km, which was insane back then."

"Like many concepts that evolve, you never throw anything away."

That very expertise was used for *MARSOC*, where landscapes could now have a higher level of visual fidelity as a result. They had to rewrite the rendering part of the engine to do it, though. "Back then, we were 'talking to the metal'," confirmed Mark. "We were literally trying to get every bit of computing we could and do all kinds of clever things per frame."

Like *Gears of War*, *MARSOC* had destructible cover that characters could jump behind. Zombie would take this concept further and have a data structure that informs the game's AI of what it should do when under attack, and that it should find an available cover node. For example, depending on the game state, certain AI sequences would play out to show you keeping your head down and firing from the side. The AI could respond to you in the game, either helping to cover you or following you to the next cover node. Both you and the AI would also be able to scale walls, either by jumping over low ones or by standing on your teammates' backs to scale over taller ones.

"It was difficult to develop. You'd get in situations like a Venn diagram, two circles where you've advanced towards an enemy but not killed enough of them, and their AI and your AI are mixing. So, your AI wants to keep up with you, but it would run to a cover node occupied by an enemy AI, and they would ridiculously stand a foot away from each other and shoot at each other!" laughed Mark. "It was really hard to debug." A tricky aspect was also the AI across multiple planes in the game, where you could have people above or below you. Determining the best cover position for the AI was tricky. Also, your team members would need to provide cover for you or independently carry out their own actions in the game, all happening alongside your own actions. These were all complex problems that the team would need to solve over time.

Controls were given careful consideration, kept very simple with basic movement, fire and grenade options through single button presses. You would be able to easily switch between weaponry, ranging from different guns, knives, and grenades, and you could also set explosive charges and trigger them with your combat PDA device. Ammo would be limited, meaning that you'd have to be resourceful, though enemies would drop ammo and weapons when killed. If available, you could also call airstrikes to parts of the map (or 'laze and blaze' as described in the plans) to help out, though these would be in limited supply too.

Finally, in an era where games demanded a multiplayer mode, *MARSOC* was no different. There were planned options for basic 'Deathmatch' or 'Capture the Flag' modes, as well as 'Assault' (one team attacks, another defends) and 'Raid' (teams compete to achieve the same objective) modes with up to four players in total (configurable as human or bot). There were plans to offer the main campaign as a multiplayer, either in a co-op mode throughout the entire campaign or by playing the *MARSOC* unit and the other the insurgents, swapping sides afterwards.

Rather than offering a fixed set of maps, the team had an ambitious plan to keep everything fresh for players. "We had a unique multiplayer idea that we had been wanting to do for a long time," Mark explained. "There were those hex-based military board games like *Squad Leader*, where the boards were cleverly designed so, no matter what way you arranged them, the hexagonal tiles all lined up. We wanted to do that with the multiplayer level design for *MARSOC*. We had the idea that there would be three panels, and, when getting ready for the next round, your team would select or vote on the panel they wanted to play within. The opposing team had their selection, and you couldn't see what they were selecting. When you were both ready, the game would select a third panel randomly in the middle. It had the advantage of reducing map fatigue, getting used to weak points and where all the advantage points were."

It wasn't perfect as there would be limited panels, so, eventually, you'd get to play all of them and get a sense for them all after a short while. Also, there were major technical hurdles to overcome for it to work, having to load in what was essentially three separate levels and join up all of their geometry and AI pathfinding in a sufficient way. Although *MARSOC* would never see the vision implemented, it would eventually be utilised for *Special Forces: Team X*.

There were also big aspirations for the music and sound design, with Inon Zur targeted to compose all of the music for the game. Mark felt he was the 'Hans Zimmer' of video games, doing virtually every big game that you can think of. A crucial part of *MARSOC*'s realism included the quality of the sound recording and the effects that would occur within the game. "I really love sound design, and an important part of *MARSOC* was going to be working with Soundelux," explained Mark. "They were the go-to guys in Hollywood for top filmmakers like Quentin Tarantino or Oliver Stone, and they came to my attention because of the movie *Heat*. Everybody remembers that gun battle outside the bank, a really great, gritty Michael Mann scene that goes on forever. But, if you watch it now, it still has this verisimilitude that is really hard to put your finger on. I swear to god, if you go and watch it now on a really good sound system, it will just blow your fucking mind – just on how the tension builds and how well it sounds."

Mark found that this was a rare film where sound designers asked to fully mic the set. Usually, sounds were added later on in the studio. Weapon sounds are super dynamic, where you cannot record a weapon realistically with a single microphone, and *Heat* had done it properly. "I read about all of this in a cinema magazine, and I was like, 'Fuck me, man, I want to work with guys who give that much thought about weapon audio'," he exclaimed. "So, over the years, we produced I think six titles with Soundelux, and we loved working with each other because, each time, we wouldn't fall back on 'let's just use your inventory of audio'. We wanted to go all out like this for *MARSOC* and wanted to do live audio in a 5.1 Dolby mix and go for a new level of verisimilitude in gear and weapon audio."

Although not able to work directly with the military, Zombie Studios was still able to go to ranges and record live rounds and grenades being fired. However, the development of *MARSOC* would never get to the stage where audio was properly recorded by Soundelux, with only brief sound recordings taken and used from Morocco. As it was expensive to purchase their time for a week to get what they needed, the game needed to be guaranteed full funding first.

After almost a year of development, the team had a prototype showing 4-5 minutes of gameplay. There were no missions or tasks present; it just gave a sense of some of the complex environment and what you could do in the game. You could see a range of animations, how movement/switching characters worked, using a selection of weapons and calling an airstrike. You could climb walls, use team members to get to higher platforms, jump down from different heights, slide down ropes, and have characters follow you. Then, you were able to seek cover, crouch behind walls and other protective areas, whilst being able to fire back at enemies. The development was wrapped up with prototype presentation screens and options, as well as temporary placeholder music composed by the team.

With concept work, documentation, a running prototype and gameplay video now complete by late 2009, Zombie Studios began looking for a publisher, needing further funds to start full development. After approaching a number of publishers, SEGA UK was the most keen, looking to try and sign a military franchise and find their own *Call of Duty*. Zombie Studios and SEGA UK would sign a deal to develop and produce the game into 2010, with crucial funding obtained. The overall aim was to complete production of the game within just over a year, with target platforms including the PC, PlayStation 3 and Xbox 360.

The funding would initially cover a further six months, with Zombie Studios dedicating more team members to the project and building upon the prototype. This included tidying up the AI, animations, textures, and tightening up the engine. Early missions started to be integrated, building storyline and content into the game. Artists began to go full force, creating meshes and structures required to form the map. Early on, builds could be created for all of the main platforms, demonstrated on core hardware as and when required. Although impressed with progress, SEGA had a dramatic change of heart. "They terminated development, thinking it was too ambitious, and couldn't agree internally to continue funding," explained Mark. "Although the UK office wanted a military franchise, the US office didn't. So, when it came to really commit to complete development, they had to put their money together to proceed – but couldn't agree. I also think the new *Call of Duty* was shown at E3, and the bar was raised so high that they weren't confident the title would perform as well."

Left with no publisher, Zombie Studios tried to save the project by showcasing it to others. This included Konami, which showed the most interest but wanted to take the idea down a completely different route, to which Zombie declined. Deciding to permanently park *MARSOC*, ideas and parts of the development would be repurposed in other productions, in particular, *Special Forces: Team X* and parts of *Blacklight: Tango Down*, *Blacklight: Retribution* and *Blackwater*.

"Like many concepts that evolve, you never throw anything away. If you couldn't get a concept picked up, then you modify and pitch it in a different way," explained Mark. "My multiplayer map tile system eventually ended up in a stripped-down way in *Special Forces: Team X*," added producer John Williamson. "Some of the designs (man jumping and multiplayer map tiles) were also in the Zombie version of *Rogue Warrior*, where Bethesda went insane, and the changes they wanted appeared in their 2009 version of the game – the lowest-rated Xbox 360 game for years. They had Mickey Rourke rapping for goodness sake!"

Due to its relatively short period of time in full-scale development, *MARSOC* has not really been heard about until now, never seeing any press coverage. As a result, finding screenshots or something of the game could have been tricky. But luckily, much of the development has been kept. However, for those wanting to get the chance to play something of the original *MARSOC* development, unfortunately, this is not going to happen anytime soon.

The release of any prototype has been denied, though most of the ideas from *MARSOC* live on in other titles anyway, so there's a chance you've already played parts of it without even knowing. Mark kindly provided assets and screenshots of *MARSOC*, many of which can be seen here for the first time. In addition to this, there will hopefully be a video on the Games That Weren't website, showing the game in action. In an intriguing twist, this isn't the first time that *MARSOC* has been seen by the public – though you wouldn't know it.

"I hired a friend of mine to write a screenplay for *Black Light* (we actually sold the rights to 20th Century Fox for a feature film). He wrote the screenplay, turned it in, and Fox Atomic shut it down, and the screenplay came back to us. That person was Jason Dean Hall," explained Mark. "He went on to write *American Sniper* and was nominated for an Oscar. Because the film performed so well, they gave him a shot at writing and directing his own movie called *Thank You for Your Service*. There is a scene where one of the soldiers gets triggered playing a video game, and he's playing video from *MARSOC*! The only light of day it ever saw."

Top: Early *MARSOC* character concept sketches, showing different equipment available.
Bottom: More detailed designs of some of the key characters and their specifications.

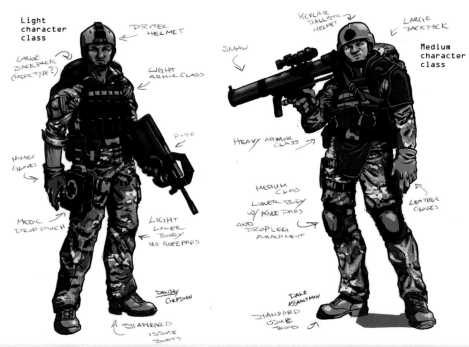

Light character class

DRTEC HELMET

LARGE BACKPACK (MEDIC TYPE?)

LIGHT ARMOR CLASS

NOMEX GLOVES

P-90

MEDIC DROP POUCH

LIGHT LOWER BODY NO KNEEPADS

DALISAY CORPSMAN

STANDARD ISSUE BOOTS

KEVLAR BALLISTIC HELMET

LARGE BACKPACK

SMAW

Medium character class

HEAVY ARMOR CLASS

MEDIUM CLASS LOWER BODY W/ KNEE PADS AND DROPLEG ATTACHMENT

LEATHER GLOVES

DALE ASSAULTMAN

STANDARD ISSUE BOOTS

Top: Comparison showing a standard equipped MARSOC and a fully levelled-up equivalent.
Bottom: Two more characters from the game, with key equipment labelled.

2a Cont...

LTC DARROW INTERUPTS,
VO- THEY KNOW WERE COMING. LZ IS RED

AS O'CONER BEGINS TO RESPOND, THE REAR
HATCH BEGINS TO OPEN,

SPILLING LIGHT INTO THE DARKEN CABIN

VIEW FROM BACK HATCH, THE CITY OF MASSAUA IS
REVEALED, PLUMES OF SMOKE & SPORADIC GUNFIRE
CAN BE SEEN. 3 TRAILING OSPREYS BREAK
OFF TO COVER TARGET LZ
(VO- O'CONER- LOOKS LIKE NAJAF,
-DARROW - TIME TO "RAISE THE RUCK"
-MARSOC - HOO-RAH)

DARROW & O'CONER EXCHANGE   AS CREW CHIEF
LOOKS OVER POINTING A FINGER IN THE AIR, SHOUTS
ABOVE VTOL NOISE (VOICE- "GET READY")

CAM CUTS BACK TO INT. MAIN CARGO BAY
AS MARSH & RM STAND & CHECK GEAR

2a)- Cont...

PILOT LEANS TOWARD CREW CHIEF,
PILOT HAS TO YELL TO BE HEARD OVER ROTORS
(VO- OP'S ARE GO, HLZ IN SIGHT) AS CREW
CHIEF NODS. CAM TRACK WITH C.C.

INT. OSPREY/CABIN; CREW CHIEF TURNS TO MAIN
CARGO AREA SHOWS & MOTIONS VIGOROUS THUMBS
UP. (VO- 30 SECONDS)

CAM TRACKS INTO MAIN CARGO BAY - PAST ROYAL MARINE
BITS OF DIALOGUE CAN BE HEARD - CAM FOLLOWS
CREW CHIEF TO

LTC DARROW RH LEANER, AS CREW CHIEF
YELLS INTO HIS EAR   CAM CONTINUES TO TRACK
PAST DARROW & CREW CHIEF
(VO- CC-HLZ's HOT, SIR)

TO REAR OF OSPREY, WHERE MARSOC TEAM
CAN BE SEEN STANDING.

MARSOC TEAM - CPT O'CONER, GUNNY BROWN, SGT
KIRBY, SSGT NELSON & CPL VASQUEZ
(VO- O'CONER- RELAYING LAST MINUTE ORDERS)

Above: Storyboards depicting part of the proposed intro sequence for the game.

Above: Mock-ups showing the heads-up display plans for moving between team members, highlighting nearby characters and how to make the selection.

Above: Screenshots from the promotional video that was created to pitch *MARSOC* to potential publishers, demonstrating actual gameplay from the PC prototype that Zombie had built.

Above: More screens from the promotional video of the PC prototype, showing navigation across the top of a building and then inside what is believed to be the Kikoni hotel.

Black Death Financial difficulties

Year: 2011
Developer: Darkworks
Platforms: Microsoft Xbox 360, PC (pictured) and Sony PlayStation 3

Available to play
◉ Yes   ○ No

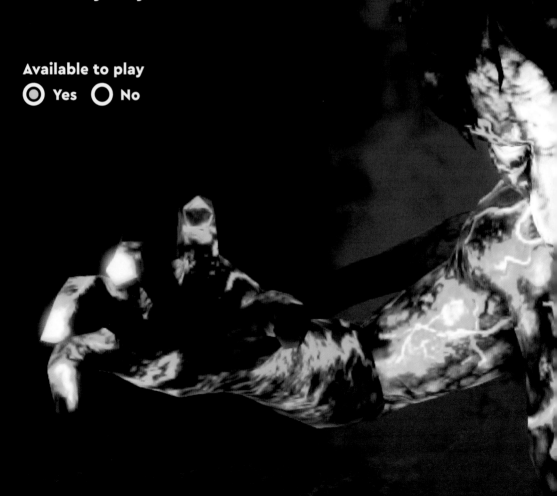

A first-person survival horror game set in New England, where a strange fog has caused humans to transform into zombie-like creatures. Attempting to survive, you can mix chemicals to create weapons to kill or cures to heal. Even though a promising demo was released, a publisher couldn't be secured before financial difficulties resulted in Darkworks closing its doors.

"The objective was to create something new in the survival genre and within a first-person semi-open world. *Black Death* drew on some of humanity's biggest fears: dirty air and noxious chemicals that interfere with the brain, turning people into violent offenders. Starting with black smoke filling the streets of Boston and contaminating everyone, *Black Death* ambitiously used procedural generation for locations, creating a dynamic fog that spreads.

The game was the first to use and showcase an engine in development for three years. Developing a game whilst developing the engine requires more time for testing and making everything work; time we didn't have, where we had to release an emergency teaser demo, representative of the game's atmosphere. Feedback was very positive, but the industry was at an inflection point, with publishers only going for AAA franchises. This period saw massive contractions in development studios, with around 100 closing during that time, Darkworks included."

*Guillaume Gouraud, general manager,
and Florian Desforges, producer*

Eye of the Moon

Developer passed away

Year: 2011
Developers: Mike Singleton and Chris Wild
Platforms: Apple iOS and other current platforms.

Available to play
 Yes ◉ No

In the days when computers allowed access to only a limited amount of memory, we were blessed by geniuses who were able to squeeze an entire world within those strict confinements. During 1984, you had an entire eight galaxies within the seminal *Elite* by David Braben and Ian Bell, and, within the very same year, you could also explore an entire land in *The Lords of Midnight*.

Created by Mike Singleton, the game was inspired by the works of J.R.R. Tolkien and by his love of war-based board games. You had to battle against Doomdark the witch king, who attempts to use a magical Ice Crown to increase his icy grip over the land. Leading with Luxor of the Free, you attempt to unite the world of Midnight, joining forces to defeat Doomdark. The clever thing was that the game could be completed in two ways, either by defeating Doomdark's army or by capturing the Ice Crown. You, as the player, had the choice which path to take, but you could decide to take on both if you were really skilful.

The game presented you with a 360-degree panoramic view, depicting trees, mountains, castles and the armies that awaited. Played over a grid-based map, the game had a total of 3,904 locations, consisting of a staggering 32,000 views using a special 'Landscaping' technique that Mike had developed. The game allowed the control of up to 32 characters in total, making it revolutionary for its time on 8-bit platforms and firmly putting Mike Singleton on the map.

With resounding success upon its release, the game saw a sequel in the form of *Doomdark's Revenge*. Some felt it was not quite as good as the first game, feeling it was a bit too random, unpredictable and had less love put into the characters, but it was still a very good and well-received game. It was enough to see a trilogy scheduled – something that had always been the plan, like Tolkien with *Lord of the Rings*. The second game would talk of the next title being called the *Eye of the Moon*, where "Mike will send Morkin down to the warmer lands which lie below Midnight itself to find the *Eye of the Moon*" – as detailed in the manual.

The game's title referred to a magical jewel that would allow the possessor to look into the future. Many years after the second chapter, Luxor is now dying and wishes to see what will happen to Midnight beyond his time. Morkin is sent to the lands of Bloodmarch, south-west of Midnight, in search of the jewel to ensure that Luxor will be able to fully rest in peace upon receiving his dying wish.

"*Eye of the Moon* was partly in development following *Doomdark's Revenge*. It was to feature an even bigger map (128×128), and I planned for the complete game to feature 12 different kingdoms, with a sub-game to win in each one before you can actually get the *Eye of the Moon* itself," Mike told journalist Martyn Carroll.

It was twice as big as *Doomdark's Revenge*, with approximately 16,000 locations and around 131,000 possible views planned. Characters would have more detail, utilising a clever police E-fit style construction done through the character set to allow different mouths, noses, eyes, etc.

Each would have their own strengths and weaknesses too, and it would be crucial to recruit the right people to help complete the game. It was intended to write the game back to back with *Quake Minus One*, but that proved to be a more difficult task than first anticipated, with Mike having to take on most of the development work himself. He was then drawn into taking on a *Star Trek* licence and then *Dark Sceptre*, meaning that *Eye of the Moon* was constantly put on ice.

Development was started on both the ZX Spectrum and Commodore 64 during the mid-to-late 1980s, the C64 version being developed by Dave Ollman whilst at Maelstrom. But, during this time, Mike got deeper involved in other projects and management, too much to continue on the Spectrum development in depth. In the end, the game never saw completion after TelecomSoft decided to move the goalposts. "They took over Beyond and wanted to change the terms of the contract – so that I personally did the coding for both the Spectrum and the C64 version but for no more cash than the advance that had already been agreed for just the Spectrum version. I refused, and they used their get-out cancellation-of-contract clause," Mike informed Martyn Carroll.

"There was an actual map, largely generated but hand-coded to give a more realistic feel," he continued. "I also had done quite a lot of work on new graphics, which would introduce more variety so that, for example, each castle would look slightly different to the other castles, allowing you to recognise a place by sight, in theory, at least. I had also been working on introducing colour into the landscape itself, using the same sort of masking principles that went into removing colour-clash in *Dark Sceptre*. And that is about as far as it went. I always intended to find another publisher for it, but Maelstrom Games was taking up too much time."

Mike was eventually given the chance to complete the trilogy with Domark but created *Lords of Midnight 3: The Citadel* instead, which just took elements from *Eye of the Moon*. The intention was still there to do *Eye of the Moon* as its own stand-alone game, but Mike felt the deal with Domark was too restrictive and that he wouldn't be able to do the game that he truly wanted. Mike wanted to save his intended end to the series for the right moment, and this wasn't it.

Unfortunately, *The Citadel* took a long time and encountered many problems, including losing its original developer. Eventually, the game surfaced without much of an impact and full of bugs too, meaning that it was panned badly by the press. The poor reception and experience would be the final nail in the coffin for *Eye of the Moon*, for now, at least.

Sadly, Mike didn't keep anything of the original project, and not much was developed apart from a prototype 'Randscape' system that generated the scenery and locations. It seems even his original notes and design documents were lost after several moves over the years. But the game would always come and go in Mike's thoughts over the following years. Later moving to Switzerland, Mike continued to work on games, but a new world of mobile gaming was about to open up a great opportunity to resurrect the final chapter.

It all started with an older brother's introduction to *Lords of Midnight* during the mid-1980s on a 48K ZX Spectrum. "I don't remember too much, just some late nights in a dark room, listening to *Street Sounds Electro 05* album," began developer Chris Wild. "My brother was an avid mapper, but, as I came to the game a little later than him, I was able to use his maps and those already published in the press. I remember being engrossed by the game and thoroughly enjoying it. I did manage to complete it with both the quest and by utilising the Xajorkith defence. But, I guess the real truth is that the technical aspect would draw me back a few years later and properly take over my life."

Chris returned to the Midnight series several years later in 1991 when he began taking apart the original classic ZX Spectrum game. "I decided to reverse-engineer *Lords of Midnight* and work out how Mike had programmed it," he explained. "I disassembled it to a file on my PC and worked my way through the assembler, documenting the code. While working on it, I had a real urge to start replaying it, but I didn't really want to use my Spectrum."

Industry veteran Jon Ritman had heard about Chris's impressive porting of both *Lords of Midnight* and *Doomdark's Revenge* to PC DOS and suggested the games industry would be a perfect fit for him. Therefore, Chris decided to take the plunge and make the shift from his job of writing business software to work in games development. Crucially, Jon would also introduce Chris to Mike Singleton, subsequently leading to permission to release the conversions, which Mike requested were included with the release of *The Citadel*.

During the late 1990s, Chris occasionally kept in touch with Mike whilst working on a Windows version of *Lords of Midnight*, named *WinLom*. A later Windows development of *Doomdark's Revenge* would not see completion but would lead on to the development of *The Midnight Engine*, allowing users to generate their own scenarios and create their own versions of Mike's games. Chris also helped with some development work and hosting for *Midnight/MU* – a multi-user online game based on both games, developed by Jean-Yves Rouffiac.

"Mike wrote a new landscaping engine that did all the maths real-time rather than using the original 8-bit lookup tables."

"Mike was happy with any Midnight work as long as it didn't move into the mobile space because he was interested in exploring that. With *Midnight/MU*, at the time, we didn't think there would be any issues because it was web-based, and mobile just wasn't up to it," explained Chris. With the release of the iPhone and excitement over iOS, Chris contacted Mike about the possibility of a *Lords of Midnight* remake on the platform. He enthused to Mike just how the iPhone was a perfect device to bring the series to mobile users. Although there was some interest from Mike, nothing really came of it.

It wasn't until a few years later in early 2011 when Mike asked Chris if he was still interested in exploring an iPhone *Lords of Midnight*. Chris jumped at the new opportunity. "I quickly ported the *Midnight Engine*, and we had a system up and running with Marmalade (Airplay at the time)," he recalled. "Mike wrote a new landscaping engine that did all the maths real-time rather than using the original 8-bit lookup tables. This also meant that it was smoother, and you were able to spin around as you looked and have movement as you moved. After that, he started work on a new landscape-rendering concept that would allow for real-time lighting, where the images would use normal maps. The nearest thing that would be like it would be *Sprite Illuminator* by CodeAndWeb. But he was also working on a concept that he called Ink or Paint-Key Normal Maps. The idea was that you could describe an image in a few colours because most buildings/etc. only have a few colours, but the image would then be made up of variations of that colour. This would allow for quick recolouring and lighting."

Chris would handle all of the development work, with daily contact online with Mike to discuss progress and any new ideas. Progress was slower perhaps than hoped for as this was a hobby project for Chris, whose day job was as a software contractor, and free time was often non-existent. There was also to be a major blow during development, with Mike receiving a devastating cancer diagnosis shortly after his 60th birthday. Whilst fighting through his very own battle, the show would go on.

The new development would once more rekindle thoughts of *Eye of the Moon*, with Mike surprising Chris one day with new details for the game, as well as the beginnings of a novella. "As we were progressing with early ideas for *The Lords of Midnight*, Mike suddenly hit me with his initial *Eye of the Moon* document, along with the idea to create a Midnight-related studio," Chris recalled. "He called the idea Games for Tomorrow, and it would be developed by Tomorrow's Midnight – a new studio which would start with the four games from the Midnight series. The idea was that the Midnight games would be available on many platforms and could be continued on any of them, including the web."

At the time, Mike had been recovering in hospital from a debilitating operation to remove a tumour from his mouth. Chris felt that it was probably this sobering moment which had compelled Mike to get some words down. The document was so detailed that it excited Chris a lot, with some ideas from the original project but new ones too. "I think much of it was Mike going back over what he had thought of before and then expanding on it," Chris reflected. "Some of the details came out of a few hours of frantic Skyping after I read his initial pitch. We talked about concepts that may or may not work. As an example, he wanted to have a large area of lava but didn't think we could manage the concept with landscaping. So I showed him the work that the team had done on water for M/MU. This really impressed him and put lava and water back to the fore."

"As we were progressing with early ideas for *The Lords of Midnight*, Mike suddenly hit me with his initial *Eye of the Moon* document."

There was suddenly now the potential to complete the original trilogy, which would no doubt cause excitement within the series fan base. It was clear from the effort that Mike had put in of his serious intention to finish the game once and for all, without the shackles of publisher interference that he had once feared from Domark. With Chris present as a strong ally, the scene was now perfectly set. Within Mike's thoughts for the game, he concluded: "The idea is to make this last game of the series a truly grand finale, with new landscape and gameplay features, new enemies and new friends, but also the potential of Midnight being assaulted by all its old enemies too. And, at the same time, the land of Midnight itself returns firmly to the gameplay, which is fitting for the end of the saga, not to mention satisfying for old fans."

The original intention for 12 kingdoms was retained with just name changes. The game no longer took place in Bloodmarch as this and most of the original regions had been used in *The Citadel*. The starting focus was now within the kingdom of Valahar, found to the west of Midnight. Each kingdom was also broken down into domains, with Valahar segmented into areas such as Midral, Halgrim and Fingnor. "I have deliberately broken up the overall map into Midnight-sized chunks," Mike explained in his plan. "As much as anything, this is to serve as a reminder to myself that each chunk should be as detailed, varied and handcrafted as the original Midnight map itself. If this is not done, it quickly becomes worse and monotonous rather than better."

Domains were also set to become a powerful tool, where taking over via a Citadel within could help bring the local population onside and bring intelligence in quickly to aid your quest. There was the consideration that, if you had a particular domain garrisoned, and there was enemy activity detailed within the domain, AI would take over on your behalf to fight back.

As with the original game plan, before being able to go and find the 'Eye of the Moon', you had to complete all sub-tasks within each realm. The tasks were either quest-based or conquest-based. Chris revealed there would be the task of having to deal with the Battle Kings of Varangor, who had been sent out to reanimate Doomdark, Shareth and Boroth. This was as well as the task of getting Morkin and Domse to meet up so that you could gain full power of the Moon Ring. The rest was still to be decided.

There were also to be some familiar faces in the form of Morkin, Rorthron and Luxor, though Luxor's involvement would be limited due to his old age and illness. Each kingdom would include their own 'Wise' to join Rorthron within the game and who can be recruited by Rorthron to help enhance his powers. Each of the Wise would have a powerful single-use spell that would need to be utilised carefully and at the right time. Although there would be many characters, there were plans to restrict how many you could directly control so as not to overcomplicate and spoil the core game.

Chris and Mike had decided to complete their *Lords of Midnight* development first, then move straight on to *Eye of the Moon*, with planned updates of *Doomdark's Revenge* and *The Citadel* pushed back until afterwards. There was still plenty of work left on *Lords of Midnight*, but the excitement of *Eye of the Moon* meant further development of that instead. Ideas were still continuously formed in the background, including fleshing out how the enemy AI was going to work and more of how the map would look.

Mike crucially wanted to avoid mistakes from previous games and have all the kingdoms carefully crafted like the original game. "We briefly spoke about what didn't work in *The Citadel* and why *The Lords of Midnight* and *Doomdark's Revenge* did work," confirmed Chris. "Mike was keen to craft all the locations and names as he was aware of the damage to *Doomdark's Revenge* by having names that were instantly unmemorable. We were also aware of how controlling all these lords could become unwieldy. The control method used in *The Citadel* didn't really work; however, he'd done a much better job of it in *Ashes of Empire*. The same with AI – Mike was aware of things that went wrong in *Doomdark's Revenge* where the AI lords would just end up killing each other. So, really, it became about going back to *The Lords of Midnight* and working out how to properly update things."

Visually, it was far too early for discussion on how the game would look. It was likely that the game would remain faithful to the originals, making use of the iconic landscaping technique once more, but with potentially more detailed and colourful characters and scenery, as was once planned for the original 8-bit developments. However, there were discussions on new features and improvements, including the ability to control battles through the night, watch representations of them and possibly even interact with them too.

"I've been very open and vocal about not wanting to develop *Eye of the Moon*."

New landscape features were still being discussed, with the map having a sea of lava as well as water. There was to be a volcano (Eldfjall), a great mountain (Horn), magical forests and glades that were only penetrable by the Fey. There would be lodges providing a place of rest and rejuvenation, dangerous wastelands, teleportation gates, watchtowers to pass news between other watchtowers about enemy movements, forges for equipping armies, and, finally, caverns inhabited by dragons that can be recruited by Farflame the Dragonlord.

So many great ideas by the duo were never to progress further, with Mike passing away suddenly from a heart attack in October 2012. The news hit Chris hard. Mike had not only been a significant part of his life through his games, but he was a good friend, too – both chatting almost daily at one point. There was a feeling that the remakes could no longer go on, with Chris even contemplating walking away from the project.

"I was completely numb. I just couldn't see myself being able to continue with the game on my own without Mike around," reflected Chris. "Mike's son, Jules, asked me to go up to his father's wake, where I met family and friends. The next morning, we sat in Starbucks on the waterfront of Wallasey, New Brighton, and talked about his dad. It was there that he gave me some of the handwritten notes and designs for *Eye of the Moon* amongst other things. Right there and then was when the decision was formed to continue the game as a dedication and in memoriam of Mike."

With the blessing of Mike's family, Chris would complete their *Lords of Midnight* remake two months later, but without making any further changes to the core game. Without Mike's input, everything was kept as faithful as possible to the original, with the exception of enhanced visuals and save options. The game saw a release with glowing reviews in December 2012, *Doomdark's Revenge* later following just a few years after.

However, *Eye of the Moon* was a different story. Not previously existing and sadly now without the input of its key creator, Chris felt the game had to be laid to rest once and for all. To him, it didn't feel right to continue the game; in the same way, he felt he couldn't add or change the original games for the previous remakes. "I've been very open and vocal about not wanting to develop *Eye of the Moon* because there is so much work to do, and it doesn't feel right to do it without Mike," confirmed Chris. "I just feel that people will always want to play Mike Singleton's *Eye of the Moon* and not Chris Wild's *Eye of the Moon: Based on an idea by Mike Singleton*."

Although a game will never happen, a novel could be on the cards instead. With a full novel written for *Lords of Midnight*, *Eye of the Moon* may see something similar. "The novels are different," Chris explained. "The *Lords of Midnight* has been written with all parts of the series in mind. It references bits of information from the whole Midnightverse, even parts from the *Eye of the Moon* design. Part of this is actually really important because only when you step back and look at the whole story do you start to see an overarching idea that Mike was playing with. There is a big difference with the concept of the magic of the Moon Ring at the start and where it ends up at the end. You also see a thread weaving its way through. By looking at this, we've been able to create a theme which gives us a four-novel story. However, should any of the later stories get told is purely down to how the first is received."

Several years on since the remakes, is there anything that can be seen of *Eye of the Moon* to give a glimpse of what was started? Chris reveals that the game was nowhere near a development stage, with the novella still needing to be finished to work out the rest of the design. There was still the hard work of handcrafting the remaining 11 kingdom maps and the people situated within, along with the design of the artificial intelligence and all of the quests and campaigns. The design was not even halfway complete. However, what both Mike and Chris did manage to formulate would be generously collated together by Chris and released to the world at www.thelordsofmidnight.com. The site includes the beginnings of the novella, handwritten notes from Mike, design ideas, and the start of the game's map.

It is a solemn end, knowing that we will now never see a proper completion of the series. It almost finally happened and was so very close; it is with much sadness that Mike personally never got to conclude things the way he wanted. Chris continues to act as a guardian and protector for Mike's legacy, treating it with the great dignity and respect that it deserves. If you haven't already, be sure to check out the remakes and future novels and help ensure that Mike's legacy lives on for many more years to come.

THE EYE OF THE MOON.

We do it as originally planned, 12 subgames, but with a grand difference; we don't tell anyone. The original objective is to complete the 1st game. Only when you have completed it do you get to know about the 2nd goal (if you watch till the end and don't leave before the material ends).

The games all share the same system, but they are otherwise more than mere levels.

(Another possibility is to randomly start the player in any one of the 12 subgames — they don't need to be linked sequentially).

However, there is a better scheme.

Perhaps even better is to use characters. One character (at least) must go through all twelve levels. Yes, that's the key! AND you can choose which one to start with, if you want!

The character dynamics then determine the story that may (or may not) unfold.

OK. The 1st game has 32 characters, any one of which can follow through.

The subsequent games also have 32, but at least one original character must survive throughout or pass the torch! A thus fundamentally decides a web of plot lines that interweave, all leading to the final goal.

$10! = ?$

$4 \times 3 \times 2 \times 1 = 24 \times 5 = 120 \times 6 = 720 \times 7 = 6040 \times 8 = 48320 \times 9 = 434880 \times 10 = 4,398,800$ ways of completing

Above: Notes written by Mike on *Eye of the Moon* that were shared with Chris, discussing the 12 subgames and how these could work.

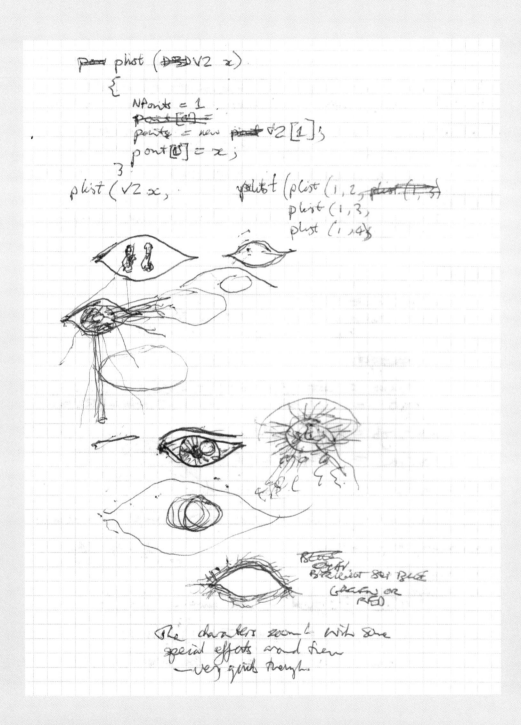

Above: More thoughts and designs from Mike, including some brief code and what seems to be initial ideas for a game logo.

So, typically from any phrase we will get quite a large number of neutral responses.)

To keep these manageable within the interface, we need to categorise them, thus creating menus and submenus.

Going back to the sheriff :—

I shot the sheriff. ⇒   Icons for each:

QUESTION   Really?
             Why?
             When?
             How?
             Did he die?

COMMENT   Great
             That's terrible
             He deserved it.
             He didn't deserve that.

PERSONAL   You're crazy
             You're joking
             You're an evil bastard.
             You're a hero

EFFECT   I don't care
             I'm not interested.
             That's interesting
             That's fascinating
             That's sickening

CONSEQUENCE   So ~~what happened after that~~ They'll come after you. etc.

Then we have some default choices such as.

CONTINUE   Carry on
             Tell me more.

CHANGE POINT / BREAK THREAD.

? ! + — =
⇒ ✗

Above: Notes from Mike on possible landscape objects and character interfacing structure ideas within the game.

Top: Screenshot of the game that started it all – *The Lords of Midnight* (ZX Spectrum).
Bottom: Artist's impression of *Eye of the Moon*, based on notes from Mike and Chris.

The Panasonic Jungle Changes in the market

Year: 2011
Developer: Panasonic

Moving on from experiences of the 3DO and M2, Panasonic decided to have another crack at the market with a portable system called the 'Jungle'. It wasn't really a handheld but closer to a small-form factor laptop with a keyboard, D-pad controller, touchpad and a high-resolution display. In many ways, it was similar to the Pandora console released around the same time.

The system was intended mainly to run online games – in particular, MMORPGs – and was rumoured to store data on remote servers rather than directly on the machine. A working prototype was created, and a handful of launch games were announced, including Bigpoint's *Battlestar Galactica*. However, in early 2011, Panasonic abruptly cancelled development, citing "changes in the market" and their own strategic direction.

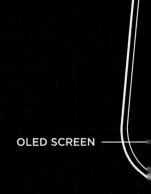

OLED SCREEN

POWER

DIRECTIONAL PAD

QWERTY KEYBOARD

BSPACE

DEL

SHIFT

ALT

MAPKEY

SD MEMORY SLOT

POWER CONNECTI

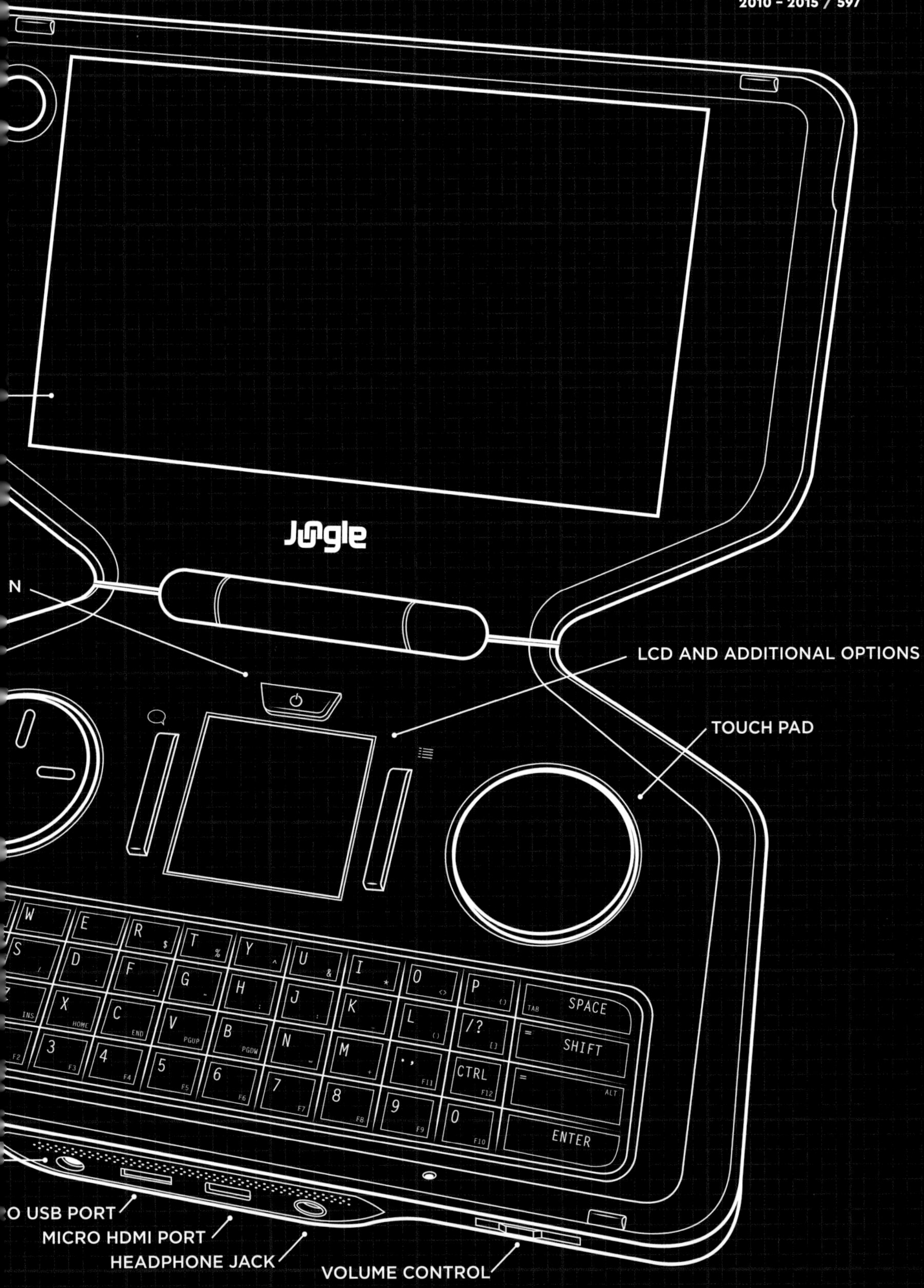

Jungle

N

LCD AND ADDITIONAL OPTIONS

TOUCH PAD

W E R T Y U I O P

S D F G H J K L TAB SPACE

X C V B N M /? SHIFT

INS HOME END PGUP PGDW CTRL ALT

F2 3 4 5 6 7 8 9 0 F11 F12 ENTER

F3 F4 F5 F6 F7 F8 F9 F10

O USB PORT

MICRO HDMI PORT

HEADPHONE JACK

VOLUME CONTROL

Discussing 'The Lizzie Borden Murders' Development issues

Year: 2011
Developer: GameShastra
Platforms: Apple Macintosh,
iOS, Android and PC

Horror-themed games have been around for decades and continue to be popular today. Recent titles such as *Layers of Fear 2* and a remake of *Resident Evil 2* use modern and realistic graphics to depict graphic and gory scenes, potentially giving more nightmares compared with early efforts, such as *Haunted House* on the Atari 2600. Our final title was yet another to add to the genre, based on the Lizzie Borden murders of her father and stepmother in 1892. Kicked off in 2011 at GameShastra and intended for release on the PC, Mac, iOS and Android, industry legend Dan Kitchen discusses a recent development felt to have had much promise (and could still); one that even triggered strange paranormal activities during its conception.

The Lizzie Borden murders is an interesting subject choice for a video game. What inspired creating a game based on events from over 100 years ago?
I've always been interested in stories about haunted houses and urban folklore. So, during a trip through Massachusetts in the fall of 2010, I noticed an exit for the town of Fall River, which I remembered being the town where Lizzie Borden committed the infamous crime of killing her father and stepmother with a hatchet in 1892.

After looking up the house which became a bed and breakfast years ago, I decided to drive by and check it out. The moment I saw it, I realised that it would be a great setting for a horror-themed game. I met the owner that day, took a tour of the house and started negotiating the rights to make the game.

Available to play
O Yes ◉ No

Above: Art concept showing the main house that you would enter.

The story goes that Lizzie was accused of murdering her parents but was later acquitted. That must have been a challenge to shape into a game concept?
That wasn't really a challenge for me as I was very familiar with the story. Lizzie actually did kill her father and stepmother; all the evidence pointed to her. But, in 1893, New England, a jury of 12 men were not going to find a Victorian spinster guilty of such a crime.

"I wanted to approach the murders as Hitchcock would have."

Additionally, much of the evidence was not allowed to be admitted during the trial due to it being mishandled by the investigating officers. To most historians Lizzie was clearly guilty. Thus, it was easy for me to formulate a story based upon the evidence.

With a story in place, what was the genre of the game and who did you control?
I conceived the game as a horror-themed Hidden Object adventure. This genre is heavily story-based, and games like this are very popular with the mature female gaming audience. So, I had the player taking on the character of a female journalist visiting the present-day house, who, through a supernatural visit by the ghost of Lizzie, is transported back in time to view the horrific events of August 4, 1892, and help the spirit of Lizzie finally find justice and rest.

Above: Artwork for the game, depicting Lizzie Borden's room within the house.

Interesting, as you could imagine the game being a 3D adventure title like *Alone in the Dark*. **What were your inspirations when designing the game?**
Our goal was actually to build two games: one version was a 3D first-person adventure, and the second was a story-based Hidden Object adventure.

The story-based Hidden Object adventure was the first game to be developed. For that game, the inspiration was any number of "Collector Edition" Hidden Object games found on the Big Fish Games portal.

There must have still been plenty of research required to draw up the structure, story and general flow for such a game. Can you tell us what this entailed?
Most of the research was done on the premises of the house itself. In fact, a colleague and I had the house to ourselves for two nights, during which time we gathered much of the photographic and video reference we needed.

We spent the first day photographing all of the rooms and taking the shots we had storyboarded ahead of time. As night came, we walked the house and made notes of the sights and sounds the character would experience. About 3am we heard creaks coming from the upstairs attic area and honestly felt a bit uneasy. After a careful examination of the attic rooms, we settled back into our respective rooms for the night.

It must have been two very sleepless nights!
It was. Around 6am, I was woken up by my colleague standing over my bed in a panic. He told me that he had heard a voice speak to him a few moments earlier. I told him he was dreaming, but the damage was already done. He was spooked, and we both stayed awake. On the second night, he refused to sleep by himself and slept on the floor of my room in a sleeping bag.

"We had full creative freedom, considering having to stay within the constraints of the story of the murders. After all, it was the overarching theme of the game, given the location."

Approximately how many hours of gameplay were there to be?
We were designing the game with about 20 hours of gameplay.

How much creative freedom did you have?
We had full creative freedom, considering having to stay within the constraints of the story of the murders. After all, it was the overarching theme of the game, given the location. The owner of the house did have approval rights over the story elements and style of the art. However, not being from the industry, he was easy to work with and was very happy with the look and feel of the game.

On the subject of freedom, how much was there in the game itself?
Since the game followed the story of the crime and the trial that followed, the game was written in a linear fashion.

Presumably, the game would have been broken up into segments/levels?
The game was to be segmented by story chapters.

Were you aiming to have gory content and visuals throughout?
The game was not designed to be a slasher title. I wanted to approach the murders as Hitchcock would have approached the material. For instance, the viewer doesn't actually see the graphic murder of Janet Leigh in the *Psycho* shower scene. Instead, during the attack, Hitchcock focuses on the image of Leigh behind the shower curtain, on the image of her face, and on the knife. Finally, he focuses on the blood going down the drain.

In the same way, I planned on presenting the murders as silhouettes and shadows cast against the wall of the house as the attacks happened. The old nursery rhyme states Lizzie Borden took an axe and gave her father 40 whacks. She actually only gave him 11 whacks, but imagine the imagery of 11 hatchet blows to a human skull. I realised that the scene would appear even more horrific if we saw this presented as a shadow on a wall without the gore to cloud our thoughts about the actions taking place.

The silhouette approach would have been potentially distinctive. Were there any other interesting features that were planned to make the game stand out?

At the time, the Lizzie Borden house had installed a series of night-vision cameras in each room which were accessible via their website. We were going to work that into our game, such that players would be able to find clues to some of the game's adventure-like challenges by viewing (by way of the game through an internet connection) these rooms.

Was there an off-the-shelf engine being used to develop the game?

The team used a proprietary engine developed internally at GameShastra.

The game just never had the internal resources needed, so eventually, art development stopped, and the game was shelved.

What problems and challenges occurred on the project?

On many games, I successfully worked with remote teams at GameShastra. In fact, many times, I travelled to India to work closely with the teams. However, at the time we started the *Lizzie Borden* game, GameShastra's management decided to focus their internal efforts on a group of Indian-related game projects, and didn't bother to inform me that I didn't have the internal resources promised.

It sounds like you had a very limited team – not enough to get things going.

Part of the problem with getting the game done was that there wasn't a dedicated team for the game at all. I felt that the Hidden Object version of the game was coming along quite well, at least from an art perspective. The code portion is where progress had stalled due to the shift of the internal resources.

Was this why the game was cancelled?

Yes. Ultimately, the game just never had the internal resources needed, so eventually, art development stopped, and the game was shelved.

It must have been far too early for any music to be composed or integrated.

None was composed, but it would have played a large part in setting the mood.

At the point of cancellation, how long had been spent working on the game?

The code portion was only worked on for a few weeks; however, the art development went on for about two months. It was very far from completion.

Interestingly, there seem to be references to a brand-new game on the Tiki Interactive website. Can you tell us if this is a fresh development on the cards?

Yes, there are references to the game on www.tikiinteractive.com. I have secured the rights to the Lizzie Borden house and will be releasing both a PC Hidden Object adventure and a tabletop board game in 2020.

Above: More artwork concepts showing a shelf within the house and the kitchen, with various objects to investigate.

Tony Hawk's Shred Session Focus on console

Year: 2014
Developer: BigBit Ltd.
Platforms: Android
and Apple iOS (pictured)

A popular franchise entertaining many for years that saw a free-to-play development for mobile platforms. Mixing skateboard action with *Temple Run*-like mechanics, Activision decided mobile wasn't for them and cancelled after a short-lived soft launch. Subsequent titles have been less than stellar – the wait continuing for the series to get back on track.

"The goal was to create a game for both skaters and casual mobile gamers. The framework was based on *The Snowman and the Snowdog*, a simple lane-switching game. First step was layering a trick system over the core game, whilst keeping it approachable. I created a simple gesture-based system where tricks could be linked. It worked well, especially when adding the ability to grind rails and ride other obstacles for additional airtime. Things went really well, and Tony was very complimentary, giving sound advice, especially on the skater animations.

Soft-launching in several countries, the feedback was good. Players got the trick system and enjoyed the game. But, shortly after, things went quiet, and we were told it wasn't going to be released worldwide. The plan now to concentrate solely on console versions. So, that was that. A shame it wasn't just released and sold for a few dollars to at least get some money back."

Gary Richards, lead designer

Available to play

◉ Yes   ○ No

Dizzy Returns Failed Kickstarter

Year: 2013
Developer: Blitz Games
Platforms: Microsoft Xbox 360, Mobile, Nintendo Wii U, PC and Sony PlayStation 3

Available to play

 Yes No

Dizzy brings many a nostalgic tear to the eye of kids growing up in the late 1980s and early 1990s. The lovable cartoon egg, with his bright-red boxing gloves and jungle hat, was an 8-bit gaming icon. It was a very popular choice amongst young budget-loving gamers, including the author of this book, who, with limited pocket money, lapped up the various 'eggcellent' adventures for a number of years.

Created by Andrew and Philip Oliver in 1987, *Dizzy* was a slow-burner to start with for Codemasters, but its popularity rapidly grew and spawned a number of new adventures and spin-off titles. *Fantasy World Dizzy* was seen by many as the ultimate of all the adventures produced, which contained the perfect mixture of fantasy storyline and puzzles.

The Oliver Twins were to separate from Codemasters due to payment issues in 1994. According to the book *The Story of the Oliver Twins*, the twins felt that Codemasters were possibly trying to change their image and move away from producing kids' games. Marketing manager Richard Eddy also made it clear that Dizzy was no longer part of their future plans. The Oliver Twins were released from their exclusivity agreement with Codemasters, but it was on the condition that they could not write anything based on previously published Codemasters games. It meant that the popular egg was laid to rest, perhaps prematurely some might feel.

Ever since Dizzy's final game appearance, there have been various campaigns to bring him back to our screens. In 2003, Blitz Games (run by the Oliver Twins) teased fans with a mock-up video, showing a 3D Dizzy game in a similar vein to *Super Mario 64*. Nothing was to result from it, but it got fans (past and present) talking again about the character and how it would be great to see him relaunched for a future generation.

Then, in 2011, a Dizzy game finally appeared on modern platforms, with the successful remake of *Dizzy: Prince of the Yolkfolk* on iOS and Android. It gave hope that the brand could finally see a long-awaited relaunch to a whole new audience. The success of the remake would finally result in an announcement to relaunch the character in an all-new adventure called *Dizzy Returns*.

"We always wanted to bring Dizzy back, but, when leaving Codemasters back in the early '90s, Dizzy was left stuck between us," Andrew began. "When the iPhone was released a few years ago, a programmer friend of ours, who had written *Dizzy: Prince of the Yolkfolk* on the Atari ST and Amiga, found his old code and graphics and recreated it on the iPhone. He asked Codemasters and us if he could publish it, and indeed it got published via Codemasters. This event got us talking with Codemasters, and we agreed that, if they could do more Dizzy games, then so could we."

What was different about this particular development was the Kickstarter approach to try and fund the project. "We wanted to do it well, and that costs a reasonable amount of money. Kickstarter came along and, with it, the idea for resurrecting retro games for new platforms. So, we figured this would be a reasonable route to raise the development funds needed. We wanted to stay true to the original with the side view, but take the modelling into 3D. The idea was to look like a leafy organic version of *Little Big Planet*," explained Andrew.

Working closely with the Oliver Twins were graphic artists Duncan Nimmo (known to many as Dunk) and Nick Myles, who were both just kids themselves around the time of the original games. "Dizzy was certainly part of my life. Looking through the cassette games, Dizzy used to catch my eye because of his clean design and bright-red gloves. When you're eight, you notice those kinds of things!" Nick recalled. "I was aware of Dizzy during my early computer gaming days but never knew of the link with the Oliver Twins, so coming to work where I do, it was a big surprise. I was more of a shot/kill kinda player (still am) and drifted toward that side of the market more than platformers," added Dunk.

"Scenarios and locations would remain faithful to the original fairytale design and rules that were set by the Oliver Twins."

Plenty of preparation would go into planning for the Kickstarter in mid-to-late 2012, and the team decided the approach to undertake. "We were mindful to look at what went before," explained Nick. "We also looked at current, trending art styles, both in games and the entertainment industry as a whole. The aim was to create something that felt like it built on the Dizzy style, so long-term fans felt like they were returning to something familiar, but that there were also many new things to see and do."

"We were respectful and took inspiration from what had gone before. But we cast a wide net to see what had gone on in design in general, and gaming design in particular, in the intervening years," added Dunk. "We also all brought years of experience from other games to the table when it came to what we could do with Dizzy."

To better fit within the ever-changing landscape of gaming, the game's structure and flow was the first thing to be pinned down. "We planned to have grouped areas. The older games would have themed areas: the Crystal caves, the Castle, etc.," recalled Andrew. "We were going to have these as distinct areas/levels in *Dizzy Returns* that spanned several screens. Then, when you completed X amount of tasks, you'd unlock another area. There's a familiarity that people like to know that, within a certain area, X out of Y tasks are complete. You can come back to complete everything, but you may not have to."

The Kickstarter campaign would launch on 23rd November. Over the space of a month, tantalising mock-ups and concept drawings would be released on its pages to attract backers. However, eyebrows were raised over the ambitious £350,000 funding target, which the Oliver Twins would try to justify throughout the course of the campaign. Both Dunk and Nick would focus all of their time and efforts on the project for the duration of the campaign. "This gave us time to explore the look of the character and respond as design ideas were generated," explained Dunk. "When getting to grips with Dizzy's rich history, the only way to do it justice was to give it your full attention," added Nick.

Dunk focused purely on character design, with a traditional approach of using layout paper and Prismacolor Col-Erase pencils to produce rough ideas for an approval process. Characters would later be scanned in and rendered up in colour using *Photoshop* in preparation for the Kickstarter pages. Nick concentrated on environments for Dizzy to exist, producing them directly in *Photoshop* to allow for image layering and easy use within promotional videos.

To inspire and guide the designs, an opening story was produced early on. It set the scene of Dizzy awakening to a world covered in dust and overgrown plants. Thinking that Zaks the evil wizard had cast the spell, Dizzy questions why he hadn't destroyed the Yolkfolk. Dizzy wakes Theodore the wizard, who gives him a device that can control the time of day.

Arriving at Zaks' castle to find out more, Dizzy finds that Zaks is also asleep, along with a giant dragon present at the castle. Whilst waking others, Dizzy accidentally wakes Zaks and the dragon in the process, with the dragon escaping to cause destruction. Flashbacks would have been shown – in the style of the 8-bit games – where Dizzy learns of exactly what happened.

Zaks had summoned the dragon 20 years ago to help him get rid of the Yolkfolk, but he lost control when it began to run wild. Casting a spell to put the dragon to sleep, it worked too well and put himself and everyone else to sleep too. It would be 20 years until the spell would begin to wear off. With the dragon now awake, Dizzy must save the world and work with Zaks to gather the ingredients for a spell that will banish the dragon for good.

And so the adventure would begin. Dizzy would have to explore various scenarios within the game to collect ingredients, solving puzzles in the process to retrieve them. Once all were collected, Zaks would cast the spell to banish the dragon. Though (spoiler alert), ultimately, it would end with Zaks betraying Dizzy, leaving a cliffhanger for a potential sequel.

Some 20 years since the last Dizzy game, a lot had changed – especially with the quality of graphics in games. Modern games were now more akin to an interactive cartoon, and Dizzy needed to be able to compete with the tough competition out there. It was important for Dizzy's iconic look to be kept, without changing so dramatically that he wasn't recognisable from the original series. The solution was simple: Dizzy's key shape and features were kept, but more character was added through his actions and expressions. In essence, the game would become like a moving version of the cover art, something that many original Dizzy fans would have always dreamed of.

However, fans wanted a game respectful of the original series, and many were hoping for something as good as (if not better than) their favourite of all the titles – *Fantasy World Dizzy*. They wanted to see Dizzy able to just carry a maximum of three items, and they didn't want him to have his own voice, but be narrated instead. Maybe there were fears of something cheesy resulting, like when the *Sonic the Hedgehog* cartoons were released (in the author's opinion, anyway).

Scenarios and locations would remain faithful to the original fairytale design and rules that were set by the Oliver Twins. There would be physics, such as the ability to drop boulders into water to raise floating platforms, and also plenty of fantasy elements where real-life dangerous animals would be friendly and not enemies. Other location ideas would be opened up to suggestions from backers.

"We were very open to people chucking in ideas, and that's why we invited it," explained Andrew. "But we had to ensure that their ideas worked within the confines of Dizzy's world and didn't break things. For example, we wanted to avoid anything from the modern day and keep things in fantasy medieval. So, if people wanted a puzzle that involved flying, we'd work out something not using motors... by building a hang glider! It kept within the boundaries set. There were cool features being toyed with, and we had yet to work out how we could use them without too many knock-on and damaging effects."

To begin with, the focus would be kept purely on internally developed ideas, building an initial solid foundation that held true to the Oliver Twins' vision. The most intriguing of all of the ideas would be the 'Day and Night' feature. With the time device provided by Theodore the wizard, Dizzy would have the ability to change between night and day at all of the locations he could visit, and on demand. Daytime could reveal characters, plants, platforms, different world characteristics (such as higher tides and different weather) and possibly other objects or puzzles. Switching to night-time could reveal monsters, but potentially other hidden objects that could help progress as well.

Dizzy was to begin his quest at 'Olivia's Cove', home to a mermaid of the same name. Here, Dizzy has been washed up on the shore, where a monkey pirate has stolen the time device. Dizzy would have to catch the monkey, chasing it towards a place called 'Goldheart's Tomb'. Travelling towards the location, a rope bridge would snap, and the monkey would drop the device and flee, leaving Dizzy to find another way to reach the tomb to progress. Olivia was to help Dizzy by revealing that he would need to go through an underwater tunnel, and she would give him diving gear if he helped her to find her comb and scales. There was to be a simple puzzle to retrieve the comb, but the scales would have involved digging up treasure and trapping fireflies in a bottle.

Eventually taking the underwater route, Dizzy would then have discovered a shipwreck that was home to a giant octopus (hiding in the wreck during the day and emerging at night). Dizzy must use parts of the boat to form platforms to find a way into Goldheart's Tomb whilst avoiding the octopus in the process. Upon reaching the tomb, designs suggested that Dizzy would have had to climb through mining tunnels by solving puzzles involving missing gears and moving cranes. By collecting idols of Goldheart, Dizzy would unleash 'Goldheart's curse', where the tomb would fill with lava, with Dizzy having to climb for his life.

Other areas were mostly just ideas on paper at this stage, with votes made by the Kickstarter backers on what new locations they would most like to see. These included the 'Tomb of Goldheart' but also: 'The Sewers of Tradeport' – a deep network of sewer tunnels, with giant rats, toxic gases and an entire underground city; 'The Lost Temple of the Yellow God' – containing treasures, stone guardians and an area which constantly rearranges itself as you move around; 'Theodore's Library' – a magical library that stretched across many dimensions; 'The Ethereal Fleet' – a complete fleet of sunken pirate ships, with an armada of ghosts; 'The Jungles of Doom' – a place so deep and dark, that no explorer has ever returned – a potential city of gold could be discovered here; 'The Lava Caves' – caves full of trolls that must be explored carefully and where a river of lava leads straight to Zaks' lair.

To bring the world fully to life, the game also needed vibrant and interesting characters throughout. We already had a pirate monkey, a mermaid and a giant octopus, but there were many others planned. Zaks' Knights were to be part of a puzzle in a town with a curfew, where you would need to switch to night-time to avoid detection by them. Rockwart the Troll would make a return with his army of trolls – switching to daytime would see the trolls move at a slower pace. Other enemies suggested were to be skeleton pirates, bats, birds and rats. No doubt, Dizzy's family would have also featured and played a key role.

Dizzy's own character was to be shown in different costumes based on the scenario found within, and which possibly could have seen him given different traits. "Initially, it was purely cosmetic, but the design may have called for that later," suggested Dunk. "I think lots of the costumes could've been rewards or 'Easter eggs' for playing the game a certain way. Dizzy is easily put into another hat." Many other ideas and suggestions were mostly scribbles on bits of paper, yet to be considered or be fully formed to present to backers.

"It was clear that the new game would respect its roots."

A key decision on whether the game would scroll or flip screen was yet to be decided. The focus early on would just keep to narrative and visual mock-ups. "Whilst discussions around mechanics had begun, they weren't yet at a stage to influence visual development," confirmed Nick. "The [one] expectation was that Dizzy would have some 3D elements to the gameplay – think along the lines of theatrical set pieces which are often layered to give the illusion of depth."

Overall, from the early designs and concepts, it was clear that the new game would respect its roots but still take bold steps to bring the game successfully to a new audience. There was still plenty to be decided, especially on how the game would fully play out and how it would build up and be presented. Funding first had to be obtained before anything more substantial could be produced.

Funding was very slow, and even after releasing more concept art and plans for the game, things didn't really pick up. Finishing at £25,620, the project fell well short of its £350,000 target. "On reflection, we probably should have had more to show at the beginning," Andrew conceded. "We had wanted to strike as Kickstarter launched in the UK, and we were advised not to let it go too near to Christmas or over the holidays. So we rushed it out shortly after the UK launch." Much to their credit, even though it was clear the project would not meet its target, the team continued to release material to fans up right until the deadline.

"I think Kickstarter is a great concept, and I fully support those thinking of doing it. I do believe you need to show quite a lot running and/or have extremely good publicity," reflected Andrew. In addition, Andrew believed that most money raised on Kickstarter projects is raised by Americans. With Dizzy being a very UK/Europe-centric character, the level of funding was never going to hit the same dizzying heights as projects with a more universal appeal.

We asked whether there was anything produced beyond the visual mock-ups and if there were any playable prototypes ever developed. "Ourselves and the designers had many meetings and came up with lots of good ideas, characters, areas, features and puzzles. But, sadly, we never got to implement them. Those that had been fully agreed on were drawn up and placed on the Kickstarter website," Andrew clarified. There was nothing playable or controllable at any stage, not even animation.

As a gift to those who backed the campaign, Blitz Games kindly produced a presentation document as a thank you for their support. This presented many of the concepts and ideas created over the course of the campaign. It was a lovely gesture, though it further added to the regret that the great egg would not be returning any time soon. "It was good fun and a privilege to work in Philip and Andrew's Dizzy sandbox for a while. The twins still have the same passion and love for their creation as they did when they first created his world, and that can be infectious," reflected Dunk.

After a disappointing campaign, we wonder if that might be it for Dizzy and his chance to grace a new generation. "We've decided to leave it for a while, unless something major changes, like someone coming forwards with a funding proposal. But we'd love to come back to it in the future," concluded Andrew with hope. However, Blitz Games would sadly close its doors in 2013 due to struggles in the changing economic climate. The Oliver Twins would resurface later with Radiant Worlds (which was purchased by Rebellion and renamed to Rebellion Warwick), and now run a game consultancy firm called Game Dragons.

However, another Dizzy game was made available thanks to the Oliver Twins, when the long-lost NES game *Wonderland Dizzy* was released in 2015, carefully pieced together from recovered source code, and even getting a physical release as part of a biography released on the Oliver Twins. So, in many ways, we have got to see a new Dizzy game of some kind.

We conclude with the message left to backers on the closure of the project, which felt apt to repeat here: "We'd like to say a sincere thank you to each and every one of you – it's been heart-warming to see all the love for Dizzy that is still out there, and we're humbled by the fond remembrances of your experiences with the original series of Dizzy games and the part they played in your lives. Regardless of whether we make a brand-new Dizzy adventure or not, there's no doubt that he has a place in gaming history. Thanks once again to all of you – a Kickstarter project is nothing without its backers, and we couldn't have asked for better supporters."

Top: Where it all began with *Dizzy: The Ultimate Cartoon Adventure* (ZX Spectrum).
Bottom: The 2011 HD remake of *Dizzy: Prince of the Yolkfolk* (iOS) that inspired *Dizzy Returns*.

Above: Various Dizzy character concepts by the art team, thinking about what kinds of actions would feature in the new game, including skydiving!

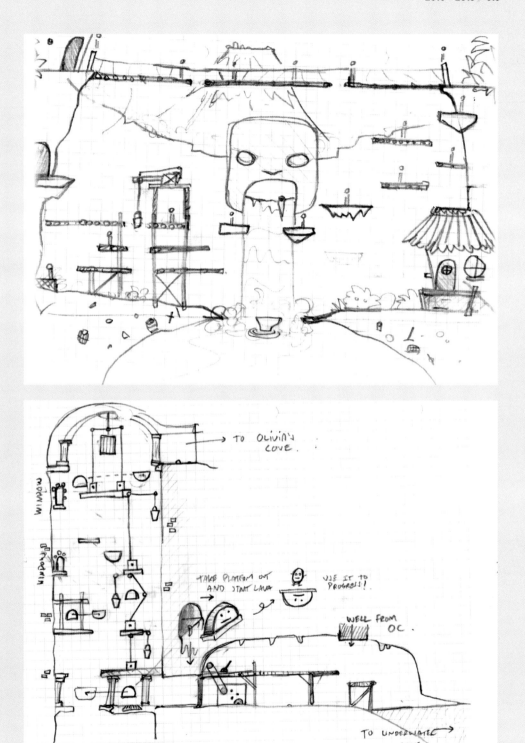

Above: Early sketches of some of the concepts planned, including the start of Olivia's Cove.
Here you can see how the level could have been broken down into separate areas and puzzles.

Top: Concept showing the Olivia's Cove location in the game. Bottom: The Crystal Cave area concept, with ladders and steps to navigate.

Above: Other environment concepts, showing possible locations that may have ended up in the game or as part of a cutscene. The last image seems to show part of the Yolkfolk village.

Human Element
Developer closed doors

Year: 2015
Developer: Robotoki
Platforms: Microsoft Xbox One, Ouya, PC (pictured) and Sony PlayStation 4

Set 35 years after the zombie apocalypse, survivors have learned to deal with the undead and now struggle to compete against the human element. An ambitious first-person multiplayer survival game set in an open-world environment, the Ouya edition was cancelled early on. Later versions were put on hiatus when Robotoki closed its doors, and they still remain that way today.

Available to play

◯ Yes ◉ No

Subtraddition Sidelined

Year: 2015
Developer: Sacred Square Games
Platforms: PC and potentially others

Available to play

○ Yes ◉ No

In an industry now dominated by big player companies, the small 'bedroom programmer' hasn't been defeated just yet. Mobile development, combined with outlets – such as the iOS app store, Google app store, Xbox Live and, of course, Steam to name a few – have all been influential in seeing the return and rise of the 'Indie developer' over the past decade or so.

With the Internet now firmly ingrained into our everyday lives and giving easy access to new games, the 'small form' way of development is even more popular than it was during the 8- and 16-bit eras, giving gamers the chance to break away from story-based games and the oversaturation of first-person shooters.

There are hundreds of thousands of small home-grown projects started, which fall by the wayside for many reasons. Although many are personal projects, they all fit under the umbrella of 'indie development', an important gaming movement today. Our next title wasn't a huge blockbuster game by any means, and would likely just have been sold by the author themselves, but it is an example of the raw talent outside of the big companies.

Developing a game is a lot easier these days, thanks not only to online communities but also the pre-made engines and code libraries readily available. One such game-changing tool has been *GameMaker Studio* by YoYo Games, enabling individuals and small teams to develop games within a short space of time without reinventing the wheel for things like creating a scrolling level engine. One person to massively benefit would be Stuart Lilford, a curriculum leader in games design at Sheffield College.

"Ever since I was about five or six years old and first loaded *Super Mario World* on the SNES, I knew that I wanted to make games as a career," explained Stuart. "I studied Game Design at university and did some volunteer work in QA for a company that made games for the Nintendo Wii. That volunteer experience allowed me to get a job working in QA at Rare and Codemasters. Eventually, I left that line of work and became a designer on a series of Augmented Reality games for the PlayStation Vita. After that, I got into teaching, but I tried to work on as much of my own stuff as I could as well."

During his free time, Stuart developed a number of small games under his own 'Scared Square Games' label. This included *Time Stone*, a short adventure game created with *Adventure Game Studio* (AGS), with vibes of classic SCUMM titles, such as *Maniac Mansion*. Stuart's clever design and imagination would see the title win an *AGS* award for the best short game in 2013. Clearly good at his craft, Stuart had the impetus to keep creating more games.

After initially developing a game called *Gravity Box* during 2015, Stuart suddenly became distracted with a new idea after playing around with the platformer mechanics within *GameMaker Studio*. "I wanted to teach my students how to make basic platformers, and so I was teaching myself how to do it first," he explained. "I found it frustrating when testing a prototype that, if I wanted to try out a specific jump (to fine-tune things like jump height and distance), then I needed to close down the game, change the level design to allow me to test it, then run the game again. So I implemented a debugging feature that allowed me to place and remove platforms during the game to fit specific test cases, which allowed me to get the feel of the game right."

What started as a debugging feature quickly became a light bulb moment for Stuart, rapidly turning into something fun that was felt could go places. *Gravity Box* was sidelined, with the new concept capturing Stuart's interest and not letting go. Right from the start, the key mechanism of adding and removing blocks ingeniously led to an early title for the game, with the theme of block subtraction and addition creating *Subtraddition* as its name.

Stuart began drawing up ideas in his notebook to take the concept forwards, noting various platformers as key inspirations, such as *Fez*, *Braid*, *Super Meat Boy*, *Limbo* and various Flash-based games. "*Fez* was a definite inspiration," confirmed Stuart. "Some of my favourite games growing up were also collection-based platformers, such as *Banjo-Kazooie*, *Jak and Daxter* and *Ratchet and Clank*. Overall though, I felt that *Fez* really encapsulated the feeling of all those games but in a beautiful, pixel-art, 2D world (well, sort of 2D). Other than that, *Birdsong* was also a massive inspiration – a game that was a platformer, used only four colours and was made in an impressive 48 hours for Ludum Dare."

One requirement was that the game would feature large levels to explore, with doors (some requiring keys to unlock) taking you to different parts of a level. Making up the levels would be different types of blocks. As well as solid blocks (rock, platforms, bridges, etc.), there would be blocks that crumbled, were icy, or disappeared/appeared through the use of switches dotted throughout the game. But one of the key components was, of course, to be 'blox' that could be picked up, used as a platform or as a defence mechanism. However, there would be variations available with different effects within the game.

"Early concepts included finding blocks with different properties that you could add to your collection, including blocks that conformed to gravity, TNT boxes that exploded, and bouncy blocks that helped you jump higher," recalled Stuart. "These would have been necessary to help you to progress through certain areas of the game. Many concepts were similar to games like *Banjo-Kazooie*, or more recently *Yooka-Laylee*, where parts of the game were inaccessible unless you learnt a specific move from another area of the game. *Subtraddition* would have mirrored this, but with unlockable blocks in place of new moves. This was meant to invoke the need for exploration within the game."

'Blox' replaced the need for weapons in a game which also featured no enemies either. Instead, there were obstacles such as spikes, fireballs and falling blocks, with nothing creature/human-based to hunt you down. Your 'blox' would act as your only form of defence against anything that could kill you. Stuart started by designing head blocks that fired flames at you and 'thwomp' blocks that could fall on you, inspired by *Super Mario World* on the SNES. There were moving platforms to get you around levels, but which could also crush you, as well as static/moving spikes that could pierce you. Further obstacles would later depend on the level, such as molten lava in a lava-themed world.

As with any initial design process, many ideas were considered and dropped early on. These included having to guide a bouncy block along a path and protecting it from deadly spikes, falling crates for puzzles involving weight-activated buttons (placing a crate to activate something in the game), and even a 'God of Death' character, who gets you to bring souls to unlock secrets, such as more blocks, characters and locations. There were also early suggestions of having to form large items very similar to 'Jiggys' from *Banjo-Kazooie* that unlocked doors to new worlds. These would have to be constructed from five components dotted around the levels, borrowing from the power cell concept in *Jak and Daxter*.

"Some of my favourite games growing up were also collection-based platformers, such as *Banjo-Kazooie*."

With the key components eventually boiled down and settled upon, Stuart began to think about puzzles to fill the worlds. "I began to invent puzzles in my mind that used the available mechanics until I had thought of enough that I could turn it into a full game," he confirmed. "The main concept was always that you have these blocks that you can add or subtract from the game scene. You can place these to allow you to jump across large gaps and navigate traps that would otherwise kill you."

For instance, in some areas, there could be spikes that are too long to jump across, so you must use your 'blox' as a temporary platform to get across. Scenarios could also include situations where you need two 'blox' to be able to get across a particular area, or you even have to use a bouncy 'blox' to reach a high-up platform or jump across a very large gap. Then there would be puzzles where you would need to use TNT to blow up pathways or blockages to progress.

Thinking of themes that could make up the game's environment, Stuart considered topics such as 'Ice', 'Lava', 'Underground Caves', 'Floating Abandoned Ships', 'Underwater Cities', and 'Floating/Mysterious Islands'. After much deliberation, the game was shortened to a final plan of just three themes – 'Grass/Wooded/Ruins', 'Industrial/Steampunk' and 'Castle/Medieval'. Each consisted of mostly visual changes, but there would be one or two items and obstacles that were unique to the world and fitted in with the general theme.

Stuart also wanted to ensure an almost *Super Mario Bros.*-style introduction to some of the main concepts. So the plan was to begin within the 'Start Zone', a sandbox area where you learn all the basic concepts without the risk of dying. Here you would be able to move on to the 'Hub Zone', which would have doors to each of the three worlds, with the 'Castle/Medieval' area featuring a hidden tomb somewhere within. Upon finding the tomb, Stuart planned to include a final boss to defeat, using just your 'blox' to deflect attacks.

Every world was to include a total of five levels, each containing unique challenges and puzzles to solve. To complete each, you would be required to find a particular object hidden away somewhere on the map. To reduce the frustration of starting from the beginning after dying, levels would be dotted with checkpoints to save new spawn points. A level map would also show the levels as you progressed, in case you get lost. If you got stuck on a particular puzzle, then you would be free to play the other levels in any order you wished within a world and come back to troublesome levels later on. However, to progress to the later worlds, you would need to collect a certain amount of cross collectables within levels to open them up.

Although the second and third worlds were locked away, Stuart's intention was for the player to have complete freedom. "The intention was always to allow players to jump around and explore as they wished," he explained. "Once a player had found two placeable blocks, they could pretty much get anywhere in the level. They could place a block, jump on it, place the second block, jump on that, remove the first block and place it again, and repeat as often as they wanted to explore every nook and cranny." To encourage that exploration, there would be a number of secret areas, with chests full of goodies to find.

Stuart started to produce a suitable story to wrap around the game to give context and purpose. "I seem to recall a story about an ancient civilisation that had powers associated with basic maths functions (the power to add, subtract, divide and multiply), but something happened which caused them to hide away underground," he began. "At the start of the game, the player would discover that they are descended from a race of people and uncover ancient ruins belonging to them. Whilst exploring these ruins, the player finds magical blocks that they can add and subtract from space and use them to help them navigate the ruins underground. The climax of the story would have seen the player uncovering a tomb of sorts, where this ancient race has been sleeping, awakening them to start a new age for magical maths people."

When it came to visuals, Stuart decided to go with a classic Game Boy style. "I perceive myself to be a novice artist and felt comfortable enough with pixel art that I could produce some OK-looking visual aesthetics for the game," explained Stuart. "The decision to go with the classic four colours of the original Game Boy was mostly down to my own personal connection. I received my first classic Game Boy as a hand-me-down from my sister's boyfriend (now husband) at the time. I remember spending a lot of time playing *The Legend of Zelda: Link's Awakening*, *Super Mario Land 2* and, of course, *Pokémon Red* and *Blue*."

Once Stuart had created some initial pixel work, he decided to open up proceedings to his blog readers to see if he should keep the restricted theme or come up with his own style. He was mostly concerned that he may be seen to be merely 'piggy-backing' onto the success of the Game Boy, and he worried that potential publishers could be scared off due to the 'Nintendo-ness' of it all.

It wasn't long though until Stuart found reassurance from his followers to carry on, so it was full steam ahead. The graphics would go through a number of iterations and adjustments once Stuart found his feet within the limitations, and he eventually came up with a style that looked accomplished. The visuals formed would not have been out of place at all during the heyday of Game Boy releases and certainly didn't look like the work of a 'novice' artist either.

With the development side, Stuart added to the prototype he had originally started for his teaching. Firstly, he wanted the user to jump straight into the game with very little training required, so focus was put on fine-tuning the controls early on. Along with the basic movement of your character, you would have a moveable target controlled separately with a mouse or stylus, with two separate buttons to add and subtract 'blox'. Another button was then left to enable you to enter doors to other rooms.

Stuart also began looking at other games for inspiration on effects to make the game feel good to play. One helpful resource was the results from a previous Ludum Dare Game Jam. "The good thing was that developers had to upload the source code for their games," explained Stuart. "The *Birdsong* game just happened to be made in the same engine I was using, so I was able to reverse-engineer how the creator had achieved certain effects and make my own attempts to apply them to *Subtraddition*. Jan Willem Niijman's Vlambeer talk on 'The art of screen shake' also aided me in creating more 'game feel' with the early prototype, and I am certainly a fan of Vlambeer's games – *Super Crate Box* in particular was a favourite."

After around three months of working most evenings, the majority of the game engine was working, with a large prototype map containing a cave/graveyard set of themes. The concept of levels was not quite in place, and you were not yet able to complete anything. You could move around and explore, navigating some basic puzzles that Stuart created to test the engine, and that was it. There were still many obstacle types yet to be implemented, as well as the different 'blox' that you could pick up and use. Only a single standard solid 'blox' was currently available, and there was no inventory system yet implemented to keep track of what you were holding in terms of 'crosses' and 'blox'.

All the character movements and animations were also complete, though background artwork was mostly placeholder-based. Music and sound effects were also still a distant thought for Stuart, though he did have options in mind. "I really liked the music by an artist known as Rushjet1," confirmed Stuart. "He writes chip music and later created three tracks for my Game Boy Jam game, *Procedrill*. He also created the music for *PewDiePie: Legend of the Brofist* and *PewDiePie's Tuber Simulator*."

"Every world was to include a total of five levels, each containing unique challenges and puzzles to solve."

With *Subtraddition* fast becoming one of the most complex titles Stuart had worked on, it was felt that it could be sold this time around, with plans to release it on the PC, with Android and iOS also considered. "I felt that there was a lot of potential to make this a commercial title, even if only for a couple of quid," he said. "The art style, the idea of the core mechanic, and the puzzles involved – I felt they would be enough to get people interested. I shared an image on Twitter of a screenshot from the game, and it got a few likes/retweets so, hopefully, people would have liked it."

On paper at least, level designs and puzzles were now complete for two of the three worlds planned, with Stuart now about to start implementing them into the actual game, producing the tilesets needed for the levels along the way. However, just as the game was about to properly hit its final stride and take form, a new arrival in the Lilford household was to about mark a welcome disruption to the project as a whole.

Stuart was to become a father that September, and he knew that it would have an impact on his time for development work. But he attributes other factors more for what would result eventually in the shelving of *Subtraddition*. "I have this awful habit of starting a new project when I am already in the middle of one," Stuart confessed. "Derek Yu, creator of *Spelunky*, wrote a great article on finishing a game, and a lot of the sentiment in there resonates with me."

"I have this awful habit of starting a new project when I am already in the middle of one."

Even when again finding time to create more games, *Subtraddition* remained on the shelf whilst other new titles such as *Procedrill* flourished and were released instead. The most recent have been the releases of *Splodey Vaders* and *The Temple of Adventure*, created for an AdventureJam event.

However, Stuart isn't ready to fully throw in the towel just yet, hinting that *Subtraddition* could someday be resurrected in some other shape or form, but only when time is perhaps kinder. "In my free time, I still try to tinker with projects when I can, but it's tricky as I have a wife, a child, two dogs, a mortgage and other family commitments," Stuart explained. "Plus I'm studying a Master's degree in Game Design part-time, distance-learning, so having the time to make an epic indie masterpiece is rare these days. I mainly find myself making shorter micro-games lately – little games that I can make in an afternoon or a couple of days."

After seeing the final prototype for ourselves in action and the promise that it had, it is hoped that Stuart does return to the game someday to reimagine and showcase more of his clear natural talent for game design. Maybe it's something Stuart could return to full-time someday? "I'll never say never," he responded. "Although teaching has its own stresses, the holidays are great – I don't have the constant pressure of crunch, plus I'm in a secure job role."

For now, be sure to check out Stuart's most recent work and updates at www.scaredsquare.com. Hopefully, someday, there will be the anticipated news of *Subtraddition* being resurrected once more and, this time, properly finished.

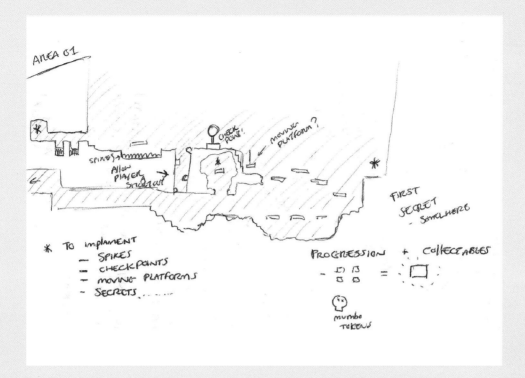

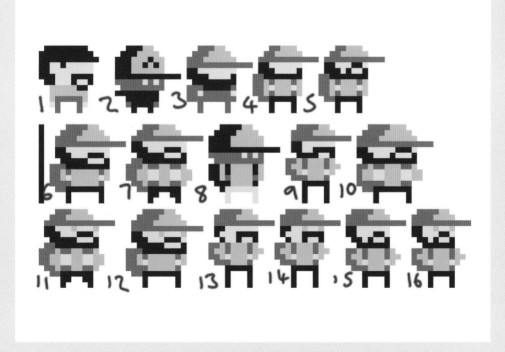

Top: An early sketched-out map of Area 1 for the game, showing some basic elements.
Bottom: Early art test by Stuart for the main character.

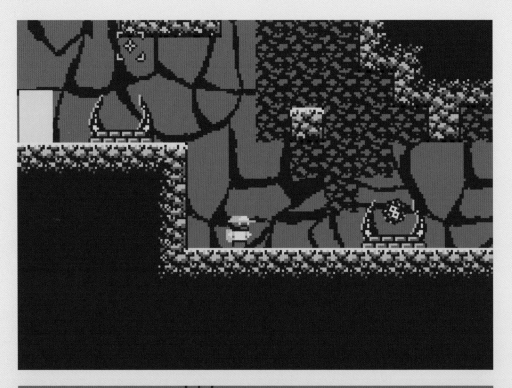

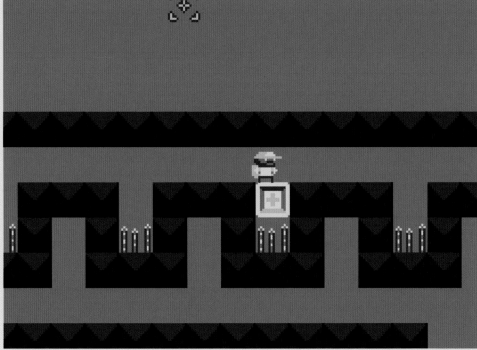

Above: *Subtraddition* (PC) – Exploring the underground cave section of the prototype and trying to navigate across some deadly spikes.

Above: *Subtraddition* (PC) – Outside with a starry night scenario and then further on in an abandoned graveyard.

Spooky
On hold

Year: 2015
Developer:
Johan Forslöf
Platform:
Commodore 64

Considering the roots of Games That
Weren't, it feels somewhat fitting to
conclude on a Commodore 64 game.
A recent development and one which
has blown all away who have seen
and experienced it, this wonderful
and atmospheric platformer had a
touch of Jonathan Blow's *Braid* about
it all. Tragically, it seems unlikely it
will ever be completed, showing that
casualties still occur even today on
classic platforms gone by.

Available to play
⊙ Yes   ○ No

Honourable mentions

It just isn't possible to include every single unreleased game in a single book; many platforms require a book to themselves. We conclude with a final selection of other notable titles in chronological order that you may wish to also investigate further through many of the digital archives out there.

Dirt Bike
Year: 1977. Developer: Atari. Platform: Arcade. *Sprint*-like game with dirt bikes instead of cars.

PT Commander
Year: 1978. Developer: Atari. Platform: Arcade. In brief: Prototype by Owen Rubin with a single screen and two boats that must attack each other.

Space Storms
Year: 1978. Developer: Atari. Platform: Arcade. In brief: Similar to *Kaboom!* on the Atari 2600. Here, you must catch incoming asteroids.

Adventures of Tron
Year: 1982. Developer: Mattel Electronics. Platform: Mattel Intellivision. In brief: Conversion from Atari 2600, reportedly rejected by marketing. Surfaced in 2011.

Donkey Kong
Year: 1982. Developer: Wayne Westmoreland and Terry Gilman. Platform: Tandy TRS-80. In brief: Remarkable conversion. Sadly, licensing problems put a stop to release.

Space Vultures
Year: 1982. Developer: Commodore. Platform: Commodore VIC-20. In brief: Full *Phoenix* clone created by Andy Finkel for cartridge release. Possible licence issue causing its cancellation.

Star Wars: Ewok Adventure
Year: 1983. Developer: Parker Brothers. Platform: Atari 2600. In brief: Hang gliding Ewok game, potentially the best *Star Wars* game on the system.

Hungry Horace
Year: 1983. Developer: Melbourne House. Platform: Commodore VIC-20. In brief: Advertised briefly but never surfaced anywhere.

Tour de France
Year: 1983. Developer: GCC. Platform: Vectrex. In brief: An incredible-for-its-time, third-person bike racing game, caught up in the Vectrex's premature demise.

Robotron 2084
Year: 1984. Developer: Atarisoft. Platform: ZX Spectrum 48K. In brief: Impressive arcade conversion that died when Atarisoft collapsed.

Moon Patrol
Year: 1984. Developer: Atarisoft. Platform: ColecoVision. In brief: Another impressive Atarisoft conversion caught up in the company's collapse.

1942
Year: 1986. Developer: Elite. Platform: Commodore 16. In brief: Believed to be cancelled due to slow sales for the platform – never resumed, even after a brief sales revival.

Jail Break
Year: 1986. Developer: Konami. Platform: MSX. In brief: Conversion from arcade. Surely couldn't be any worse than the other home conversions either.

Mire Mare
Year: 1986. Developer: Ultimate Play The Game. Platform: ZX Spectrum 48K. In brief: The 'Holy Grail' of the ZX Spectrum world, which may sadly never see a release.

Firetrack 2
Year: 1987. Developer: Nick Pelling. Platform: BBC Micro. In brief: A more 3D-feeling sequel to *Firetrack*, with very smooth scrolling.

The Bubbler
Year: 1987. Developer: Lynsoft. Platform: Commodore 64. In brief: Painfully slow-moving conversion of Ultimate's Spectrum title – cancelled for that reason.

Cyber Tank
Year: 1988. Developer: Coreland. Platform: Arcade. In brief: On-rails tank shooter with a neat two-screen display. Tested poorly and consigned to the scrap heap.

Knight Orc
Year: 1988. Developer: Level 9. Platform BBC Micro. In brief: Long rumoured conversion of the graphic text adventure, finally recovered in 2019.

Silvern Castle
Year: 1988. Developer: Jeff Fink. Platform: Apple II. In brief: *Wizardry*-like RPG. Never released due to a dwindling market.

D-Generation
Year: 1989. Developer: Robert Cook. Platform: Apple II. In brief: Began life on the Apple II – canned when the platform became unprofitable and moved to other platforms.

Last Ninja 2
Year: 1989. Developer: Attention to Detail. Platform: Konix Multi-System. In brief: Simple conversion of the popular sequel, unreleased for a platform also unreleased.

Electrocop
Year: 1989–1990. Developer: ICC. Platform: Atari 7800. In brief: A very different version of the popular Atari Lynx game that was apparently finished. Still waiting to be found by enthusiasts.

Arctic Moves
Year: 1991. Developer: Dinamic Software. Platform: Atari ST. In brief: Final chapter of *Moves* trilogy, travelling to the Arctic to destroy a base controlled by aliens.

SimCity
Year: 1991. Developer: Intelligent Systems. Platform: Nintendo Entertainment System. In brief: Conversion of Will Wright's seminal game, cancelled to focus on SNES release.

Death Track
Year: 1992. Developer: Argonaut Software. Platform: Nintendo Game Boy. In brief: A rather *Stunt Car Racer*-looking title with combat elements and upgrades. Recently recovered.

Flood 2 – Quiffy's Revenge
Year: 1992. Developer: Insight. Platform: Atari ST, Commodore Amiga and PC. In brief: Similar to the first game, with many improvements and new features.

Marble Madness
Year: 1992. Developer: Tengen. Platform: PC Engine. In brief: Impressive conversion of Atari's classic arcade which was unreleased for reasons unknown.

Ninja Gaiden
Year: 1992. Developer: Opus. Platform: SEGA Mega Drive. In brief: Misjudged title in the *Gaiden* series, attempting to replicate the 1988 arcade but ending up becoming a broken mess instead.

Nobby the Aardvark
Year: 1992. Developer: Genesis Software. Platform: Commodore Amiga. In brief: Half-completed conversion of a classic C64 game that was shaping up well.

Street Fighter 2
Year: 1992. Developer: Creative Materials. Platform: Amstrad CPC. In brief: Long-awaited home conversion that never was and continues to haunt CPC fans today after many promises in magazines at the time.

Star Wars
Year: 1993. Developer: SEGA Interactive. Platform: PC (DOS) and SEGA Mega Drive + CD. In brief: Abandoned port of SNES LucasArts game. Early prototype recovered in late 2019 by Hidden Palace.

Eddie's Puzzle Time
Year: 1994. Developer: Hookstone. Platform: Nintendo Game Boy. In brief: In development for around four months, publishers found it too risky and didn't take it on. Prototype can be found online to download.

Yogi Bear's Gold Rush
Year: 1994. Developer: Twilight. Platform: SEGA Game Gear. In brief: Released on the Nintendo Game Boy. Unknown why the SEGA handheld version never surfaced.

Alien Trilogy
Year: 1995. Developer: Probe. Platforms: SEGA 32X and SEGA CD. In brief: Planned conversion of popular PlayStation/Saturn game to SEGA's misguided platforms.

Mr Nutz: Hoppin' Mad
Year: 1995. Developer: Neon Software. Platform: SEGA Mega Drive. In brief: Fully complete conversion of Amiga sequel cancelled due to the dwindling platform market.

Rayman
Year: 1995. Developer: Ubisoft. Platform: Super Nintendo. In brief: Starting out on Nintendo's ageing 16-bit platform, development switched to newer platforms.

X-Men: Mind Games
Year: 1995. Developer: Scavenger. Platform: SEGA 32X. In brief: Impressive 3D title based on Marvel *X-Men* comics. Apparently cancelled due to poor 32X sales.

GoldenEye
Year: 1996. Developer: Rare. Platform: Nintendo Virtual Boy. In brief: Not a conversion of the N64 game, but a racing game that got quite far along before its untimely cancellation.

Phase Zero
Year: 1996. Developer: Hyper Image Productions. Platforms: Atari Jaguar and SEGA Saturn. In brief: Impressive 3D game on platforms not as 3D-strong as the Sony PlayStation.

Power Crystal
Year: 1997. Developer: Perceptions. Platform: 3DO M2. In brief: Starting as a PC RPG game called Artemis, before being moved to the 3DO M2. Canned when the target platform was cancelled.

Return Fire
Year: 1997. Developer: Silence Software. Platform: SEGA Saturn. In brief: Solid conversion of classic 3DO tank game that was fully complete and, thankfully, leaked.

Quintessential Art of Destruction
Year: 1998. Developer: Cranberry Source. Platforms: Sony PlayStation and SEGA Saturn. In brief: Combat flight sim with the early Saturn attempt cancelled. PlayStation edition was also not up to scratch.

Turrican 3D
Year: 1999. Developer: Factor 5. Platforms: PC + supposedly SEGA Dreamcast. In brief: Aborted attempt at trying to move *Turrican* into a 3D environment. Later attempts were also canned.

Titan A.E.
Year: 2000. Developer: Blitz Games. Platforms: Sony PlayStation and PC. In brief: Film bombed at the box office. Game swiftly cancelled. A PS1 demo sneaked out.

Katakis 3D
Year: 2001. Developer: Factor 5. Platform: Nintendo Game Boy Color. In brief: Completed sequel to the classic C64 shooter. Publisher couldn't be found.

ToeJam and Earl 3
Year: 2001. Developer: ToeJam and Earl Productions and Visual Concepts Entertainment. Platform: SEGA Dreamcast (+ Nintendo 64 in 1998). In brief: Third instalment of popular series. Cancelled due to both platforms dying.

Demon Hunter
Year: 2002. Developer: Independent Arts Software. Platform: Nintendo Game Boy Advance. In brief: RPG title with large procedurally generated areas to explore.

Starcraft Ghost
Year: 2002–2006. Developer: Nihilistic Software (later Swingin' Ape Studios). Platforms: Microsoft Xbox, Nintendo GameCube and Sony PlayStation 2. In brief: third-person sci-fi game put on indefinite hold by Blizzard.

Animal Crossing 2
Year: 2004. Developer: Nintendo. Platform: Nintendo GameCube. In brief: Sequel to the popular life simulation game which was cancelled for reasons unknown.

Deus Ex: Insurrection
Year: 2004. Developer: Ion Storm. Platforms: Microsoft Xbox and PC. In brief: An alternative *Deus Ex 3* game that was canned at concept stage. Read more at Unseen64.

Far Cry
Year: 2006. Developer: Ubisoft Montreal. Platform: Sony PlayStation Portable. In brief: Only known due to an information leak. Unclear if a conversion or unique game.

Super Mario Spikers
Year: 2007. Developer: Next Level Games. Platform: Nintendo Wii. In brief: An interesting wresting/volleyball mix featuring the lovable plumber but rejected by Nintendo.

Star Wars Battlefront 3
Year: 2008. Developer: Free Radical Design. Platform: Microsoft Xbox 360. In brief: Cancellation that hit fans of the franchise hard due to the promise that it had.

Hellion: Mystery of the Inquisition
Year: 2009. Developer: Flying Fish Works. Platforms: PC, Sony PlayStation 3 and Microsoft Xbox 360. In brief: Impressive medieval RPG set across European locations.

Saints Row: Undercover
Year: 2009. Developer: Mass Media Games, then Savage Entertainment. Platform: Sony PlayStation Portable. In brief: *Saints Row 2* port that evolved into a completely new title.

Nano Street Racers
Year: 2011. Developer: Firebrand Games. Platforms: Microsoft Xbox 360, Sony PlayStation 3 and PC. In brief: *Super Sprint*-inspired racing game with weapons. No publisher found.

Family Guy: Back to the Multiverse
Year: 2011–2012. Developer: Heavy Iron. Platforms: Nintendo 3DS and Wii. In brief: Released on other platforms, believed to be cancelled due to performance concerns.

Star Wars: First Assault
Year: 2012. Developer: LucasArts. Platforms: Microsoft Xbox 360 and Sony PlayStation 3. In brief: Another lost *Star Wars* title. Cancelled when LucasArts closed.

The Avengers
Year: 2012. Developer: THQ Australia and Blue Tongue Entertainment. Platforms: Microsoft Xbox 360, Nintendo Wii U, PC and Sony PlayStation 3. In brief: First-person fighting game, canned due to studio closures.

Fez 2
Year: 2013. Developer: Polytron. Platforms: Unknown. In brief: Sequel to the beautiful puzzler, canned due to its creator becoming disillusioned with the industry.

Know Your Friends
Year: 2013. Developer: Ubisoft. Platform: Nintendo Wii U. In brief: A party game that Ubisoft had completed but did not release due to the poor sales of the platform.

Warrior's Lair
Year: 2013. Developer: Idol Minds. Platforms: Sony PlayStation 3 and PlayStation Vita. In brief: Medieval RPG where you play PS3 copy at home then continue on Vita.

Rimini
Year: 2015. Developer: Robotoki. Platforms: PC, Sony PlayStation 4 and Xbox One. In brief: Impressive sci-fi title, progressing well until the developer had to close its doors.

Contributions and thanks

Thank you to the following people for help and support throughout:
Sam Dyer, Vinny Mainolfi, Paul Drury, Mark Hardisty and Neil Grayson for advice, guidance and constant encouragement. Craig Stevenson for the wonderful ZX Spectrum *Last Ninja* loading screen implementation. Gonçalo Lopes for the improved PlayStation screenshots. Mat Allen for additional fact-checking. Pascal Welsing for the glossary help. Amanda Purdom for the proofreading. Hidden Palace, Atari Protos, Lost Levels, Unseen64 and others, whose preservation work made it possible to screenshot many of the titles in the first place. Finally, thank you to the following people for their contributions and assets, helping to make this publication possible:

100 Bullets
Eduardo Risso
and Scott Brocker

8 Kings
Martin Piper
and Oscar Ferrero

Akka Arrh
John Salwitz

Attack of the Mutant Camels '89
Frédéric Letellier (scans), Jeff Minter, Jon Dean, Lee Hammerton, Mark Campbell, Steinar Lund (artwork) and Stephen Stuttard (scans)

Attack of the Mutant Zombie Flesh Eating Chickens from Mars
Gerard Sweeney, John Darnell, Keith Ainsworth, Matthew Smith, Paul Drury, Ste Cork, Steve Leyland, Steve Brown and Vinny Mainolfi

Bandersnatch
John Gibson

Black Death
Florian Desforges and Guillaume Gouraud

Black Hawk
Aric Wilmunder, Charlie Kellner and Noah Falstein

Blackjack
Dave Nutting, Dan Hower (flyer from Flyer Fever archive) and Jamie Fenton

Blaster
Eugene Jarvis
and Larry DeMar

Boggle
David Crane
and Matt Reichert

Boxer
Mike Albaugh

Bubble Bobble
Martin Kelsey, Peter Gillett and Richard Hewison

Burnt Out Cop
Dan Malone, John Rowlands, Logi26, Mitchell Goodwin, Nick Lee, Robin Ellis, Robin Levy and Steve Rowlands

Cannonball
Owen Rubin

Captain Seahawk
Dan Moss, Dave Stubben and Mike Albaugh

Carmageddon TV
Damien Djaouti (images), David Guthrie, Grant Clarke, Iain Anderson, Ian Moody, Jim Thompson, Justin Castle, Ken Fee, Kevin Martin, Lez Andrew, Mark Traynor, Neil Barnden, Patrick Buckland, Pat McGovern, Paul Walker, Steve Haggerty and Will McCourt

CCTV
Jon Hare and
Volodymyr Kyselov

Chip's Challenge
Chuck Sommerville, Jim Smart, Karl Jeffery, Rex and Stephen Bedser

Conquest
Eugene Jarvis, Jeff Vavasour, Larry DeMar and Sam Dicker

Creation
Glenn Corpes

Daffy Duck – Starring in the Great Paint Caper
Ashley Routledge, Alan Benson, Ben Walshaw, Craig Wight, David Palmer, David Saunders, Gary Antcliffe, Mat Allen (scans), Nigel Speight, Paul Tankard, Pete Frith and Richard Morton

Dark Seed
Brian Hargrove

Dark Tower
Chris Romero, Gary Bergmann, Helmut Müller, John Hall, Jim Francis, Mark Indictor, Paul Allen Newell, Robert Hoffberg, Sean Kelly and Thomas McDonald

Deadlock
Robin Levy

Deathwatch
Ben Whitlock, Darren Wood, Dale Johnstone, Eamonn Barr, John Court, Lee Chapman, Richard Priest, Ross Sillifant, Scott Stilphen, Stewart Green, Simeon Hankins and Urs Koenig

Dick Special
Angela Sutherland, Alastair Hearsum, Brendan Phoenix, Graeme Ashton, Gordon Leggatt, James Hutchby, Paul Drury, Patricia Curtis, Richard Hewison and Sandy White

Dizzy Returns
Andrew Oliver, Duncan (Dunk) Nimmo, Nick Myles and Philip Oliver

Eye of the Moon
Chris Wild and Martyn Carroll (quotes)

Fallout 3: Van Buren
Feargus Urquhart and Josh Sawyer

Frogger 2: Swampy's Revenge
Andrew Oliver, Andy Eder, Darren Wood, Matt Cloy, Philip Oliver and Steve Bond

Gazza 2
Adam Waring, Chris Pink, David Colley, Dean Hickingbottom, John Pickford, Julian Rignall, Matthew Regan, Mark R. Cobley-Jones, Paul Clansey, Ross Sillifant, Rik Yapp, Richard Leadbetter, Simon Butler and Ste Pickford

Gauntlet
Adam Rippon, David Sullivan, Gerald Broas, Micah Russo, Tracey King and Yannis Brown

Green Lantern
Bobby Earl, Dean Evans, Gary Bracey, Ian Turnbull, Ivan Horn, John Tatlock, John Lomax, John Reitze, Myron Rumsey, Mike Delves, Mike Marshall, Ray Coffey and Roy Fielding

Half-Life
Austin Malcolm, Brian Martel, Brian Kraack, Chris Faylor, Dan Amrich, Jeff Skal, Jeff Pobst, Marc Laidlaw, Randy Pitchford, Robert Morgan and Tiffany Hillary

Hard Drivin'
Mark Morris

Heart of Yesod
Colin Grunes, Marc Wilding, Mark McCubbin and Steve Wetherill

Human Element
Robert Bowling (information and screenshot)

Keystone Kannonball
Dan Kitchen and National Videogame Museum USA

Lemmings 2
Matt Taylor

Lethal Weapon
Gary Bracey, Ivan Horn, Jeroen Tel, Mick West and Paul Hughes

Mail Plane
Mark Indictor

MARSOC
Erik Bretz, John Williamson, Jared Gerritzen and Mark Long

Mega Twins
Wayne Billingham

Millipede
Curt Vendel, Doug Macrae, Dave Staugas, Ed Logg, Jed Margolin (Vax Mail quotes for Ed Logg), Michael Feinstein, Steve Golson and Steve Szymanski (photos)

Mini Golf
Dan Moss, Dennis Koble, Ed Rotberg, John Ray, Lyle Rains, Mike Albaugh, Owen Rubin, Paul Drury, Roger Hector and Victoria Gray + Jeremy Saucier (photo – The Strong Museum)

Oops!
Dan Sunday, Flora Johnson, Jonathan Koolpe, James Hague, Larry Rosenthal, Shawn Rosenthal, Scott Boden and Zonn Moore

Primal Rage 2
Chris Tang and Stephen Riesenberger

Putty Squad
Andy Roberts, Ashley Routledge, Gary Tonge, Galahad, Jon Colling, Jon Wells, John Twiddy, Michael Smith, Martin Oliver, Nick Lee, Phil Thornton and Robin Levy

Rescue on Fractalus!
Lars Jensen and Steve Golson

Resident Evil
Simon Butler

Ridge Racer
Andy Satterthwaite, Gary Burley, Jed Adams, John Dwyer and Mike Clarke

Safire
Scott Adams

Sebring
BillySeven, Jed Margolin, Owen Rubin, Paul Mancuso and Victoria Gray + Jeremy Saucier (photo – The Strong Museum)

Sex 'n' Drugs 'n' Rock 'n' Roll
Jon Hare and Robert Trevellyan

SimMars
Alex Zvenigorodsky, B.J. West, Dan Brazelton, Jason Shankel and Sean Baity

Sonic X-treme
Christian Senn

Solar Jetman
Dave Broadhurst, Geoff Follin, Haydn Dalton, John Buckley, Martin Holland, Pete Andrew, Rob Whitaker, Rob Henderson, Simon Street, Ste Pickford and Tony Williams

Spitfire Fury
Andrew Hutchings, David Hartburn, Mark Ferguson, Richard Hanson and Stephen Scott

Star Fox 2
Dylan Cuthbert, John Davis
and Matt Almanza

Starring Charlie Chaplin
Charles Cecil, Donald
Campbell, Danielle Woodyatt,
Dawn Hollywood (nee Drake),
Jon Grimshaw, Matt Biebly,
Martin Holland, Martin Calvert,
Paul Clansey, Richard Tidsall,
Ross Sillifant, Sean Townsend,
Stephen Ward, Simon Butler
and Tim Chaney

Stunt Car Racer Pro
Alex Trowers, Anthony
Caulfield, Ben Carter, Geoff
Crammond, Glenn Corpes,
John Cook, Jon Ritman and
Nicola Caulfield

Subtraddition
Stuart Lilford

Super Mario's Wacky Worlds
Nina Stanley

The Last Ninja
Alan Huffman, Mevlut Dinc,
Marc Rosocha, Nick Cook, Phil
Churchyard and Rick Adams

The Lizzie Borden Murders
Dan Kitchen

The Terminator
David Siller

Thrill Kill
Kevin Mulhall

Time Bomb
Chris Downend, John Ray,
Lyle Rains and Scott Evans

Tony Hawk's Shred Session
Gary Richards

Tork
Andy Onions, Michael Smith
and Neil Millstone

USSA
Eugene Jarvis, John
Newcomer, Ken Fedesna
and Warren Davis

**Vindicators
and Rolling Thunder**
Adam Harvey, Al Baker,
Chuck Ernst, David Kurensky,
Harry Dodgson (screenshots),
Ian Baronofsky, Joel Seider,
Mark Wickart, Robb Mariani,
Ross Sillifant, Scott Stilphen
and Ted Tahquechi

Virtua Hamster
Ben Palmer, David Palmer, Eric
Quakenbush, Ken Horowitz,
Nick Kimberley, Paul Tankard
and Roddy McMillan

Virtual Tank
Barry Leitch, Hans Piwenitzky,
Rob Povey, Seth Mendelsohn,
Todd Downing and Warrick
Holfeld

Waterworld
Carleton Handley, Frédéric
Letellier (scans), Greg Holt,
Lorraine Starr, Peter Scott,
Ross Sillifant, Ste Pickford
and Steve Woita

Wolf Pack
Dan Moss, Dave Sherman,
Dennis Koble and Mike
Albaugh

Glossary

Struggling to know the difference between your bits and bytes? We've created this handy guide to help explain some of the more technical terms and concepts mentioned throughout this book.

10NES
Lock-out chip within the Nintendo Entertainment System to prevent imported and unofficial/pirated games.

6502
8-bit processor created by MOS Technology that helped spark the home computer revolution. Contemporary of the Z80 (see Z80).

AirPlay
Software development kit created by Apple to aid developers in creating applications for iOS.

Alpha build
First working build of software ready for initial testing, containing at least the core features. Expected to contain bugs at this stage.

ARM
Widely used processor architecture first released by Acorn in 1985, found in modern-day devices, such as mobile devices.

Assembly language
Human-readable programming language which makes it easier to write machine code.

BASIC (Beginners' All-purpose Symbolic Instruction Code)
Very simple-to-use programming language, using English-like commands that give beginners a good entry into programming.

Beta build
First software build available outside of the development team, mostly complete but requiring testing to iron out remaining bugs.

Bezel (arcade)
The border around an arcade screen, often featuring artwork/logos as part of the design.

Bit (binary digit)
The smallest unit of data within a computer, consisting of a single binary value of 0 (off) or 1 (on).

Bitmap/Raster graphics
Grid of pixels (see Pixel) which make up the visual display. Higher resolutions result in more pixels displayed on the screen.

C/C++
Both programming languages, with C++ being an extension of C and including a number of major features and additions.

CGI (Computer-Generated Imagery)
Images created with a computer, often with the use of a 2D/3D graphics package.

Clipping
Procedure that determines if parts of an image or 3D object are outside or inside a specified area of space.

ComLynx
The Atari Lynx system for networking units together over a cable for multiplayer games.

CPU (Central Processing Unit)/Processor
Core part of computer/device that executes the instructions from a program, e.g. handling logic, maths and input/output functions.

CRT (Cathode-Ray Tube)
Vacuum tube component found within old display screens using one or more electron guns and a phosphor screen to display images.

DOS (Disk Operating System)
A command line/text-based operating system that runs from a disk drive, allowing you to navigate and run software.

Double buffering
A fast, memory-hungry technique of updating a screen's display. Whilst one image is displayed on the screen, the next is prepared elsewhere in memory, ready to be swapped in.

Emulator
Hardware/software enabling a computer to replicate functions of another system.

Engine/Game engine
Environment or base for developers to create games, consisting of functions/libraries to try and make the process easier.

Field test
Test of a product within the environment where it is eventually to be used, e.g. an arcade field test often occurs within an actual arcade.

FMV (Full Motion Video)
Pre-recorded video used within games, often used as cutscenes or part of the game itself. Games using this technology are called FMV games.

Forth
Early high-level programming language.

FPS (Frames Per Second)/Frame rate
Measure of how frequently a display screen is updated every second. A standard computer monitor is typically 60 FPS.

Fractal graphics
Graphics generated by mathematical formulas and loops, rather than by hand.

Gouraud shading
Named after Henri Gouraud. Method of shading to simulate light and shading gradient effects, making polygons appear smoother.

GUI (Graphical User Interface)
Visual components a user can interact with (often with a mouse) to carry out particular tasks within software or an operating system.

HAM (Hold and Modify)
Display mode on the Commodore Amiga, allowing many colours at once on the screen.

Hex/Hexadecimal
A numerical system that consists of 16 symbols, allowing for large binary numbers to be represented in a smaller amount of hexadecimal digits.

HUD (Heads-up Display)
A way of presenting information without having to shift gaze away from your main viewpoint. In a game, this could be simply presenting available lives/ammo/energy, etc.

Hz (Hertz)/MHz (Megahertz)/GHz (Gigahertz)
Units of speed for a CPU (see CPU). 1000Hz = 1MHz, 1000 MHz = 1GHz. The higher the Hz, the faster the CPU can process instructions.

JPEG (Joint Photographic Experts Group)
A common standard for compressing images to smaller file sizes but with a trade-off on image quality due to its lossy compression algorithm.

K/KB (Kilobyte)
Unit of storage in computing consisting of 1,024 bytes (1 byte = 8 bits – see Bit). E.g. a text file may be 5–10KB.

Kernel
Central part of a computer operating system that has control over everything, overseeing interactions between software and hardware.

Logic board
A printed circuit board, consisting of other components that make up the hardware.

LZW (Lempel-Ziv-Welch)
A lossless compression technique that uses a table lookup algorithm. A GIF image uses the technique for its compression.

Mainframe computer
Large and powerful computers often used for complex/large data processing. Would often use a lower-powered device to access and carry out particular functions.

MB (Megabyte)
A unit of storage in computing consisting of 1,024 kilobytes (see Kilobyte). E.g. a 4-minute MP3 sound file may take up approximately 4MB.

Microprocessor
A single-chip CPU (see CPU).

MIDI (Musical Instrument Digital Interface)
A way for computers and musical instruments to communicate using a set standard.

MMORPG (Massively Multiplayer Online Role-Playing Game)
An online role-playing game (see RPG) where a very large number of game players play together in a large virtual world.

Mode 7
Graphics mode on the Super Nintendo, where a background layer can be scaled and rotated to create a number of clever effects, including perspective and zooming.

NPC (Non-Player Character)
A character who is not controlled by a human player within a game. Often, it refers to a character controlled by the computer.

On rails
Where the player travels along a pre-determined route without the freedom to go anywhere, like a train, hence the name.

Parallax scrolling
An illusion of depth on a computer created by moving background objects at a slower speed than foreground objects.

Parser
Interpreting input by looking at certain keywords or structures to work out the required function.

PCB (Printed Circuit Board)
A board of conductive tracks allowing the connection of electrical components, such as chips and capacitors to be mounted together to produce a particular piece of hardware, such as a computer.

Pixel
The smallest controllable element of a raster display. E.g. a digital photo can be made up of millions of different-coloured pixels arranged in a grid.

Playfield

The area within a game where the action all takes place.

Plexiglass/Plexiglas

A plastic alternative to glass which is strong and shatter-proof, and is often printed onto.

Procedural generation

Creation of data using algorithms, such as images, sound or level data, for example, within a very small memory footprint.

Prototype

A working example of a product used to test a particular idea or concept early on, helping to establish if the direction being taken is reliable.

Push-scrolling

The process where scrolling occurs when a character or cursor reaches a particular point of a static display.

R&D (Research and Development)

Process of innovating and creating new ideas, often developing a proof of concept early on.

RAM (Random Access Memory)

Volatile storage space where data is stored temporarily whilst a system is powered up. Data can be read and written to.

ROM (Read-Only Memory)

Permanent storage space, where data is still present even when a system is powered off. Data can only be read and not written to.

RPG (Role-Playing Game)

A genre of game – taking roles of characters within a fantasy world, typically consisting of a number of quests and an in-depth story.

RTS (Real-Time Strategy)

A genre of strategy game where everything happens in real time, without each event happening incrementally in turns.

Sandbox

Where a gamer can freely roam and explore, without being forced down a particular path. Also known as open-world or free-roaming.

Scanline

One line or row of a raster display.

SCUMM (Script Creation Utility for Maniac Mansion)

An engine created by Lucasfilm Games initially to help the development of *Maniac Mansion* but then used for later titles.

Source code

Instructions/code written by a programmer whilst developing their software. Later compiled into a code that a system can execute.

Sprite

A 2D bitmap object that can be animated, moved and manipulated on a display, often used for player characters or enemies.

Sprite multiplexor

A technique for displaying more sprites (see Sprite) than usually allowed on a system.

Stereoscopics/Stereoscopy

A technique for creating an illusion of depth by two offset images presented separately to the left and right eyes.

Super FX chip

A coprocessor that provides advanced maths capabilities within a Super Nintendo game cartridge to enable faster 3D graphics and advanced 2D effects.

Texture mapping

The process of mapping a 2D texture/surface around a 3D object.

Trackball

A pointing device where the pointer is controlled by moving a ball, allowing control over the speed of movement the faster it is rolled.

UI (User Interface)

What the user interacts with to carry out particular functions within a piece of software.

UX (User Experience)

Focus on understanding what the user needs from a design, in order to create an experience which is both enjoyable and beneficial overall.

Vector graphics

Graphics defined by points and paths to form polygons and other various shapes, rather than a grid of pixels.

Venetian Blind technique

Atari 2600 technique created by Bob Whitehead to get more than six sprites (see Sprite) to appear on a line by displaying each object on every other scanline (see Scanline).

VGA (Video Graphics Array)

A graphics standard widely used before the likes of HDMI and DVI, allowing for high-resolutions and colour display.

Z80

An 8-bit processor which was fast and cheap and made its way into many products over the years. A contemporary of the 6502 (see 6502).

Do you have an unreleased game sitting around gathering dust? If so, get in touch on www.gamesthatwerent.com

First published in 2020 by Bitmap Books Ltd.

To get in touch, please email us at hello@bitmapbooks.co.uk

Accept no imitations... we are the world's no. 1!